"Information through Innovation"

Mastering and Using LOTUS 1-2-3

Release 3.4

H. Albert Napier

Rice University and
Napier & Judd, Inc.

Philip J. Judd

Napier & Judd, Inc.

boyd & fraser publishing company

Senior Acquisitions Editor: James H. Edwards
Production Editor: Barbara Worth
Marketing Manager: Eileen Pfeffer
Manufacturing Coordinator: Tracy Megison
Composition: Michael & Sigrid Wile
Cover Design: Hannus Design Associates

© 1994 by boyd & fraser publishing company
A Division of South-Western Publishing Co.
One Corporate Place • Ferncroft Village
Danvers, Massachusetts 01923

I(T)P

International Thomson Publishing
boyd & fraser publishing company is an ITP Company.
The ITP trademark is used under license.

Manufactured in the United States of America

Library of Congress Cataloging-in-Publication Data

Napier, H. Albert, 1944–
    Mastering and using Lotus 1-2-3 : release 3.4 / H. Albert Napier,
Philip J. Judd.
        p.   cm.
    Includes index.
    ISBN 0–87709–299–0
    1. Lotus 1-2-3 (Computer program)   2. Electronic spreadsheets
3. Business--Computer programs.   I. Judd, Philip J., 1953– .
II. Title.   III. Title: Mastering and using Lotus one-two-three.
HF5548.4.L67N365   1993
650'.0285'5369--dc20   93-5260
                                                        CIP

2 3 4 5 6 7 8 9 10 D 7 6 5

Dedication

This book is dedicated to our families for their loving support and patience.
Liz, J.B. and Lanham
Valerie, Michelle, Jacob and Heather

BRIEF CONTENTS

CONTENTS

Chapter Three
Designing Spreadsheets Properly   41

Chapter Four
Creating and Printing a Spreadsheet   51

Chapter Five
Improving the Appearance of a Spreadsheet

Chapter Six
Useful Lotus Commands

Chapter Seven
Creating and Printing Graphs

PREFACE

■ INTRODUCTION

Today, there are literally millions of people using personal computers. One of the most popular uses for personal computers is creating spreadsheets. Prior to the use of computers, spreadsheets were typically completed on what are called "columnar pad" sheets of paper. Spreadsheets are used extensively in accounting, financial analysis, and many other business planning and analysis situations.

■ OBJECTIVES OF THIS BOOK

This book was developed specifically for an introductory course on personal computers or spreadsheet analysis that utilizes IBM PCs or compatible hardware on which Lotus 1-2-3 can be used. The objectives of this book are as follows:

- To acquaint the user with the process of using personal computers to solve spreadsheet analysis type problems.
- To provide a working knowledge of the basic and advanced capabilities of 1-2-3.
- To encourage the use of good problem-solving techniques for situations in which spreadsheet solutions are appropriate.
- To permit learning through examples using an exercise-oriented approach.
- To provide the user with an excellent reference source to advance in the knowledge of 1-2-3.

■ LEVEL OF INSTRUCTION

This book is designed to introduce the beginning, intermediate, and advanced capabilities available in Lotus 1-2-3. It is pedagogically designed. First, the basic skills needed to create a spreadsheet are discussed. Subsequent chapters build on previously presented concepts and developed skills. A variety of practical examples provides an understanding of how Lotus 1-2-3 can be used. The book assumes the user has little or no personal computer experience. However, individuals with some previous experience can also advance their knowledge of 1-2-3. The book is characterized by its continuity, simplicity, and practicality. This book does not replace the Lotus 1-2-3 reference manual that accompanies the software package. Used in conjunction with the reference manual, this book will provide the user with a complete understanding of the capabilities of Lotus 1-2-3.

■ AUTHORS' EXPERIENCE

The authors have worked with personal computers since they were introduced. More than 40,000 people have participated in personal computer seminars for which the authors have been responsible for providing instruction. Insights from this experience are implicit throughout the book. In addition, the authors have more than 38 years of combined experience in teaching and consulting in the field of information systems.

■ LOTUS AUTHORIZED TRAINING COMPANY

The authors' consulting company, Napier & Judd, Inc., is a Lotus Authorized Training Company. The company's training materials, instructors, and facilities have been evaluated and approved by Lotus Development Corporation. Only a small number of companies in the United States and Canada have been designated as a Lotus Authorized Training Company. This book is based on materials that have been used in the company's training activities in which more than 15,000 participants have been trained on Lotus 1-2-3.

■ DISTINGUISHING FEATURES

The distinguishing features of this book include the following:

Research-Based Material

The design of the book is based on how experienced 1-2-3 users actually utilize the software. Napier, Batsell, Lane, and Guadagno at Rice University completed a study of 40 experienced 1-2-3 users from eight large organizations and determined the set of commands used most often by the individuals. The users studied had an average of 2.5 years experience and worked in a variety of corporations and governmental agencies.

The research indicates that 27 commands accounted for 85 percent of the commands issued by the experienced individuals. The materials in this book have been carefully planned to provide extensive coverage of these 27 most frequently used commands.

New Access Method for Lotus 1-2-3

This book features a unique parallel treatment of Lotus 1-2-3 Release 3.4's two user interfaces. Students may choose either the traditional keyboard method or use a mouse to select commands from menus or the SmartIcon palettes, specify ranges, and navigate around a worksheet.

Learning through Examples

The book is designed for learning through examples rather than learning a series of commands. The materials are built around a series of example problems. Commands are learned for one example, then reinforced. New commands are learned on subsequent examples. The example problems are logically related and integrated throughout the book.

Step-by-Step Instructions and Screen Illustrations

All examples include step-by-step instructions. Screen illustrations are used extensively to assist the user while learning 1-2-3.

Extensive Exercises

Exercises at the end of each chapter provide comprehensive coverage of the topics introduced in the chapter.

Emphasis on Business and Organizational Problem Solving

The book includes many example problems that may be encountered in a business or other type of organization.

Three-Dimensional Worksheets

Extensive coverage of the use of multiple worksheets in a file is presented. The process for linking worksheets between files is illustrated.

What You Should Know Concept Lists

Each chapter includes a list of key concepts emphasizing what should be learned in the chapter.

Emphasis on Proper Spreadsheet Design

Proper design of a spreadsheet can make its use more effective and reduce the probability of errors in a spreadsheet. Numerous comments are made to help in spreadsheet design.

Comprehensive Coverage

Major topics represented are: creating and printing worksheets and graphs; templates; using 3-D worksheets; combining and consolidating worksheets; database management; special functions; and macros.

Graphics

One of the most powerful options available in 1-2-3 is graphics. Graphs can be useful in business analysis and presentations. The user learns how to create and print bar, line, stacked bar, XY, pie, high-low-close-open, mixed bar and line, horizontal bar, area, and horizontal stacked bar graphs.

Templates

Most experienced users of 1-2-3 make extensive use of template worksheets. This book covers the process of building and using template worksheets.

Database Capabilities

While 1-2-3 is not a database management system, it does have many database-like commands that can be applied to data in a worksheet. For example, we discuss how to sort data, complete queries on information in a worksheet, fill spreadsheets with sequences of data, create tables for decision-making purposes, use data tables created by external database management systems, and create frequency distributions.

Add-In Programs

This book includes coverage of the Wysiwyg add-in for improving the appearance of spreadsheets and graphs. The book illustrates the Viewer add-in for examining the contents of a file before retrieving; delineates the Auditor add-in for analyzing the formulas in a spreadsheet. The Bsolver add-in calculates a formula where a given value for the result of the formula is desired. The Solver add-in determines the maximum or minimum value for a cell based on a set of constraints and adjustable cells.

Macros

With experience in using 1-2-3, the use of macros increases. Much of the power of 1-2-3 is really available to users of macros. This book introduces the process of building and using macros both at the simple and advanced levels. A method for automatically recording macro instructions is included.

Combining Information Between Worksheets

Many spreadsheet applications require movement of data from one worksheet to another or the combining of data from several worksheets into one worksheet. The process of using templates to create such "detail" worksheets and then combining information into a "summary" worksheet is covered. A method for linking worksheets in different files through the use of formulas is also presented.

Proven Materials

This book is based on proven materials that have been used in college and university classes as well as training seminars. More than 25,000 individuals have learned to use 1-2-3 utilizing materials on which this book is based. For example, the authors have been responsible for training more than 6,000 members of the Texas Society of CPAs employing materials from this book.

■ ORGANIZATION/FLEXIBILITY

The book is organized in a manner that takes the user through the fundamentals of Lotus 1-2-3 and then builds on the solid foundation to cover more advanced subjects. The book is useful for college courses, training classes, individual learning, and as a reference manual.

In Chapter 1, the Lotus 1-2-3 package is described and explained. Typical applications are presented. The process of loading the software package is explained. The various parts of the 1-2-3 worksheet screen are detailed along with methods to move around the worksheet. The meaning of the function keys is summarized. The process for exiting 1-2-3 is explained.

Chapter 2 gives a quick overview of the processes for creating, editing, printing, and saving a spreadsheet. The methods for using the 1-2-3 menu structure are explained and illustrated.

When you create spreadsheets, it is important to use good design principles. Chapter 3 explains how to design a spreadsheet properly.

Chapter 4 contains a step-by-step process for creating, building, and printing a spreadsheet. Operations included are: entering labels, numbers and formulas; copying numbers, formulas and labels; widening columns; inserting rows; entering headings; selecting formats for numeric data; saving and retrieving a spreadsheet; correcting rounding errors, and more. A method for completing "What-if" analysis is illustrated.

Chapter 5 discusses how to improve the appearance of a spreadsheet. Some of the topics covered are boldfacing text, changing the font size of text, creating a shadow box, changing the print orientation, and creating named styles.

A variety of useful Lotus 1-2-3 commands is presented in Chapter 6. Some of the topics include: keeping a cell constant in a formula; attaching, invoking, and detaching an add-in program; using SmartIcons; using the Auditor add-in program; using the File command; erasing cells; correcting cell errors; automatic formatting; moving cell contents; using the Undo feature; widening multiple columns; inserting and deleting columns, rows, and worksheets; aligning labels; creating page breaks; printing borders, headers and footers, and cell formulas; using the background printing feature; and protecting data. Other topics presented are: creating range names; checking the status of a worksheet; using the System command; viewing a worksheet before retrieving the worksheet file; freezing titles; creating windows; using the Backsolver and Solver add-in programs; recalculation of a worksheet; providing worksheet documentation; and suppressing zero values.

Numerous types of graphs can be prepared using 1-2-3. In Chapter 7, some graphics capabilities are covered, including bar graph, line graph, mixed graph (combined bar and line graphs), stacked-bar graph, pie graph, and XY graph. Other topics discussed are printing a graph, viewing the current graph, selecting a graph to view, deleting a named graph, and erasing graph files from the disk.

In Chapter 8, additional graphics capabilities are discussed. Included topics are creating a high-low-close-open graph, creating an area graph, specifying a 3-D effect for a graph, specifying a horizontal and vertical orientation, specifying the appearance of the graph frame, removing the scale indicator from a graph, group graphing, and displaying a graph in a window.

Chapter 9 discusses how to enhance the appearance of a graph. Topics include adding and removing a graph to/from a worksheet, editing a graphic, sizing and moving a graphic, and printing a worksheet and graph.

In Chapter 10, the process for building and using template worksheets is discussed. A template is a worksheet that is constructed and saved as a "shell" for the creation of worksheets at a later time containing the same formulas and/or text.

Sometimes it is useful to have more than one worksheet in a file. Chapter 11 includes a discussion of the use of multiple worksheets in a file and the three-dimensional capabilities. Topics incorporated are: adding worksheets to a file, moving between worksheets, copying information from one worksheet to other worksheets, and formatting data in multiple worksheets. The process of using multiple worksheet files at the same time is also presented.

Many practical applications of spreadsheets require that information be combined from one or more spreadsheets into one or more other spreadsheets. The process for consolidating information from one or several worksheets into a summary worksheet is illustrated in Chapter 12. Methods for linking worksheets in different files are also covered.

While 1-2-3 does not provide all the capabilities of a database management system, many database-like operations can be applied to data in a worksheet. Chapter 13 includes a discussion of sorting data, completing a query, and computing information based on a query. Chapter 14 contains the following topics: filling cells with data, creating data tables that can be used in decision-making situations, combining information from multiple database tables, and creating and graphing a frequency distribution.

There are many preprogrammed functions available in Lotus 1-2-3. In Chapter 15, most of the special functions available in 1-2-3 such as the functions for statistical analysis, financial analysis, date and time data, logical analysis, database operations, mathematical computations, special analyses such as lookup table calculations, and string functions are discussed and illustrated.

In many situations, the same steps are applied to the development of a worksheet each time it is used. For example, an organization may summarize the budget expenditures of three departments into one worksheet. In 1-2-3, a macro can be developed that instructs the computer to repeat the steps automatically rather than have the user enter the set of steps each time the spreadsheets are summarized. An introduction to the process of creating and using macros appears in Chapter 16. A method for recording macro keystrokes is discussed and illustrated. The concept of using a macro library file for storing macros that are used in many types of applications is presented.

Advanced macro commands and examples of using the commands are described in Chapter 17. Some types of macros illustrated are: sorting data, restricting data entry to specific cells, automatically executing macros, interactive macros, changing program flow and looping, and using subroutines. User-designed menus are also created.

Appendix A contains a list of SmartIcons available in Lotus 1-2-3 Release 3.4.

■ ACKNOWLEDGEMENTS

We would like to thank and express our appreciation to the many fine and talented individuals who have contributed to the completion of this book. Special thanks go to: Cristal D. Ewald, Iowa State University and Sheryl Rose.

No book is possible without the motivation and support of an editorial staff. Therefore, we wish to acknowledge with great appreciation the following people at boyd & fraser: Tom Walker, vice-president and publisher, for the opportunity to write this book and for his constant encouragement; Jim Edwards and Barbara Worth, for their keen assistance in the editing process; and the production staff for support in completing the book.

We are very appreciative of the personnel at Napier & Judd, Inc. who helped prepare this book. We acknowledge, with great appreciation the assistance provided by Nancy Onarheim, Joyce Sarahan, and Robyn Yahola in preparing and checking the many drafts of this book.

H. Albert Napier
Philip J. Judd
Houston, Texas

CHAPTER ONE

GETTING STARTED WITH LOTUS 1-2-3

OBJECTIVES

In this chapter, you will learn to:

- Define spreadsheets and the Lotus 1-2-3 program
- Determine hardware and software requirements
- Load the Lotus 1-2-3 program into the computer memory
- Identify the basic features of the 1-2-3 worksheet screen
- Move the cell pointer around the worksheet
- Identify the use of the function keys in Lotus 1-2-3
- Exit Lotus 1-2-3

■ CHAPTER OVERVIEW

This book assumes that you have little or no knowledge of Lotus 1-2-3. Chapter 1 introduces you to the capabilities of 1-2-3 and typical applications. The chapter explains the hardware requirements for using 1-2-3 and the process for loading the software into the memory of a personal computer; discusses the basic items that appear on the worksheet screen; defines the process of moving around the 1-2-3 worksheet; and presents an overview of the special functions associated with the function keys. Finally, the chapter specifies the process for exiting the software package.

■ DEFINING SPREADSHEETS AND THE LOTUS 1-2-3 PROGRAM

Lotus 1-2-3 is an integrated software package. The term "integrated" means that Lotus has more than one basic capability. Lotus 1-2-3 can be used for creating spreadsheets (also referred to as worksheets), creating graphs, and manipulating information within and between spreadsheets. In this book, it is assumed that you are using Lotus 1-2-3 Release 3.4. However, if you are using an earlier version of Lotus 1-2-3, much of the material presented in this book is still applicable.

An example of a worksheet appears in Figure 1-1. The next chapter shows you how to create and print a spreadsheet. Figure 1-2 is a bar graph that includes some information from the worksheet in Figure 1-1. You will create this graph in Chapter 7.

Figure 1-1

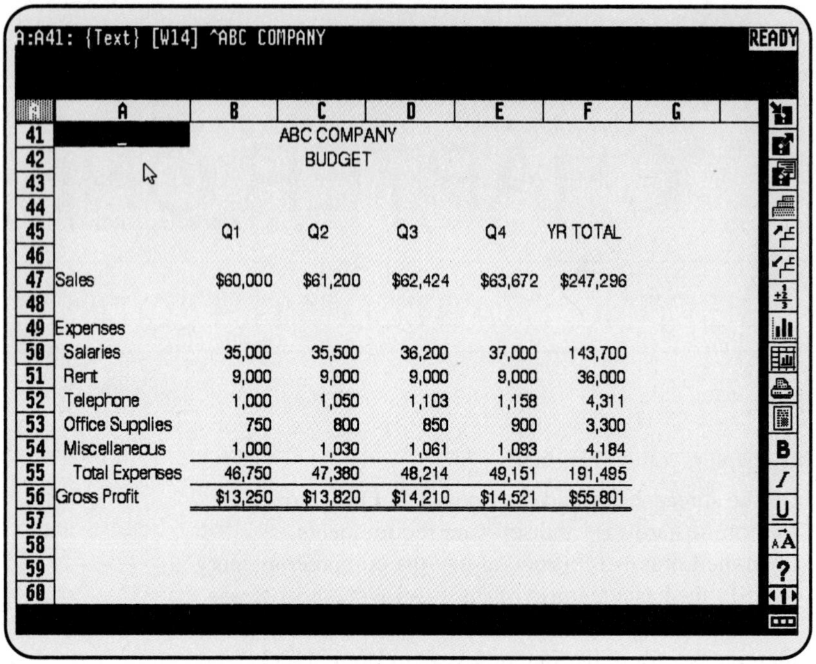

	A	B	C	D	E	F	G
41			ABC COMPANY				
42			BUDGET				
43							
44							
45		Q1	Q2	Q3	Q4	YR TOTAL	
46							
47	Sales	$60,000	$61,200	$62,424	$63,672	$247,296	
48							
49	Expenses						
50	Salaries	35,000	35,500	36,200	37,000	143,700	
51	Rent	9,000	9,000	9,000	9,000	36,000	
52	Telephone	1,000	1,050	1,103	1,158	4,311	
53	Office Supplies	750	800	850	900	3,300	
54	Miscellaneous	1,000	1,030	1,061	1,093	4,184	
55	Total Expenses	46,750	47,380	48,214	49,151	191,495	
56	Gross Profit	$13,250	$13,820	$14,210	$14,521	$55,801	
57							
58							
59							
60							

`A:A41: {Text} [W14] ^ABC COMPANY`   `READY`

Up to six items such as SALES can appear on a graph. Lotus 1-2-3 has seven types of graphs available: bar, line, XY, stacked-bar, pie, high-low-close-open, and mixed graphs.

Figure 1-2

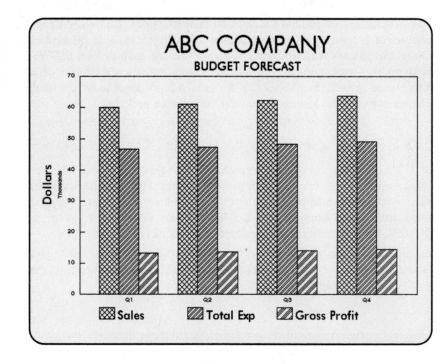

Lotus 1-2-3 can be used to perform operations on a worksheet. For example, information in a worksheet can be sorted by various criteria. Figure 1-3 is a worksheet that has information about salaries for a group of individuals. The information is not sorted in any particular order.

Figure 1-3

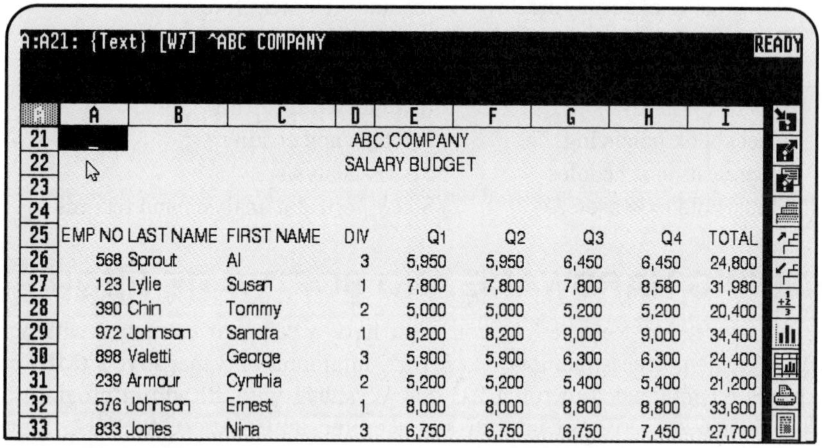

```
A:A21: {Text} [W7] ^ABC COMPANY                                          READY
```

	A	B	C	D	E	F	G	H	I
21					ABC COMPANY				
22					SALARY BUDGET				
23									
24									
25	EMP NO	LAST NAME	FIRST NAME	DIV	Q1	Q2	Q3	Q4	TOTAL
26	568	Sprout	Al	3	5,950	5,950	6,450	6,450	24,800
27	123	Lylie	Susan	1	7,800	7,800	7,800	8,580	31,980
28	390	Chin	Tommy	2	5,000	5,000	5,200	5,200	20,400
29	972	Johnson	Sandra	1	8,200	8,200	9,000	9,000	34,400
30	898	Valetti	George	3	5,900	5,900	6,300	6,300	24,400
31	239	Armour	Cynthia	2	5,200	5,200	5,400	5,400	21,200
32	576	Johnson	Ernest	1	8,000	8,000	8,800	8,800	33,600
33	833	Jones	Nina	3	6,750	6,750	6,750	7,450	27,700

Sometimes it is desirable to sort the information in a particular order. In Figure 1-4, the data that appear in Figure 1-3 have been sorted in ascending order by division number.

Figure 1-4

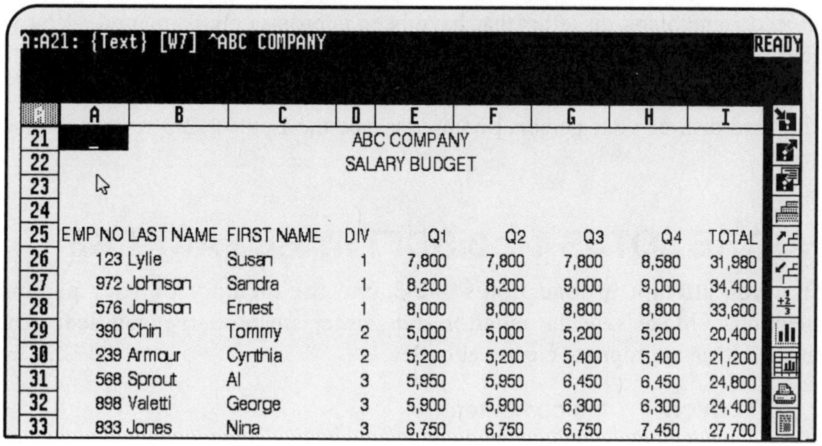

```
A:A21: {Text} [W7] ^ABC COMPANY                                          READY
```

	A	B	C	D	E	F	G	H	I
21					ABC COMPANY				
22					SALARY BUDGET				
23									
24									
25	EMP NO	LAST NAME	FIRST NAME	DIV	Q1	Q2	Q3	Q4	TOTAL
26	123	Lylie	Susan	1	7,800	7,800	7,800	8,580	31,980
27	972	Johnson	Sandra	1	8,200	8,200	9,000	9,000	34,400
28	576	Johnson	Ernest	1	8,000	8,000	8,800	8,800	33,600
29	390	Chin	Tommy	2	5,000	5,000	5,200	5,200	20,400
30	239	Armour	Cynthia	2	5,200	5,200	5,400	5,400	21,200
31	568	Sprout	Al	3	5,950	5,950	6,450	6,450	24,800
32	898	Valetti	George	3	5,900	5,900	6,300	6,300	24,400
33	833	Jones	Nina	3	6,750	6,750	6,750	7,450	27,700

You will learn the process for sorting the data in Chapter 13.

Typical Applications

Lotus 1-2-3 is used in many organizations as well as by individuals. Some examples of Lotus 1-2-3 applications include:

Advertising expense forecasts	Income statement forecasts
Balance sheet forecasts	Income tax projections
Budgets	Income tax records
Cash flow analysis	Inventory forecasting
Checkbook balancing	Job bids and costing
Depreciation schedules	Sports analysis
Household expenses	Stock portfolio analysis and records

■ DETERMINING HARDWARE AND SOFTWARE REQUIREMENTS

To run Lotus 1-2-3 Release 3.4, you must have a personal computer with a minimum of 1 megabyte (MB) of random access memory (RAM). A minimum of 3 megabytes (MB) of random access memory (RAM) is recommended to run 1-2-3 and Wysiwyg with all add-in programs; DOS 3.0 and higher; at least 5 megabytes (MB) of hard disk space; and an EGA, VGA, XGA, Super VGA, high resolution CGA, or high resolution Hercules adapter monitor.

A printer is necessary. A dot matrix printer can print spreadsheets as well as graphs. Most laser printers provide a full range of graphics printing capabilities. If you want to print high quality graphics, you will need a plotter.

You need some blank diskettes that have been appropriately formatted. You will use these diskettes to store spreadsheet and graph files so you can use them at a later time.

You must have the Lotus 1-2-3 diskettes on which the software is stored. To install the 1-2-3 software on the hard disk of your personal computer, see the Lotus 1-2-3 reference manual that came with your software.

■ LOADING THE LOTUS 1-2-3 SOFTWARE PACKAGE

Before you attempt to load Lotus 1-2-3 into the memory of your personal computer, check all connections. Make sure the monitor and printer are properly installed. The power cord should be connected to an appropriate electrical outlet.

Turn on   the computer

Assuming that 1-2-3 Release 3.4 is installed in the directory 123R34 on the C drive, use the following steps to load the software.

Type   cd\123R34   (cd is a DOS command used to make the 123R34
                                        directory the active directory)

Press   ←Enter

Type   Lotus

Press   ←Enter

In many situations, you may have a menu from which to select 1-2-3 Release 3.4 or some other process for invoking the use of 1-2-3 Release 3.4. In a few seconds your screen will look like Figure 1-5.

Figure 1-5

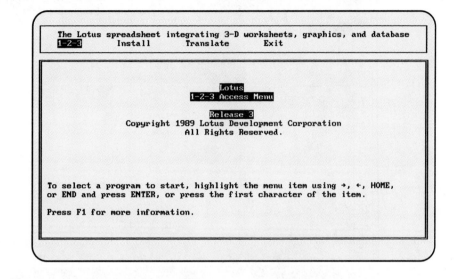

```
┌──────────────────────────────────────────────────────────────┐
│  The Lotus spreadsheet integrating 3-D worksheets, graphics, and database │
│  1-2-3        Install        Translate        Exit            │
├──────────────────────────────────────────────────────────────┤
│                                                                │
│                          Lotus                                 │
│                    1-2-3 Access Menu                           │
│                                                                │
│                        Release 3                               │
│            Copyright 1989 Lotus Development Corporation         │
│                    All Rights Reserved.                        │
│                                                                │
│                                                                │
│  To select a program to start, highlight the menu item using →, ←, HOME, │
│  or END and press ENTER, or press the first character of the item. │
│                                                                │
│  Press F1 for more information.                                │
│                                                                │
└──────────────────────────────────────────────────────────────┘
```

The menu at the top of the screen has the choices of 1-2-3, Install, Translate, and Exit. Notice that the characters 1-2-3 are highlighted with a rectangle that is referred to as a menu pointer. Above 1-2-3 appears the message "The Lotus spreadsheet integrating 3-D worksheets, graphics, and database." This indicates that you will enter the Lotus 1-2-3 program if you select the 1-2-3 option from the menu.

To select the The Lotus spreadsheet integrating 3-D worksheets, graphics, and database option:

Press   `←Enter`

A message with copyright and licensing information briefly appears on the screen. In another few seconds, a blank worksheet like the one in Figure 1-6 appears on your screen.

Figure 1-6

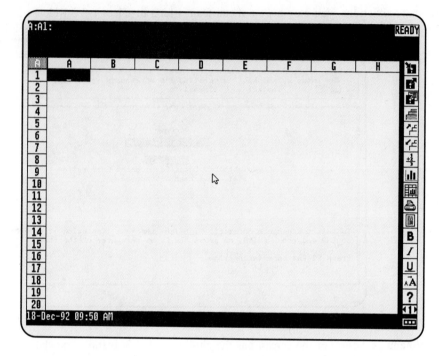

■ IDENTIFYING FEATURES OF THE LOTUS 1-2-3 WORKSHEET SCREEN

Figure 1-6 is the standard form of the initial **worksheet** used by Lotus 1-2-3. In some situations, a worksheet is referred to as a **spreadsheet**. The terms **worksheet** and **spreadsheet** are used interchangeably in this book. A worksheet is a gridlike structure consisting of rows and columns.

Figure 1-7 is a worksheet screen with the Lotus 1-2-3 main menu visible across the top.

Figure 1-7

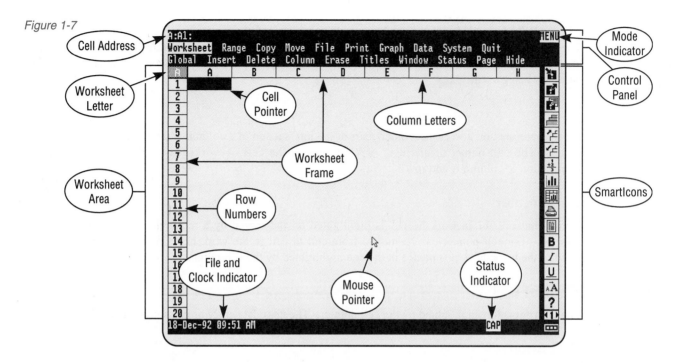

This section describes the various items that appear on the worksheet screen in Figure 1-7.

Worksheet Letter

A maximum of 256 worksheets can be used at one time. The worksheets are labeled A through Z, AA through AZ, BA through BZ and so forth, until the letter IV is reached. In Figure 1-7, the **worksheet letter** is A. It appears at the intersection of the horizontal and vertical borders near the top left corner of the screen. The use of multiple worksheets is discussed in Chapter 11.

Worksheet Frame

Above and to the left of the worksheet is the **worksheet frame**. This portion of the worksheet includes the row number and column letter borders.

Column Letters

Across the top border of the worksheet are the letters A through H. These are the **column letters**. There are 256 columns in the worksheet. The columns are identified with the letters A through Z, AA through AZ, BA through BZ, and so forth until the letters IV are reached.

Row Numbers

On the left border of the worksheet are numbers called **row numbers**. Note that 20 rows appear on the screen. A total of 8,192 rows are available in the worksheet.

Worksheet Area

The **worksheet area** includes: (1) the column letters, (2) the row numbers, and (3) the blank area below and to the right of these borders. The worksheet area displays only that portion of the worksheet that is currently being used.

Cell

A **cell** is the area on a worksheet that occurs at the intersection of a column and a row. Data are stored in a cell. The cell name, or address, A:A1, refers to the cell in worksheet A that is located at the intersection of column A and row 1.

Cell Pointer

Notice that cell A1 in worksheet A is highlighted on the screen by a rectangle referred to as the **cell pointer**. The cell pointer can be moved from cell to cell in the worksheet. Whenever information is input to the worksheet, it is placed in the cell highlighted by the cell pointer.

Current Cell

The **current cell** is highlighted by the cell pointer. The next data entry or operation affects this cell.

Cell Address

The location of a cell is called the **cell address**. A cell address is defined by a column letter followed by a row number. For example, A:B2 is the cell address for the cell that occurs at the intersection of column B and row 2 in worksheet A.

Mouse Pointer

The **mouse pointer** is usually an arrow. Its position on your screen changes when you move the mouse.

Control Panel

Above the worksheet at the top of the screen is an area called the **control panel**. The control panel consists of three lines. The first line has the cell address for the current cell and the contents of the cell. Notice the cell address at the top left corner of the screen. Assuming you have a blank worksheet and the cell pointer is in cell A:A1, the cell address area on the first line of the control panel contains A:A1:. Nothing appears to the right of A:A1:, because no data have been entered in the cell.

When the contents of a cell are being created or edited, the second line of the control panel displays the current data. As shown in Figure 1-7, it is also used to display the Lotus 1-2-3 menus.

The third line of the control panel will display either a submenu or a one-line description of the command item currently highlighted on the second line of the control panel.

Even though the control panel always includes the worksheet letter (e.g., A:H1: or D:B4:), in most cases this book refers to the cell address appearing in the control panel using only the column and row location (e.g., H1 or B4).

Mode Indicator

The **mode indicator** appears at the top right corner of the first line in the control panel. It indicates the current operating mode. For example, it may say READY, indicating that 1-2-3 is ready for you to input information or create a formula. It may say MENU, indicating that a menu appears in the control panel and you may make a selection from the menu.

Status Indicator

The **status indicator** specifies the condition of certain keys or of the program. For example, if you press the CAPS LOCK key, the characters CAP will appear in the right corner below the worksheet indicating that all alphabetic characters subsequently used are automatically capitalized. To remove the CAP specification, you press the CAPS LOCK key again and the CAP indicator no longer appears on the screen.

File and Clock Indicators

At the bottom left corner of the screen the **file** and **clock** indicators appear. Assuming the current date and time have been entered properly, the current date and time should appear. Lotus 1-2-3 has an option that allows you to suppress the clock indicator from view. If the current file has been saved, or if the current file has been retrieved, the file name will appear instead of the date and time. Note that in this book the file name, date and time will not appear in the screen illustrations.

SmartIcons

Located to the right of the worksheet area is the **SmartIcon palette**. The palette contains a set of **SmartIcons**. The SmartIcons are used to improve your efficiency as you use 1-2-3. The number at the bottom right corner of your screen indicates the current SmartIcon palette being used. There are a total of eight SmartIcon palettes available. You can select a SmartIcon using a mouse or the keyboard. You will learn more about this feature in Chapter 2.

■ MOVING THROUGH THE WORKSHEET

As mentioned earlier in this chapter, the cell pointer is the highlighted rectangle on the screen that indicates the location on the worksheet. The cell address of the cell pointer's location always appears in the top left corner of the screen. This section discusses and illustrates methods to move the cell pointer through the worksheet.

Using Pointer-Movement Keys or a Mouse to Move the Cell Pointer

The cursor movement keys, which are the basic keys used to move the cell pointer from cell to cell on the worksheet, are located on the right side of the keyboard (see Figure 1-8). The cursor movement keys are placed on the numeric keypad (sometimes called "the ten key") and/or they may be in a separate location as depicted in Figure 1-8. In Lotus 1-2-3 Release 3.4, these keys are referred to as the **pointer-movement keys**.

A mouse can also be used to move the cell pointer. A **mouse** is an optional piece of hardware connected to your computer. With a mouse, you can perform various operations otherwise done with the keyboard. The mouse pointer, usually represented by a small arrow on the screen, is controlled by the mouse. The mouse pointer moves on the screen in the same direction and the same distance as your hand moves the mouse.

In This Book

When referring to a mouse operation, **[click]** means to press a mouse button and then release it. **[Drag]** means to press and hold the mouse button down and then move the mouse. When the instructions for using a mouse tell you to press the mouse button, they assume the left mouse button. The alternate mouse button refers to the right mouse button. If you switch the mouse buttons in the Install process, press the right mouse button when the instructions refer to the mouse button, and press the left mouse button when the instructions refer to the alternate mouse button.

Figure 1-8

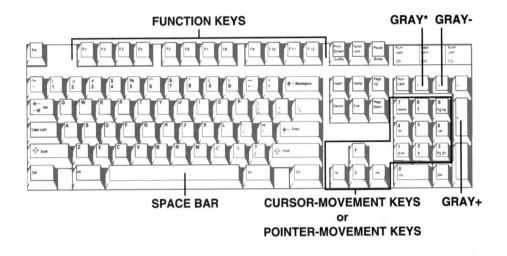

FUNCTION KEYS   GRAY* GRAY-

SPACE BAR   CURSOR-MOVEMENT KEYS   GRAY+
                           or
                  POINTER-MOVEMENT KEYS

In This Book

The use of the keyboard method and the mouse method are shown in two columns. The directions in the left column are for the keyboard method. They appear in normal type. The instructions for using the mouse appear in the second column in *italics*.

To illustrate the use of the pointer-movement keys:

Locate	the pointer-movement keys	*Move*	*the mouse pointer to cell H1*
Press	the [→] key seven times	*Click*	*the mouse button*

As shown in Figure 1-9, the cell pointer is now in cell H1. This fact is indicated on the first line of the control panel. The process of moving around the screen is sometimes called scrolling.

Figure 1-9

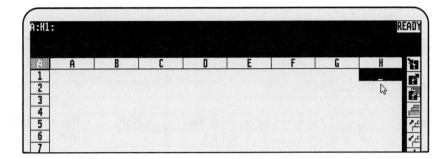

To move the cell pointer to cell I1:

Press   the → key one time

Move   *the mouse pointer to the left or right arrow beside the palette number at the bottom right corner of the screen*

Click   *the mouse button until the pointer-movement SmartIcons appear*

Move   *the mouse pointer to the ➡ SmartIcon*

Click   *the mouse button*

As illustrated in Figure 1-10, the cell pointer has been moved to column I and column A has disappeared. 1-2-3 can only display a total of 72 characters across the screen.

Figure 1-10

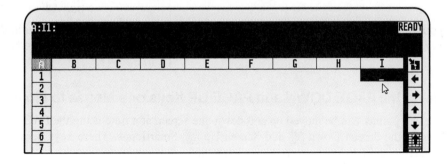

To move to cell A1:

Locate	the ⟵ key
Press	the ⟵ key eight times until the cell pointer appears in cell A1

If you press the ⟵ key too many times, you will hear a "beep" sound indicating that you are trying to move to the left of column A. The "beep" sound means that you are trying to perform some type of operation that is not permitted at that point.

Move	*the mouse pointer to the* ⟵ *SmartIcon*
Click	*the mouse button eight times until the cell pointer appears in cell A1*

If you click the ⟵ *SmartIcon too many times, you will hear a "beep" sound indicating that you are trying to move to the left of column A. The "beep" sound means that you are trying to perform some type of operation that is not permitted at that point.*

To move the cell pointer rapidly:

Locate	the ↓ key
Press	the ↓ key and hold it down

Move	*the mouse pointer to the* ↓ *SmartIcon*
Press	*and hold down the mouse button*

After the cell pointer has moved down 20 or 30 rows, stop pressing the ↓ key or release the mouse button. To return the cell pointer to cell A1:

Locate	the ↑ key
Press	the ↑ key until the cell pointer appears in cell A1

You hear a "beep" sound if you press the ↑ key after the cell pointer appears in cell A1.

Move	*the mouse pointer to the* ↑ *SmartIcon*
Press	*and hold down the mouse button until the cell pointer appears in cell A1*

You hear a "beep" sound if you press the ↑ *SmartIcon after the cell pointer appears in cell A1.*

Using the PAGE DOWN and PAGE UP Keys or a Mouse to Move the Cell Pointer

The cell pointer can be moved up and down one screen at a time using the PAGE DOWN and PAGE UP keys or the Screen Down ▦ and Screen Up ▦ SmartIcons. These keys permit you to move the cell pointer up and down the screen 20 rows at a time.

To use the PAGE DOWN key or the Screen Down ▦ SmartIcon:

Locate	the Page Down key
Press	Page Down

Move	*the mouse pointer to the Screen Down* ▦ *SmartIcon*
Click	*the mouse button*

Assuming that the cell pointer was in cell A1 before you pressed the PAGE DOWN key or clicked the Screen Down 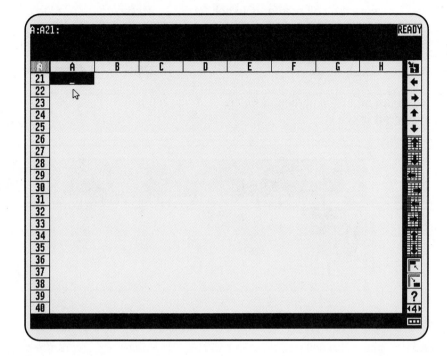 SmartIcon, the cell pointer is now in cell A21. See Figure 1-11. If the cell pointer was not in cell A1, then the cell pointer has now moved 20 rows down in the worksheet from the cell it was in before you pressed the PAGE DOWN key or clicked the Screen Down SmartIcon.

Figure 1-11

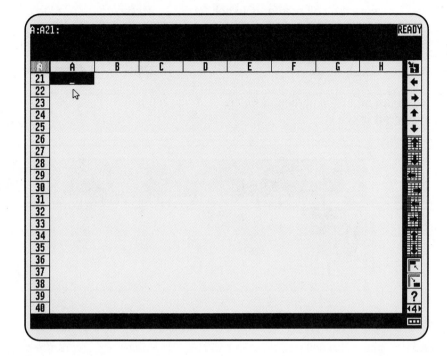

To use the PAGE UP key or Screen Up SmartIcon:

Locate	the `Page Up` key	
Press	`Page Up`	

Move	*the mouse pointer to the Screen Up SmartIcon*
Click	*the mouse button*

Assuming that the cell pointer was in cell A21 before you pressed the PAGE UP key or clicked the Screen Up SmartIcon, the cell pointer should now be in cell A1.

Using the TAB Key or the Mouse to Move the Cell Pointer

The cell pointer can be moved to the right or left one screen at a time using the TAB key or clicking Tab Left or Tab Right SmartIcons.

To move the cell pointer one screen to the right:

Make	sure the cell pointer is in cell A1	*Make*	*sure the cell pointer is in cell A1*
Locate	the Tab⇆ key	*Move*	*the mouse pointer to the Tab Right ▦ SmartIcon*
Press	Tab⇆	*Click*	*the mouse button*

As illustrated in the top portion of Figure 1-12, the cell pointer has been moved to the right one screen and it appears in cell I1.

Figure 1-12

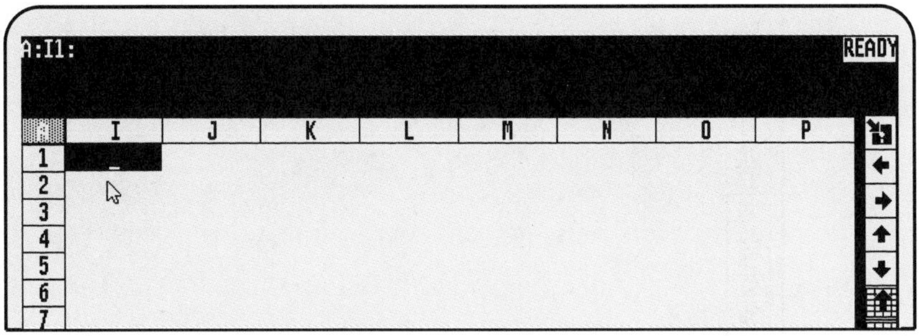

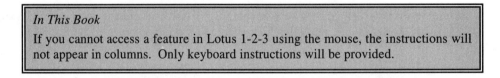

To move the cell pointer one screen to the left:

Make	sure the cell pointer is in cell I1	*Make*	*sure the cell pointer is in cell I1*
Locate	the Tab⇆ key	*Move*	*the mouse pointer to the Tab Left ▦ SmartIcon*
Press	the Shift key and hold it down, then	*Click*	*the mouse button*
Press	Tab⇆		

The cell pointer has been moved to cell A1 or one screen to the left. The SHIFT key is marked with the word Shift. There are two shift keys on a keyboard. Either one can be used.

> *In This Book*
> If you cannot access a feature in Lotus 1-2-3 using the mouse, the instructions will not appear in columns. Only keyboard instructions will be provided.

Another way to move the cell pointer one screen to the right or left is:

Make	sure the cell pointer is in cell A1
Locate	the Ctrl key

Press   the ⌨Ctrl⌨ key and hold it down, then
Press   ⌨→⌨

The cell pointer should now be in cell I1. To return to cell A1:

Press   the ⌨Ctrl⌨ key and hold it down, then
Press   ⌨←⌨

Using the GoTo Key (the F5 Function Key) or the GoTo SmartIcon to Move the Cell Pointer

Sometimes it is necessary to move the cell pointer to a particular cell in the worksheet. For example, to move the cursor to cell IV8192:

Make	sure the cell pointer is in cell A1	*Make*	*sure the cell pointer is in cell A1*
Locate	the ⌨F5⌨ function key (The ⌨F5⌨ key is at the top of the keyboard or on the left side of the keyboard.)	*Move*	*the mouse pointer to the left or right arrow beside the palette number*
Press	⌨F5⌨	*Click*	*the mouse button until the GoTo SmartIcon 🚗 appears*
		Move	*the mouse pointer to the 🚗 SmartIcon*
		Click	*the mouse button*

As displayed in the top portion of Figure 1-13, the screen now has a message in the control panel prompting you to enter the desired cell address.

Figure 1-13

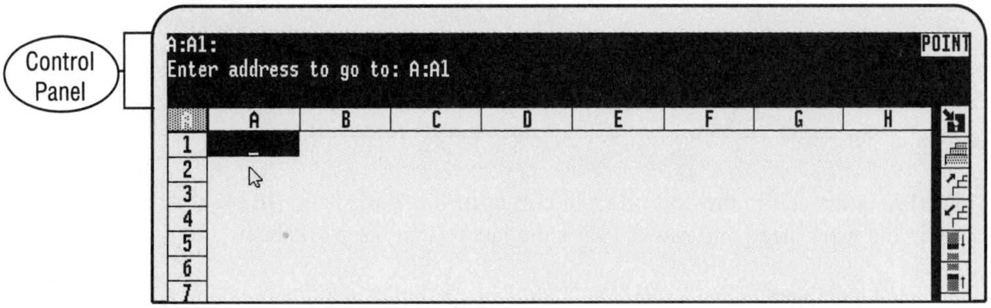

Control Panel

```
A:A1:                                              POINT
Enter address to go to: A:A1

     A      B      C      D      E      F      G      H
 1   _
 2    ▷
 3
 4
 5
 6
 7
```

| Type | IV8192 | *Type* | *IV8192* |

Note that lowercase or uppercase letters can be used when you type the cell address.

The top part of Figure 1-14 depicts the entering of cell address IV8192.

Figure 1-14

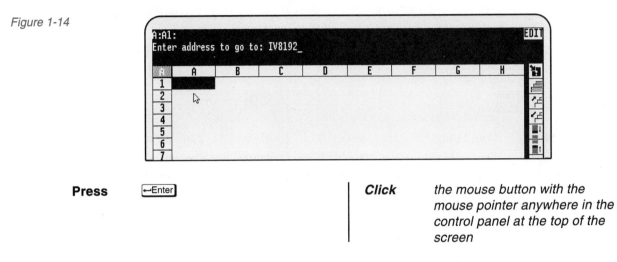

| **Press** | ⏎Enter | ***Click*** | *the mouse button with the mouse pointer anywhere in the control panel at the top of the screen* |

As illustrated in the top part of Figure 1-15, the cell pointer is in cell IV8192.

Figure 1-15

Cell IV8192 is the cell in the bottom right corner of the worksheet. In other words, column IV is the last column in the worksheet, and row 8,192 is the last row in the worksheet.

Using the HOME Key or the Home SmartIcon to Move the Cell Pointer

The cell pointer can be moved to the top left corner of the worksheet by pressing the HOME key or clicking the Home [K] SmartIcon.

To return the cell pointer to the top left corner of the worksheet:

Locate	the Home key	**Move**	the mouse pointer to the left or right arrow beside the palette number
Press	Home	**Click**	the mouse button until the Home ⬚ SmartIcon appears
		Move	the mouse pointer to the ⬚ SmartIcon
		Click	the mouse button

The cell pointer is now in cell A1.

■ IDENTIFYING THE FUNCTION KEYS IN LOTUS 1-2-3

The **function keys** have been "programmed" in Lotus 1-2-3 to perform specific operations. One of these operations is the GoTo function, associated with the F5 key, which was presented earlier in this chapter.

The 1-2-3 HELP system allows you to access an on-line reference for 1-2-3 features. To access the Help system:

Press	F1	**Move**	the mouse pointer to the Help ? SmartIcon
		Click	the mouse button

To get assistance on specific topics, choose one of the menu options listed on the screen. Use the arrow keys to move the pointer to the desired option. When the desired option is highlighted, press the ←Enter key.

If you are using a mouse, move the mouse pointer to the desired option and click the mouse button.

To leave the Help system and return to the worksheet currently in use:

Press	Esc	**Click**	the alternate mouse button

A brief description of the operations programmed for all the function keys follows.

F1: **Help**   Display the Help screens that are available in Lotus 1-2-3
F2: **Edit**   Switch to/from EDIT mode for current entry
F3: **Name**   Display menu of names depending on what command is being used

F4:	**Abs**	Make/Unmake cell address "absolute" in a formula or specify a range of cells prior to issuing a command
F5:	**GoTo**	Move the cell pointer to a particular cell in a worksheet
F6:	**Window**	Move the cell pointer when "windows" appear on the screen
F7:	**Query**	Repeat most recent Data Query operation
F8:	**Table**	Repeat most recent Data Table operation
F9:	**Calc**	Recalculate worksheet values
F10:	**Graph**	Draw graph on screen using the most recent graph specifications
Alt F1:	**Compose**	Use in conjunction with keystrokes to input characters that are not on the standard keyboard
Alt F2:	**Record**	Turn STEP mode on or off or use contents of the record buffer
Alt F3:	**Run**	Select a macro to process
Alt F4:	**UNDO**	Cancel any changes made since 1-2-3 was last in READY mode
Alt F6:	**Zoom**	Enlarges the current window or reduces it to its original size
Alt F7:	**APP1**	Start an available add-in application assigned to the key or access SmartIcon palette
Alt F8:	**APP2**	Start an available add-in application assigned to the key
Alt F9:	**APP3**	Start an available add-in application assigned to the key
Alt F10:	**Addin**	Display menu of available add-in applications

Many of these function keys will be used in subsequent chapters.

■ EXITING LOTUS 1-2-3

To quit using 1-2-3, you must use the Lotus 1-2-3 menu structure. The menu structure is explained in more detail in the next chapter.

To initiate the use of the menu structure:

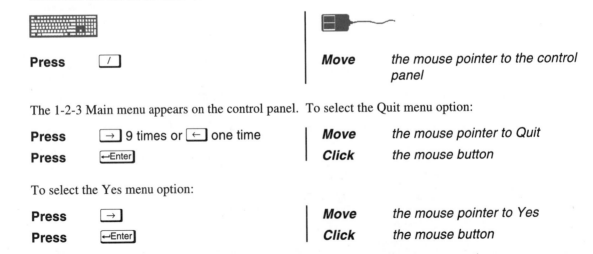

Press   /

Move   *the mouse pointer to the control panel*

The 1-2-3 Main menu appears on the control panel. To select the Quit menu option:

Press   → 9 times or ← one time

Press   ←Enter

Move   *the mouse pointer to Quit*

Click   *the mouse button*

To select the Yes menu option:

Press   →

Press   ←Enter

Move   *the mouse pointer to Yes*

Click   *the mouse button*

You will need to select Yes twice if you have entered data into the current worksheet.

To select the Exit option on the Lotus 1-2-3 Access Menu:

Press	$\boxed{\rightarrow}$ three times or $\boxed{\leftarrow}$ one time
Press	$\boxed{\leftarrow\text{Enter}}$

You should now have a familiar prompt or menu on the screen.

SUMMARY

This chapter presented an overview of Lotus 1-2-3. Lotus 1-2-3 is often used for business, government, and personal applications. Lotus 1-2-3 can be executed on IBM or IBM-compatible PCs. The actual Lotus 1-2-3 software is on a set of diskettes. The software can be loaded into the memory of your personal computer by reading from a hard disk. The key items on the worksheet screen are the worksheet letter, worksheet frame, column letters, row numbers, worksheet area, cells, cell pointer, current cell, cell address, mouse pointer, control panel, mode indicator, status indicator, file and clock indicators, and SmartIcon palette. Move the cell pointer around the worksheet by using the arrow keys, the PAGE DOWN and PAGE UP keys, the TAB key, the F5 function key, and a mouse. A set of function keys (F1 through F10) is preprogrammed in Lotus 1-2-3 to perform specific operations such as moving the cell pointer to a specific cell in a worksheet.

KEY CONCEPTS

Cell	Mouse
Cell address	Mouse pointer
Cell pointer	Pointer-movement keys
Clock indicator	Row numbers
Column letters	SmartIcon
Control panel	SmartIcon palette
Current cell	Software requirements for 1-2-3
Escape $\boxed{\text{Esc}}$ key	Spreadsheet
File indicator	Status indicator
Function keys	Worksheet
GoTo $\boxed{\text{F5}}$ key	Worksheet area
Hardware requirements for 1-2-3	Worksheet frame
Help $\boxed{\text{F1}}$ key	Worksheet letter
Mode indicator	

EXERCISE 1

INSTRUCTIONS: Answer the following questions in the space provided.

1. Define the following terms:

a. Worksheet letter _____

_____

b. Column letters _____

_____

c. Row numbers _____

_____

d. Cell _____

_____

e. Cell pointer _____

_____

f. Current cell _____

_____

g. Cell address _____

_____

h. Control panel _____

_____

i. Mode indicator _____

_____

j Status indicator _____

_____

k. Clock indicator _____

_____

l. File indicator _____

_____

m. Worksheet area _____

_____

n. SmartIcon _____

_____

o. Mouse pointer _____

_____

p. Mouse _____

_____

q. SmartIcon palette _____

_____

r. Worksheet frame _____

_____

2. Describe the purpose of using the function keys F1 through F10. _____

_____

_____

_____

3. Describe the value of using SmartIcons. _____

_____

_____

_____

EXERCISE 2

INSTRUCTIONS: Identify the circles and enclosed items on the worksheet in Figure 1-16.

Figure 1-16

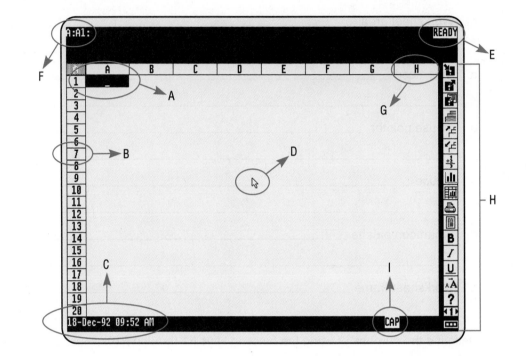

EXERCISE 3

INSTRUCTIONS: Initiate the use of Lotus 1-2-3.

Exit from Lotus 1-2-3 using the keyboard method.

EXERCISE 4

INSTRUCTIONS: Initiate the use of Lotus 1-2-3.

Exit from Lotus 1-2-3 using a mouse.

CHAPTER TWO

QUICK START FOR LOTUS 1-2-3

OBJECTIVES

In this chapter, you will learn to:
- Create a simple spreadsheet
- Edit a spreadsheet
- Use the Lotus 1-2-3 menu structure
- Print a spreadsheet
- Save a spreadsheet
- Erase a spreadsheet
- Retrieve a spreadsheet
- Exit Lotus 1-2-3

■ CHAPTER OVERVIEW

When you create a spreadsheet using Lotus 1-2-3, you usually go through the following steps:

1. Access the 1-2-3 software.
2. Create a spreadsheet by keying in the data.
3. Make modifications or changes to the spreadsheet.
4. Print the spreadsheet.
5. Save the spreadsheet in a file on a disk.

In other situations, you may retrieve an existing spreadsheet from a disk and make changes to it on the screen. After completing the changes, you save the document again. You may also print it.

When you are finished using one spreadsheet, you need to erase the material on your screen before you start working on another spreadsheet. Finally, you must exit the Lotus 1-2-3 software when you are finished using the software.

In this chapter, you are given a quick overview of the processes of creating, editing, printing, and saving a spreadsheet. You are also introduced to the process of erasing the spreadsheet on your screen. You will retrieve a spreadsheet from a file on a disk, make some changes, and save the document again. The procedure for exiting 1-2-3 is also presented.

■ CREATING A SIMPLE SPREADSHEET

Access the Lotus 1-2-3 software on your computer. If you are unfamiliar with this task, refer to Chapter 1. In this exercise, you will create the spreadsheet in Figure 2-1.

Figure 2-1

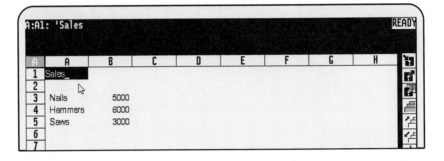

In This Book

To save space, the symbols representing the keyboard and mouse are omitted in the remainder of the book. The directions remain in the same columns. The directions in the left column are for the keyboard method. They appear in normal type. The directions in the second column are for using the mouse. They appear in *italic* type.

To enter information in cell A1:

Make	sure the cell pointer is in cell A1	***Move***	*the mouse pointer to cell A1*
Type	Sales	***Click***	*the mouse button*
		Type	*Sales*

See the top part of Figure 2-2. The word Sales appears on the second line of the control panel. Notice that when you type the first character, the word LABEL appears in the mode indicator specifying that a label is being entered.

Figure 2-2

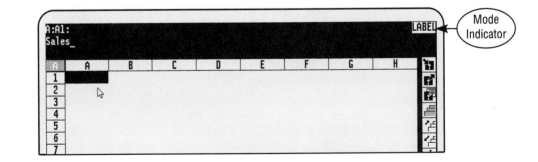

To accept the information in cell A1:

| **Press** | ←Enter | | *Click* | *the mouse button* |

See the top part of Figure 2-3. The word Sales appears in cell A1.

Figure 2-3

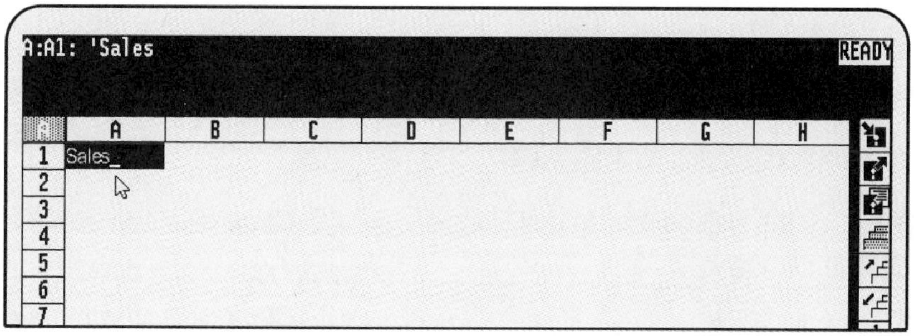

```
A:A1: 'Sales                                                    READY

        A       B       C       D       E       F       G       H
   1  Sales_
   2        ▷
   3
   4
   5
   6
   7
```

Note that all labels are **left aligned** in a cell. Left aligned means that the characters begin at the leftmost position of the cell. When a number is entered, the word VALUE appears in the mode indicator and the number is **right aligned**. That is, the number appears in the rightmost portion of the cell. Notice that the characters **'Sales** are visible next to the cell address A1: on the first line of the control panel. The **'** is one of the symbols that means **label** in 1-2-3, and **Sales** is the information stored in cell A1.

To place the labels Nails and Hammers in cells A3 and A4:

| **Move** | the cell pointer to cell A3 | | *Move* | *the mouse pointer to cell A3* |
| | | | *Click* | *the mouse button* |

To indent the product names two spaces:

Press	the space bar twice		*Press*	*the space bar twice*
Type	Nails		*Type*	*Nails*
Press	←Enter		*Click*	*the mouse button*
Move	the cell pointer to cell A4		*Move*	*the mouse pointer to cell A4*
Press	the space bar twice		*Click*	*the mouse button*
Type	Hammers		*Press*	*the space bar twice*
Press	←Enter		*Type*	*Hammers*
			Click	*the mouse button*

In This Book
To select a specific cell using a mouse, you have been instructed to move the mouse pointer to the cell and then click the mouse button. For the remainder of the book, these two steps are combined by asking you to click on the cell.

To enter the sales amount for Nails:

Move	the cell pointer to cell B3		***Click***	*on cell B3*
Type	4000		***Type***	*4000*

Because 4000 is numeric, it is interpreted by Lotus 1-2-3 as a **value**. The mode indicator displays the word VALUE. To enter the number:

Press	⏎Enter		***Click***	*the mouse button*

To input the sales value for Hammers:

Move	the cell pointer to cell B4		***Click***	*on cell B4*
Type	6000		***Type***	*6000*
Press	⏎Enter		***Click***	*the mouse button*

Your screen should look like Figure 2-4.

Figure 2-4

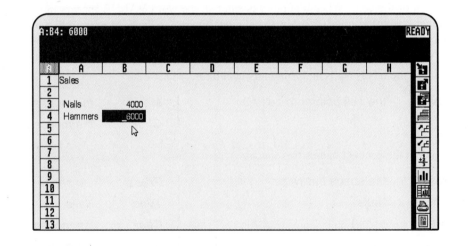

■ EDITING A SPREADSHEET

Suppose the sales value for Nails should have been 5000. To change the number:

Move	the cell pointer to cell B3		***Click***	*on cell B3*
Type	5000		***Type***	*5000*
Press	⏎Enter		***Click***	*the mouse button*

The sales value for Nails is changed. Your screen should look like Figure 2-5.

Figure 2-5

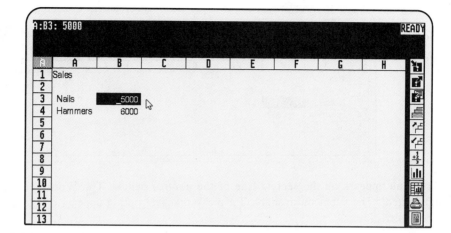

Additional editing methods are presented in Chapter 6.

> *User Tip*
>
> The F2 function key is often referred to as the EDIT key. When you press the F2 key, a cursor appears at the end of the entry in the control panel. The left and right pointer-movement keys as well as the HOME and END keys can be used to move the cursor to various characters in an entry. To delete a character, move the cursor under the character you wish to delete and then press the DELETE key. You can also delete a character by placing the cursor to the right of the character you wish to delete and then press the BACKSPACE key. To insert a character, move the cursor where you wish the new character(s) to appear and then type the data. After you edit the data, press ENTER or click the mouse button with the mouse pointer in the control panel.

■ USING THE MENU STRUCTURE

In Chapter 1, the term **menu structure** was mentioned. This section briefly discusses the menu structure. You use the menu structure in the next section to print the spreadsheet you have created.

To display the 1-2-3 main menu:

Press ⌷ / ⌷

Move the mouse pointer to the control panel

The main menu is now on your screen. Notice the word MENU appears in the mode indicator. See the top part of Figure 2-6.

Figure 2-6

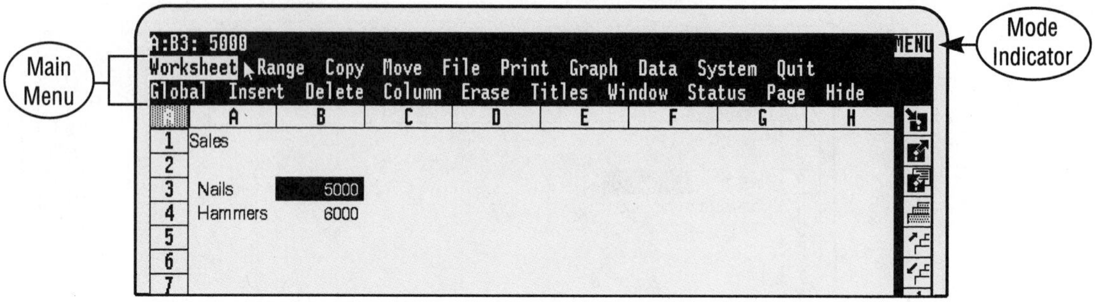

The menu appears on the second line of the control panel. The Worksheet option on the menu is highlighted. The submenu available for the Worksheet option appears on the third line of the control panel.

The **menu pointer** is a rectangular shape that is similar to the cell pointer. It is used to highlight an option on the menu.

Other options on the main menu include Range, Copy, Move, File, Print, Graph, Data, System, and Quit. These options are used to perform a variety of operations on a worksheet. Many of the operations are presented in the remainder of this book.

To remove the main menu from your screen:

Press	Esc	**Move**	*the mouse pointer to the worksheet area*

An additional control menu is available through the **Wysiwyg** add-in program. Wysiwyg is the acronym for *What You See Is What You Get*, which means that the screen is able to represent what the printed page will look like. The Wysiwyg feature is used to enhance your spreadsheet in a number of ways. These enhancements will be discussed in greater detail in Chapter 5. For now, we will use the Wysiwyg feature to print the spreadsheet.

To display the Wysiwyg menu:

Press	:	**Move**	*the mouse pointer to the control panel*
		Click	*the alternate mouse button*

The Wysiwyg menu is now on your screen. Notice the text WYSIWYG appears in the mode indicator at the top right corner of the screen. In addition, the menu pointer has changed color. See the top part of Figure 2-7.

Figure 2-7

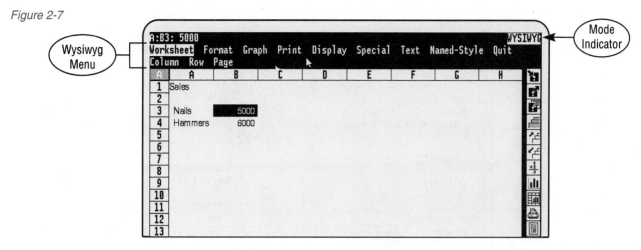

The menu appears on the second line of the control panel. The Worksheet option on the menu is highlighted. The submenu available for the Worksheet option appears on the third line of the control panel.

Other options on the Wysiwyg menu include Format, Graph, Print, Display, Special, Text, Named-Style, and Quit. These options are used to perform a variety of operations on a worksheet.

To remove the Wysiwyg menu from your screen:

Press	Esc	***Move***	*the mouse pointer to the worksheet area*

■ PRINTING A SPREADSHEET

To initiate the printing process:

Press	:	***Move***	*the mouse pointer to the control panel*
Move	the menu pointer to Print	***Move***	*the mouse pointer to Print*
Press	←Enter	***Click***	*the mouse button*

Notice the Print Settings sheet appears on your screen. See Figure 2-8.

Figure 2-8

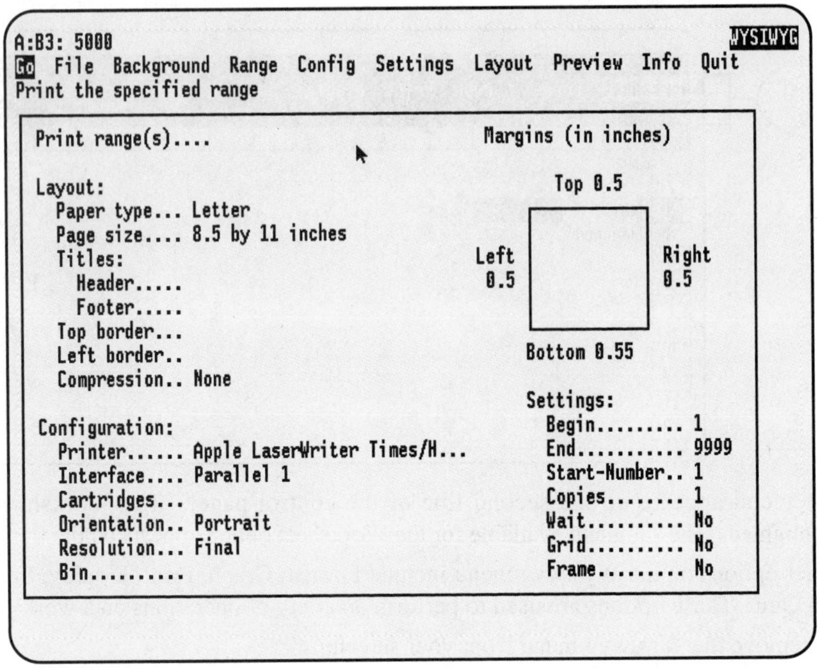

```
A:B3: 5000                                                        WYSIWYG
Go File Background Range Config Settings Layout Preview Info Quit
Print the specified range

  ┌────────────────────────────────────────────────────────────────────┐
  │  Print range(s)....                    Margins (in inches)           │
  │                                                                      │
  │  Layout:                                    Top 0.5                  │
  │    Paper type... Letter                  ┌──────────┐                │
  │    Page size.... 8.5 by 11 inches        │          │                │
  │    Titles:                        Left   │          │   Right        │
  │       Header.....                 0.5    │          │   0.5          │
  │       Footer.....                        │          │                │
  │    Top border...                         └──────────┘                │
  │    Left border..                          Bottom 0.55               │
  │    Compression.. None                                                │
  │                                           Settings:                  │
  │  Configuration:                           Begin......... 1           │
  │    Printer...... Apple LaserWriter Times/H...   End........... 9999  │
  │    Interface.... Parallel 1               Start-Number.. 1           │
  │    Cartridges...                          Copies........ 1           │
  │    Orientation.. Portrait                 Wait.......... No          │
  │    Resolution... Final                    Grid.......... No          │
  │    Bin..........                          Frame......... No          │
  └────────────────────────────────────────────────────────────────────┘
```

Now you specify the range of cells you desire to print.

Move	the menu pointer to Range	‖	*Move*	*the mouse pointer to Range*
Press	←Enter	‖	*Click*	*the mouse button*
Move	the menu pointer to Set	‖	*Move*	*the mouse pointer to Set*
Press	←Enter	‖	*Click*	*the mouse button*
Move	the cell pointer to cell A1	‖	*Click*	*on cell A1 and*
Type	.	‖	*Drag*	*the mouse pointer to cell B4*
Move	the cell pointer to cell B4	‖		

The spreadsheet you created is now highlighted.

To complete the specification of the range of cells to print:

| **Press** | ←Enter | ‖ | *Click* | *the mouse button* |

To print the range of cells:

| **Move** | the menu pointer to Go | ‖ | *Move* | *the mouse pointer to Go* |
| **Press** | ←Enter | ‖ | *Click* | *the mouse button* |

The printer should print your worksheet.

> *User Tip*
>
> The concept of a **range** appears frequently in 1-2-3. The word "range" designates any rectangular block of adjacent cells. A range may consist of cells within several columns or rows, single columns or rows, or even a single cell.
>
> A range can be specified in several ways: by using the pointer-movement keys to highlight the cells in the range, by using the mouse to drag across the desired cells, or by typing the range address.
>
> A range address consists of the cell addresses of two diagonally opposite corners of the range separated by two periods. Normally, the upper left and lower right corners are chosen. For example, the address B2..C10 indicates a range of cells extending from row 2 through row 10 in columns B and C. If you think of the two periods as standing for the word "through," we would call the range of cells "B2 through C10." The address B1..B1 denotes a range consisting of the single cell B1.
>
> Pointing is preferable to typing, because fewer errors are made when the actual cell addresses are highlighted than when trying to determine the correct column and row visually.
>
> After issuing the **R**ange command, highlight the first desired cell (usually the upper left corner of the range). Then press a period. Pressing the period anchors the cell pointer in the cell and permits extending the highlighting in any direction adjacent to the first highlighted cell. When the desired rectangular range is highlighted, lock in the range by pressing the ENTER key or clicking the mouse

■ SAVING A SPREADSHEET

While creating or editing a spreadsheet, any changes you make are stored in your computer's memory. If the power to the computer fails, or if you turn off the computer, your work will be lost. You can prevent such a loss by using the **F**ile **S**ave command to place the spreadsheet in a file on a disk. The disk can be either a floppy disk or a hard disk. The **F**ile **S**ave command allows you to save a spreadsheet without losing your place on the screen and then to continue creating or editing the spreadsheet. As you work, it is a good idea to save the spreadsheet every 10 to 15 minutes.

Pressing the HOME key or clicking the Home ⬚ SmartIcon prior to saving a spreadsheet to a file on a disk is an optional step. If you press the HOME key or click the Home ⬚ SmartIcon, the file is saved with the cell pointer located in cell A1. When the file is later retrieved, the cell pointer appears in cell A1.

To save the spreadsheet:

Press   [Home]

Move   *the mouse pointer to the left or right arrow beside the palette number*

Press	/	*Click*	*the mouse button until the Home* ▣ *SmartIcon appears*
		Move	*the mouse pointer to the* ▣ *SmartIcon*
		Click	*the mouse button*
		Move	*the mouse pointer to the control panel*
		Click	*the alternate mouse button until the 1-2-3 main menu appears*

At this point the main menu appears in the control panel as shown in the top part of Figure 2-9. Then you select the desired menu option with the menu pointer or the mouse pointer.

Figure 2-9

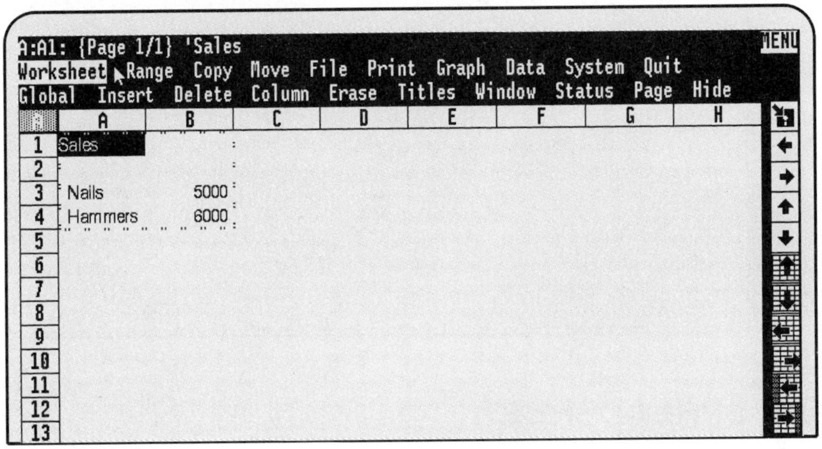

To select the **File Save** command:

Move	the menu pointer to File		*Move*	*the mouse pointer to File*
Press	←Enter		*Click*	*the mouse button*
Move	the menu pointer to Save		*Move*	*the mouse pointer to Save*
Press	←Enter		*Click*	*the mouse button*

When prompted for the file name:

Type	EXAMPLE		*Type*	*EXAMPLE*
Press	←Enter		*Click*	*the mouse button*

User Tip

Another method for saving a worksheet to a file is to click the File Save ▦ SmartIcon. Then type the filename and click the mouse button with the mouse pointer in the control panel.

Filenames can be a maximum of eight characters long. Any character except a period or a space can be used in a filename. The EXAMPLE file contains the information you have entered into your spreadsheet.

Notice that the name of the file (EXAMPLE) and its extension (WK3) now appear on the status line and replace the date and time indicator.

In This Book

Note that you may set up 1-2-3 to save files on a different disk or directory other than the one in which 1-2-3 is installed. In this book, it is assumed that you have specified an appropriate directory to save your spreadsheet files. As you use this book, save a spreadsheet to a file only when you are instructed to do so.

User Tip

An alternative method for selecting a menu option using the keyboard is to press the letter corresponding to the first character in the menu option. This approach saves time in the creation and editing of worksheets. Initially, it may be advantageous for you to use the pointer-movement keys to move the menu pointer to the appropriate menu option and then press the ENTER key. Once you are comfortable with the way the menus are structured, you can use first letters for selecting menu options. After working with Lotus 1-2-3 for a short while, most individuals use the first letter approach for selecting menu options when they use the keyboard method.

■ ERASING A SPREADSHEET

You should clear your screen before starting to work on another spreadsheet. You can erase the spreadsheet from your screen and remove it from the memory of your computer by using the **Worksheet Erase Yes** command.

> *In This Book*
>
> In selecting items from the menus utilizing the keyboard, you may use either the standard method (using pointer-movement keys to move the menu pointer to a menu option and pressing the ENTER key) or the alternative method (pressing the character corresponding to the first character in a menu option). For the remainder of this book, you are simply instructed to select the menu option and are not told what method to use for selecting a menu option.
>
> When using a mouse, it is a common practice to choose an option from a menu by moving the mouse pointer to the desired option and clicking the mouse button. For the remainder of this book, you are instructed to simply choose a command rather than be given the set of instructions to move the mouse pointer to the menu option and click the mouse button.

To erase the spreadsheet from your screen:

Press	☐ /		***Move***	*the mouse pointer to the control panel*
Select	Worksheet		***Choose***	*Worksheet*
Select	Erase		***Choose***	*Erase*
Select	Yes		***Choose***	*Yes*

Note that the **W**orksheet **E**rase **Y**es command does **not** delete the EXAMPLE spreadsheet from the disk where it was previously saved. The **W**orksheet **E**rase **Y**es command only removes the spreadsheet from the memory of your computer and clears the screen.

■ RETRIEVING A SPREADSHEET

The spreadsheets you create in Lotus 1-2-3 are saved in files. When you want to edit a spreadsheet, you need to retrieve a copy of the file from a disk and place it in the memory of your computer. It will then appear on your screen.

The spreadsheet is then active in your computer's memory, and you can edit it. However, the changes you make will affect only the spreadsheet on the screen. They will not be recorded on the disk until you save them.

You can retrieve a spreadsheet from any directory or from any disk. If the spreadsheet is stored in the current directory, just enter the name of the spreadsheet. When the spreadsheet is stored in another directory, you must include the drive and directory name before the spreadsheet name.

To retrieve your EXAMPLE spreadsheet:

Press	☐ /		***Move***	*the mouse pointer to the control panel*
Select	File		***Choose***	*File*

Select	Retrieve		***Choose***	*Retrieve*

When prompted for the name of the file to retrieve:

Type	EXAMPLE		***Type***	*EXAMPLE*
Press	⟮←Enter⟯		***Click***	*the mouse button*

User Tip

Another method for retrieving a worksheet from a file is to click the File Retrieve SmartIcon. Then you enter the file name and click the mouse button.

Your screen should look like Figure 2-10.

Figure 2-10

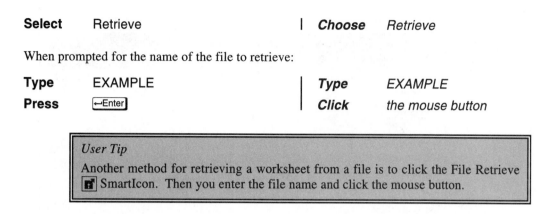

User Tip

After issuing the **F**ile **R**etrieve command, an alternative to typing the file name is to press the F3 key and use the pointer-movement keys to highlight the desired file with the pointer. Once the desired file is highlighted, press the ENTER key. If you are using a mouse, you move the mouse pointer to the desired file name and click the mouse button.

The EXAMPLE spreadsheet is visible on your screen. Now enter the additional information that appears in Figure 2-11.

Figure 2-11

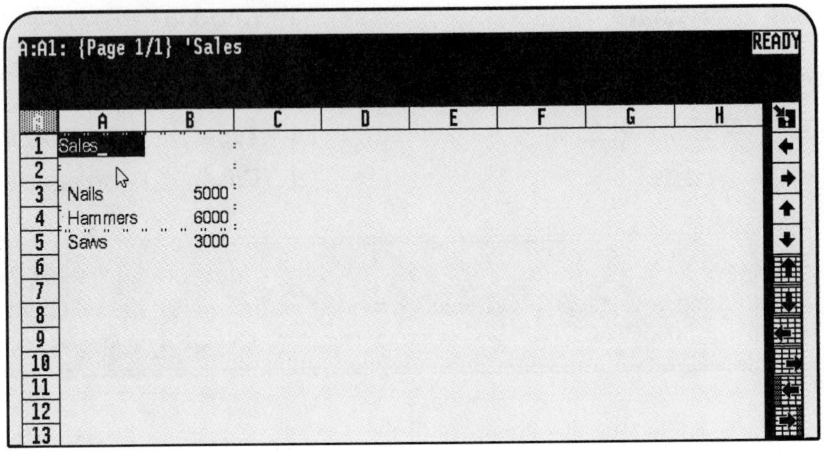

Move	the cell pointer to cell A5		***Click***	*on cell A5*
Press	the space bar twice		***Press***	*the space bar twice*
Type	Saws		***Type***	*Saws*
Press	⌐Enter		***Click***	*the mouse button*
Move	the cell pointer to cell B5		***Click***	*on cell B5*
Type	3000		***Type***	*3000*
Press	⌐Enter		***Click***	*the mouse button*

After changing a spreadsheet, you usually save it again using the same name for the spreadsheet file.

To save the spreadsheet with the same name:

Press	Home		***Move***	*the mouse pointer to the Home SmartIcon*
Press	/		***Click***	*the mouse button*
Select	File		***Move***	*the mouse pointer to the control panel*
Select	Save		***Choose***	*File*
			Choose	*Save*

When you are prompted for the file name, the name for the current spreadsheet appears in the control panel. The extension .WK3 is automatically added to the end of the file name when the spreadsheet is saved. In this case, EXAMPLE.WK3 appears. To continue using the same file name:

Press	⌐Enter	***Click***	*the mouse button*

When prompted to **C**ancel, **R**eplace, or **B**ackup:

Select	Replace	***Choose***	*Replace*

The previously saved version of EXAMPLE has been replaced with the updated version that is displayed on your screen. You will learn more about the other choices in Chapter 4.

■ EXITING LOTUS 1-2-3

When you finish using Lotus 1-2-3, you will need to exit from the software.

To exit Lotus 1-2-3:

Press	⌨ /		***Move***	*the mouse pointer to the control panel*
Select	Quit		***Choose***	*Quit*
Select	Yes		***Choose***	*Yes*

You may need to select **Yes** twice if you have not saved the worksheet.

To select Exit from the 1-2-3 Access Menu:

Select	Exit		*The mouse does not work in the Access menu*

SUMMARY

This chapter presented an overview of the processes for creating, editing, saving, printing, erasing, and retrieving a spreadsheet. The method for exiting Lotus 1-2-3 was also illustrated.

KEY CONCEPTS

File Retrieve	Print Range
File Save	Range
Label	Right aligned
Left aligned	Value
Menu pointer	Worksheet Erase
Menu structure	Wysiwyg
Print Go	

EXERCISE 1

INSTRUCTIONS: Circle T if the statement is true and F if the statement is false.

T   F   1.   The only way to edit an entry in a spreadsheet is to type the entry again and press the ENTER key.

T   F   2.   When the first character typed for an entry in a cell is a number, the mode indicator changes to LABEL.

T   F   3.   A spreadsheet can be saved to a file on a diskette, but not on a hard disk.

T   F   4.   The maximum number of characters that can appear in a file name is eight.

T   F   5.   A period can be used in a spreadsheet file name.

T   F   6.   A spreadsheet can be saved to a file only one time.

T   F   7.   It is a good idea to save a spreadsheet to a file about every 10 to 15 minutes.

T   F   8.   In order to print a spreadsheet, you need to specify a range of cells to print.

T   F   9.   The Quit menu option is used to exit the 1-2-3 Access Menu.

T   F   10.   The File Save command is used to retrieve a spreadsheet file.-

---

EXERCISE 2

INSTRUCTIONS: Explain a typical situation when the following commands are used.

Problem 1:   [/] **File Save Replace**   *Problem 5:*   [/] **Worksheet Erase**

Problem 2:   [:] **Print Range**   *Problem 6:*   [:] **Print Go**

Problem 3:   [/] **File Retrieve**   *Problem 7:*   [:] **Print Quit**

Problem 4:   [/] **File Save**

EXERCISE 3

INSTRUCTIONS: Create the spreadsheet in Figure 2-12.

Figure 2-12

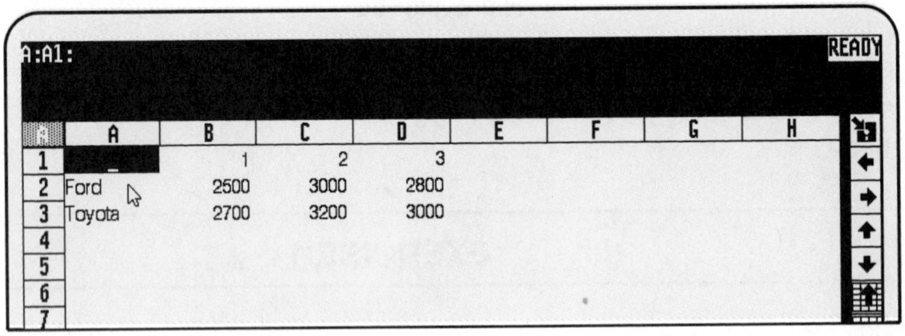

1. Print the spreadsheet.

2. Save the spreadsheet to a file using the name CARS.

3. Erase the worksheet from your screen.

EXERCISE 4

INSTRUCTIONS: Create the spreadsheet in Figure 2-13.

Figure 2-13

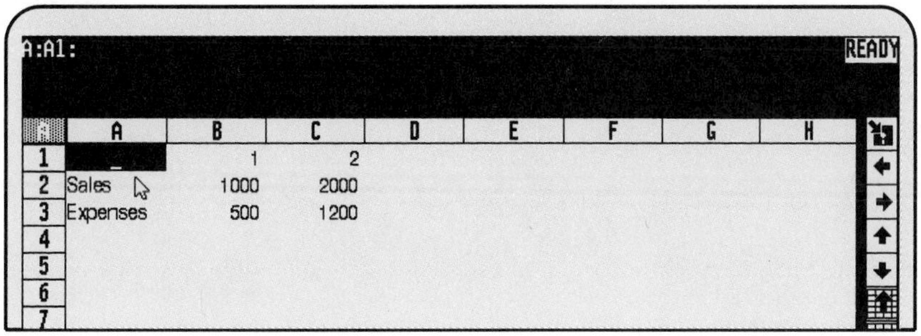

1. Print the spreadsheet.

2. Save the spreadsheet to a file using the name INCOME.

3. Erase the worksheet from your screen.

EXERCISE 5

INSTRUCTIONS: Retrieve the CARS file created in Exercise 3.

1. Change the values for Ford sales to 4000, 4200, and 4800.

2. Save the spreadsheet to a file using the name CARS1.

3. Print the spreadsheet.

4. Erase the worksheet from your screen.

EXERCISE 6

INSTRUCTIONS: Retrieve the INCOME file created in Exercise 4.

1. Change the values for Expenses to 300 and 900.

2. Save the spreadsheet to a file using the name INCOME1.

3. Print the spreadsheet.

4. Erase the worksheet from your screen.

CHAPTER THREE

DESIGNING SPREADSHEETS PROPERLY

OBJECTIVES

In this chapter, you learn to:

- Design a spreadsheet
- Format a spreadsheet
- Save a spreadsheet

■ CHAPTER OVERVIEW

When you create spreadsheets, it is important to use good design principles. Properly designed spreadsheets are easier to modify at a later date. Furthermore, if a spreadsheet is designed properly, less effort is required to understand how a spreadsheet prepared by someone else actually works.

■ DESIGNING A SPREADSHEET

Spreadsheet software provides individuals with a tool that enhances their productivity. Spreadsheets should be designed so they are useful for the individuals who create them as well as for other persons who may utilize the spreadsheet. A spreadsheet should be designed so that it is easy for the developer of the spreadsheet and others to make modifications to the spreadsheet in the future.

In designing a spreadsheet, Thommes (1992) has suggested several criteria to consider. These criteria include (1) accuracy, (2) clarity, (3) flexibility, (4) efficiency, and (5) auditability.

The first criterion is accuracy. If a spreadsheet does not provide its user with correct results, it is worthless. As you will see later in this book, there are many situations in which you may enter a wrong formula or value that leads to incorrect answers. The formulas and functions used in 1-2-3 are not immediately visible to a user of a spreadsheet. Proper design and documentation can improve the comprehension of the spreadsheet to users and reduce the likelihood of improper utilization of the spreadsheet.

Clarity is the second criterion for designing a spreadsheet. It is important that the creator and designer of the spreadsheet understand how the spreadsheet works. Proper spreadsheet layout and documentation improve the clarity for everyone who uses the worksheet.

The third criterion is flexibility. When a spreadsheet is designed and developed, consideration should be given to adapting the spreadsheet when changes or modifications are required in the future.

Efficiency is the fourth criterion. A spreadsheet needs to be efficient from the perspective of how much computer memory is required to process the spreadsheet, and how much time it takes the computer to process the spreadsheet. Also, the user of the spreadsheet should be able to easily find the important sections of the spreadsheet.

The final criterion is auditability. In many situations, spreadsheets may need to be audited for accuracy. At a minimum, an individual should be able to determine what items are used to calculate the value in a cell. Proper spreadsheet layout and documentation can permit individuals to effectively audit spreadsheets.

■ FORMATTING A SPREADSHEET

Thommes (1992) and Ronen, Palley, and Lucas (1989) discuss some formats to use in designing the layout of a spreadsheet. The format suggested by Ronen, Palley, and Lucas, which is discussed in the work by Thommes, has been adopted and slightly adapted for use in this book. The suggested layout appears in Figure 3-1.

Figure 3-1

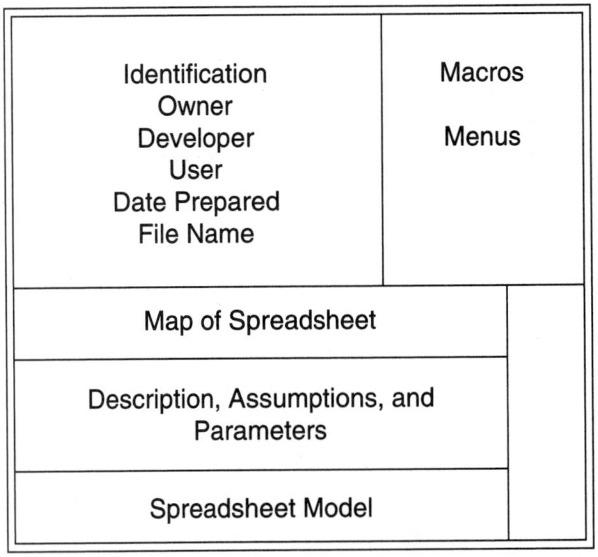

Identification Owner Developer User Date Prepared File Name	Macros Menus
Map of Spreadsheet	
Description, Assumptions, and Parameters	
Spreadsheet Model	

Source. "Spreadsheet Analysis and Design," Communications of the ACM, January, 1989 by Boaz Ronen, Michael A. Palley, and Henry C. Lucas, Jr. Used by permission.

Use of this "block-structured" format can assist a person developing a spreadsheet to satisfy the five criteria for proper spreadsheet design.

The identification block includes information on the owner, developer, and user of the spreadsheet. The date the spreadsheet was created and last revised, and the file on which the spreadsheet is stored are also specified in the identification block.

The macros and menus block is to the right of the identification block. Macros are used to improve the efficiency of processing a spreadsheet and are discussed more thoroughly in Chapter 16. Menus improve the clarity of spreadsheets for users and allow spreadsheet developers to customize spreadsheet applications. The macros/menu block is placed in the indicated location to alert the user to macros and menus used in a spreadsheet. Being aware of them can help to prevent cells from being erased or blank cells from being introduced into the spreadsheet. If either error occurs, the macros and menus may not work correctly.

A map of the spreadsheet appears below the identification block which indicates the order the various blocks appear in the spreadsheet. For example, the identification block appears before the map of the spreadsheet.

The next block consists of documentation about the spreadsheet. Documentation includes a general description of the spreadsheet and specifies parameters and assumptions. For example, growth rates and interest rates might be indicated.

The final block contains the spreadsheet model. In this block the actual rows and columns of the spreadsheet appear. Formulas are included to calculate values based on the parameters and assumptions specified for the spreadsheet.

Example Problem

Suppose you are asked to create a spreadsheet for ABC Company that projects various budget items for the last three quarters of a year based on data from the first quarter. The information from the first quarter and the projections are as follows:

	1st Quarter	Projected Increases Per Quarter
Sales	$60,000	2%
Salaries	35,000	(given below)
Rent	9,000	(constant for all periods)
Telephone	1,000	5%
Office Supplies	750	$50
Miscellaneous	1,000	3%

The salary amounts for each quarter are: $35,000; $35,500; $36,200; $37,000.

You will create and print the spreadsheet model itself in the next chapter. In the remaining portion of this chapter, you will create (1) the identification block, (2) a map of the spreadsheet block, and (3) the description, assumptions, and parameters block.

Prior to entering the data for the identification block, it is a good idea to place the name of the company at the beginning of the worksheet.

Move	the cell pointer to cell A1		*Click*	*on cell A1*
Type	ABC Company		*Type*	*ABC COMPANY*
Press	⏎Enter		*Click*	*the mouse button*

In the identification block, you include (1) information on the owner of the spreadsheet, (2) the person who developed the spreadsheet, (3) the user of the spreadsheet, (4) the date the spreadsheet was completed (5)the date the spreadsheet was last revised, and (6) the file name used to save the spreadsheet.

To enter the data for the identification block:

Move	the cell pointer to cell A3		*Click*	*on cell A3*
Type	Identification:		*Type*	*Identification:*
Press	⏎Enter		*Click*	*the mouse button*
Move	the cell pointer to cell A4		*Click*	*on cell A4*
Press	the space bar twice		*Press*	*the space bar twice*
Type	Owner: Financial Planning Department		*Type*	*Owner: Financial Planning Department*
Press	⏎Enter		*Click*	*the mouse button*
Move	the cell pointer to cell A5		*Click*	*on cell A5*
Press	the space bar twice		*Press*	*the space bar twice*
Type	Developer: Your name		*Type*	*Developer: Your name*
Press	⏎Enter		*Click*	*the mouse button*
Move	the cell pointer to cell A6		*Click*	*on cell A6*
Press	the space bar twice		*Press*	*the space bar twice*
Type	User: Marsha Thompson		*Type*	*User: Marsha Thompson*

In This Book

Note that from this point on, the instructions utilize a "shortcut" for entering labels. Instead of pressing the ENTER key, you can press a pointer-movement key to enter a label and move to the next cell. If you use a mouse, you can click the appropriate pointer-movement SmartIcon and move to the next cell.

Press	the ↓ key		*Click*	*the ↓ SmartIcon*

The cell pointer is in cell A7. To enter the next portion of the identification block:

Press	the space bar twice		*Press*	*the space bar twice*
Type	Date: 9/14/92		*Type*	*Date: 9/14/92*
Press	the space bar 10 times		*Press*	*the space bar 10 times*

Type	Revised: 4/3/93		***Type***	*Revised: 4/3/93*
Press	↓ twice		***Click***	*the ⬇ SmartIcon twice*

The cell pointer is now in cell A9. To enter the file name where the spreadsheet will be stored:

Type	File: BUDGET		***Type***	*File: BUDGET*
Press	↓ twice		***Click***	*the ⬇ SmartIcon twice*

The cell pointer is now in cell A11. Your screen should look similar to Figure 3-2.

Figure 3-2

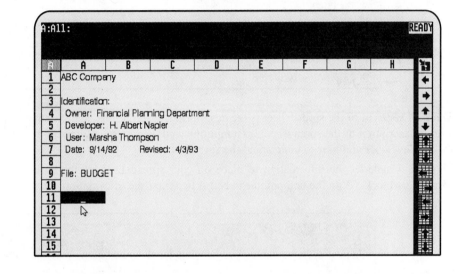

You now enter the data for the map of the spreadsheet. This block in the spreadsheet specifies the order in which the various portions of the spreadsheet appear.

Use the information in Figure 3-3 to enter the data for the map of the spreadsheet block. You will use cells A11 through A15.

Figure 3-3

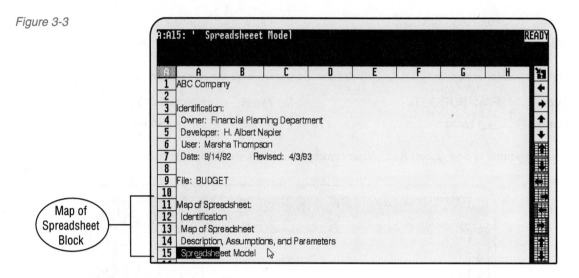

The next segment of the spreadsheet is the description, assumptions, and parameters block. By including a brief description of the spreadsheet, assumptions, and parameters utilized in the spreadsheet, it is easier for the developer and user to understand the spreadsheet.

Figure 3-4 includes the information to place on your spreadsheet for the description, assumptions, and parameters block. With the cell pointer in cell A18, enter the information shown in Figure 3-4.

Figure 3-4

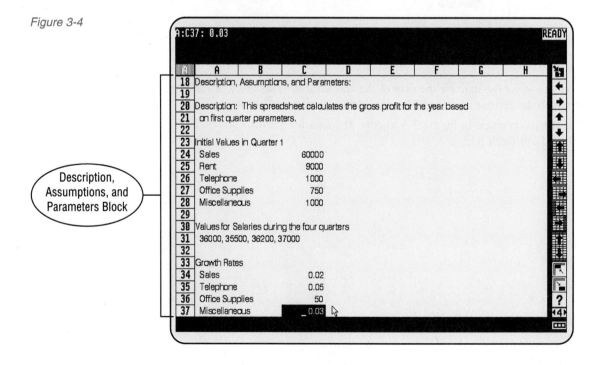

In Chapter 4, you will learn how to format the various values so their appearance is improved. For example, you will change the format for the growth rates of Sales, Telephone, and Miscellaneous expenses so they appear as percentages rather than decimal values.

The last block is the spreadsheet model. This block includes the actual spreadsheet. Various data and formulas are contained in the block. You will create the spreadsheet model in the next chapter.

To specify the beginning of the spreadsheet model block:

Move	the cell pointer to cell A39		*Click*	*on cell A39*
Type	Spreadsheet Model:		*Type*	*Spreadsheet Model:*
Press	⏎Enter		*Click*	*the mouse button*

The bottom part of your screen should look like Figure 3-5.

Figure 3-5

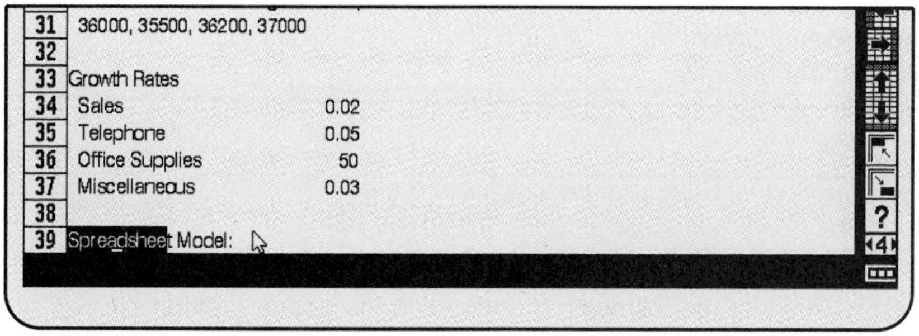

■ SAVING A SPREADSHEET

To save the spreadsheet:

Press	Home		*Click*	*the Home ▣ SmartIcon*
Press	/		*Click*	*the File Save ▣ SmartIcon*
Select	File			
Select	Save			

When prompted for the file name:

Type	BUDGET		*Type*	*BUDGET*
Press	⏎Enter		*Click*	*the mouse button*

SUMMARY

This chapter described the basics of spreadsheet design. The five criteria for good spreadsheet design are accuracy, clarity, flexibility, efficiency, and auditability. A popular spreadsheet format used by many individuals is the "block-structured" format. The primary blocks in the "block-structured" format are the identification; macros and menus; map of the spreadsheet; description, assumptions, and parameters; and the spreadsheet model. For more detailed information on designing spreadsheets, see the references at the end of this chapter.

KEY CONCEPTS

Block-structured format
Design criteria
Spreadsheet format
Spreadsheet design

EXERCISE 1

INSTRUCTIONS: Answer the following questions in the space provided.

1. Briefly describe the following criteria for good spreadsheet design:

   a. Accuracy _____

   _____

   b. Clarity _____

   _____

   c. Flexibility _____

   _____

   d. Efficiency _____

   _____

   e. Auditability _____

   _____

2. Briefly describe the following blocks of a "block-structured" spreadsheet:

a. Identification _____

_____

b. Macros and menus _____

_____

c. Map of spreadsheet _____

_____

d. Description, assumptions, and parameters _____

_____

e. Spreadsheet model _____

_____

EXERCISE 2

INSTRUCTIONS: Circle T if the statement is true and F if the statement is false.

T	F	1.	It is important to design a spreadsheet properly.
T	F	2.	There are six criteria to consider when designing a spreadsheet.
T	F	3.	It is important to include documentation to describe the parameters and assumptions in a spreadsheet.
T	F	4.	Formulas cannot be included in a spreadsheet.
T	F	5.	The name of the developer of a spreadsheet should not be specified.
T	F	6.	The last date a spreadsheet was changed should be noted on the spreadsheet.

References

Ronen, B., Palley, M. A., Lucas, Jr., H. C., "Spreadsheet Analysis and Design," *Communications of the ACM,* Volume 32, No. 1 (January, 1989), pp. 84-93.

Thommes, M.C., *Proper Spreadsheet Design,* Boyd & Fraser Publishing Company, Danvers, MA, 1992.

CHAPTER FOUR

CREATING AND PRINTING A SPREADSHEET

OBJECTIVES

In this chapter, you will learn to:

- Retrieve a spreadsheet
- Build a spreadsheet
- Save and replace a spreadsheet
- Correct rounding errors
- Prepare the printer, preview, and print a spreadsheet
- Change the font used in printing
- Use another format for a spreadsheet
- Use the rounding option
- Make a backup of a spreadsheet file
- Change the assumptions to complete a "what-if" analysis
- Use formulas in Lotus 1-2-3

■ CHAPTER OVERVIEW

One of the difficulties facing you as a beginning Lotus 1-2-3 user in learning to create a spreadsheet is how to begin! Chapter 4 cites the example problem from Chapter 3, and provides step-by-step procedures on solving the problem with a properly designed Lotus 1-2-3 spreadsheet. While guiding you through the process for building the spreadsheet, the instructions will provide details about 1-2-3 capabilities as you need them.

The instructions address typical problems you may have as a beginning user, such as how to solve rounding problems, change the numeric display of the spreadsheet, and make a backup copy of the spreadsheet file.

■ EXAMPLE PROBLEM

In Chapter 3, you entered some information about the spreadsheet you will create in this chapter. The description of the problem is included again for clarity.

The spreadsheet you create in this chapter will project sales for the last three quarters of a year based upon data from the first quarter. The information from the first quarter and the assumptions for making projections are as follows:

	1st Quarter	Projected Increases Per Quarter
Sales	$60,000	2%
Salaries	35,000	(given below)
Rent	9,000	(constant for all periods)
Telephone	1,000	5%
Office Supplies	750	$50
Miscellaneous	1,000	3%

The salary amounts for each quarter are as follows: $35,000; $35,500; $36,200; $37,000.

To complete the problem cited above, a common procedure for creating a spreadsheet using 1-2-3 is shown below:

Creating labels for the spreadsheet

Expanding the width of a column

Entering assumptions

Entering numbers, formulas, and copying information in a spreadsheet

Selecting a format for the data

Centering the worksheet title

Inserting blank rows in a spreadsheet

Entering underlines and double underlines

In this chapter, you create the spreadsheet model to complete the spreadsheet you started in Chapter 3. The completed spreadsheet model is displayed in Figures 4-1 and 4-2.

Figure 4-1

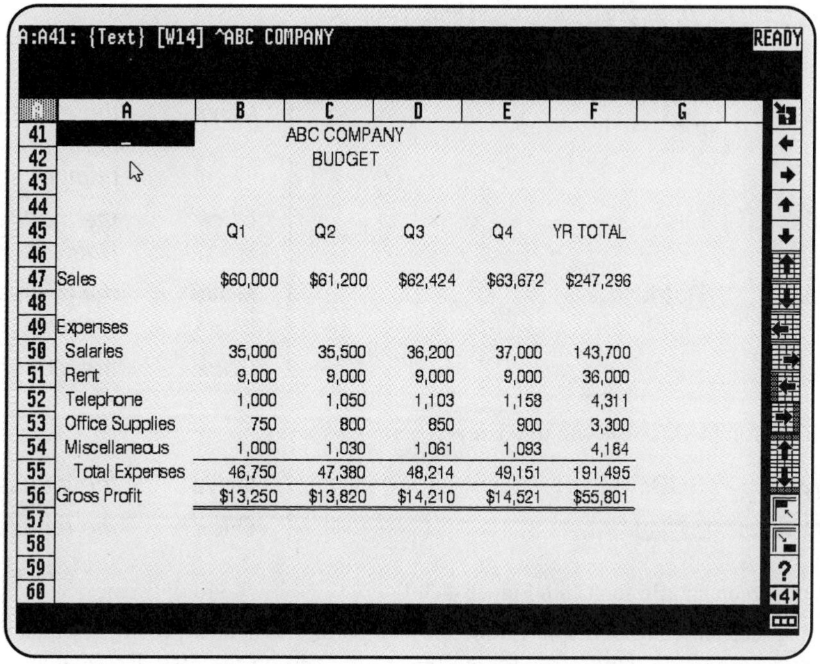

```
A:A41: {Text} [W14] ^ABC COMPANY                                    READY

        A          B         C         D         E         F         G
 41  __                  ABC COMPANY
 42                        BUDGET
 43
 44
 45                  Q1        Q2        Q3        Q4     YR TOTAL
 46
 47  Sales        $60,000   $61,200   $62,424   $63,672  $247,296
 48
 49  Expenses
 50   Salaries     35,000    35,500    36,200    37,000   143,700
 51   Rent          9,000     9,000     9,000     9,000    36,000
 52   Telephone     1,000     1,050     1,103     1,158     4,311
 53   Office Supplies  750      800       850       900     3,300
 54   Miscellaneous  1,000     1,030     1,061     1,093     4,184
 55    Total Expenses 46,750   47,380    48,214    49,151   191,495
 56  Gross Profit  $13,250   $13,820   $14,210   $14,521   $55,801
 57
 58
 59
 60
```

Figure 4-2

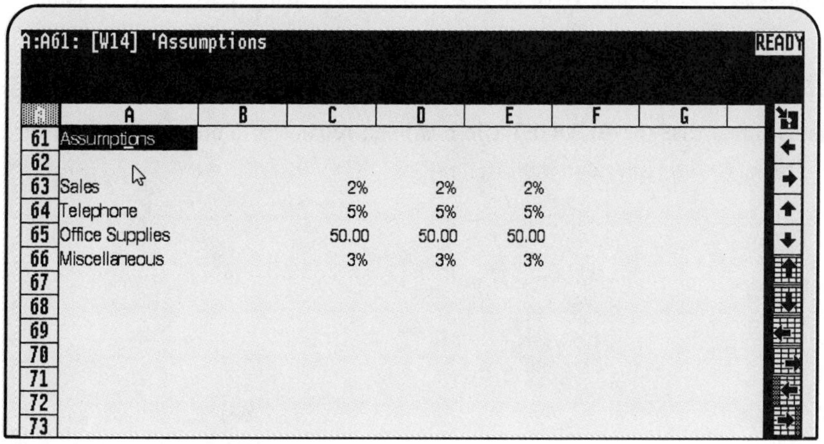

```
A:A61: [W14] 'Assumptions                                           READY

        A          B         C         D         E         F         G
 61  Assumptions
 62
 63  Sales                             2%        2%        2%
 64  Telephone                         5%        5%        5%
 65  Office Supplies                 50.00     50.00     50.00
 66  Miscellaneous                     3%        3%        3%
 67
 68
 69
 70
 71
 72
 73
```

■ RETRIEVING A SPREADSHEET

To retrieve the BUDGET file:

Press	⌞ / ⌟	*Move*	*the mouse pointer to the left or right arrow beside the palette number*
Select	File	*Click*	*the mouse button until the File Retrieve ▣ SmartIcon appears*
Select	Retrieve	*Move*	*the mouse pointer to the File Retrieve ▣ SmartIcon*
		Click	*the mouse button*

When prompted for the file to retrieve:

Type	BUDGET	*Move*	*the mouse pointer to BUDGET*
Press	⌞←Enter⌟	*Click*	*the mouse button*

Your screen should look like Figure 4-3.

The spreadsheet BUDGET is visible on your screen. It is now possible to make revisions or print it. Any changes are made only to the screen, not to the file on the disk. To save any changes to the BUDGET file, go through the process of saving and replacing the file that was presented in Chapter 2. To save revisions as a completely separate file, save the file using a different file name.

■ BUILDING THE SPREADSHEET

It is assumed that the BUDGET file has been retrieved. Your spreadsheet should look like Figures 4-3 and 4-4.

Figure 4-3

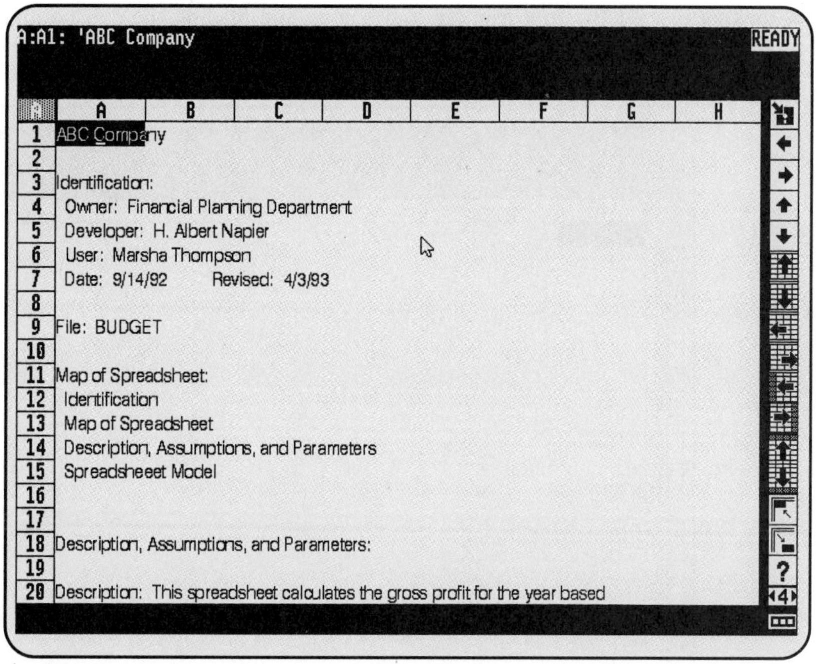

```
A:A1: 'ABC Company                                              READY

       A        B        C        D        E        F        G        H
 1  ABC Company
 2
 3  Identification:
 4   Owner: Financial Planning Department
 5   Developer: H. Albert Napier
 6   User: Marsha Thompson
 7   Date: 9/14/92      Revised: 4/3/93
 8
 9  File: BUDGET
10
11  Map of Spreadsheet:
12   Identification
13   Map of Spreadsheet
14   Description, Assumptions, and Parameters
15   Spreadsheeet Model
16
17
18  Description, Assumptions, and Parameters:
19
20  Description: This spreadsheet calculates the gross profit for the year based
```

Figure 4-4

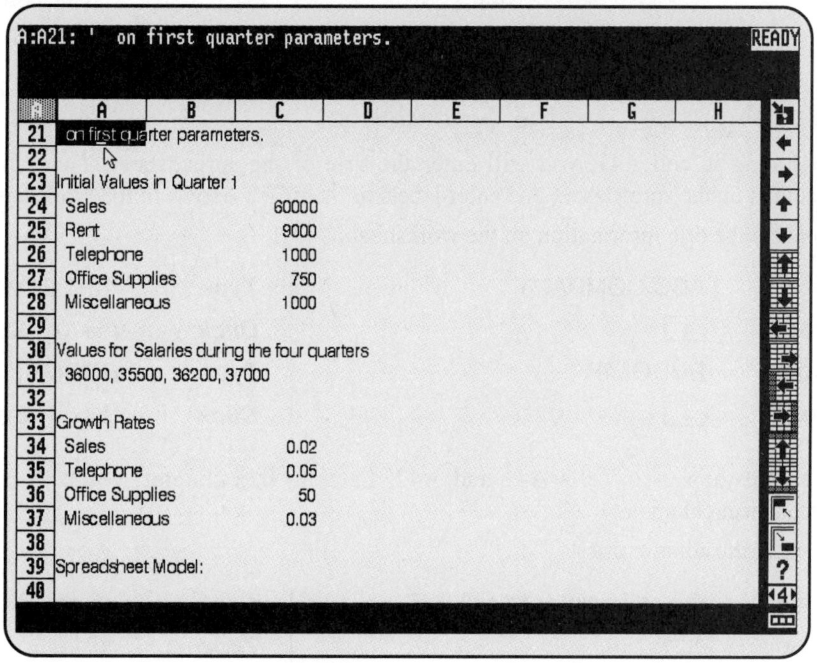

```
A:A21: '   on first quarter parameters.                          READY

       A        B        C        D        E        F        G        H
21  on first quarter parameters.
22
23  Initial Values in Quarter 1
24   Sales              60000
25   Rent                9000
26   Telephone           1000
27   Office Supplies      750
28   Miscellaneous       1000
29
30  Values for Salaries during the four quarters
31   36000, 35500, 36200, 37000
32
33  Growth Rates
34   Sales               0.02
35   Telephone           0.05
36   Office Supplies       50
37   Miscellaneous       0.03
38
39  Spreadsheet Model:
40
```

After making row 41 the first row on your screen and placing the cell pointer in cell A41, your screen should look like Figure 4-5.

Figure 4-5

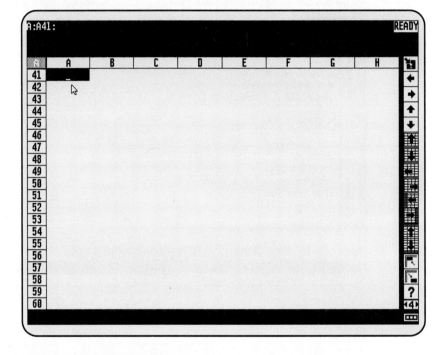

Creating Labels for the Spreadsheet

Beginning in cell A41, you will enter the title of the spreadsheet. Then you will place the column headings on the spreadsheet and enter labels to identify the rows in the worksheet.

To place the title information on the worksheet:

Type	ABC COMPANY	**Type**	*ABC COMPANY*
Press	↓	*Click*	*the ↓ SmartIcon*
Type	BUDGET	*Type*	*BUDGET*
Press	↓	*Click*	*the ↓ SmartIcon*

The titles appear in cells A41 and A42. Later in this chapter, you will center the titles over the spreadsheet columns.

To enter the column titles:

Move	the cell pointer to cell B45	*Click*	*on cell B45*
Type	^Q1	*Type*	*^Q1*
Press	→	*Click*	*the → SmartIcon*

The ^ symbol causes a label to be **centered** within the column; a **double quote mark** (") before the label causes the label to be **right-aligned** in the cell.

Notice that you did not have to press the ENTER key. Pressing the RIGHT ARROW key or clicking the RIGHT ARROW SmartIcon after typing ^Q1 did two things: entered ^Q1 and moved the cell pointer to cell C45.

To enter the column titles for the last three columns:

Type	^Q2		*Type*	*^Q2*
Press	→		*Click*	*the* → *SmartIcon*
Type	^Q3		*Type*	*^Q3*
Press	→		*Click*	*the* → *SmartIcon*
Type	^Q4		*Type*	*^Q4*
Press	→		*Click*	*the* → *SmartIcon*

To enter the column title for the year total column:

Type	^YR TOTAL		*Type*	*^YR TOTAL*
Press	←Enter		*Click*	*the mouse button*

Your screen should look like Figure 4-6.

Figure 4-6

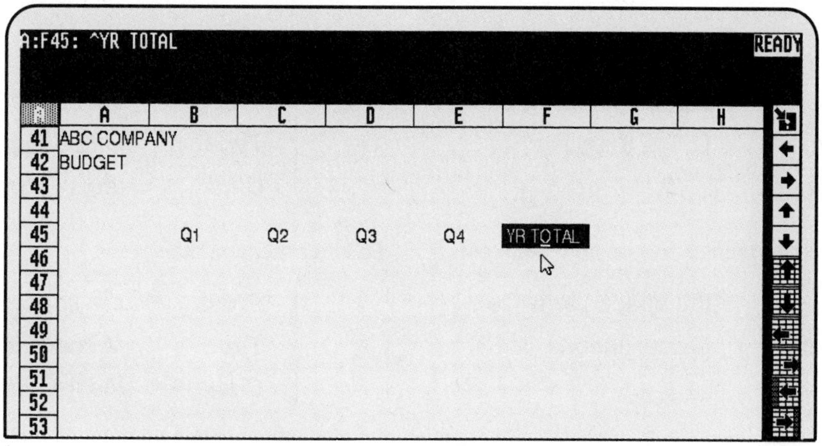

Beginning in cell A47, you enter the labels that describe the contents of the rows.

To input the label Sales in cell A47:

Move	the cell pointer to cell A47		*Click*	*on cell A47*
Type	Sales		*Type*	*Sales*
Press	↓		*Click*	*the* ↓ *SmartIcon*

To input the label Expenses in cell A48:

Type	Expenses		*Type*	*Expenses*
Press	⬚↓		*Click*	*the* ⬚↓ *SmartIcon*

To input the label Salaries in cell A49:

Press	the space bar twice		*Press*	*the space bar twice*
Type	Salaries		*Type*	*Salaries*
Press	⬚↓		*Click*	*the* ⬚↓ *SmartIcon*

The cell pointer should now be in cell A50. To enter the next label:

Press	the space bar twice		*Press*	*the space bar twice*
Type	Rent		*Type*	*Rent*
Press	⬚↓		*Click*	*the* ⬚↓ *SmartIcon*

The cell pointer should now be in cell A51. To enter the next label:

Press	the space bar twice		*Press*	*the space bar twice*
Type	Telephone		*Type*	*Telephone*
Press	⬚↓		*Click*	*the* ⬚↓ *SmartIcon*

The cell pointer should now be in cell A52. To enter the next label:

Press	the space bar twice		*Press*	*the space bar twice*
Type	Office Supplies		*Type*	*Office Supplies*
Press	⬚↓		*Click*	*the* ⬚↓ *SmartIcon*

The cell pointer should now be in cell A53. To enter the next label:

Press	the space bar twice		*Press*	*the space bar twice*
Type	Miscellaneous		*Type*	*Miscellaneous*
Press	⬚↓		*Click*	*the* ⬚↓ *SmartIcon*

The cell pointer should now be in cell A54. To enter the next label:

Press	the space bar four times		*Press*	*the space bar four times*
Type	Total Expenses		*Type*	*Total Expenses*
Press	⬚↓		*Click*	*the* ⬚↓ *SmartIcon*

The cell pointer should now be in cell A55. To enter the next label:

Type	Gross Profit	**Type**	*Gross Profit*
Press	⏎Enter	**Click**	*the mouse button*

You did not have to press the DOWN ARROW key or click on the ⬇ SmartIcon because Gross Profit is the last label on the spreadsheet. Your worksheet should look like Figure 4-7.

Figure 4-7

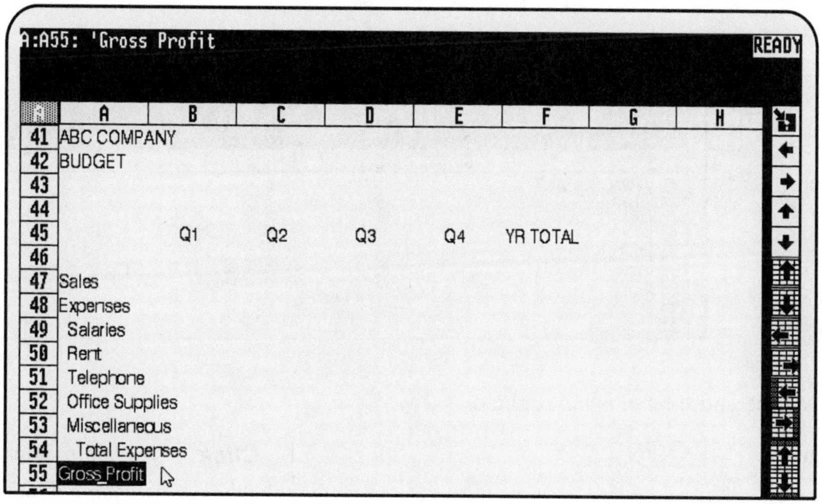

Expanding the Width of a Column

Note that several labels extend into column B. To enter data in column B but still see all the labels in column A, you must widen column A. To widen column A:

Move	the cell pointer to the cell containing the longest label in the column	**Click**	*on the cell containing the longest label in the column*

In this example, move the cell pointer to cell A54, which has the indented label Total Expenses.

Access the Lotus 1-2-3 menu and select the menu options for expanding a column.

Press	⬜ /	**Move**	*the mouse pointer to the control panel*
Select	Worksheet	**Choose**	*Worksheet*

Select	Column		**_Choose_**	_Column_
Select	Set-Width		**_Choose_**	_Set-Width_
Press	⟶ until the entire label is highlighted by the cell pointer		**_Click_**	_the_ ➡ _SmartIcon until the entire label is highlighted by the cell pointer_

In the control panel, the message "Enter column width (1..240): 14" should be displayed as shown in the top part of Figure 4-8.

Figure 4-8

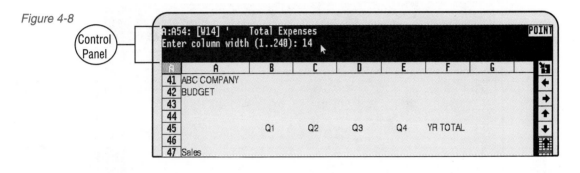

```
A:A54: [W14] '    Total Expenses                              POINT
Enter column width (1..240): 14   ▸
```

	A	B	C	D	E	F	G	
41	ABC COMPANY							←
42	BUDGET							→
43								↑
44								↓
45		Q1	Q2	Q3	Q4	YR TOTAL		
46								
47	Sales							

When the entire label is highlighted:

Press	⟵Enter		**_Click_**	_the mouse button with the mouse pointer in the control panel_

Note that when the prompt "Enter column width (1..240):" appears, you do not have to highlight the desired width, but rather you can type the desired column width (such as 14) and press ENTER. The column width can be set from 1 character to 240 characters. The width of column A is now 14 characters. Because column A occupies more screen space, column B has shifted to the right and part of column H no longer appears on the screen.

When the cell pointer is in any cell in column A, the control panel will display [W14], indicating that a column width of 14 has been set for the column. See the top part of Figure 4-9.

Figure 4-9

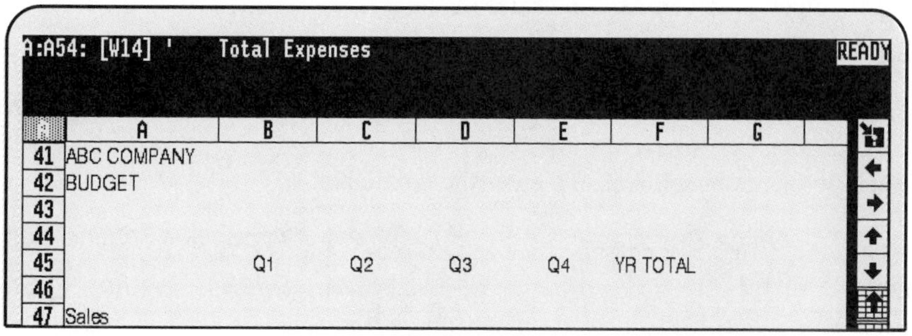

```
A:A54: [W14] '    Total Expenses                                    READY

          A         B        C        D        E        F        G
   41  ABC COMPANY
   42  BUDGET
   43
   44
   45              Q1       Q2       Q3       Q4    YR TOTAL
   46
   47  Sales
```

User Tip

An alternative method for expanding the width of a column is to move the mouse pointer to the boundary line of columns A and B. Then press and hold the mouse button down. A two-headed horizontal arrow appears. Drag the two-headed arrow to the right until the boundary line is to the right of the last letter in the longest label in the column. When you release the mouse button, the column width is changed.

Entering the Assumptions

Design Tip

Whenever you create a spreadsheet, it is a good idea to include the assumptions you use in a separate portion of the spreadsheet. If someone else looks at the worksheet, it is then much easier for the person to determine how the values appearing in the spreadsheet are computed. "What-if" analysis is also facilitated by placing the assumptions in a separate location of the spreadsheet. In this example worksheet, you will place the assumptions below the worksheet.

To enter the labels for the Assumptions:

Move	the cell pointer to cell A58		*Click*	*on cell A58*
Type	Assumptions		*Type*	*Assumptions*
Press	⬇ twice		*Click*	*the* ⬇ *SmartIcon twice*

The cell pointer is in cell A60. To enter the next label:

Type	Sales		*Type*	*Sales*
Press	⬇		*Click*	*the* ⬇ *SmartIcon*

The cell pointer is in cell A61. To enter the next label:

Type	Telephone	**Type**	Telephone
Press	⬇	**Click**	the ⬇ SmartIcon

The cell pointer is in cell A62. To enter the next label:

Type	Office Supplies	**Type**	Office Supplies
Press	⬇	**Click**	the ⬇ SmartIcon

The cell pointer is in cell A63. To enter the next label:

Type	Miscellaneous	**Type**	Miscellaneous
Press	⏎Enter	**Click**	the mouse button

The bottom part of your screen should look like Figure 4-10.

Figure 4-10

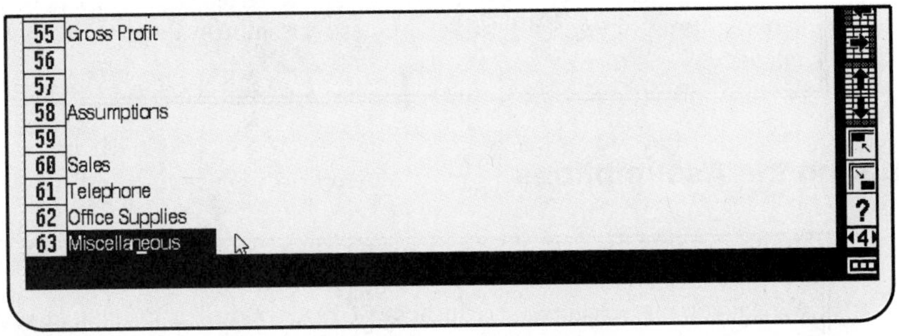

55	Gross Profit
56	
57	
58	Assumptions
59	
60	Sales
61	Telephone
62	Office Supplies
63	Miscellaneous

To input the assumed Sales growth rate for Quarters 2, 3, and 4 in columns C, D, and E:

Move	the cell pointer to cell C60	**Click**	on cell C60
Type	.02	**Type**	.02

Because 0.02 is numeric, it is interpreted by Lotus 1-2-3 as a **value**. The mode indicator at the top right corner of the screen displays the word VALUE. To enter the number:

Press	➡	**Click**	the ➡ SmartIcon

The cell pointer is in cell D60.

Type	.02	**Type**	.02
Press	➡	**Click**	the ➡ SmartIcon

With the cell pointer in cell E60:

Type	.02	**Type**	.02

Press	⎣←Enter⎦		*Click*	*the mouse button*

The Sales rate is not placed in column B because the rate is not needed for the first quarter.

Move	the cell pointer to cell C61		*Click*	*on cell C61*

To input the Telephone, Office Supplies, and Miscellaneous expense rates for Q2:

Type	.05		*Type*	*.05*
Press	⎣↓⎦		*Click*	*the* ⊞ *SmartIcon*

The cell pointer is in cell C62.

Type	50		*Type*	*50*
Press	⎣↓⎦		*Click*	*the* ⊞ *SmartIcon*

The cell pointer is in cell C63.

Type	.03		*Type*	*.03*
Press	⎣←Enter⎦		*Click*	*the mouse button*

You will enter the remaining quarterly assumptions for Telephone, Office Supplies, and Miscellaneous expenses using a more efficient process in the next section. The bottom part of your screen should look like Figure 4-11.

Figure 4-11

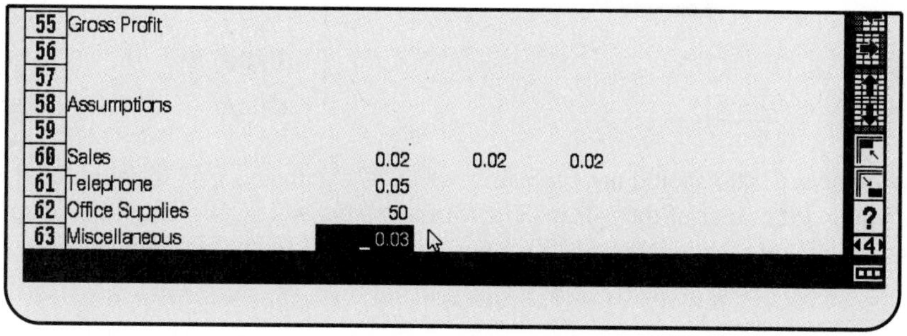

Entering Numbers and Formulas and Copying Information in a Spreadsheet[1]

To enter the Sales amount for the first quarter:

Move	the cell pointer to cell B47		*Click*	*on cell B47*
Type	60000		*Type*	*60000*
Press	⎣←Enter⎦		*Click*	*the mouse button*

[1]See the section at the end of this chapter for additional information on using formulas in Lotus 1-2-3.

A formula is an effective way to compute values in Lotus 1-2-3. Cell addresses, numbers, arithmetic operators, and parentheses are included in a formula to specify the calculations necessary to place an appropriate value in a specific cell on your screen.

To enter the sales amount for the second quarter, you need to show a 2% increase over the first quarter. The formula for the second quarter of Sales multiplies the Sales amount in the first quarter by (1 + .02) or 1.02 to show a 2% projected increase.

First place the cell pointer in the cell where the formula will be entered.

Move	the cell pointer to cell C47	*Click*	*on cell C47*

Begin typing the formula:

Type	+	*Type*	*+*

A plus sign (+) is used to indicate that a value is being calculated.

Move	the cell pointer to cell B47 (First Quarter Sales)	**Click**	*the ◄ SmartIcon to move the cell pointer to cell B47 (First Quarter Sales)*
Type	*	*Type*	*＊*

The asterisk (＊) is the symbol for multiplication.

Type	(1+	*Type*	*(1+*
Move	the cell pointer to cell C60	**Click**	*the ▼ SmartIcon until the cell pointer is in cell C60*
Type	)	*Type*	*)*
Press	◄─Enter	**Click**	*the mouse button*

The number 61200 should now appear in cell C47. With cell C47 highlighted, look at the control panel at the upper left corner of the screen. The formula +B47＊(1+C60) should be displayed. This is the formula used to compute the number 61200. Your screen should look like Figure 4-12.

Figure 4-12

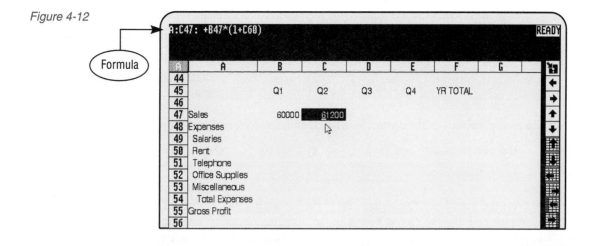

Formula

A:C47: +B47*(1+C60)   READY

	A	B	C	D	E	F	G
44							
45		Q1	Q2	Q3	Q4	YR TOTAL	
46							
47	Sales	60000	61200				
48	Expenses						
49	Salaries						
50	Rent						
51	Telephone						
52	Office Supplies						
53	Miscellaneous						
54	Total Expenses						
55	Gross Profit						
56							

Design Tip

A formula can be typed directly into a cell. For example, by typing +B47*(1+C60) with the cell pointer in cell C47 and pressing the ENTER key or clicking the mouse button with the mouse pointer in the control panel, you would obtain the same result. It is best to point to the cells when creating a formula, because you tend to make fewer errors in specifying the formula.

The formulas in Lotus 1-2-3 are based on **relative cell location**. For example, the formula in cell C47, +B47*(1+C60), is interpreted by Lotus 1-2-3 as "multiply the contents of the cell immediately to the left of the formula location by 1 and add the number appearing 13 cells below the formula location." The Sales for Quarters 3 and 4 are projected to increase from the previous quarter (the previous cell) by 2 percent. Therefore, the formula +B47*(1+C60) can be **copied** to cells D47 and E47 and adjusted to read +C47*(1+D60) and +D47*(1+E60), respectively. 1-2-3 makes the adjustments automatically.

To copy the formula in cell C47 to cells D47 and E47, the cell pointer should be highlighting cell C47. If not, move the cell pointer to cell C47.

| **Press** | `/` | | ***Move*** | *the mouse pointer to the control panel* |
| **Select** | Copy | | ***Choose*** | *Copy* |

The **C**opy command consists of two prompts. One prompt requires you to indicate what cells are to be copied. An easy way to do this is to highlight the cells to copy and press the ENTER key or click the mouse button. When you press the ENTER key or click the mouse button, the second prompt requires you to specify the area to where the cell or cells will be copied. When you press the ENTER key or click the mouse button after the second prompt, the Copy command is completed.

In the control panel, the first prompt requests "Enter range to copy FROM:". Make sure that the cell or cells to be copied are highlighted. Since C47 is the cell to copy and it is already highlighted:

Press `←Enter`	**Click**	*the mouse button with the mouse pointer in the control panel*

The second prompt appears in the control panel and requests "Enter range to copy TO:".

Move the cell pointer to cell D47	**Move**	*the mouse pointer to cell D47*
Type . (the period key)		

When you press the period key, notice that "D47" (in the control panel) changes to "D47..D47". Pressing the period key or pressing the mouse button in the dragging operation **anchors** the cell pointer so that more than one cell can be highlighted at a time. In this example, the cell pointer is **anchored** at cell D47 and can be **stretched** to cell E47.

Move the cell pointer to cell E47	**Drag**	*the mouse pointer to cell E47 to highlight cells D47 through E47*
Press `←Enter`	**Click**	*the mouse button*

The formula in cell C47 has now been copied to cells D47 and E47 (Quarters 3 and 4). Refer to Parts 1 through 5 of Figure 4-13 for an illustration of the copy process.

USING THE COPY COMMAND - ENTER RANGE TO COPY FROM

Step 1 of Copy Procedure: Highlight the cell(s) to copy, press `/`, select Copy, and press `←Enter`.

With the mouse pointer in the control panel, choose Copy, and click the mouse button.

Figure 4-13 Part 1

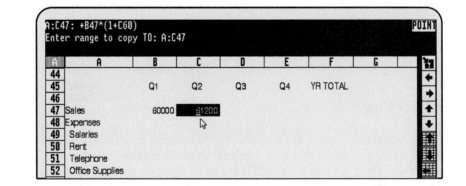

USING THE COPY PROCEDURE - ENTER RANGE TO COPY TO

Step 2 of Copy Procedure: Highlight the first cell where the cell(s) will be copied.

Move the mouse pointer to the first cell where the cell(s) will be copied.

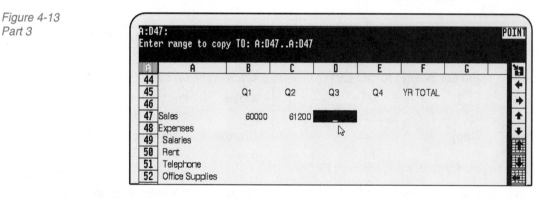

Step 3 of Copy Procedure: When copying to more than one cell, press the period key to **anchor** the cell pointer.

Press and hold down the mouse button.

Step 4 of Copy Procedure: **Stretch** the cell pointer from its anchored position to the rest of the area where the cell will be copied.

Drag the mouse pointer to highlight the rest of the area where the cell will be copied.

Step 5 of Copy Procedure: Press ⏎Enter to copy the desired cell(s) and complete the Copy Procedure.

Click the mouse button to copy the desired cell(s) and complete the Copy Procedure.

Figure 4-13
Part 5

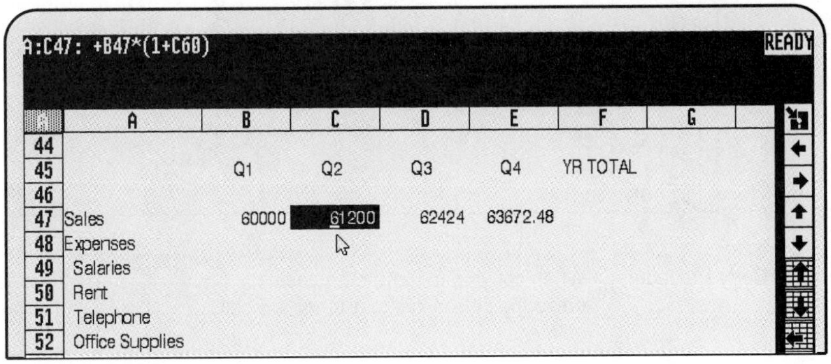

```
A:C47: +B47*(1+C60)                                          READY

           A        B        C        D        E        F        G

  44
  45                Q1       Q2       Q3       Q4     YR TOTAL
  46
  47   Sales       60000    61200    62424   63672.48
  48   Expenses
  49   Salaries
  50   Rent
  51   Telephone
  52   Office Supplies
```

To copy the assumptions for Telephone, Office Supplies, and Miscellaneous expense categories from Quarter 2 to Quarter 3 and Quarter 4:

Move	the cell pointer to cell C61		*Click*	*on cell C61*
Press	/		*Move*	*the mouse pointer to the control panel*
Select	Copy		*Choose*	*Copy*

When prompted for "Enter range to copy FROM:"

Move	the cell pointer to cell C63		*Move*	*the mouse pointer to cell C61*
			Drag	*the mouse pointer to cell C63*

You do not have to press the period key, because 1-2-3 automatically anchors the cell pointer at its current position when prompting for "Enter range to copy FROM:". In this example, the cell pointer is anchored at cell C61 and is **stretched** to highlight cells C61 through C63.

Press	⏎Enter		*Click*	*the mouse button*

When prompted for "Enter range to copy TO:"

Move	the cell pointer to cell D61		*Move*	*the mouse pointer to cell D61*
Type	.			

The period anchors the cell pointer at cell D61.

Move	the cell pointer to cell E63		*Drag*	*the mouse pointer to cell E63*
Press	⏎Enter		*Click*	*the mouse button*

The expense assumptions have now been copied to cells D61 through E63. Refer to Parts 1 through 3 of Figure 4-14 for an illustration of the process for copying several cells.

COPYING MULTIPLE CELLS TO A RANGE

Figure 4-14
Part 1

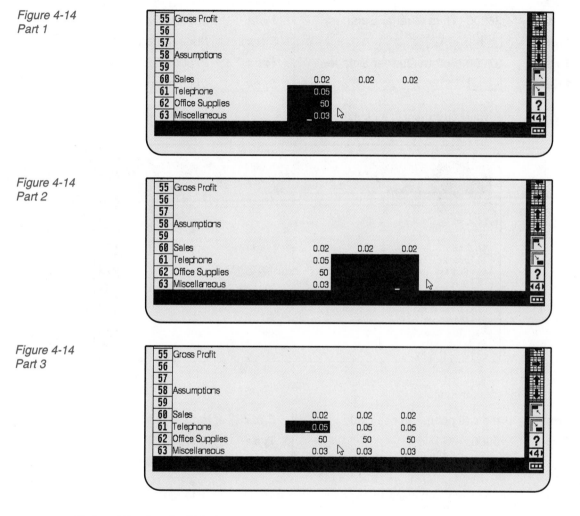

Figure 4-14
Part 2

Figure 4-14
Part 3

To input the data for Salaries:

Move	the cell pointer to cell B49	*Click*	*on cell B49*
Type	35000 (First Quarter Salaries)	*Type*	*35000 (First Quarter Salaries)*
Press	→	*Click*	*the* → *SmartIcon*

The cell pointer is now on cell C49.

To enter the salary amounts for Quarters 2, 3, and 4:

Type	35500 (Second Quarter Salaries)		*Type*	*35500 (Second Quarter Salaries)*
Press	→		*Click*	*the* ➡ *SmartIcon*
Type	36200 (Third Quarter Salaries)		*Type*	*36200 (Third Quarter Salaries)*
Press	→		*Click*	*the* ➡ *SmartIcon*
Type	37000 (Fourth Quarter Salaries)		*Type*	*37000 (Fourth Quarter Salaries)*
Press	←Enter		*Click*	*the mouse button*

The top part of your screen should look like Figure 4-15.

Figure 4-15

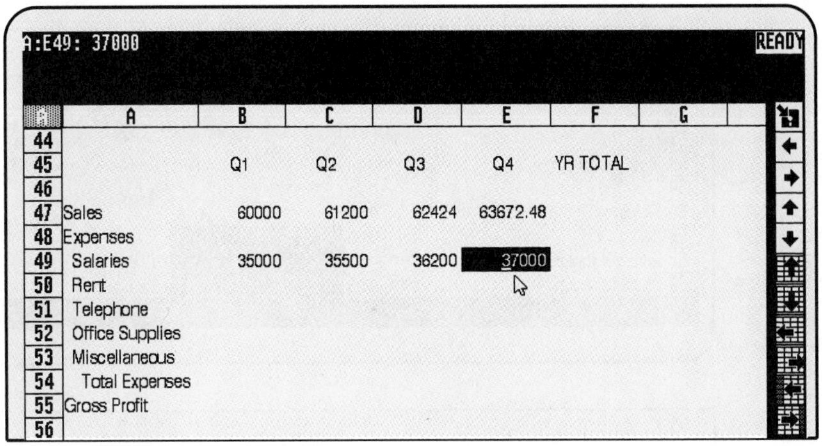

To input the data for Rent:

Move	the cell pointer to cell B50		*Click*	*on cell B50*
Type	9000		*Type*	*9000*
Press	←Enter		*Click*	*the mouse button*

You can use the Copy command to copy the 9000 from Quarter 1 to Quarters 2, 3, and 4. The cell pointer should be in cell B50.

To copy the Rent amount to the other quarters:

Press	/		*Move*	*the mouse pointer to the control panel*
Select	Copy		*Choose*	*Copy*

When prompted for "Enter range to copy FROM:" note that the cell pointer is highlighting cell B50, which is the cell to copy. To indicate that B50 is the cell to copy:

Press	[←Enter]	**Click**	the mouse button with the mouse pointer in the control panel

When prompted for "Enter range to copy TO:"

Move	the cell pointer to cell C50	**Move**	the mouse pointer to cell C50
Type	.	**Drag**	the mouse pointer to cell E50
Move	the cell pointer to cell E50	**Click**	the mouse button
Press	[←Enter]		

The number 9000 should now be copied to Quarters 2, 3, and 4. The top part of your screen should look like Figure 4-16.

Figure 4-16

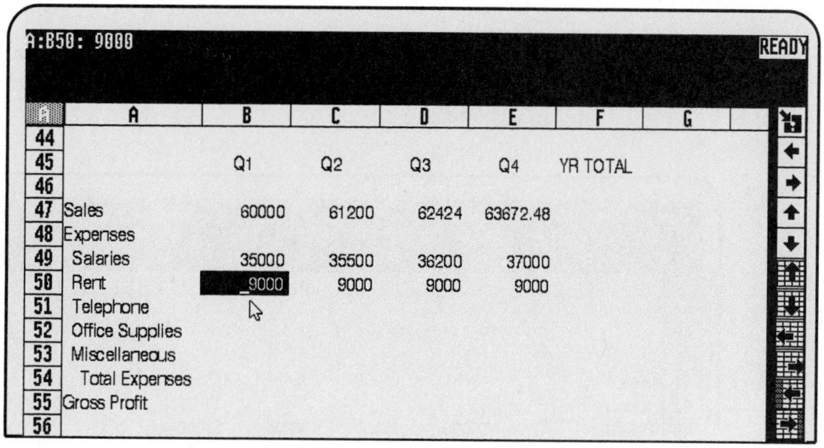

To input the data for Telephone expenses for the first quarter:

Move	the cell pointer to cell B51	**Click**	on cell B51
Type	1000	**Type**	1000
Press	[←Enter]	**Click**	the mouse button

> *In This Book*
> Up to this point, you have been instructed to move the mouse pointer to a cell and then click the mouse button to include a cell in a formula. In the remainder of the book, these instructions are combined by asking you to click on the cell you want to include in a formula.

You can enter the following formula to indicate that Telephone expenses will increase by 5 percent for the remaining quarters:

Move	the cell pointer to cell C51		**Click**	on cell C51
Type	+		**Type**	+
Move	the cell pointer to cell B51 (Telephone expenses for Quarter1)		**Click**	the ← SmartIcon to move the cell pointer to cell B51 (Telephone expenses for Quarter1)
Type	*(1+		**Type**	*(1+
Move	the cell pointer to cell C61 (Growth Rate factor for Telephone expense)		**Click**	the ↓ SmartIcon until the cell pointer is in cell C61 (Growth Rate factor for Telephone expense)
Type	)		**Type**	)
Press	⊢Enter		**Click**	the mouse button

The number 1050 should appear in cell C51. The formula +B51*(1+C61) should be displayed in the control panel, and the top part of your screen should look like Figure 4-17. The formulas for Quarters 3 and 4 will be completed later in this chapter.

Figure 4-17

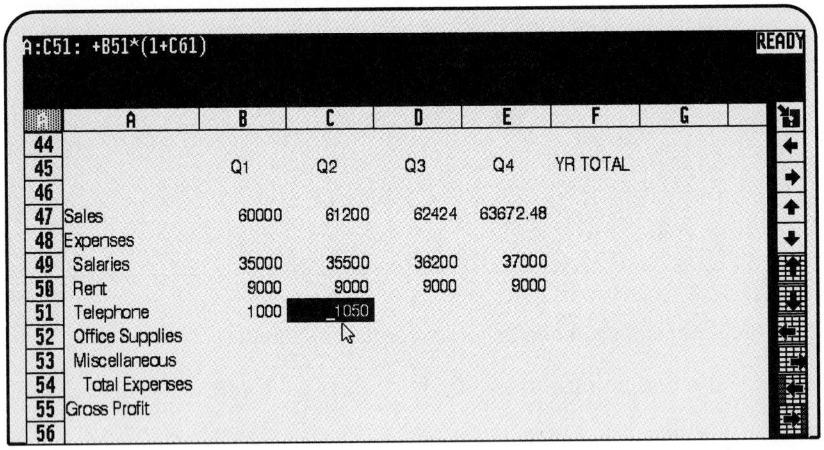

```
A:C51: +B51*(1+C61)                                              READY

        A           B        C        D        E         F       G
44
45                  Q1       Q2       Q3       Q4     YR TOTAL
46
47  Sales          60000    61200    62424   63672.48
48  Expenses
49   Salaries      35000    35500    36200   37000
50   Rent           9000     9000     9000    9000
51   Telephone      1000     1050
52   Office Supplies
53   Miscellaneous
54    Total Expenses
55  Gross Profit
56
```

To input the data for Office Supplies expenses for the first quarter:

Move	the cell pointer to cell B52		**Click**	on cell B52
Type	750		**Type**	750
Press	⊢Enter		**Click**	the mouse button

Office Supplies expenses increase by $50 for the remaining quarters. To enter the appropriate formula:

Move	the cell pointer to cell C52		*Click*	*on cell C52*
Type	+		*Type*	*+*
Move	the cell pointer to cell B52		*Click*	*the ◄ SmartIcon to move the cell pointer to cell B52*
Type	+		*Type*	*+*
Move	the cell pointer to cell C62		*Click*	*the ▼ SmartIcon until the cell pointer is in cell C62*
Press	⮐Enter		*Click*	*the mouse button with the mouse pointer in the control panel*

The number 800 appears in cell C52. The formula +B52+C62 is now displayed in the control panel. The top part of your screen should look like Figure 4-18. The formulas for Quarters 3 and 4 are completed later in this chapter.

Figure 4-18

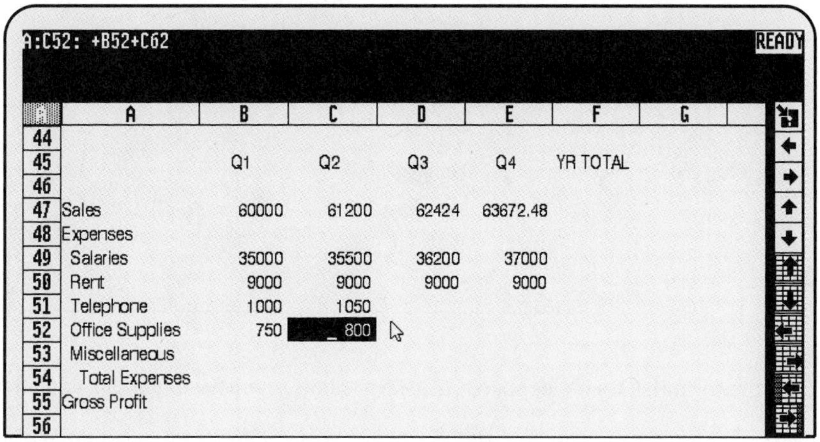

To input the data for Miscellaneous expenses for the first quarter:

Move	the cell pointer to cell B53		*Click*	*on cell B53*
Type	1000		*Type*	*1000*
Press	⮐Enter		*Click*	*the mouse button*

To enter the formula that indicates Miscellaneous expenses are to increase by 3%:

Move	the cell pointer to cell C53		*Click*	*on cell C53*
Type	+		*Type*	*+*

Move	the cell pointer to cell B53		*Click*	the ◄ *SmartIcon to move the cell pointer to cell B53*
Type	∗(1+		*Type*	*∗(1+*
Move	the cell pointer to cell C63		*Click*	the ▼ *SmartIcon until the cell pointer is in cell C63*
Type	)		*Type*	*)*
Press	⌐←Enter⌐		*Click*	*the mouse button*

The number 1030 now appears in cell C53. The formula +B53∗(1+C63) is displayed in the control panel, and the top part of your screen should look like Figure 4-19.

Figure 4-19

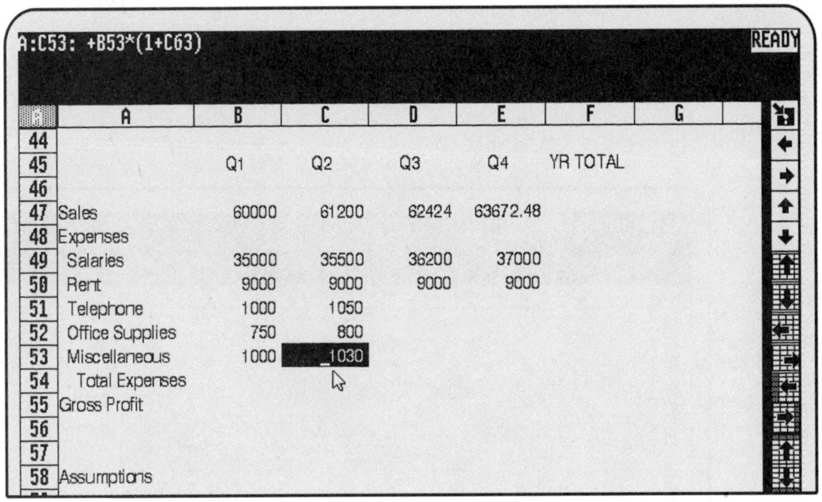

To copy the formulas for Telephone, Office Supplies, and Miscellaneous expenses to Quarters 3 and 4:

Move	the cell pointer to cell C51 (the formula for projecting Telephone expenses)		*Click*	*on cell C51 (the formula for projecting Telephone expenses)*
Press	⌐ / ⌐		*Move*	*the mouse pointer to the control panel*
Select	Copy		*Choose*	*Copy*

When prompted for "Enter range to copy FROM:"

Move	the cell pointer to cell C53 (the formula for projecting Miscellaneous expenses)	*Move*	*the mouse pointer to cell C51*
		Drag	*the mouse pointer to cell C53*

You did not have to press the period key because 1-2-3 automatically anchors the cell pointer at its current position when prompting for "Enter range to copy FROM:". In this example, the cell pointer is anchored at cell C51 and is stretched to highlight cells C51 through C53.

Press	[←Enter]	*Click*	*the mouse button*

When prompted for "Enter range to copy TO:"

Move	the cell pointer to cell D51	**Move**	the mouse pointer to cell D51
Type	.	**Drag**	the mouse pointer to cell E53
Pressing the period key anchors the cell pointer at cell D51.		*Pressing the mouse button anchors the cell pointer at cell D51.*	
Move	the cell pointer to cell E53		

The screen currently displays a highlighted rectangle that covers cells D51 through E53.

Press	[←Enter]	*Click*	*the mouse button*

The formulas in cells C51 through C53 that project Telephone, Office Supplies, and Miscellaneous expenses have been copied to cells D51 through E53. The top part of your screen should look like Figure 4-20.

Figure 4-20

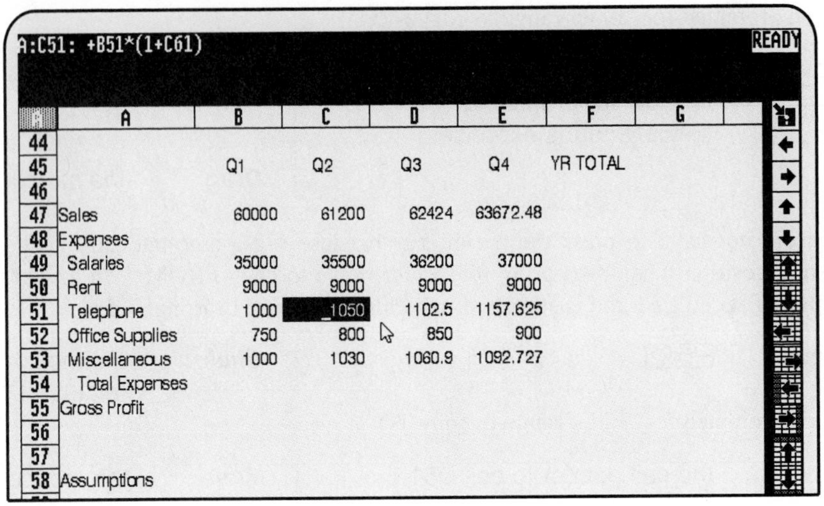
A:C51: +B51*(1+C61) READY

	A	B	C	D	E	F	G
44							
45		Q1	Q2	Q3	Q4	YR TOTAL	
46							
47	Sales	60000	61200	62424	63672.48		
48	Expenses						
49	Salaries	35000	35500	36200	37000		
50	Rent	9000	9000	9000	9000		
51	Telephone	1000	1050	1102.5	1157.625		
52	Office Supplies	750	800	850	900		
53	Miscellaneous	1000	1030	1060.9	1092.727		
54	Total Expenses						
55	Gross Profit						
56							
57							
58	Assumptions						

Using a Special Function

You now need to sum the quarterly values for the various items to obtain the Total Expenses for the first quarter. Lotus 1-2-3 has a special function that makes it easy to sum the expense values. The SUM function is used to add a series of numbers together. The general format for the SUM function is:

@SUM(first cell..last cell)

Note that a range of cells is specified within the set of parentheses. By placing the @ character prior to the word SUM, you have indicated that you want to use the special function @SUM. The many other special functions available in 1-2-3 are discussed in Chapter 15.

To enter the @SUM function for calculating Total Expenses for the first quarter:

Move	the cell pointer to cell B54	***Click***	*on cell B54*
Type	@SUM(	***Type***	*@SUM(*
Move	the cell pointer to cell B49 (the first item in column B to total, which is Salaries)	***Click***	*the [↑] SmartIcon until the cell pointer is in cell B49 (the first item in column B to total, which is Salaries)*
Type	.	**Type**	.
Pressing the period key anchors the cell pointer in cell B49.		*Pressing the period key anchors the cell pointer in cell B49.*	

Move	the cell pointer to cell B53	*Click*	*the ⬇ SmartIcon until the cell pointer is in cell B53*
Type	)	*Type*	*)*
Press	←Enter	*Click*	*the mouse button*

The number 46750 should appear in cell B54. The formula @SUM(B49..B53) is displayed in the control panel, and the top part of your screen should look like Figure 4-21.

Figure 4-21

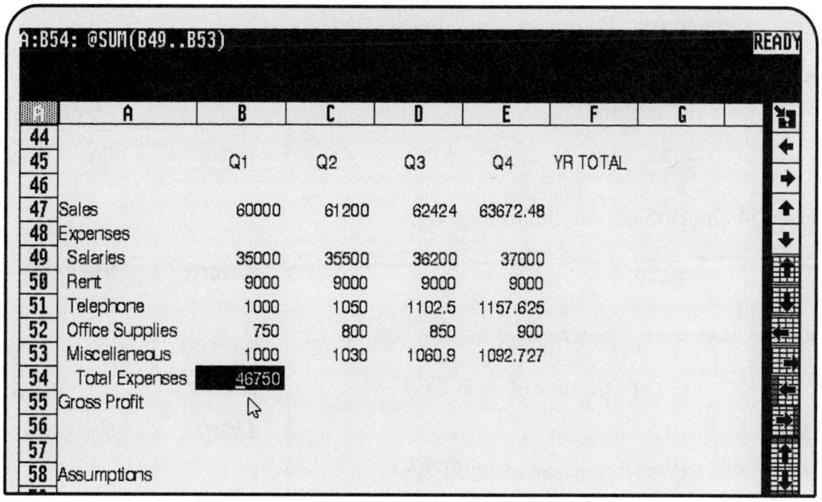

To compute Gross Profit, you must create a formula that subtracts Total Expenses from Sales.

Move	the cell pointer to cell B55	*Click*	*on cell B55*
Type	+	*Type*	*+*
Move	the cell pointer to cell B47 (Sales)	*Click*	*the ⬆ SmartIcon until the cell pointer is in cell B47 (Sales)*
Type	-	*Type*	*-*
Move	the cell pointer to cell B54 (Total Expenses)	*Click*	*the ⬆ SmartIcon to move the cell pointer to cell B54 (Total Expenses)*
Press	←Enter	*Click*	*the mouse button with the mouse pointer in the control panel*

The number 13250 should appear in cell B55. The formula +B47-B54 is displayed in the control panel.

You can use the Copy command to copy the formulas for computing Total Expenses and Gross Profit to the remaining three quarters.

Move	the cell pointer to cell B54 (Total Expenses)		*Click*	*on cell B54 (Total Expenses)*
Press	☐ / ☐		*Move*	*the mouse pointer to the control panel*
Select	Copy		*Choose*	*Copy*

When prompted for "Enter range to copy FROM:"

Move	the cell pointer to cell B55 (Gross Profit)		*Move*	*the mouse pointer to cell B54 (Total Expenses)*
			Drag	*the mouse pointer to cell B55*

Cells B54 and B55 should be highlighted.

Press	⌐Enter		*Click*	*the mouse button*

When prompted for "Enter range to copy TO:"

Move	the cell pointer to cell C54		*Move*	*the mouse pointer to cell C54*
Type	.		*Drag*	*the mouse pointer to cell E55*
Move	the cell pointer to cell E55			

Cells C54 through E55 are highlighted.

Press	⌐Enter		*Click*	*the mouse button*

Your screen should look like Figure 4-22.

Figure 4-22

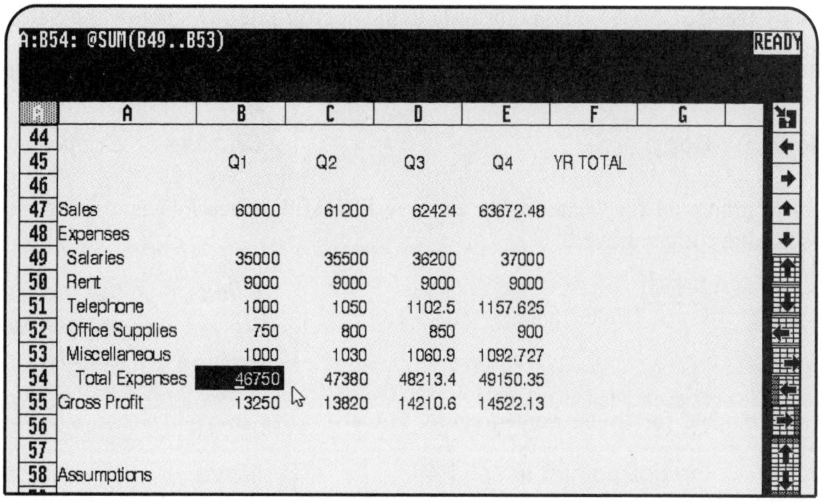

User Tip

An alternative method for summing the contents of contiguous cells is to use the SUM ⊞ SmartIcon.

To compute the total Sales for the year:

Move	the cell pointer to cell F47		*Click*	*on cell F47*
Type	@SUM(		*Move*	*the mouse pointer to the left or right arrow beside the palette number*
Move	the cell pointer to cell B47		*Click*	*the mouse button until the SUM ⊞ SmartIcon appears*
Type	.		*Move*	*the mouse pointer to the SUM ⊞ SmartIcon*
Move	the cell pointer to cell E47		*Click*	*the mouse button*
Type	)			
Press	←Enter			

The number 247296.5 appears in cell F47. The formula @SUM(B47..E47) appears in the control panel.

To copy the @SUM(B47..E47) formula to the appropriate rows below the Sales row:

Press	☐ /		***Move***	*the mouse pointer to the control panel*
Select	Copy		***Choose***	*Copy*

You are prompted for "Enter range to copy FROM:" Since F47 is already highlighted, the cell pointer does not have to be moved.

Press	⟵Enter		***Click***	*the mouse button with the mouse pointer in the control panel*

When prompted for "Enter range to copy TO:"

Move	the cell pointer to cell F49		***Move***	*the mouse pointer to cell F49*
Type	.		***Drag***	*the mouse pointer to cell F55*
Move	the cell pointer to cell F55		***Click***	*the mouse button*
Press	⟵Enter			

The formula @SUM(B47..E47) has been copied from cells F47 to cells F49 through F55. Your screen should look like Figure 4-23.

Figure 4-23

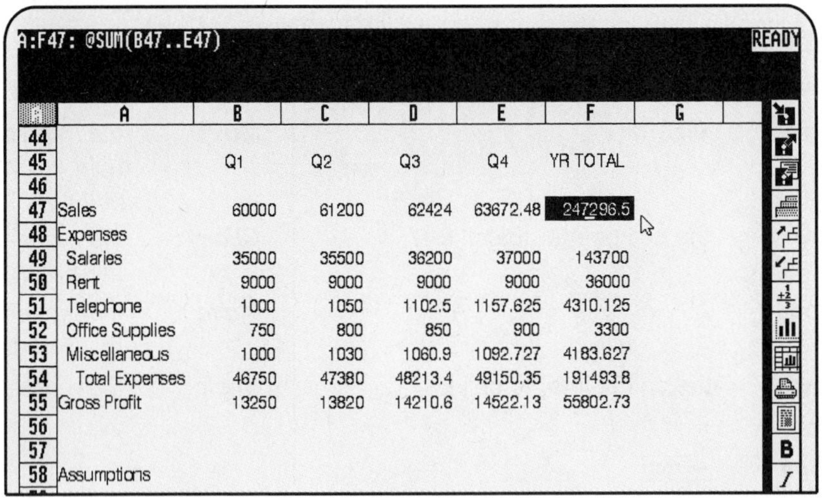

	A	B	C	D	E	F	G
44							
45		Q1	Q2	Q3	Q4	YR TOTAL	
46							
47	Sales	60000	61200	62424	63672.48	247296.5	
48	Expenses						
49	Salaries	35000	35500	36200	37000	143700	
50	Rent	9000	9000	9000	9000	36000	
51	Telephone	1000	1050	1102.5	1157.625	4310.125	
52	Office Supplies	750	800	850	900	3300	
53	Miscellaneous	1000	1030	1060.9	1092.727	4183.627	
54	Total Expenses	46750	47380	48213.4	49150.35	191493.8	
55	Gross Profit	13250	13820	14210.6	14522.13	55802.73	
56							
57							
58	Assumptions						

A:F47: @SUM(B47..E47) — READY

Selecting a Format for the Data

To choose a numeric **format** (commas, dollar signs, the number of decimal places, and so forth) for the worksheet:

Press	`/`		***Move***	*the mouse pointer to the control panel*
Select	Worksheet		***Choose***	*Worksheet*
Select	Global		***Choose***	*Global*
Select	Format		***Choose***	*Format*

You will now change the global format from General to Comma with no decimal places.

Select	, (for comma)		***Choose***	*, (for comma)*

Global means that the format chosen will be used as the default for the spreadsheet, unless another numeric format is specified. The , represents the comma format.

When prompted for the number of decimal places:

Type	0		***Type***	*0*
Press	←Enter		***Click***	*the mouse button with the mouse pointer in the control panel*

Be sure to type the number "zero" and not the letter "O." Your screen should look like Figure 4-24.

Figure 4-24

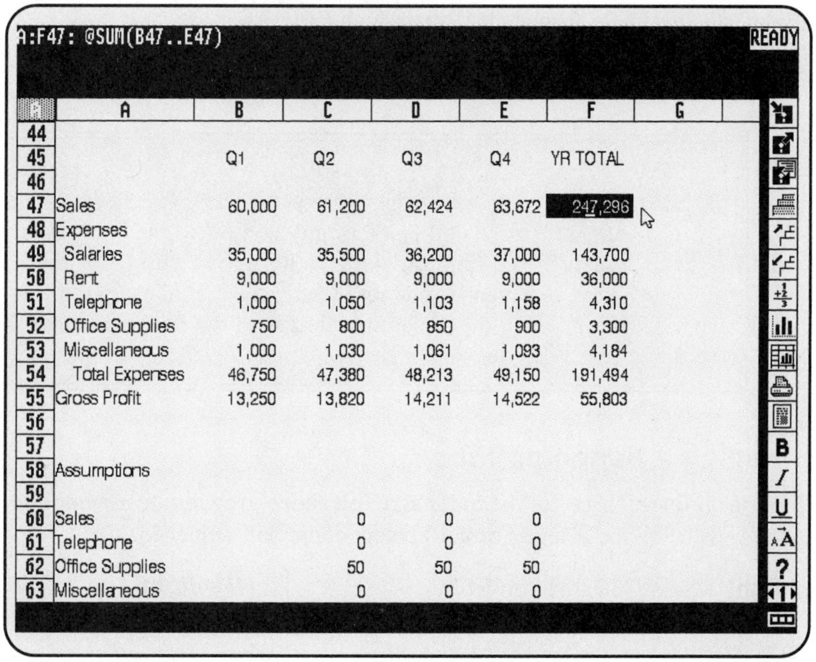

Notice that the various growth rates no longer have decimal numbers on the screen, because the format command indicated that the format for all numbers does not include any characters to the right of the decimal point. Later in this chapter, you will learn how to format only a range of cells instead of the entire spreadsheet.

Notice that rounding errors occur (e.g., Sales of 247,296 minus Total Expenses of 191,494 should equal 55,802 rather than 55,803). The rounding error occurred because the numbers are *formatted* to *show* 0 decimal places on your screen, but the *values* in the cells are not truly *rounded* to 0 decimal places. Rounding errors are resolved later in this chapter.

Highlighting a Range of Cells Before Issuing a Command

In all commands used to this point, the command has been issued prior to highlighting the range of cells to which the command is applicable. 1-2-3 provides you the alternative of highlighting the cells before you complete the command.

To illustrate the steps, suppose you want to highlight the values for the growth rate assumptions for Sales and Telephone expenses before you format them to include a percent sign.

To highlight the cells including the growth rate assumptions for Sales and Telephone:

Move	the cell pointer to cell C60		*Move*	*the mouse pointer to cell C60*
Press	`F4`		*Drag*	*the mouse pointer to cell E61*
Move	the cell pointer to cell E61			
Press	`←Enter`			

Notice that cells C60 through E61 are highlighted. You can remove the highlight of the cells by pressing a pointer-movement key, ESCAPE, or clicking the alternate mouse button.

To remove the highlight from cells C60 through E61:

Press	`Esc`		*Click*	*the alternate mouse button*

> *In This Book*
> When you have selected a range of cells, you have been asked to move to a specific cell, anchor the cell pointer, and then move the cell pointer to the last cell to be included in the range. Another alternative you have used is to move the mouse pointer to a specific cell and then drag the mouse pointer to the last cell in the desired range. For the remaining portion of the book, you are asked to highlight the range.

Formatting a Range of Cells

To have the proper format for the Sales and Telephone growth rate assumption values, you must format a range of cells using the **R**ange **F**ormat **P**ercent command sequence.

Highlight	cells C60 through E61		*Highlight*	*cells C60 through E61*

Press	⬚ / ⬚
Select	Range
Select	Format
Select	Percent
Type	0
Press	⬚←Enter⬚ to accept 0 decimal places

Move	*the mouse pointer to the control panel*
Choose	*Range*
Choose	*Format*
Choose	*Percent*
Type	*0*
Click	*the mouse button with the mouse pointer in the control panel to accept 0 decimal places*

Sales and Telephone growth rate assumptions should now be represented with a percent sign.

To have the proper format for the Office Supplies growth rate assumption values, you must format a range of cells using the **R**ange **F**ormat **F**ixed command sequence.

Highlight	cells C62 through E62
Press	⬚ / ⬚
Select	Range
Select	Format
Select	Fixed
Press	⬚←Enter⬚ to accept 2 decimal places

Highlight	*cells C62 through E62*
Move	*the mouse pointer to the control panel*
Choose	*Range*
Choose	*Format*
Choose	*Fixed*
Click	*the mouse button with the mouse pointer in the control panel to accept 2 decimal places*

To have the proper format for the Miscellaneous growth rate assumption values, you must format the range of cells C63 through E63 using the **R**ange **F**ormat **P**ercent command sequence.

Highlight	cells C63 through E63
Press	⬚ / ⬚
Select	Range
Select	Format
Select	Percent
Type	0
Press	⬚←Enter⬚ to accept 0 decimal places

Highlight	*cells C63 through E63*
Move	*the mouse pointer to the control panel*
Choose	*Range*
Choose	*Format*
Choose	*Percent*
Type	*0*
Click	*the mouse button with the mouse pointer in the control panel to accept 0 decimal places*

After moving to cell C63, the bottom part of your screen should look like Figure 4-25.

Figure 4-25

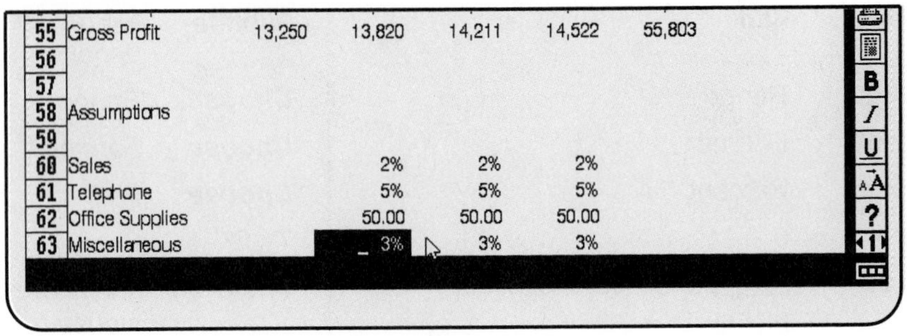

To format the Sales and Telephone growth rate values in the description, assumptions, and parameters block of your spreadsheet:

Highlight	cells C34 through C35		*Highlight*	*cells C34 through C35*
Press	⬜ /		*Move*	*the mouse pointer to the control panel*
Select	Range		*Choose*	*Range*
Select	Format		*Choose*	*Format*
Select	Percent		*Choose*	*Percent*
Type	0		*Type*	*0*
Press	⬅Enter		*Click*	*the mouse button with the mouse pointer in the control panel*

To format the Office Supplies growth rate:

Move	the cell pointer to cell C36		*Click*	*on cell C36*
Press	⬜ /		*Move*	*the mouse pointer to the control panel*
Select	Range		*Choose*	*Range*
Select	Format		*Choose*	*Format*
Select	Fixed		*Choose*	*Fixed*
Press	⬅Enter twice to accept 2 decimal places		*Click*	*the mouse button twice with the mouse pointer in the control panel to accept 2 decimal places*

To format the Miscellaneous growth rate:

Move	the cell pointer to cell C37		*Click*	*on cell C37*
Press	⬜ /		*Move*	*the mouse pointer to the control panel*

Select	Range		*Choose*	Range
Select	Format		*Choose*	Format
Select	Percent		*Choose*	Percent
Type	0		**Type**	0
Press	⟵Enter twice		**Click**	the mouse button twice with the mouse pointer in the control panel

Notice that the initial values in Quarter 1 for Sales, Salaries, Rent, Telephone, Office Supplies, and Miscellaneous expenses in cells C24 through C28 were formatted appropriately when you formatted the entire worksheet.

> *User Tip*
>
> An alternative method for formatting a range of cells with the percent format is to highlight the cells and then click the Percent Format % SmartIcon. Note that two decimal places are automatically included in the format.

Inserting Blank Rows in a Spreadsheet

Before starting this exercise, make sure row 41 is the first row appearing on your screen.

To insert a blank row between Sales and Expenses:

Move	the cell pointer to cell A48 (Expenses)		*Click*	on cell A48 (Expenses)
Press	/		*Click*	the mouse pointer to the control panel
Select	Worksheet		*Choose*	Worksheet
Select	Insert		*Choose*	Insert
Select	Row		*Choose*	Row

When prompted for the range of rows to insert:

Press	⟵Enter		*Move*	the mouse pointer to cell A48
			Click	the mouse button twice

Since the cell pointer was already highlighting cell A48, pressing the ENTER key or clicking the mouse button twice at this point caused one row to be inserted at row 48. The top part of your screen should look like Figure 4-26.

Figure 4-26

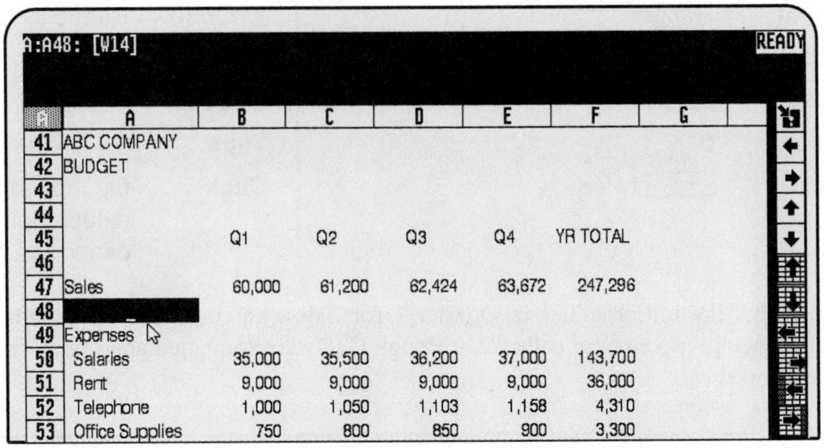

	A	B	C	D	E	F	G	
41	ABC COMPANY							
42	BUDGET							
43								
44								
45		Q1	Q2	Q3	Q4	YR TOTAL		
46								
47	Sales	60,000	61,200	62,424	63,672	247,296		
48								
49	Expenses							
50	Salaries	35,000	35,500	36,200	37,000	143,700		
51	Rent	9,000	9,000	9,000	9,000	36,000		
52	Telephone	1,000	1,050	1,103	1,158	4,310		
53	Office Supplies	750	800	850	900	3,300		

A:A48: [W14] — READY

> *User Tip*
>
> An alternative method for inserting a row is to place the cell pointer in the row in which you want to insert a blank row. Then click the Row Insert ▦ SmartIcon. If you want to insert more than one row, highlight cells in more than one row before you click the Row Insert ▦ SmartIcon.

Entering Underlines and Double Underlines

To underline a cell, you use the Wysiwyg (What You See Is What You Get) add-in menu. You access this menu by pressing the COLON key or by clicking the alternate mouse button with the mouse pointer in the control panel. Further information on the Wysiwyg add-in is provided in Chapter 5.

To input subtotal underlines for the Miscellaneous expense cells:

Highlight	cells B54 through F54	*Highlight*	*cells B54 through F54*
Press	[:]	*Move*	*the mouse pointer to the control panel*
Select	Format	*Click*	*the alternate mouse button to access the Wysiwyg menu*
Select	Lines	*Choose*	*Format*
Select	Bottom	*Choose*	*Lines*
		Choose	*Bottom*

After moving to cell A54, the bottom part of your screen should look like Figure 4-27.

Figure 4-27

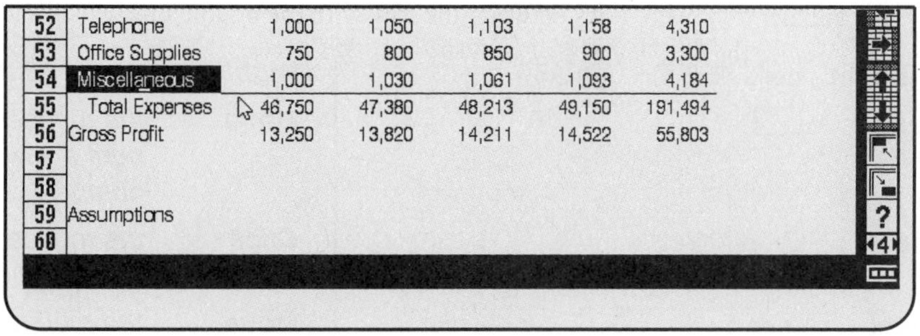

Notice that the bottom of cells B54 through F54 appear as underlines.

To place single underlines under the Total Expenses cells:

Highlight	cells B55 through F55	**Highlight**	cells B55 through F55
Press	⬚:⬚	**Move**	the mouse pointer to the control panel
Select	Format	**Choose**	Format
Select	Lines	**Choose**	Lines
Select	Bottom	**Choose**	Bottom

To place double underlines on the Gross Profit cells:

Highlight	cells B56 through F56	**Highlight**	cells B56 through F56
Press	⬚:⬚	**Move**	the mouse pointer to the control panel
Select	Format	**Choose**	Format
Select	Lines	**Choose**	Lines
Select	Double	**Choose**	Double
Select	Bottom	**Choose**	Bottom

Note that double underlines appear at the bottom of cells B56 through F56.

After moving to cell A56, the bottom part of your screen should look like Figure 4-28.

Figure 4-28

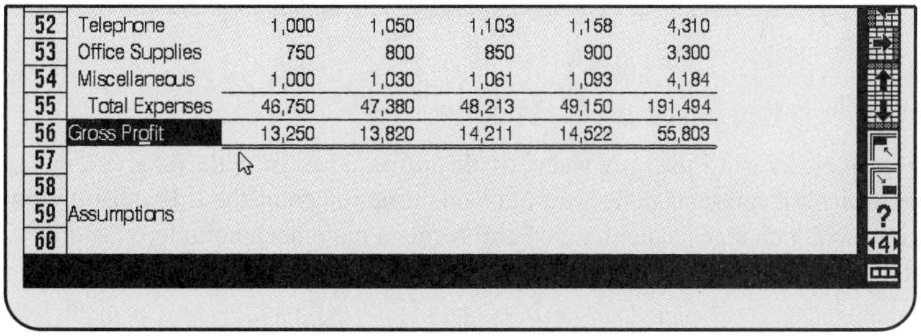

To place another two blank lines between the row with the double underlines and the Assumptions:

Highlight	cells A58 through A59		**Highlight**	cells A58 through A59
Press	[/]		**Move**	the mouse pointer to the left or right arrow beside the palette number
Select	Worksheet		**Click**	the mouse button until the Row Insert ▦ SmartIcon appears
Select	Insert		**Move**	the mouse pointer to the Row Insert ▦ SmartIcon
Select	Row		**Click**	the mouse button

The bottom part of your screen should look like Figure 4-29 and the assumptions should begin on row 61.

Figure 4-29

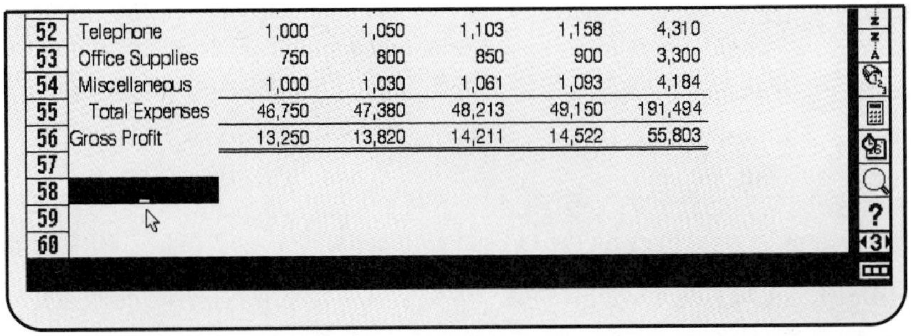

52	Telephone	1,000	1,050	1,103	1,158	4,310
53	Office Supplies	750	800	850	900	3,300
54	Miscellaneous	1,000	1,030	1,061	1,093	4,184
55	Total Expenses	46,750	47,380	48,213	49,150	191,494
56	Gross Profit	13,250	13,820	14,211	14,522	55,803
57						
58						
59						
60						

User Tip

Another method of underlining values is to select the Underline option on the Format menu. Then you can choose a single or double underline. Unfortunately, the single and double underlines only include the underline for the number of characters of the value in the affected cell. In most situations, it is desirable for the underline to have at least the same number of characters as the longest value in the column. To avoid having columns with different underline widths, most individuals use the Lines option on the Format menu to cover the entire width of each column.

Centering the Spreadsheet Title

Except for centering the spreadsheet title information in cells A41 and A42, you have completed the worksheet. It is appropriate to wait until this time to center the title information, because at this point, all column width changes, calculations, and formats have been completed and you know the true boundaries of the spreadsheet.

To center the spreadsheet title information:

Move	the cell pointer to cell A41		*Click*	*on cell A41*
Highlight	cells A41 through F42		*Highlight*	*cells A41 through F42*
Press	:		*Move*	*the mouse pointer to the control panel*
Select	Text		*Choose*	*Text*
Select	Align		*Choose*	*Align*
Select	Center		*Choose*	*Center*

The spreadsheet title information is centered above the rest of the spreadsheet model. Your screen should look like Figure 4-30.

Figure 4-30

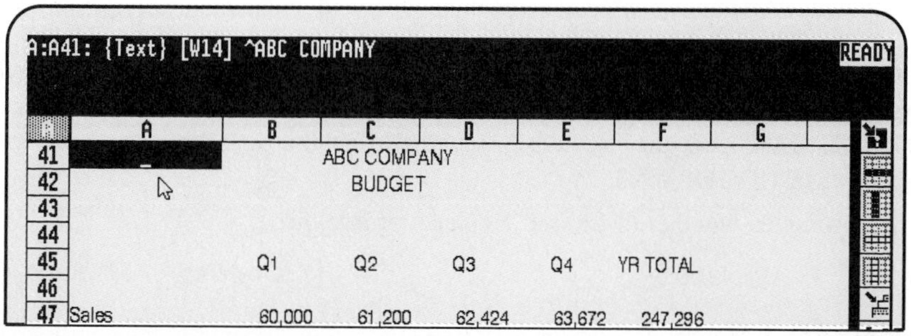

```
A:A41: {Text} [W14] ^ABC COMPANY                                    READY

          A         B        C        D        E        F        G
   41                            ABC COMPANY
   42                              BUDGET
   43
   44
   45                 Q1        Q2       Q3       Q4     YR TOTAL
   46
   47  Sales        60,000    61,200   62,424   63,672   247,296
```

> *User Tip*
> Another method for aligning text in a range of cells is to first highlight the range of cells. Then click the Align Text ▦ SmartIcon to center the text in the range. You can left align, right align, or return the text to its original alignment by continuing to click the Align Text ▦ SmartIcon.

■ SAVING AND REPLACING A SPREADSHEET

To have a particular cell in your spreadsheet model appear as the first cell on your screen when you retrieve a spreadsheet file, you must place the cell pointer in the desired cell before you save the spreadsheet. The first row of the spreadsheet model should also appear as the first row on your screen prior to saving the spreadsheet.

Make sure row 41 is the first row on your screen.

The spreadsheet previously saved did not include the spreadsheet model. To save the spreadsheet model, you must save the spreadsheet to your disk again.

To replace the BUDGET spreadsheet file that was previously saved:

Move	the cell pointer to cell A41		*Click*	*on cell A41*

Press	☐ /
Select	File
Select	Save

Move	*the mouse pointer to the control panel*
Click	*the alternate mouse button until the 1-2-3 main menu appears*
Choose	*File*
Choose	*Save*

After initiating the save command, the prompt for the file name appears in the control panel followed by the file name of the spreadsheet. In this example, the BUDGET file name appears. To save the current spreadsheet to the BUDGET file:

Press	⏎Enter

Click	*the mouse button with the mouse pointer in the control panel*

Since the BUDGET file already exists on the disk, a prompt appears asking whether to cancel the **S**ave command, replace the BUDGET file with the version in memory, or create a backup file named BUDGET.BAK from the previously saved file on the disk, and also save the file that is currently in memory as BUDGET.WK3.

When prompted whether to **C**ancel, **R**eplace, or **B**ackup:

Select	Replace

Choose	*Replace*

The previously saved version of BUDGET has now been replaced with the updated version that is currently displayed on your screen.

User Tip

If a worksheet has already been saved to a file, an alternative method for saving changes to the current worksheet and replacing the contents of the current file is to click the File Save 🗎 SmartIcon. Then click the Replace menu option. When you click the File Save 🗎 SmartIcon, the file name does not appear in the control panel. If you need to rename the file, click the alternate mouse button. Then enter the new file name and click the mouse button.

■ CORRECTING ROUNDING ERRORS

The worksheet that was just completed did not **foot** or balance correctly. The result in the YR TOTAL column is shown below:

Sales	247,296	
− Total Expenses	191,494	
Gross Profit	55,803	(does not foot correctly)

When multiplication, division or exponents are used in a formula, the @ROUND function can be used to round a number to a specified number of decimal places. Otherwise, 1-2-3 uses the "hidden" decimal places in calculation, resulting in rounding errors. The @ROUND function will be explained in more detail later in this chapter. For now, the following steps can be used for rounding the appropriate formulas where necessary in this example.

Note that you should *immediately* use the @ROUND function when creating formulas rather than going back to edit them later. This example was done differently to show the results of not using the @ROUND function.

The three sets of formulas for Sales, Telephone, and Miscellaneous expenses need to be edited to use the @ROUND function because the three lines contain multiplication.

Note that the only way rounding errors can occur in a spreadsheet is through multiplying, dividing, using exponents, or through the use of special functions such as the square root.

The @ROUND function's format is as follows:

@ROUND(number or formula,number of digits to round to)

Sales is the first formula to be edited. The formula in cell C47 for the Sales projection for the Second Quarter is +B47*(1+C63). To round the Sales projection to 0 decimal places:

Move	the cell pointer to cell C47		*Click*	*on cell C47*
Type	@ROUND(		*Type*	*@ROUND(*
Move	the cell pointer to cell B47		*Click*	*the* ⬅ *SmartIcon to move the cell pointer to cell B47*
Type	*(1+		*Type*	**(1+*
Move	the cell pointer to cell C63		*Click*	*the* ⬇ *SmartIcon until the cell pointer is in cell C63*
Type	),		*Type*	*),*

To indicate zero decimal places:

Type	0		*Type*	*0*
Type	)		*Type*	*)*
Press	⟵Enter		*Click*	*the mouse button with the mouse pointer in the control panel*

The formula @ROUND(B47*(1+C63),0) is now in cell C47. The formula "B47*(1+C63)" is rounded to 0 decimal places. Your screen should look like Figure 4-31.

Figure 4-31

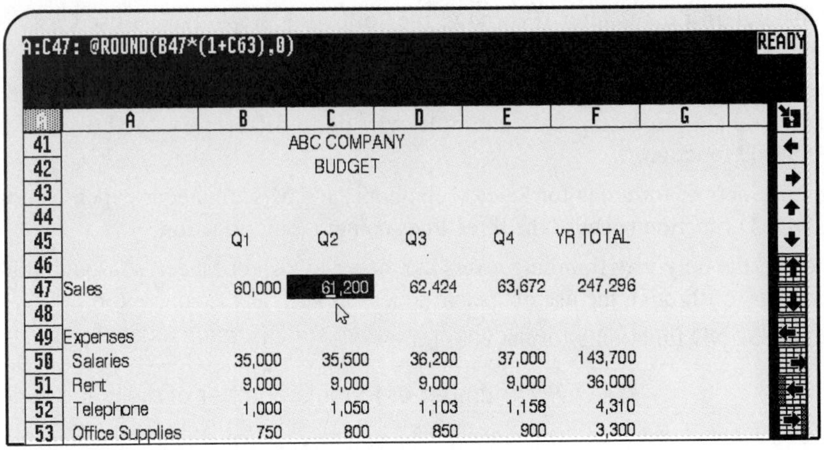

To copy the rounded formula for Sales to the remaining quarters:

Press	☐/	**Move**	the mouse pointer to the control panel
		Choose	Copy
Select	Copy		

When prompted for "Enter range to copy FROM:"

| **Press** | ⏎Enter | **Click** | the mouse button with the mouse pointer in the control panel |

By pressing the ENTER key or clicking the mouse button, you selected C47 as the cell to copy.

When prompted for "Enter range to copy TO:"

Move	the cell pointer to cell D47	**Move**	the mouse pointer to cell D47
Type	.	**Drag**	the mouse pointer to cell E47
Move	the cell pointer to cell E47	**Click**	the mouse button
Press	⏎Enter		

The projections for Sales are now rounded to 0 decimal places.

Telephone Expenses is the second set of formulas you need to round. The formula for Telephone expenses in the Second Quarter is +B52*(1+C64). To round the Telephone expenses to 0 decimal places:

| **Move** | the cell pointer to cell C52 | **Click** | on cell C52 |

Rather than retyping the formula, use a shortcut to edit the current formula.

| **Press** | the F2 key | **Press** | the F2 key |

The F2 function key is often referred to as the EDIT key when using 1-2-3.

Press	the ⬅ key until the cursor is under the **+** sign at the front of the formula–an alternative is to press the Home key to move to the beginning of the formula		*Click*	the ◄ SmartIcon until the cursor is under the **+** sign at the front of the formula–an alternative is to press the Home key to move to the beginning of the formula
Type	@ROUND(		*Type*	@ROUND(
Press	the Delete key one time to delete the **+** sign if desired		*Press*	the Delete key one time to delete the **+** sign if desired
Press	the → key to move the cell pointer to the end of the formula–an alternative is to press the End key to move to the end of the formula		*Click*	the ► SmartIcon to move the cell pointer to the end of the formula–an alternative is to press the End key to move to the end of the formula
Type	,0)		*Type*	,0)
Press	←Enter		*Click*	the mouse button with the mouse pointer in the control panel

The formula @ROUND(B52∗(1+C64),0) is now in cell C52.

To copy the formula for Telephone expenses to the remaining quarters:

Press	/		*Click*	the mouse pointer to the control panel
Select	Copy		*Choose*	Copy

When prompted for "Enter range to copy FROM:"

Press	←Enter		*Click*	the mouse button with the mouse pointer in the control panel

By pressing the ENTER key or clicking the mouse button, you selected cell C52 as the cell to copy.

When prompted for "Enter range to copy TO:"

Move	the cell pointer to cell D52		*Move*	the mouse pointer to cell D52
Type	.		*Drag*	the mouse pointer to cell E52
Move	the cell pointer to cell E52		*Click*	the mouse button
Press	←Enter			

Telephone expenses are now rounded to 0 decimal places.

The next set of formulas to be rounded is for Miscellaneous expenses. The formula for Miscellaneous expenses in the second quarter is +B54*(1+C66). To round the Miscellaneous expenses to 0 decimal places:

Move	the cell pointer to cell C54		*Click*	*on cell C54*
Press	F2 to edit the formula in cell C54		*Press*	*F2 to edit the formula in cell C54*
Press	Home to move to the beginning of the formula		*Press*	*Home to move to the beginning of the formula*
Type	@ROUND(		*Type*	*@ROUND(*
Press	Delete one time to delete the + sign if desired		*Press*	*Delete one time to delete the + sign if desired*
Press	End to move the end of the formula		*Press*	*End to move the end of the formula*
Type	,0)		*Type*	*,0)*
Press	←Enter		*Click*	*the mouse button with the mouse pointer in the control panel*

The rounded formula @ROUND(B54*(1+C66),0) is now in cell C54.

To copy the rounded formula to the remaining quarters:

Press	/		*Click*	*the mouse pointer to the control panel*
Select	Copy		*Choose*	*Copy*

When prompted for "Enter range to copy FROM:"

Press	←Enter		*Click*	*the mouse button with the mouse pointer in the control panel*

By pressing the ENTER key or clicking the mouse button, you selected cell C54 as the cell to copy.

When prompted for "Enter range to copy TO:"

Move	the cell pointer to cell D54		*Move*	*the mouse pointer to cell D54*
Type	.		*Drag*	*the mouse pointer to cell E54*
Move	the cell pointer to cell E54		*Click*	*the mouse button*
Press	←Enter			

The projections for Miscellaneous expenses are rounded to 0 decimal places. The rounding error in the worksheet has been corrected. The corrected results in the YR TOTAL column are shown below:

Sales	247,296
− Total Expenses	191,495
Gross Profit	55,801

Your screen should look like Figure 4-32.

Figure 4-32

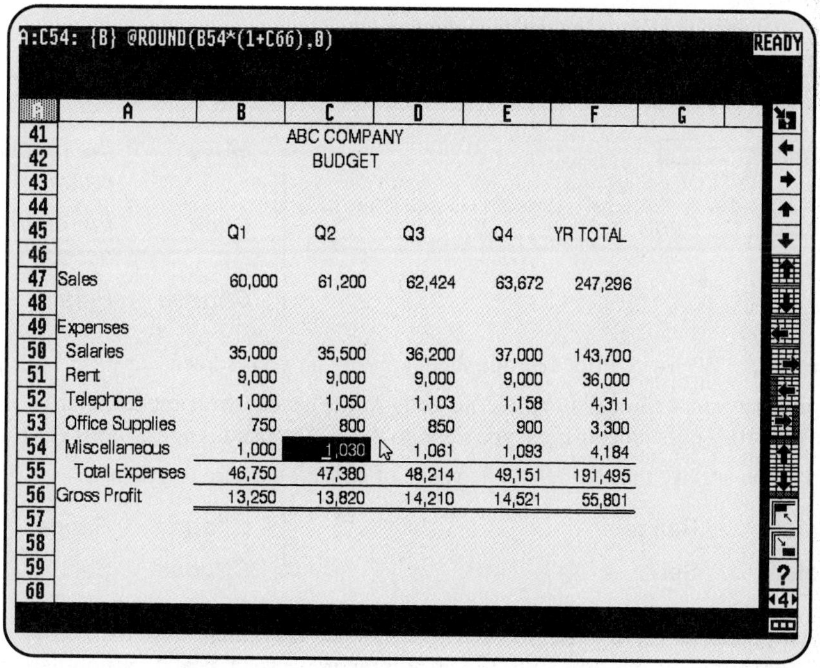

```
A:C54: {B} @ROUND(B54*(1+C66),0)                                    READY

         A         B        C        D        E        F        G
  41              ABC COMPANY
  42                BUDGET
  43
  44
  45            Q1       Q2       Q3       Q4    YR TOTAL
  46
  47  Sales      60,000   61,200   62,424   63,672   247,296
  48
  49  Expenses
  50  Salaries   35,000   35,500   36,200   37,000   143,700
  51  Rent        9,000    9,000    9,000    9,000    36,000
  52  Telephone   1,000    1,050    1,103    1,158     4,311
  53  Office Supplies 750    800      850      900      3,300
  54  Miscellaneous 1,000   1,030    1,061    1,093     4,184
  55    Total Expenses 46,750 47,380  48,214   49,151   191,495
  56  Gross Profit 13,250  13,820   14,210   14,521    55,801
  57
  58
  59
  60
```

Save the spreadsheet to the BUDGET file using the **F**ile **S**ave **R**eplace command sequence.

■ PREPARING THE PRINTER, PREVIEWING, AND PRINTING A SPREADSHEET

The following steps outline how to print the spreadsheet.

Prepare the Printer for Use

If you are using a dot matrix printer and the paper needs to be aligned, perform the following step before turning on the printer:

Turn the cylinder that moves the paper so the paper perforation is directly above the print head and ribbon

The gears of many printers can be damaged if the cylinder is turned manually while the motor is running. If you are using a laser printer, no paper alignment steps are required.

Before printing:

Check   to see that the printer is connected to the computer

Turn   on the printer

Your printer should now be on.

Previewing the Spreadsheet

You can preview the range of cells you want to print on your screen before you print it. To specify the range of cells to preview:

Press	`:`		***Move***	*the mouse pointer to the control panel*
			Click	*the alternate mouse button to access the Wysiwyg menu*
Select	Print		***Choose***	*Print*

Notice the Wysiwyg Print settings sheet appears on your screen.

Note that you will only preview the cells in the spreadsheet model, that is, cells A41 through F66. To include the entire spreadsheet, you need to define the print range as cells A1 through F66.

Now you specify the setting for the range of cells you desire to preview.

Select	Range		***Choose***	*Range*
Select	Set		***Choose***	*Set*

If you press the END key followed by a pointer-movement key, the cell pointer will move to the first nonblank cell in the direction of the pointer-movement key. If a nonblank cell does not exist in the selected direction, the cell pointer will move to the last cell in the selected direction. When the cell pointer is in a nonblank cell and you repeat the above action, the cell pointer will move to the next nonblank cell in the direction selected. If nonblank cells do not exist in the selected direction, the cell pointer will move to the last cell in the selected direction.

If you press the END key followed by the HOME key, the cell pointer moves to the last cell in the worksheet, which is defined by the last column and row that have a nonblank entry.

Note that the status indicator END appears on the status line when you press the END key. If you decide not to press a pointer-movement key after pressing the END key, you can remove the END status indicator from the screen by pressing the END key again. The END status indicator automatically disappears when you press a pointer-movement key.

When prompted for the print range:

Move	the cell pointer to cell A41		***Move***	*the mouse pointer to cell A41*
Type	.		***Drag***	*the mouse pointer to cell F66*

Press	End
Press	Home

The spreadsheet model is now highlighted.

Press	←Enter		*Click*	*the mouse button*

To preview the range:

Select	Preview		*Choose*	*Preview*

Your screen should look like Figure 4-33.

Figure 4-33

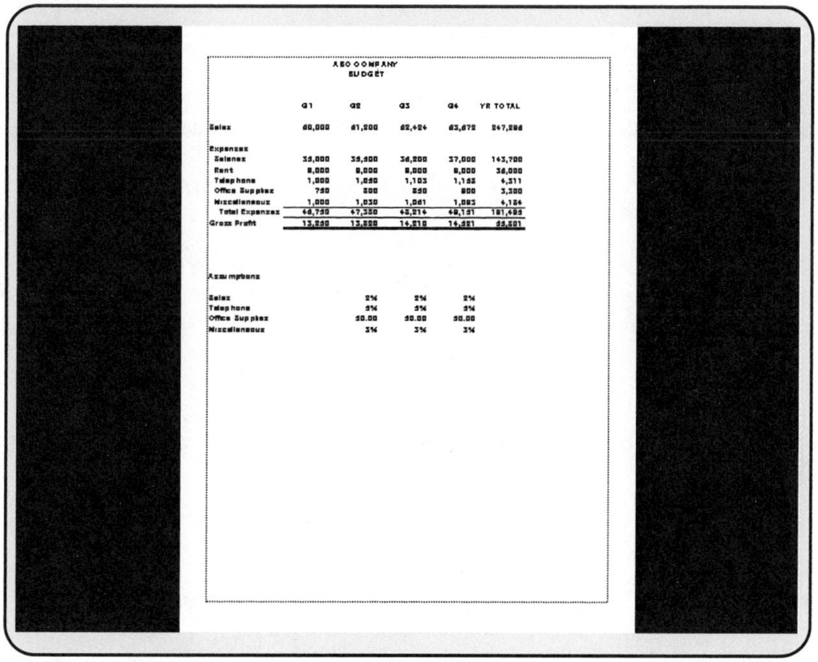

To exit the preview screen:

Press	←Enter		*Click*	*the mouse button*

Printing the Spreadsheet

To begin printing the range:

Select	Go		**Choose**	Go

The printout should appear similar to the printout in Figure 4-34.

Figure 4-34

ABC COMPANY
BUDGET

	Q1	Q2	Q3	Q4	YR TOTAL
Sales	60,000	61,200	62,424	63,672	247,296
Expenses					
Salaries	35,000	35,500	36,200	37,000	143,700
Rent	9,000	9,000	9,000	9,000	36,000
Telephone	1,000	1,050	1,103	1,158	4,311
Office Supplies	750	800	850	900	3,300
Miscellaneous	1,000	1,030	1,061	1,093	4,184
Total Expenses	46,750	47,380	48,214	49,151	191,495
Gross Profit	13,250	13,820	14,210	14,521	55,801
Assumptions					
Sales		2%	2%	2%	
Telephone		5%	5%	5%	
Office Supplies		50.00	50.00	50.00	
Miscellaneous		3%	3%	3%	

You may not want to have the print range outlined on your screen. To clear the print range from your screen:

Press	`:`	***Move***	*the mouse pointer to the control panel*
Select	Print	***Choose***	*Print*
Select	Range	***Choose***	*Range*
Select	Clear	***Choose***	*Clear*
Select	Quit	***Choose***	*Quit*

User Tip

An alternative method for printing a worksheet is to highlight the appropriate range and then click the Print 🖨 SmartIcon.

If you want to preview the appearance of the worksheet prior to printing it, highlight the appropriate cells and then click the Print Preview 🖺 SmartIcon.

> *User Tip*
>
> If you do not choose to attach Wysiwyg or are unable to do so because of the large size of a spreadsheet, it is possible to print the worksheet from the 1-2-3 main menu. The command sequence is **Print Printer Range Align Go**. If the printed data does not fill a complete page, you will need to select **P**age to eject the page from the printer.
>
> When using the standard mode for printing, "page creeping" might occur. Page creeping means that each subsequent page prints lower than the previous page. To prevent "page creep," use the **Print Printer Options Pg Length** command sequence. Set the default page length appropriately for your printer. For laser jet printers, default page length should be 60 lines per page. For dot matrix printers, default page length should be 66 lines per page.
>
> Changing the page orientation to landscape is printer dependent and is accomplished with a printer setup string. The command sequence is **Print Printer Options Setup**. Consult the Lotus 1-2-3 reference manual for more details.
>
> Margins, headers, footers, and borders are created and adjusted with the command sequence **Print Printer Options**.
>
> Compression of text and changing fonts is done with the command sequence **Print Printer Options Setup**. Consult the Lotus 1-2-3 reference manual for more details.
>
> Many of the other features like shading, drawing lines and previewing are not available in the standard print mode. For ease of printing and variety of features, use Wysiwyg whenever possible.

■ CHANGING THE FONT USED IN PRINTING

In some situations, it may be desirable to change the **font** used when a spreadsheet is printed. You can change the fonts and the appearance of a worksheet using the Wysiwyg add-in option. See Chapter 5 for additional instructions on using Wysiwyg.

■ USING ANOTHER FORMAT FOR A SPREADSHEET

When building the spreadsheet BUDGET, you chose the numeric format **Worksheet Global Format , 0** to display numbers with commas and no decimal places. The instructions in this section demonstrate how to use some of the other available format specifications.

Setting the Entire Spreadsheet with Dollar Signs

It is assumed that the BUDGET spreadsheet is displayed on your screen. If not, retrieve the file BUDGET before continuing. Make sure the cell pointer is in cell A41.

To change the numeric format in BUDGET so that dollar signs are added and two decimal places are shown, use the Currency format.

Press	[/]		**Move**	the mouse pointer to the control panel
Select	Worksheet		**Click**	the alternate mouse button until the 1-2-3 main menu appears
Select	Global		**Choose**	Worksheet
Select	Format		**Choose**	Global
Select	Currency		**Choose**	Format
			Choose	Currency

When prompted for the number of decimal places:

Press	[←Enter]		**Click**	the mouse button with the mouse pointer in the control panel

When you press the ENTER key, the default of two decimal places is accepted. Notice that asterisks fill some of the cells instead of numbers. Because of the addition of a dollar sign, a period, and two decimal places to each cell containing a value or formula, **column F is no longer wide enough to display all of the numbers** in currency format. Sometimes asterisks may appear in only one or two cells in a column, rather than throughout the entire worksheet. The columns need to be widened for you to see the contents of the cell(s) containing asterisks (refer to Figure 4-35). Make sure your cell pointer is in cell F41.

Figure 4-35

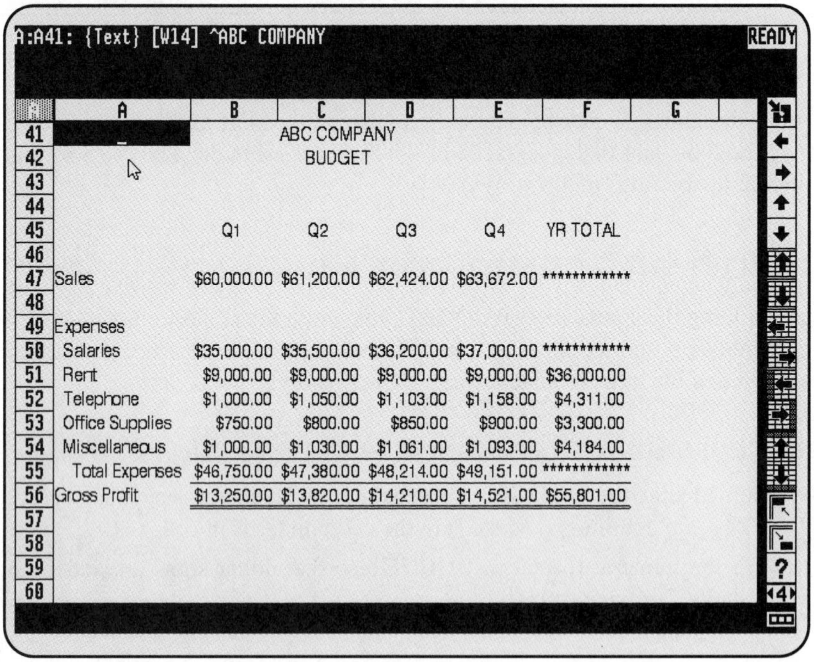

To widen all the columns in a spreadsheet so that the numbers are visible and the columns containing values remain a constant width:

Press	[/]	***Move***	*the mouse pointer to the control panel*
Select	Worksheet	***Choose***	*Worksheet*
Select	Global	***Choose***	*Global*
Select	Col-Width	***Choose***	*Col-Width*
Press	[→] until the numbers can be seen in their entirety	***Click***	*the [➜] SmartIcon until the numbers can be seen in their entirety*
Press	[↵Enter]	***Click***	*the mouse button with the mouse pointer in the control panel*

The column width should be set to 10 characters. Your screen should look like Figure 4-36.

Figure 4-36

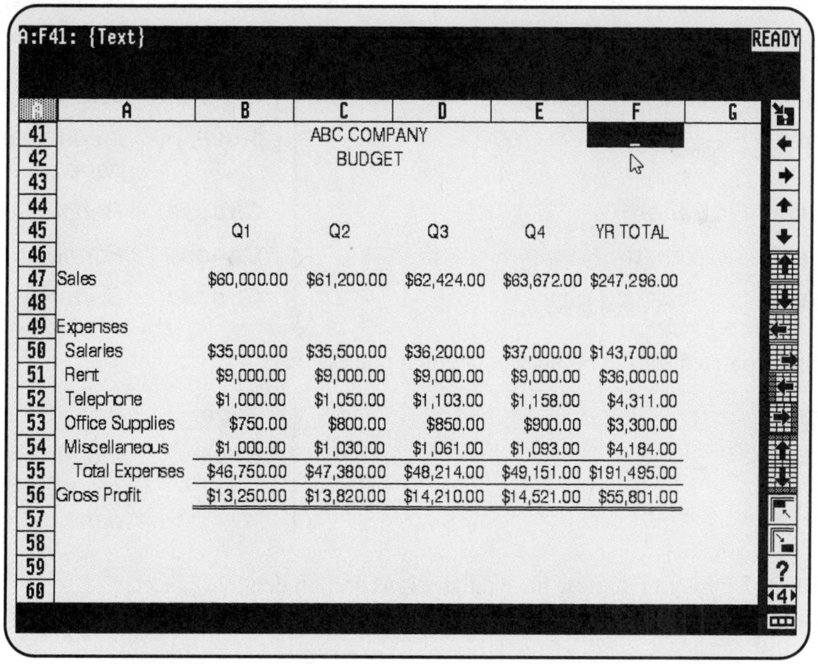
A:F41: {Text} READY

	A	B	C	D	E	F	G
41			ABC COMPANY				
42			BUDGET				
43							
44							
45		Q1	Q2	Q3	Q4	YR TOTAL	
46							
47	Sales	$60,000.00	$61,200.00	$62,424.00	$63,672.00	$247,296.00	
48							
49	Expenses						
50	Salaries	$35,000.00	$35,500.00	$36,200.00	$37,000.00	$143,700.00	
51	Rent	$9,000.00	$9,000.00	$9,000.00	$9,000.00	$36,000.00	
52	Telephone	$1,000.00	$1,050.00	$1,103.00	$1,158.00	$4,311.00	
53	Office Supplies	$750.00	$800.00	$850.00	$900.00	$3,300.00	
54	Miscellaneous	$1,000.00	$1,030.00	$1,061.00	$1,093.00	$4,184.00	
55	Total Expenses	$46,750.00	$47,380.00	$48,214.00	$49,151.00	$191,495.00	
56	Gross Profit	$13,250.00	$13,820.00	$14,210.00	$14,521.00	$55,801.00	
57							
58							
59							
60							

When the global column width is set, any columns that have been set individually using the **W**orksheet **C**olumn **S**et-Width command are *not* affected. This is the reason why the width of column A did not change.

> *User Tip*
> An alternative method for formatting the cells with the currency format option is to highlight the cells and then click the Currency Format $ SmartIcon. If this SmartIcon is utilized, two decimal places are included.

Using the **W**orksheet **E**rase command sequence, erase the BUDGET file from your screen. Do not save any changes.

Using More Than One Numeric Format in a Spreadsheet

You can also alter the BUDGET spreadsheet so that only the top and bottom rows of the spreadsheet display dollar signs.

Retrieve the BUDGET file before continuing and make sure the cell pointer is in cell A41.

The BUDGET spreadsheet's format was previously set by **W**orksheet **G**lobal **F**ormat **, 0** which displays all numbers in the spreadsheet with commas and no decimal places. For the majority of the spreadsheet, this format is more appropriate than dollar signs and decimals in each cell. However, another command is needed to change the top and bottom rows of the spreadsheet to show dollar signs.

To change the numeric format of the top row in BUDGET:

Highlight	cells B47 through F47		*Highlight*	*cells B47 through F47*
Press	☐ / ☐		*Move*	*the mouse pointer to the control panel*
Select	Range		*Choose*	*Range*
Select	Format		*Choose*	*Format*
Select	Currency		*Choose*	*Currency*

When prompted for the number of decimal places:

Type	0		*Type*	*0*
Press	⏎Enter		*Click*	*the mouse button with the mouse pointer in the control panel*

Cells B47 through F47 now have dollar signs and no decimal places.

To change the numeric format of the Gross Profit values:

Highlight	cells B56 through F56		*Highlight*	*cells B56 through F56*
Press	☐ / ☐		*Move*	*the mouse pointer to the control panel*
Select	Range		*Choose*	*Range*

Select	Format		***Choose***	*Format*
Select	Currency		***Choose***	*Currency*

When prompted for the number of decimal places:

Type	0		***Type***	*0*
Press	⎡←Enter⎤		***Click***	*the mouse button with the mouse pointer in the control panel*

After moving to cell A56, your screen should look like Figure 4-37.

Figure 4-37

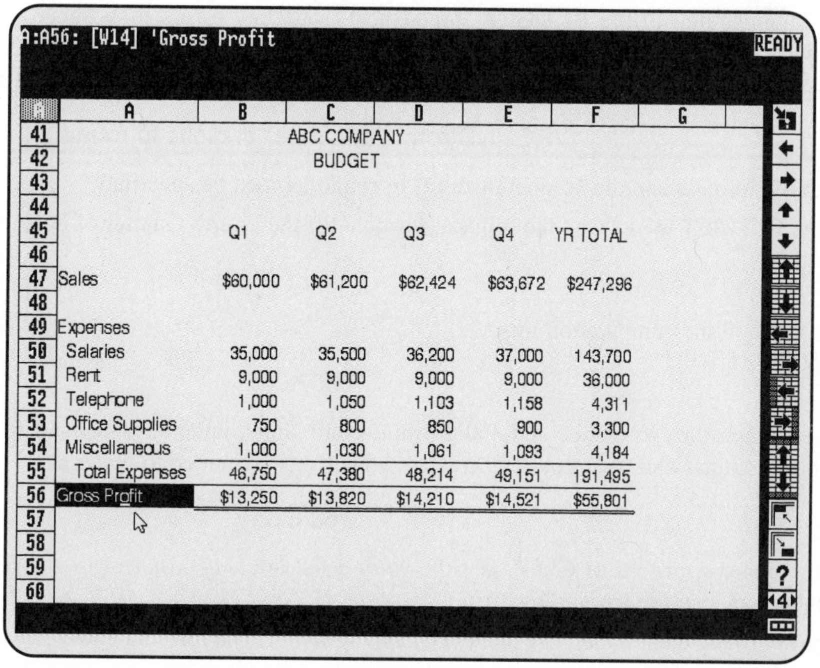

```
A:A56: [W14] 'Gross Profit                                          READY

         A        B        C        D        E        F        G
 41              ABC COMPANY
 42                BUDGET
 43
 44
 45              Q1       Q2       Q3       Q4     YR TOTAL
 46
 47 Sales      $60,000  $61,200  $62,424  $63,672  $247,296
 48
 49 Expenses
 50  Salaries   35,000   35,500   36,200   37,000   143,700
 51  Rent        9,000    9,000    9,000    9,000    36,000
 52  Telephone   1,000    1,050    1,103    1,158     4,311
 53  Office Supplies 750    800      850      900     3,300
 54  Miscellaneous 1,000  1,030    1,061    1,093     4,184
 55   Total Expenses 46,750 47,380  48,214   49,151  191,495
 56 Gross Profit $13,250 $13,820  $14,210  $14,521  $55,801
 57
 58
 59
 60
```

The dollar signs in the Currency format do not align with each other in a column; the dollar signs are placed flush to the formatted number. If the dollar signs need to be aligned, it is not appropriate to use the Currency format. Instead, one-character columns must be inserted before each column of values, and the dollar sign "$" must be typed manually. The dollar sign must be entered with a label prefix such as the apostrophe for left alignment (e.g., '$).

Comparing Worksheet Global Format to Range Format

The **W**orksheet **G**lobal **F**ormat command sequence is used to set the format of how *most* of the numbers in the spreadsheet are to be displayed. The **R**ange **F**ormat command sequence is used to set the format of **specified ranges** of numbers in the spreadsheet.

In the BUDGET worksheet, most of the numbers were set to display commas. Therefore, the **W**orksheet **G**lobal **F**ormat command sequence was used. The **R**ange **F**ormat command could have been used, but the former command sequence is faster. Two specified ranges, the top and bottom row of numbers, were set to display dollar signs. Therefore, the **R**ange **F**ormat command sequence was used.

With the cell pointer in cell B56, look at the information in the control panel. "(C0)" is displayed, indicating that the **C**urrency format with **0** decimal places was chosen with **R**ange **F**ormat. All cells formatted with the **R**ange **F**ormat command will display a similar message in the control panel when highlighted by the cell pointer. No format specification appears in the control panel for cells when the **W**orksheet **G**lobal **F**ormat command is used.

■ USING THE ROUNDING OPTION

As demonstrated in the BUDGET spreadsheet, rounding errors may occur in spreadsheets that have growth rates or percentages. To prevent this problem, use the @ROUND function whenever a formula includes multiplication, division, or exponents. The format for the @ROUND function is as follows:

@ROUND(formula,number of digits to round to)

Both the formula and the number of digits to round to must be specified.

In the BUDGET worksheet, the original formula for the Fourth Quarter of Sales was:

+D47*(1+E63)

The value of the computation was:

63672.48

Later, when the **W**orksheet **G**lobal **F**ormat command sequence was used to format the numbers to display commas and 0 decimal places, the number was formatted to *appear* as:

63,672

The number *appeared* as 63,672 but the *value used in computation* was still 63672.48. The use of this number can result in a rounding error.

To truly round the number, use the @ROUND function. The formula above must be entered as:

@ROUND(+D47*(1+E63),0)

A summary of the differences is below:

Formula	Value	Global Format Appears as Comma 0	Number Used in Computation
+D47*(1+E63)	63672.48	63,672	63672.48
@ROUND(+D47*(1+.02),0)	63672	63,672	63672

The @ROUND function may not remove rounding errors properly for all situations (e.g., percentages). It may be necessary to "plug in" a number to get the desired results.

■ MAKING A BACKUP OF A SPREADSHEET FILE

In 1-2-3 you can make a backup worksheet file on the disk with the **File Save Backup** command sequence. You can also place the worksheet on a separate diskette to create a backup file.

To make a backup file on the same disk on which your active files reside:

Move	the cell pointer to cell A41		*Click*	*on cell A41*
Press	☐ / ☐		*Click*	*the File Save* 🛅 *SmartIcon*
Select	File			
Select	Save			
Press	⏎Enter			

When prompted to **C**ancel, **R**eplace, or **B**ackup:

Select	Backup	*Select*	*Backup*

A BAK file has been created using the same file name.

When you use the Backup menu option again for the BUDGET file, 1-2-3 changes the file extension of the file on the disk from WK3 to BAK and saves the active version of the file as BUDGET.WK3.

To see that a BAK file has been created:

Press	☐ / ☐		*Move*	*the mouse pointer to the control panel*
Select	File		*Choose*	*File*
Select	List		*Choose*	*List*
Select	Other		*Choose*	*Other*

BUDGET.BAK now appears on the list of files with BUDGET.WK3.

To continue to the next exercise:

Press	⏎Enter	*Press*	⏎Enter

To save the BUDGET worksheet on a separate diskette in drive A, you first need to insert a formatted disk in drive A. Then you can save the worksheet using the following instructions:

Press	☐ / ☐		*Click*	*the File Save* 🛅 *SmartIcon*
Select	File		*Click*	*the alternate mouse button three times*

Select	Save
Press	[Esc] three times

By pressing the ESC key three times or clicking the alternate mouse button three times, you clear the current directory and file name from the control panel.

Type	A:BUDGET	*Type*	*A:BUDGET*
Press	[←Enter]	*Click*	*the mouse button*

You now have saved a copy of BUDGET on the diskette in drive A. It can be used in case you have a problem with your hard disk. Note that the extension ".WK3" file has been used. The ".WK3" extension is always used except when you select the Backup menu option mentioned earlier in this section.

■ CHANGING THE ASSUMPTIONS TO COMPLETE A "WHAT-IF" ANALYSIS

One of the advantages of using 1-2-3 is the ability to change some of the assumptions and see the impact of the changes on the other values in the worksheet. For example, suppose you show your supervisor the BUDGET spreadsheet results. Your supervisor may then ask some "what-if" questions, and ask you to complete some further analysis.

Assume that you are asked to determine the impact on Gross Profit if the growth rates for Sales are 5%, 9%, and 6% in Quarters 2 through 4 respectively.

To enter the new growth rates for Sales:

Move	the cell pointer to cell C63	*Click*	*on cell C63*
Type	.05	*Type*	*.05*
Press	[→]	*Click*	*the* [→] *SmartIcon*
Type	.09	*Type*	*.09*
Press	[→]	*Click*	*the* [→] *SmartIcon*
Type	.06	*Type*	*.06*
Press	[←Enter]	*Click*	*the mouse button*

The worksheet is recalculated to reflect the new growth rates each time you change one of them. You can now see the new values for Gross Profit that were computed using the new assumptions. If desired, you can change some of the other assumptions. Your screen should now look like Figure 4-38 if you made no additional changes. Remember, any changes are only temporary in the memory of your computer until you resave the spreadsheet, but do not resave at this time.

Figure 4-38

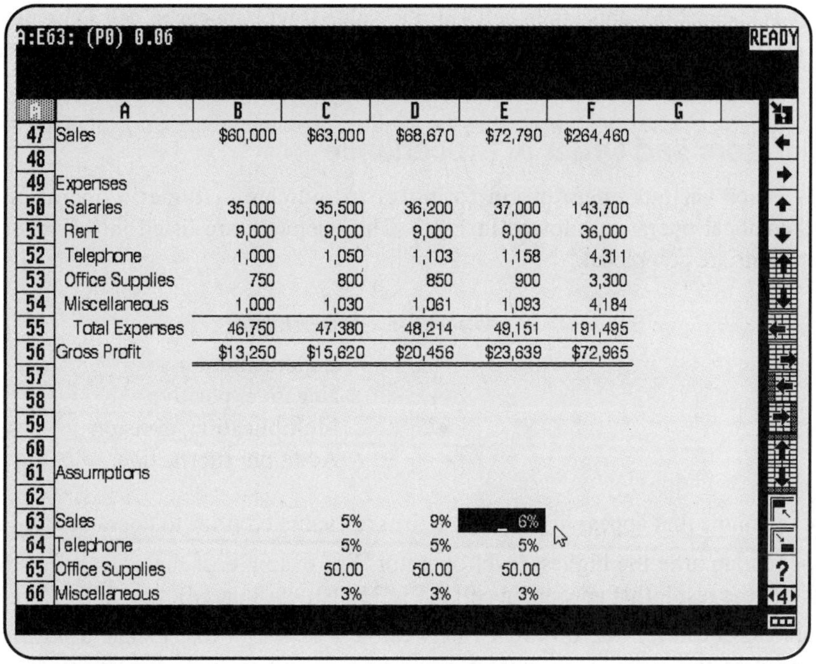

```
A:E63: (P0) 0.06                                                    READY
```

	A	B	C	D	E	F	G
47	Sales	$60,000	$63,000	$68,670	$72,790	$264,460	
48							
49	Expenses						
50	Salaries	35,000	35,500	36,200	37,000	143,700	
51	Rent	9,000	9,000	9,000	9,000	36,000	
52	Telephone	1,000	1,050	1,103	1,158	4,311	
53	Office Supplies	750	800	850	900	3,300	
54	Miscellaneous	1,000	1,030	1,061	1,093	4,184	
55	Total Expenses	46,750	47,380	48,214	49,151	191,495	
56	Gross Profit	$13,250	$15,620	$20,456	$23,639	$72,965	
57							
58							
59							
60							
61	Assumptions						
62							
63	Sales		5%	9%	6%		
64	Telephone		5%	5%	5%		
65	Office Supplies		50.00	50.00	50.00		
66	Miscellaneous		3%	3%	3%		

■ USING FORMULAS IN LOTUS 1-2-3

Lotus 1-2-3 allows the use of formulas to indicate operations such as addition and subtraction. This section discusses the types of formulas and the order in which operations occur in formulas.

Types of Formulas

The three types of formulas that can be entered into a cell in 1-2-3 are arithmetic, text, and logical.

Arithmetic Formulas

Arithmetic formulas are used to compute numeric values using arithmetic operators. For example, if the cell formula +A3-10 appears in B5, the value 10 is subtracted from the number appearing in cell A3, and the result will appear in cell B5.

Text Formulas

Text formulas are used to calculate labels using the text operator (&). For example, if the text formula +C5&"EXPENSES" appears in cell K7, the label that results from combining the label in cell C5 with EXPENSES will appear in cell K7.

Logical Formulas

Logical formulas are used to compare values in two or more cells using logical operators. A logical formula calculates a value of 0 (meaning false) or 1 (meaning true). For example, if the formula

+C3<=25000 appears in cell D3, the value 0 will appear in cell D3 whenever the value in cell C3 is greater than 25,000. A value of 1 will appear in cell D3 if the value in cell C3 is less than or equal to 25,000.

Operators and Order of Precedence

1-2-3 uses various operators in formulas to indicate arithmetic operations. Listed below are the mathematical operators allowed in 1-2-3. The operators are listed in the order of precedence by which operations are completed.

Operator	Definition
^	Exponentiation
- +	Negative, positive
*/	Multiplication, division
+ -	Addition, subtraction

The operators that appear higher on the list are evaluated prior to operators that are lower on the list.

Exponentiation is the highest level operator. For example, if the arithmetic formula 10+5^2 is used for cell A5, the result that appears in cell A5 is 35 (10 + 5 squared), not 225 (15 raised to the power of two).

Lotus 1-2-3 can tell the difference between a + or - sign that means a positive or negative number as opposed to the + or - sign meaning addition or subtraction. For example, if the formula 10/-5+10 appears in cell B8, the result that appears in the cell is 8 (-2+10), not 2 (10/5).

Multiplication and division operators are evaluated before addition and subtraction operators. For example, if cell C8 contains the formula 7-3/2, the value that appears in cell C8 is 5.5 (7-(3/2)), not 2 ((7-3)/2).

The order of precedence can be overridden using sets of parentheses. If more than one set of parentheses is included in a formula, the order of execution begins with the innermost set of parentheses and proceeds to the outermost set of parentheses. For example, suppose the formula ((10/2) + 3) * 4 is used for cell E1; the result appearing in cell E1 is 32.

SUMMARY

Creating spreadsheets is faster and more effective using a spreadsheet software package such as Lotus 1-2-3. Creating formulas and values that can be copied, inserting and deleting entire rows and columns with menu commands, and saving the file for easy editing are just a few advantages of the Lotus 1-2-3 spreadsheet software package.

KEY CONCEPTS

Assumptions	Preview
@ROUND	Print Go
@SUM	Print Range
Backup	Range Format Currency
Centering labels	Range Format Fixed
Copy	Range Format Percent
Esc	Relative cell location
File Retrieve	Replacing a spreadsheet file
File Save	Saving a worksheet
Font	Value
Format	Worksheet Column Set-Width
Formula	Worksheet Global Col-Width
Function	Worksheet Global Format
Label	Worksheet Insert Row

EXERCISE 1

INSTRUCTIONS: Circle T if the statement is true and F if the statement is false.

T F 1. One way to correct data is to move the cell pointer to the incorrect cell, retype the data correctly, and press the ENTER key to enter the correction.

T F 2. The formula SUM(A..A7) will add the data in cells A1 through A7.

T F 3. To round a number to two decimal places, use the **R**ange **F**ormat command.

T F 4. The **W**orksheet **E**rase **Y**es command sequence erases the worksheet currently in use from the computer's memory.

T F 5. A print range must be specified before a spreadsheet can be printed.

T F 6. The "@" character must precede special functions such as the SUM and ROUND functions.

T F 7. Lotus 1-2-3 will automatically save changes that are made to a spreadsheet file.

T F 8. The **F**ile **R**etrieve command is used to look at a previously saved file.

T F 9. "BUDGET 1" is an acceptable file name.

T F 10. The letter "X" is the symbol for multiplication when using Lotus 1-2-3.

EXERCISE 2

INSTRUCTIONS: Explain a typical situation when the following keystrokes or Lotus 1-2-3 commands are used.

Problem 1:   ☐/ **F**ile **S**ave

Problem 2:   ☐/ **W**orksheet **I**nsert **R**ow

Problem 3:   +B1∗1.09

Problem 4:   ☐/ **W**orksheet **G**lobal **C**ol-Width

Problem 5:   ☐/ **W**orksheet **C**olumn **S**et-Width

Problem 6:   ☐/ **W**orksheet **E**rase **Y**es

Problem 7:   ☐: **P**rint **R**ange

Problem 8:   ☐: **P**rint **G**o

Problem 9:   ☐F2

Problem 10:   +B7-B6

Problem 11:   @ROUND(+B7∗B8,0)

Problem 12:   @SUM(B1..B25)

Problem 13:   ☐/ **W**orksheet **G**lobal **F**ormat **, 2**

Problem 14:   ☐/ **R**ange **F**ormat **C**urrency **2**

Problem 15:   ☐/ **F**ile **R**etrieve

Problem 16:   ☐/ **C**opy

Problem 17:   ☐/ **R**ange **F**ormat **F**ixed **2**

Problem 18:   ☐/ **F**ile **S**ave **R**eplace

EXERCISE 3 — Correcting a Spreadsheet

INSTRUCTIONS: The following example illustrates a common error. Follow the instructions below to create the error and answer the questions.

Clear the screen (use the **W**orksheet **E**rase **Y**es command).

In cell A1, type 52 and press ☐←Enter.
In cell A2, type 30 and press ☐←Enter.
In cell A3, type A1-A2 and press ☐←Enter.

The top part of your screen should look like Figure 4-39.

Figure 4-39

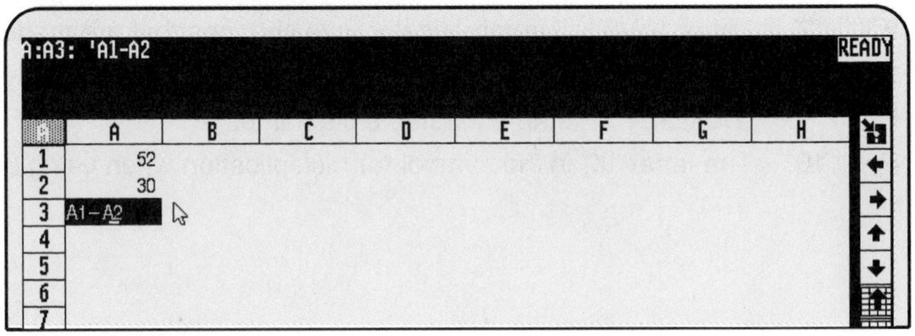

1. What caused the error in cell A3?

2. How can the error be corrected?

EXERCISE 4 — Correcting a Spreadsheet

INSTRUCTIONS: The following example illustrates a common error. Follow the instructions below to create the error and answer the questions.

Clear the screen (use the **W**orksheet **E**rase **Y**es command).

In cell A1, type 52 and press ⏎Enter.
In cell A2, press the space bar one time. Type 30 and press ⏎Enter.
In cell A3, type +A1-A2 and press ⏎Enter.

The screen should look like Figure 4-40.

Figure 4-40

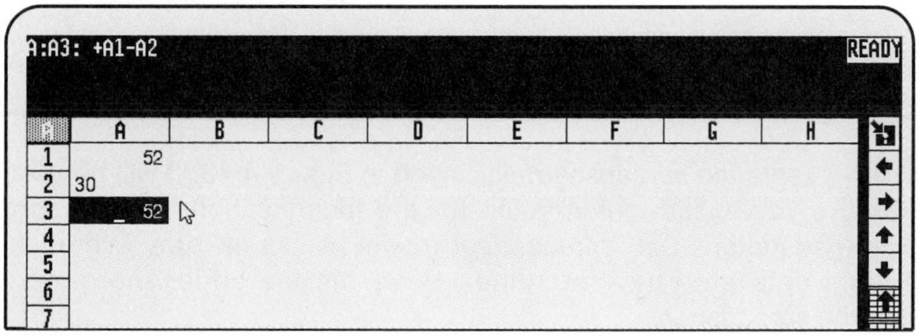

1. What caused the error in computing A1-A2?

2. How can the error be corrected?

EXERCISE 5 — Correcting a Spreadsheet

INSTRUCTIONS: The following example illustrates a common error. Use the instructions below to create the error and answer the questions.

Clear the screen (use the **W**orksheet **E**rase **Y**es command).

In cell A1, type 52 and press ⏎Enter.
In cell A2, type 30 and press ⏎Enter.
In cell A3, type +A1 and press ⏎Enter. Then type -A2 and press ⏎Enter.

The screen should look like Figure 4-41.

Figure 4-41

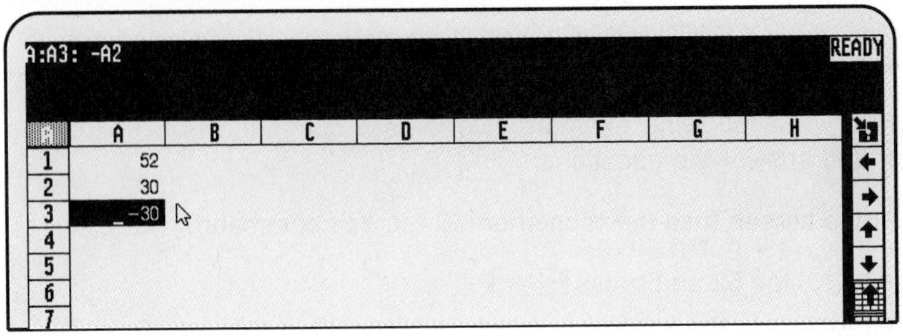

1. What caused the error in computing A1-A2?

2. How can the error be corrected?

EXERCISE 6 — Creating a Spreadsheet

INSTRUCTIONS: Create the spreadsheet displayed in Figure 4-42. It will be used for exercises in other chapters. Make sure you include information for the identification; map of spreadsheet; description, assumptions, and parameters; and spreadsheet model blocks in rows 1 through 40. The spreadsheet consists of straight data entry (no formulas). Save the file under the name UNITPROD (for Unit Production). Print the spreadsheet.

Figure 4-42

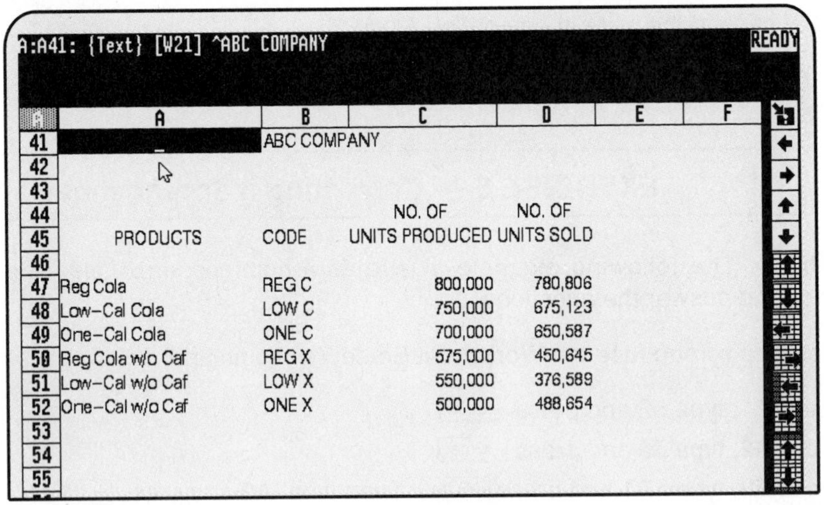

EXERCISE 7 — Creating a Spreadsheet

INSTRUCTIONS: Create the spreadsheet displayed in Figure 4-43. It will be used for an exercise in a later chapter. Make sure you include information for the identification; map of spreadsheet; description, assumptions, and parameters; and spreadsheet model blocks in rows 1 through 40. The spreadsheet consists of straight data entry except for the SUM formula in cell C54. Save the file under the name SALES. Format cells C48 through C54. Print the spreadsheet.

Figure 4-43

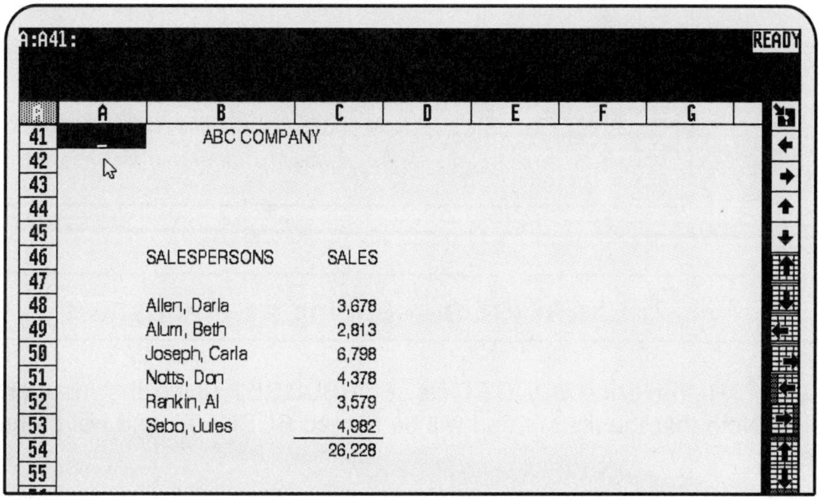

EXERCISE 8 — Creating a Spreadsheet

INSTRUCTIONS: Create and print the spreadsheet displayed in Figure 4-44.

Revenue is 25,000 in YEAR 1 and projected to increase by 6 percent for years 2 through 5. Expenses are 9,500 in YEAR 1 and projected to be 25 percent of Revenue in YEARS 2 through 5 . Profit Before Tax is Revenue minus Expenses. Taxes are 40 percent of Profit Before Tax. Profit After Tax is Profit Before Tax less Taxes. Save the file under the name PRACTICE. Make sure you include information for the identification; map of spreadsheet; description, assumptions, and parameters; and spreadsheet model blocks in rows 1 through 40. This file will be used in an exercise in a subsequent chapter.

Figure 4-44

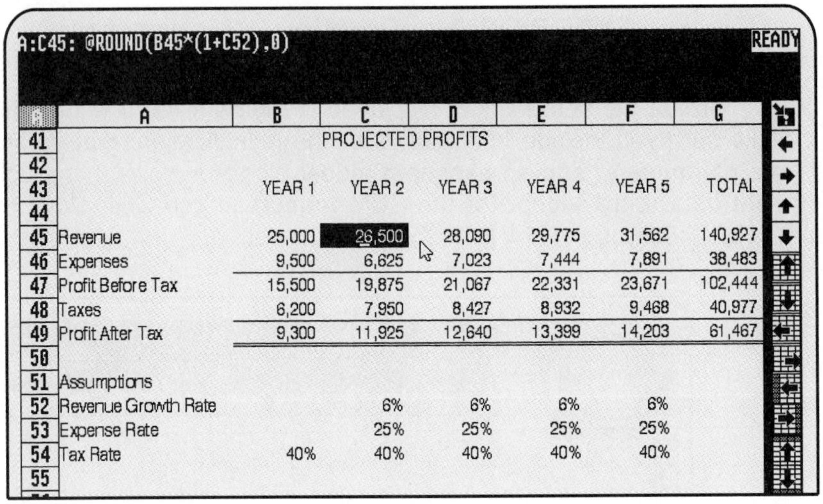

```
A:C45: @ROUND(B45*(1+C52),0)                                    READY
```

	A	B	C	D	E	F	G
41			PROJECTED PROFITS				
42							
43		YEAR 1	YEAR 2	YEAR 3	YEAR 4	YEAR 5	TOTAL
44							
45	Revenue	25,000	26,500	28,090	29,775	31,562	140,927
46	Expenses	9,500	6,625	7,023	7,444	7,891	38,483
47	Profit Before Tax	15,500	19,875	21,067	22,331	23,671	102,444
48	Taxes	6,200	7,950	8,427	8,932	9,468	40,977
49	Profit After Tax	9,300	11,925	12,640	13,399	14,203	61,467
50							
51	Assumptions						
52	Revenue Growth Rate		6%	6%	6%	6%	
53	Expense Rate		25%	25%	25%	25%	
54	Tax Rate	40%	40%	40%	40%	40%	
55							

EXERCISE 9 — Editing a Spreadsheet

INSTRUCTIONS: Retrieve the BUDGET file. Edit BUDGET using the instructions below. Use Figure 4-45 as a guide. Note that the file created will be named BUDGET2 and will be needed for an exercise in a later chapter.

Expand the worksheet to include projections through YEAR 10. Insert six columns (F-K) between Q4 and YR TOTAL using the **W**orksheet **I**nsert **C**olumn command sequence. Rename the headings Q1 through Q4 with the headings YEAR 1 through YEAR 4 and continue the headings through YEAR 10. Copy the growth rate information to YEARS 5 through 10. Copy the formulas, values, and total lines from YEAR 4 (E47..E56) to YEAR 5 through YEAR 10 (F47..K56).

Change the sums under YR TOTAL to reflect the additional years. Change the formula in cell L47 from @SUM(B47..E47) to @SUM(B47..K47). Copy the formula in cell L47 to cells L50..L56.

Center the spreadsheet title information ABC COMPANY and BUDGET over columns A throughL.

Save the spreadsheet, being sure to name the new spreadsheet BUDGET2. BUDGET and BUDGET2 are two separate files on the disk. The final result should look like Figure 4-45 (the entire spreadsheet will not be visible on the screen at one time).

Figure 4-45

	YEAR 1	YEAR 2	YEAR 3	YEAR 4	YEAR 5	YEAR 6	YEAR 7	YEAR 8	YEAR 9	YEAR 10	YR TOTAL
				ABC COMPANY							
				BUDGET							
Sales	$60,000	$61,200	$62,424	$63,672	$64,945	$66,244	$67,569	$68,920	$70,298	$71,704	$656,976
Expenses											
Salaries	35,000	35,500	36,200	37,000	37,000	37,000	37,000	37,000	37,000	37,000	$365,700
Rent	9,000	9,000	9,000	9,000	9,000	9,000	9,000	9,000	9,000	9,000	$90,000
Telephone	1,000	1,050	1,103	1,158	1,216	1,277	1,341	1,408	1,478	1,552	$12,583
Office Supplies	750	800	850	900	950	1,000	1,050	1,100	1,150	1,200	$9,750
Miscellaneous	1,000	1,030	1,061	1,093	1,126	1,160	1,195	1,231	1,268	1,306	$11,470
Total Expenses	46,750	47,380	48,214	49,151	49,292	49,437	49,586	49,739	49,896	50,058	$489,503
Gross Profit	$13,250	$13,820	$14,210	$14,521	$15,653	$16,807	$17,983	$19,181	$20,402	$21,646	$167,473
Assumptions											
Sales		2%	2%	2%	2%	2%	2%	2%	2%	2%	
Telephone		5%	5%	5%	5%	5%	5%	5%	5%	5%	
Office Supplies		50.00	50.00	50.00	50.00	50.00	50.00	50.00	50.00	50.00	
Miscellaneous		3%	3%	3%	3%	3%	3%	3%	3%	3%	

EXERCISE 10

INSTRUCTIONS: Work the following set of problems using the information provided to make sure you understand the order of precedence in the calculation of formulas. Assume that cell A1=3, cell B2=4, and cell C4=8.

	Formula	Order of Evaluation	Answer
a.	+C4-B2*2	8-(4*2)	_____
b.	+B2-A1-C4/B2	4-3-(8/4)	_____
c.	+B2-(A1-C4)/B2	4-((3-8)/4)	_____
d.	+A1/-3+3	(3/-3)+3	_____
e.	+A1-4*C4/B2^2	3-((4*8)/4^2)	_____
f.	(A1-4)*C4/B2^2	(3-4)*(8/4^2)	_____
g.	+A1*B2/C4-10/2	((3*4)/8-(10/2))	_____

CHAPTER FIVE

IMPROVING THE APPEARANCE
OF A SPREADSHEET

OBJECTIVES

In this chapter, you will learn to:

- Define Wysiwyg (What You See Is What You Get) and other basic terms and concepts
- Select commands from the Wysiwyg menu
- Use the Display mode
- Improve the appearance of a spreadsheet
- Use a named-style command
- Use additional printing features

■ CHAPTER OVERVIEW

Some prior releases of 1-2-3 do not have the ability to prepare presentation-quality documents. Lotus 1-2-3 Release 3.4 has the Wysiwyg Publishing and Presentation software included in the software as an add-in. This add-in allows you to format, view, and print presentation-quality documents.

■ DEFINING WYSIWYG AND OTHER BASIC TERMS AND CONCEPTS

Wysiwyg can be used only if you are using a personal computer that has a minimum of 1.5 megabytes (MB) of random access memory (RAM); DOS 3.0 or above, or Microsoft Windows Version 3.0 or above; at least 5 megabytes (MB) of hard disk space; and a VGA, XGA, EGA, high resolution CGA monitor, or high resolution Hercules adapter.

The following are some of the enhancements available with Wysiwyg:

Include a maximum of eight fonts on any printed document

Boldface text and numbers

Add various degrees of shading to areas on a worksheet

Place a box around one cell or outline a range of cells

Print color documents when a color printer is available

With these capabilities you can enhance your reports and presentations with improved quality documents. Note that you should only use Wysiwyg if you have a printer that will produce graphics.

When you install 1-2-3 in the standard manner, the Wysiwyg add-in is attached to the memory and is automatically invoked. If you do not wish to use the Wysiwyg add-in to improve the appearance of your documents, you can detach it from memory. Attaching and detaching add-ins is discussed in Chapter 6.

Other Basic Terms and Concepts

There are several types of text styles that can be used. **Typeface** refers to the design of the characters on a printed document. **Font** is used to indicate a specific typeface with a particular size. A font set is a collection of fonts you select for a particular printout.

By using Wysiwyg, the format of a cell can be changed dramatically. Some of the additional format options available include changing the font and typeface, boldfacing characters, specifying colors for numbers and text, placing solid lines on the edges of a cell, placing double underlines on a cell, and creating various degrees of shading. When you use Wysiwyg, you can also modify the column width and row height.

■ SELECTING COMMANDS FROM THE WYSIWYG MENU

You can select commands from the Wysiwyg menu by:

Press   :

| **Move** | the mouse pointer to the control panel |
| **Press** | the alternative mouse button (if necessary) |

To exit the Wysiwyg menu:

Press   Esc

| **Move** | the mouse pointer into the worksheet area |

■ THE DISPLAY MODE

Once Wysiwyg is in memory, you can change the display of your screen. The Display Mode commands allow you to select graphic display mode, text display mode, color display, or black and white display.

In graphic display mode, the screen displays the text as it will look when it is printed. When you make formatting changes, you will see them change on the screen.

In text display mode, the screen appears as it does when Wysiwyg is not attached. You can apply formatting changes, but you will not see them change on the screen. The changes will appear when you print.

The color display command allows you to change the color of the worksheet background, data, unprotected ranges, the cell pointer, the worksheet frame, negative numbers, lines, and drop shadows.

The black and white display command allows you to change the screen display from color to black and white.

To change from graphics to text mode:

Press	⬚:⬚		**Move**	*the mouse pointer to the control panel*
Select	Display		**Choose**	*Display*
Select	Mode		**Choose**	*Mode*
Select	Text		**Choose**	*Text*
Select	Quit		**Choose**	*Quit*

Your screen should look similar to Figure 5-1.

Figure 5-1

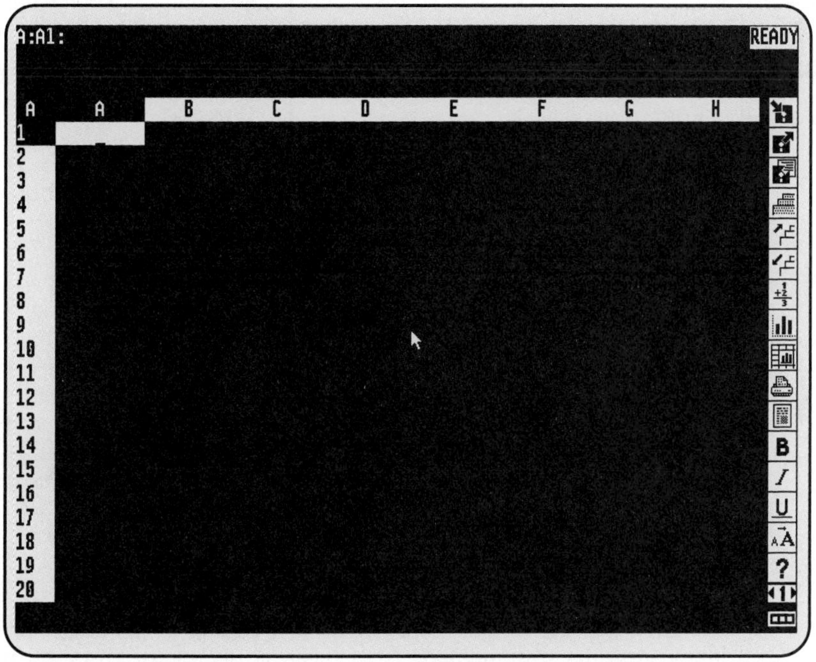

To change from text to graphics mode:

Press	⬚:⬚		**Move**	*the mouse pointer to the control panel*
Select	Display		**Choose**	*Display*
Select	Mode		**Choose**	*Mode*
Select	Graphics		**Choose**	*Graphics*
Select	Quit		**Choose**	*Quit*

■ IMPROVING THE APPEARANCE OF A SPREADSHEET

To illustrate the process for improving the appearance of a spreadsheet, retrieve the BUDGET file.

Note: Mouse users will need to press the alternate mouse button to return to the 1-2-3 main menu.

Suppose you want to change the appearance of the spreadsheet as follows:

Change the font of the worksheet titles

Boldface the worksheet titles, column titles, and row labels

Add shading to the column titles

Place an outline around the cells containing the assumptions

To change the font of the worksheet titles:

Highlight	cells A41 through A42		*Highlight*	*cells A41 through A42*
Press	[:]		*Move*	*the mouse pointer to the control panel*
			Click	*the alternate mouse button*
Select	Format		*Choose*	*Format*
Select	Font		*Choose*	*Font*

To select Swiss 14 point:

Select	2		*Choose*	*2*

The top part of your screen should look like Figure 5-2.

Figure 5-2

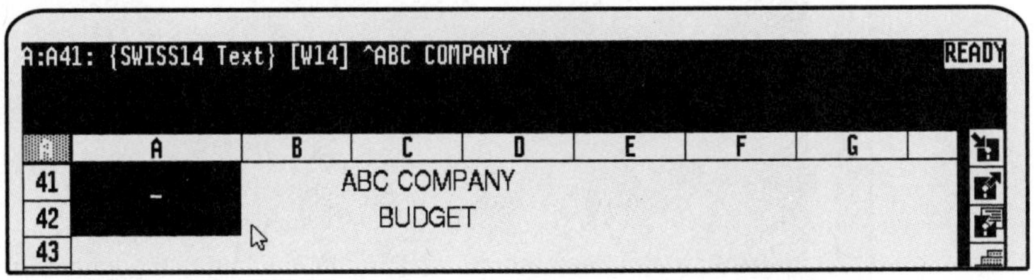

```
A:A41: {SWISS14 Text} [W14] ^ABC COMPANY                        READY

      A           A       B     C      D     E     F     G
     41                         ABC COMPANY
     42                            BUDGET
     43
```

Notice, by observing the row numbers, that the row height for rows 41 and 42 was automatically increased when the font size was changed. The new font selection appears in the control panel.

To boldface the worksheet titles:

Highlight	cells A41 through A42		*Highlight*	*cells A41 through A42*
Press	[:]		*Move*	*the mouse pointer to the control panel*

Select	Format		***Choose***	*Format*
Select	Bold		***Choose***	*Bold*

To add boldface to the worksheet titles:

Select	Set		***Choose***	*Set*

The top part of your screen should look like Figure 5-3.

Figure 5-3

```
A:A41: {SWISS14 Bold Text} [W14] ^ABC COMPANY              READY

          A        B       C       D       E       F       G
    41              -              ABC COMPANY
    42                              BUDGET
    43
```

> *User Tip*
> An alternative method for boldfacing the contents of a cell or range of cells is to
> highlight the cell or range of cells, and then click the Bold ⃞B⃞ SmartIcon.

To boldface the column titles:

Highlight	cells B45 through F45		***Highlight***	*cells B45 through F45*
Press	⃞ : ⃞		***Click***	*the Bold* ⃞B⃞ *SmartIcon*
Select	Format			
Select	Bold			
Select	Set			

Repeat the **F**ormat **B**old **S**et command sequence to boldface the row labels in cells A47 through A66.
After moving the cell pointer to cell A46, your screen should look like Figure 5-4.

Figure 5-4

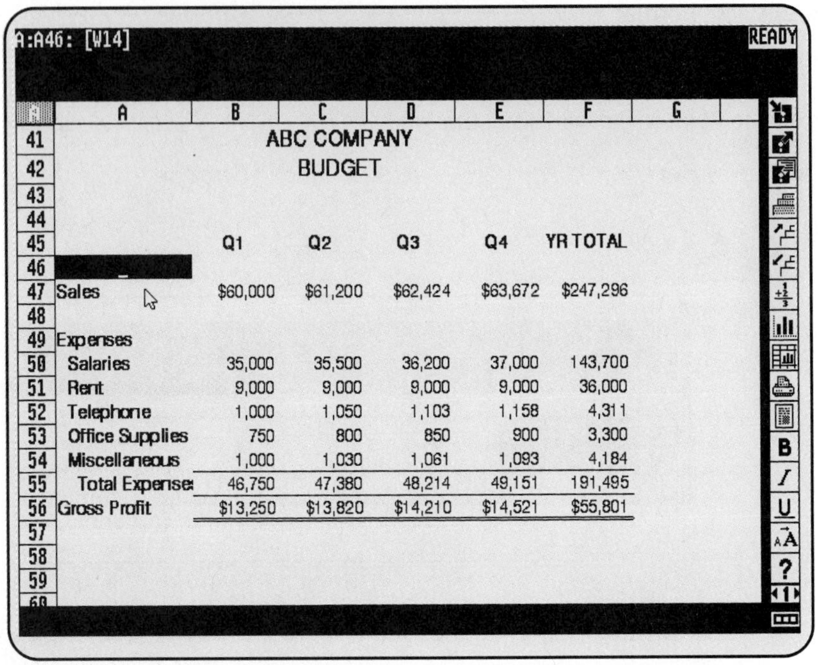

```
A:A46: [W14]                                                    READY

         A        B       C        D       E        F      G
  41             ABC COMPANY
  42               BUDGET
  43
  44
  45             Q1      Q2       Q3      Q4      YR TOTAL
  46
  47 Sales       $60,000 $61,200  $62,424 $63,672 $247,296
  48
  49 Expenses
  50  Salaries    35,000  35,500   36,200  37,000  143,700
  51  Rent         9,000   9,000    9,000   9,000   36,000
  52  Telephone    1,000   1,050    1,103   1,158    4,311
  53  Office Supplies 750    800      850     900    3,300
  54  Miscellaneous 1,000   1,030    1,061   1,093    4,184
  55   Total Expense: 46,750 47,380  48,214  49,151  191,495
  56 Gross Profit $13,250 $13,820  $14,210 $14,521  $55,801
  57
  58
  59
  60
```

Notice the "s" in Total Expenses in cell A55 is partially displayed. In order to fully display Total Expenses, you need to widen column A to 15 characters.

To widen column A to 15 characters:

Press	⌐/⌐	***Move***	*the mouse pointer to the control panel*
Select	Worksheet	***Click***	*the alternate mouse button*
Select	Column	***Choose***	*Worksheet*
Select	Set-Width	***Choose***	*Column*
Type	15	***Choose***	*Set-Width*
Press	←Enter	***Type***	*15*
		Click	*the mouse button*

Your screen should look like Figure 5-5.

Figure 5-5

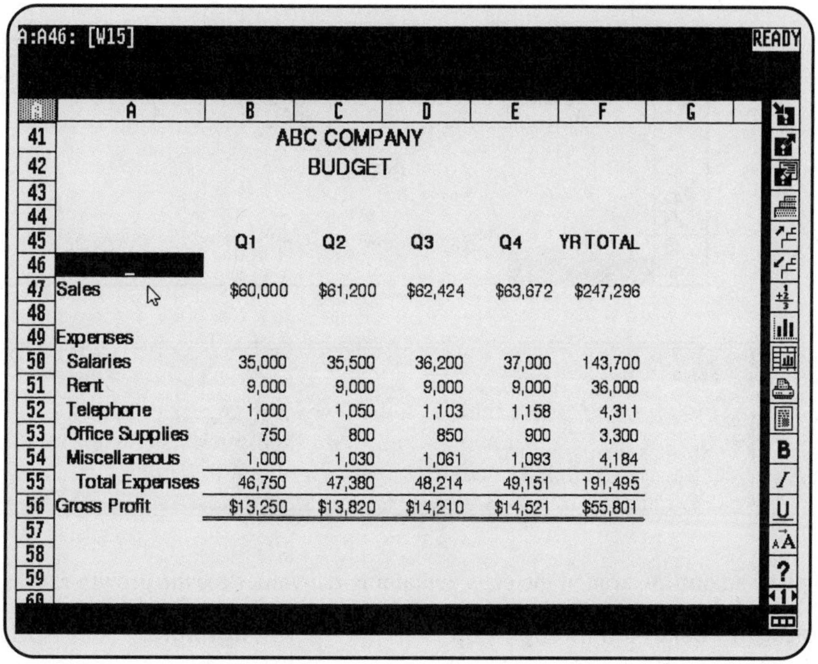

```
A:A46: [W15]                                                      READY
         A          B        C        D        E        F        G
 41               ABC COMPANY
 42                 BUDGET
 43
 44
 45              Q1       Q2       Q3       Q4    YR TOTAL
 46
 47  Sales       $60,000  $61,200  $62,424  $63,672  $247,296
 48
 49  Expenses
 50    Salaries   35,000   35,500   36,200   37,000   143,700
 51    Rent        9,000    9,000    9,000    9,000    36,000
 52    Telephone   1,000    1,050    1,103    1,158     4,311
 53    Office Supplies 750    800      850      900     3,300
 54    Miscellaneous 1,000  1,030    1,061    1,093     4,184
 55    Total Expenses 46,750 47,380  48,214   49,151  191,495
 56  Gross Profit $13,250  $13,820  $14,210  $14,521  $55,801
 57
 58
 59
 60
```

To place a light shading in the cells containing the column titles:

Highlight	cells B45 through F45		**Highlight**	*cells B45 through F45*
Press	`:`		**Move**	*the mouse pointer to the control panel*
Select	Format		**Click**	*the alternate mouse button*
Select	Shade		**Choose**	*Format*
			Choose	*Shade*

To indicate the use of a light shading:

Select	Light		**Choose**	*Light*

After moving the cell pointer to cell A46, the top part of your screen should look like Figure 5-6.

Figure 5-6

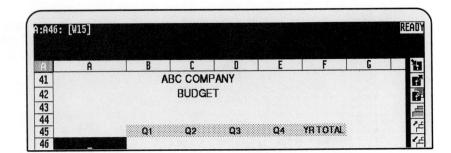

> *User Tip*
> An alternative approach for lightly shading a cell or range of cells is to first highlight the cell or range of cells, and then click the Shade ▦ SmartIcon. By continuing to click the SmartIcon you can select light, dark, solid, or no shading.

To place an **outline** around the cells containing the values for the growth rate assumptions:

Highlight	cells A63 through E66	*Highlight*	*cells A63 through E66*
Press	〔 : 〕	*Move*	*the mouse pointer to the control panel*
Select	Format	*Choose*	*Format*
Select	Lines	*Choose*	*Lines*

To specify an outline:

Select	Outline	*Select*	*Outline*

After moving the cell pointer to cell A68, the bottom part of your screen should look like Figure 5-7.

Figure 5-7

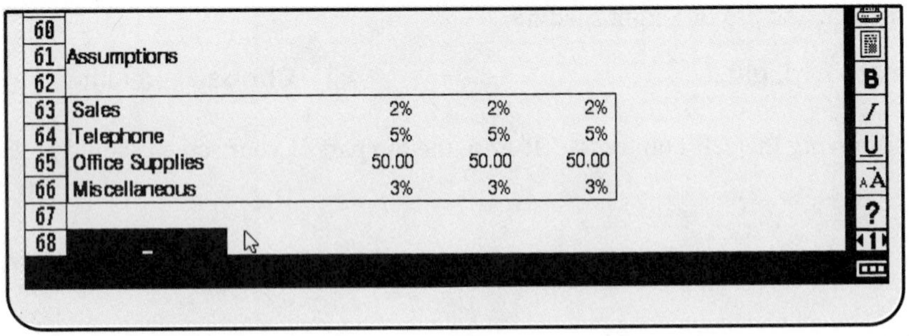

60				
61	Assumptions			
62				
63	Sales	2%	2%	2%
64	Telephone	5%	5%	5%
65	Office Supplies	50.00	50.00	50.00
66	Miscellaneous	3%	3%	3%
67				
68				

> *User Tip*
> Another method for outlining a range of cells is to first highlight the range of cells. Then click the Outline ▢ SmartIcon. By pressing the Drop Shadow ▣ SmartIcon, you can place a drop shadow below and to the right of the range of cells. To remove the outline or drop shadow click the same SmartIcon you used to place the outline or drop shadow on the range of cells.

The first time you print in Wysiwyg, you may need to configure or specify the printer to use.

Move	the cell pointer to cell A41		*Click*	*on cell A41*
Press	⬚ : ⬚		*Move*	*the mouse pointer to the control panel*
Select	Print		*Choose*	*Print*
Select	Config		*Choose*	*Config*
Select	Printer		*Choose*	*Printer*
Select	your printer		*Choose*	*your printer*
Select	Quit twice		*Choose*	*Quit twice*

To print the enhanced version of the worksheet, make sure the cell pointer is in cell A41.

Press	⬚ : ⬚		*Move*	*the mouse pointer to the control panel*
Select	Print		*Choose*	*Print*
Select	Range		*Choose*	*Range*
Select	Set		*Choose*	*Set*
Press	.		*Move*	*the mouse pointer to cell A41*
Move	the cell pointer to cell F66		*Drag*	*the mouse pointer to cell F66*
Press	⬚←Enter⬚		*Click*	*the mouse button*

To print the worksheet:

Select	Go	|	*Choose*	*Go*

Your printout should look like Figure 5-8.

Figure 5-8

```
                        ABC COMPANY
                           BUDGET


                    Q1       Q2       Q3       Q4    YR TOTAL

    Sales        $60,000  $61,200  $62,424  $63,672  $247,296

    Expenses
      Salaries    35,000   35,500   36,200   37,000   143,700
      Rent         9,000    9,000    9,000    9,000    36,000
      Telephone    1,000    1,050    1,103    1,158     4,311
      Office Supplies 750     800      850      900     3,300
      Miscellaneous  1,000   1,030    1,061    1,093     4,184
      Total Expenses 46,750  47,380   48,214   49,151   191,495
    Gross Profit  $13,250  $13,820  $14,210  $14,521   $55,801




    Assumptions

    Sales                    2%       2%       2%
    Telephone                5%       5%       5%
    Office Supplies        50.00    50.00    50.00
    Miscellaneous            3%       3%       3%
```

■ NAMED-STYLE COMMAND

A **named style** is a set of Wysiwyg formats copied from a single cell. Named styles save a particular combination of formatting options for reuse. Named styles can be applied to one or more ranges of cells. Each worksheet can contain a maximum of eight named styles. A named style can have a six-character name and a 37-character description.

To define a named style to boldface and place a light shading on text:

Move	the cell pointer to cell A41		*Click*	*on cell A41*
Press	⬚ : ⬚		*Move*	*the mouse pointer to the control panel*
Select	Named-Style		*Choose*	*Named-Style*
Select	Define		*Choose*	*Define*

To specify the number for the named style:

Select	1:Normal		*Choose*	*1:Normal*

To specify the cell containing the format:

Move	the cell pointer to cell B45		*Click*	*on cell B45 twice*
Press	⎗Enter			

To give the style a name:

Press	Esc to delete the current name	*Click*	*the alternate mouse button to delete the current name*
Type	Titles	*Type*	*Titles*
Press	←Enter	*Click*	*the mouse button*

To give the style a description:

Type	Bold and Light Shading	*Type*	*Bold and Light Shading*
Press	←Enter	*Click*	*the mouse button*

To apply the Titles named style to cells A47 through A56:

Highlight	cells A47 through A56	*Highlight*	*cells A47 through A56*
Press	:	*Move*	*the mouse pointer to the control panel*
Select	Named-Style	*Choose*	*Named-Style*
Select	1:Titles	*Choose*	*1:Titles*

After moving the cell pointer to cell A46, your screen should look like Figure 5-9.

Figure 5-9

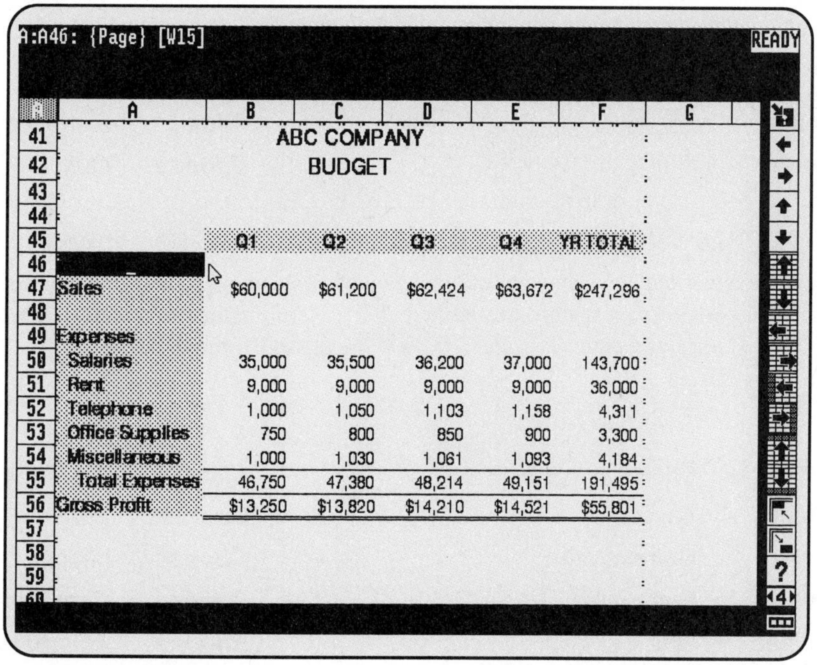

Save the worksheet using the file name BUDGETWY.

■ USING ADDITIONAL PRINTING FEATURES

Printing Orientation

Worksheets can be printed either horizontally or vertically on the page. The vertical printing position (from top to bottom of the page) is called **portrait** mode, and it is the default selection. The horizontal printing position (sideways on the page) is called **landscape** mode.

To illustrate the use of landscape mode, retrieve the BUDGET file. Then,

Press	⬚ : ⬚		*Move*	*the mouse pointer to the control panel*
Select	Print		*Click*	*the alternate mouse button*
Select	Config		*Choose*	*Print*
Select	Orientation		*Choose*	*Config*
Select	Landscape		*Choose*	*Orientation*
Select	Quit		*Choose*	*Landscape*
Specify	the range of cells to print as A41 through F66		*Choose*	*Quit*
Select	Preview		*Specify*	*the range of cells to print as A41 through F66*
			Choose	*Preview*

Notice the horizontal or landscape orientation of the worksheet on the paper.

To exit Preview and the print menu:

Press	←Enter		*Click*	*the mouse button*
Select	Quit		*Choose*	*Quit*

Printing a Wide Range of Cells

In some situations, you may have a great many cells to print on a line. In such a situation, you can use the print compression feature available in 1-2-3. To illustrate this feature, erase any worksheet you have on your screen, and enter the value 100,000 in cells A1 through M1.

Press	⬚ : ⬚		*Move*	*the mouse pointer to the control panel*
Select	Print		*Click*	*the alternate mouse button*
Select	Layout		*Choose*	*Print*
Select	Compression		*Choose*	*Layout*
Select	Automatic		*Choose*	*Compression*
Select	Quit		*Choose*	*Automatic*

Specify	the range of cells to print as A1 through M1		*Choose*	*Quit*
Select	Preview		*Specify*	*the range of cells to print as A1 through M1*
			Choose	*Preview*

Notice that the characters have been compressed so the entire range of numbers appears on one line of the page.

To exit Preview and the print menu:

Press	←Enter		*Click*	*the mouse button*
Select	Quit		*Choose*	*Quit*

SUMMARY

By using the Wysiwyg add-in that comes with the Lotus 1-2-3 Release 3.4 software, you can improve the format of 1-2-3 worksheets to the level of presentation-quality documents. You can include various fonts, boldface the contents of a cell, shade a cell, and include boxes around a cell.

KEY CONCEPTS

Boldface	Portrait
Font	Shade
Landscape	Typeface
Named style	Wysiwyg
Outline	

EXERCISE 1

INSTRUCTIONS: Circle T if the statement is true and F if the statement is false.

T   F   1. By using Wysiwyg, the appearance of worksheets can be significantly improved.

T   F   2. At most, six named styles can be used on a worksheet.

T   F   3. You cannot shade the background of a cell.

T   F   4. Typeface refers to the design of the characters on a printed document.

T   F   5. In text display mode, the screen displays the text as it will look when it is printed.

T   F   6. Font indicates a specific typeface with a particular size.

T   F   7. The vertical printing position (from top to bottom of page) is called landscape mode.

T   F   8. The horizontal printing position (sideways on the page) is called portrait mode.-

---

EXERCISE 2

INSTRUCTIONS: Explain a typical situation when the following keystrokes or Lotus 1-2-3 commands are used.

Problem 1:   : **D**isplay **M**ode **G**raphics
Problem 2:   : **F**ormat **F**ont **B**old
Problem 3:   : **F**ormat **S**hade

Problem 4:   : **F**ormat **L**ines **O**utline
Problem 5:   : **N**amed-Style
Problem 6:   : **P**rint **C**onfig **O**rientation **L**andscape

---

EXERCISE 3 — Improving the Appearance of a Spreadsheet

INSTRUCTIONS: Retrieve the UNITPROD file you created as an exercise in Chapter 4. Complete the following items to improve the appearance of the spreadsheet.

1. Change the font of the worksheet title to Swiss 14 point.

2. Boldface the worksheet title, column titles, and row labels.

3. Widen columns as necessary to fully display labels.

4. Print the worksheet.

EXERCISE 4 — Improving the Appearance of a Spreadsheet

INSTRUCTIONS: Retrieve the PRACTICE file you created as an exercise in Chapter 4. Complete the following items to improve the appearance of the spreadsheet.

1. Change the font of the worksheet title to Swiss 14 point.

2. Lightly shade and boldface the column titles.

3. Create a named style using YEAR 1.

4. Apply the style name created in step 3 to the cells containing row labels (cells A45 through A54).

5. Widen columns as necessary to fully display labels.

6. Place an outline around the cells containing the assumptions.

7. Save the spreadsheet using the file name PRACTAPP.

8. Print the spreadsheet.

EXERCISE 5 — Improving the Appearance of a Spreadsheet

INSTRUCTIONS: Retrieve the SALES file you created as an exercise in Chapter 4.

1. Change the font for the worksheet title to Swiss 24 point.

2. Boldface the worksheet title and the column titles.

3. Boldface the salespersons' names.

4. Place a light shade in the cells containing the salespersons' names.

5. Print the spreadsheet.

CHAPTER SIX

USEFUL LOTUS COMMANDS

OBJECTIVES

In this chapter, you will learn to:

- Use absolute and relative cell addresses
- Use add-in programs
- Use SmartIcons
- Audit considerations
- Use File commands
- Erase data
- Use automatic formatting
- Move cell contents
- Use the Undo feature
- Widen multiple columns on a spreadsheet
- Insert and delete columns, rows, and worksheets
- Align labels
- Insert page breaks
- Print borders, headers and footers, and cell formulas
- Store a printing job in memory
- Protect data
- Hide and redisplay a column
- Hide and redisplay a range of cells
- Name ranges
- Search and replace data
- Display worksheet status
- Execute a System command
- View a worksheet before retrieving the worksheet file
- Keep titles on the screen
- Create windows
- Use the Backsolver and Solver add-ins for problem solving
- Recalculate a spreadsheet
- Document a worksheet
- Suppress zero values

■ CHAPTER OVERVIEW

Chapter 4 provided general procedures for building spreadsheets. Chapter 6 describes a variety of 1-2-3 commands that are often indispensable when creating and maintaining spreadsheets. For example, one exercise demonstrates how to use the **Worksheet Titles** command so that column headings and row labels do not scroll off the screen when you move the cell pointer through a large spreadsheet.

Since the problems in this chapter are small, the documentation necessary for proper spreadsheet design is omitted.

■ USING ABSOLUTE AND RELATIVE CELL ADDRESSES

Retrieve the SALES file for this example. The SALES worksheet was created in an exercise at the end of Chapter 4.

To enter a formula that will compute the percentage of sales for each salesperson:

Move	the cell pointer to cell D48		*Click*	*on cell D48*
Type	+		*Type*	*+*
Move	the cell pointer to cell C48		*Click*	*the ◄ SmartIcon to move the cell pointer to cell C48*
Type	/		*Type*	*/*
Move	the cell pointer to cell C54		*Click*	*the ▼ and ◄ SmartIcons until the cell pointer is in cell C54*
Press	⟵Enter		*Click*	*the mouse button with the mouse pointer in the control panel*

Cell D48 should now display the following number: 0.140232.

To copy the formula for the rest of the SALESPERSONS:

Press	/		*Move*	*the mouse pointer to the control panel*
Select	Copy		*Choose*	*Copy*

When prompted for Enter range to copy FROM:

Press	⟵Enter		*Click*	*the mouse button with the mouse pointer in the control panel*

Since the cell pointer was highlighting cell D48, it is now designated as the range of cells to copy.

When prompted for "Enter range to copy TO:"

Move	the cell pointer to cell D49		*Move*	*the mouse pointer to cell D49*
Type	.		*Drag*	*the mouse pointer to cell D53*
Move	the cell pointer to cell D53		*Click*	*the mouse button*
Press	←Enter			

ERR (Error) appears in cells D49 through D53. Your screen should look like Figure 6-1.

Figure 6-1

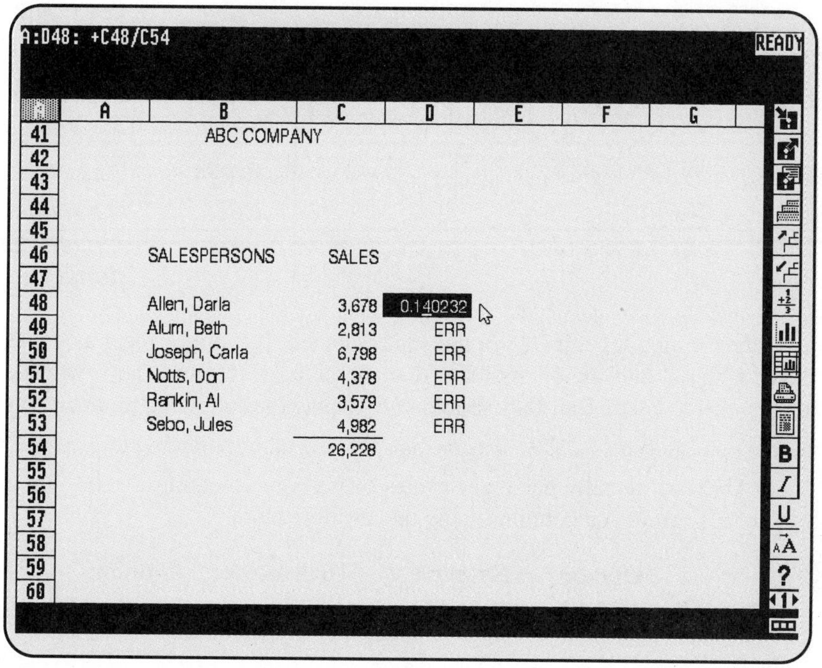

```
A:D48: +C48/C54                                                    READY

      A        B          C        D       E       F       G
 41            ABC COMPANY
 42
 43
 44
 45
 46       SALESPERSONS    SALES
 47
 48       Allen, Darla    3,678   0.140232
 49       Alum, Beth      2,813   ERR
 50       Joseph, Carla   6,798   ERR
 51       Notts, Don      4,378   ERR
 52       Rankin, Al      3,579   ERR
 53       Sebo, Jules     4,982   ERR
 54                      26,228
 55
 56
 57
 58
 59
 60
```

To see why the formula +C48/C54, when copied, did not compute the expected amount:

Move	the cell pointer to cell D49		*Click*	*on cell D49*

Look in the control panel to see the formula in cell D49. The formula that was *intended* to be copied was **+C49/C54**. However, when the formula was copied, it became **+C49/C55**. The same results occurred for the formulas in cells D50 through D53 (**+C50/C56, +C51/C57,** and so on). Formulas are based on **relative location** in Lotus 1-2-3. Lotus 1-2-3 interprets the formula that was copied not as **C48/C54** but as "divide the number one cell to the left by the number to the left one column and *six rows down*." The problem occurs when the formula is copied; cell C54 is not . . . to the left and six rows down for cells D49 through D53. Furthermore, since the cells C55, C56, and so forth are blank and a number cannot be divided by zero, the ERR message appears.

To solve the problem encountered above, you must keep cell C54 (the address for Total Sales) *constant* in the formula, even when the formula is copied to other cells. Lotus 1-2-3 refers to constant cells as being **absolute**.

To enter a formula that computes the percentage of SALES for each salesperson and keeps the cell representing Total Sales constant:

Move	the cell pointer to cell D48		*Click*	*on cell D48*
Type	+		*Type*	*+*
Move	the cell pointer to cell C48		*Click*	*the ⬇ SmartIcon to move the cell pointer to cell C48*
Type	/		*Type*	*/*
Move	the cell pointer to cell C54		*Click*	*the ⬇ and ⬅ SmartIcons until the cell pointer is in cell C54*
Press	F4		*Press*	*F4*
Press	←Enter		*Click*	*the mouse button with the mouse pointer in the control panel*

Look at the formula for cell D48 in the control panel. It should appear as **+C48/$C$54**. The dollar signs in front of the C and the 54 indicate that the column (C) and the row (54) will remain constant, or absolute, when copied. Cell D48 should still display the following number: 0.140232.

Note that you can type $C$54 directly into the cell without having to use the F4 (Abs) key.

The F4 (Abs) key actually has eight **cycles** or ways of changing a cell. The following options provide ways to change rows and columns using the absolute feature.

Option	Example	Worksheet	Column	Row
1	$A:$C$8	Absolute	Absolute	Absolute
2	$A:C$8	Absolute	Relative	Absolute
3	$A:$C8	Absolute	Absolute	Relative
4	$A:C8	Absolute	Relative	Relative
5	A:$C$8	Relative	Absolute	Absolute
6	A:C$8	Relative	Relative	Absolute
7	A:$C8	Relative	Absolute	Relative
8	A:C8	Relative	Relative	Relative

You can continue pressing the F4 (Abs) key until the desired format has been selected.

To copy the formula to the rest of the SALESPERSONS:

Press	/		*Move*	*the mouse pointer to the control panel*
Select	Copy		*Choose*	*Copy*

When prompted for "Enter range to copy FROM:"

| **Press**   ⎵Enter⎦ | **Click** | the mouse button with the mouse pointer in the control panel |

Since the cell pointer was highlighting cell D48, it is now designated as the range of cells to copy.

When prompted for "Enter range to copy TO:"

Move	the cell pointer to cell D49	**Move**	the mouse pointer to cell D49
Type	.	**Drag**	the mouse pointer to cell D53
Move	the cell pointer to cell D53	**Click**	the mouse button
Press	⎵Enter⎦		

The correct computation occurs. Your screen should look like Figure 6-2.

Figure 6-2

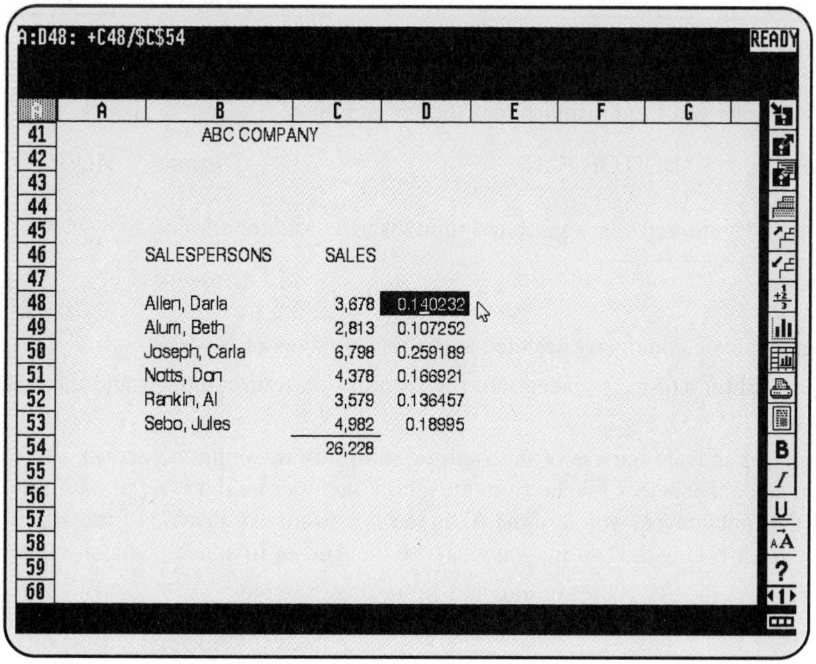

```
A:D48: +C48/$C$54                                          READY

      A         B          C       D       E     F     G
 41              ABC COMPANY
 42
 43
 44
 45
 46          SALESPERSONS     SALES
 47
 48          Allen, Darla     3,678   0.140232
 49          Alum, Beth       2,813   0.107252
 50          Joseph, Carla    6,798   0.259189
 51          Notts, Don       4,378   0.166921
 52          Rankin, Al       3,579   0.136457
 53          Sebo, Jules      4,982   0.18995
 54                          26,228
 55
 56
 57
 58
 59
 60
```

To see how the formula +C48/$C$54 was copied correctly:

| **Move** | the cell pointer to cell D49 | **Click** | on cell D49 |

The formula +C49/$C$54 should be visible in the control panel; $C$54 is held constant. If you so desire, move to cells D50 through D53 to see that $C$54 is held constant in the formulas for the cells.

■ USING ADD-IN PROGRAMS

Lotus 1-2-3 provides several add-in programs that expand the functionality of the software. There are several add-in commands that help you use the add-in programs. The following add-in programs are available in 1-2-3.

Auditor: provides a method to analyze the contents of cells in a worksheet.

Viewer: permits the viewing of files prior to retrieval.

Wysiwyg: provides the ability to improve the appearance of worksheets and graphs.

Bsolver: calculates a formula where a given value for the result of the formula is desired by changing one or more variables that affect the calculation of the formula.

Solver: determines the maximum or minimum value for a cell based on a set of constraints and adjustable cells.

To use an add-in, you must first attach the add-in and then invoke the add-in. Suppose you want to attach the Auditor add-in (load it into your personal computer's memory):

Press	Alt + F10		**Press**	Alt + F10
Select	Load		**Choose**	Load

To indicate you want to attach the Auditor add-in:

Select	AUDITOR.PLC		**Choose**	AUDITOR.PLC

To specify the key you want to use to invoke the Auditor add-in:

Select	1		**Choose**	1

Note that you could have selected any of the numbers or No-Key.

The Auditor add-in is loaded into the memory of your computer and the add-in menu appears on your screen.

You can activate the use of the Auditor add-in by invoking the add-in. To activate the Auditor add-in, you can either select **I**nvoke from the add-in menu or hold down the ALT key and then press the number of the function key you designated as the key to invoke the use of the add-in. If you did not specify a key for invoking the add-in, you must use the Add-In **I**nvoke command sequence.

To invoke the use of the Auditor add-in for this example:

Select	Invoke		**Choose**	Invoke

A list of available add-ins appears in the control panel. To specify that you want to use the Auditor add-in:

Select	Auditor		**Choose**	Auditor

The Auditor add-in menu appears on the screen. The top part of your screen should look like Figure 6-3.

Figure 6-3

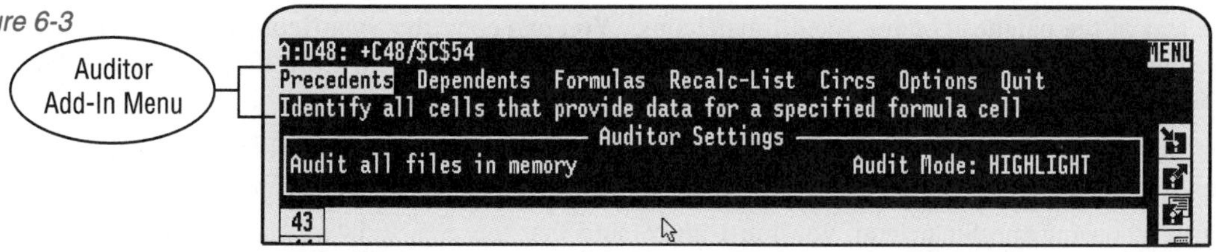

Auditor
Add-In Menu

```
A:D48: +C48/$C$54                                              MENU
Precedents  Dependents  Formulas  Recalc-List  Circs  Options  Quit
Identify all cells that provide data for a specified formula cell
┌────────────────────────── Auditor Settings ──────────────────────────┐
│ Audit all files in memory                      Audit Mode: HIGHLIGHT  │
└───────────────────────────────────────────────────────────────────────┘
   43                              ⌖
```

To exit the Auditor add-in:

Select   Quit | ***Choose***   *Quit*

To detach or remove an add-in from your computer's memory:

Press   Alt + F10 | ***Press***   *Alt + F10*
Select   Remove | ***Choose***   *Remove*

To indicate that you want to detach the Auditor add-in:

Select   Auditor | ***Choose***   *Auditor*

To exit the add-in menu:

Select   Quit | ***Choose***   *Quit*

Assuming you installed Lotus 1-2-3 using the standard procedure, the Wysiwyg add-in is automatically loaded into the memory of your computer. If you do not desire to use Wysiwyg, you can detach it from the memory of your computer in exactly the same manner as for the Auditor add-in.

■ USING SMARTICONS

1-2-3 provides a set of **SmartIcons** that improves the efficiency of utilizing the software. By using these SmartIcons, you can access many of the popular features available by selecting the SmartIcon rather than going through the standard command sequence.

There are 93 SmartIcons available for your use in 1-2-3 Release 3.4. The SmartIcons are arranged in a series of palettes and appear when the Wysiwyg add-in is invoked. The number of palettes available is determined by what type of monitor you are using and whether the Wysiwyg add-in is attached. You can remove the SmartIcon palettes from your screen by clicking the Toggle ▦ SmartIcon in the bottom right corner of the screen. To restore the SmartIcon palettes, click the Toggle ▦ SmartIcon again. See the Lotus 1-2-3 reference manual that came with your software or Appendix A for a complete list of the SmartIcons, their appearance, and their function.

Palette number 1 is used to create your own custom palette of those SmartIcons that you use most or need for a particular spreadsheet application. The last palette contains the SmartIcons U1 through U12. These SmartIcons are called user icons. They are used to assign macros for 1-2-3 to execute. This process is covered in Chapter 16 when macros are introduced.

The rest of the palettes contain fixed SmartIcons. You can copy the SmartIcons to your custom palette, but you cannot move the SmartIcons to another palette or delete them from the palette on which they appear.

The SmartIcons are selected by using the keyboard or a mouse. Whenever the SmartIcon you want to use affects a range of cells, you must highlight the range of cells prior to selecting the SmartIcon.

Before choosing the SmartIcon, you must make sure that the appropriate SmartIcon palette is on your screen. Then you can select the desired SmartIcon.

To select a SmartIcon:

Press	Ctrl + F10	*Click*	*the left or right arrow beside the palette number until the desired SmartIcon appears on the SmartIcon palette*
Press	→ or ← until the desired SmartIcon appears on the SmartIcon palette	*Click*	*the desired SmartIcon*
Press	↑ or ↓ to move to the desired SmartIcon		
Press	←Enter		

To illustrate the use of the SmartIcons, make sure you have a blank worksheet on your screen. Enter the value .02 in cells A1 through C1. Suppose these are percents and you want to display them with a percent sign and two decimal places.

Highlight	cells A1 through C1	*Highlight*	*cells A1 through C1*
Press	Ctrl + F10	*Click*	*the left or right arrow beside the palette number until the Percent % SmartIcon appears*
Press	→ or ← until the Percent % SmartIcon appears	*Click*	*the % SmartIcon*
Press	↑ or ↓ until the % SmartIcon is highlighted		
Press	←Enter		

Your screen should look like Figure 6-4.

Figure 6-4

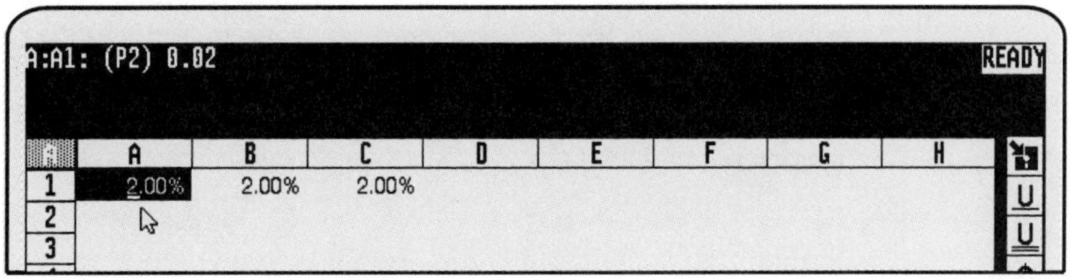

```
A:A1: (P2) 0.02                                              READY

      A      B       C      D      E      F      G      H
 1  2.00%  2.00%  2.00%
 2     ▷
 3
```

Adding SmartIcons to the Custom Palette

You can add or remove SmartIcons from your custom icon palette. The custom palette is always palette 1. When you add a SmartIcon to your custom palette, the SmartIcon is always placed at the bottom of the custom palette. If the custom palette is full, then the last SmartIcon on the custom palette is removed and the one you specify is added.

To illustrate the process of adding a SmartIcon, make sure you have a blank worksheet on your screen. Suppose you want to place the Comma Format [0,0] SmartIcon on your custom palette. The Comma Format [0,0] SmartIcon is used to format a cell or range of cells using the , format and 0 decimal places.

Press Ctrl + F10

Press → or ← until the Add SmartIcon appears

Press ↑ or ↓ until the Add SmartIcon is highlighted

Press ←Enter

Press → or ← until the Comma Format [0,0] SmartIcon appears

Press ↑ or ↓ until the [0,0] SmartIcon is highlighted

Press ←Enter

Press Ctrl + F10

Press → or ← until palette number 1 appears

Press Esc

Click the left or right arrow beside the palette number until the Add SmartIcon appears

Click the Add SmartIcon

Click the left or right arrow beside the palette number until the Comma Format [0,0] SmartIcon appears

Click the [0,0] SmartIcon

Click the left or right arrow beside the palette number until palette 1 appears

The Comma Format [0,0] SmartIcon appears at the bottom of your custom palette. Your screen should look similar to Figure 6-5.

Figure 6-5

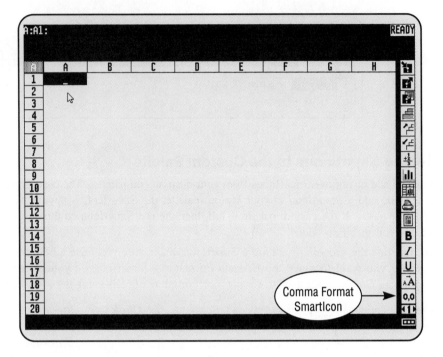

Removing SmartIcons from the Custom Palette

In some situations, you may want to remove a SmartIcon from your custom palette. Suppose you want to remove the Comma Format 0,0 SmartIcon from your custom palette.

Press	Ctrl + F10	**Click**	the left or right arrow beside the palette number until the Delete SmartIcon appears
Press	→ or ← until the Delete SmartIcon appears	**Click**	the Delete SmartIcon
Press	↑ or ↓ until the Delete SmartIcon is highlighted	**Click**	the 0,0 SmartIcon
Press	←Enter	**Click**	the left or right arrow beside the palette number until palette number 1 appears
Press	↑ or ↓ until the 0,0 SmartIcon is highlighted		
Press	←Enter		
Press	Ctrl + F10		

| **Press** | → or ← until palette number 1 appears |
| **Press** | Esc |

Notice that the Comma Format ⊞0,0 SmartIcon has been removed from your custom icon palette.

Add the Help ? SmartIcon to your custom palette.

Rearranging the Location of SmartIcons on the Custom Palette

You can change the position of a SmartIcon on your custom palette. For example, suppose you want to move the Help ? SmartIcon above the Bold B SmartIcon.

Press	Ctrl + F10		**Click**	the left or right arrow beside the palette number until the Move ▦ SmartIcon appears
Press	← or → until the Move ▦ SmartIcon appears		**Click**	the Move ▦ SmartIcon
Press	↑ or ↓ until the Move ▦ SmartIcon is highlighted		**Click**	the Help ? SmartIcon
Press	←Enter		**Click**	the Bold B SmartIcon
Press	↑ or ↓ until the Help ? SmartIcon is highlighted		**Click**	the left or right arrow beside the palette number until palette number 1 appears
Press	←Enter			
Press	↑ or ↓ until the Bold B SmartIcon is highlighted			
Press	←Enter			
Press	Ctrl + F10			
Press	← or → until palette number 1 appears			

Notice that the Help ? SmartIcon is now above the Bold B SmartIcon.

Rearrange your custom palette by moving the Help ? SmartIcon to the bottom of the palette.

■ AUDITING CONSIDERATIONS

Lotus 1-2-3 includes an Auditor add-in that provides you with assistance in analyzing a worksheet and its contents. This add-in can be particularly helpful when you are trying to understand the formulas used in a worksheet completed by another individual. The Auditor add-in can also be helpful when you are trying to find computational errors in a worksheet. The available options are:

Precedents: specifies the cells that are used in a formula.

Dependents: indicates all formulas that use a specified cell.

  Formulas: specifies all formulas in the worksheet or audit range that you define.

  Circs: identifies cells that are included in a circular reference (cells that are included in a formula).

  Audit-Range: denotes the range of cells examined when the Auditor add-in is used.

To illustrate the use of the Auditor add-in, retrieve the BUDGET file and invoke the Auditor add-in. If you are not familiar with using an add-in, see the section on Add-ins earlier in this chapter. After you invoke the Auditor add-in, the top part of your screen should look like Figure 6-6.

Figure 6-6

```
A:A41: {Text} [W14] ^ABC COMPANY                                        MENU
Precedents Dependents Formulas Recalc-List Circs Options Quit
Identify all cells that provide data for a specified formula cell
─────────────────────────── Auditor Settings ───────────────────────────
Audit all files in memory                        Audit Mode: HIGHLIGHT

  43
```

Note that an Auditor Settings dialog box appears on your screen indicating the current audit range and the report method being used. You can change these items by using the **O**ptions menu option.

To illustrate the Precedents command:

Select	Precedents		***Choose***	*Precedents*
Move	the cell pointer to cell D47		***Click***	*on cell D47 twice*
Press	⏎Enter		***Choose***	*Quit*
Select	Quit			

Notice that cells B47, C47, C63, and D63 are a different color or appear to be more intense. These cells provide data used in the calculation of cell D47.

To illustrate the use of the Dependents command, retrieve the BUDGET file, invoke the Auditor add-in and then:

Select	Dependents		***Choose***	*Dependents*
Move	the cell pointer to cell B50		***Click***	*on cell B50 twice*
Press	⏎Enter		***Choose***	*Quit*
Select	Quit			

Cells F50, B55, F55, B56, and F56 are a different color or appear to be more intense. The data in cell B50 is used in calculating the formulas for these cells.

To specify the cells in the worksheet that include formulas, retrieve the BUDGET file, invoke the Auditor add-in and then:

| **Select** | Formulas | | ***Choose*** | *Formulas* |
| **Select** | Quit | | ***Choose*** | *Quit* |

All cells in the worksheet that include formulas are a different color or appear to be more intense.

In some situations, you may see the characters CIRC appear in the lower right portion of your screen. When CIRC appears, it means that a cell in the worksheet contains a formula that refers to that particular cell. To illustrate how you might create a circular reference, retrieve the BUDGET file and enter @SUM(B56..F56) in cell F56. Since cell F56 is used in the calculation of cell F56, the characters CIRC now appear on your screen.

To identify the cell that is used as part of a circular reference, invoke the Auditor add-in and then:

Select	Circs		***Choose***	*Circs*

A list appears on your monitor identifying cells used in a circular reference. In this case, cell F56 appears in the list. To return to the worksheet:

Press	←Enter		***Click***	*the alternate mouse button*
Select	Quit		***Choose***	*Quit*

To remove the characters CIRC from your screen, enter the correct formula @SUM(B56..E56) in cell F56. There are other options available in the Auditor add-in. For additional information, see the Lotus 1-2-3 reference manual that came with your software.

Before continuing to the next section, detach the Auditor add-in.

■ USING FILE COMMANDS

File Directory

The **F**ile **D**irectory command temporarily changes the drive and path specifications from the files that are retrieved and saved. To change from drive C to drive A, for example:

Press	/		***Move***	*the mouse pointer to the control panel*
Select	File		***Choose***	*File*
Select	Directory		***Choose***	*Directory*

The top part of your screen should look similar to Figure 6-7.

Figure 6-7

```
A:A41: {Text} [W14] ^ABC COMPANY                                    EDIT
Enter current directory: C:\123R34

        A        B        C        D        E        F        G
41                        ABC COMPANY
42                         BUDGET
43
```

The current directory (where data files are being retrieved and saved) should be displayed. If you are currently saving the data in the root directory on drive C, your directory setting is C:\ .

To change the directory to drive A, for example, you could type A:\ and press ENTER (do **not** do so at this time). For the rest of this work session using 1-2-3, all data files will automatically be retrieved from and saved to the A drive.

To avoid changing the directory from its present setting:

| **Press** | [Esc] until the menus disappear from the control panel | **Click** | *the alternate mouse button until the menus disappear from the control panel* |

Note: To permanently change the default directory, issue the **W**orksheet **G**lobal **D**efault **D**irectory sequence. Change the directory to the desired drive or path, press the ENTER key or click the mouse button with the mouse pointer in the control panel and select **U**pdate to permanently save the directory as a default. Choose **Q**uit to exit the menu.

File Erase

The **F**ile **E**rase command sequence erases a previously saved file from the disk. To permanently erase a worksheet file:

Press	[/]	**Move**	*the mouse pointer to the control panel*
Select	File	**Choose**	*File*
Select	Erase	**Choose**	*Erase*

Four types of files are listed on the menu: Worksheet, Print, Graph, and Other. When prompted for the type of file to erase:

| **Select** | Worksheet | **Choose** | *Worksheet* |

The top part of your screen should look similar to Figure 6-8.

Figure 6-8

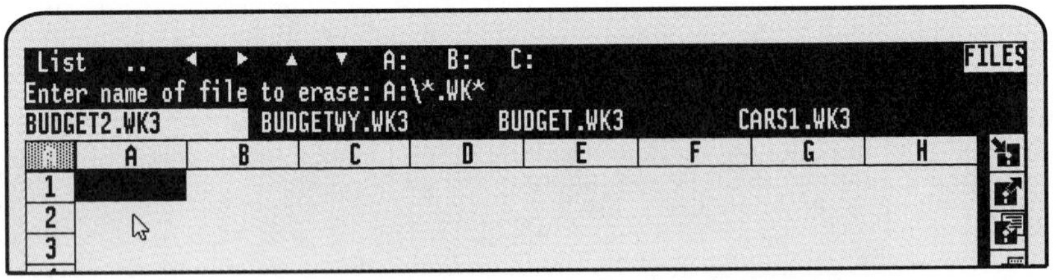

To permanently erase a file from the disk, you can press the F3 key, use the pointer-movement keys to highlight the file to erase, and press ENTER (do **not** do so at this time). To escape from this process and not erase a file:

Press	Esc until the menus disappear	**Click**	the alternate mouse button until the menus disappear

File List

The **F**ile **L**ist command sequence lists the files in the directory being used. To list the worksheet files:

Press	/	**Move**	the mouse pointer to the control panel
Select	File	**Choose**	File
Select	List	**Choose**	List

Note the six options—Worksheet, Print, Graph, Other, Active, or Linked.

Worksheet:	lists the worksheet files.
Print:	lists print files (created using the **P**rint **F**ile command sequence and printing a range to a file).
Graph:	lists graph files (created using the **G**raph **S**ave command sequence to print a graph from the graph settings in the current file).
Other:	lists all files in the directory being used including those that were not created with Lotus 1-2-3.
Active:	lists files in the computer's memory.
Linked:	lists the files that are linked to the current file.

Select	Worksheet	**Choose**	Worksheet

The top part of your screen should look like Figure 6-9.

Figure 6-9

```
List  ..  ◄  ►  ▲  ▼  A:  B:  C:                         FILES
Enter names of files to list: A:\*.WK*
          BUDGET2.WK3    08-Dec-92      03:55 AM      5301
 BUDGET2.WK3     BUDGETWY.WK3     BUDGET.WK3      CARS1.WK3
 CARS.WK3        EXAMPLE.WK3      INCOME1.WK3     INCOME.WK3
 PRACTICE.WK3    SALES.WK3        UNITPROD.WK3
              ▸
```

To return to the worksheet:

Press	←Enter	**Press**	←Enter

File Admin Seal

In a multiuser situation, several persons may be using a file at the same time. Only one user at a time may make changes to a file. 1-2-3 has a **reservation-setting** that guarantees your changes to a file can be saved. If you do not have a file's reservation status, changes to that file cannot be saved. A read only (RO) indicator alerts you that the reservation status is currently not available.

The Seal feature prevents changes from being made to worksheets, ranges, graphs, or print settings. A file is sealed using the **File Admin Seal** command sequence. The entire file or just the reservation-settings can be sealed.

The file or reservation-settings are sealed from general use with a password. Only users who know the password can make changes to the file. The password is case sensitive. It is important to remember or keep a record of the exact password and the combination of uppercase or lowercase letters that you need.

When a password is entered at the prompt, 1-2-3 displays an asterisk for each character. Upon entering the password, 1-2-3 again asks you to verify the password. You must enter the exact password again. A password can have a maximum of 15 characters.

Three options appear when selecting the **S**eal feature. The available options are:

File:	seals the File and the Reservation-Settings.
Reservation-Setting:	seals the Settings only.
Disable:	permits the unsealing of the File or Reservation-Settings.

Retrieve the BUDGET file and use the following commands to seal the file's reservation-settings so they cannot be changed.

Press	⌞ / ⌟		*Move*	*the mouse pointer to the control panel*
Select	File		*Choose*	*File*
Select	Admin		*Choose*	*Admin*
Select	Seal		*Choose*	*Seal*
Select	Reservation-Setting		*Choose*	*Reservation-Setting*

When prompted to enter a password, choose a suitable word and make a notation of it exactly as it was entered.

Press	⌞←Enter⌟		*Click*	*the mouse button*

When prompted to verify the password, enter the same password exactly as you did before. The top part of your screen should look similar to Figure 6-10.

Figure 6-10

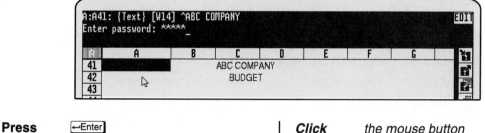

```
A:A41: {Text} [W14] ^ABC COMPANY                                    EDIT
Enter password: *****              Verify password: *****_

      A        B        C        D        E        F        G
 41                          ABC COMPANY
 42          ↳                 BUDGET
 43
```

Press   `←Enter` | ***Click***   *the mouse button*

To remove the password, the procedure is similar. Use the following commands:

Press   `/` | ***Move***   *the mouse pointer to the control panel*

Select   File | ***Choose***   *File*
Select   Admin | ***Choose***   *Admin*
Select   Seal | ***Choose***   *Seal*
Select   Disable | ***Choose***   *Disable*

When prompted to enter the password, use the password you used before to seal the file or reservation-settings. The top part of your screen should look like Figure 6-11.

Figure 6-11

```
A:A41: {Text} [W14] ^ABC COMPANY                                    EDIT
Enter password: *****_

      A        B        C        D        E        F        G
 41                          ABC COMPANY
 42          ↳                 BUDGET
 43
```

Press   `←Enter` | ***Click***   *the mouse button*

Whether a file is sealed or just the reservation-setting is sealed, the following commands will not make changes to the file:

File Admin Reservation
Graph Name
Print Encoded/File/Printer Options Name
Range Format
Range Label
Range Name
Range Name Note
Range Prot
Range Unprot

Worksheet Column
Worksheet Column Hide
Worksheet Global

When the reservation-setting is sealed, changes can be made to everything in the file except the reservation-setting.

Before sealing the entire file, it is wise to unprotect the cells that may have data changes. Use the **R**ange **U**nprot command sequence. If the file is globally protected, data can only be changed in the unprotected cells.

File Save Backup

When saving a file, 1-2-3 will automatically add a three-character extension to a file name.

The **F**ile **S**ave **B**ackup command is useful when you want to save the last version of a file without renaming the file. Before using this command, retrieve the BUDGET file. To use this feature, follow these commands:

Press	`/`	***Click***	the File Save SmartIcon
Select	File		
Select	Save		

When prompted to enter the file name, you will see that a file name already appears in the control panel.

Press   `←Enter`

Three choices appear on the screen as shown in Figure 6-12.

Cancel: cancels the Save command.

Replace: replaces the original file with the file on the screen.

Backup: creates a second file with a backup (BAK) extension.

Figure 6-12

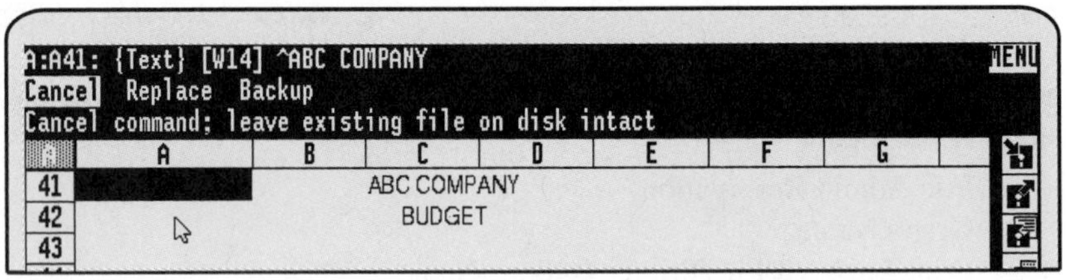

```
A:A41: {Text} [W14] ^ABC COMPANY                              MENU
Cancel  Replace  Backup
Cancel command; leave existing file on disk intact
        A        B       C       D       E       F       G
  41                        ABC COMPANY
  42              ▷            BUDGET
  43
```

Select	Backup	***Choose***	Backup

The file is now saved with its original extension "WK3", and also as a backup file is created with the extension "BAK". The file name remains the same. You can use the **F**ile **L**ist **O**ther command sequence to see that a BAK file has been created.

File Admin Table

One of the features of the **F**ile **A**dmin **T**able command sequence is its capability to create information in table form about files on the disk. From the following six selections, tables can be created.

Worksheet: worksheet files in a specific directory.

Print: files in a specific directory with a "PRN" extension.

Graph: graph files in a specific directory.

Other: all files in a specific directory.

Active: all the active files in memory.

Linked: all files linked by formula references to the current file.

Clear your screen using the **W**orksheet **E**rase **Y**es command sequence.

To create a table showing all the files on the disk in the root directory of Drive C:

Press	/	**Move**	the mouse pointer to the control panel
Select	File	**Choose**	File
Select	Admin	**Choose**	Admin
Select	Table	**Choose**	Table
Select	Other	**Choose**	Other

When prompted to enter the current directory:

Press	Esc until the current directory disappears	**Click**	the alternate mouse button until the current directory disappears
Type	C:*.* (or your directory)	**Type**	C:*.* (or your directory)
Press	←Enter	**Click**	the mouse button

Note: Existing data will be written over by the table. When prompted to enter a range, move the cell pointer to a blank area.

Press	←Enter	**Click**	the mouse button twice

A sample of a table appears in Figure 6-13.

Figure 6-13

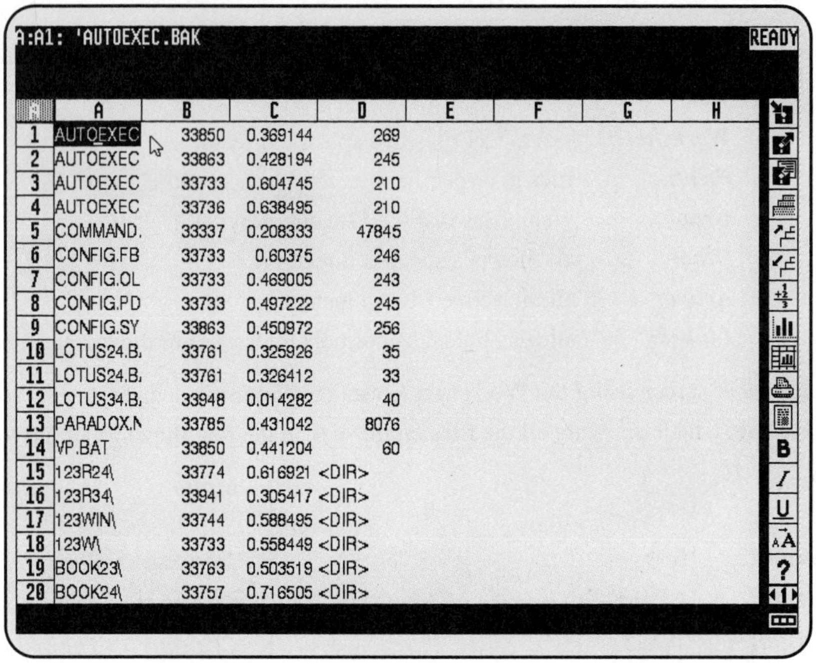

A:A1: 'AUTOEXEC.BAK READY

	A	B	C	D
1	AUTOEXEC	33850	0.369144	269
2	AUTOEXEC	33863	0.428194	245
3	AUTOEXEC	33733	0.604745	210
4	AUTOEXEC	33736	0.638495	210
5	COMMAND.	33337	0.208333	47845
6	CONFIG.FB	33733	0.60375	246
7	CONFIG.OL	33733	0.469005	243
8	CONFIG.PD	33733	0.497222	245
9	CONFIG.SY	33863	0.450972	256
10	LOTUS24.B.	33761	0.325926	35
11	LOTUS24.B.	33761	0.326412	33
12	LOTUS34.B.	33948	0.014282	40
13	PARADOX.N	33785	0.431042	8076
14	VP.BAT	33850	0.441204	60
15	123R24\	33774	0.616921	<DIR>
16	123R34\	33941	0.305417	<DIR>
17	123WIN\	33744	0.588495	<DIR>
18	123W\	33733	0.558449	<DIR>
19	BOOK23\	33763	0.503519	<DIR>
20	BOOK24\	33757	0.716505	<DIR>

The first column indicates the file name; the second and third columns show the date and time before they are formatted. The last column indicates the file size.

Once the date and time are formatted and the columns have been widened to display the information, your table should look similar to Figure 6-14. The process of formatting the date and time is covered in Chapter 15.

Figure 6-14

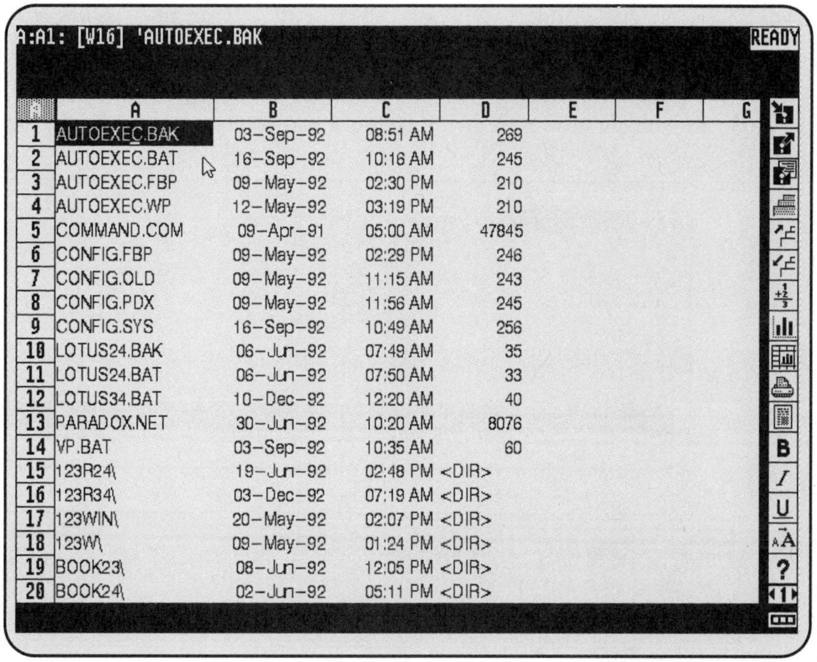

```
A:A1: [W16] 'AUTOEXEC.BAK                                          READY
```

	A	B	C	D	E	F	G
1	AUTOEXEC.BAK	03–Sep–92	08:51 AM	269			
2	AUTOEXEC.BAT	16–Sep–92	10:16 AM	245			
3	AUTOEXEC.FBP	09–May–92	02:30 PM	210			
4	AUTOEXEC.WP	12–May–92	03:19 PM	210			
5	COMMAND.COM	09–Apr–91	05:00 AM	47845			
6	CONFIG.FBP	09–May–92	02:29 PM	246			
7	CONFIG.OLD	09–May–92	11:15 AM	243			
8	CONFIG.PDX	09–May–92	11:56 AM	245			
9	CONFIG.SYS	16–Sep–92	10:49 AM	256			
10	LOTUS24.BAK	06–Jun–92	07:49 AM	35			
11	LOTUS24.BAT	06–Jun–92	07:50 AM	33			
12	LOTUS34.BAT	10–Dec–92	12:20 AM	40			
13	PARADOX.NET	30–Jun–92	10:20 AM	8076			
14	VP.BAT	03–Sep–92	10:35 AM	60			
15	123R24\	19–Jun–92	02:48 PM	\<DIR>			
16	123R34\	03–Dec–92	07:19 AM	\<DIR>			
17	123WIN\	20–May–92	02:07 PM	\<DIR>			
18	123W\	09–May–92	01:24 PM	\<DIR>			
19	BOOK23\	08–Jun–92	12:05 PM	\<DIR>			
20	BOOK24\	02–Jun–92	05:11 PM	\<DIR>			

File View

If the Viewer add-in is attached and invoked, you can browse and retrieve files by:

Press	⬚/		***Move***	*the mouse pointer to the control panel*
Select	File		***Choose***	*File*
Select	View		***Choose***	*View*

An example of viewing files prior to retrieving a specific file appears later in this chapter.

■ EDITING DATA

Erasing Cells

Retrieve the BUDGET file for this exercise.

To erase the labels in cells A63 through A66:

Highlight	cells A63 through A66		***Highlight***	*cells A63 through A66*
Press	⬚/		***Move***	*the mouse pointer to the control panel*

Select	Range		***Choose***	*Range*
Select	Erase		***Choose***	*Erase*

Cells A63 and A66 are now erased. The bottom part of your screen should look like Figure 6-15.

Figure 6-15

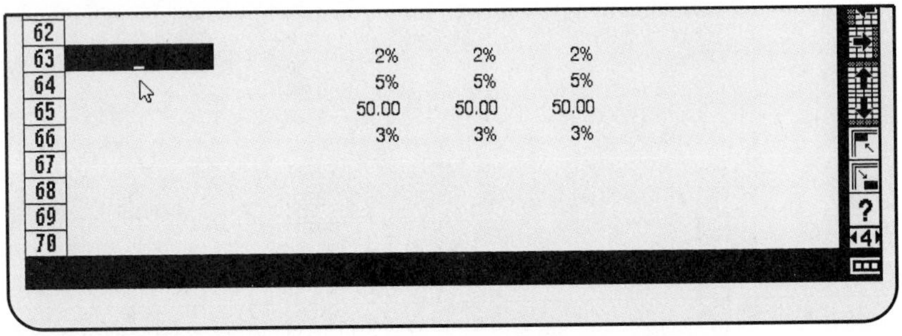

User Tip

An alternative method for erasing a range of cells is to first highlight the cells. Then press the DELETE key or click the Delete SmartIcon.

Error Correction and Cell Editing

There are various ways to correct errors on a worksheet. Two commonly used methods are illustrated below.

Replacing an Erroneous Entry

Clear your screen using the **W**orksheet **E**rase **Y**es command sequence.

In cell A1:

Type	100		***Type***	*100*
Press	⏎Enter		***Click***	*the mouse button*

The top part of your screen should now look like Figure 6-16, Part 1.

Figure 6-16
Part 1

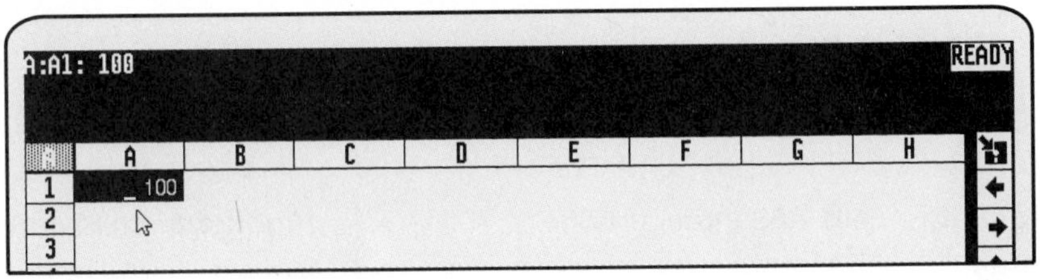

To change the entry to 1000:

Type	1000		*Type*	*1000*
Press	⌐⏎Enter⌐		*Click*	*the mouse button*

To replace an item that is incorrect, make sure the cell pointer is highlighting the cell with the incorrect entry and retype the entry. The top part of your screen should look like Figure 6-16, Part 2.

Figure 6-16
Part 2

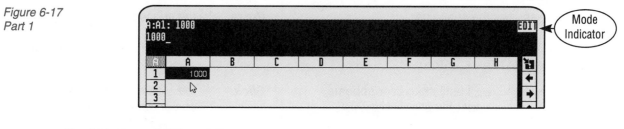

Editing an Entry Using the F2 Key

To change the cell entry in cell A1 from 1000 to 1000*1.03:

Move	the cell pointer to cell A1		*Click*	*on cell A1*
Press	F2		*Press*	*F2*

The entry is displayed in the control panel and a cursor appears at the end of the entry. EDIT appears in the mode indicator to indicate that the EDIT mode has been activated. The top part of your screen should look like Figure 6-17, Part 1.

Figure 6-17
Part 1

To add to the end of the existing entry:

Type	*1.03		*Type*	**1.03*
Press	⌐⏎Enter⌐		*Click*	*the mouse button*

The entry in cell A1 has now been changed from 1000 to 1000*1.03 or 1030. The top part of your screen should look like Figure 6-17, Part 2.

Figure 6-17
Part 2

When the EDIT mode is activated, the left and right pointer-movement keys as well as the HOME and END keys can also be used to move the cursor to various characters in an entry.

Clear your screen by using the **Worksheet Erase Yes** command sequence.

Move	the cell pointer to cell C3	*Click*	*on cell C3*
Type	ABC COMPANY	*Type*	*ABC COMPANY*
Press	⏎Enter	*Click*	*the mouse button*

To change the entry to THE ABC MANUFACTURING COMPANY, INC.:

Press	F2	*Press*	*F2*
Press	Home	*Press*	*Home*

The cursor is now under the apostrophe, which is the left-aligned default label prefix. The HOME key places the cursor at the first position of the cell entry.

Press	→ to move the cursor to the letter A in ABC	*Click*	*the ➡ SmartIcon to move the cursor to the letter A in ABC*
Type	THE	*Type*	*THE*
Press	the space bar	*Press*	*the space bar*

When the additional text is typed, the remaining text moves over so that the new text is inserted. To insert MANUFACTURING:

Press	→ until the cursor appears under the space after ABC	*Click*	*the ➡ SmartIcon until the cursor appears under the space after ABC*
Press	the space bar	*Press*	*the space bar*
Type	MANUFACTURING	*Type*	*MANUFACTURING*

To move quickly to the end of the line, you can use the END key so that , INC. can be added:

Press	End	*Press*	*End*
Type	, INC.	*Type*	*, INC.*

Since the entry is completely edited:

Press   [←Enter] | *Click*   *the mouse button*

The top part of your screen should look like Figure 6-18.

Figure 6-18

As illustrated in the previous example, when you are in EDIT mode, additional text can be typed and the existing text is moved over.

The INSERT key can be pressed to activate the Overstrike (OVR will appear on the status line) feature.

If the Overstrike function is activated, the new text will overstrike or type over the existing text. For example, to replace the letters ABC with XYZ:

Move   the cell pointer to cell C3 | *Click*   *on cell C3*
Press   [F2] | *Press*   [F2]
Press   [←] to move the cursor to the | *Click*   *the [←] SmartIcon to move the*
             A in ABC (or use the [Home] | *cursor to the letter A in ABC (or*
             key and the [→] key to achieve | *use the [Home] key and click the*
             the same result) | *[→] SmartIcon to achieve the*
                                                           | *same result)*

Press   [Insert] | *Press*   [Insert]

OVR appears in the status line.

Type   XYZ | *Type*   *XYZ*
Press   [←Enter] | *Click*   *the mouse button*

The letters ABC have now been replaced with the letters XYZ. The top part of your screen should look like Figure 6-19.

Figure 6-19

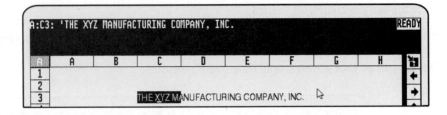

■ USING AUTOMATIC FORMATTING

Regular formatting uses two operations. First the value is entered; then the cell is formatted. With **automatic formatting,** data can be entered and formatted at the same time. Automatic formatting can be applied to the entire worksheet or it can be used for a specific range of cells.

With automatic formatting, 1-2-3 recognizes data as it is entered and formats cells in a logical way. Existing numbers are formatted in General format. When a new entry is made, 1-2-3 looks at the number and then formats that cell according to the format specified for the cell.

Clear your screen. To format a worksheet globally using the Automatic feature:

Press	/	***Move***	*the mouse pointer to the control panel*	
Select	Worksheet	***Choose***	*Worksheet*	
Select	Global	***Choose***	*Global*	
Select	Format	***Choose***	*Format*	
Select	Other	***Choose***	*Other*	
Select	Automatic	***Choose***	*Automatic*	

Widen column A to 15 characters. Then place the cell pointer in cell A1. Include the comma and decimal point as you enter a number.

Type	35,000.00	***Type***	*35,000.00*
Press	←Enter	***Click***	*the mouse button*

Additional entries are formatted according to the previous cell unless the new entry uses a different format. If a different format is used, 1-2-3 changes to that format and continues to use it for subsequent entries until a new format is encountered.

Move the cell pointer down column A of the worksheet as you enter these numbers. Include the commas and decimal points.

Type	9,000.00	***Type***	*9,000.00*
Type	0,750.00	***Type***	*0,750.00*
Type	1,000.00	***Type***	*1,000.00*

The top part of your screen should look like Figure 6-20.

Figure 6-20

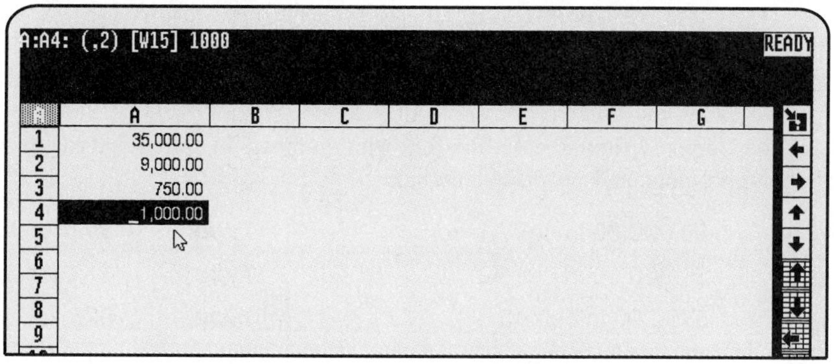

```
A:A4: (,2) [W15] 1000                                    READY

        A           B      C      D      E      F      G
  1   35,000.00
  2    9,000.00
  3      750.00
  4    _1,000.00
  5           ▷
  6
  7
  8
  9
```

In cell A4 0,750.00 was entered. The zero and comma in front of the number 750 are place holders. The numbers have been entered in the Comma format with two decimal places. 1-2-3 immediately recognized the format and displayed (,2) in the control panel before the value. Another format such as the Currency format could have been used.

To illustrate how you can change formats, move the cell pointer to cell A6.

Type	25%		*Type*	*25%*
Press	←Enter		*Click*	*the mouse button*

Look at the control panel in Figure 6-21 and notice that 1-2-3 recognized the format change to Percent with zero decimal places (P0) and stored the number as .25 in cell A6.

Figure 6-21

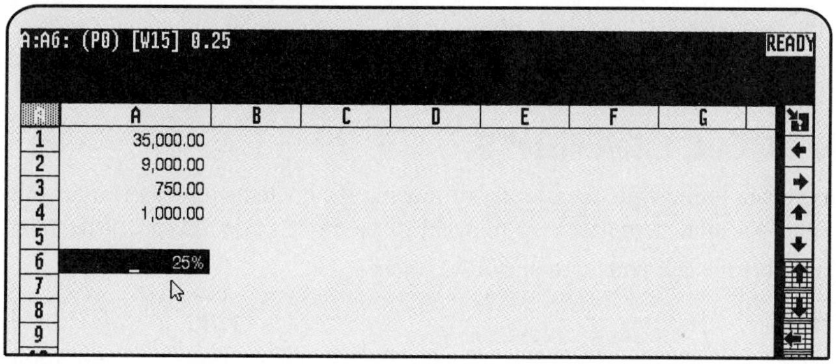

```
A:A6: (P0) [W15] 0.25                                    READY

        A           B      C      D      E      F      G
  1   35,000.00
  2    9,000.00
  3      750.00
  4    1,000.00
  5
  6       _ 25%
  7         ▷
  8
  9
```

Ranges can also be formatted automatically. Erase the current worksheet, then widen column A to 15. To format a range automatically:

Highlight	cells A1 through A4		*Highlight*	*cells A1 through A4*
Press	/		*Move*	*the mouse pointer to the control panel*

Select	Range		***Choose***	*Range*
Select	Format		***Choose***	*Format*
Select	Other		***Choose***	*Other*
Select	Automatic		***Choose***	*Automatic*

Using the Currency format, enter the following numbers in cells A1 through A4 making certain that the dollar sign, comma, and periods are included.

Type	$9,000.00 in cell A1		***Type***	*$9,000.00 in cell A1*
Type	$1,000.00 in cell A2		***Type***	*$1,000.00 in cell A2*
Type	$750.00 in cell A3		***Type***	*$750.00 in cell A3*
Type	$1,000.00 in cell A4		***Type***	*$1,000.00 in cell A4*

The screen should look like Figure 6-22. Notice that 1-2-3 recognized the format as Currency with two decimal places (C2) as shown in the control panel.

Figure 6-22

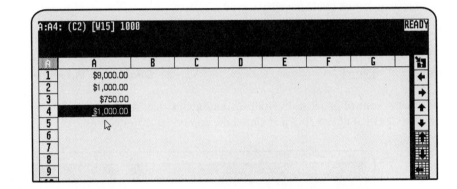

■ MOVING CELL CONTENTS

To prepare to illustrate the process of moving the contents of cells from one location on a spreadsheet to another location, complete the following steps. First, erase the spreadsheet on your screen.

Make sure the cell pointer is in cell A1; then:

Type	100		***Type***	*100*
Press	⏎Enter		***Click***	*the mouse button*
Move	the cell pointer to cell A4		***Click***	*on cell A4*
Type	50		***Type***	*50*
Press	→		***Click***	*the mouse button*
Type	25		***Click***	*the* ➡ *SmartIcon*

Press	←Enter		**Type**	25
			Click	the mouse button

Make sure the top part of your screen looks like Figure 6-23.

Figure 6-23

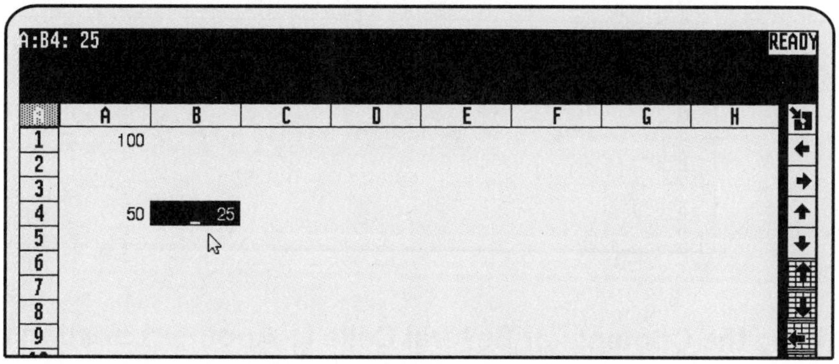

Moving the Contents of One Cell to Another Cell

To move the contents of cell A1 to cell H1:

Move	the cell pointer to cell A1		**Click**	on cell A1

When the cell pointer is already highlighting the cell to move, it is easier to use the **Move** command.

Press	/		**Move**	the mouse pointer to the control panel
Select	Move		**Choose**	Move

When prompted for "Enter range to move FROM:"

Press	←Enter		**Click**	the mouse button with the mouse pointer in the control panel

The cell to move (cell A1) was already highlighted, so only the ←Enter key has to be pressed.

The cell to move (cell A1) was already highlighted, so you only had to click the mouse button with the mouse pointer in the control panel.

When prompted for "Enter range to move TO:"

Move	the cell pointer to cell H1		**Move**	the mouse pointer to cell H1
Press	←Enter		**Click**	the mouse button twice

The top part of your screen should look like Figure 6-24.

Figure 6-24

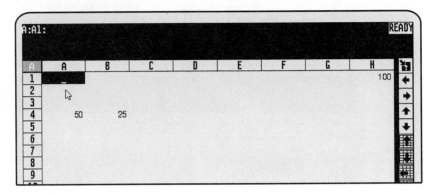

Moving the Contents of Several Cells to Another Location on the Worksheet

To move the contents of cells A4 through B4 to cells A14 through B14:

Move	the cell pointer to cell A4	*Click*	*on cell A4*
Press	⎡ / ⎤	*Move*	*the mouse pointer to the control panel*
Select	Move	*Choose*	*Move*

When prompted for "Enter range to move FROM:"

Move	the cell pointer to cell B4	*Move*	*the cell pointer to cell A4*
		Drag	*the mouse pointer to cell B4*

Cells A4 through B4 are now highlighted and therefore specified as the cells to move.

Press	⎡←Enter⎤	*Click*	*the mouse button*

When prompted for "Enter range to move TO:"

Move	the cell pointer to cell A14	*Move*	*the mouse pointer to cell A14*
Press	⎡←Enter⎤	*Click*	*the mouse button twice*

The contents of cells A4 through B4 have now been moved to cells A14 through B14. Note that it was only necessary to specify the upper left corner of the range to move to. Your screen should look like Figure 6-25.

Figure 6-25

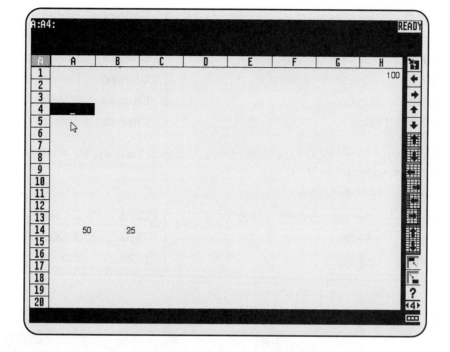

■ USING THE UNDO FEATURE

1-2-3 makes it possible to restore work to its original condition. The Undo feature creates a temporary copy of both the data and settings. The primary purpose of Undo is to save time redoing procedures. The ALT + F4 key combination and the Undo ⤶ SmartIcon operate the Undo feature. It works like a toggle switch and restores canceled changes.

At times when only a small amount of memory is available, 1-2-3 will display a menu to turn Undo off with three possible choices. These choices are:

Disable:	turns off Undo; completes procedure.
Proceed:	turns off Undo; completes procedure; turns Undo on.
Quit:	quits procedure; saves changes made; Undo stays on.

Note: Using CTRL + BREAK or ESC produces the same results as the third choice, **Quit**.

Undo does not work with all commands. For a complete description of the operations that you cannot undo, see the Lotus 1-2-3 reference manual.

Note: The Undo option is initially disabled when you install Lotus 1-2-3 Release 3.4.

If the Undo feature is disabled, use these commands to activate it:

Press	/	**Move**	the mouse pointer to the control panel
Select	Worksheet	**Choose**	Worksheet

Select	Global		**Choose**	*Global*
Select	Default		**Choose**	*Default*
Select	Other		**Choose**	*Other*
Select	Undo		**Choose**	*Undo*
Select	Enable		**Choose**	*Enable*
Select	Quit		**Choose**	*Quit*

Note: If you want UNDO to be enabled on a permanent basis, use the **W**orksheet **G**lobal **D**efault **U**pdate command sequence.

Retrieve the BUDGET file.

Move	the cell pointer to cell B50		**Click**	*on cell B50*
Type	50000		**Type**	*50000*
Press	⏎Enter		**Click**	*the mouse button*

The worksheet now appears like Figure 6-26, Part 1.

Figure 6-26 Part 1

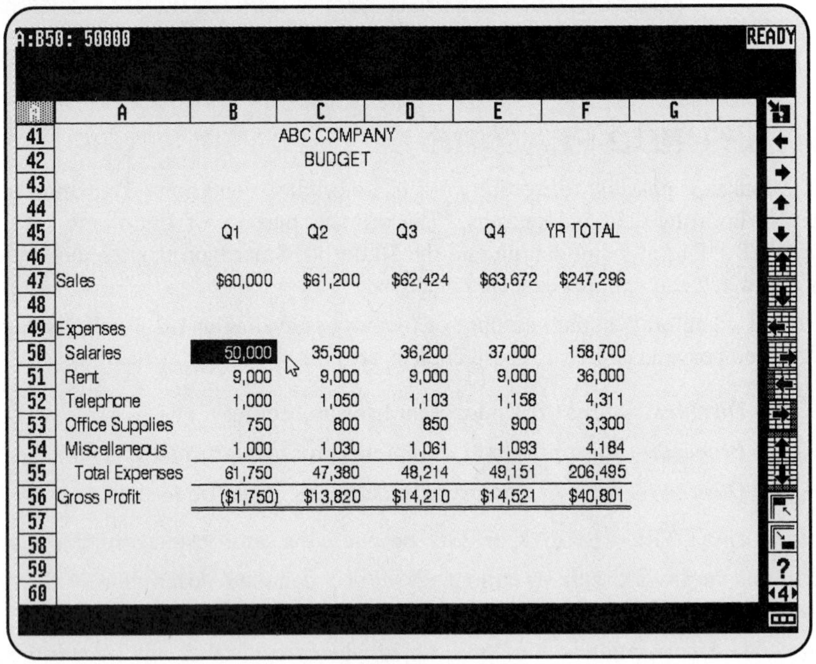

To restore the figure in cell B50 to its original amount:

| **Press** | Alt + F4 | | **Click** | *the Undo ⮌ SmartIcon* |
| **Select** | Yes | | **Choose** | *Yes* |

Your screen should look like Figure 6-26, Part 2.

Figure 6-26
Part 2

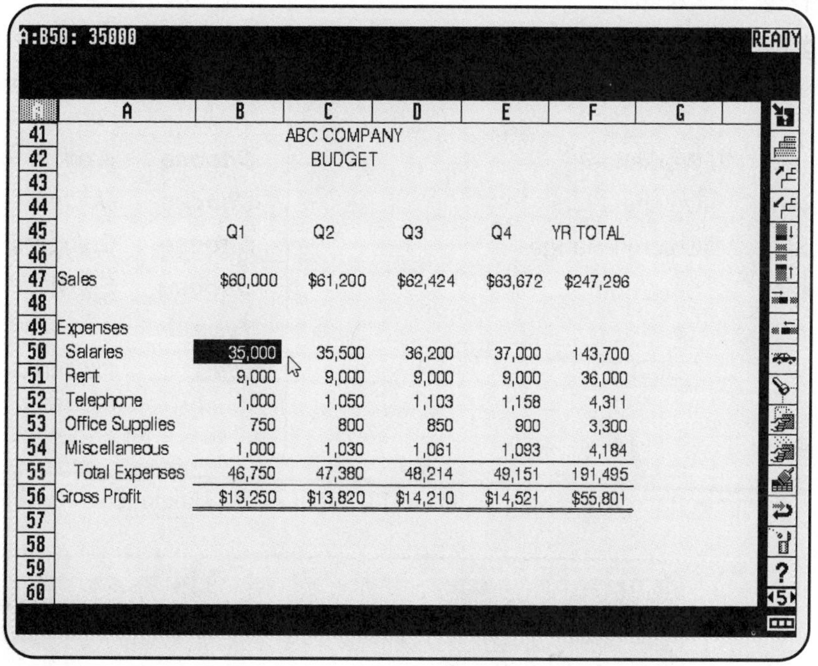
A:B50: 35000 READY

	A	B	C	D	E	F	G
41			ABC COMPANY				
42			BUDGET				
43							
44							
45		Q1	Q2	Q3	Q4	YR TOTAL	
46							
47	Sales	$60,000	$61,200	$62,424	$63,672	$247,296	
48							
49	Expenses						
50	Salaries	35,000	35,500	36,200	37,000	143,700	
51	Rent	9,000	9,000	9,000	9,000	36,000	
52	Telephone	1,000	1,050	1,103	1,158	4,311	
53	Office Supplies	750	800	850	900	3,300	
54	Miscellaneous	1,000	1,030	1,061	1,093	4,184	
55	Total Expenses	46,750	47,380	48,214	49,151	191,495	
56	Gross Profit	$13,250	$13,820	$14,210	$14,521	$55,801	
57							
58							
59							
60							

Now the figure in cell B50 is restored to its original amount of 35,000.

To disable the **U**ndo feature for the present example:

Press	/	***Move***	*the mouse pointer to the control panel*
Select	Worksheet	***Choose***	*Worksheet*
Select	Global	***Choose***	*Global*
Select	Default	***Choose***	*Default*
Select	Other	***Choose***	*Other*
Select	Undo	***Choose***	*Undo*
Select	Disable	***Choose***	*Disable*
Select	Quit	***Choose***	*Quit*

■ WIDENING MULTIPLE COLUMNS ON THE WORKSHEET

When you plan to place data in cells requiring more space than allowed by the nine-character default, you need to widen the columns. Otherwise, the cells will display asterisks each time the data exceeds the column width. This situation may occur in several contiguous columns.

Retrieve the BUDGET file. To widen columns B through E to 11 characters:

Highlight	cells B41 through E41	**Highlight**	cells B41 through E41
Press	`/`	**Move**	the mouse pointer to the control panel
Select	Worksheet	**Choose**	Worksheet
Select	Column	**Choose**	Column
Select	Column-Range	**Choose**	Column-Range
Select	Set-Width	**Choose**	Set-Width
Type	11	**Type**	11
Press	`←Enter`	**Click**	the mouse button with the mouse pointer in the control panel

Now columns B through E have widths of 11. Your screen should look like Figure 6-27.

Figure 6-27

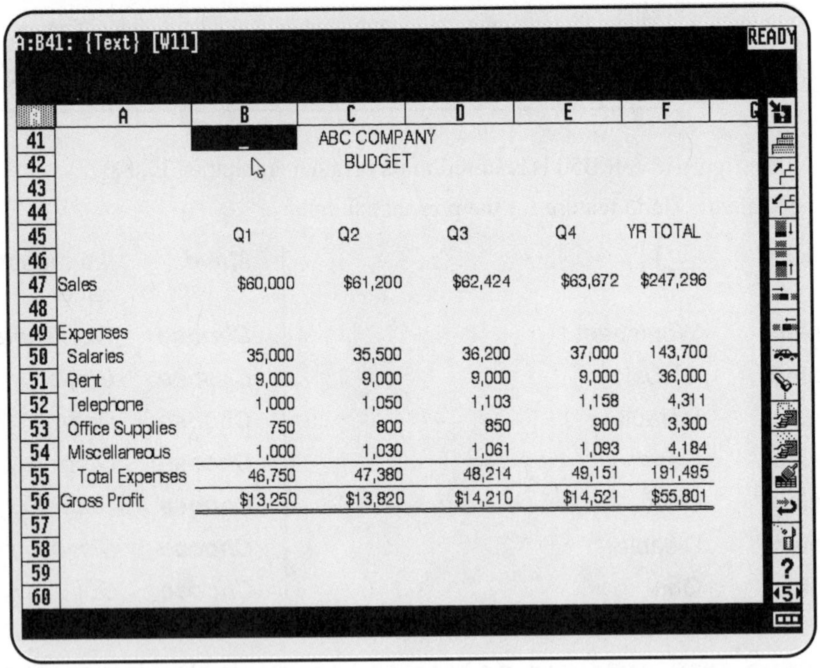

By using a **Worksheet Global** command, you can widen all the columns at one time. However, this global command does not change any columns set with the **Column-Range** command illustrated above.

■ INSERTING AND DELETING COLUMNS, ROWS, AND WORKSHEETS

Columns and rows can be inserted into a worksheet after the worksheet has been created. They can also be deleted whenever necessary.

Inserting and Deleting Columns

To complete this exercise, create the worksheet in Figure 6-28, Part 1 and save the worksheet using the file name BOATSALE.

Figure 6-28
Part 1

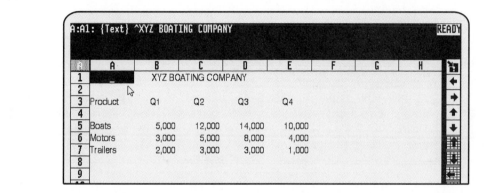

To insert a column between the Q3 and Q4 columns:

Move	the cell pointer to cell E3	*Click*	*on cell E3*
Press	⟨ / ⟩	*Move*	*the mouse pointer to the control panel*
Select	Worksheet	*Choose*	*Worksheet*
Select	Insert	*Choose*	*Insert*
Select	Column	*Choose*	*Column*
Press	⟨←Enter⟩	*Click*	*the mouse button with the mouse pointer in the control panel*

The top part of your screen should now look like Figure 6-28, Part 2.

Figure 6-28
Part 2

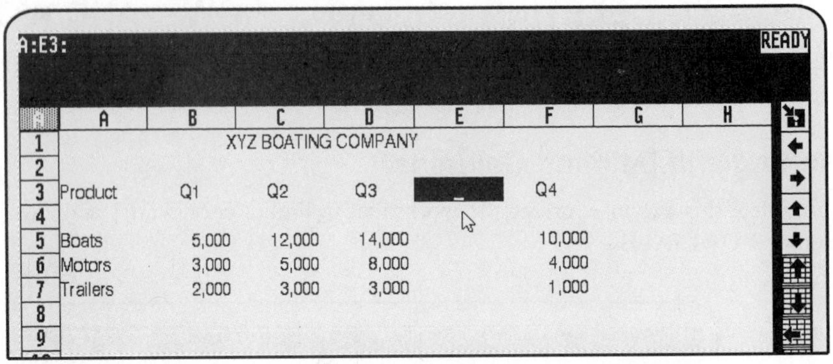

A:E3:								READY

	A	B	C	D	E	F	G	H
1			XYZ BOATING COMPANY					
2								
3	Product	Q1	Q2	Q3		Q4		
4								
5	Boats	5,000	12,000	14,000		10,000		
6	Motors	3,000	5,000	8,000		4,000		
7	Trailers	2,000	3,000	3,000		1,000		
8								
9								

User Tip

An alternative method for inserting a column is to place the cell pointer in a cell in the column where you want to insert a column. Then click the Column Insert ▓ SmartIcon. If you want to insert more than one column, highlight cells in more than one column before you click the Column Insert ▓ SmartIcon.

To remove column E from the worksheet:

Move	the cell pointer to cell E3		***Click***	*on cell E3*
Press	⌿		***Move***	*the mouse pointer to the control panel*
Select	Worksheet		***Choose***	*Worksheet*
Select	Delete		***Choose***	*Delete*
Select	Column		***Choose***	*Column*
Press	←Enter		***Click***	*the mouse button with the mouse pointer in the control panel*

The top part of your screen should look like Figure 6-28, Part 1 again. If you want to delete more than one column, you can highlight the columns to be deleted with the cell pointer whenever they are adjacent to one another.

Note: When data appear in columns to be deleted, there is no warning that data will be lost. Thus, when worksheets are larger than what appears on the screen, it is a good idea to first confirm that the column is empty by pressing END and then the DOWN ARROW key. The cell pointer should move to row 8192.

> *User Tip*
>
> An alternative method for deleting a column is to place the cell pointer in any cell within the column you want to delete. Then click the Column Delete ▦ SmartIcon. Click the OK command button and then the column is deleted. If you want to delete more than one column, highlight cells in more than one column before you click the Column Delete ▦ SmartIcon.

Inserting and Deleting Rows

Retrieve the BOATSALE file. To insert a blank row in the worksheet:

Move	the cell pointer to cell A3	***Click***	*on cell A3*
Press	⟋	***Click***	*the Row Insert* ▦ *SmartIcon*
Select	Worksheet		
Select	Insert		
Select	Row		
Press	⏎Enter		

The top part of your screen should look like Figure 6-29. If more than one row is to be inserted, move the cell pointer down an additional time for each desired row.

Figure 6-29

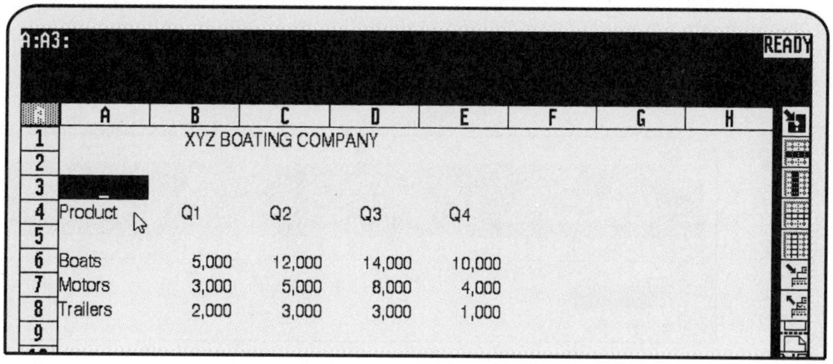

Rows can be deleted in a similar manner by using **D**elete instead of **I**nsert or by clicking on the Row Delete ▦ SmartIcon.

Note: When data appear in rows to be deleted, there is no warning that data will be lost. Thus, when worksheets are larger than what appears on the screen, it is a good idea to first confirm that the row is empty by pressing END and then the RIGHT ARROW key. The cell pointer is in column IV.

Inserting and Deleting Worksheets

Sheet is a choice on the **W**orksheet **I**nsert and **W**orksheet **D**elete menus. Sheets can be added or deleted when working with multiple worksheets. The procedure for adding worksheets is discussed in detail in Chapter 11.

■ ALIGNING LABELS

Aligning Cell Contents

In some situations, you may want to change the alignment of the labels of the various cells in a worksheet. The labels can be right aligned, left aligned, or centered by using the **R**ange **L**abel command. Create the worksheet in Figure 6-30.

Figure 6-30

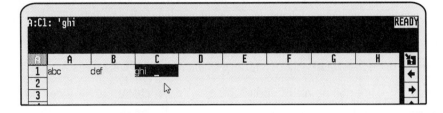

Since the entry in each cell is a label, 1-2-3 automatically left aligns the content of each cell.

To right align the data in cells A1, B1, and C1:

Highlight	cells A1 through C1		**Highlight**	cell A1 through C1
Press	⌨ /		**Click**	the Right Align ▤ SmartIcon
Select	Range			
Select	Label			
Select	Right			

The contents of cells A1 through C1 are now right aligned. After moving to cell A2, the top part of your screen should look like Figure 6-31.

Figure 6-31

```
A:A2:                                                    READY

      A      B      C      D      E      F      G      H
  1        abc    def    ghi
  2
  3
```

You can center or left align the contents of cells A1 through C1 by selecting the Center or Left menu option respectively if you are using the keyboard.

> *User Tip*
> A cell or range of cells can be left aligned or centered by highlighting the range and then clicking the Left Align ▤ or Center ▤ SmartIcon.

Label Prefixes

The use of the caret (the ^ symbol) to center labels was illustrated in Chapter 4. The caret is a **label prefix**. 1-2-3 has four label prefixes that affect the appearance of labels both on the screen and when they are printed. This section discusses and demonstrates the label prefixes. Before starting the following exercise, erase your screen.

The apostrophe (the ' symbol located on the double-quote key) is the default label prefix in 1-2-3. When a nonnumeric character is the first character of an entry, 1-2-3 automatically places an apostrophe as the prefix to the label. The entry then appears at the left of the cell in which it is input. Enter the following label in cell A1:

Type	USA		*Type*	*USA*
Press	←Enter		*Click*	*the mouse button*

Look at the control panel. Notice that an apostrophe appears before USA in the control panel. In the worksheet, notice that USA appears on the left side of cell A1. Because you did not specify a label prefix and you typed non-numeric characters, the apostrophe was used. The top part of your screen should look like Figure 6-32.

Figure 6-32

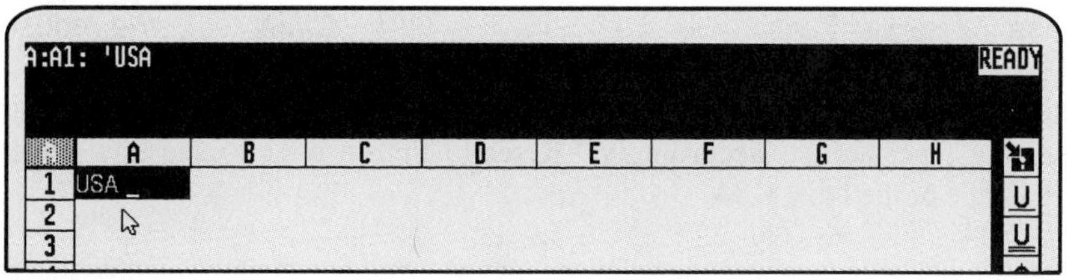

Erase the contents of cell A1 by using the **R**ange **E**rase command sequence. In cell A1, manually input the apostrophe before entering USA.

Type	'USA		*Type*	*'USA*
Press	←Enter		*Click*	*the mouse button*

Again, USA appears at the left side of the cell. The apostrophe appears before USA in the control panel when cell A1 is highlighted.

The caret symbol causes a label to appear in the center of a cell. The caret must be typed as the first character of the entry.

To center a label in a cell:

Move	the cell pointer to cell A2		*Click*	*on cell A2*
Type	^USA		*Type*	*^USA*
Press	←Enter		*Click*	*the mouse button*

USA appears in the center of the cell. The caret appears before USA in the control panel when cell A2 is highlighted.

The double-quote symbol (") causes a label to appear at the right side of the cell. The double-quote must be typed as the first character of the entry.

To right-justify a label:

Move	the cell pointer to cell A3		**Click**	on cell A3
Type	"USA		**Type**	"USA
Press	⮐Enter		**Click**	the mouse button

USA appears in the rightmost portion of the cell. The double-quote appears before USA in the control panel when cell A3 is highlighted.

The backslash symbol (\ ) causes the characters entered after the backslash to be repeated in the cell.

To cause the label USA to be repeated in a cell:

Move	the cell pointer to cell A4		**Click**	on cell A4
Type	\USA		**Type**	\USA
Press	⮐Enter		**Click**	the mouse button

Cell A4 displays USA throughout the cell. If the width of column A is shortened or lengthened, the repeating label adjusts accordingly. Refer to Figure 6-33 to see how the label prefixes altered the appearance of the label USA.

Figure 6-33

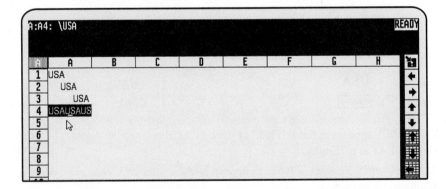

User Tip

Note that label prefixes are to be used only for **labels**. If ^123 is entered in a cell, for example, 123 is centered, treated as a label, and cannot be used for computation.

■ INSERTING PAGE BREAKS

When you print a spreadsheet in Lotus 1-2-3, Lotus prints as much as it can on a single page based on the default page length. The remaining rows are printed on the next page or set of pages. Sometimes you may wish to specify where you want page breaks to occur. The Worksheet **P**age command from the Wysiwyg menu can be used in such situations to manually create row or column page breaks.

Retrieve the BUDGET2 file for use in the following exercise. To set a print range:

Press	`:`		**Move**	*the mouse pointer to the control panel*
Select	Print		**Click**	*the alternate mouse button*
Select	Range		**Choose**	*Print*
Select	Set		**Choose**	*Range*
If necessary, press the `Esc` key to delete the current print range			**Choose**	*Set*
			If necessary, press the alternate mouse button to delete the current print range.	

When prompted for the range to print:

Move	the cell pointer to cell A41		**Click**	*on cell A41*
Type	.		**Drag**	*the mouse pointer to cell G66*
Move	the cell pointer to cell G66			

Cells A41..G66 (the descriptions, data, and assumptions for YEAR 1 through YEAR 6) are now highlighted.

Press	`←Enter`		**Click**	*the mouse button*
Select	Quit		**Choose**	*Quit*

To insert a page break at cell A52:

Move	the cell pointer to cell A52		**Click**	*on cell A52*
Press	`:`		**Move**	*the mouse pointer to the control panel*
Select	Worksheet		**Choose**	*Worksheet*
Select	Page		**Choose**	*Page*
Select	Row		**Choose**	*Row*
Select	Quit		**Choose**	*Quit*

Note that a dashed line appears above row 52. If the print range for BUDGET2 is printed, the data in row 52 (Telephone expenses) will be printed at the top of the second page. Note that {MPage} appears in the control panel in cell A52.

To erase the page break, use the **W**orksheet **P**age **D**elete command sequence. Do **not** erase the page break at this time. Your screen should look like Figure 6-34.

Figure 6-34

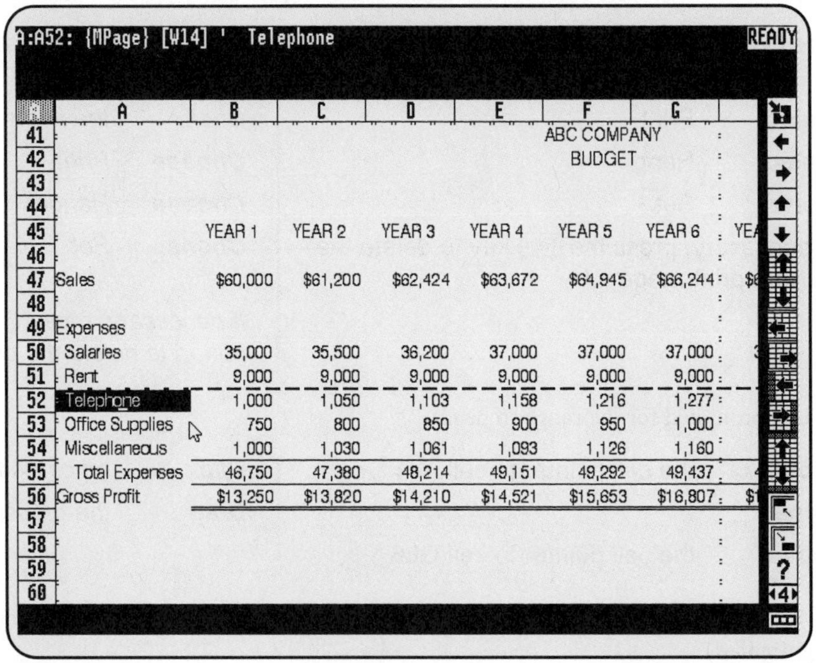

```
A:A52: {MPage} [W14] '  Telephone                                      READY

         A        B        C        D        E        F        G
  41                                                   ABC COMPANY      :
  42                                                     BUDGET         :
  43                                                                    :
  44                                                                    :
  45              YEAR 1   YEAR 2   YEAR 3   YEAR 4   YEAR 5   YEAR 6  : YEA
  46                                                                    :
  47 Sales        $60,000  $61,200  $62,424  $63,672  $64,945  $66,244 : $6
  48                                                                    :
  49 Expenses                                                           :
  50   Salaries   35,000   35,500   36,200   37,000   37,000   37,000  :
  51   Rent       9,000    9,000    9,000    9,000    9,000    9,000   :
  52   Telephone  1,000    1,050    1,103    1,158    1,216    1,277   :
  53   Office Supplies 750 800      850      900      950      1,000   :
  54   Miscellaneous 1,000 1,030    1,061    1,093    1,126    1,160   :
  55     Total Expenses 46,750 47,380 48,214 49,151 49,292  49,437    :
  56 Gross Profit $13,250  $13,820  $14,210  $14,521  $15,653  $16,807 : $1
  57                                                                    :
  58                                                                    :
  59                                                                    :
  60                                                                    :
```

User Tip

An alternative method for inserting a page break is to move the cell pointer to a cell in the row where you want to place a page break. Then click the Row Page Break ▦ SmartIcon. To insert a column page break, move the cell pointer to any cell in a column in which you want to start a new page. Then click the Column Page Break ▥ SmartIcon.

> *User Tip*
>
> If you are not using Wysiwyg to print and wish to insert a page break, use the 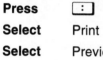 **W**orksheet **P**age command sequence.
>
> Two colons (: :) will appear in the current cell and any data previously in the row will be moved down one row. The symbols | : : (the pipe symbol and two colons) appear in the control panel.
>
> The page break symbol can be erased just as though it were a typical data entry. One option is the **R**ange **E**rase command sequence. Another option is the **W**orksheet **D**elete **R**ow command sequence. The second option may be preferable because it eliminates the row that was added to accommodate the page break symbol.

To preview the spreadsheet:

Press	`:`		***Click***	the Print Preview ▦ SmartIcon
Select	Print			
Select	Preview			

Your screen should look like Figure 6-35, Part 1.

Figure 6-35
Part 1

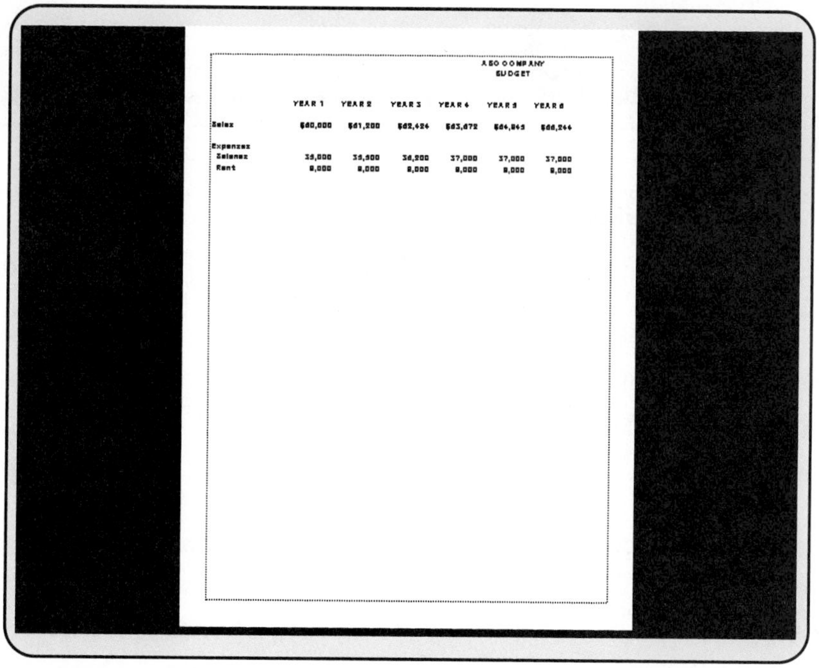

To view page 2:

Press [Page Down] | **Click** *the mouse button*

Your screen should look like Figure 6-35, Part 2.

Figure 6-35
Part 2

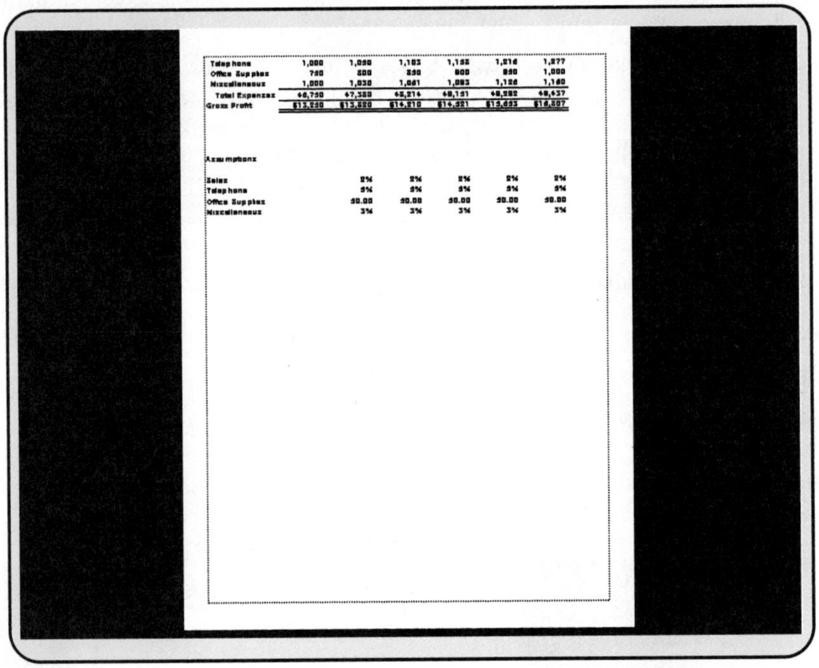

To exit preview and return to **READY** mode:

Press [←Enter] | **Click** *the mouse button*
Select Quit |

To delete the page break:

Move	the cell pointer to cell A52	**Click**	*on cell A52*
Press	[:]	**Move**	*the mouse pointer to the control panel*
Select	Worksheet	**Choose**	*Worksheet*
Select	Page	**Choose**	*Page*
Select	Delete	**Choose**	*Delete*
Select	Quit	**Choose**	*Quit*

The page break symbol {MPage} no longer appears in the control panel on your screen.

■ PRINTING BORDERS, HEADERS AND FOOTERS, AND CELL FORMULAS

Borders

The **B**orders option is useful when working with large spreadsheets or worksheets of more than one page. This command places headings or labels from the worksheet on every page either to the left of the data or at the top of the page, or both.

When using the **B**orders feature, there are two options to choose from:

> *Rows:*   horizontal headings above each print range and at the top of each page.
>
> *Columns:*   vertical headings to the left of each print range and at the left side of each page.

Before starting this exercise, retrieve the BUDGET2 file.

To print columns on every page of the worksheet:

Press	☐ : ☐		*Move*	*the mouse pointer to the control panel*
Select	Print		*Click*	*the alternate mouse button*
Select	Layout		*Choose*	*Print*
Select	Borders		*Choose*	*Layout*
Select	Left		*Choose*	*Borders*
			Choose	*Left*

To make the labels in column A appear on every page, highlight any cell in column A; then:

Move	the cell pointer to cell A41		*Click*	*on cell A41*
Press	⏎Enter		*Click*	*the mouse button*
Select	Quit		*Choose*	*Quit*
Select	Quit		*Choose*	*Quit*

When selecting the print range, do not include the borders. This would cause a double printing of the border on each page. For this example:

Select	Range		*Choose*	*Range*
Select	Set		*Choose*	*Set*

To clear the current print range if necessary:

Press	Esc		*Click*	*the alternate mouse button*

To specify the new print range:

Highlight	cells B41 through L66		*Highlight*	*cells B41 through L66*
Press	◄─Enter		*Click*	*the mouse button*

To undo a border selection, use the **Print Layout Borders Clear** command sequence. Do **not** undo the border selection at this time.

Headers and Footers

The **header** is a line of text entered below the top margin of every page. The default setting reserves three lines for a header: one line for the text followed by two blank lines before the worksheet data. Headers may be placed at the left margin, right margin, or centered. Although headers are normally short, they may contain as many as 240 characters.

To place a header at the top of each page, use the following procedure:

Select	Layout		*Choose*	*Layout*
Select	Titles		*Choose*	*Titles*
Select	Header		*Choose*	*Header*

When prompted to enter the header:

Type	ABC COMPANY		*Type*	*ABC COMPANY*

Notice the control panel in Figure 6-36.

Figure 6-36

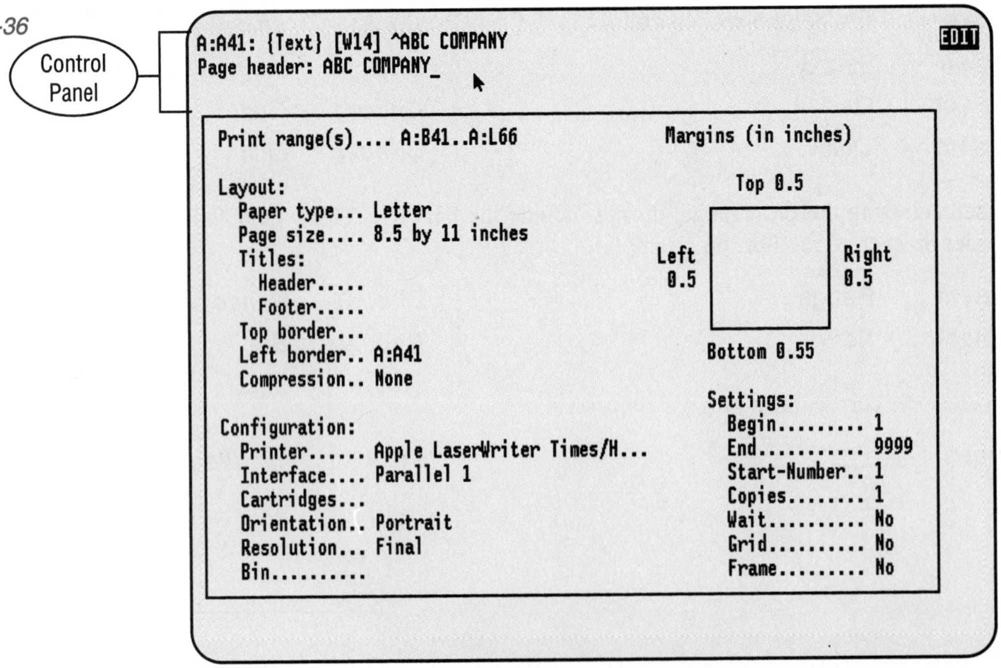

Control Panel

```
A:A41: {Text} [W14] ^ABC COMPANY                            EDIT
Page header: ABC COMPANY_        ▸

   Print range(s).... A:B41..A:L66        Margins (in inches)

   Layout:                                    Top 0.5
     Paper type... Letter
     Page size.... 8.5 by 11 inches
     Titles:                            Left            Right
       Header.....                      0.5             0.5
       Footer.....
     Top border...
     Left border.. A:A41                Bottom 0.55
     Compression.. None
                                        Settings:
   Configuration:                         Begin......... 1
     Printer...... Apple LaserWriter Times/H...   End........... 9999
     Interface.... Parallel 1             Start-Number.. 1
     Cartridges...                        Copies........ 1
     Orientation.. Portrait               Wait.......... No
     Resolution... Final                  Grid.......... No
     Bin..........                        Frame......... No
```

Press | ***Click***   *the mouse button*

Headers are entered only once, but they are reproduced on each printed page. Headers can be changed by repeating the procedure. They can be deleted by repeating the procedure and then pressing the ESC key or clicking the alternate mouse button when you are prompted to enter the heading.

Headers and footers may also be entered by using special characters and symbols. The following symbols can be used to format headers and footers:

> \#   (pound sign) places the page number on every page.
>
> \#\#   (double pound sign) when followed by a page number specifies that page number as the first page of the printout.
>
> @   (at sign) places current date (DD-MM-YY) on every page.
>
> | (vertical bar or pipe symbol) separates footer or header text and aligns the text left, centered, or right.
>
> \\   (backslash) followed by a cell address or range name. Contents of specified cell or range of cells become the header or footer text.

The vertical bar controls the position of the header or footer text on the page. Without the vertical bar, the text is left-justified. With one vertical bar preceding the text, it is centered. With two vertical bars preceding the text, it is right-justified.

To create a footer that will result in a right-justified page number:

Select   Footer | ***Choose***   *Footer*

When prompted to enter the footer:

Type ||\# | ***Type***   *||\#*

Your control panel should match the one shown in Figure 6-37.

Figure 6-37

Control
Panel

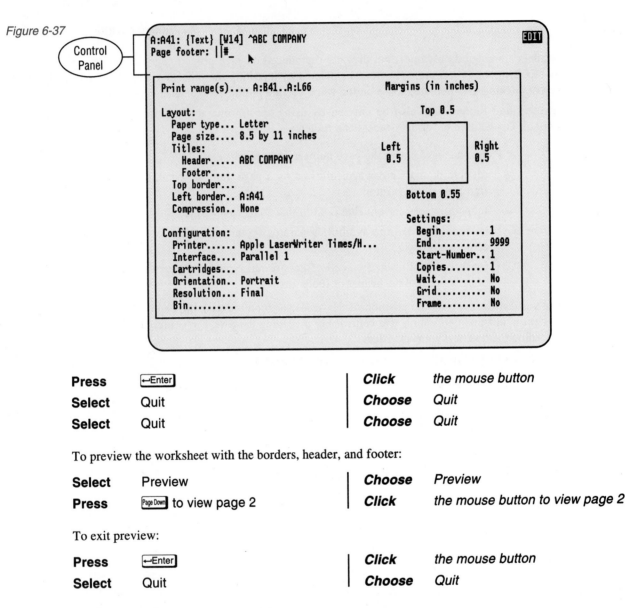

```
A:A41: {Text} [W14] ^ABC COMPANY                                   EDIT
Page footer: ||#_
                        ▸

  ┌─────────────────────────────────────────────────────────────────┐
  │ Print range(s).... A:B41..A:L66          Margins (in inches)      │
  │                                                                   │
  │ Layout:                                    Top 0.5                 │
  │   Paper type... Letter                                            │
  │   Page size.... 8.5 by 11 inches        ┌──────────┐             │
  │   Titles:                          Left │          │  Right       │
  │     Header..... ABC COMPANY        0.5  │          │  0.5         │
  │     Footer.....                         │          │             │
  │   Top border...                         └──────────┘             │
  │   Left border.. A:A41                    Bottom 0.55              │
  │   Compression.. None                                             │
  │                                          Settings:               │
  │ Configuration:                             Begin......... 1       │
  │   Printer...... Apple LaserWriter Times/H...  End........... 9999 │
  │   Interface.... Parallel 1                 Start-Number.. 1       │
  │   Cartridges...                            Copies........ 1       │
  │   Orientation.. Portrait                   Wait.......... No      │
  │   Resolution... Final                      Grid.......... No      │
  │   Bin..........                            Frame......... No      │
  └─────────────────────────────────────────────────────────────────┘
```

Press	←Enter		**Click**	*the mouse button*
Select	Quit		**Choose**	*Quit*
Select	Quit		**Choose**	*Quit*

To preview the worksheet with the borders, header, and footer:

Select	Preview		**Choose**	*Preview*
Press	Page Down to view page 2		**Click**	*the mouse button to view page 2*

To exit preview:

Press	←Enter		**Click**	*the mouse button*
Select	Quit		**Choose**	*Quit*

Cell Formulas of a Spreadsheet

At times you may want to see the cell formulas that comprise a spreadsheet. To print the cell formulas used to create the BUDGET spreadsheet, retrieve the BUDGET file and then follow the steps below. It is assumed that a print range for BUDGET has previously been set.

If you want to print the cell formulas for the spreadsheet model, then the print range should be A41..F66. If you want to print the cell formulas for the entire spreadsheet and not just the spreadsheet model, then the print range should be A1..F66.

Press	[/]		***Move***	*the mouse pointer to the control panel*
Select	Print		***Click***	*the alternate mouse button*
Select	Printer		***Choose***	*Print*
Select	Options		***Choose***	*Printer*
Select	Other		***Choose***	*Options*
Select	Cell-Formulas		***Choose***	*Other*
Select	Quit		***Choose***	*Cell-Formulas*
Select	Align		***Choose***	*Quit*
Select	Go		***Choose***	*Align*
			Choose	*Go*

Assuming that the print range has been set previously, the printer will print the contents of each nonblank cell.

To eject the printout when it is complete, and also to eject a second page (if necessary) to keep the paper aligned in the printer:

Select	Page		***Choose***	*Page*
Select	Page		***Choose***	*Page*

The printout should look like Figure 6-38, Parts 1 and 2.

Figure 6-38
Part 1

A:A41: {Text} [W14] ^ABC COMPANY
A:A42: {Text} [W14] ^BUDGET
A:B45: ^Q1
A:C45: ^Q2
A:D45: ^Q3
A:E45: ^Q4
A:F45: ^YR TOTAL
A:A47: [W14] 'Sales
A:B47: (C0) 60000
A:C47: (C0) @ROUND(B47*(1+C63),0)
A:D47: (C0) @ROUND(C47*(1+D63),0)
A:E47: (C0) @ROUND(D47*(1+E63),0)
A:F47: (C0) @SUM(B47..E47)
A:A49: [W14] 'Expenses
A:A50: [W14] ' Salaries
A:B50: 35000
A:C50: 35500
A:D50: 36200
A:E50: 37000
A:F50: @SUM(B50..E50)
A:A51: [W14] ' Rent
A:B51: 9000
A:C51: 9000

Figure 6-38
Part 2

A:D51: 9000
A:E51: 9000
A:F51: @SUM(B51..E51)
A:A52: [W14] ' Telephone
A:B52: 1000
A:C52: @ROUND(B52*(1+C64),0)
A:D52: @ROUND(C52*(1+D64),0)
A:E52: @ROUND(D52*(1+E64),0)
A:F52: @SUM(B52..E52)
A:A53: [W14] ' Office Supplies
A:B53: 750
A:C53: +B53+C65
A:D53: +C53+D65
A:E53: +D53+E65
A:F53: @SUM(B53..E53)
A:A54: [W14] ' Miscellaneous
A:B54: {B} 1000
A:C54: {B} @ROUND(B54*(1+C66),0)
A:D54: {B} @ROUND(C54*(1+D66),0)
A:E54: {B} @ROUND(D54*(1+E66),0)
A:F54: {B} @SUM(B54..E54)
A:A55: [W14] '   Total Expenses
A:B55: {B} @SUM(B50..B54)
A:C55: {B} @SUM(C50..C54)
A:D55: {B} @SUM(D50..D54)
A:E55: {B} @SUM(E50..E54)
A:F55: {B} @SUM(B55..E55)
A:A56: [W14] 'Gross Profit
A:B56: {B} (C0) +B47-B55
A:C56: {B} (C0) +C47-C55
A:D56: {B} (C0) +D47-D55
A:E56: {B} (C0) +E47-E55
A:F56: {B} (C0) @SUM(B56..E56)
A:A61: [W14] 'Assumptions
A:A63: [W14] 'Sales
A:C63: (P0) 0.02
A:D63: (P0) 0.02
A:E63: (P0) 0.02
A:A64: [W14] 'Telephone
A:C64: (P0) 0.05
A:D64: (P0) 0.05
A:E64: (P0) 0.05
A:A65: [W14] 'Office Supplies
A:C65: (F2) 50
A:D65: (F2) 50
A:E65: (F2) 50
A:A66: [W14] 'Miscellaneous
A:C66: (P0) 0.03
A:D66: (P0) 0.03
A:E66: (P0) 0.03

Note: If you are using a laser printer, you will only need to select **P**age once.

To return the print settings to their previous setting (i.e., so that when **G**o is selected, the spreadsheet will be printed rather than the cell formulas):

Select	Options		*Choose*	*Options*
Select	Other		*Choose*	*Other*
Select	As-Displayed		*Choose*	*As-Displayed*

To leave the current menu:

Select	Quit		*Choose*	*Quit*

To leave the Print menu:

Select	Quit		*Choose*	*Quit*

The print settings have now been returned to their previous setting.

Cell Formulas of a Spreadsheet in Tabular Form

To display cell formulas exactly where they appear on the spreadsheet model requires changing the format of the spreadsheet. Before changing the format to see the cell formulas, make sure the file has been saved to the disk in the desired numeric format. In this way, the "final version" of the spreadsheet is safely saved on the disk and can be retrieved for later use.

Before starting this exercise, retrieve the BUDGET file.

To change the format of the spreadsheet to see the cell formulas:

Press	⌷ / ⌷		*Move*	*the mouse pointer to the control panel*
Select	Worksheet		*Choose*	*Worksheet*
Select	Global		*Choose*	*Global*
Select	Format		*Choose*	*Format*
Select	Text		*Choose*	*Text*

The formulas are now displayed on the spreadsheet itself. However, some cell formulas are not fully displayed because the column width is not wide enough to accommodate them. For example, column B is not large enough to fully display the @SUM formula. In row 55, the @SUM command is not displayed fully. Your screen should look like Figure 6-39.

Figure 6-39

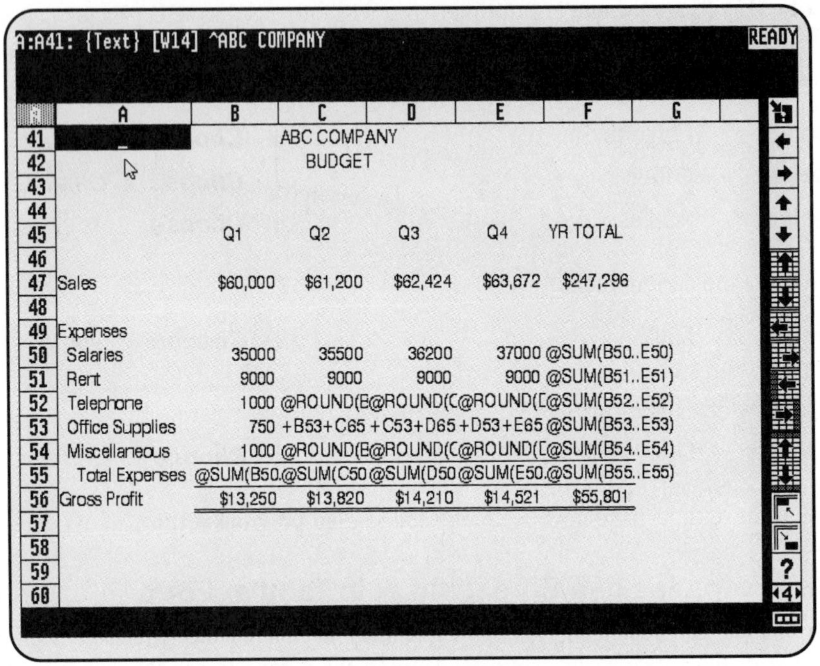

```
A:A41: {Text} [W14] ^ABC COMPANY                                         READY
```

	A	B	C	D	E	F	G
41			ABC COMPANY				
42			BUDGET				
43							
44							
45		Q1	Q2	Q3	Q4	YR TOTAL	
46							
47	Sales	$60,000	$61,200	$62,424	$63,672	$247,296	
48							
49	Expenses						
50	Salaries	35000	35500	36200	37000 @SUM(B50..E50)		
51	Rent	9000	9000	9000	9000 @SUM(B51..E51)		
52	Telephone	1000 @ROUND(B@ROUND(C@ROUND(D@SUM(B52..E52)					
53	Office Supplies	750 +B53+C65 +C53+D65 +D53+E65 @SUM(B53..E53)					
54	Miscellaneous	1000 @ROUND(B@ROUND(C@ROUND(D@SUM(B54..E54)					
55	Total Expenses	@SUM(B50.@SUM(C50.@SUM(D50.@SUM(E50.@SUM(B55..E55)					
56	Gross Profit	$13,250	$13,820	$14,210	$14,521	$55,801	
57							
58							
59							
60							

For this example, you will widen columns B through E in order to ensure the view of the full formulas.

To widen columns B through E:

Move	the cell pointer to cell B41 (or any other cell in column B)	*Click*	*on cell B41 (or any other cell in column B)*
Press	/	*Move*	*the mouse pointer to the control panel*
Select	Worksheet	*Choose*	*Worksheet*
Select	Column	*Choose*	*Column*
Select	Column-Range	*Choose*	*Column-Range*
Select	Set-Width	*Choose*	*Set-Width*

When prompted for the columns to change:

Highlight	cells B41 through E41	*Highlight*	*cells B41 through E41*
Press	←Enter	*Click*	*the mouse button*

When prompted for the column width:

Press	the → key until the formulas are fully displayed	*Click*	*the ➡ SmartIcon until the formulas are fully displayed*

| **Press** | ←Enter | | **Click** | the mouse button with the mouse pointer in the control panel |

The entire formulas for each cell in columns B through E are now displayed.

To preview the cells in tabular form:

Press	:		**Click**	the Print Preview ▦ SmartIcon
Select	Print			
Select	Preview			

The print range did not need to be specified because it was specified earlier.

The preview should look like Figure 6-40, Parts 1 and 2.

Figure 6-40
Part 1

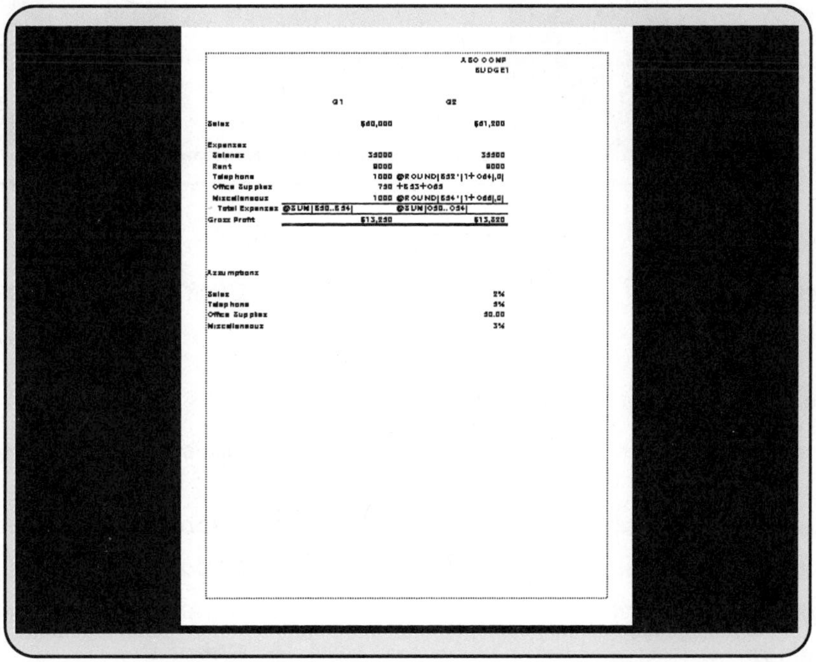

Figure 6-40
Part 2

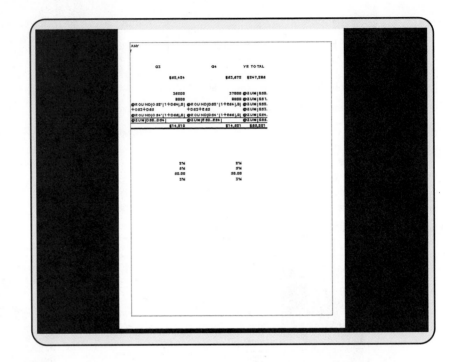

To exit the preview:

Press	←Enter		*Click*	*the mouse button*
Select	Quit			

To return the format to its original setting:

Press	/		*Move*	*the mouse pointer to the control panel*
Select	Worksheet		*Choose*	*Worksheet*
Select	Global		*Choose*	*Global*
Select	Format		*Choose*	*Format*
Select	,		*Choose*	*,*

When prompted for the number of decimal places:

Type	0		*Type*	*0*
Press	←Enter		*Click*	*the mouse button*

Columns B through E need to be reset so that they once again have a column width of 9. To return columns B through E to their original column width, make sure the cell pointer is within column B.

Press	⏍ /		***Move***	*the mouse pointer to the control panel*
Select	Worksheet		***Choose***	*Worksheet*
Select	Column		***Choose***	*Column*
Select	Column-Range		***Choose***	*Column-Range*
Select	Reset-Width		***Choose***	*Reset-Width*
Highlight	cells B41 through E41		***Highlight***	*cells B41 through E41*
Press	⏎Enter		***Click***	*the mouse button*

The width for columns B through E is returned to the default size of 9 characters. Your screen should look like Figure 6-41.

Figure 6-41

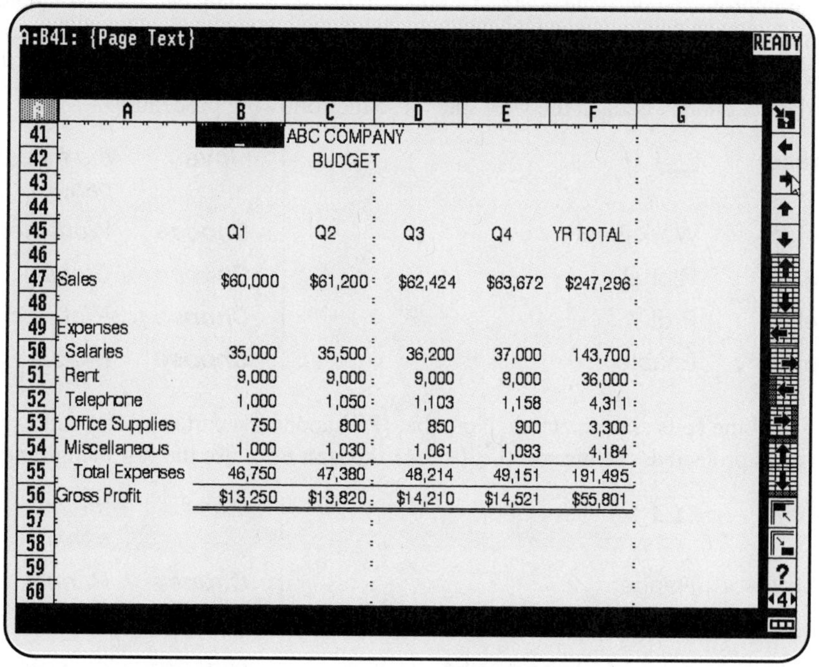

```
A:B41: {Page Text}                                                    READY

        A          B          C          D          E          F          G
 41                          ABC COMPANY                        :
 42                            BUDGET                           :
 43                                     :                       :
 44                                     :                       :
 45                 Q1         Q2      : Q3         Q4    YR TOTAL :
 46                                     :                       :
 47  Sales       $60,000    $61,200 : $62,424    $63,672   $247,296 :
 48                                     :                       :
 49  Expenses                          :                       :
 50    Salaries  35,000     35,500 :   36,200     37,000    143,700 :
 51    Rent       9,000      9,000 :    9,000      9,000     36,000 :
 52    Telephone  1,000      1,050 :    1,103      1,158      4,311 :
 53    Office Supplies 750      800 :     850        900      3,300 :
 54    Miscellaneous 1,000     1,030 :    1,061      1,093      4,184 :
 55      Total Expenses 46,750  47,380 :  48,214     49,151    191,495 :
 56  Gross Profit $13,250    $13,820 : $14,210    $14,521    $55,801 :
 57                                     :                       :
 58                                     :                       :
 59                                     :                       :
 60                                     :                       :
```

■ USING THE BACKGROUND PRINTING FEATURE

Background printing stores a printing job in memory so you can continue to work on another activity without having to wait for the printing job to finish. Print jobs are processed in the order in which they are created unless they have been marked with one of the print priority options.

The Background printing feature works automatically unless you are printing to a file. In that situation, you must first select the **H**old option before leaving the print menu. See the Lotus 1-2-3 reference manual for additional information.

■ PROTECTING DATA

You can protect your worksheet data by restricting access to the worksheet or to parts of the worksheet. Lotus 1-2-3 allows you to protect cells and to hide data in order to prevent changes.

Before starting this example, retrieve the BUDGET file.

Cell Protection

Cells can be locked to prevent changes from being made to them. This protection is accomplished through the **W**orksheet **G**lobal **P**rot **E**nable command sequence for the whole spreadsheet or through a range command for a specific group of cells.

The **W**orksheet **G**lobal **P**rot **E**nable command activates the worksheet protection. Only when cells have been unprotected with the **R**ange **U**nprot command can they be changed. When you try to enter data or make changes in protected cells, an error message is displayed. 1-2-3 also uses screen colors or highlighting to distinguish between protected and unprotected cells.

To protect all the cells in the worksheet, use the following procedure:

Press	/	***Move***	*the mouse pointer to the control panel*
Select	Worksheet	***Choose***	*Worksheet*
Select	Global	***Choose***	*Global*
Select	Prot	***Choose***	*Prot*
Select	Enable	***Choose***	*Enable*

Now all the cells are protected. Note that [PR] appears next to the cell address in the control panel when a cell is protected. To unprotect cells A41 through B54, use the following range commands:

Press	/	***Move***	*the mouse pointer to the control panel*
Select	Range	***Choose***	*Range*
Select	Unprot	***Choose***	*Unprot*
Highlight	cells A41 through B54	***Highlight***	*cells A41 through B54*

The unprotected cells are a different color or highlighted depending on the type of monitor being used.

Move	the cell pointer to cell C50	***Click***	*on cell C50*
Type	36000	***Type***	*36000*
Press	←Enter	***Click***	*the mouse button*

The computer sounds a "beep" and a message appears on the screen informing you that the cell is protected.

Press	Esc		***Click***	*the alternate mouse button*
Move	the cell pointer to cell B50		***Click***	*on cell B50*
Type	36000		***Type***	*36000*
Press	←Enter		***Click***	*the mouse button*

Notice that you are able to change the data in the unprotected cell and the worksheet recalculates.

Using the range commands, return the unprotected cells to a protected status.

Highlight	cells A41 through B54		***Highlight***	*cells A41 through B54*
Press	/		***Move***	*the mouse pointer to the control panel*
Select	Range		***Choose***	*Range*
Select	Prot		***Choose***	*Prot*

The entire worksheet is protected again and changes cannot be made to any of the cells.

Design Tip

Use the cell protection capabilities of 1-2-3 liberally in your worksheet. For example, protect all cells that include formulas. By protecting such cells, you can avoid accidental changes to your worksheet.

Hiding a Column

One or more columns of a worksheet can be suppressed so that any data in them is not displayed or printed, but the data continues to be used in calculations.

Retrieve the BUDGET file. To hide column E:

Press	/		***Move***	*the mouse pointer to the control panel*
Select	Worksheet		***Choose***	*Worksheet*
Select	Column		***Choose***	*Column*
Select	Hide		***Choose***	*Hide*

When prompted for the column(s) to hide:

Move	the cell pointer to any cell in column E		***Click***	*on any cell in column E*
Press	←Enter		***Click***	*the mouse button with the mouse pointer in the control panel*

Column E is no longer visible on the screen. Your screen should look like Figure 6-42.

Figure 6-42

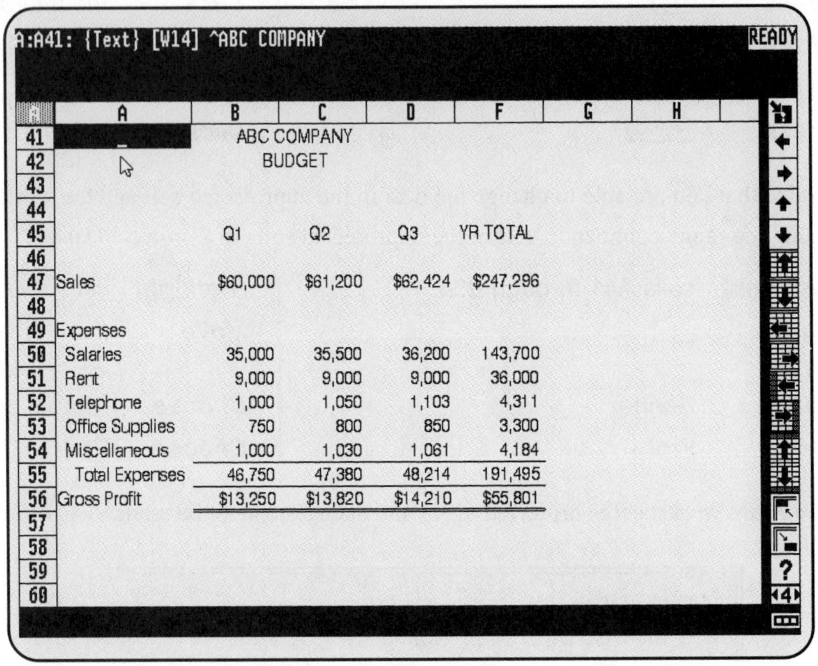

```
A:A41: {Text} [W14] ^ABC COMPANY                                    READY

        ┌──────┬────────┬────────┬──────┬─────────┬──────┬──────┐
        │  A   │   B    │   C    │  D   │    F    │  G   │  H   │
   41 │      _            ABC COMPANY                             │
   42 │      ▷              BUDGET                                │
   43 │                                                          │
   44 │                                                          │
   45 │              Q1       Q2      Q3    YR TOTAL              │
   46 │                                                          │
   47 │Sales       $60,000  $61,200  $62,424  $247,296           │
   48 │                                                          │
   49 │Expenses                                                  │
   50 │  Salaries   35,000   35,500   36,200   143,700           │
   51 │  Rent        9,000    9,000    9,000    36,000           │
   52 │  Telephone   1,000    1,050    1,103     4,311           │
   53 │  Office Supplies  750    800      850     3,300           │
   54 │  Miscellaneous  1,000  1,030    1,061     4,184           │
   55 │   Total Expenses 46,750 47,380  48,214   191,495          │
   56 │Gross Profit $13,250 $13,820  $14,210   $55,801           │
   57 │                                                          │
   58 │                                                          │
   59 │                                                          │
   60 │                                                          │
```

Redisplaying a Hidden Column

To make column E visible on your screen again:

Press	⬚ / ⬚	**Move**	the mouse pointer to the control panel
Select	Worksheet	**Choose**	Worksheet
Select	Column	**Choose**	Column
Select	Display	**Choose**	Display

Any column that is hidden is now visible and has an asterisk beside the letter in the column heading to indicate it is a hidden column.

When prompted for the column(s) to redisplay:

Move	the cell pointer to any cell in column E	**Click**	on any cell in column E
Press	←Enter	**Click**	the mouse button with the mouse pointer in the control panel

Column E appears on your screen again.

Hiding a Range of Cells

To hide the Gross Profit label and values:

Highlight	cells A56 through F56		*Highlight*	*cells A56 through F56*
Press	☐ / ☐		*Move*	*the mouse pointer to the control panel*
Select	Range		*Choose*	*Range*
Select	Format		*Choose*	*Format*
Select	Hidden		*Choose*	*Hidden*

The Gross Profit label and associated values have been hidden. Note that the double underline remains on your screen.

Redisplaying a Range of Cells

To restore the hidden information to your screen:

Highlight	cells A56 through F56		*Highlight*	*cells A56 through F56*
Press	☐ / ☐		*Move*	*the mouse pointer to the control panel*
Select	Range		*Choose*	*Range*
Select	Format		*Choose*	*Format*
Select	Reset		*Choose*	*Reset*

The hidden data now appears on your screen. Note that the format of the cells is reset to the **Worksheet Global , 0** format setting. The dollar signs present before hiding the cells are gone.

■ NAMING RANGES

Creating a Range Name

Range names can be used rather than cell addresses to make it easier to remember the location of cells. A range name is associated with cell addresses.

Retrieve the BUDGET worksheet. To assign a range name to the cells containing the values of Total Expenses for the four quarters:

Highlight	cells B55 through E55		*Highlight*	*cells B55 through E55*
Press	☐ / ☐		*Move*	*the mouse pointer to the control panel*
Select	Range		*Choose*	*Range*

Select	Name		*Choose*	*Name*
Select	Create		*Choose*	*Create*

When prompted for the range name:

Type	TOTAL_EXP		*Type*	*TOTAL_EXP*
Press	⏎Enter		*Click*	*the mouse button*

Range names are used in formulas in place of cell addresses. Cell addresses in formulas are changed to reflect that you have defined a range name.

Move	the cell pointer to cell F55		*Click*	*on cell F55*

The top part of your screen should look like Figure 6-43.

Figure 6-43

```
A:F55: {B} @SUM(TOTAL_EXP)                          READY

        A          B        C        D      E      F      G
  41                     ABC COMPANY                          ←
  42                       BUDGET                             →
  43
```

Note that TOTAL_EXP has replaced the B55..E55 in the @SUM function in cell F55.

Range names may be up to 15 characters in length.

> *Design Tip*
> In some situations, you may need to specify several ranges of cells to print for a worksheet. By defining and using range names, you do not need to remember the cell ranges, but can refer to the range names instead.

Deleting a Range Name

When a range name is deleted, the range name is replaced in formulas with the cell address. It does not change the range. Remember to delete the name for a range of cells before assigning that name to a different set of cells.

To delete a range name for a range of cells:

Press	/		*Move*	*the mouse pointer to the control panel*
Select	Range		*Choose*	*Range*
Select	Name		*Choose*	*Name*

Select	Delete		**Choose**	Delete
Press	F3		**Press**	F3

Specify that the range name TOTAL_EXP is to be deleted by highlighting it.

Press	←Enter		**Move**	the mouse pointer to TOTAL_EXP
			Click	the mouse button

Notice in the control panel that TOTAL_EXP in cell F55 has been replaced with B55..E55.

Table of Range Names

An alphabetical list of range names can be created by using the **R**ange **N**ame **T**able command. Decide on a location for the table before beginning the command. Because the table will overwrite existing data, be sure to use a blank area.

Before creating a table of range names, create range names for Sales and Salaries that include the values for Q1 through Q4 for each item. Then create an alphabetical list of the range names by using the following procedure:

Move	the cell pointer to cell A70		**Click**	on cell A70
Press	/		**Move**	the mouse pointer to the control panel
Select	Range		**Choose**	Range
Select	Name		**Choose**	Name
Select	Table		**Choose**	Table
Press	←Enter		**Click**	the mouse button with the mouse pointer in the control panel

The table should be placed below the worksheet assumptions. After moving the cell pointer to cell A73, the bottom part of your screen should look like Figure 6-44.

Figure 6-44

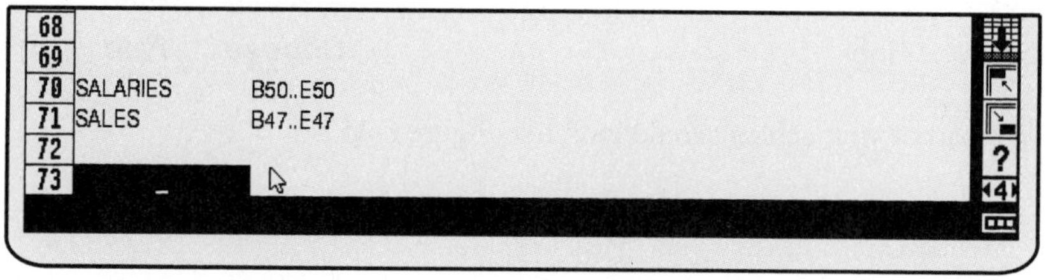

Search and Replace

The **R**ange **S**earch command finds a string of characters in a label, formula, or both and highlights the string. Uppercase and lowercase letters are treated without sensitivity. If you specify the command to **R**eplace the string, 1-2-3 finds the string and then replaces it with the exact string of characters that you enter. In the **F**ind option, you are given the choice of continuing the search or quitting.

The **R**eplace option highlights the matching cell. It provides the following four options:

> *Replace:* inserts the replacement and moves to the next occurrence.
>
> *All:* replaces each occurrence of the string.
>
> *Next:* finds the next matching string without replacing the current one.
>
> *Quit:* quits the search and replace procedure.

When there are no further matching strings, an error message is displayed. When this occurs, press ENTER, ESC, or the mouse button to return to **READY** mode.

Retrieve the BUDGET file and search for the word Sales.

Highlight	cells A41 through F66		*Highlight*	*cells A41 through F66*
Press	[/]		*Move*	*the mouse pointer to the control panel*
Select	Range		*Choose*	*Range*
Select	Search		*Choose*	*Search*

> *User Tip*
> An alternative method for initiating the **R**ange **S**earch command is to click the Find 🔍 SmartIcon.

When the prompt asks for the search string:

Type	Sales		*Type*	*Sales*
Press	[←Enter]		*Click*	*the mouse button*
Select	Both		*Choose*	*Both*
Select	Find		*Choose*	*Find*

The top part of your screen should look like Figure 6-45.

Figure 6-45

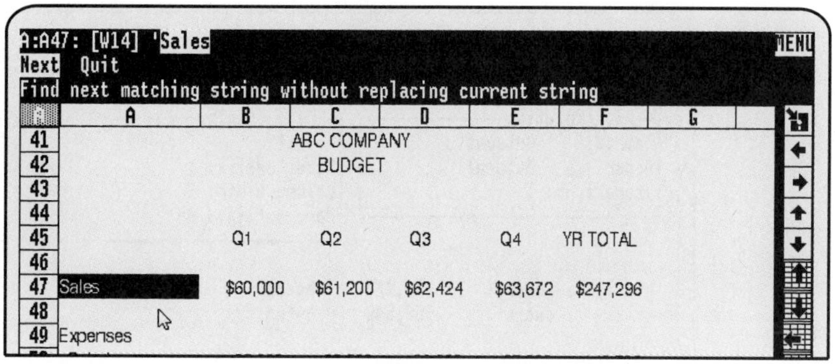

```
A:A47: [W14] 'Sales                                          MENU
Next  Quit
Find next matching string without replacing current string
        A        B        C        D        E        F        G
  41                   ABC COMPANY
  42                     BUDGET
  43
  44
  45              Q1       Q2       Q3       Q4    YR TOTAL
  46
  47  Sales       $60,000  $61,200  $62,424  $63,672  $247,296
  48
  49  Expenses
```

Note that the cell pointer is in cell A47 where the Sales label is located.

Select	Next	**Choose**	Next

until you hear a beep indicating there are no additional matches. A message will also appear on the screen. When there are no other matching strings, press ENTER, ESC, or click the mouse button to return to **READY** mode.

To replace a string, choose **R**eplace and type the replacement string at the prompt. You may then proceed in the same manner as with the **F**ind option.

■ DISPLAYING THE STATUS OF A WORKSHEET

In some situations, you may want to know how much memory is being used for a worksheet. The status of other items can also be determined.

To illustrate the process of checking on the status of some worksheet items, retrieve the BUDGET file.

To look at the **Status** (settings) of the worksheet:

Press	/	**Move**	the mouse pointer to the control panel
Select	Worksheet	**Choose**	Worksheet
Select	Status	**Choose**	Status

The Worksheet Status settings sheet appears. Various settings are displayed. The displayed settings indicate available conventional memory, whether a math coprocessor is used, and whether circular references exist. Your screen should look similar to Figure 6-46. The available memory and math coprocessor settings depend on the system being used.

Figure 6-46

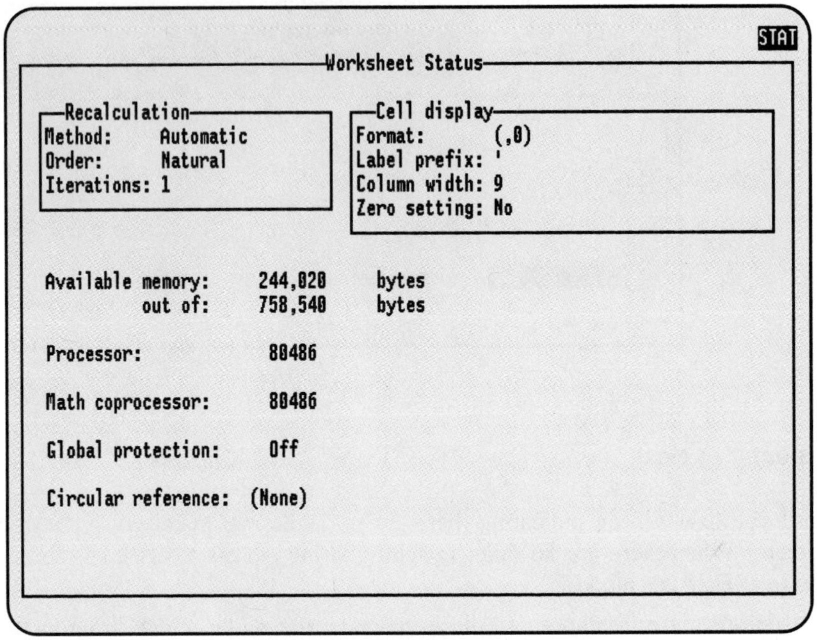

```
                                                                    STAT
                        ─────Worksheet Status─────
  ┌───────────────────────────┐  ┌──────────────────────────────┐
  │ ─Recalculation─           │  │ ─Cell display─               │
  │ Method:    Automatic       │  │ Format:       (,0)           │
  │ Order:     Natural         │  │ Label prefix: '              │
  │ Iterations: 1              │  │ Column width: 9              │
  │                            │  │ Zero setting: No             │
  └───────────────────────────┘  └──────────────────────────────┘


     Available memory:     244,020    bytes
               out of:     758,540    bytes

     Processor:            80486

     Math coprocessor:     80486

     Global protection:    Off

     Circular reference:   (None)
```

To remove the Worksheet Status setting sheet from your screen:

Press Esc | *Click*   *the alternate mouse button*

Pressing the ENTER key or clicking the mouse button can also be used to eliminate the Worksheet Status settings sheet from your screen.

■ EXECUTING SYSTEM COMMANDS

You may exit Lotus 1-2-3 temporarily to issue operating system level commands by using the **System** command.

To access the **System** command:

Press / | *Move*   *the mouse pointer to the control panel*

Select System | *Choose*   *System*

Lotus is still in memory, but the cursor is blinking at the operating system prompt. At this point, you can issue operating system commands, such as FORMAT to format a floppy diskette.

The top part of your screen should look similar to Figure 6-47.

Figure 6-47

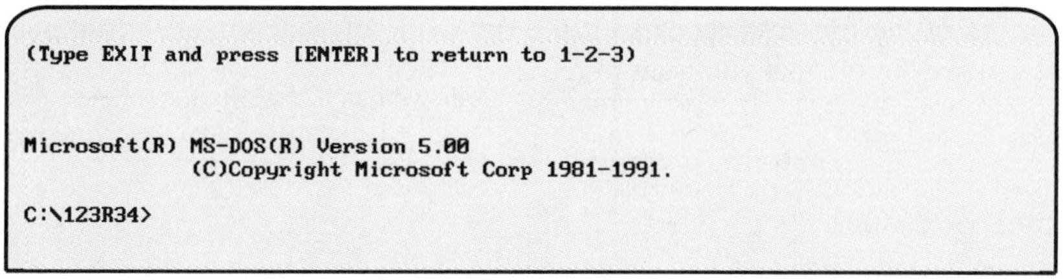

```
(Type EXIT and press [ENTER] to return to 1-2-3)


Microsoft(R) MS-DOS(R) Version 5.00
          (C)Copyright Microsoft Corp 1981-1991.

C:\123R34>
```

To return to Lotus 1-2-3:

Type	EXIT		*Type*	*EXIT*
Press	[←Enter]		*Press*	[←Enter]

The cell pointer will appear in the same position as it was before you used the System command.

■ VIEWING A WORKSHEET BEFORE RETRIEVING THE WORKSHEET FILE

In some situations, you may want to browse through your worksheet files before you retrieve a particular worksheet. 1-2-3 includes a Viewer add-in program that allows you to retrieve, open, link, or browse through your worksheet files. The Viewer add-in can be particularly useful if you do not remember the name of the file that contains a worksheet that you would like to retrieve.

Assume that you want to view the files on your current directory. First invoke the Viewer add-in. If you are not familiar with using an add-in, see the section on Add-ins earlier in this chapter. After invoking the Viewer add-in, the top part of your screen should look like Figure 6-48.

Figure 6-48

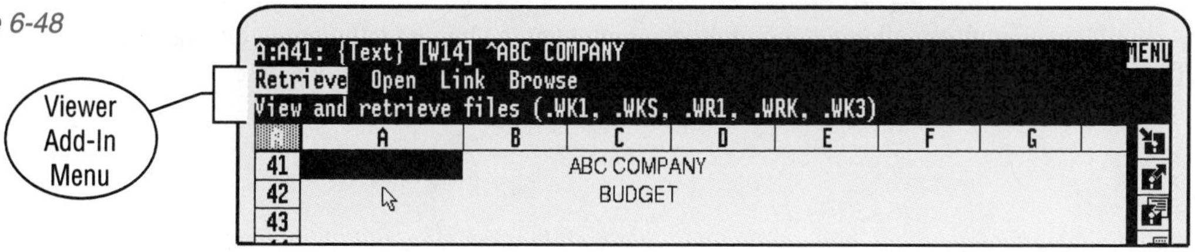

Viewer Add-In Menu

```
A:A41: {Text} [W14] ^ABC COMPANY                          MENU
Retrieve  Open  Link  Browse
View and retrieve files (.WK1, .WKS, .WR1, .WRK, .WK3)
        A        B        C        D        E        F        G
41                        ABC COMPANY
42                          BUDGET
43
```

Note that a menu appears giving you the options **Retrieve**, **Open**, **Link**, and **Browse**. To illustrate the process of browsing through the files on the current directory:

Select	Browse		*Choose*	*Browse*

Note: You cannot select a file using the mouse.

A list of files appears on the left part of your screen. To select the BUDGET2 file to view:

Move	the pointer to BUDGET2.WK3		*Move*	*the pointer to BUDGET2.WK3*

A portion of the file now appears on the right side of your screen. Continue pointing at various files until you see the file that you want to retrieve. Then:

Press	Esc	**Click**	*the alternate mouse button*

To retrieve the file:

Select	Retrieve	**Choose**	*Retrieve*
Move	the pointer to BUDGET2.WK3	**Move**	*the pointer to BUDGET2.WK3*
Press	←Enter	**Press**	←Enter

The BUDGET2 file now appears on your screen.

■ MANIPULATING DATA

Titles

When working on a large spreadsheet and moving the cell pointer to a distant row or column, you may see headings and row labels "scroll" off the screen. When this happens, it is difficult to see exactly where data is to be input. The following example demonstrates how such a problem may occur, and how to solve the problem by "freezing" **titles** on your screen. Retrieve the BUDGET2 file.

To move to a "distant" cell location:

Move	the cell pointer to cell H66	**Move**	*the cell pointer to cell H66*

(In this example, use the pointer-movement keys or the pointer-movement SmartIcons and **not** the F5 (GOTO) key to move to H66.)

Note that it is difficult to tell what the numbers represent, because neither the column titles nor the labels in column A are displayed on the screen as guides. Your screen should look like Figure 6-49.

Figure 6-49

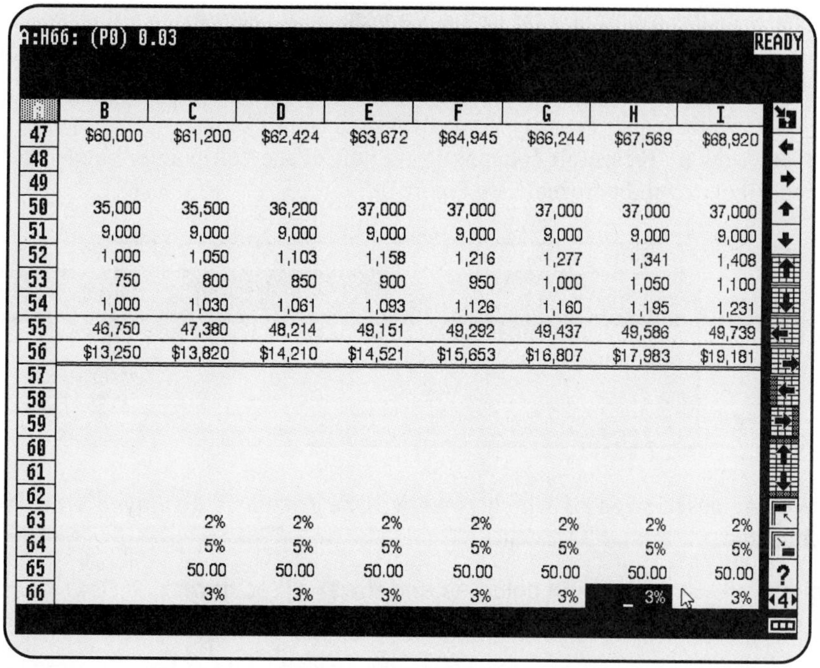

To position the cell pointer so that the appropriate headings and descriptive labels are visible on the screen:

Move	the cell pointer to cell A41	*Click*	on cell A41
Move	the cell pointer to cell B46	*Click*	on cell B46

Before you use the menu to freeze the title, the cell pointer must be in the correct position as described below:

The column(s) you wish to keep displayed on the screen must be directly to the *left* of the cell pointer (in this example, column A will remain on the screen because the cell pointer is in column B).

The row(s) you desire to keep displayed on the screen must be directly *above* the cell pointer (in this example, rows 41 through 45 will remain on the screen, because the cell pointer is in row 46).

To access the menu commands to freeze the titles and descriptive labels:

Press	/	*Move*	the mouse pointer to the control panel
Select	Worksheet	*Choose*	Worksheet
Select	Titles	*Choose*	Titles

Move	the menu pointer to the Vertical menu option		*Move*	*the menu pointer to the Vertical menu option*
	(Do **NOT** press **V** for **Vertical**)			*(Do **NOT** choose **Vertical**)*

The description "Freeze all columns to the left of the cell pointer" under the **Vertical** option explains which columns will be frozen. See Figure 6-50.

Figure 6-50

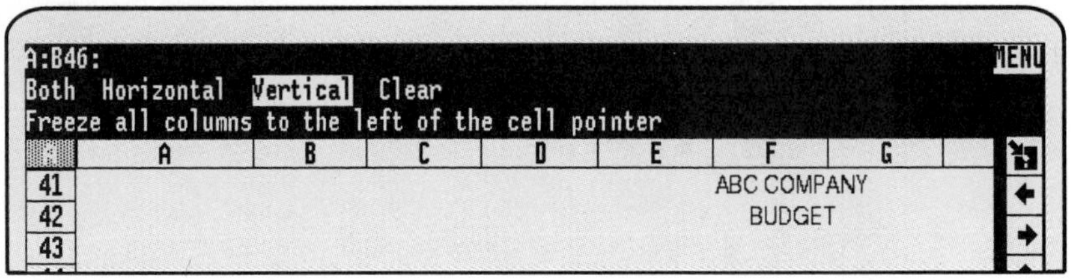

A similar description of which rows will be frozen is displayed when the **Horizontal** option is highlighted.

Select	Both (for both columns and rows)		*Choose*	*Both (for both columns and rows)*

Note that you can choose to freeze only the columns, only the rows, or both rows and columns as mentioned above.

To see the results of freezing the screen:

Move	the cell pointer to cell H66 (use the → or ↓ pointer-movement keys to move to cell H66)		*Move*	*the cell pointer to cell H66 (use the → and ↓ SmartIcons to move to cell H66)*

Note that even though the cell pointer has been moved to a "distant" area of the spreadsheet, rows 41 through 45 and column A remain frozen on the screen. By using this option, it is possible to see the column and row descriptions and understand the content of the spreadsheet. For example, H56 contains the contents of Gross Profit for YEAR 7. Your screen should look like Figure 6-51.

Figure 6-51

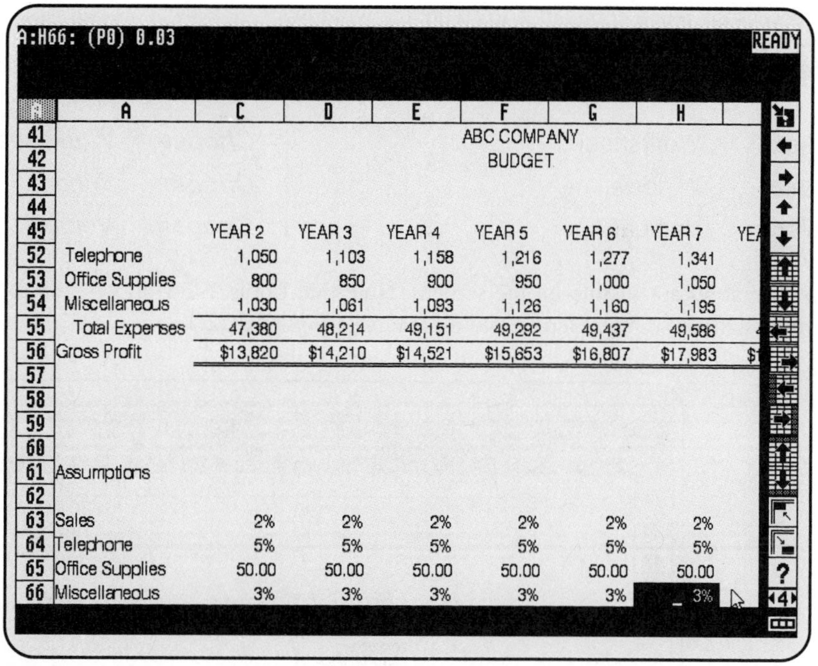

```
A:H66: (P0) 0.03                                                      READY
```

	A	C	D	E	F	G	H	
41					ABC COMPANY			
42					BUDGET			
43								
44								
45		YEAR 2	YEAR 3	YEAR 4	YEAR 5	YEAR 6	YEAR 7	YEA
52	Telephone	1,050	1,103	1,158	1,216	1,277	1,341	
53	Office Supplies	800	850	900	950	1,000	1,050	
54	Miscellaneous	1,030	1,061	1,093	1,126	1,160	1,195	
55	Total Expenses	47,380	48,214	49,151	49,292	49,437	49,586	4
56	Gross Profit	$13,820	$14,210	$14,521	$15,653	$16,807	$17,983	$1
57								
58								
59								
60								
61	Assumptions							
62								
63	Sales	2%	2%	2%	2%	2%	2%	
64	Telephone	5%	5%	5%	5%	5%	5%	
65	Office Supplies	50.00	50.00	50.00	50.00	50.00	50.00	
66	Miscellaneous	3%	3%	3%	3%	3%	3%	

Press	Home		***Press***	Home

Note that the cell pointer cannot move to cell A1 because the titles are frozen, but rather moves only to cell B46.

To cancel the title settings:

Press	/		***Move***	*the mouse pointer to the control panel*
Select	Worksheet		***Choose***	*Worksheet*
Select	Titles		***Choose***	*Titles*
Select	Clear		***Choose***	*Clear*
Press	Home		***Press***	Home

Notice the cell pointer is in cell A1.

Windows

Lotus 1-2-3 allows you to view two different areas of the spreadsheet on the screen at the same time by using the Windows command. Retrieve the BUDGET2 file for use in the following example.

When creating windows, the cell pointer must be in the desired position before the menus are accessed. To position the cell pointer so that the screen will be divided at column D:

Move	the cell pointer to cell D47		***Click***	*on cell D47*

To access the menu commands to create the windows:

Press	⌷/⌷		**Move**	the mouse pointer to the control panel
Select	Worksheet		**Choose**	Worksheet
Select	Window		**Choose**	Window
Select	Vertical		**Choose**	Vertical

Two windows are visible on the screen. Note that Lotus 1-2-3 allows you to make either horizontal or vertical windows. Your screen should look like Figure 6-52.

Figure 6-52

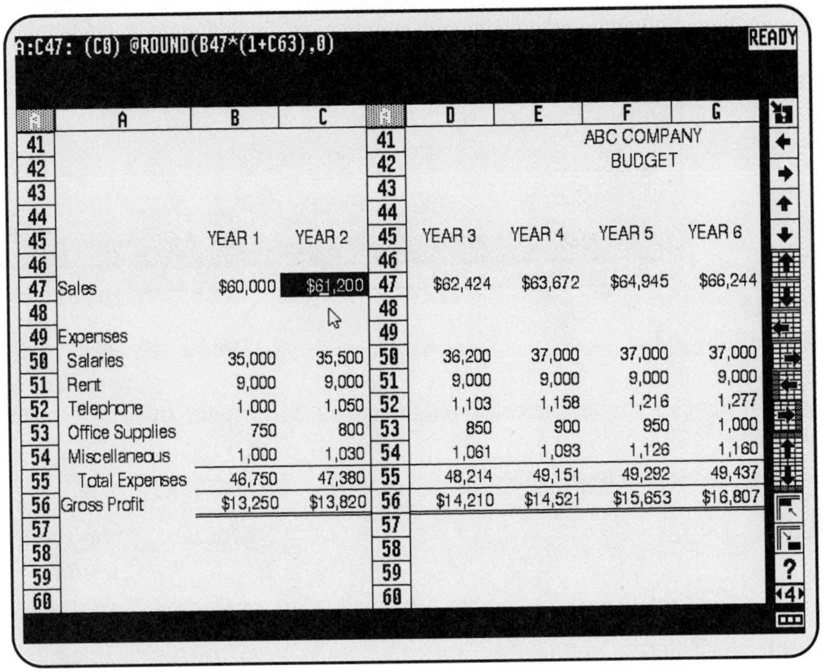

To move around in the left window:

Move	the cell pointer to cell B47		**Click**	on cell B47

Notice that the cell pointer can be moved anywhere in the spreadsheet in the left window.

To move to the right window:

Press	⌷F6⌷		**Click**	on cell D47 in the right window

Move	the cell pointer to cell L47 (YR TOTAL for Sales)		*Click*	*the* → *SmartIcon until the cell pointer highlights cell L47 (YR TOTAL for Sales)*

The F6 key is sometimes referred to as the **window** key.

To return to the left window:

Press	F6		*Click*	*on cell B47 in the left window*
Move	the cell pointer to cell B47		*Type*	*65000*
Type	65000		*Click*	*the mouse button*
Press	←Enter			

By using windows, you are able to see the effect of changing a cell's contents on another area of the worksheet. In this example, you can see the updated amount for the YR TOTAL of Sales when the value for Sales in YEAR 1 is changed.

Your worksheet should look similar to Figure 6-53.

Figure 6-53

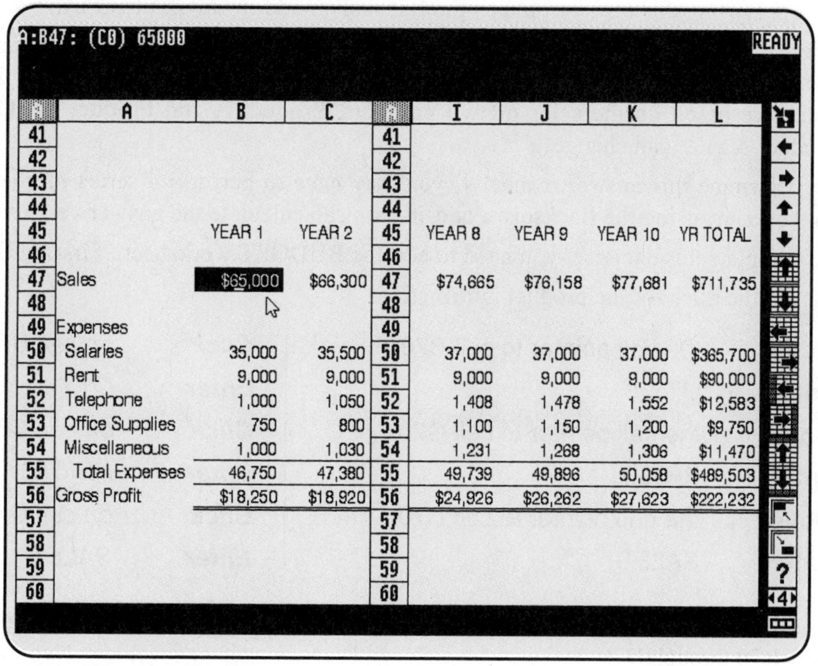

To clear the window setting:

Press	/		*Move*	*the mouse pointer to the control panel*

Select	Worksheet		*Choose*	*Worksheet*	
Select	Window		*Choose*	*Window*	
Select	Clear		*Choose*	*Clear*	

The windows are now deleted from your screen.

> *In This Book*
> For the remaining portion of the book, you are asked to enter values or labels rather than being instructed to type the information and then press the ENTER key or click the mouse button with the mouse pointer in the control panel.

■ PROBLEM SOLVING

Backsolver

1-2-3 allows you to perform complicated "what-if" analysis by using the Backsolver add-in program. Before starting this exercise, attach the Backsolver add-in BSOLVER.PLC.

The **Backsolver** add-in helps you calculate a particular outcome by changing one variable. For example, suppose you want to determine how to reach Total Sales in Q1 of $73,000 for the ABC Company. Total Sales are based on the sales of two products, Product A and Product B. Of the two products only Product A sales can change.

To determine this answer manually, you may have to perform a series of guesses for Product A sales. However, by using the Backsolver add-in, you can calculate the answer very easily.

To complete this exercise, you need to edit the BUDGET worksheet. First, retrieve the BUDGET file.

To add the titles for the product information:

Move	the cell pointer to cell B70		*Click*	*on cell B70*
Enter	QTY		*Enter*	*QTY*
Move	the cell pointer to cell C70		*Click*	*on cell C70*
Enter	PRICE		*Enter*	*PRICE*
Move	the cell pointer to cell D70		*Click*	*on cell D70*
Enter	SALES		*Enter*	*SALES*

Use the **R**ange **L**abel **R**ight command or the Right Align ▤ SmartIcon to right align the information in cells B70 through D70.

To add the data for Product A:

Move	the cell pointer to cell A71		*Click*	*on cell A71*
Enter	Product A		*Enter*	*Product A*

Move	the cell pointer to cell B71		*Click*	*on cell B71*
Enter	5000		*Enter*	*5000*
Move	the cell pointer to cell C71		*Click*	*on cell C71*
Enter	2		*Enter*	*2*

To add the data for Product B:

Move	the cell pointer to cell A72		*Click*	*on cell A72*
Enter	Product B		*Enter*	*Product B*
Move	the cell pointer to cell B72		*Click*	*on cell B72*
Enter	10000		*Enter*	*10000*
Move	the cell pointer to cell C72		*Click*	*on cell C72*
Enter	5		*Enter*	*5*

To compute the sales of each product:

Move	the cell pointer to cell D71		*Click*	*on cell D71*
Enter	the formula +B71∗C71		*Enter*	*the formula +B71∗C71*
Copy	the formula in cell D71 to cell D72		*Copy*	*the formula in cell D71 to cell D72*

The bottom part of your screen should look like Figure 6-54.

Figure 6-54

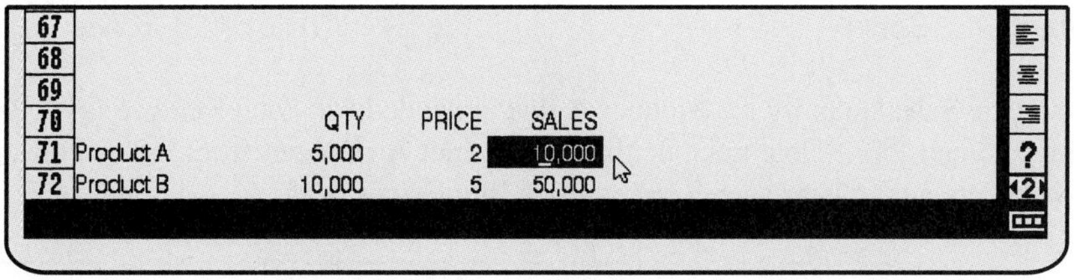

Q1 Sales needs to be a formula that reflects the sales of Product A and Product B. To change the Q1 Sales to a formula:

| **Move** | the cell pointer to cell B47 | | *Click* | *on cell B47* |
| **Enter** | the formula +D71+D72 | | *Enter* | *the formula +D71+D72* |

Save this new worksheet using the file name PRODUCT.

To solve the sales problem:

| **Invoke** | the BSOLVER add-in | | *Invoke* | *the BSOLVER add-in* |

First, you must enter the cell that contains the formula for Q1 Sales:

Select	Formula-Cell		*Choose*	*Formula-Cell*
Move	the cell pointer to cell B47		*Click*	*on cell B47*
Press	⏎Enter		*Click*	*the mouse button with the mouse pointer in the control panel*

Next, you must enter the goal for the result of this formula. To make Q1 Sales equal to $73,000:

Select	Value		*Choose*	*Value*
Type	73000		*Type*	*73000*
Press	⏎Enter		*Click*	*the mouse button*

Finally, you must tell the Backsolver add-in which cell you want to change to reach this goal. To change Product A quantity:

Select	Adjustable		*Choose*	*Adjustable*
Move	the cell pointer to cell B71		*Move*	*the mouse pointer to cell B71*
Press	⏎Enter		*Click*	*the mouse button with the mouse pointer in the control panel*

To solve the problem:

Select	Solve		*Choose*	*Solve*

To see the Sales quantity for Product A that is needed for Total Sales in Q1 to be $73,000, move the cell pointer to cell B73. Note the quantity for Product A changed from the original value of 5,000 to 11,500. The bottom part of your screen should look like Figure 6-55.

Figure 6-55

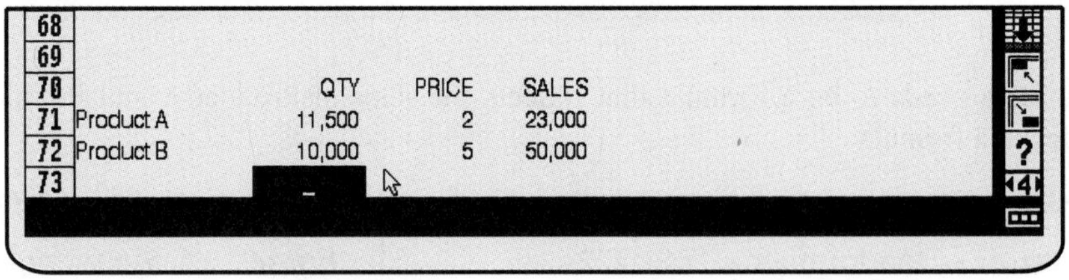

Do not save the changes to your worksheet.

The Backsolver add-in can also be used to change several variables so that a specific outcome can be obtained for a formula in a cell. Backsolver changes the variables by the same percent.

For example, suppose you want to lower the initial values for the various expense categories in the BUDGET worksheet so that Total Expenses in Q1 is $45,000. Before starting this exercise, retrieve the BUDGET file.

To reduce the expenses appropriately:

Invoke	the BSOLVER add-in		*Invoke*	*the BSOLVER add-in*

First, you must specify the cell that contains the Q1 Total Expenses:

Select	Formula-Cell		*Choose*	*Formula-Cell*
Move	the cell pointer to cell B55		*Click*	*on cell B55 twice*
Press	[←Enter]			

Next, you must enter the desired outcome of the Total Expenses formula for Q1. To make Q1 Total Expenses equal to $45,000:

Select	Value		*Choose*	*Value*
Type	45000		*Type*	*45000*
Press	[←Enter]		*Click*	*the mouse button*

Finally, you must specify to the Backsolver add-in which cells you want to change to reach this outcome. To specify the range of expense cells in Q1:

Select	Adjustable		*Choose*	*Adjustable*
Highlight	cells B50 through B54		*Highlight*	*cells B50 through B54*
Press	[←Enter]		*Click*	*the mouse button*

To solve the problem:

Select	Solve		*Choose*	*Solve*

Your screen should look like Figure 6-56.

Figure 6-56

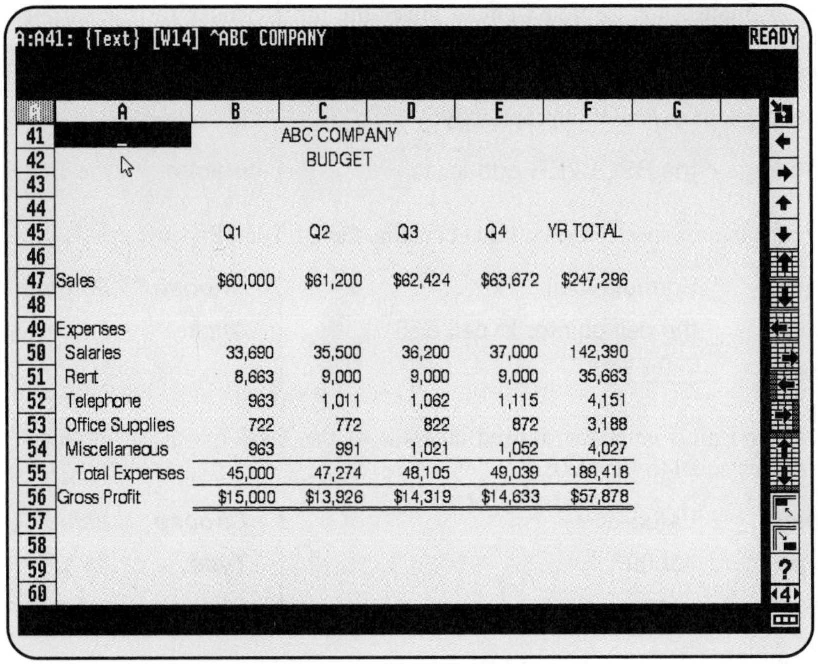

```
A:A41: {Text} [W14] ^ABC COMPANY                                      READY
```

	A	B	C	D	E	F	G
41			ABC COMPANY				
42			BUDGET				
43							
44							
45		Q1	Q2	Q3	Q4	YR TOTAL	
46							
47	Sales	$60,000	$61,200	$62,424	$63,672	$247,296	
48							
49	Expenses						
50	Salaries	33,690	35,500	36,200	37,000	142,390	
51	Rent	8,663	9,000	9,000	9,000	35,663	
52	Telephone	963	1,011	1,062	1,115	4,151	
53	Office Supplies	722	772	822	872	3,188	
54	Miscellaneous	963	991	1,021	1,052	4,027	
55	Total Expenses	45,000	47,274	48,105	49,039	189,418	
56	Gross Profit	$15,000	$13,926	$14,319	$14,633	$57,878	
57							
58							
59							
60							

The expenses in cells B50 through B54 have each been reduced by 3.74% to obtain a Q1 Total Expenses outcome of $45,000.

Detach the Backsolver add-in from your computer's memory. Do not save the changes to the worksheet.

Solver

Before starting this exercise, attach the Solver add-in SOLVER.PLC.

The **Solver** allows you to determine the maximum or minimum value for a cell based on a set of constraints and adjustable cells which you specify. For example, you can compute the maximum value for Q1 Sales when both Products A and B change.

Because there are limits to how much you can possibly sell in one quarter, the Solver allows you to set constraints. To determine the answer to this problem, you will use the following constraints:

Q1 Sales can be no less than or equal to $65,000

Q1 Sales can be no more than or equal to $80,000

Production of Product A can be greater than or equal to 6,000 units

Production of Product B can be less than or equal to 12,000 units

To begin the example, retrieve the PRODUCT file you created in the previous section.

First, you need to place the constraints of the problem in the worksheet. The constraints must be entered as logical formulas.

To enter the first constraint:

Move	the cell pointer to cell A74		*Click*	*on cell A74*
Enter	Q1 Sales not less than $65,000		*Enter*	*Q1 Sales not less than $65,000*
Move	the cell pointer to cell E74		*Click*	*on cell E74*
Enter	+B47>=65000		*Enter*	*+B47>=65000*

Note that a zero appears in cell E74, because the value in cell B47 is not greater than or equal to 65,000. If the value in cell B47 is greater than or equal to 65,000, the number 1 appears in cell D74.

To enter the formula that Sales cannot be more than $80,000:

Move	the cell pointer to cell A75		*Click*	*on cell A75*
Enter	Q1 Sales not more than $80,000		*Enter*	*Q1 Sales not more than $80,000*
Move	the cell pointer to cell E75		*Click*	*on cell E75*
Enter	+B47<=80000		*Enter*	*+B47<=80000*

To enter the Product A constraint:

Move	the cell pointer to cell A76		*Click*	*on cell A76*
Enter	Product A greater than or equal to 6,000 units		*Enter*	*Product A greater than or equal to 6,000 units*
Move	the cell pointer to cell E76		*Click*	*on cell E76*
Enter	+B71>=6000		*Enter*	*+B71>=6000*

To enter the Product B constraint:

Move	the cell pointer to cell A77		*Click*	*on cell A77*
Enter	Product B less than or equal to 12,000 units		*Enter*	*Product B less than or equal to 12,000 units*
Move	the cell pointer to cell E77		*Click*	*on cell E77*
Enter	+B72<=12000		*Enter*	*+B72<=12000*

To view the formulas in text form:

Highlight	cells E74 through E77		*Highlight*	*cells E74 through E77*
Press	⌑ / ⌑		*Move*	*the mouse pointer to the control panel*
Select	Range		*Choose*	*Range*
Select	Format		*Choose*	*Format*
Select	Text		*Choose*	*Text*

The bottom part of your screen should look like Figure 6-57.

Figure 6-57

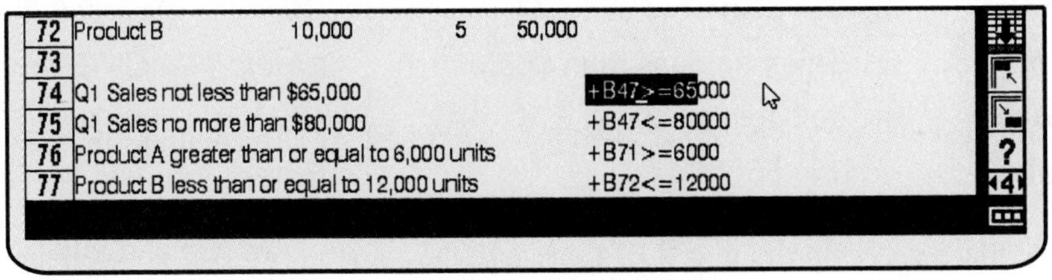

72	Product B	10,000	5	50,000		
73						
74	Q1 Sales not less than $65,000				+B47>=65000	
75	Q1 Sales no more than $80,000				+B47<=80000	
76	Product A greater than or equal to 6,000 units				+B71>=6000	
77	Product B less than or equal to 12,000 units				+B72<=12000	

Before invoking the Solver add-in, move the cell pointer to cell B47.

To start the Solver:

Invoke	the SOLVER add-in		*Invoke*	*the SOLVER add-in*

First, you define the adjustable cell or cells that the solver can change. Adjustable cells must be cells that contain values. The Solver will not perform correctly if an adjustable cell contains text or a formula. To enter more than one adjustable cell, separate the cells or ranges with a comma.

To define Q1 Sales as an adjustable cell:

Select	Define		*Choose*	*Define*
Select	Adjustable		*Choose*	*Adjustable*
Move	the cell pointer to cell B47		*Click*	*on cell B47*
Type	a comma (,)		*Type*	*a comma (,)*

To define Product A and Product B quantity as adjustable cells:

Highlight	cells B71 through B72		*Highlight*	*cells B71 through B72*
Press	←Enter		*Click*	*the mouse button*

The constraint cells must be entered next. Constraint cells contain logical formulas that restrict the Solver to use certain boundaries. You placed the constraints in cells E74 through E77.

Select	Constraints		*Choose*	*Constraints*
Highlight	cells E74 through E77		*Highlight*	*cells E74 through E77*
Press	←Enter		*Click*	*the mouse button*

The optimal cell is the cell for which you want the Solver to find the highest or lowest answer. To specify that the Solver should find the maximum value for Q1 Sales:

Select	Optimal		*Choose*	*Optimal*
Select	X Maximize		*Choose*	*X Maximize*

Move	the cell pointer to cell B47		***Click***	*on cell B47*
Press	←Enter		***Click***	*the mouse button*
Select	Quit		***Choose***	*Quit*

The Solver allows you to select the maximum number of solutions that should be found. The default number of solutions is 10. To change the maximum number of solutions to 6:

Select	Options		***Choose***	*Options*
Select	Number-Answers		***Choose***	*Number-Answers*
Type	6		***Type***	*6*
Press	←Enter		***Click***	*the mouse button*

To find the possible solutions to this problem:

Select	Solve		***Choose***	*Solve*
Select	Problem		***Choose***	*Problem*

Your screen should look like Figure 6-58.

Figure 6-58

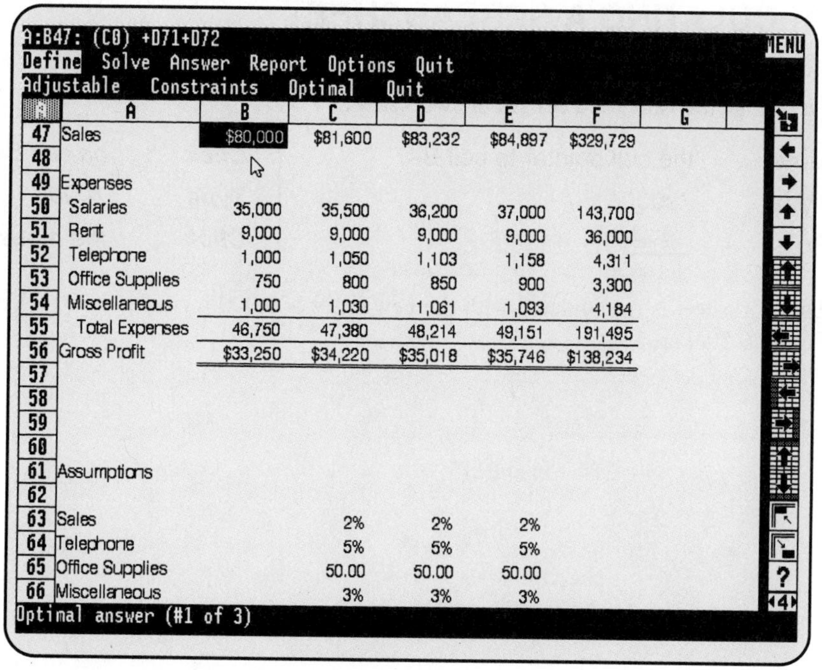

```
A:B47: (C0) +D71+D72                                          MENU
Define  Solve  Answer  Report  Options  Quit
Adjustable   Constraints   Optimal   Quit
        A            B         C        D        E        F        G
 47 Sales        $80,000   $81,600  $83,232  $84,897  $329,729
 48                   ↳
 49 Expenses
 50  Salaries     35,000    35,500   36,200   37,000  143,700
 51  Rent          9,000     9,000    9,000    9,000   36,000
 52  Telephone     1,000     1,050    1,103    1,158    4,311
 53  Office Supplies  750      800      850      900    3,300
 54  Miscellaneous 1,000     1,030    1,061    1,093    4,184
 55   Total Expenses 46,750  47,380   48,214   49,151  191,495
 56 Gross Profit  $33,250   $34,220  $35,018  $35,746  $138,234
 57
 58
 59
 60
 61 Assumptions
 62
 63 Sales                       2%       2%       2%
 64 Telephone                   5%       5%       5%
 65 Office Supplies          50.00    50.00    50.00
 66 Miscellaneous               3%       3%       3%
Optimal answer (#1 of 3)
```

The Solver should find three answers to this problem. The total number of answers appears at the bottom of the screen. The best answer is designated as Answer #1 and is displayed in the worksheet.

To view the other answers in the worksheet:

Select	Answer		***Choose***	*Answer*
Select	Next		***Choose***	*Next*

The new answer will display each time the Next option is selected. If you do not want to keep any of the Solver solutions and would like to return to the original data, select the **R**eset option. To return to the first, or best, answer and use this data in your worksheet:

Select	First		***Choose***	*First*

Notice that the values in the worksheet now reflect the best answer. To keep these values and return to the worksheet:

Select	Quit twice		***Choose***	*Quit twice*

Detach the Solver add-in from your computer's memory. Do not save the changes to the worksheet.

■ RECALCULATING A SPREADSHEET

Retrieve the BUDGET file for this example.

To change the value of a cell on the worksheet:

Move	the cell pointer to cell B47		***Click***	*on cell B47*
Type	70000		***Type***	*70000*
Press	[←Enter]		***Click***	*the mouse button*

The worksheet is recalculated with the new entry $70,000 for Sales in Q1. Your screen should look like Figure 6-59, Part 1.

Figure 6-59
Part 1

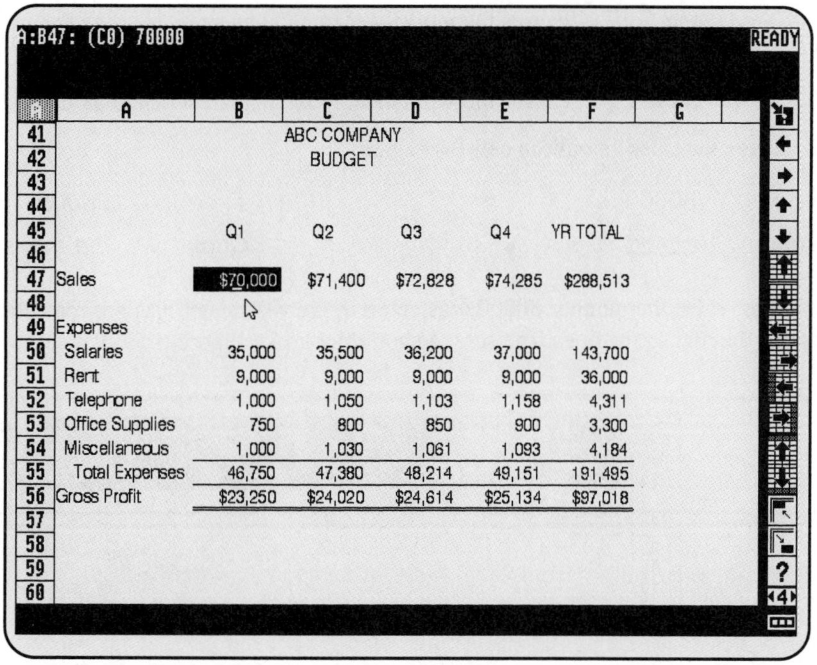

```
A:B47: (C0) 70000                                              READY

         A        B        C        D        E        F      G
  41                    ABC COMPANY
  42                       BUDGET
  43
  44
  45                   Q1       Q2       Q3       Q4    YR TOTAL
  46
  47  Sales        $70,000  $71,400  $72,828  $74,285  $288,513
  48
  49  Expenses
  50   Salaries     35,000   35,500   36,200   37,000   143,700
  51   Rent          9,000    9,000    9,000    9,000    36,000
  52   Telephone     1,000    1,050    1,103    1,158     4,311
  53   Office Supplies 750      800      850      900     3,300
  54   Miscellaneous  1,000    1,030    1,061    1,093    4,184
  55    Total Expenses 46,750  47,380   48,214   49,151  191,495
  56  Gross Profit  $23,250  $24,020  $24,614  $25,134  $97,018
  57
  58
  59
  60
```

The initial settings for recalculation are **A**utomatic and **N**atural; the worksheet recalculates automatically and in natural order every time any cell is changed. Sometimes when new data are input into a large spreadsheet, it may take several seconds or even minutes for the worksheet to recalculate. If you have several changes to make, time will be wasted while you wait for 1-2-3 to recalculate the worksheet as you make each change. A way to reduce the amount of waiting time is to set the **R**ecalculation option to **M**anual.

To control the recalculation in a worksheet manually:

Press		*Move*	*the mouse pointer to the control panel*
Select	Worksheet	*Choose*	*Worksheet*
Select	Global	*Choose*	*Global*
Select	Recalc	*Choose*	*Recalc*
Select	Manual	*Choose*	*Manual*

The recalculation options are described below.

Natural:	first recalculates other formulas upon which a particular formula depends.
Columnwise:	causes the worksheet to recalculate column by column.
Rowwise:	causes the worksheet to recalculate row by row.

>*Automatic:*   causes the worksheet to recalculate every time the worksheet data is changed.
>
>*Manual:*   causes the worksheet to recalculate only by pressing the F9 function key.
>
>*Iteration:*   causes the worksheet to recalculate a designated number of times or iterations.

To change the sales amount in cell B47 again:

Type   80000   **Type**   *80000*

Press   `←Enter`   **Click**   *the mouse button*

Note that when the number 80000 was entered, the worksheet was not recalculated and the letters **CALC** appeared in the status line. The screen should look like Figure 6-59, Part 2.

*Figure 6-59
Part 2*

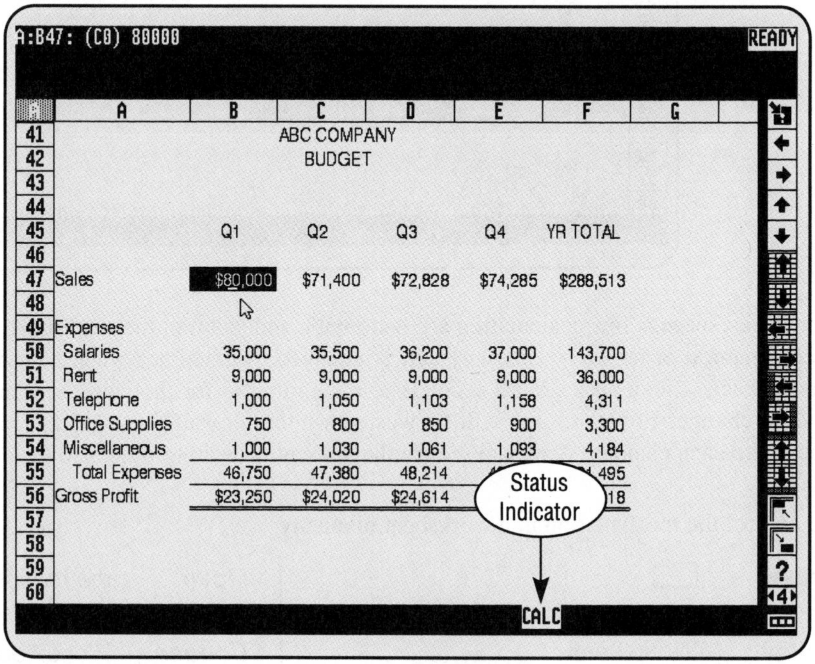

To recalculate the worksheet:

Press   `F9`   **Click**   *the Calc* ▦ *SmartIcon*

The F9 key is sometimes referred to as the **CALC** key.

Your worksheet is now recalculated. If another number is changed at this point, **CALC** will reappear on the status line. Multiple entries can be made without the worksheet recalculating after each new entry. You must press the F9 key again or click the Calc ▦ SmartIcon before the worksheet will be recalculated. Your screen should look like Figure 6-59, Part 3.

Figure 6-59
Part 3

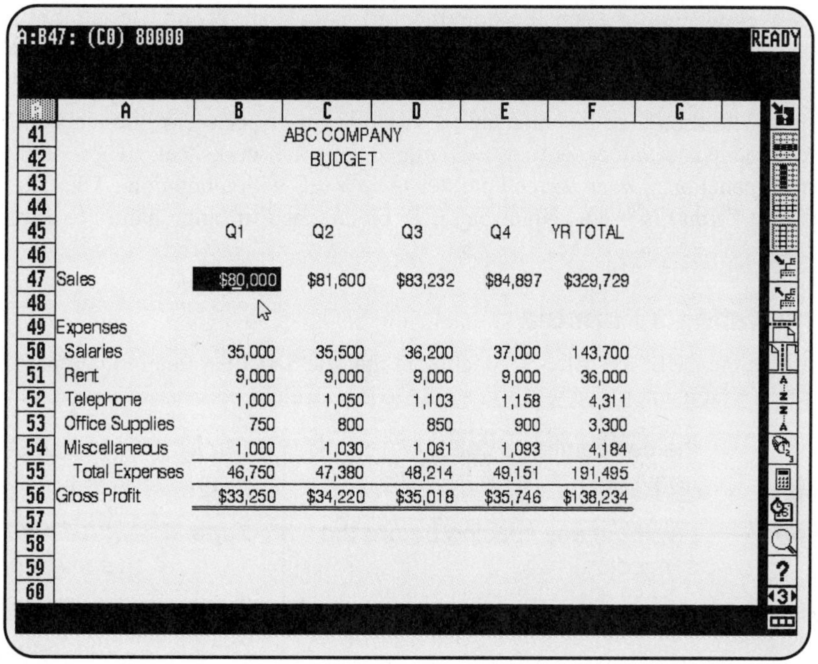

```
A:B47: (C0) 80000                                              READY

        A        B         C         D         E         F        G
 41              ABC COMPANY
 42                BUDGET
 43
 44
 45              Q1        Q2        Q3        Q4      YR TOTAL
 46
 47  Sales      $80,000   $81,600   $83,232   $84,897  $329,729
 48                ⤷
 49  Expenses
 50   Salaries   35,000    35,500    36,200    37,000   143,700
 51   Rent        9,000     9,000     9,000     9,000    36,000
 52   Telephone   1,000     1,050     1,103     1,158     4,311
 53   Office Supplies 750     800       850       900     3,300
 54   Miscellaneous 1,000    1,030     1,061     1,093     4,184
 55    Total Expenses 46,750  47,380   48,214    49,151   191,495
 56  Gross Profit $33,250   $34,220   $35,018   $35,746  $138,234
 57
 58
 59
 60
```

To cause the worksheet to recalculate automatically when the contents of a cell are changed or new data is entered:

Press	/		**Move**	the mouse pointer to the control panel
Select	Worksheet		**Choose**	Worksheet
Select	Global		**Choose**	Global
Select	Recalc		**Choose**	Recalc
Select	Automatic		**Choose**	Automatic

Your worksheet will now recalculate automatically whenever a change is made.

■ DOCUMENTING A WORKSHEET

After a worksheet is completed, it should be documented. Minimum documentation should include: (1) a printout of the worksheet, (2) a printout of the worksheet cell formulas, (3) a copy of the worksheet on a diskette, (4) information on the purpose of the worksheet, (5) the source of the input data, and (6) the destination and users of the output information. Documentation is particularly useful when a worksheet must be changed or a worksheet file is destroyed.

It is a good idea to keep the documentation in a fireproof file cabinet or at a separate location. Additional assistance on documentation and backup precautions can usually be obtained from the information systems department in an organization.

Worksheets should be documented so that other users may easily understand them. Explanatory notes can be added to values as they are entered into the worksheet. These annotations will appear in the control panel only when the cell pointer is on a cell with a notation. They do not show in the cell unless the Text format is used. Notes can also be attached to range names to explain the data in the named range.

Annotating a Formula

Retrieve the BUDGET file. To document that the SALES value in Q2 represents a two percent increase over the first quarter, you will add a note to the formula.

Move	the cell pointer to cell C47		***Click***	*on cell C47*
Press	F2		***Press***	*F2*
Type	; (without any spacing before the semicolon)		***Type***	*; (without any spacing before the semicolon)*
Type	represents a 2% increase		***Type***	*represents a 2% increase*
Press	←Enter		***Click***	*the mouse button with the mouse pointer in the control panel*

Your screen should look like Figure 6-60.

Figure 6-60

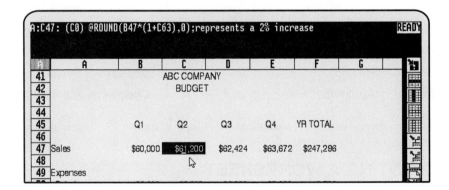

Annotating a Range

Range names that have notes provide an explanation of the data for others. The notes are attached to the range name by using the **R**ange **N**ame **N**ote **C**reate command.

Before illustrating the process for annotating a range name, you need to create a range name that includes cells B47 through E47.

Highlight	cells B47 through E47		*Highlight*	*cells B47 through E47*
Press	[/]		*Move*	*the mouse pointer to the control panel*
Select	Range		*Choose*	*Range*
Select	Name		*Choose*	*Name*
Select	Create		*Choose*	*Create*

When prompted for the range name:

Type	SALES		*Type*	*SALES*
Press	[←Enter]		*Click*	*the mouse button*

Additional information on creating range names is included in the Range Names section earlier in this chapter.

To add a notation to the previously named SALES range in the BUDGET worksheet, use the following commands:

Press	[/]		*Move*	*the mouse pointer to the control panel*
Select	Range		*Choose*	*Range*
Select	Name		*Choose*	*Name*
Select	Note		*Choose*	*Note*
Select	Create		*Choose*	*Create*
Select	SALES		*Choose*	*SALES*

When prompted to enter the note:

Type	Quarterly Sales increased 2 percent		*Type*	*Quarterly Sales increased 2 percent*

Your screen should look like Figure 6-61.

Figure 6-61

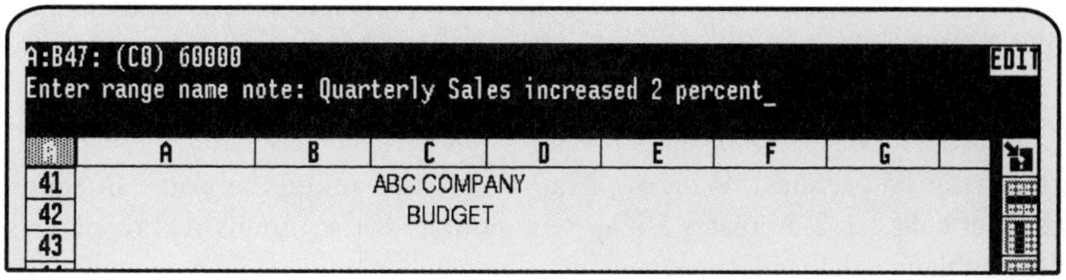

To complete the command:

Press	⌐Enter⌐		***Click***	*the mouse button*
Select	Quit		***Choose***	*Quit*

If you wish to view the notes and range name in a worksheet, use the **R**ange **N**ame **N**ote **T**able command.

Press	/		***Move***	*the mouse pointer to the control panel*
Select	Range		***Choose***	*Range*
Select	Name		***Choose***	*Name*
Select	Note		***Choose***	*Note*
Select	Table		***Choose***	*Table*
Press	Esc		***Click***	*the alternate mouse button*
Move	the cell pointer to cell A70 (the first cell selected for the table range)		***Click***	*on cell A70 (the first cell selected for the table range)*
Press	⌐Enter⌐		***Click***	*the mouse button with the mouse pointer in the control panel*
Select	Quit		***Choose***	*Quit*
Move	the cell pointer to cell A70		***Click***	*on cell A70*

The table appears in a three-column format with the range name, cell addresses, and range notes. The table location selected should be blank because 1-2-3 writes over any existing data when it generates the table. When there are at least two range names, they are listed in alphabetical order. The bottom part of your screen should look like Figure 6-62.

Figure 6-62

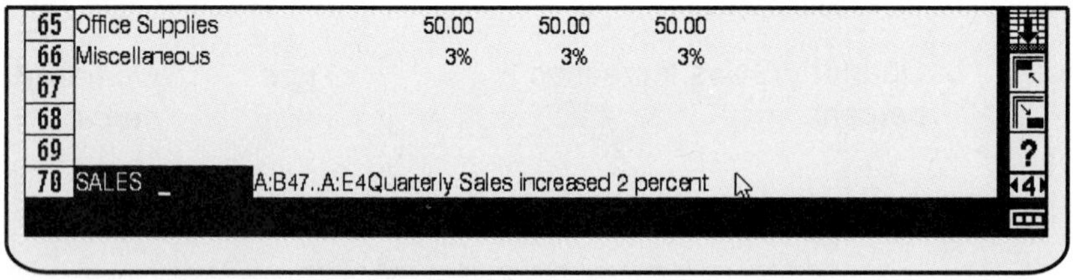

Mapping a Spreadsheet

Through the **W**orksheet **W**indow **M**ap command sequence you can view the type of data in the worksheet cells. 1-2-3 creates a map with compressed columns that displays symbols for what appears in the nonblank cells.

Make sure the BUDGET worksheet appears on your screen.

To create a map of the cell information:

Press	/	**Move**	the mouse pointer to the control panel
Select	Worksheet	**Choose**	Worksheet
Select	Window	**Choose**	Window
Select	Map	**Choose**	Map
Select	Enable	**Choose**	Enable

Your screen now appears like Figure 6-63 showing the cell data using these symbols:

" label cells

\# number cells

+ formulas or annotated numbers

Figure 6-63

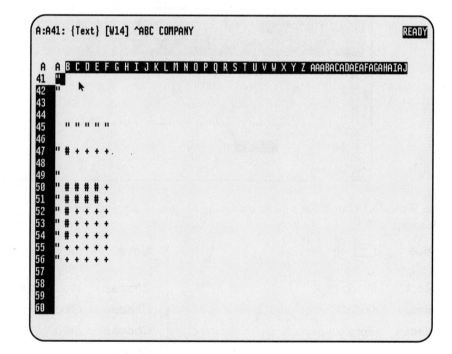

To return to the worksheet, you must disable the Map feature.

Press	Esc	**Click**	the alternate mouse button

Your screen should now display the BUDGET worksheet again.

■ SUPPRESSING ZERO VALUES

The **Z**ero Value **S**uppression command sequence in Lotus 1-2-3 allows you to eliminate the display of all zero values in a worksheet. This command places a blank in place of a cell entry of zero whether the cell entry consists of the number zero or a cell formula that currently evaluates to zero.

Retrieve the BUDGET file for this example.

For the purposes of this example, a zero will be placed in the entry for Sales in Q1. All of the projections for Sales in the following years are based on this number and, therefore, will also display zeros.

Move	the cell pointer to cell B47	*Click*	*on cell B47*
Type	0	*Type*	*0*
Press	←Enter	*Click*	*the mouse button*

The entire row displaying the Sales data now contains zeros. The top part of your screen should look like Figure 6-64.

Figure 6-64

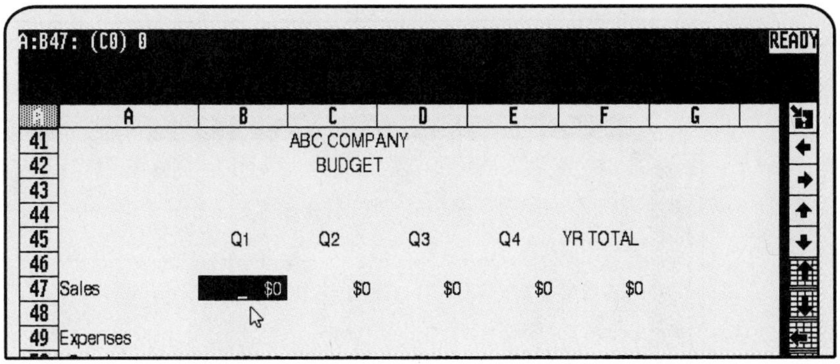

The **W**orksheet **G**lobal **Z**ero menu option allows you to suppress zeros from your screen. To suppress the zeros:

Press	/	*Move*	*the mouse pointer to the control panel*
Select	Worksheet	*Choose*	*Worksheet*
Select	Global	*Choose*	*Global*
Select	Zero	*Choose*	*Zero*
Select	Yes	*Choose*	*Yes*
Move	the cell pointer to cell C47	*Click*	*on cell C47*

The zeros are now suppressed. Notice that even though the zero value is suppressed, the formula for cell C47 still appears in the control panel. The top part of your screen should look like Figure 6-65.

Figure 6-65

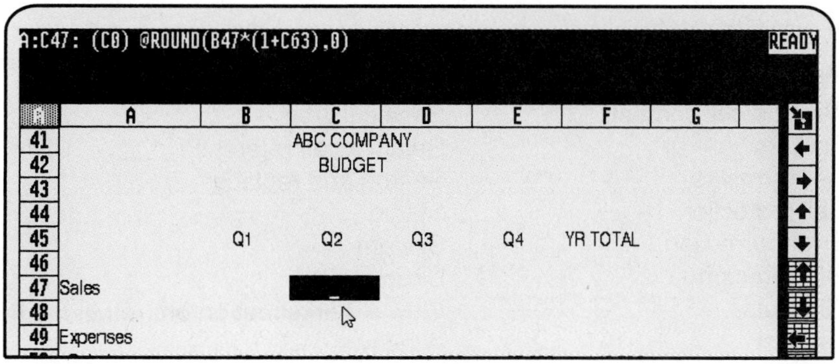

```
A:C47: (C0) @ROUND(B47*(1+C63),0)                              READY

         A        B        C        D        E        F        G
  41                      ABC COMPANY
  42                       BUDGET
  43
  44
  45               Q1       Q2       Q3       Q4     YR TOTAL
  46
  47  Sales
  48                                 ▷
  49  Expenses
```

To make the zeros visible on your screen again:

Press	/	**Move**	the mouse pointer to the control panel
Select	Worksheet	**Choose**	Worksheet
Select	Global	**Choose**	Global
Select	Zero	**Choose**	Zero
Select	No	**Choose**	No

The zeros should now be visible again. The top part of your screen should look like Figure 6-66.

Figure 6-66

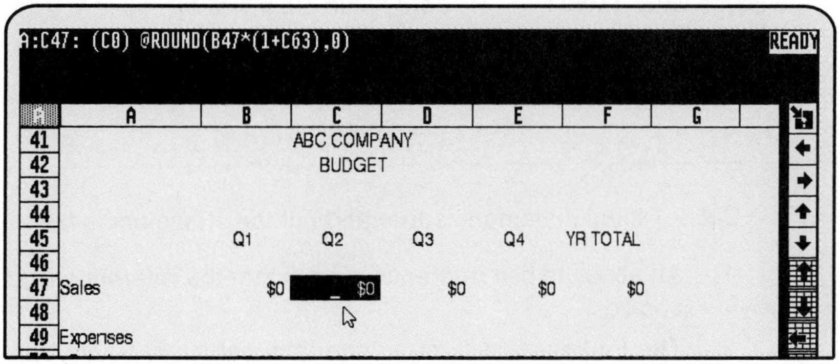

```
A:C47: (C0) @ROUND(B47*(1+C63),0)                              READY

         A        B        C        D        E        F        G
  41                      ABC COMPANY
  42                       BUDGET
  43
  44
  45               Q1       Q2       Q3       Q4     YR TOTAL
  46
  47  Sales        $0       _   $0   $0       $0       $0
  48                                 ▷
  49  Expenses
```

SUMMARY

Lotus 1-2-3 has various menu options and features that allow you to control how data is entered and viewed. These 1-2-3 commands allow you to work more effectively and efficiently when you are creating, editing, or analyzing spreadsheets.

KEY CONCEPTS

Absolute cell reference	Range Search
Aligning cell contents	Recalculation
Borders	Relative cell reference
Cell formulas	Search and replace
Cell protection	Status
Error correction	System
File Directory	Undo
File Erase	View a worksheet before retrieving the worksheet file
File List	Windows
File Save Backup	Widening multiple columns
File Admin Table	Worksheet Column Hide
File View	Worksheet Delete Column
Footers	Worksheet Delete Row
Headers	Worksheet Global Recalc Manual
Hiding cells	Worksheet Global Zero
Hiding columns	Worksheet Insert Column
Label prefix	Worksheet Insert Row
Move	Worksheet Page
Page break	Worksheet Status
Range Erase	Worksheet Titles
Range Name	Worksheet Window
Range Name Note Create	Worksheet Window Map
Range Name Note Table	Zero value suppressing
Range Name Table	

EXERCISE 1

INSTRUCTIONS: Circle T if the statement is true and F if the statement is false.

T F 1. An absolute cell reference means that the reference is kept constant, even when copied.

T F 2. The F2 key allows you to correct a cell entry without having to retype the entire entry.

T F 3 **W**orksheet **T**itles allows you to center titles on a spreadsheet.

T F 4. **W**orksheet **W**indow allows you to view two different areas of a spreadsheet at the same time.

T F 5. **W**orksheet **P**age creates a page break in a spreadsheet.

T F 6. If column D is hidden on a worksheet using **W**orksheet **C**olumn **H**ide, column D will not appear if the worksheet is printed.

T	F	7.	Worksheet **G**lobal **R**ecalc **M**anual is activated so that data can be entered without the worksheet recalculating after each new entry.
T	F	8.	Changing the **F**ile **D**irectory changes the drive designation or path to which 1-2-3 saves and retrieves files.
T	F	9.	**F**ile **E**rase erases a file from memory.
T	F	10.	The **S**ystem command permanently returns you to the operating system command.
T	F	11.	Only one cell at a time can be erased.
T	F	12.	The width for multiple contiguous columns can be changed to the same width at the same time.

EXERCISE 2

INSTRUCTIONS: Explain a typical situation when the following keystrokes or Lotus 1-2-3 commands are used.

Problem 1: F4

Problem 2: / **R**ange **N**ame **C**reate

Problem 3: / **W**orksheet **T**itles

Problem 4: / **W**orksheet **W**indows

Problem 5: F6

Problem 6: / **W**orksheet **I**nsert **R**ow

Problem 7: / **W**orksheet **D**elete **C**olumn

Problem 8: / **W**orksheet **C**olumn **H**ide

Problem 9: : **W**orksheet **P**age

Problem 10: / **W**orksheet **G**lobal **R**ecalc **M**anual

Problem 11: F9

Problem 12: / **W**orksheet **G**lobal **Z**ero

Problem 13: / Range **E**rase

Problem 14: / **F**ile **L**ist

Problem 15: / **F**ile **E**rase

Problem 16: / **F**ile **D**irectory

Problem 17: / **S**ystem

Problem 18: F2

Problem 19: Insert in EDIT mode

Problem 20: / **W**orksheet **C**olumn **C**olumn-Range **S**et-Width

Problem 21: / **W**orksheet **G**lobal **D**efault **O**ther **U**ndo **E**nable

Problem 22: / Range **S**earch

Problem 23: : **P**rint **L**ayout **T**itles **H**eader

Problem 24: : **P**rint **L**ayout **T**itles **F**ooter

EXERCISE 3 — Making a Cell Entry Absolute

INSTRUCTIONS: The following example illustrates a common error. Follow the instructions below to create the error and solve the problem.

Clear the screen.

In cell A1, enter Revenue.

In cell A2, enter Assumed Rev Rate.

Widen column A to 16 characters.

In cell B1, enter 10000.

In cell B2, enter .15.

In cell C1, enter +B1*(1+B2).

Copy the formula in cell C1 to cells D1 and E1.

The top part of your screen should look like Figure 6-67.

Figure 6-67

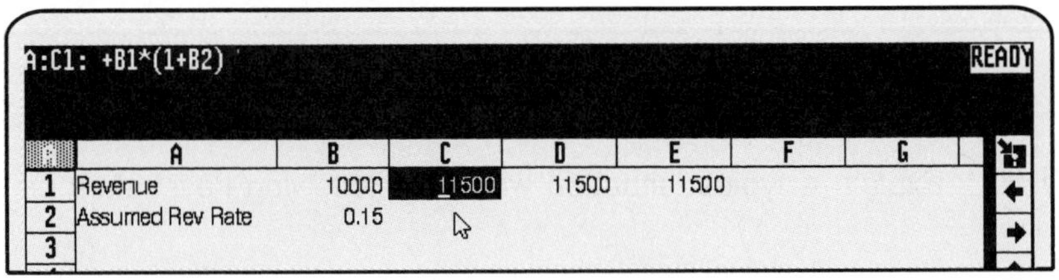

Change the formula in cell C1 and copy it again so that the formulas in cells D1 and E1 also refer to cell B2 for the projected revenue rate.

Print the worksheet.

EXERCISE 4 — Protecting Cells in a Worksheet

INSTRUCTIONS: Retrieve the PRACTICE file you created as an exercise in Chapter 4.

Protect all cells in the worksheet.

Try to change the value of any cell on the worksheet. What happens?

Unprotect the cells containing the revenue growth rates.

Change the revenue growth rates to 8%, 5%, 10%, and 7% respectively for Year 2 through Year 5.

Print the worksheet after changing the growth rates.

EXERCISE 5 — Erasing Cells

INSTRUCTIONS: Retrieve the PRACTICE file.

Erase the title line "PROJECTED PROFITS."

Print the worksheet after you erase the title line.

EXERCISE 6 — Hiding and Displaying a Column

INSTRUCTIONS: Retrieve the BUDGET file that was created in Chapter 4.

Hide columns B and F.
Print the worksheet.
Display columns B and F on the screen.
Print the worksheet.

EXERCISE 7 — Label Prefixes

INSTRUCTIONS: Clear your screen.

In cell B1, enter the value 123.
In cell B3, enter 123 as a label and left-justify the characters.
Right-justify the characters ABC in cell B5.
Repeat the characters XYZ in cell B7.
Center the characters ABC in cell B9.
Print the worksheet.

EXERCISE 8 — Entering Page Breaks in a Spreadsheet

INSTRUCTIONS: Retrieve the BUDGET file.

Create a page break after Total Expenses.
Print the spreadsheet.

EXERCISE 9 — Printing Headers and Footers

INSTRUCTIONS: Retrieve the SALES file that was created as an exercise in Chapter 4.

Create and center the following header and footer:

Header:
SALES RESULTS

Footer:
ANNUAL SALES—CURRENT YEAR

Include the current date right aligned in the footer.

Print the worksheet.

EXERCISE 10 — Range Names

INSTRUCTIONS: Retrieve the BUDGET2 file that was created as an exercise in Chapter 4.

Create the range name SALES and include the cells containing the Sales amounts for the 10 years as its range.

Create the range name TOTAL_EXPENSES and include the cells containing the Total Expenses values for the 10 years as its range.

Create the range name GROSS_PROFIT and include the cells containing the Gross Profit amounts for the 10 years as its range.

Place a table of the range names beginning in cell A70 at the bottom of the worksheet and print the table containing the range names and cells contained in the named ranges.

Print the worksheet.

EXERCISE 11 — Search and Replace

INSTRUCTIONS: Retrieve the BUDGET file.

Use the **S**earch and **R**eplace command to change the name ABC COMPANY to ABC, INC.

Change the word Sales to Revenues using the **S**earch and **R**eplace command.

Print the worksheet.

EXERCISE 12 — Widening Multiple Columns in One Worksheet

INSTRUCTIONS: Retrieve the BUDGET file.

Change the column width of columns B through E to 11 using the multiple column width option.

Print the worksheet.

EXERCISE 13 — Inserting and Deleting Rows and Columns

INSTRUCTIONS: Retrieve the SALES file.

Insert a column at column C.
Insert two rows at row 52.
Print the worksheet.
Delete the column you inserted.
Delete the rows you inserted.
Print the worksheet.

EXERCISE 14 — Suppressing Zero Values

INSTRUCTIONS: Retrieve the PRACTICE file.

Enter the value 0 for the revenue in Year 1.
Suppress the zero values in the worksheet so that no zeros appear.
Print the worksheet.

EXERCISE 15 — Printing Cell Formulas

INSTRUCTIONS: Retrieve the PRACTICE file.

Print the cell formulas where the contents of each cell appear on a separate line.
Print the cell formulas in tabular form.

EXERCISE 16 — Backsolver

INSTRUCTIONS: Retrieve the PRACTICE file.

Assume you need to achieve a first-year After Tax Profit of $15,000.
Use the Backsolver add-in to determine the proportional increase in Revenue and Expenses required to achieve this projected profit.

EXERCISE 17 — Using SmartIcons

INSTRUCTIONS: Add the Calc 🔲 SmartIcon to your custom palette. Note the icon that is removed when you add the Calc 🔲 SmartIcon to your custom palette.

Make the Calc 🔲 SmartIcon the first icon on your custom palette.

Remove the Calc 🔲 SmartIcon from your custom palette.

Add the SmartIcon back to the custom palette that 1-2-3 removed when you placed the Calc 🔲 SmartIcon on your custom palette.

CHAPTER SEVEN

CREATING AND PRINTING GRAPHS

OBJECTIVES

In this chapter, you will learn to:

- ■ Create different types of graphs
- ■ Name, save, and view graphs
- ■ Print a graph
- ■ Delete a named graph

■ CHAPTER OVERVIEW

If a spreadsheet contains a large amount of data, it can be very difficult to detect trends and see relationships among various numbers. A **graph** depicting key elements of a spreadsheet can facilitate a more accurate analysis. Graphs can be created easily in Lotus 1-2-3 by using the spreadsheet data. The graphic image can be viewed on the screen and may also be printed.

> *Design Tip*
>
> In creating a graph, it is usually a good idea to specify the type of graph to be used and the information to identify the X-axis units, and then designate which data to graph. After viewing your graph, you should then specify legend and graph title information.

■ CREATING DIFFERENT TYPES OF GRAPHS

Lotus 1-2-3 has seven types of graphs available: bar, line, XY, stacked-bar, pie, high-low-close-open, and mixed graphs. The BUDGET worksheet will be used to create some of the graphs. Retrieve the BUDGET file.

Creating a Bar Graph

The first graph you will create in this chapter is a bar graph based on data in the BUDGET worksheet that you created in Chapter 4.

The BUDGET worksheet should now be visible on your screen (Figure 7-1).

Figure 7-1

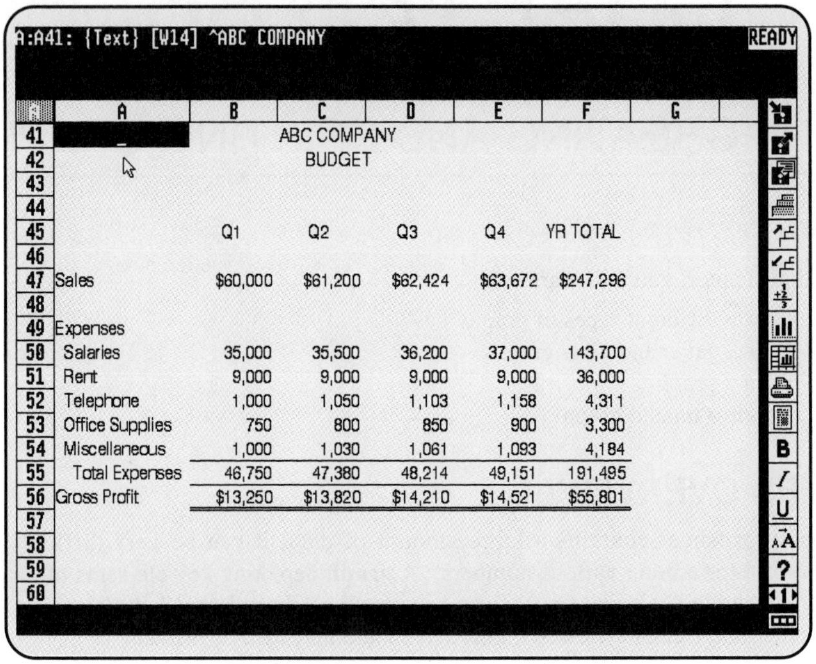

```
A:A41: {Text} [W14] ^ABC COMPANY                                    READY
```

	A	B	C	D	E	F	G
41	_		ABC COMPANY				
42			BUDGET				
43							
44							
45		Q1	Q2	Q3	Q4	YR TOTAL	
46							
47	Sales	$60,000	$61,200	$62,424	$63,672	$247,296	
48							
49	Expenses						
50	Salaries	35,000	35,500	36,200	37,000	143,700	
51	Rent	9,000	9,000	9,000	9,000	36,000	
52	Telephone	1,000	1,050	1,103	1,158	4,311	
53	Office Supplies	750	800	850	900	3,300	
54	Miscellaneous	1,000	1,030	1,061	1,093	4,184	
55	Total Expenses	46,750	47,380	48,214	49,151	191,495	
56	Gross Profit	$13,250	$13,820	$14,210	$14,521	$55,801	
57							
58							
59							
60							

You will first create a **bar graph**. The bars will represent the Sales, Total Expenses, and Gross Profit variables for the four quarters. When the graph is completed, it will look like Figure 7-2.

Figure 7-2

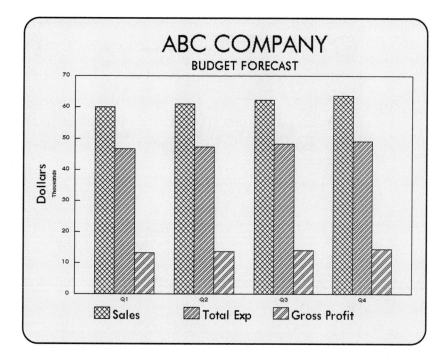

Specifying the Type of Graph

To specify the type of graph to create:

Press	⌐ / ⌐		**Move**	*the mouse pointer to the control panel*
Select	Graph		**Choose**	*Graph*

The main graph menu and the Graph Settings sheet appear on your screen.

Select	Type		**Choose**	*Type*
Select	Bar		**Choose**	*Bar*

Note that an "x" appears to the left of the word Bar in the Graph Type box to indicate that the type of graph is a Bar graph. Your screen should look like Figure 7-3.

Figure 7-3

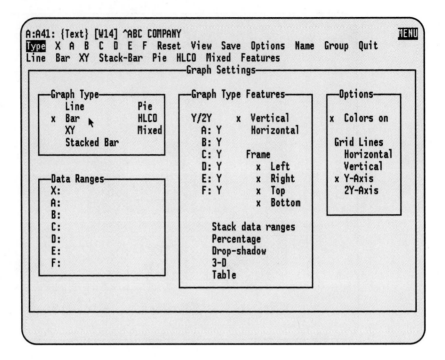

Specifying the X-axis and Data Ranges

To specify the labels that will be on the **X-axis**:

Select	X		*Choose*	*X*

When prompted for the X-axis range:

Highlight	cells B45 through E45		*Highlight*	*cells B45 through E45*

Do not include the YR TOTAL label. If you accidentally highlighted this label, choose **X** again from the menu to reset the range. Press the ESC key or the alternate mouse button to cancel the previous setting. Cells B45 through E45 contain the labels Q1 through Q4 that will be used for the X-axis of the graph. See Figure 7-4, Part 1.

Figure 7-4
Part 1

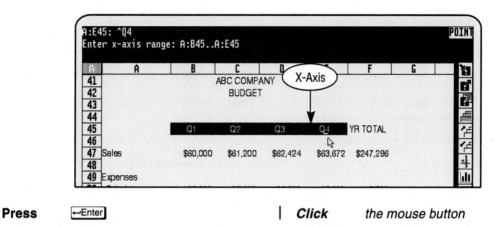

Press   `←Enter` | ***Click***   *the mouse button*

To indicate the data to display, use the menu options A through F. In this exercise, you use menu options A through C to specify the data for Sales, Total Expenses, and Gross Profit. To specify the first data range for the Y-axis:

Select   A | ***Choose***   *A*

When prompted to enter the first data range:

Highlight   cells B47 through E47 | ***Highlight***   *cells B47 through E47*

Cells B47 through E47 contain the data for Sales. The data for Sales for all four quarters will be the first data range displayed on the graph. See Figure 7-4, Part 2.

Figure 7-4
Part 2

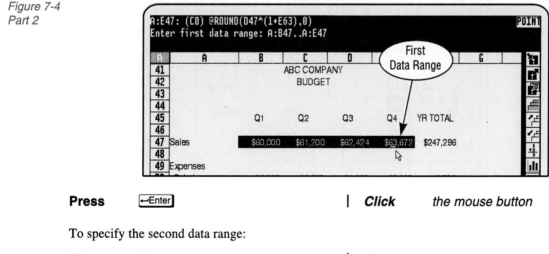

Press   `←Enter` | ***Click***   *the mouse button*

To specify the second data range:

Select   B | ***Choose***   *B*

When prompted to enter the second data range:

Highlight	cells B55 through E55	*Highlight*	*cells B55 through E55*
Press	⌐Enter	*Click*	*the mouse button*

Cells B55 through E55 contain the data for Total Expenses. The data for Total Expenses will be the second data range displayed on the graph.

To specify the third data range:

Select	C	*Choose*	*C*

When prompted to enter the third data range:

Highlight	cells B56 through E56	*Highlight*	*cells B56 through E56*
Press	⌐Enter	*Click*	*the mouse button*

The data for Gross Profit for all four quarters will be the third data range displayed on the graph.

Notice the type of graph and data range specifications in the Graph Settings sheet. Your screen should look like Figure 7-5.

Figure 7-5

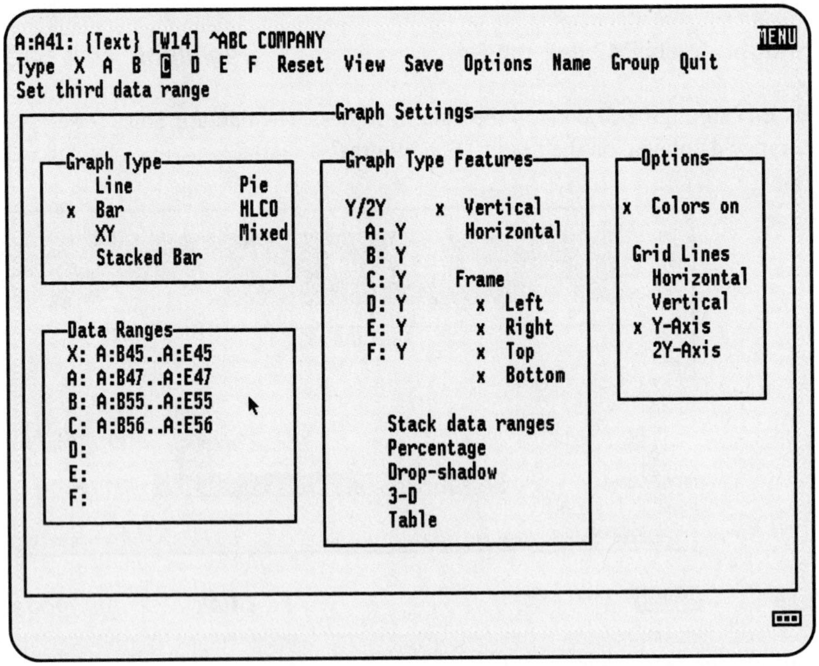

```
A:A41: {Text} [W14] ^ABC COMPANY                                    MENU
Type X A B C D E F  Reset  View  Save  Options  Name  Group  Quit
Set third data range
                              ┌Graph Settings─────────────────────
 ┌─────────────────────────────────────────────────────────────────┐
 │  ┌Graph Type──────┐     ┌Graph Type Features──┐    ┌Options──────┐│
 │     Line       Pie                                                │
 │   x Bar        HLCO     Y/2Y   x Vertical       x Colors on       │
 │     XY         Mixed    A: Y      Horizontal                      │
 │     Stacked Bar         B: Y                     Grid Lines       │
 │                         C: Y      Frame            Horizontal     │
 │                         D: Y    x Left             Vertical       │
 │  ┌Data Ranges─────┐     E: Y    x Right          x Y-Axis         │
 │   X: A:B45..A:E45       F: Y    x Top              2Y-Axis        │
 │   A: A:B47..A:E47               x Bottom                          │
 │   B: A:B55..A:E55   ▶                                             │
 │   C: A:B56..A:E56               Stack data ranges                 │
 │   D:                           Percentage                        │
 │   E:                           Drop-shadow                       │
 │   F:                           3-D                               │
 │                                Table                             │
 └─────────────────────────────────────────────────────────────────┘
```

Viewing the Graph

To view the graph:

Select   View | *Choose*   *View*

The graph should look similar to Figure 7-6. If you are using a color monitor, you may see solid colors rather than hatching patterns. If the screen does not display a graph, it may be because the computer you are using does not have a graphics card. If this is the case, you cannot see a graph on the screen, but you can still create and print it.

Figure 7-6

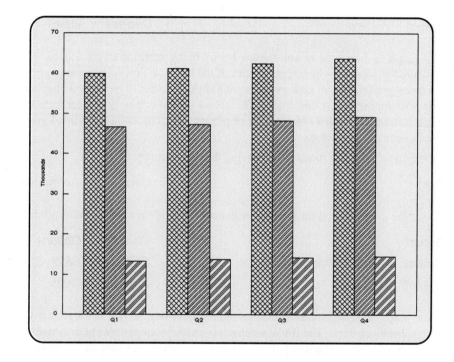

To return to the graph menu after viewing the graph:

Press   ⎵Enter or Esc | *Click*   *the mouse button*

Actually, you can use any key on the keyboard.

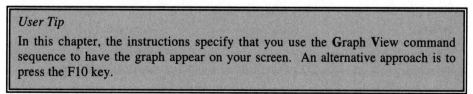

User Tip
In this chapter, the instructions specify that you use the **Graph View** command sequence to have the graph appear on your screen. An alternative approach is to press the F10 key.

The basic settings for the graph have been specified. Now you will add the **titles**, **legends**, and other details necessary to complete the graph.

If you are using a color monitor, you can display the graph in color. To display a color graph:

Select	Options		***Choose***	*Options*
Select	Color		***Choose***	*Color*
Select	Quit		***Choose***	*Quit*

To view the color graph:

Select	View		***Choose***	*View*

The graph is displayed in solid color bars. If the monitor is not a color monitor, the graph may be displayed as solid bars in varying shades of the monitor's primary color (e.g., green or amber). Note that the color graph is not an appropriate setting if the graph is to be printed on a one-color printer because all bars will appear in just one color. The colors on the screen do *not* indicate the color the graph will be when it is printed with a color printer or plotter. The colors on the printed graph depend on the *printer's* available ink or pen colors.

To return to the graph menu after viewing the color graph:

Press	⏎Enter		***Click***	*the mouse button*

To set the graph to print on a printer with only black ink (i.e., not a color plotter):

Select	Options		***Choose***	*Options*
Select	B&W (Black and White)		***Choose***	*B&W (Black and White)*
Select	Quit		***Choose***	*Quit*

If the graph remained set as a color graph, a printer with only a black ribbon would have printed a graph with solid black bars. The B&W setting sets cross-hatch patterns to distinguish the bars from each other. If you want to continue using the color option as you complete this chapter, repeat the **Graph Options Color** command sequence.

Entering the Titles for the Graph

Graphs can have two title lines, which appear centered at the top of the graph.

Using the main graph menu, to enter the first title for the graph:

Select	Options		***Choose***	*Options*
Select	Titles		***Choose***	*Titles*
Select	First		***Choose***	*First*

The Graph Legends and Titles dialog box appears on your screen.

When prompted to enter the first line of the graph title:

Type	ABC COMPANY		*Type*	*ABC COMPANY*
Press	[←Enter]		*Click*	*the mouse button*

To enter the second title:

Select	Titles		*Choose*	*Titles*
Select	Second		*Choose*	*Second*

When prompted to enter the second line of the graph title:

Type	BUDGET FORECAST		*Type*	*BUDGET FORECAST*
Press	[←Enter]		*Click*	*the mouse button*

To enter a title for the Y-axis:

Select	Titles		*Choose*	*Titles*
Select	Y-Axis		*Choose*	*Y-Axis*

When prompted to enter the Y-axis title:

Type	Dollars		*Type*	*Dollars*
Press	[←Enter]		*Click*	*the mouse button*

To view the graph with titles on it:

Select	Quit		*Choose*	*Quit*
Select	View		*Choose*	*View*

The graph should look like Figure 7-7.

Figure 7-7

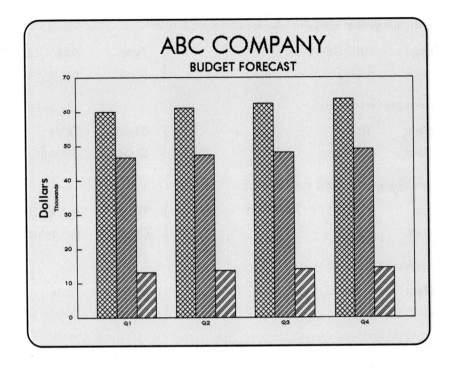

To return to the graph menu after viewing the graph:

Press	←Enter	*Click* the mouse button

Specifying the Legends

To enter the legend for the first data range (highlighted as data range A earlier in this exercise):

Select	Options	*Choose* Options
Select	Legend	*Choose* Legend
Select	A	*Choose* A

When prompted to enter the legend for data range A:

Type	Sales	*Type* Sales
Press	←Enter	*Click* the mouse button

To enter the legend for the second data range (placed in data range B earlier in this exercise):

Select	Legend	*Choose* Legend
Select	B	*Choose* B

When prompted for the legend for data range B:

Type	Total Exp	**Type**	*Total Exp*
Press	⎡←Enter⎤	**Click**	*the mouse button*

To enter the legend for the third data range (placed in data range C earlier in this exercise):

Select	Legend	***Choose***	*Legend*
Select	C	***Choose***	*C*

When prompted for the legend for data range C:

Type	Gross Profit	**Type**	*Gross Profit*
Press	⎡←Enter⎤	**Click**	*the mouse button*

To view the graph with titles and legends:

Select	Quit	***Choose***	*Quit*
Select	View	***Choose***	*View*

Your screen should look like Figure 7-8.

Figure 7-8

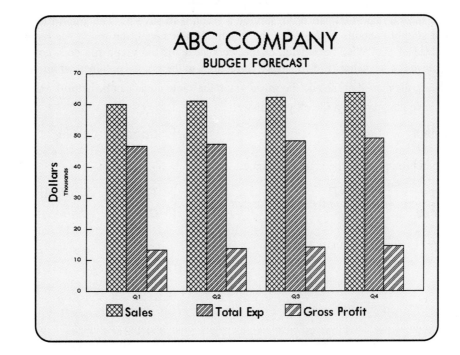

To return to the graph menu:

Press [←Enter] | ***Click*** *the mouse button*

Naming and Saving the Graph

There are three important parts of the process of preserving a graph for later use. First is **naming** the graph. Naming the graph protects the graph settings in the worksheet. This is especially important if more than one graph will be created from the worksheet data.

To name the graph:

Select	Name		***Choose***	*Name*
Select	Create		***Choose***	*Create*

When prompted for the graph name:

Type	BUDBAR		***Type***	*BUDBAR*
Press	[←Enter]		***Click***	*the mouse button*

The graph name can consist of up to 15 characters.

When a particular graph is needed, the **G**raph **N**ame **U**se command sequence displays all graph names so that the desired graph can be selected and viewed.

The second important part of preserving a graph is to **save** it. The graph file has no settings of its own and simply contains a picture of the graph. When saved, the graph file has a "CGM" file extension instead of the "WK3" extension of the worksheet. If the graph file does not print correctly, you must retrieve the worksheet file and make corrections to the graph contained within the worksheet.

Giving the *named* graph and the *saved* graph the same name can be helpful when editing is required.

To save the graph as a file on your disk:

Select	Save		***Choose***	*Save*

When prompted for the graph file name:

Type	BUDBAR		***Type***	*BUDBAR*
Press	[←Enter]		***Click***	*the mouse button*

Refer to Figure 7-9, Parts 1 and 2.

Graph **N**ame **C**reate assigns a name to the graph settings for a graph. (**File S**ave will permanently save the graph settings as part of the worksheet file.)

Figure 7-9
Part 1

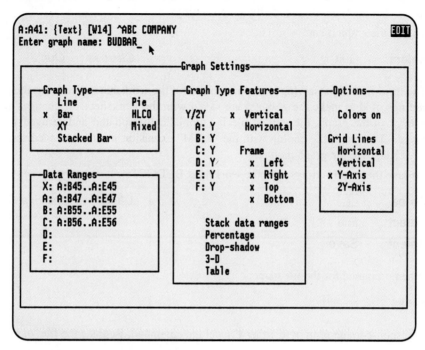

Graph **S**ave saves the graph in a .CGM file for later printing.

Figure 7-9
Part 2

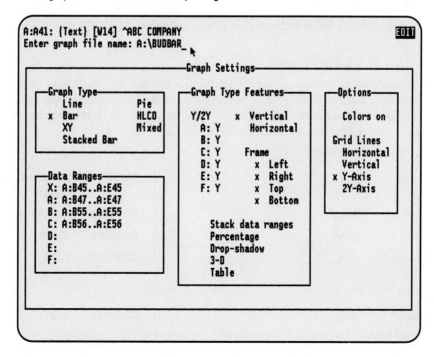

The settings used to make the graph should be saved with the worksheet file BUDGET.WK3 in the event that changes will be made later. For this reason, the next step is to save and replace the BUDGET.WK3 file so that the file will include the graph settings.

To exit the graph menu:

Select Quit	**Choose** Quit

The third part of preserving a graph is to *resave* the worksheet containing the graph(s). In doing so, the settings used to make the graph(s) are saved with the worksheet. If changes are made to the worksheet data or to the graph, the *named* file is automatically updated and resaved when the worksheet file is saved. The graph file ending with the "CGM" extension must be resaved separately in order to protect any changes to the graph picture.

To save the graph settings with the worksheet BUDGET:

Press [/]	**Click** the File Save 🔲 SmartIcon
Select File	
Select Save	

When prompted for the file name:

Press [←Enter]	

In response to the prompt to either **C**ancel the command, **R**eplace the file, or create a **B**ackup file:

Select Replace	**Choose** Replace

The graph specifications and name are now saved on the BUDGET worksheet file.

Creating a Line Graph

The graph settings saved on the BUDGET file contain the graph data range specifications for Sales, Total Expenses, and Gross Profit. Because the graph settings are already designated, they can be used to redisplay the same data as a **line graph**. Only the graph type has to be changed. The newly designated graph can then be given a different graph name.

To create a line graph:

Press [/]	**Move** the mouse pointer to the control panel
Select Graph	**Choose** Graph
Select Type	**Choose** Type
Select Line	**Choose** Line

To view the graph:

Select View	**Choose** View

The lines on the screen appear more jagged than they are when printed. Your screen should look similar to Figure 7-10.

Figure 7-10

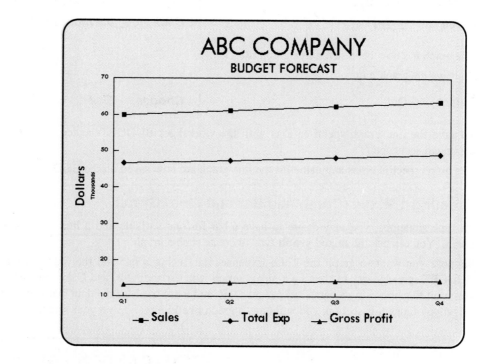

To return to the graph menu:

Press   ⏎Enter | ***Click***   *the mouse button*

Notice that since the graph settings were established in an earlier exercise, specifications such as data ranges, titles, and legends do not have to be set again.

To name the graph:

Select   Name | ***Choose***   *Name*
Select   Create | ***Choose***   *Create*

When prompted for the graph name:

Type   BUDLINE | ***Type***   *BUDLINE*
Press   ⏎Enter | ***Click***   *the mouse button*

To save the graph image in a file:

Select   Save | ***Choose***   *Save*

When prompted for the graph file name:

Type	BUDLINE		*Type*	*BUDLINE*
Press	⟨←Enter⟩		*Click*	*the mouse button*

The graph has now been saved to a graph file.

To leave the graph menu:

Select	Quit		*Choose*	*Quit*

To save the line graph specifications with the worksheet BUDGET, execute the **File Save Replace** command sequence.

The graph specifications and name for the line graph are now saved on the BUDGET worksheet file.

Creating a Mixed (Combined Bar and Line) Graph

In some situations, you may desire to have a bar for one variable and a line for another variable on a graph. You can use the **mixed graph** type to create such a graph.

Suppose you want to graph the Total Expenses data using a bar and the Sales data as a line for the BUDGET spreadsheet. In creating a mixed graph, you use the A, B, and C data ranges for the items that you want to graph using a bar. Data ranges D, E, and F are used for the data that is depicted using a line. When you finish this section, you will have a graph like Figure 7-11 on your screen.

Figure 7-11

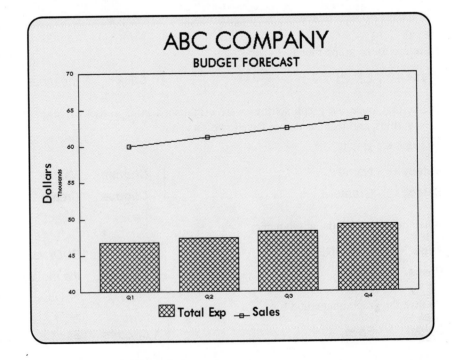

Make sure the BUDGET worksheet appears on your screen. Before creating the mixed graph, you need to delete the previous data ranges using the **Graph R**eset command sequence.

To delete the ranges:

Press	⊘		*Move*	*the mouse pointer to the control panel*
Select	Graph		*Choose*	*Graph*
Select	Reset		*Choose*	*Reset*
Select	Ranges		*Choose*	*Ranges*

To return to the main graph menu:

Select	Quit		*Choose*	*Quit*

To specify that a mixed graph is desired:

Select	Type		*Choose*	*Type*
Select	Mixed		*Choose*	*Mixed*

To indicate the four quarters as the X-axis data range:

Select	X		*Choose*	*X*
Highlight	cells B45 through E45		*Highlight*	*cells B45 through E45*
Press	←Enter		*Click*	*the mouse button*

To specify Total Expenses as the data to display with a bar:

Select	A		*Choose*	*A*
Highlight	cells B55 through E55		*Highlight*	*cells B55 through E55*
Press	←Enter		*Click*	*the mouse button*

To designate the legend for Total Expenses:

Select	Options		*Choose*	*Options*
Select	Legend		*Choose*	*Legend*
Select	A		*Choose*	*A*

To erase the current legend:

Press	Esc		*Click*	*the alternate mouse button*
Type	Total Exp		*Type*	*Total Exp*
Press	←Enter		*Click*	*the mouse button*
Select	Quit		*Choose*	*Quit*

To specify Sales as the data to illustrate with a line:

Select	D		***Choose***	*D*
Highlight	cells B47 through E47		***Highlight***	*cells B47 through E47*
Press	⏎Enter		***Click***	*the mouse button*

To designate the legend for Sales:

Select	Options		***Choose***	*Options*
Select	Legend		***Choose***	*Legend*
Select	D		***Choose***	*D*
Type	Sales		***Type***	*Sales*
Press	⏎Enter		***Click***	*the mouse button*
Select	Quit		***Choose***	*Quit*

To display graphs on your screen:

Select	View		***Choose***	*View*

Your screen now should look like Figure 7-12.

Figure 7-12

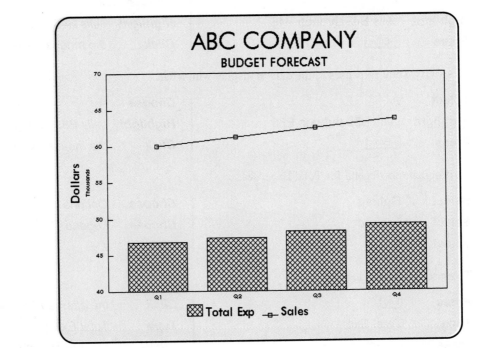

To return to the worksheet:

Press	[←Enter]		***Click***	*the mouse button*

To name the graph:

Select	Name		***Choose***	*Name*
Select	Create		***Choose***	*Create*

When prompted for the graph name:

Type	BUDMIXED		***Type***	*BUDMIXED*
Press	[←Enter]		***Click***	*the mouse button*

To save the graph image on a file:

Select	Save		***Choose***	*Save*

When prompted for the graph file name:

Type	BUDMIXED		***Type***	*BUDMIXED*
Press	[←Enter]		***Click***	*the mouse button*

The graph now has been saved as a separate file.

To exit the graph menu:

Select	Quit		***Choose***	*Quit*

To save the mixed graph specifications with the worksheet BUDGET, execute the **F**ile **S**ave **R**eplace command sequence.

The graph specifications and the name for the mixed graph are now saved on the BUDGET worksheet file.

Creating a Stacked-Bar Graph

The BUDGET worksheet is again used in this exercise. The graph settings for the graph named BUDBAR saved on the BUDGET file contain the graph range specifications for Sales, Total Expenses, and Gross Profit. Because the graph settings are already set, they can be used to redisplay the same data as a **stacked-bar** graph. Only the graph type has to be changed. The newly designated graph will be given a different graph name. When you finish, your graph will look like Figure 7-13.

To use the BUDBAR graph, first retrieve the BUDGET file and then:

Press	[/]		***Move***	*the mouse pointer to the control panel*
Select	Graph		***Choose***	*Graph*

Select	Name		*Choose*	*Name*
Select	Use		*Choose*	*Use*
Select	BUDBAR		*Move*	*the mouse pointer to BUDBAR*
Press	⏎Enter		*Click*	*the mouse button*

To return to the graph menu:

Press	⏎Enter		*Click*	*the mouse button*

To create a stacked-bar graph:

Select	Type		*Choose*	*Type*
Select	Stack-Bar		*Choose*	*Stack-Bar*

To view the graph:

Select	View		*Choose*	*View*

Your screen should look similar to Figure 7-13.

Figure 7-13

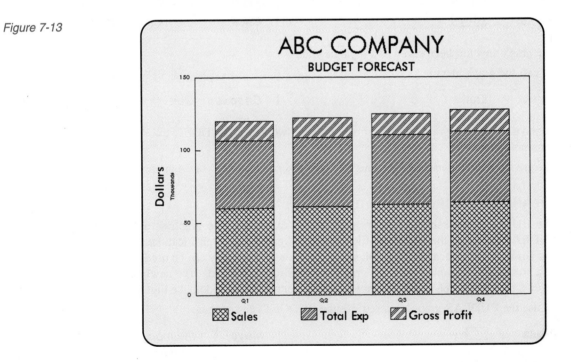

To return to the graph menu:

Press	⏎Enter		*Click*	*the mouse button*

Because the graph settings were established in the earlier bar graph exercise, specifications such as data ranges, titles, and legends are already set.

In the following exercise, data range and legend settings will be changed to depict a different stacked-bar graph. The newly created graph will offer a visual representation of Gross Profits and Expenses adding up to Total Sales.

To reset data ranges:

Select	Reset		*Choose*	*Reset*

When prompted for the ranges to reset:

Select	A		*Choose*	*A*
Select	C		*Choose*	*C*

Data range B does not need to be changed because it already represents Total Expenses.

To leave the Reset menu:

Select	Quit		*Choose*	*Quit*

To specify range A as Gross Profit:

Select	A		*Choose*	*A*

When prompted for the first data range:

Highlight	cells B56 through E56		*Highlight*	*cells B56 through E56*
Press	⏎Enter		*Click*	*the mouse button*

Data range A now contains the data for Gross Profit.

The data have been rearranged as follows: data range A was changed to the data for Gross Profit; data range B was left as Total Expenses; data range C was canceled. In this way the stacked-bar stacks ranges A and B (Gross Profit and Total Expenses) will add up to Total Sales.

To change the legends:

Select	Options		*Choose*	*Options*
Select	Legend		*Choose*	*Legend*
Select	A		*Choose*	*A*

The current legend is Sales. To replace the legend for range A:

Press	Esc		*Click*	*the alternate mouse button*
Type	Gross Profit		*Type*	*Gross Profit*
Press	⏎Enter		*Click*	*the mouse button*

To eliminate the legend for range C:

Select	Legend		***Choose***	*Legend*
Select	C		***Choose***	*C*
Press	Esc		***Click***	*the alternate mouse button*
Press	←Enter		***Click***	*the mouse button*

The ESC key or the alternate mouse button was pressed to cancel the legend for the C range.

To return to the main graph menu:

Select	Quit		***Choose***	*Quit*

To view the graph:

Select	View		***Choose***	*View*

Note that the data ranges are now appropriate. Data range A (Gross Profit) and data range B (Total Expenses) are stacked and result in a pictorial representation of Sales. A third data range is not needed. Refer to Figure 7-14.

Figure 7-14

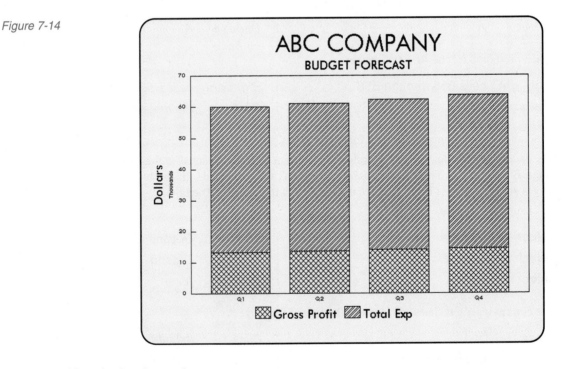

After viewing the graph:

Press	←Enter		***Click***	*the mouse button*

To name the graph:

Select	Name		***Choose***	*Name*
Select	Create		***Choose***	*Create*

When prompted for the graph name:

Type	BUDSTBAR		***Type***	*BUDSTBAR*
Press	⏎Enter		***Click***	*the mouse button*

To save the graph image on a file:

Select	Save		***Choose***	*Save*

When prompted for the graph file name:

Type	BUDSTBAR		***Type***	*BUDSTBAR*
Press	⏎Enter		***Click***	*the mouse button*

The graph now has been saved as a separate file.

To exit the graph menu:

Select	Quit		***Choose***	*Quit*

To save the stacked-bar graph specifications with the worksheet BUDGET, execute the **F**ile **S**ave **R**eplace command sequence.

The graph specifications and the name for the stacked-bar graph are now saved on the BUDGET worksheet file.

Creating a Pie Graph

The BUDGET worksheet is again used in this exercise. You will create a **pie graph**, name it, and save it for later use. The pie graph will depict the first quarter's expenses for Salaries, Rent, and Telephone. When you complete the graph, your screen should look like Figure 7-15.

Before creating the pie graph, you need to reset all the previously defined graph data and option ranges.

Press	☐ /		***Move***	*the mouse pointer to the control panel*
Select	Graph		***Choose***	*Graph*
Select	Reset		***Choose***	*Reset*

To reset all previously defined graph settings:

Select	Graph		**Select**	*Graph*

You will create a pie graph to show the breakdown of some of the expense items for Q1.

To create the pie graph:

Select	Type		*Choose*	*Type*
Select	Pie		*Choose*	*Pie*

To specify the labels for the pie segments:

Select	X		*Choose*	*X*
Highlight	cells A50 through A52		*Highlight*	*cells A50 through A52*
Press	⏎Enter		*Click*	*the mouse button*

To indicate the Q1 expense data to graph:

Select	A		*Choose*	*A*
Highlight	cells B50 through B52		*Highlight*	*cells B50 through B52*
Press	⏎Enter		*Click*	*the mouse button*

To add titles to the graph:

Select	Options		*Choose*	*Options*
Select	Titles		*Choose*	*Titles*
Select	First		*Choose*	*First*
Type	ABC COMPANY		*Type*	*ABC COMPANY*
Press	⏎Enter		*Click*	*the mouse button*
Select	Titles		*Choose*	*Titles*
Select	Second		*Choose*	*Second*
Type	PARTIAL EXPENSE ANALYSIS		*Type*	*PARTIAL EXPENSE ANALYSIS*
Press	⏎Enter		*Click*	*the mouse button*

To view the graph:

Select	Quit		*Choose*	*Quit*
Select	View		*Choose*	*View*

Your screen should look like Figure 7-15.

Figure 7-15

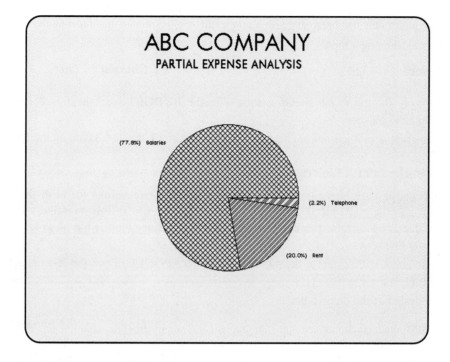

After viewing the graph:

| **Press** | ←Enter | | ***Click*** | *the mouse button* |

To name the graph:

| **Select** | Name | | ***Choose*** | *Name* |
| **Select** | Create | | ***Choose*** | *Create* |

When prompted for the graph name:

| **Type** | BUDPIE | | ***Type*** | *BUDPIE* |
| **Press** | ←Enter | | ***Click*** | *the mouse button* |

To save the graph image on a file:

| **Select** | Save | | ***Choose*** | *Save* |

When prompted for the graph file name:

| **Type** | BUDPIE | | ***Type*** | *BUDPIE* |
| **Press** | ←Enter | | ***Click*** | *the mouse button* |

The graph now has been saved on a graph file.

To exit the graph menu:

Select	Quit	**|** *Choose* *Quit*

To save the pie graph specifications with the BUDGET worksheet, execute the **File Save Replace** command sequence.

The graph specifications and the name for the pie graph are now saved on the BUDGET worksheet file.

Creating an XY Graph

XY graphs are basically line graphs that use numeric values for both the X-axis and the Y-axis. Retrieve the UNITPROD (Unit Production) file for use in this exercise. The UNITPROD file was created in an exercise you completed in Chapter 4. Since the file has no graph settings, you will need to create them.

This graph will represent the number of UNITS PRODUCED on the X-axis and the number of UNITS SOLD on the Y-axis.

To designate the graph type:

Press	⬚ / ⬚	**|** *Move* the mouse pointer to the control panel
Select	Graph	**|** *Choose* Graph
Select	Type	**|** *Choose* Type

When prompted for the graph type:

Select	XY	**|** *Choose* XY

To designate the data for the X-axis:

Select	X	**|** *Select* X

When prompted for the X-axis range:

Highlight	cells C47 through C52	**|** *Highlight* cells C47 through C52
Press	⬚←Enter⬚	**|** *Click* the mouse button

To designate the data for the Y-axis:

Select	A	**|** *Select* A

When prompted to enter the A range:

Highlight	cells D47 through D52	**|** *Highlight* cells D47 through D52
Press	⬚←Enter⬚	**|** *Click* the mouse button

A helpful menu option is **Data-Labels**. For clarification, labels are placed near each data point:

Select	Options		*Choose*	*Options*
Select	Data-Labels		*Choose*	*Data-Labels*
Select	A		*Choose*	*A*
Highlight	cells B47 through B52		*Highlight*	*cells B47 through B52*
Press	⮐Enter		*Click*	*the mouse button*
Select	Below		*Choose*	*Below*

To exit the current menu:

Select	Quit		*Choose*	*Quit*

To enter a title for the graph:

Select	Titles		*Choose*	*Titles*
Select	First		*Choose*	*First*

When prompted to enter the top line of the graph title:

Type	ABC COMPANY		*Type*	*ABC COMPANY*
Press	⮐Enter		*Click*	*the mouse button*

To enter an X-axis title:

Select	Titles		*Choose*	*Titles*
Select	X-Axis		*Choose*	*X-Axis*

When prompted for the title:

Type	UNITS PRODUCED		*Type*	*UNITS PRODUCED*
Press	⮐Enter		*Click*	*the mouse button*

To enter a Y-axis title:

Select	Titles		*Choose*	*Titles*
Select	Y-Axis		*Choose*	*Y-Axis*

When prompted for the title:

Type	UNITS SOLD		*Type*	*UNITS SOLD*
Press	⮐Enter		*Click*	*the mouse button*

To exit the current menu:

Select Quit | *Choose*   *Quit*

To view the graph:

Select View | *Choose*   *View*

The graph should look like Figure 7-16. Note that the graph on the screen and the printed graph may look slightly different since the scale on the printout may vary from the scale on the screen display.

Figure 7-16

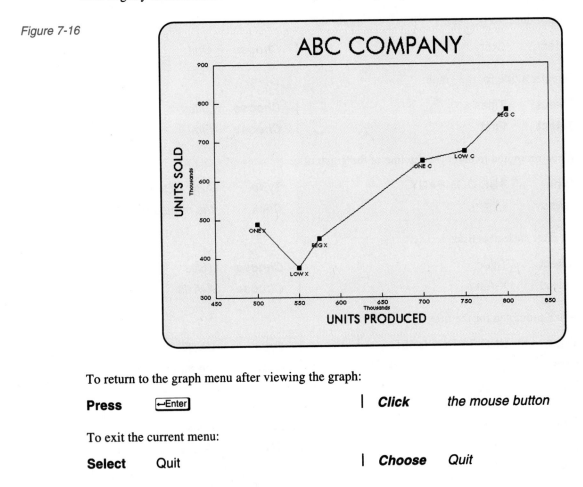

To return to the graph menu after viewing the graph:

Press   ⏎Enter | *Click*   *the mouse button*

To exit the current menu:

Select Quit | *Choose*   *Quit*

You do not need to save the graph settings.

■ PRINTING A GRAPH

After creating a graph, you will most likely want to print the graph. In some instances, you may want to print a graph that you created in an earlier 1-2-3 work session. Furthermore, you may want to print a graph in conjunction with data from a worksheet. In this section, you will learn how to print graphs for each of these situations and examine some advanced printing options.

Printing the Current Graph

Before printing a graph, retrieve the BUDGET file.

To select the BUDBAR graph you created:

Press	`/`		*Move*	*the mouse pointer to the control panel*
Select	Graph		*Choose*	*Graph*
Select	Name		*Choose*	*Name*
Select	Use		*Choose*	*Use*
Select	BUDBAR		*Choose*	*BUDBAR*

The graph will appear on your screen. To leave the graph menu:

Press	`←Enter`		*Click*	*the mouse button*
Select	Quit		*Choose*	*Quit*

To print the current graph associated with the BUDGET worksheet:

Press	`/`		*Move*	*the mouse pointer to the control panel*
Select	Print		*Choose*	*Print*
Select	Printer		*Choose*	*Printer*

The Print Settings sheet appears on your screen.

Select	Image		*Choose*	*Image*
Select	Current		*Choose*	*Current*
Select	Align		*Choose*	*Align*
Select	Go		*Choose*	*Go*
Select	Page		*Choose*	*Page*

The graph will now be printed. Assuming you are using the BUDBAR graph, your output will look like Figure 7-17.

Figure 7-17

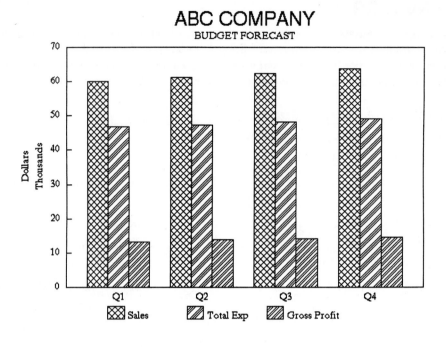

To exit the graph menu:

Select	Quit		*Choose*	*Quit*

Printing a Named Graph

Assuming that you still have the BUDGET worksheet on the screen that was used when you created, named, and saved the various types of graphs in an earlier section of this chapter, the steps necessary to print the pie graph are:

Press	[/]		*Move*	*the mouse pointer to the control panel*
Select	Print		*Choose*	*Print*
Select	Printer		*Choose*	*Printer*
Select	Image		*Choose*	*Image*
Select	Named-Graph		*Choose*	*Named-Graph*
Press	[F3]		*Press*	*[F3]*
Select	BUDPIE		*Choose*	*BUDPIE*
Select	Align		*Choose*	*Align*
Select	Go		*Choose*	*Go*
Select	Page		*Choose*	*Page*
Select	Quit		*Choose*	*Quit*

Printing Different Sized Graphs

You can print various sized graphs. For example, you can indicate that a graph is to fill the page from the left to the right margin or specify the length of the graph on the page. You can also reshape the graph by specifying the width and length for the graph. In this section, you will print a full-page graph. It is assumed that you are using a printer with 8 1/2 by 11-inch paper.

Make sure you have the BUDGET worksheet on the screen.

You can print a full-page bar graph by completing the following steps:

Press	`/`		*Move*	*the mouse pointer to the control panel*
Select	Print		*Choose*	*Print*
Select	Printer		*Choose*	*Printer*
Select	Image		*Choose*	*Image*
Select	Named-Graph		*Choose*	*Named-Graph*
Select	BUDBAR		*Choose*	*BUDBAR*
Select	Options		*Choose*	*Options*
Select	Advanced		*Choose*	*Advanced*
Select	Image		*Choose*	*Image*
Select	Image-Sz		*Choose*	*Image-Sz*
Select	Length-Fill		*Choose*	*Length-Fill*
Press	`←Enter`		*Click*	*the mouse button with the mouse pointer in the control panel*

You have indicated that your printer has 66 available lines for printing. If your printer has a different number of lines that can be printed on an 8 1/2 by 11-inch sheet of paper or your paper length is not 11 inches, you will need to type a different number after you select the Length-Fill option.

To complete the printing process:

Select	Quit three times		*Choose*	*Quit three times*
Select	Align		*Choose*	*Align*
Select	Go		*Choose*	*Go*
Select	Page		*Choose*	*Page*
Select	Quit		*Choose*	*Quit*

Your printout should look similar to Figure 7-18.

Figure 7-18

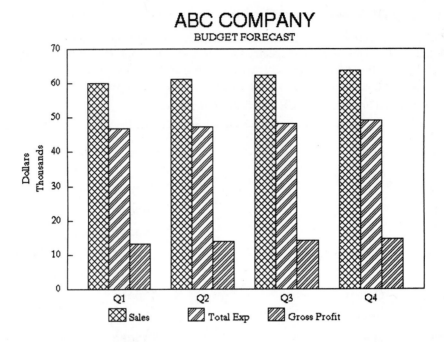

Printing a Graph with Advanced Options (Colors, Fonts, Sizes, and Hatches)

If desired, you can use advanced options to specify colors, fonts, and sizes for various groups of items on a graph when it is printed. There are three groups of graph parameters.

Graph-text Group	Items Included
1	First line of the graph title
2	Second line of the graph title, axes titles, and legend text
3	Scale indicators, axes labels, data labels, and footnotes

There are many possible combinations of colors, fonts, sizes, and hatches that you can select. In this section, you will specify the fonts for the three groups using the default options for your printer. For additional information on these advanced options, see the command reference in the appendix.

Make sure you have the BUDGET worksheet on your screen. Select the BUDBAR named-graph using the **Graph Name Use** command sequence.

You must first specify the fonts desired using the graph menus and then print the graph.

To indicate the font desired for the first graph-text group:

Press	⊏ / ⊐		***Move***	*the mouse pointer to the control panel*
Select	Graph		***Choose***	*Graph*
Select	Options		***Choose***	*Options*

Select	Advanced		*Choose*	*Advanced*
Select	Text		*Choose*	*Text*
Select	First		*Choose*	*First*
Select	Font		*Choose*	*Font*
Select	Default		*Choose*	*Default*
Select	Quit		*Choose*	*Quit*

Note that you can select one of the numbers 1 through 8 instead of the default if you know the fonts that have been assigned to those numbers for your printer.

To specify the font to use with the second graph-text group:

Select	Second		*Choose*	*Second*
Select	Font		*Choose*	*Font*
Select	Default		*Choose*	*Default*
Select	Quit		*Choose*	*Quit*

To define the font to use with the third graph-text group:

Select	Third		*Choose*	*Third*
Select	Font		*Choose*	*Font*
Select	Default		*Choose*	*Default*
Select	Quit		*Choose*	*Quit*

To exit the graph menus:

Select	Quit four times		*Choose*	*Quit four times*

To print the graph with the specified fonts for the graph-text groups:

Press	`/`		*Move*	*the mouse pointer to the control panel*
Select	Print		*Choose*	*Print*
Select	Printer		*Choose*	*Printer*
Select	Image		*Choose*	*Image*
Select	Named-Graph		*Choose*	*Named-Graph*
Select	BUDBAR		*Choose*	*BUDBAR*
Select	Align		*Choose*	*Align*
Select	Go		*Choose*	*Go*
Select	Page		*Choose*	*Page*
Select	Quit		*Choose*	*Quit*

Your printout should be similar to Figure 7-19. The fonts may be different because your set of fonts may be different from those used in preparing this example.

Figure 7-19

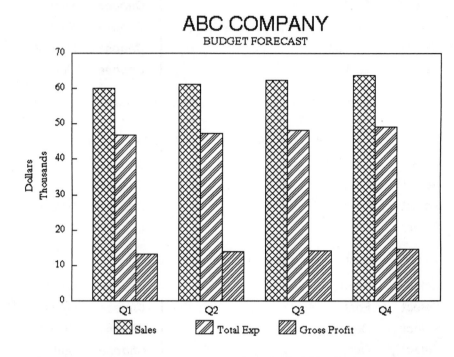

> *User Tip*
>
> If your graph shows solid color bars and you do not have a color plotter, all the bars will print in black. You will need to change the bars to appear as crosshatch patterns.
>
> To change the graph to a black and white image, issue the **Options B&W** command sequence.
>
> You will then need to rename the graph, resave the graph, and resave the worksheet for printing. When the bars appear as cross-hatch patterns, the bars will print properly on a black and white printer.

■ OTHER GRAPH COMMANDS

A summary of commonly used graph commands is included here for your reference. Tasks such as viewing a particular graph, deleting graph settings, and erasing graph files are discussed.

Viewing the Current Graph

Retrieve the BUDGET file for this exercise. It is assumed that the previous exercises in this chapter have been completed. There are two ways to view the current graph in a worksheet.

Press	F10		***Press***	F10
	or			*or*
Press	/		***Move***	*the mouse pointer to the control panel*
Select	Graph		***Choose***	*Graph*
Select	View		***Choose***	*View*

The current graph appears on your screen.

> *User Tip*
> Another alternative for viewing the current graph is to click the Graph View 📖 SmartIcon.

To return to the worksheet after viewing the graph:

Press	←Enter		***Click***	*the mouse button*

To exit the current menu if one appears on your screen:

Select	Quit		***Choose***	*Quit*

Selecting a Graph to View

In order to assign two or more graphs to a worksheet, each graph must be named and saved with the worksheet, just as BUDBAR and BUDLINE were two of the graphs named in the BUDGET file. As an example, you earlier named the bar graph BUDBAR and the line graph BUDLINE. Then you saved the graph specifications and names on the BUDGET file.

To choose the graph to view:

Press	/		***Move***	*the mouse pointer to the control panel*
Select	Graph		***Choose***	*Graph*
Select	Name		***Choose***	*Name*
Select	Use		***Choose***	*Use*
Press	F3 (graph names are listed)		***Press***	*F3 (graph names are listed)*
Move	the pointer to the graph name to view		***Move***	*the mouse pointer to the graph name to view*

In this example, highlight the name BUDBAR. When BUDBAR is highlighted:

Press	←Enter		***Click***	*the mouse button*

The graph will appear on the screen. Your screen should look like Figure 7-20.

Figure 7-20

To return to the worksheet after viewing the graph:

Press   ⌷←Enter⌷ | *Click*   the mouse button

To exit the graph menu:

Select   Quit | *Choose*   Quit

Note: The following steps give further information about graphs and are not part of the exercise. If the exercises are completed, graphs that were created earlier will be erased. This will not cause a problem because the graphs are not used again in this book.

Deleting a Named Graph

To delete a named graph that was saved on a worksheet:

Press   ⌷ / ⌷ | *Move*   the mouse pointer to the control panel

Select   Graph | *Choose*   Graph

Select   Name | *Choose*   Name

Select	Delete	**Choose**	Delete
Move	the pointer to the name of the graph to erase (in this case, BUDLINE)	**Move**	the mouse pointer to the name of the graph to erase (in this case, BUDLINE)
Press	⏎Enter	**Click**	the mouse button

To exit the menu:

Select	Quit	**Choose**	Quit

To delete the graph specifications for BUDLINE from the BUDGET file, you will need to complete the **F**ile **S**ave **R**eplace command sequence for the BUDGET file.

Erasing Graph Files from the Disk

Even if the BUDGET worksheet file is erased from the disk, any files saved as graph files will remain on the disk. To list the graph files on the disk for the current directory:

Press	/	**Move**	the mouse pointer to the control panel
Select	File	**Choose**	File
Select	List	**Choose**	List
Select	Graph	**Choose**	Graph

If there are any graph files in the directory, the graph file names will appear on your screen. If there are none saved, no name will appear on the screen, and you will need to press the ESC key several times to exit the menu structure. Your screen should look like Figure 7-21.

Figure 7-21

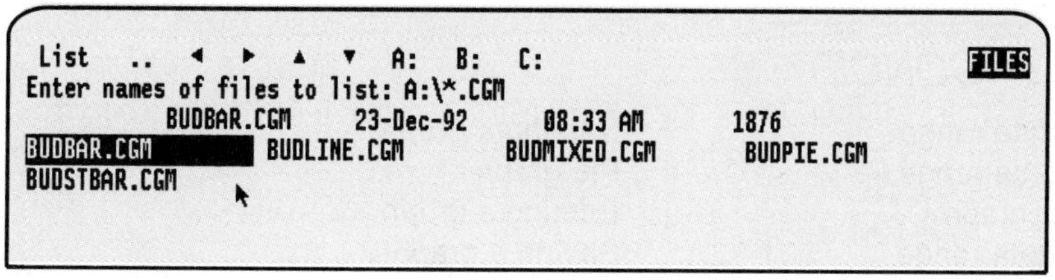

```
List  ..  ◄  ►  ▲  ▼  A:  B:  C:                        FILES
Enter names of files to list: A:\*.CGM
              BUDBAR.CGM    23-Dec-92      08:33 AM      1876
BUDBAR.CGM        BUDLINE.CGM      BUDMIXED.CGM      BUDPIE.CGM
BUDSTBAR.CGM        ▸
```

To return to the worksheet screen:

Press	⏎Enter	**Click**	the mouse button

To erase a graph file:

Press	/	**Move**	the mouse pointer to the control panel

Select	File		***Choose***	*File*
Select	Erase		***Choose***	*Erase*
Select	Graph		***Choose***	*Graph*
Press	F3		***Press***	*F3*

A list of the graph files appears.

Move	the pointer to the graph file to erase (BUDLINE in this case)		***Move***	*the mouse pointer to the graph file to erase (BUDLINE in this case)*
Press	←Enter		***Click***	*the mouse button*

Menu choices of **No** and **Yes** appear. To erase the graph file:

Select	Yes		***Choose***	*Yes*

The graph file has been erased from the disk. To check if the file has been erased, complete the **File List Graph** command sequence again.

SUMMARY

1-2-3 allows you to integrate graphics with worksheets. Creating graphics using worksheet data is easy to do because the data to be graphed does not have to be entered a second time. In fact, if the data on a worksheet are changed and the worksheet is recalculated, the graph reflects the changes in the data the next time the graph is viewed. Graphic representations of data on a worksheet allow you to use graphs as an aid not only in analyzing worksheet data, but in presenting the data to others.

KEY CONCEPTS

A data range
B data range
Bar graph
C data range
D data range
E data range
F data range
Graph
Legend
Line graph
Mixed graph

Naming a graph
Pie graph
Printing a graph
Saving a graph
Stacked-bar graph
Titles
Type of graph
Viewing a graph
X-axis
XY graph
Y-axis

EXERCISE 1

INSTRUCTIONS: Circle T if the statement is true and F if the statement is false.

T   F   1.   A Lotus 1-2-3 graph can contain up to six different data ranges.

T   F   2.   To change a bar graph into a line graph, change the **G**raph **T**ype from **B**ar to **L**ine.

T   F   3.   If numbers are changed on the spreadsheet, the graph will reflect the changes when the graph is viewed again on the screen.

T   F   4.   If numbers are changed on the spreadsheet, the changes will be automatically reflected on any graph file that was previously created from the worksheet.

T   F   5.   It is possible to create three completely different graphs with data from one worksheet.

T   F   6.   If **F**ile **S**ave is not executed after a graph is made, the graph settings will not be saved.

T   F   7.   If a computer is not configured to show graphics on the screen, it is not possible to create and print a Lotus 1-2-3 graph.

T   F   8.   A color graph on the screen displays the colors in which the graph will be printed on a color printer or plotter.

T   F   9.   A pie graph displays the data in data range A.

T   F   10.   An XY graph is different from other Lotus graphs because it includes data for variable X.

EXERCISE 2

INSTRUCTIONS: Explain a typical situation when the following keystrokes or Lotus 1-2-3 commands are used.

Problem 1:   ☐ **G**raph **A**

Problem 2:   ☐ **G**raph **N**ame **U**se

Problem 3:   ☐ **G**raph **V**iew

Problem 4:   ☐ **G**raph **N**ame **C**reate

Problem 5:   ☐ **G**raph **O**ptions **L**egends

Problem 6:   ☐ **G**raph **O**ptions **T**itles

Problem 7:   ☐ **G**raph **O**ptions **D**ata-Labels

Problem 8:   ☐ **G**raph **T**ype **P**ie

EXERCISE 3 — Creating a Bar Graph

INSTRUCTIONS: Retrieve the PRACTICE file.

Create a bar graph that includes Revenue, Expenses, and Profit Before Tax for 5 years as the graph ranges.

Include the Year 1 through Year 5 captions on the X-axis.

Place legend and title information on the graph.

Name and save the graph using the name PROFIT.

Print the graph.

Save the PRACTICE file.

EXERCISE 4 — Creating a Stacked-Bar Graph

INSTRUCTIONS: Retrieve the PRACTICE file.

Create a stacked-bar graph for the Revenue, Profit Before Tax, and Profit After Tax data for the five-year period.

Include appropriate information for the X-axis range, legends, and graph titles.

Name and save the graph using the name PROFSTBR.

Print the graph.

Save the PRACTICE file.

EXERCISE 5 — Creating a Pie Graph

INSTRUCTIONS: Retrieve the SALES file.

Create a pie graph using the data for the individual salespersons.

Place appropriate titles on the graph.

Name and save the graph using the name SALESPCT.

Print the graph.

Save the SALES file.

EXERCISE 6 — Creating a Mixed Graph

INSTRUCTIONS: Retrieve the PRACTICE file.

Create a mixed graph using Profit Before Tax and Profit After Tax values for the five-year period.

The Profit After Tax values should appear as bars and the Profit Before Tax amounts should appear as a line.

Place appropriate title, legend, and X-axis range information on the graph.

Name and save the graph using the name MIXED.

Print the graph.

Save the PRACTICE file.

EXERCISE 7 — Creating an XY Graph

INSTRUCTIONS: Create the worksheet displayed in Figure 7-22. Make sure you include information for the identification; map of spreadsheet; description, assumptions, and parameters; and spreadsheet model blocks in rows 1 through 40.

Figure 7-22

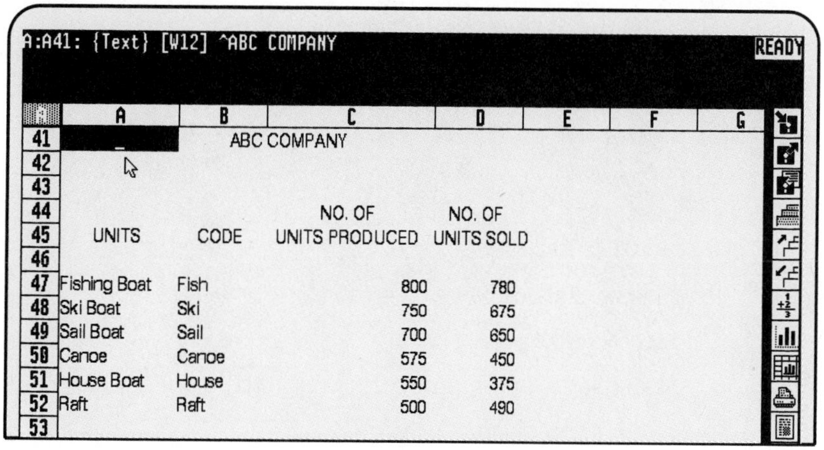

```
A:A41: {Text} [W12] ^ABC COMPANY                                    READY
```

	A	B	C	D	E	F	G
41	_		ABC COMPANY				
42							
43							
44			NO. OF	NO. OF			
45	UNITS	CODE	UNITS PRODUCED	UNITS SOLD			
46							
47	Fishing Boat	Fish	800	780			
48	Ski Boat	Ski	750	675			
49	Sail Boat	Sail	700	650			
50	Canoe	Canoe	575	450			
51	House Boat	House	550	375			
52	Raft	Raft	500	490			
53							

Create an XY graph using the number of units produced as the X item and the number of units sold as the Y item.

Include the code information on the graph to the right of each point to identify the points.

Place appropriate title, X-axis, and Y-axis information on the graph.

Name and save the graph using the name XYGRAPH.

Print the graph.

Save the file using the name XYGRAPH.

CHAPTER EIGHT

ADDITIONAL GRAPH TOPICS

OBJECTIVES

- Create a high-low-close-open-graph
- Create an area graph
- Use special features with various types of graphs
- Use the Graph Group feature
- Display a graph in a window

■ CHAPTER OVERVIEW

In the previous chapter, the basics of creating graphs were covered. The processes for preparing bar, line, mixed, XY, pie, and stacked-bar graphs were illustrated. This chapter includes instructions for completing high-low-close-open, area, and 3-D graphs. Additional useful commands associated with graphs are also discussed.

Since the problems in this chapter are small, the documentation to include for proper spreadsheet design is omitted.

■ CREATING A HIGH-LOW-CLOSE-OPEN GRAPH

Many individuals who use 1-2-3 may have investments in stocks and bonds. The **high-low-close-open** (HLCO) graph provides a convenient way to track prices.

Suppose you are given the information in Figure 8-1.

Figure 8-1

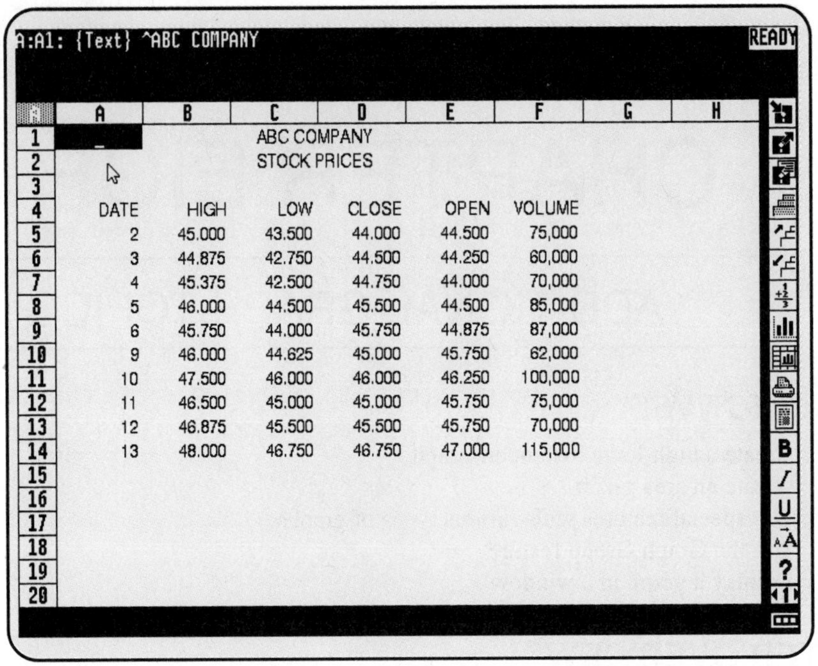

Assume that you have purchased some ABC Company stock, and desire to follow the price of the stock using an HLCO graph.

Before creating the graph, you will need to construct a worksheet like the one in Figure 8-1. After you finish the worksheet, save the worksheet using the file name ABCHLCO.

To create the HLCO graph:

Press	/		***Move***	*the mouse pointer to the control panel*
Select	Graph		***Choose***	*Graph*
Select	Type		***Choose***	*Type*
Select	HLCO		***Choose***	*HLCO*

The following table indicates what information to place in the various data ranges:

Data Range	Item
X	Date
A	High price for the date
B	Low price for the date
C	Closing price for the date
D	Opening price for the date
E	Volume of stock traded

To enter the DATES in the X data range:

Select	X		*Choose*	*X*
Highlight	cells A5 through A14		*Highlight*	*cells A5 through A14*
Press	⏎Enter		*Click*	*the mouse button*

To enter the HIGH prices for the dates in the A data range:

Select	A		*Choose*	*A*
Highlight	cells B5 through B14		*Highlight*	*cells B5 through B14*
Press	⏎Enter		*Click*	*the mouse button*

To place the LOW prices for the dates in the B data range:

Select	B		*Choose*	*B*
Highlight	cells C5 through C14		*Highlight*	*cells C5 through C14*
Press	⏎Enter		*Click*	*the mouse button*

To specify the CLOSE prices for the dates in the C data range:

Select	C		*Choose*	*C*
Highlight	cells D5 through D14		*Highlight*	*cells D5 through D14*
Press	⏎Enter		*Click*	*the mouse button*

To enter the OPEN prices for the dates in the D data range:

Select	D		*Choose*	*D*
Highlight	cells E5 through E14		*Highlight*	*cells E5 through E14*
Press	⏎Enter		*Click*	*the mouse button*

To place the VOLUME dates in the E data range:

Select	E		*Choose*	*E*
Highlight	cells F5 through F14		*Highlight*	*cells F5 through F14*
Press	⏎Enter		*Click*	*the mouse button*

To view the HLCO graph:

Select	View		*Choose*	*View*

Your screen should look similar to Figure 8-2.

Figure 8-2

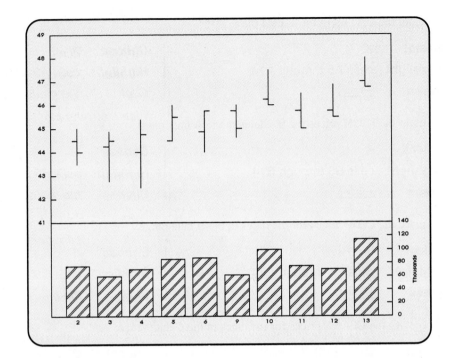

Notice that the Y-axis represents the stock prices and a vertical line is drawn for each date. The highest point on the line is the high price for that date. Likewise, the lowest point on the line is the lowest price. The left tick mark on each line represents the opening price. The right tick mark indicates the closing price. At the bottom of the graph the volume data are drawn. The second Y-axis is used to indicate the scale for the volume.

To return to the worksheet:

| **Press** | ←Enter | | ***Click*** | *the mouse button* |

To specify the graph titles:

Select	Options		***Choose***	*Options*
Select	Titles		***Choose***	*Titles*
Select	First		***Choose***	*First*
Type	ABC COMPANY		***Type***	*ABC COMPANY*
Press	←Enter		***Click***	*the mouse button*
Select	Titles		***Choose***	*Titles*
Select	Second		***Choose***	*Second*
Type	STOCK PRICES		***Type***	*STOCK PRICES*
Press	←Enter		***Click***	*the mouse button*

To specify DATE as the X-axis title:

Select	Titles		*Choose*	*Titles*
Select	X-Axis		*Choose*	*X-Axis*
Type	DATE		*Type*	*DATE*
Press	⏎Enter		*Click*	*the mouse button*

To indicate that PRICE is the Y-axis title:

Select	Titles		*Choose*	*Titles*
Select	Y-Axis		*Choose*	*Y-Axis*
Type	PRICE		*Type*	*PRICE*
Press	⏎Enter		*Click*	*the mouse button*

To denote that VOLUME is the title for the second Y-axis:

Select	Titles		*Choose*	*Titles*
Select	2Y-Axis		*Choose*	*2Y-Axis*
Type	VOLUME		*Type*	*VOLUME*
Press	⏎Enter		*Click*	*the mouse button*

To place a footnote on the graph:

Select	Titles		*Choose*	*Titles*
Select	Note		*Choose*	*Note*
Type	Prepared on February 14		*Type*	*Prepared on February 14*
Press	⏎Enter		*Click*	*the mouse button*
Select	Titles		*Choose*	*Titles*
Select	Other-Note		*Choose*	*Other-Note*
Type	YOUR NAME (insert your name here)		*Type*	*YOUR NAME (insert your name here)*
Press	⏎Enter		*Click*	*the mouse button*

To view the HLCO graph at this point:

Select	Quit		*Choose*	*Quit*
Select	View		*Choose*	*View*

Your screen should look like Figure 8-3.

Figure 8-3

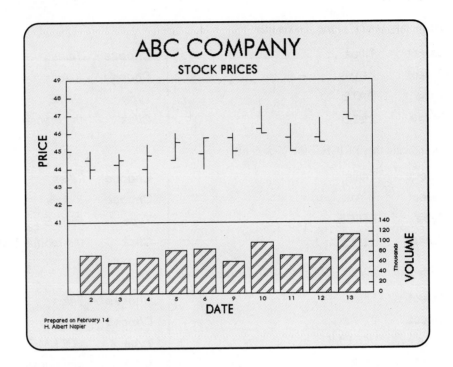

To return to the worksheet:

Press	←Enter		*Click*	*the mouse button*

To format the Y-axis to include a $ sign by each price:

Select	Options		*Choose*	*Options*
Select	Scale		*Choose*	*Scale*
Select	Y-Scale		*Choose*	*Y-Scale*
Select	Format		*Choose*	*Format*
Select	Currency		*Choose*	*Currency*

When prompted for the number of decimal places:

Type	0		*Type*	*0*
Press	←Enter		*Click*	*the mouse button*
Select	Quit		*Choose*	*Quit*
Select	Quit		*Choose*	*Quit*

To view the completed graph:

Select	View		*Choose*	*View*

Your screen should look similar to Figure 8-4.

Figure 8-4

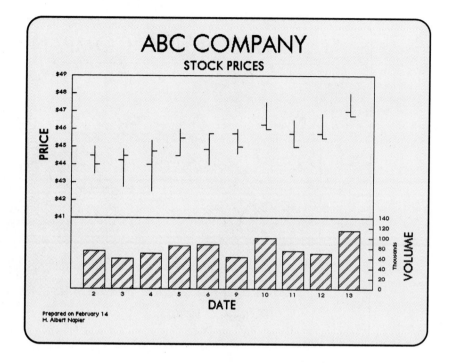

To return to the worksheet:

Press   [←Enter] | *Click*   the mouse button

To exit the graph menus:

Select   Quit | *Choose*   Quit

It is important to save the HLCO graph for future use. Recall from Chapter 7 that protecting a graph is a three-part process: (1) Name the graph ABCHLCO using the Name Create command sequence. (2) Using the same name, ABCHLCO, save the graph using the Save command sequence. Remember that it will be saved separately from the worksheet with a "CGM" extension and is nothing more than a picture of the graph. (3) Save and replace the existing worksheet using the **F**ile **S**ave **R**eplace command sequence. This will protect the graph settings in the spreadsheet.

■ CREATING AN AREA GRAPH

One additional graph option available that can be very useful is the capability to fill the **area** between the items included in a line graph.

When you finish this exercise, you will have completed a graph that looks like the one in Figure 8-5.

Figure 8-5

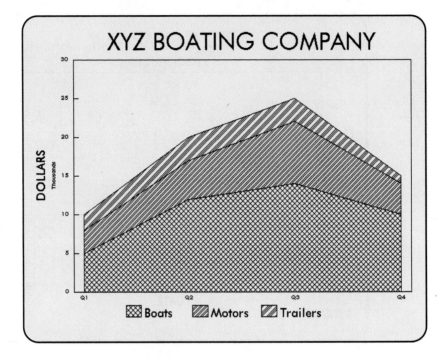

Retrieve the BOATSALE file for this exercise.

To specify the type of graph:

Press	⟋		**Move**	the mouse pointer to the control panel
Select	Graph		**Choose**	Graph
Select	Type		**Choose**	Type
Select	Line		**Choose**	Line

To indicate the data ranges:

Select	X		**Choose**	X
Highlight	cells B3 through E3		**Highlight**	cells B3 through E3
Press	←Enter		**Click**	the mouse button
Select	A		**Choose**	A
Highlight	cells B5 through E5		**Highlight**	cells B5 through E5
Press	←Enter		**Click**	the mouse button
Select	B		**Choose**	B

Highlight	cells B6 through E6		*Highlight*	*cells B6 through E6*
Press	`←Enter`		*Click*	*the mouse button*
Select	C		*Choose*	*C*
Highlight	cells B7 through E7		*Highlight*	*cells B7 through E7*
Press	`←Enter`		*Click*	*the mouse button*

To view the graph:

Select	View		*Choose*	*View*

A line graph should appear on your screen and look like Figure 8-6.

Figure 8-6

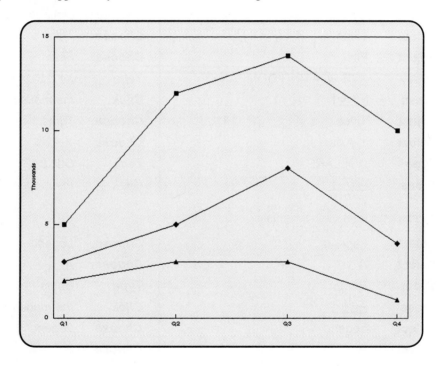

To return to the main graph menu:

Press	`←Enter`		*Click*	*the mouse button*

To delineate the data that are being graphed more effectively by filling the areas between the lines:

Select	Options		*Choose*	*Options*
Select	Format		*Choose*	*Format*
Select	Graph		*Choose*	*Graph*

Select	Area		*Choose*	*Area*

To view the line graph with the areas filled:

Select	Quit twice		*Choose*	*Quit twice*
Select	View		*Choose*	*View*

To return to the graph menu:

Press	`←Enter`		*Click*	*the mouse button*

To complete the graph by placing titles and legends on it:

Select	Options		*Choose*	*Options*
Select	Titles		*Choose*	*Titles*
Select	First		*Choose*	*First*
Type	XYZ BOATING COMPANY		*Type*	*XYZ BOATING COMPANY*
Press	`←Enter`		*Click*	*the mouse button*
Select	Titles		*Choose*	*Titles*
Select	Y-Axis		*Choose*	*Y-Axis*
Type	DOLLARS		*Type*	*DOLLARS*
Press	`←Enter`		*Click*	*the mouse button*

To place the legends on the graph:

Select	Legend		*Choose*	*Legend*
Select	A		*Choose*	*A*
Type	Boats		*Type*	*Boats*
Press	`←Enter`		*Click*	*the mouse button*
Select	Legend		*Choose*	*Legend*
Select	B		*Choose*	*B*
Type	Motors		*Type*	*Motors*
Press	`←Enter`		*Click*	*the mouse button*
Select	Legend		*Choose*	*Legend*
Select	C		*Choose*	*C*
Type	Trailers		*Type*	*Trailers*
Press	`←Enter`		*Click*	*the mouse button*

To view the completed graph:

Select	Quit		***Choose***	*Quit*
Select	View		***Choose***	*View*

Your screen should look like Figure 8-7.

Figure 8-7

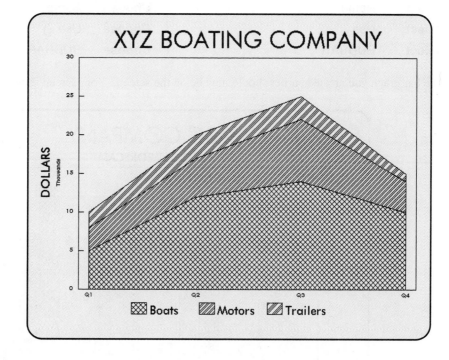

To return to the worksheet and exit the graph menus:

Press	⏎Enter		***Click***	*the mouse button*
Select	Quit		***Choose***	*Quit*

It is important to save the area graph for future use. Name the graph BOATSALE using the **Name Create** command sequence. Using the same name, BOATSALE, save the graph using the **Save** command sequence. Save and replace the existing worksheet using the **File Save Replace** command sequence.

■ USING SPECIAL FEATURES WITH VARIOUS TYPES OF GRAPHS

Specifying a 3-D Effect for a Bar Graph

There are several features that can be used with the various types of graphs available in 1-2-3. For example, you can have 3-D effects on bar graphs. You can also print bar and stacked bar graphs with a horizontal orientation.

In some situations, you may want to have a 3-D effect on a bar graph. To select the bar graph you saved in Chapter 7, first retrieve the BUDGET file, and then:

Press	⬚ /		***Move***	*the mouse pointer to the control panel*
Select	Graph		***Choose***	*Graph*
Select	Name		***Choose***	*Name*
Select	Use		***Choose***	*Use*
Select	BUDBAR		***Choose***	*BUDBAR*

The bar graph you created earlier should now be on the screen. Your screen should look like Figure 8-8.

Figure 8-8

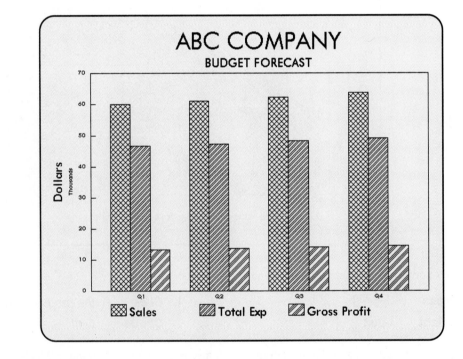

To return to the worksheet and main graph menu:

Press	←Enter		***Click***	*the mouse button*

To use the 3D-effect feature:

Select	Type		***Choose***	*Type*
Select	Features		***Choose***	*Features*

Select	3D	**Choose**	*3D*
Select	Yes	**Choose**	*Yes*

To view the graph:

Select	Quit	**Choose**	*Quit*
Select	View	**Choose**	*View*

The graph now has a 3-D effect on the bars. Your screen should look like Figure 8-9.

Figure 8-9

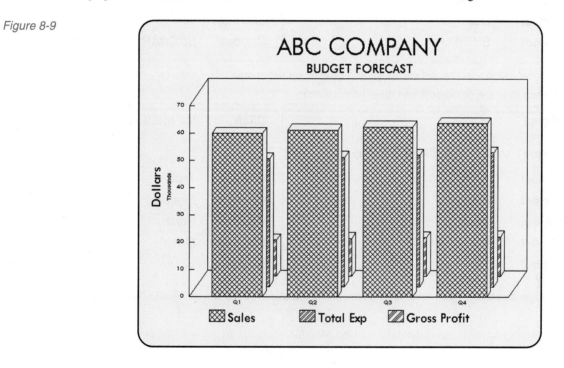

To return to the worksheet and exit the graph menus:

Press		**Click**	*the mouse button*
Select	Quit	**Choose**	*Quit*

Do not save any changes.

Specifying a Horizontal Orientation for a Bar Graph

In 1-2-3, the default orientation for bar graphs is vertical. In some situations, you may want to display a bar graph **horizontally**. To select the bar graph you created earlier, first retrieve the BUDGET file and then:

Press	⌐ /		***Move***	*the mouse pointer to the control panel*
Select	Graph		***Choose***	*Graph*
Select	Name		***Choose***	*Name*
Select	Use		***Choose***	*Use*
Select	BUDBAR		***Choose***	*BUDBAR*

The bar graph you created earlier should now be on the screen.

To return to the worksheet and main graph menu:

Press	←Enter		***Click***	*the mouse button*

To use a horizontal or sideways display orientation:

Select	Type		***Choose***	*Type*
Select	Features		***Choose***	*Features*
Select	Horiz		***Choose***	*Horiz*
Select	Quit		***Choose***	*Quit*
Select	View		***Choose***	*View*

Notice the change from vertical to horizontal orientation. Your screen should look like Figure 8-10.

Figure 8-10

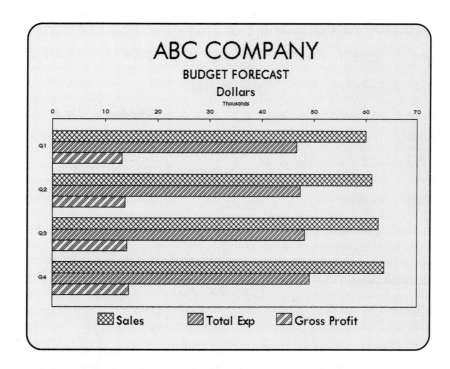

To return to the worksheet and exit the graph menus:

Press	⎵Enter		***Click***	*the mouse button*
Select	Quit		***Choose***	*Quit*

Do not save any changes.

Specifying a Horizontal Orientation for a Stacked-Bar Graph

In 1-2-3, the default orientation for stacked-bar graphs is vertical. In some situations, you may want to display a stacked-bar graph horizontally.

To select the stacked-bar graph you created in Chapter 7, first retrieve the BUDGET file, and then:

Press	/		***Move***	*the mouse pointer to the control panel*
Select	Graph		***Choose***	*Graph*
Select	Name		***Choose***	*Name*
Select	Use		***Choose***	*Use*
Select	BUDSTBAR		***Choose***	*BUDSTBAR*

The stacked-bar graph you created earlier should now be on the screen.

To return to the worksheet and main graph menu:

| **Press** | [←Enter] | | *Click* | *the mouse button* |

To use a horizontal or sideways display orientation:

Select	Type		*Choose*	*Type*
Select	Features		*Choose*	*Features*
Select	Horiz		*Choose*	*Horiz*
Select	Quit		*Choose*	*Quit*
Select	View		*Choose*	*View*

Notice the change from vertical to horizontal orientation. Your screen should look like Figure 8-11.

Figure 8-11

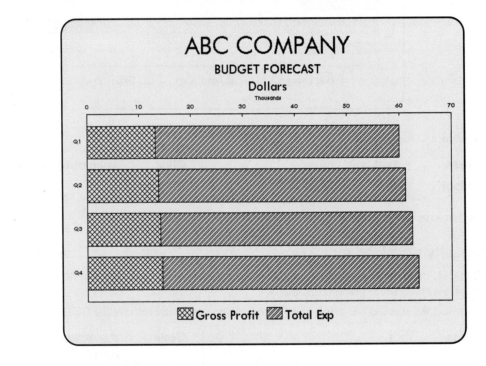

To return to the worksheet and exit the graph menus:

| **Press** | [←Enter] | | *Click* | *the mouse button* |
| **Select** | Quit | | *Choose* | *Quit* |

Do not save any changes.

Specifying the Appearance of the Graph Frame

The default condition for the frame on a graph is to include a frame. In some situations, you may want to omit a portion or the entire frame of a graph. To delete the frame from the bar graph you created earlier, retrieve the BUDGET file, and then:

Press	☐ /		*Move*	*the mouse pointer to the control panel*
Select	Graph		*Choose*	*Graph*
Select	Name		*Choose*	*Name*
Select	Use		*Choose*	*Use*
Select	BUDBAR		*Choose*	*BUDBAR*

The bar graph you created earlier should now be on your screen.

To return to the main graph menu:

Press	←Enter		*Click*	*the mouse button*

To omit the frame and view the graph:

Select	Type		*Choose*	*Type*
Select	Features		*Choose*	*Features*
Select	Frame		*Choose*	*Frame*
Select	None		*Choose*	*None*
Select	Quit		*Choose*	*Quit*
Select	View		*Choose*	*View*

Your screen should look like Figure 8-12.

Figure 8-12

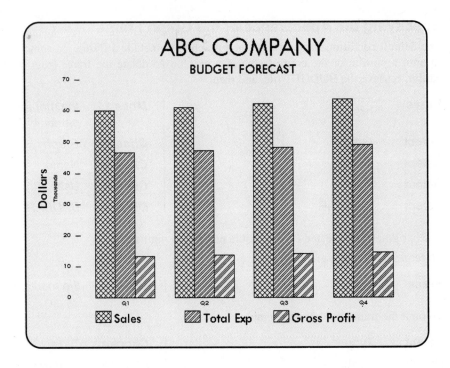

To return to the worksheet and exit the graph menus:

Press	←Enter		***Click***	*the mouse button*
Select	Quit		***Choose***	*Quit*

Do not save any changes.

Removing the Scale Indicator from a Graph

In some situations, you may want to remove the **scale indicator**.

Retrieve the BUDGET file for use in this exercise.

To pick a graph for use:

Press	/		***Move***	*the mouse pointer to the control panel*
Select	Graph		***Choose***	*Graph*
Select	Name		***Choose***	*Name*
Select	Use		***Choose***	*Use*
Select	BUDBAR		***Choose***	*BUDBAR*

On the Y-scale the word (**Thousands**) is displayed as the scale indicator as shown in Figure 8-13.

Figure 8-13

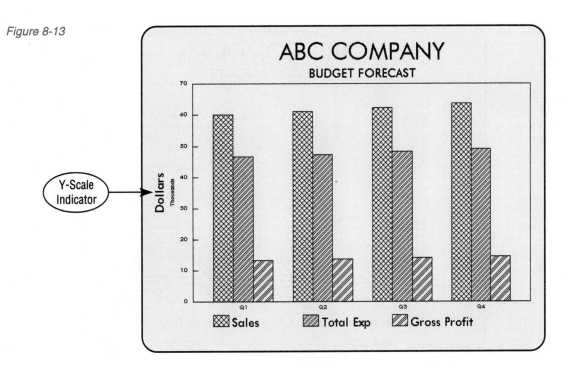

To return to the worksheet:

Press	⏎Enter	*Click*	*the mouse button*

To remove the indicator from the Y-scale, select the following menu options:

Select	Options	*Choose*	*Options*
Select	Scale	*Choose*	*Scale*
Select	Y-Scale	*Choose*	*Y-Scale*
Select	Indicator	*Choose*	*Indicator*
Select	None	*Choose*	*None*

To view the graph:

Select	Quit twice	*Choose*	*Quit twice*
Select	View	*Choose*	*View*

The Y-scale indicator no longer appears on the graph, and your screen should look like Figure 8-14.

Figure 8-14

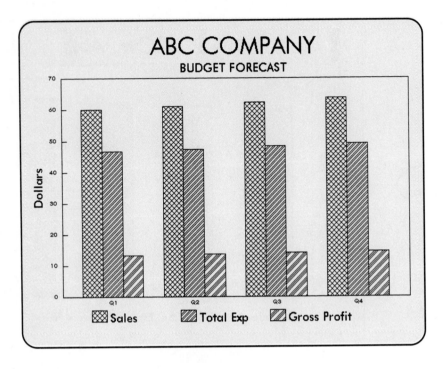

To return to the worksheet after viewing the graph, and exit the graph menus:

Press	⟵Enter		**Click**	*the mouse button*
Select	Quit		**Choose**	*Quit*

Do not save any changes.

■ USING THE GRAPH GROUP FEATURE

In the previous section, you created graphs by specifying the type of graph and the individual data ranges to include on the graph.

Another way to quickly create a graph is through the **Graph Group** command sequence. If you use this option, the data ranges X and A through F are specified simultaneously. The X and A through F ranges must be in consecutive rows or columns in a range. When you finish this section, a graph like the one in Figure 8-17 will be displayed on your screen.

Before creating the graph, prepare the worksheet in Figure 8-15 and save it using the file name AUTOMATI.

Figure 8-15

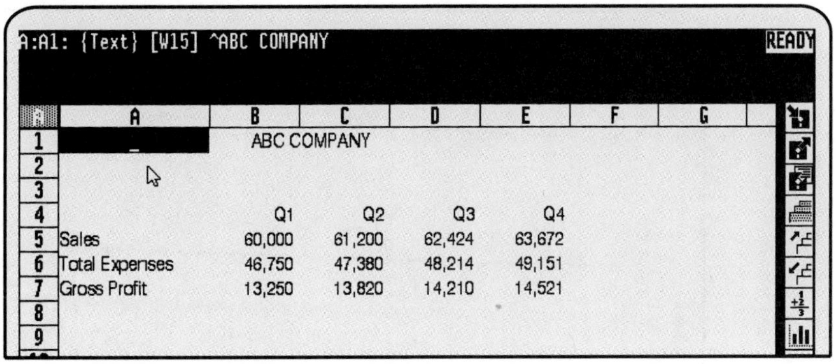

Selecting Graph Data Ranges

To create a graph using the **group graphing** option:

Press	☐/☐		***Move***	*the mouse pointer to the control panel*
Select	Graph		***Choose***	*Graph*
Select	Group		***Choose***	*Group*

To enter the group range of cells:

Highlight	cell B4 through E7		***Highlight***	*cells B4 through E7*
Press	⏎Enter		***Click***	*the mouse button*

To specify that rows are to be used as the data ranges:

Select	Rowwise		***Choose***	*Rowwise*

You have indicated that the X data range consists of cells B4 through E4 (Q1 through Q4). You have also specified that the A, B, and C data ranges include the data for Sales, Total Expenses, and Gross Profit respectively.

To view the graph you have created:

Select	View		***Choose***	*View*

Your screen should look like Figure 8-16.

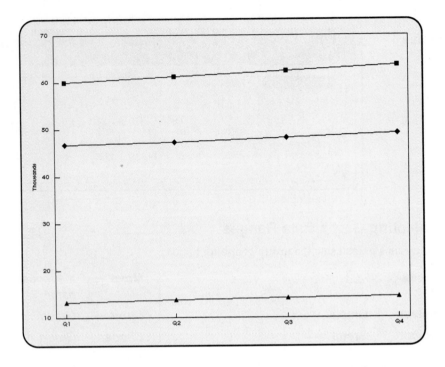

Figure 8-16

To return to the graph menu:

Press   ←Enter | **Click**   *the mouse button*

Notice that since you did not indicate the type of graph to draw, 1-2-3 defaults to the line graph option.

User Tip

An alternative method for creating a group graph is to first highlight the range of cells to graph. Then click the Quick Graph SmartIcon. The QuickGraph Settings dialog box appears. Select the Rows option and then click the OK command button. A graph appears on your screen.

Selecting a Group of Graph Legends

To indicate the legends in one step:

Select Options | **Choose** *Options*
Select Legend | **Choose** *Legend*
Select Range | **Choose** *Range*

Highlight	cells A5 through A7		*Highlight*	*cells A5 through A7*
Press	⏎Enter		*Click*	*the mouse button*

To leave the graph options menu and view the graph:

Select	Quit		*Choose*	*Quit*
Select	View		*Choose*	*View*

Your screen should look like Figure 8-17.

Figure 8-17

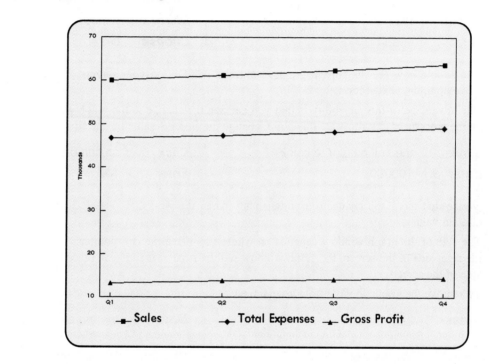

To return to the graph menu:

Press	⏎Enter		*Click*	*the mouse button*

To exit the graph menu:

Select	Quit		*Choose*	*Quit*

Save the AUTOMATI file.

■ DISPLAYING A GRAPH IN A WINDOW

You can display a graph on the screen along with a worksheet if you are using a high resolution monitor or a monochrome monitor with a graphics card. To include the current graph on the BUDGET spreadsheet, first retrieve the file BUDGET. Then you need to complete the following steps:

Move	the cell pointer to cell D41		*Click*	*on cell D41*
Press	/		*Move*	*the mouse pointer to the control panel*
Select	Worksheet		*Choose*	*Worksheet*
Select	Window		*Choose*	*Window*
Select	Graph		*Choose*	*Graph*

You should now see the current graph in a graph window on your screen. If you cannot see a graph, move on to the next section.

One advantage of this capability is that you can see the change in the graph when you change a number on the worksheet. To illustrate this point, change the SALES value for the first quarter to 100,000:

Move	the cell pointer to cell B47		*Click*	*on cell B47*
Enter	100000		*Enter*	*100000*

Notice that the graph changed instantaneously when the worksheet was recalculated based on the new SALES values.

The size of the graph window depends on where you place the cell pointer. If you place it in a cell on the right side of the screen, the graph window will be smaller than if you place the cell pointer on the left side of the screen.

To remove the graph window from your screen:

Press	/		*Move*	*the mouse pointer to the control panel*
Select	Worksheet		*Choose*	*Worksheet*
Select	Window		*Choose*	*Window*
Select	Clear		*Choose*	*Clear*

Do not save any changes.

SUMMARY

1-2-3 allows you to prepare high-low-close-open graphs, area graphs, and various types of 3D graphs. The orientation for a graph can be horizontal or vertical. The scale indicator can be removed. Group graphing is available for efficiently creating graphs for data in contiguous cells.

KEY CONCEPTS

3D
Area graph
Group graphing
High-low-close-open graph
Horizontal bar graph
Horizontal stacked-bar graph
Scale indicator

EXERCISE 1

INSTRUCTIONS: Circle T if the statement is true and F if the statement is false.

T   F   1.   High-low-close-open graphs cannot be created using 1-2-3.

T   F   2.   The Y-scale indicator can be changed.

T   F   3.   The default orientation for a graph is always horizontal.

T   F   4.   An area graph provides a convenient way to track prices and sales volumes for stocks and bonds.

T   F   5.   1-2-3 has the capability of filling the area between the items included in a line graph.

EXERCISE 2 — Creating a High-Low-Close-Open Graph

INSTRUCTIONS: Create the worksheet displayed in Figure 8-18.

Figure 8-18

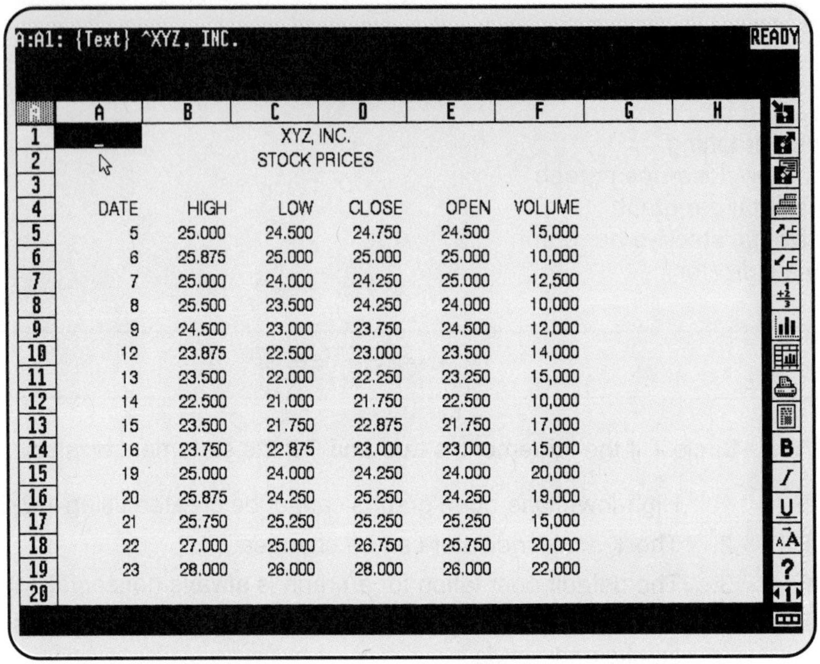

A:A1: {Text} ^XYZ, INC. READY

	A	B	C	D	E	F	G	H
1			XYZ, INC.					
2			STOCK PRICES					
3								
4	DATE	HIGH	LOW	CLOSE	OPEN	VOLUME		
5	5	25.000	24.500	24.750	24.500	15,000		
6	6	25.875	25.000	25.000	25.000	10,000		
7	7	25.000	24.000	24.250	25.000	12,500		
8	8	25.500	23.500	24.250	24.000	10,000		
9	9	24.500	23.000	23.750	24.500	12,000		
10	12	23.875	22.500	23.000	23.500	14,000		
11	13	23.500	22.000	22.250	23.250	15,000		
12	14	22.500	21.000	21.750	22.500	10,000		
13	15	23.500	21.750	22.875	21.750	17,000		
14	16	23.750	22.875	23.000	23.000	15,000		
15	19	25.000	24.000	24.250	24.000	20,000		
16	20	25.875	24.250	25.250	24.250	19,000		
17	21	25.750	25.250	25.250	25.250	15,000		
18	22	27.000	25.000	26.750	25.750	20,000		
19	23	28.000	26.000	28.000	26.000	22,000		
20								

Create a high-low-close-open graph for the stock price data of XYZ, Inc.

Include appropriate documentation on the graph.

Name and save the graph using the name XYZHLCO.

Save the worksheet using the file name XYZHLCO.

Print the graph.

EXERCISE 3 — Creating a Bar Graph with 3-D Effects

INSTRUCTIONS: Retrieve the PRACTICE file.

Use the bar graph PROFIT completed in Exercise 3 in Chapter 7 to create a bar graph with a 3-D effect.

Name and save the graph using the name PROFIT3D.

Save the PRACTICE file.

Print the graph.

EXERCISE 4 — Creating a Bar Graph with Horizontal Orientation

INSTRUCTIONS: Retrieve the PRACTICE file.

Use the bar graph PROFIT completed in Exercise 3 in Chapter 7 to create a bar graph with horizontal orientation.

Name and save the graph using the name PROFITHO.

Save the PRACTICE file.

Print the graph.

EXERCISE 5 — Creating a Stacked-Bar Graph with Horizontal Orientation

INSTRUCTIONS: Retrieve the PRACTICE file.

Use the stacked-bar graph PROFSTBR completed in Exercise 4 in Chapter 7 to create a stacked-bar graph with horizontal orientation.

Name and save the graph using the name PROFSBHO.

Save the PRACTICE file.

Print the graph.

EXERCISE 6 — Creating a Line Graph

INSTRUCTIONS: Retrieve the PRACTICE file.

Create a line graph that includes Revenue, Expenses, and Profit Before Tax for 5 years as the graph ranges.

Include the YEAR1 through YEAR5 captions on the X-axis.

Place legend and title information on the graph.

Name and save the graph using the name PROFLINE.

Save the PRACTICE file.

Print the graph.

EXERCISE 7 — Creating an Area Graph

INSTRUCTIONS: Retrieve the PRACTICE file.

Use the line graph PROFLINE completed in Exercise 6 to create an area graph.

Name and save the graph using the name PROFAREA.

Save the PRACTICE file.

Print the graph.

CHAPTER NINE

ENHANCING THE APPEARANCE OF A GRAPH

OBJECTIVES

In this chapter, you will learn to:

- Add a graph to a worksheet
- Edit a graphic
- Size and move a graphic
- Print a worksheet and graph in Wysiwyg
- Add text and graphic objects to a graph

■ CHAPTER OVERVIEW

In some situations, you may need to change the appearance of a graph you create in 1-2-3. With options available in 1-2-3, text and graphic objects can be added to a graph. You can change the fonts and appearance of text in a graph. You can also edit, size, and move a graphic.

■ USING WYSIWYG TO IMPROVE THE APPEARANCE OF A GRAPH

By using Wysiwyg, you can enhance the appearance of a graph. In this section, you will improve the appearance of the BUDBAR graph you prepared in Chapter 7. Retrieve the BUDGET worksheet you created in Chapter 4 and make sure BUDBAR is the current graph.

Adding a Graph to a Worksheet

A graph can be included on a worksheet. You specify the size of the graph by highlighting a range of cells. Then you add the graph to the worksheet.

To add the graph BUDBAR to your worksheet:

Highlight	cells A70 through F89		***Highlight***	*cell A70 through F89*
Press	:		***Move***	*the mouse pointer to the control panel*

Select	Graph		***Click***	*the alternate mouse button until the Wysiwyg menu appears*
Select	Add		***Choose***	*Graph*
Select	Current		***Choose***	*Add*
			Choose	*Current*

The **Graph** command lets you add the current or other named graph to a worksheet.

To exit the Graph menu:

Select	Quit		***Choose***	*Quit*

After making row 70 the first row on your screen, your screen should look like Figure 9-1.

Figure 9-1

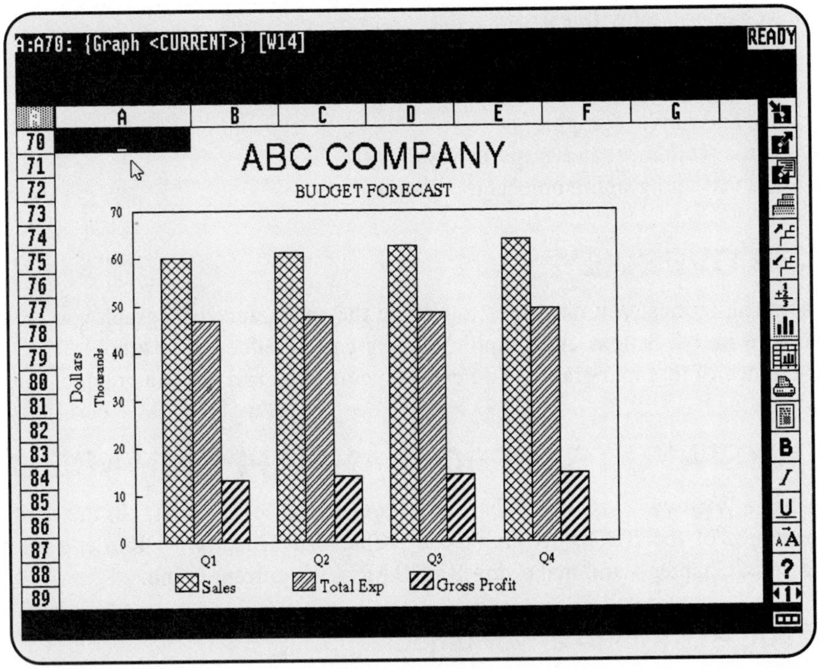

Note that Wysiwyg adjusts the size of your graph to fit in the graph range that you specified.

User Tip

An alternative method for adding the current graph to a worksheet is to first highlight the range in which the graph is to appear. Then click the Add Graph ⊞ SmartIcon. The current graph is then displayed in the designated range on your worksheet.

Editing a Graphic

Before you can change any graphic details, you must move the graphic to the **graphics editing window**. The graphics editing window displays the graphic on a full screen in which you can edit and enhance the graphic.

An **object** is any text, geometric shape, or freehand drawing that you add to a graphic. You must select an object before you can edit it. The Select menu option allows you to select an object. When you select an object, small filled squares called **selection indicators** appear around the object.

When you move or size an object, a boundary box appears around the object. The **boundary box** is used by Wysiwyg to outline each object you add to a graphic. The boundary boxes do not print.

To move the graph to the graphics editing window:

Highlight	cells A70 through F89		*Highlight*	*cell A70 through F89*
Press	☐ : ☐		*Move*	*the mouse pointer to the control panel*
Select	Graph		*Choose*	*Graph*
Select	Edit		*Choose*	*Edit*

Your screen should look like Figure 9-2.

Figure 9-2

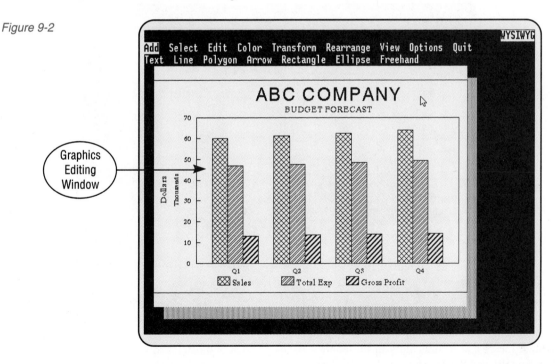

Graphics Editing Window

To add text above Q1:

Select	Add		***Choose***	*Add*
Select	Text		***Choose***	*Text*
Type	Actual		***Type***	*Actual*
Press	←Enter		***Click***	*the mouse button*

To place the text:

Press	the pointer-movement keys so **"Actual"** is centered above the three bars for Q1		***Move***	*the mouse pointer so* ***"Actual"*** *is centered above the three bar for Q1*

Your screen should look like Figure 9-3.

Figure 9-3

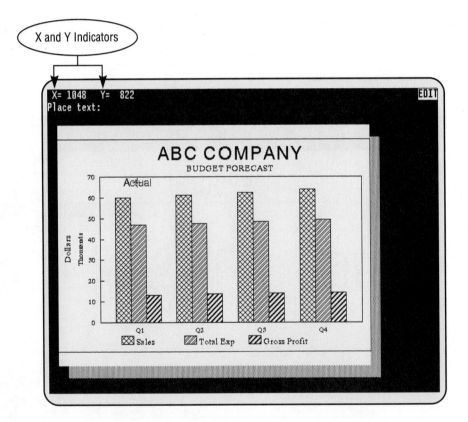

Notice the X and Y indicators in the control panel. The X indicator shows where the text is placed horizontally and the Y indicator shows where the text is placed vertically. On a typical color monitor, the pixel pattern is 640 increments horizontally and 480 pixels vertically. Thus, the X and Y values represent the pixel location on the screen. If you want an item to line up at the same place vertically or horizontally with some other item on the screen, be sure the X or Y indicators match appropriately.

To accept the placement of the text:

| **Press** | ←Enter | | ***Click*** | *the mouse button* |

Your screen should look like Figure 9-4.

Figure 9-4

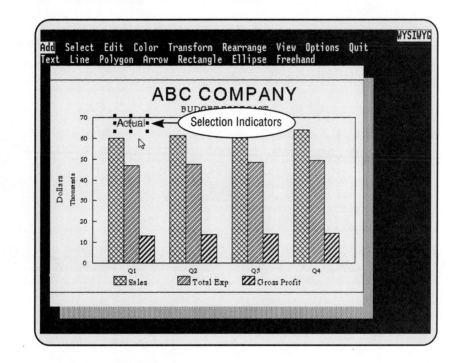

Notice the selection indicators around the text.

To add text above Q2:

Select	Add		***Choose***	*Add*
Select	Text		***Choose***	*Text*
Type	Projected		***Type***	*Projected*
Press	←Enter		***Click***	*the mouse button*

To place the text:

| **Press** | the pointer-movement keys so **"Projected"** is centered above the three bars for Q2 | | ***Move*** | *the mouse pointer so* ***"Projected"*** *is centered above the three bar for Q2* |

Press	←Enter	**Click** the mouse button

Your screen should look like Figure 9-5.

Figure 9-5

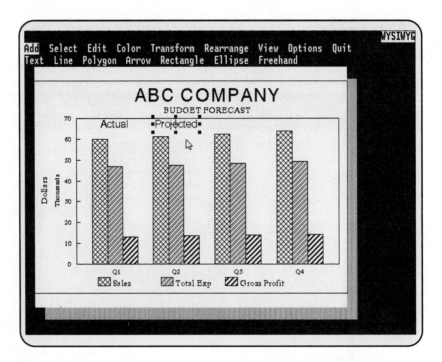

To copy **"Projected"** to Q3:

Select	Rearrange		*Choose*	*Rearrange*
Select	Copy		*Choose*	*Copy*

To move the copy:

Select	Rearrange		*Move*	*the mouse pointer to the copied text*
Select	Move		*Drag*	*the copied text so it is centered above the three bars for Q3*
Press	the pointer-movement keys so **"Projected"** is centered above the three bars for Q3		*Release*	*the mouse button*
Press	←Enter			

Repeat the Copy command sequence to copy **"Projected"** to Q4.

To select the text to edit and make smaller:

Select	Select		***Choose***	*Select*
Select	All		***Choose***	*All*

Notice the selection indicators around each piece of text.

To change the font of the text:

Select	Edit		***Choose***	*Edit*
Select	Font		***Choose***	*Font*
Select	6 (Dutch 10 point)		***Choose***	*6 (Dutch 10 point)*

Your screen should look like Figure 9-6.

Figure 9-6

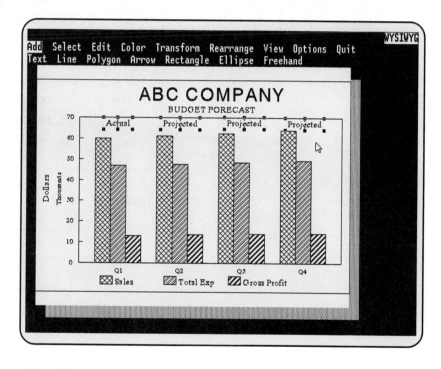

To exit the graphics editing window:

Select	Quit		***Choose***	*Quit*

Sizing and Moving a Graphic

To resize a graph:

Move	the cell pointer to cell A70
Press	[:]
Select	Graph
Select	Settings
Select	Range

Click	*on cell A70*
Move	*the mouse pointer to the control panel*
Choose	*Graph*
Choose	*Settings*
Choose	*Range*

To indicate the range of the graphic:

Type	.
Move	the cell pointer to cell F89
Press	[←Enter]

Move	*the mouse pointer to cell A70*
Drag	*the mouse pointer to cell F89*
Click	*the mouse button*

To specify the new graphic display range:

Press	[Esc]
Type	.
Move	the cell pointer to cell F84
Press	[←Enter]

Click	*the alternate mouse button*
Move	*the mouse pointer to cell A70*
Drag	*the mouse pointer to cell F84*
Click	*the mouse button*

To exit the Settings menu:

Select	Quit

Choose	*Quit*

Your screen should look like Figure 9-7.

Figure 9-7

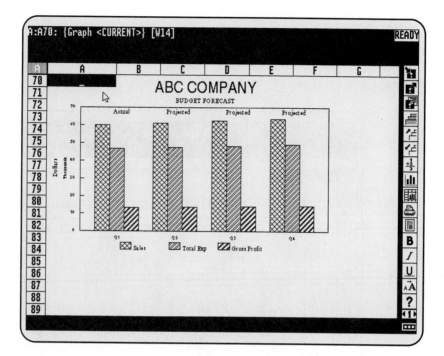

To move a graphic:

Press	:		*Move*	*the mouse pointer to the control panel*
Select	Graph		*Choose*	*Graph*
Select	Move		*Choose*	*Move*

To indicate the range of the graphic:

Move	the cell pointer to cell A70		*Move*	*the mouse pointer to cell A70*
Type	.		*Drag*	*the mouse pointer to cell F84*
Move	the cell pointer to cell F84		*Click*	*the mouse button*
Press	←Enter			

To specify the new location of the graphic:

Move	the cell pointer to cell A72		*Move*	*the mouse pointer to cell A72*
Press	←Enter		*Click*	*the mouse button twice*

To exit the Graph menu:

| **Select** | Quit | | ***Choose*** | *Quit* |

Your screen should look like Figure 9-8.

Figure 9-8

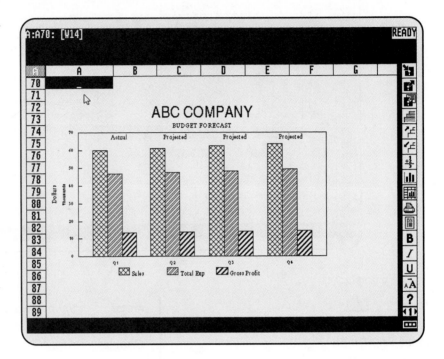

■ PRINTING A WORKSHEET AND GRAPH

You can use Wysiwyg to print a worksheet and graph on the same page.

To print the worksheet and graph:

Press			***Move***	*the mouse pointer to the control panel*
Select	Print		***Choose***	*Print*
Select	Range		***Choose***	*Range*

To remove any previously set print ranges:

| **Select** | Clear | | ***Choose*** | *Clear* |

To specify the worksheet and graph print range:

Select	Range		*Choose*	*Range*	
Select	Set		*Choose*	*Set*	
Move	the cell pointer to cell A41		*Move*	*the mouse pointer to cell A41*	
Type	.		*Drag*	*the mouse pointer to cell F86*	
Move	the cell pointer to cell F86		*Click*	*the mouse button*	
Press	←Enter				

To print the worksheet:

Select	Go		*Choose*	*Go*

Your printout should look like Figure 9-9.

Figure 9-9

ABC COMPANY
BUDGET

	Q1	Q2	Q3	Q4	YR TOTAL
Sales	$60,000	$61,200	$62,424	$63,672	$247,296
Expenses					
Salaries	35,000	35,500	36,200	37,000	143,700
Rent	9,000	9,000	9,000	9,000	36,000
Telephone	1,000	1,050	1,103	1,158	4,311
Office Supplies	750	800	850	900	3,300
Miscellaneous	1,000	1,030	1,061	1,093	4,184
Total Expenses	46,750	47,380	48,214	49,151	191,495
Gross Profit	$13,250	$13,820	$14,210	$14,521	$55,801

Assumptions

		Q2	Q3	Q4
Sales		2%	2%	2%
Telephone		5%	5%	5%
Office Supplies		50.00	50.00	50.00
Miscellaneous		3%	3%	3%

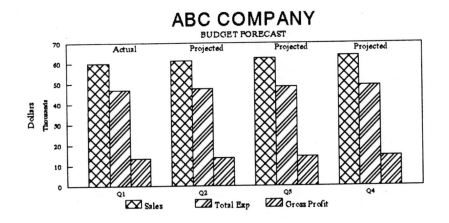

Save the worksheet using the file name BUDWYGPH.

■ OTHER CAPABILITIES OF WYSIWYG

Wysiwyg allows you to improve the appearance of worksheets and graphs in other ways than those described in this chapter. The Lotus 1-2-3 reference manual contains additional information on using Wysiwyg.

SUMMARY

By using the Wysiwyg add-in, you can improve the appearance of 1-2-3 worksheets and graphs. For example, you can add text and graphic objects to a graph. A graph can be changed to a different size or moved to another location. You can also use Wysiwyg to print a worksheet and a graph together.

KEY CONCEPTS

Boundary box
Graphics editing window
Object
Selection indicators

EXERCISE 1

INSTRUCTIONS: Circle T if the statement is true and F if the statement is false.

T   F   1.   By using Wysiwyg, you can enhance the appearance of a graph.

T   F   2.   The **G**raph command lets you add the current or a named graph.

T   F   3.   When you move or size an object, selection indicators appear around the object.

T   F   4.   An object is text, a geometric shape, or a freehand drawing that you add to a graphic.

T   F   5.   When you select an object, a boundary box appears around the object.

T   F   6.   You must move a graphic to the graphics editing window before you can change it.

EXERCISE 2

INSTRUCTIONS: Explain a typical situation when the following keystrokes or 1-2-3 commands are used.

Problem 1:   [:] **G**raph **A**dd   *Problem 3:*   [:] **G**raph **S**ettings

Problem 2:   [:] **G**raph **E**dit   *Problem 4:*   [:] **P**rint **R**ange

---

EXERCISE 3

INSTRUCTIONS: Retrieve the PRACTICE file.

Add the PROFIT graph to the worksheet.

Place the text "Actual" over the Year 1 data points. Place the text "Forecast" over the data points for Year 2 through Year 5.

Save the file using the file name PRACTBAR.

CHAPTER TEN

CREATING AND USING A TEMPLATE

OBJECTIVES

In this chapter, you will learn to:

■ Create and use a template

■ CHAPTER OVERVIEW

In Lotus 1-2-3, the term **template** describes a worksheet that can be used to create a series of other worksheets. A template usually consists of the general format (headings, labels, numeric format) and formulas that will be common to all the worksheets. When you enter data in the template, the worksheet formulas calculate accordingly. The new data are then saved under a different file name. The use of a template can save hours of time and effort in creating worksheets.

The template you will create in this chapter computes the total salaries for employees in various divisions of the ABC Company example used earlier. Since the salaries for each division will be on a separate worksheet, you will build a template that can be used for the various divisions of ABC Company. When you complete the template, your screen will look like Figure 10-1.

Figure 10-1

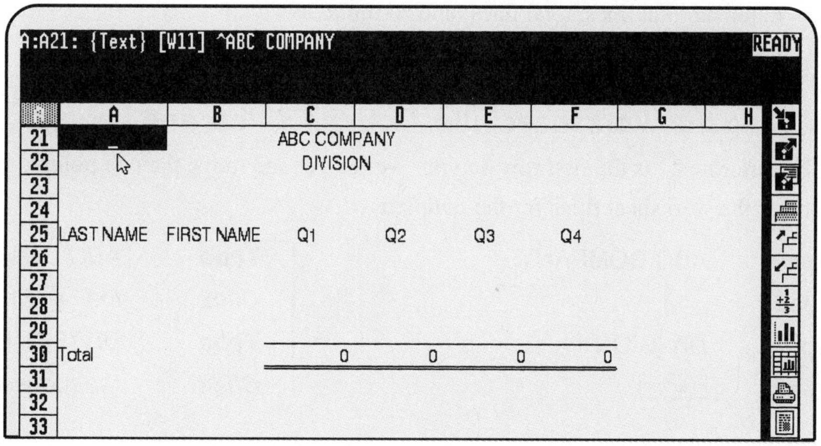

■ CREATING A TEMPLATE

Before creating the actual template, make sure there is a blank worksheet on your screen. Then enter the documentation information in Figure 10-2 on your worksheet.

Figure 10-2

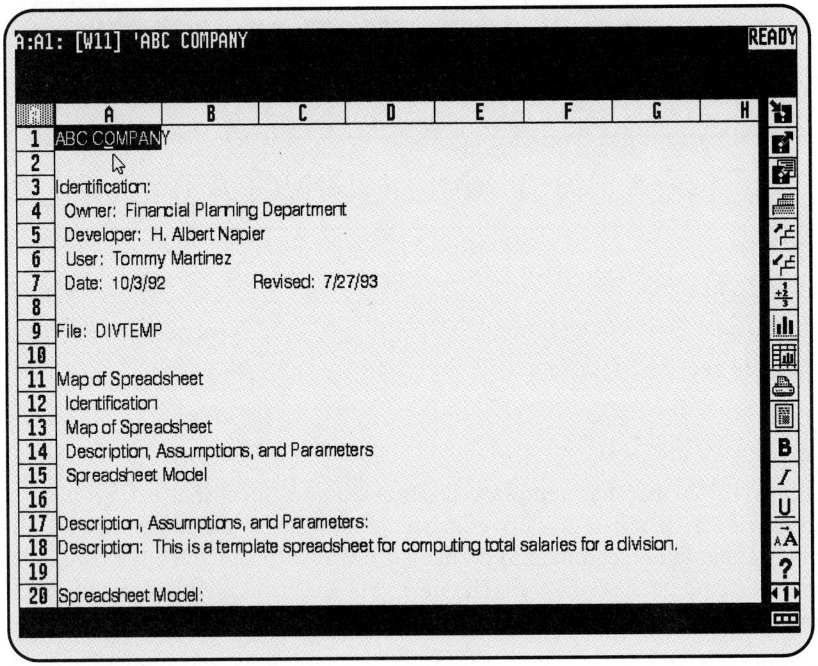

```
A:A1: [W11] 'ABC COMPANY                                              READY
┌───┬─────────┬───────┬───────┬───────┬───────┬───────┬───────┬───┐
│   │    A    │   B   │   C   │   D   │   E   │   F   │   G   │ H │
│ 1 │ABC COMPANY│
│ 2 │
│ 3 │Identification:
│ 4 │ Owner: Financial Planning Department
│ 5 │ Developer: H. Albert Napier
│ 6 │ User: Tommy Martinez
│ 7 │ Date: 10/3/92            Revised: 7/27/93
│ 8 │
│ 9 │File: DIVTEMP
│10 │
│11 │Map of Spreadsheet
│12 │ Identification
│13 │ Map of Spreadsheet
│14 │ Description, Assumptions, and Parameters
│15 │ Spreadsheet Model
│16 │
│17 │Description, Assumptions, and Parameters:
│18 │Description: This is a template spreadsheet for computing total salaries for a division.
│19 │
│20 │Spreadsheet Model:
```

There are three steps for creating the template:

1. Create the worksheet title, column titles, and labels.
2. Enter subtotal lines, total lines, and formulas.
3. Set the numeric format for the worksheet.

Creating the Worksheet Title, Column Titles, and Labels

Make sure row 21 is the first row on your worksheet and move the cell pointer to cell A21.

To enter the worksheet titles for the template:

Type	ABC COMPANY		**Type**	*ABC COMPANY*
Press	⬇		**Click**	*the ⬇ SmartIcon*
Type	DIVISION		**Type**	*DIVISION*
Press	←Enter		**Click**	*the mouse button*

Later in this chapter, you will center the titles over the spreadsheet columns.

> *In the Remainder of This Book*
> By this point, you should be thoroughly familiar with entering labels and data. Therefore, the remainder of the text uses the shortcut instruction "Enter label or data." It is assumed that you will type the label or data and press the ENTER key or click the mouse button with the mouse pointer in the control panel when asked to enter the information.

To enter the column titles in cells A25 through F25, respectively:

Enter	LAST NAME in cell A25		*Enter*	*LAST NAME in cell A25*
Enter	FIRST NAME in cell B25		*Enter*	*FIRST NAME in cell B25*
Enter	^Q1 in cell C25		*Enter*	*^Q1 in cell C25*
Enter	^Q2 in cell D25		*Enter*	*^Q2 in cell D25*
Enter	^Q3 in cell E25		*Enter*	*^Q3 in cell E25*
Enter	^Q4 in cell F25		*Enter*	*^Q4 in cell F25*

To widen column A to 11 characters:

Move	the cell pointer to any cell in column A		*Click*	*on any cell in column A*
Press	⌐/⌐		*Move*	*the mouse pointer to the control panel*
Select	Worksheet		*Choose*	*Worksheet*
Select	Column		*Choose*	*Column*
Select	Set-Width		*Choose*	*Set-Width*
Enter	11		*Enter*	*11*

To widen column B to 10 characters:

Move	the cell pointer to any cell in column B		*Click*	*on any cell in column B*
Press	⌐/⌐		*Move*	*the mouse pointer to the control panel*
Select	Worksheet		*Choose*	*Worksheet*
Select	Column		*Choose*	*Column*
Select	Set-Width		*Choose*	*Set-Width*
Enter	10		*Enter*	*10*

To enter the label Total:

Move	the cell pointer to cell A30	**Click**	on cell A30
Enter	Total	**Enter**	Total

Your screen should look like Figure 10-3.

Figure 10-3

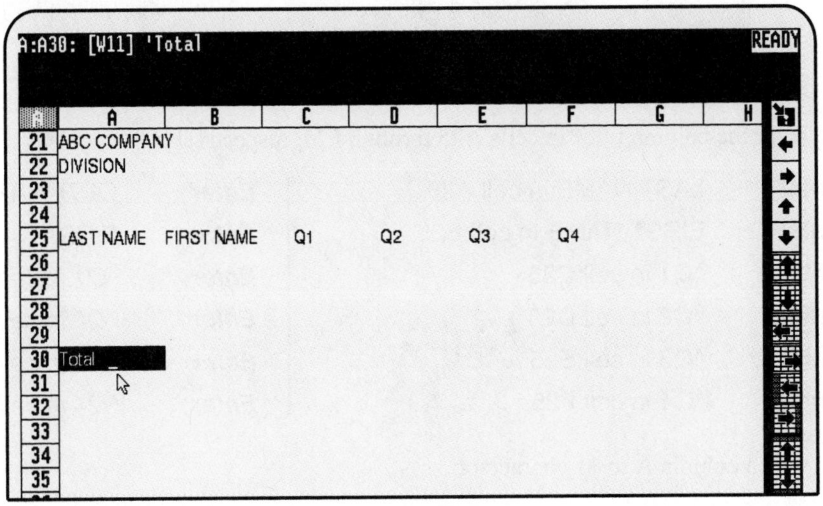

Entering Subtotal Lines and Formulas

To enter subtotal lines:

Highlight	cells C29 through F29	**Highlight**	cells C29 through F29
Press	`:`	**Move**	the mouse pointer to the control panel
Select	Format	**Click**	the alternate mouse button
Select	Lines	**Choose**	Format
Select	Bottom	**Choose**	Lines
		Choose	Bottom

> *Design Tip*
> You can use the @SUM special function to add values in contiguous cells in a
> column or a row. After completing a worksheet, you may later need to insert a row
> or column at the beginning or end of the range of cells included in an @SUM cell
> entry. To make sure you include the new cells in the @SUM cell entry, you must
> include the cell above and below the actual cells you want to include in the original
> @SUM entry. Otherwise, the cells in the row or column you insert will not be
> included in the @SUM cell entry.

To enter the formula to sum the salaries:

Move	the cell pointer to cell C30		*Click*	*on cell C30*
Type	@SUM(		*Type*	*@SUM(*
Move	the cell pointer to cell C25		*Move*	*the mouse pointer to cell C25*
Type	.		*Drag*	*the mouse pointer to cell C29*
Move	the cell pointer to cell C29		*Type*	*)*
Type	)		*Click*	*the mouse button*
Press	←Enter			

Because the template does not contain any numbers to add, a zero (0) should appear in cell C30.
Including the rows above and below where data is input allows the @SUM formula to adjust correctly in
the event rows of data are inserted or deleted. Since the cells in row 25 contain a label and the cells in
row 29 are not used, their **values** are assumed to be zero, and therefore will not cause the @SUM
formula results to be incorrect.

To copy the formula to the rest of the row:

Press	/		*Move*	*the mouse pointer to the control panel*
Select	Copy		*Click*	*the alternate mouse button*
			Choose	*Copy*

When prompted for "Enter range to copy FROM":

Press	←Enter		*Click*	*the mouse button with the mouse pointer in the control panel*

Cell C30 (the @SUM formula) is the selection for the cell to copy. When prompted for "Enter range to
copy TO":

Highlight	cells D30 through F30		*Highlight*	*cells D30 through F30*
Press	←Enter		*Click*	*the mouse button*

To place a double underline on the Total cells:

Highlight	cells C30 through F30	*Highlight*	*cells C30 through F30*
Press	☐ : ☐	*Move*	*the mouse pointer to the control panel*
		Click	*the alternate mouse button*
Select	Format	*Choose*	*Format*
Select	Lines	*Choose*	*Lines*
Select	Double	*Choose*	*Double*
Select	Bottom	*Choose*	*Bottom*

Setting the Numeric Format for the Worksheet

To set the global format:

Press	☐ / ☐	*Move*	*the mouse pointer to the control panel*
		Click	*the alternate mouse button*
Select	Worksheet	*Choose*	*Worksheet*
Select	Global	*Choose*	*Global*
Select	Format	*Choose*	*Format*
Select	, (for comma)	*Choose*	*, (for comma)*
Type	0	*Type*	*0*
Press	☐←Enter☐	*Click*	*the mouse button*

When numbers are entered, they will be formatted with commas and no decimal places.

Centering the Spreadsheet Title

To center the spreadsheet title information:

Highlight	cells A21 through F22	*Highlight*	*cells A21 through F22*
Press	☐ : ☐	*Move*	*the mouse pointer to the control panel*
		Click	*the alternate mouse button*
Select	Text	*Choose*	*Text*
Select	Align	*Choose*	*Align*
Select	Center	*Choose*	*Center*

The template worksheet is now complete. Your screen should look like Figure 10-4.

Figure 10-4

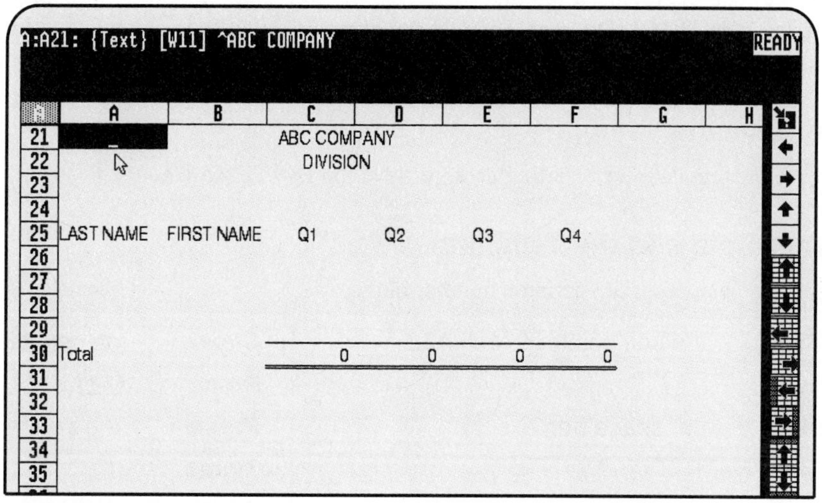

```
A:A21: {Text} [W11] ^ABC COMPANY                                    READY

        A          B          C        D       E       F       G       H
   21                              ABC COMPANY
   22                                DIVISION
   23
   24
   25  LAST NAME   FIRST NAME    Q1       Q2       Q3      Q4
   26
   27
   28
   29
   30  Total                          0        0        0       0
   31
   32
   33
   34
   35
```

Saving the Template on a File

To save the file:

Move	the cell pointer to cell A21		*Click*	*on cell A21*
Press	⎧ / ⎫		*Click*	*the File Save ⚏ SmartIcon*
Select	File			
Select	Save			

When prompted for the file name:

Type	DIVTEMP		*Type*	*DIVTEMP*
Press	⎡←Enter⎤		*Click*	*the mouse button*

Your worksheet has now been saved and can be used as a template for the various division worksheets.

Erase the template from your screen.

An alternative way to create the template is to first create a spreadsheet for a division. After creating the file and making sure that all the formulas and other elements of the worksheet are correct, save the file. Then erase the data for all the cells that will be different for the other detail worksheets and save the **shell** (data remaining) as the template. In this example, the names, salary data, and division number would be erased. This method may be preferable in some cases because it makes it easier to check the appearance and accuracy of the worksheet, especially if it is large and complex.

■ USING A TEMPLATE

The purpose of having a template is to use it as a shell for other spreadsheets. In this section, the template DIVTEMP (Division Template) that was created in the previous section will be used to create the spreadsheet for Division 1.

Retrieve the Template

To use the template for inserting data, retrieve the DIVTEMP file.

Enter Data into the Template

To enter the appropriate division number in the title:

Move	the cell pointer to cell A22		**Click**	on cell A22
Press	F2		**Press**	F2
Press	the space bar		**Press**	the space bar
Type	1		**Type**	1
Press	←Enter		**Click**	the mouse button

To enter the data for Division 1:

Move	the cell pointer to cell A26		**Click**	on cell A26

Using the data in Figure 10-5 as a reference, type the names and the quarterly salary information in rows 26 and 27 of columns A through F. The formulas in the Total row will compute the totals as the data for each quarter are input. Notice that the appropriate numeric format is used for the values.

Figure 10-5

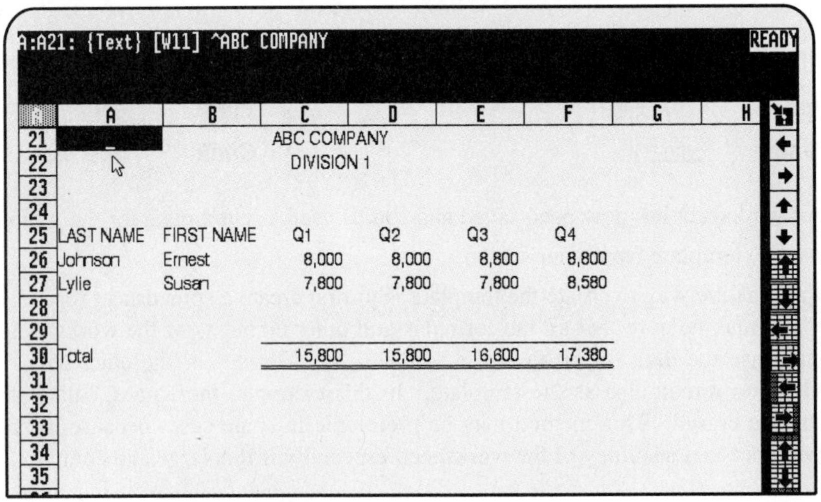

Save the Worksheet Under Another Name

Use the **F**ile **S**ave command sequence to save the salary data for DIVISION 1 as DIV1.

Move	the cell pointer to cell A21		*Click*	*on cell A21*
Press	/		*Click*	*the File Save ▉ SmartIcon*
Select	File		*Click*	*the alternate mouse button*
Select	Save		*Type*	*DIV1*
Type	DIV1		*Click*	*the mouse button*
Press	←Enter			

Two files now exist. DIVTEMP is the template, which can be used for creating worksheets of additional divisions. DIV1 contains the data for DIVISION 1. When a copy of DIVTEMP is in **memory**, it can be altered and saved under a different file name. The DIVTEMP file on the **disk** is not altered *unless* a **F**ile **S**ave **R**eplace command is executed.

> *User Tip*
>
> If you are not careful to give the worksheet a new file name, you may inadvertently save the data you entered on the template worksheet to the template file. Here are two suggestions to avoid this situation.
>
> You can save the worksheet using a different file name immediately after you retrieve the template. In the example used in this chapter, you could have named the file DIV1 before entering any divisional data. This action preserves the DIVTEMP template.
>
> Secondly, since it is very easy to accidentally replace a template, it is wise to keep an extra copy of the template file as a backup.

SUMMARY

A template is a shell document that can be used to create multiple spreadsheets with the same basic format. The template contains the features that will be common to all other worksheets having a similar appearance. For example, titles, descriptions, formulas, range names, and even print settings may be created in the template. When data are entered into the template, the results should be saved under a separate name so the template may be used to create additional worksheets.

KEY CONCEPTS

Shell
Template
Values
Worksheet in memory
Worksheet on disk

EXERCISE 1

INSTRUCTIONS: Circle T if the statement is true and F if the statement is false.

T   F   1.   In Lotus 1-2-3, a template file must be combined with another file containing data to generate a new spreadsheet.

T   F   2.   A template is a good way to keep spreadsheets standardized.

T   F   3.   When data are added to a template in memory, they are automatically added to the template file on the disk.

T   F   4.   A template can be used to create multiple worksheets.

T   F   5.   After adding data to a template in order to create a new spreadsheet, the worksheet should be saved using a name other than the template file name.

EXERCISE 2 — Creating a Template from an Existing Worksheet

INSTRUCTIONS: Retrieve the file DIV1. Erase the number 1 from the title DIVISION 1.

Erase the data for LAST NAME, FIRST NAME, and all four quarters for Ernest Johnson and Susan Lylie.

Save the file as DIVTEMP2. The file DIVTEMP2 should be identical to the file DIVTEMP that was created in this chapter. The screen should look like Figure 10-6.

Figure 10-6

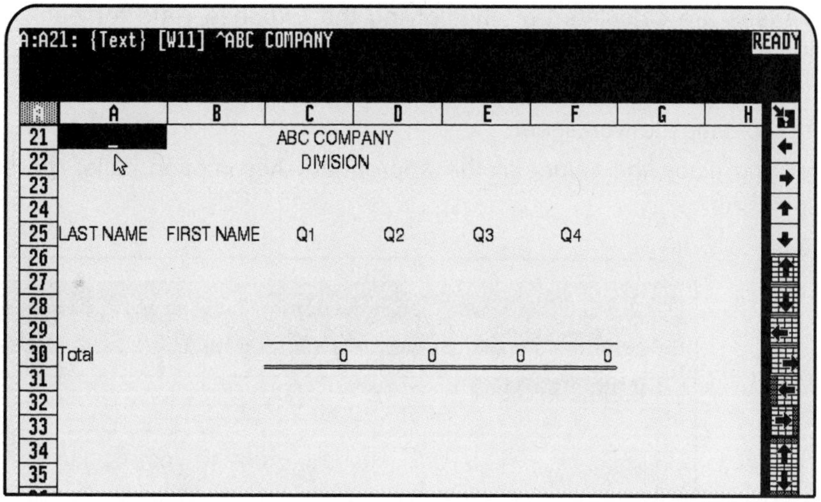

```
A:A21: {Text} [W11] ^ABC COMPANY                          READY

        A       B        C        D      E      F      G      H
  21  _                 ABC COMPANY
  22    ▷                 DIVISION
  23
  24
  25 LAST NAME  FIRST NAME    Q1      Q2      Q3      Q4
  26
  27
  28
  29
  30 Total                         0       0       0       0
  31
  32
  33
  34
  35
```

EXERCISE 3 — Creating a Template

INSTRUCTIONS: Create the template displayed in Figure 10-7. Make sure you include information for the identification; map of spreadsheet; description, assumptions, and parameters; and spreadsheet model blocks in rows 1 through 40.

Figure 10-7

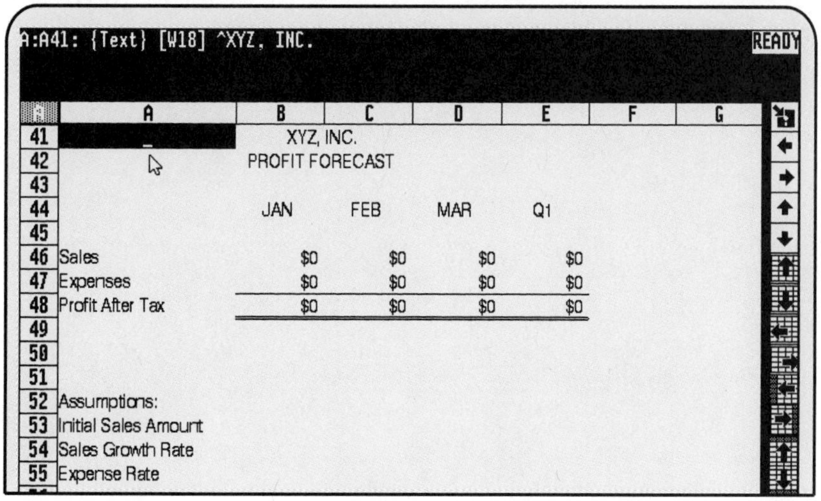

```
A:A41: {Text} [W18] ^XYZ, INC.                           READY

        A            B       C       D       E      F      G
  41  _              XYZ, INC.
  42    ▷            PROFIT FORECAST
  43
  44                 JAN     FEB     MAR     Q1
  45
  46 Sales           $0      $0      $0      $0
  47 Expenses        $0      $0      $0      $0
  48 Profit After Tax $0     $0      $0      $0
  49
  50
  51
  52 Assumptions:
  53 Initial Sales Amount
  54 Sales Growth Rate
  55 Expense Rate
```

Sales for the month of January are determined from the amount entered in cell B53 by placing the formula +B53 in cell B46. The values for Sales in February and March are computed by multiplying the Sales amount for the previous month times the Growth Rate for the current month.

Expenses are calculated by multiplying the Expense Rate for each month times the **Sales** amount for the month.

Save the template using the file name PROFTEMP.

Print the template worksheet.

After you place the values in the appropriate Assumption cells, the screen should look like Figure 10-8.

Figure 10-8

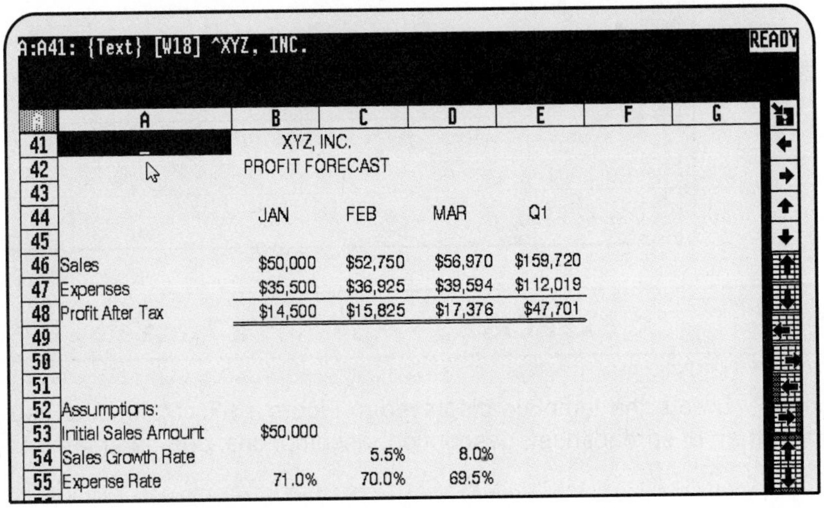

A:A41: {Text} [W18] ^XYZ, INC.							READY
	A	**B**	**C**	**D**	**E**	**F**	**G**
41			XYZ, INC.				
42			PROFIT FORECAST				
43							
44		JAN	FEB	MAR	Q1		
45							
46	Sales	$50,000	$52,750	$56,970	$159,720		
47	Expenses	$35,500	$36,925	$39,594	$112,019		
48	Profit After Tax	$14,500	$15,825	$17,376	$47,701		
49							
50							
51							
52	Assumptions:						
53	Initial Sales Amount	$50,000					
54	Sales Growth Rate		5.5%	8.0%			
55	Expense Rate	71.0%	70.0%	69.5%			

Print the results after you use the template worksheet.

CHAPTER ELEVEN

CREATING AND USING MULTIPLE WORKSHEETS AND FILES

OBJECTIVES

In this chapter, you will learn to:

- ■ Create multiple worksheets in a file
- ■ Add worksheets to a file
- ■ Move between multiple worksheets
- ■ Copy information between worksheets
- ■ Enter data and formulas into multiple worksheets
- ■ Format multiple worksheets
- ■ Print multiple worksheet data
- ■ Use multiple files

■ CHAPTER OVERVIEW

In the previous chapters, you worked with files that contained only one worksheet. The worksheets had only two dimensions. In this chapter, you are introduced to the concept of **multiple worksheets** and **files**. Essentially, a third dimension is added. Instead of having only one worksheet with a set of rows and columns, you may have multiple worksheets in a file. Another option available is to open several files and place them in your computer's memory.

The ability to have multiple worksheets or multiple files in memory at one time provides you with additional flexibility in organizing and using the data available to you. Multiple worksheets and files are particularly useful when you want to summarize and consolidate information from several worksheets.

A maximum of 256 worksheets can be in one file. Likewise, 256 files are the maximum that can be in memory at one time. The actual number of worksheets and files that you can use depends on the memory size of your computer and the number and the size of the worksheets.

■ EXAMPLE PROBLEM

Suppose ABC Company has three operating divisions and sells two products in each of the divisions. Data for projected sales in the three divisions are as follows.

Division 1:	Q1	Q2	Q3	Q4
Mowers	5,000	12,000	14,000	10,000
Edgers	3,000	5,000	8,000	4,000

Division 2:	Q1	Q2	Q3	Q4
Mowers	7,000	14,000	16,000	11,000
Edgers	2,000	4,000	7,000	5,000

Division 3:	Q1	Q2	Q3	Q4
Mowers	6,000	12,000	15,000	8,000
Edgers	1,000	7,000	8,000	3,000

You need to create a file that includes the data for the divisions on individual worksheets. Companywide totals for each quarter and for annual sales also need to be computed.

■ CREATING THE INITIAL WORKSHEET

Since you have completed many worksheets as you progressed through the earlier chapters, the instructions for creating the worksheet for DIVISION 1 are abbreviated and do not include all of the steps. Also, the documentation to include for proper spreadsheet design is omitted.

Figure 11-1 includes the spreadsheet for DIVISION 1. Create the worksheet and enter all of the data for sales of the two products for each of the quarters. Use the @SUM function to compute the quarterly and annual totals. Do not format the data.

Figure 11-1

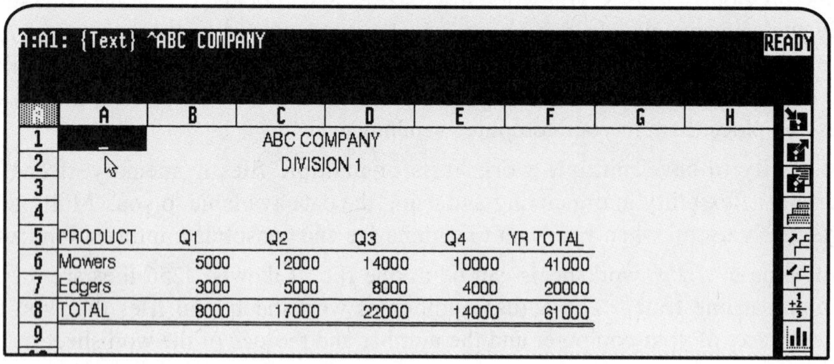

Save the worksheet as file DIVSALES using the **F**ile **S**ave command sequence.

■ ADDING WORKSHEETS TO A FILE

Before inserting a worksheet, you need to have the ability to see more than one worksheet on your screen.

To see multiple worksheets on your screen:

Press	⌴/⌴		***Move***	*the mouse pointer to the control panel*
Select	Worksheet		***Choose***	*Worksheet*
Select	Window		***Choose***	*Window*
Select	Perspective		***Choose***	*Perspective*

Three worksheets now appear on your screen, but the last two do not have a worksheet letter, column letters, or row numbers. Your screen should look like Figure 11-2.

Figure 11-2

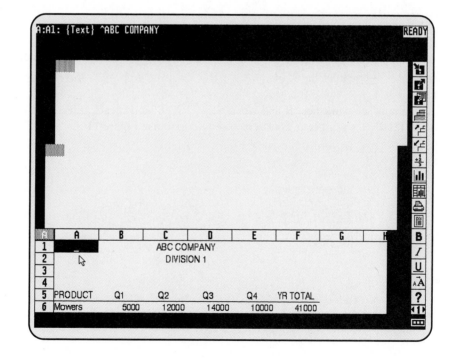

User Tip

An alternative to using the Worksheet Window Perspective command sequence is to click the Perspective ⊞ SmartIcon.

If you click the Perspective ⊞ SmartIcon a second time, the perspective view is removed and only one worksheet appears in the worksheet window.

To add worksheets for DIVISIONS 2 and 3:

Press	▭ / ▭		***Move***	*the mouse pointer to the control panel*
Select	Worksheet		***Choose***	*Worksheet*
Select	Insert		***Choose***	*Insert*
Select	Sheet		***Choose***	*Sheet*
Select	After		***Choose***	*After*

You are now asked to "Enter the number of worksheets to insert."

Type	2 (to indicate two worksheets are to be added)		***Type***	*2 (to indicate two worksheets are to be added)*
Press	◁─Enter		***Click***	*the mouse button*

You can now see worksheet B and worksheet C. The worksheets, referred to as sheets, are added after the DIVISION 1 worksheet. Your screen should look like Figure 11-3.

Figure 11-3

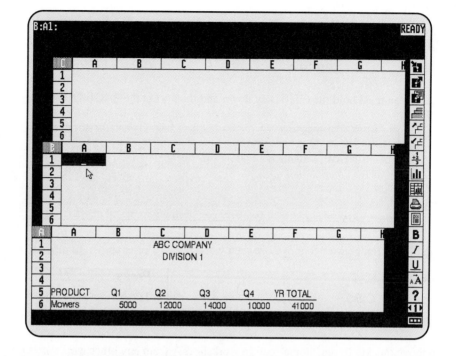

User Tip

An alternative method for inserting a new worksheet after the current worksheet is to click the Insert Sheet SmartIcon.

■ MOVING AMONG MULTIPLE WORKSHEETS

To move the cell pointer between worksheets, you can use combinations of the CTRL key and the PAGE UP, PAGE DOWN, and END keys. You can also use the mouse and the F5 (GoTo) key.

For example, to move the cell pointer from B:A1 (cell A1 in worksheet B) to C:A1:

Press   Ctrl + Page Up | **Click**   *on cell C:A1*

You must hold the CTRL key down and then press the PAGE UP key once.

The pointer-movement keys and mouse can also be used to move around worksheet C. Move the cell pointer to cell C:C10. Notice the rows and columns in the other worksheets move in a synchronous manner, and the same segments of all of the worksheets appear on the screen. If you want to scroll through worksheet C only and not have the rows and columns in the other worksheets move, you can execute the **W**orksheet **W**indow **U**nsync command sequence. To return to the synchronous movement process, you need to execute the **W**orksheet **W**indow **S**ync command sequence.

To return to cell A:A1:

Move	the cell pointer to cell C:A1	**Click**	the worksheet letter C
Press	Ctrl + Page Down twice	**Click**	on cell A:A1

Again, you must hold the CTRL key down and then press the PAGE DOWN key two times.

> *User Tip*
> An alternative method to move to the next worksheet is to click the Next Sheet
> SmartIcon. To move to the previous worksheet, click on the Previous Sheet
> SmartIcon.

The F5 key can be used to move between worksheets. For example, to move to cell B5 in worksheet C:

Press	F5	**Press**	F5
Type	C:B5	**Type**	C:B5
Press	←Enter	**Click**	the mouse button

To move quickly to the "home" cell in worksheet A from any other worksheet:

Press	Ctrl + Home	**Click**	the worksheet letter A

Similarly, you can move to the last worksheet in the file as follows:

Press	End	**Click**	the worksheet letter C
Press	Ctrl + Page Up		

> *User Tip*
> When the perspective option is not used, you can still move between worksheets
> with the combination of the CTRL key with the PAGE UP and PAGE DOWN
> keys. You can also use the Next Sheet SmartIcon and the Previous Sheet
> SmartIcon.

■ COPYING INFORMATION BETWEEN WORKSHEETS

To copy the worksheet titles and column headings from worksheet A to worksheets B and C:

Press	Ctrl + Home to move to cell A:A1	**Click**	the worksheet letter A to move to cell A:A1

| **Press** | ☐ / | | ***Move*** | *the mouse pointer to the control panel* |

| **Select** | Copy | | ***Choose*** | *Copy* |

When prompted for the "Enter range to copy FROM":

| **Highlight** | cells A:A1 through A:F5 | | ***Highlight*** | *cells A:A1 through A:F5* |

Cells A1 through F5 on worksheet A are now highlighted as the cells to be copied. On the control panel, the characters A:A1..A:F5 appear to indicate the desired range of cells to copy. Your screen should look like Figure 11-4, Part 1.

Figure 11-4
Part 1

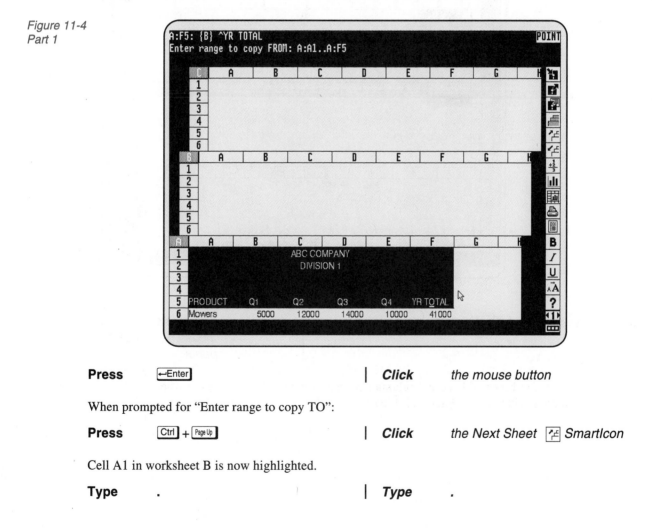

| **Press** | ⟵Enter | | ***Click*** | *the mouse button* |

When prompted for "Enter range to copy TO":

| **Press** | Ctrl + Page Up | | ***Click*** | *the Next Sheet* 🔁 *SmartIcon* |

Cell A1 in worksheet B is now highlighted.

| **Type** | . | | ***Type*** | *.* |

The period key anchors the cell pointer in B:A1.

Press   Ctrl + Page Up | **Click**   the Next Sheet ⁷⌐ SmartIcon

By pressing the Ctrl + Page Up keys or clicking the Next Sheet ⁷⌐ SmartIcon, the cell pointer is moved to cell A1 in worksheet C. You have now indicated the range to copy TO. Notice in the control panel the range is identified as B:A1..C:A1. Your screen should look like Figure 11-4, Part 2.

Figure 11-4
Part 2

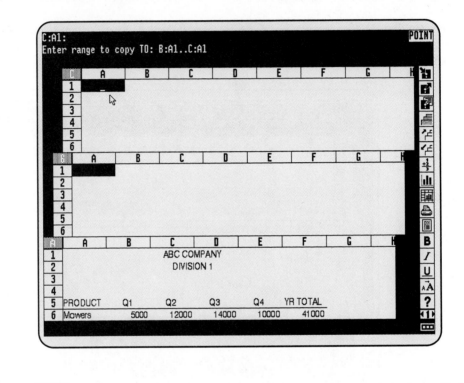

Press   ←Enter | **Click**   *the mouse button with the mouse pointer in the control panel*

The spreadsheet title lines and column headings now have been copied to worksheets B and C and your screen should look like Figure 11-4, Part 3.

Figure 11-4
Part 3

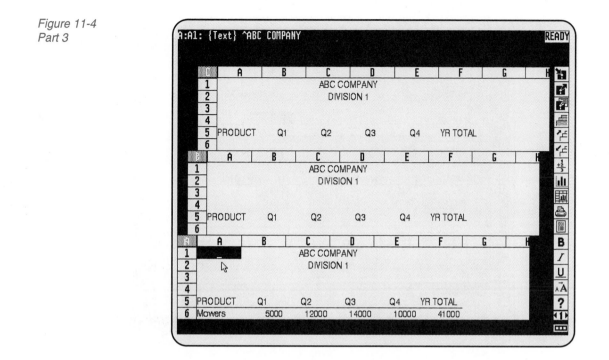

■ ENTERING DATA AND FORMULAS IN MULTIPLE WORKSHEETS

Enter the labels Mowers, Edgers, and TOTAL in cells A6, A7, and A8 respectively in worksheets B and C. Make the bottom of cells A5 through F5 and A7 through F7 in worksheets B and C appear as a solid line, and make the bottom of cells A8 through F8 appear as solid double lines in worksheets B and C. Edit the division titles so that DIVISION 2 appears in worksheet B and DIVISION 3 appears in worksheet C. You may copy the labels to further practice the process of copying information from one worksheet to other worksheets.

In worksheets B and C, enter the quarterly sales data for DIVISION 2 and DIVISION 3 respectively. Your screen should look like Figure 11-5.

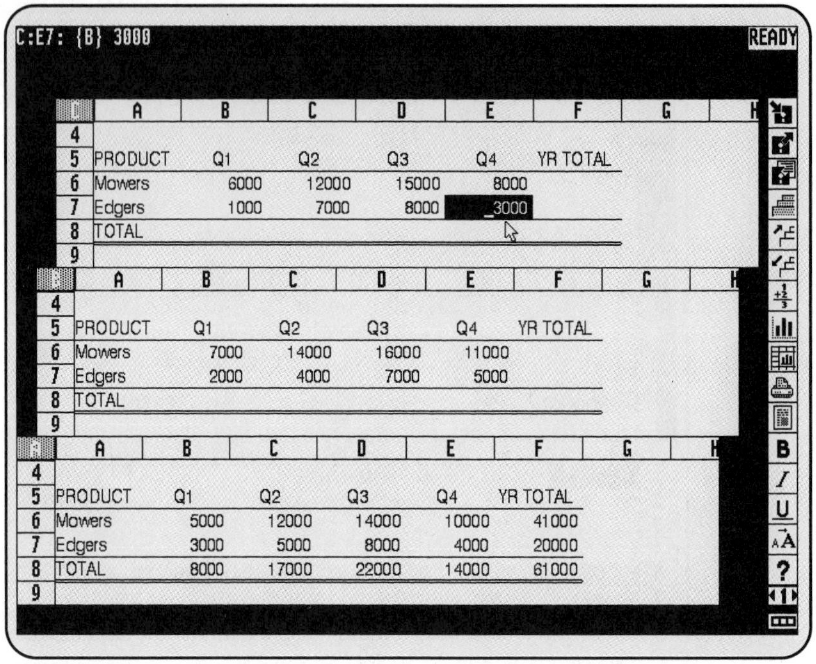

Figure 11-5

To examine the formulas for determining annual sales for each of the products.

| **Press** | Ctrl + Home | | *Click* | *the worksheet letter A* |

Your cell pointer now appears in cell A1 of worksheet A.

| **Move** | the cell pointer to cell F6 | | *Click* | *on cell F6* |

The formula for computing the annual total for the Mower sales @SUM(B6..E6) appears in the control panel. A similar formula for Edgers appears in cell F7.

| **Press** | ↓ until row 7 appears in each worksheet | | *Click* | *the ↓ SmartIcon until row 7 appears in each worksheet* |

To copy the formulas for computing the annual sales for the products from worksheet A to worksheets B and C:

Move	the cell pointer to cell F6		*Click*	*on cell F6*
Press	/		*Move*	*the mouse pointer to the control panel*
Select	Copy		*Click*	*the alternate mouse button until the 1-2-3 menu appears*

Highlight cells A:F6 through A:F7	*Choose* *Copy*
	Highlight *cells A:F6 through A:F7*

The cells F6 through F7 are now highlighted as the range of cells to copy FROM.

Press ⏎Enter	*Click* *the mouse button with the mouse pointer in the control panel*

When prompted for "Enter range to copy TO":

Press Ctrl + Page Up	*Click* *the Next Sheet ⬚ SmartIcon*
Type .	*Type* .
Press Ctrl + Page Up	*Click* *the Next Sheet ⬚ SmartIcon*

The range B:F6..C:F6 appearing in the control panel indicates the formulas will be copied to worksheets B and C.

Press ⏎Enter	*Click* *the mouse button with the mouse pointer in the control panel*

The formulas for computing annual sales have been copied and the appropriate values now appear in all of the worksheets. Your screen should look like Figure 11-6.

Figure 11-6

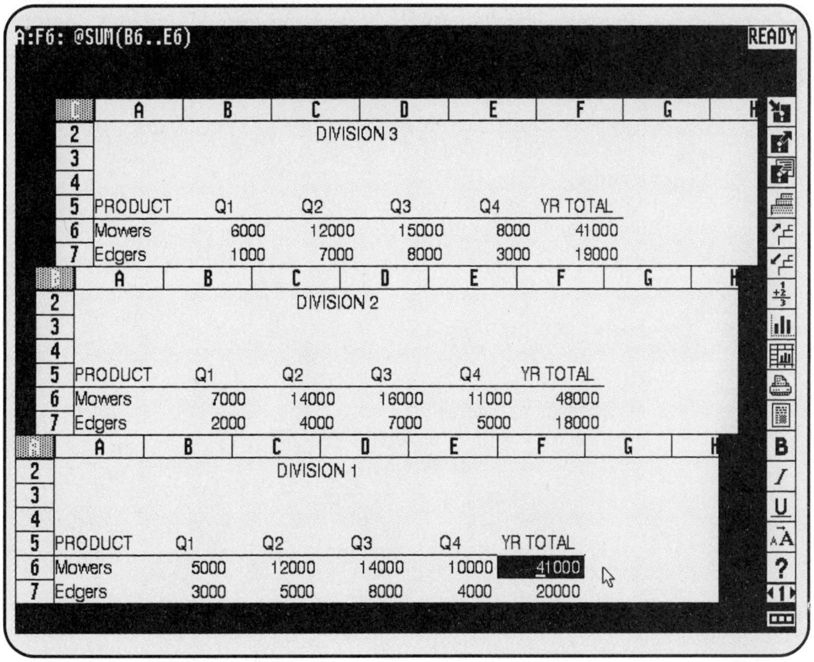

To place the formulas for determining the total sales for each quarter in worksheets B and C:

Move	the cell pointer to cell A:B8		*Click*	on cell A:B8
Press	⬚ /		*Move*	the mouse pointer to the control panel
Select	Copy		*Choose*	Copy
Highlight	cells A:B8 through A:F8		*Highlight*	cells A:B8 through A:F8
Press	⬚←Enter		*Click*	the mouse button with the mouse pointer in the control panel

The cells B8 through F8 have been designated as the cells to be copied FROM.

When prompted for "Enter range to copy TO":

Press	⬚Ctrl + ⬚Page Up		*Click*	the Next Sheet ⬚ SmartIcon
Type	.		*Type*	.
Press	⬚Ctrl + ⬚Page Up		*Click*	Next Sheet ⬚ SmartIcon

The range to copy TO is now highlighted.

Press	⬚←Enter		*Click*	the mouse button with the mouse pointer in the control panel

The formulas for quarterly product totals have been copied and the appropriate values now appear in each of the worksheets. Refer to Figure 11-7.

Figure 11-7

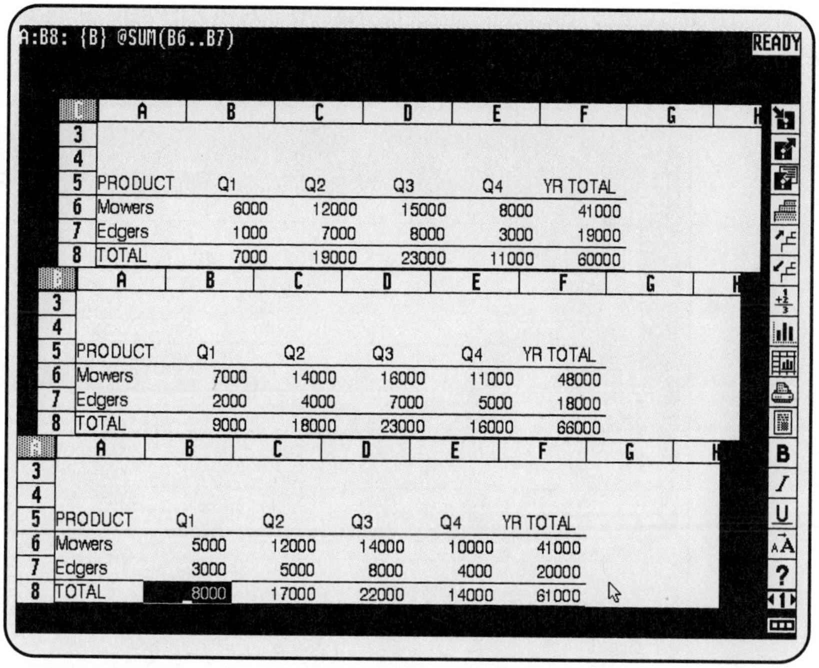

A:B8: {B} @SUM(B6..B7)   READY

	A	B	C	D	E	F	G	H
3								
4								
5	PRODUCT	Q1	Q2	Q3	Q4	YR TOTAL		
6	Mowers	6000	12000	15000	8000	41000		
7	Edgers	1000	7000	8000	3000	19000		
8	TOTAL	7000	19000	23000	11000	60000		

	A	B	C	D	E	F	G	H
3								
4								
5	PRODUCT	Q1	Q2	Q3	Q4	YR TOTAL		
6	Mowers	7000	14000	16000	11000	48000		
7	Edgers	2000	4000	7000	5000	18000		
8	TOTAL	9000	18000	23000	16000	66000		

	A	B	C	D	E	F	G	H
3								
4								
5	PRODUCT	Q1	Q2	Q3	Q4	YR TOTAL		
6	Mowers	5000	12000	14000	10000	41000		
7	Edgers	3000	5000	8000	4000	20000		
8	TOTAL	8000	17000	22000	14000	61000		

■ FORMATTING MULTIPLE WORKSHEETS

For this example, the format specifications need to be the same for all of the worksheets. Rather than format each worksheet individually, you can use the GROUP mode capability in 1-2-3. When this option is activated, you can format multiple worksheets at the same time.

Prior to using GROUP, make sure you are in the proper worksheet since 1-2-3 changes the format for all worksheets in the file based on the format change made to the current worksheet.

You must first turn on the GROUP mode and then format worksheet A. When the formatting process is completed, worksheets B and C will be formatted automatically using the format specification selected for worksheet A.

First, position the cell pointer so rows 4 through 9 for each worksheet appear on the screen.

Move	the cell pointer to cell A:B6		***Click***	*on cell A:B6*
Press	⬚ /		***Move***	*the mouse pointer to the control panel*
Select	Worksheet		***Choose***	*Worksheet*
Select	Global		***Choose***	*Global*
Select	Group		***Choose***	*Group*
Select	Enable		***Choose***	*Enable*

The GROUP mode has now been initiated. Note that **GROUP** appears in the status line. Your screen should look like Figure 11-8.

Figure 11-8

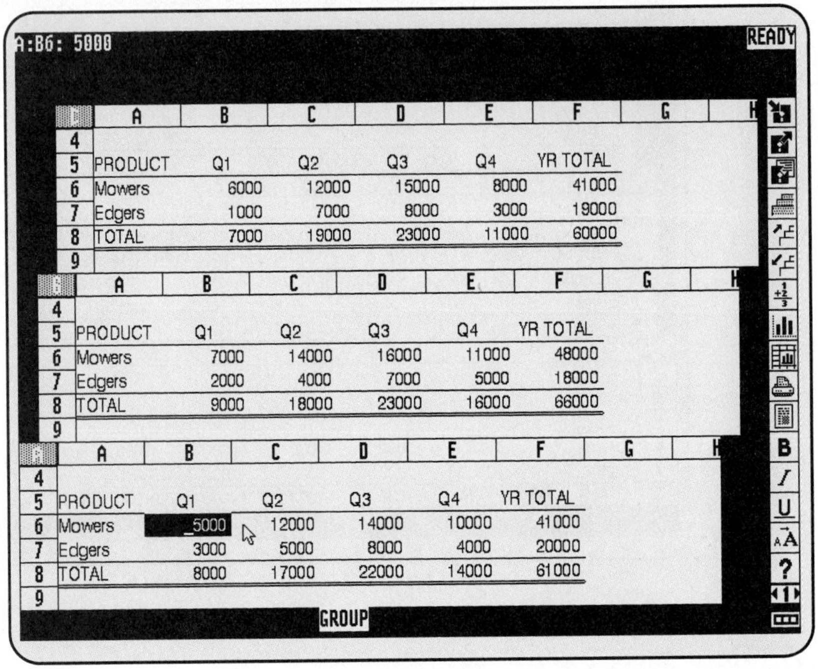

To specify the format:

Highlight	cells A:B6 through A:F8		**Highlight**	cells A:B6 through A:F8
Press	/		**Move**	the mouse pointer to the control panel
Select	Range		**Choose**	Range
Select	Format		**Choose**	Format
Select	, (comma)		**Choose**	, (comma)

When prompted for the number of decimal places:

Type	0		**Type**	0
Press	←Enter		**Click**	the mouse button

Notice that all of the worksheets have been formatted using the same format specification.

To stop using the GROUP mode:

Press	/		**Move**	the mouse pointer to the control panel

Select	Worksheet		Choose	Worksheet
Select	Global		Choose	Global
Select	Group		Choose	Group
Select	Disable		Choose	Disable

The GROUP indicator no longer appears on the screen. Your screen should look like Figure 11-9.

Figure 11-9

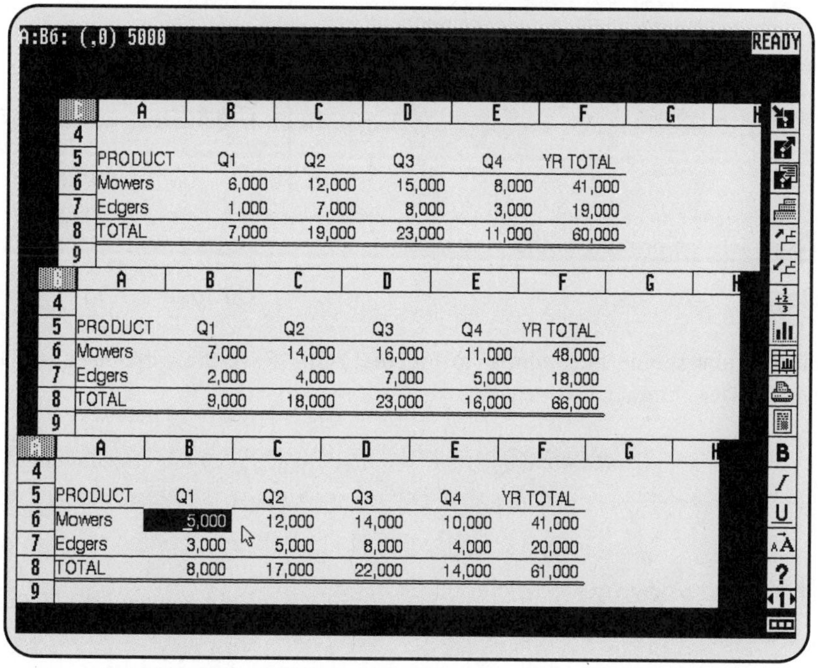

■ PRINTING MULTIPLE WORKSHEET DATA

Just as it was convenient to format all worksheets at one time, you may want to print ranges of cells from several worksheets at one time. To print worksheets A, B, and C:

Move	the cell pointer to cell A:A1		Click	the worksheet letter A
Press	`:`		Move	the mouse pointer to the control panel
Select	Print		Click	the alternate mouse button until the Wysiwyg menu appears
Select	Range		Choose	Print
Select	Set		Choose	Range

Type	.		*Choose*	*Set*
Press	End		*Highlight*	*cells A:A1 through A:F8*
Press	Home			

The print range for worksheet A is now highlighted and contains cells A1 through F8.

To extend the specify print range to worksheets B and C:

Press	Ctrl + Page Up twice		*Press*	*Ctrl + Page Up twice*

The print range is now extended to include worksheets B and C.

Press	←Enter		*Click*	*the mouse button with the mouse pointer in the control panel*

To complete the printing of the worksheets:

Select	Go		*Choose*	*Go*

Your printout should look similar to Figure 11-10. Save the worksheets as DIVSALES using the **F**ile **S**ave **R**eplace command sequence.

Figure 11-10

ABC COMPANY
DIVISION 1

PRODUCT	Q1	Q2	Q3	Q4	YR TOTAL
Mowers	5,000	12,000	14,000	10,000	41,000
Edgers	3,000	5,000	8,000	4,000	20,000
TOTAL	8,000	17,000	22,000	14,000	61,000

ABC COMPANY
DIVISION 2

PRODUCT	Q1	Q2	Q3	Q4	YR TOTAL
Mowers	7,000	14,000	16,000	11,000	48,000
Edgers	2,000	4,000	7,000	5,000	18,000
TOTAL	9,000	18,000	23,000	16,000	66,000

ABC COMPANY
DIVISION 3

PRODUCT	Q1	Q2	Q3	Q4	YR TOTAL
Mowers	6,000	12,000	15,000	8,000	41,000
Edgers	1,000	7,000	8,000	3,000	19,000
TOTAL	7,000	19,000	23,000	11,000	60,000

In some situations, you may want to print only selected ranges from each worksheet. To print a group of print ranges, you select all of the ranges you want to print separated by commas and with no spaces.

For the example problem, suppose you want to print only the total sales values by quarters and the annual sales total for each of the divisions. To accomplish this objective, complete the following steps.

Move	the cell pointer to cell A:A1		*Click*	*the worksheet letter A*
Press	$\boxed{:}$		*Move*	*the cell pointer to the control panel*
Select	Print		*Choose*	*Print*
Select	Range		*Choose*	*Range*

To erase the current print range:

Select	Clear		*Choose*	*Clear*

To include the title in the print range:

Select	Range		*Choose*	*Range*
Select	Set		*Choose*	*Set*
Highlight	cells A:A1 through A:F1		*Highlight*	*cells A:A1 through A:F1*

To specify the column titles:

Type	, (comma)		*Type*	*, (comma)*
Highlight	cells A:A5 through A:F5		*Highlight*	*cells A:A5 through A:F5*

To specify the totals for the divisions:

Type	, (comma)		*Type*	*, (comma)*
Highlight	cells A:A8 through A:F8		*Highlight*	*cells A:A8 through A:F8*
Type	.		*Type*	*.*
Press	$\boxed{\text{Ctrl}}$ + $\boxed{\text{Page Up}}$ twice		*Press*	*$\boxed{\text{Ctrl}}$ + $\boxed{\text{Page Up}}$ twice*

Your screen should look like Figure 11-11.

Figure 11-11

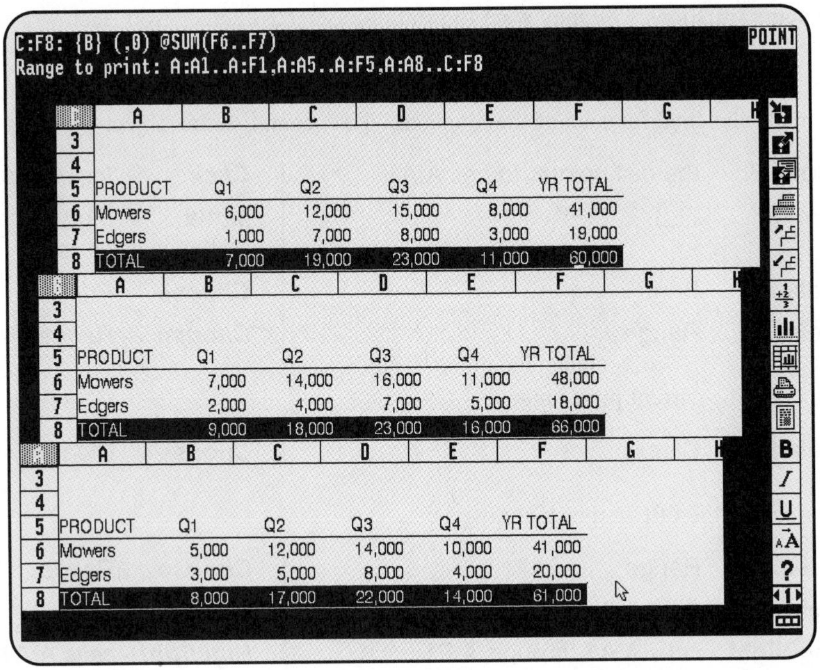

To print the selected ranges:

Press [←Enter]

Select Go

Click	the mouse button with the mouse pointer in the control panel
Choose	Go

Your printout should look similar to Figure 11-12.

Figure 11-12

		ABC COMPANY			
PRODUCT	Q1	Q2	Q3	Q4	YR TOTAL
TOTAL	8,000	17,000	22,000	14,000	61,000
TOTAL	9,000	18,000	23,000	16,000	66,000
TOTAL	7,000	19,000	23,000	11,000	60,000

If you do not want the double underlines to appear on your printout, you can use the Format Lines Clear All command sequence to remove them prior to printing.

■ USING MULTIPLE FILES

In 1-2-3, you can have several files open at the same time. When more than one file is open in memory, you can copy data between the open files. However, you cannot format multiple files using the GROUP mode, and you cannot print multiple files at one time.

To illustrate the process for using multiple files, retrieve the SALES file. To open the existing UNITPROD file and place it after the SALES file:

Press	/		*Move*	the mouse pointer to the control panel
Select	File		*Click*	the alternate mouse button until the 1-2-3 menu appears
Select	Open		*Choose*	File
Select	After		*Choose*	Open
Press	F3		*Choose*	After
Select	the UNITPROD file		*Press*	F3
Press	←Enter		*Choose*	the UNITPROD file
			Click	the mouse button

> *User Tip*
>
> An alternative method for opening an existing file is to click the File Open [icon] SmartIcon. Then move the mouse pointer to the appropriate file name and click the mouse button.

To see portions of both files on your screen:

Press	/		*Click*	the Perspective [icon] SmartIcon
Select	Worksheet			
Select	Window			
Select	Perspective			

The screen now contains the six rows of the SALES and UNITPROD worksheets. Your screen should look like Figure 11-13. Notice that each worksheet on the screen is worksheet A of the respective files.

Figure 11-13

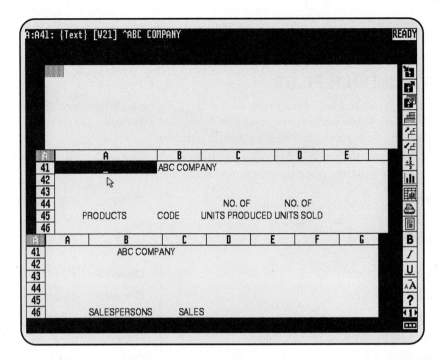

To move between files, you can use the combinations of CTRL+PAGE UP and CTRL+PAGE DOWN keys or use the mouse to click on a cell. The Next Sheet [icon] and Previous Sheet [icon] SmartIcons can also be used. The contents of cells can be copied from one file to another. Notice the file indicator changes when you move to a different file.

One of the advantages of having multiple files open is the capability to link files together. This concept is illustrated in the next chapter.

SUMMARY

Using multiple worksheets provides flexibility to individuals creating worksheet applications that have similar structures and formats. The capability of having multiple files open in memory at the same time provides you with more options for worksheet applications.

KEY CONCEPTS

Adding a worksheet to a file
Copying information between files
Copying data between worksheets
File Open
Formatting multiple worksheets
GROUP mode
Multiple files

Multiple worksheets
Opening additional files
Printing multiple worksheets
Worksheet Global Group
Worksheet Insert Sheet
Worksheet Window Perspective

EXERCISE 1

INSTRUCTIONS: Circle T if the statement is true and F if the statement is false.

T   F   1. At most three worksheets can be placed in a 1-2-3 file.

T   F   2. One or more worksheets can be inserted before or after a worksheet existing in the memory of a computer.

T   F   3. The F5 key can be used to move between multiple worksheets in a file.

T   F   4. Cells can be copied from one worksheet to another.

T   F   5. Cells cannot be copied from one file to another.

T   F   6. When multiple worksheets exist in a file, only one worksheet at a time can be viewed on the screen.

T   F   7. More than one file can be open at one time.

T   F   8. The GROUP mode option available in 1-2-3 allows you to format more than one worksheet or file at one time.

T   F   9. The Next Sheet 🗟 SmartIcon cannot be clicked several times in succession.

T   F   10. At most four worksheets can be seen on a screen at one time.

EXERCISE 2

INSTRUCTIONS: Explain a typical situation when the following keystrokes, 1-2-3 commands, or SmartIcon are used.

Problem 1:   `/` File Open

Problem 2:   `/` Worksheet Insert Sheet

Problem 3:   `/` Worksheet Window Perspective

Problem 4:   `/` Worksheet Window Perspective Clear

Problem 5:   `/` Worksheet Global Group

Problem 6:   `Ctrl` + `Page Up`

Problem 7:   `Ctrl` + `Page Down`

Problem 8:   `Ctrl` + `Home`

Problem 9:   🗟

EXERCISE 3

INSTRUCTIONS: XYZ Consulting Company provides computer training, computer consulting and system documentation services. The company has offices in New York, Chicago, Houston, and Los Angeles. Data on sales for the months of June, July, and August for each of the locations follow:

New York:	June	July	August
Training	15,000	19,000	17,000
Consulting	9,000	8,000	10,000
Documentation	5,000	7,000	9,000

Chicago:	June	July	August
Training	12,000	15,000	14,000
Consulting	12,000	18,000	11,000
Documentation	3,000	5,000	7,000

Houston:	June	July	August
Training	20,000	15,000	22,000
Consulting	17,000	18,000	19,000
Documentation	8,000	6,000	4,000

Los Angeles:	June	July	August
Training	13,000	12,000	15,000
Consulting	11,000	9,000	14,000
Documentation	10,000	10,000	12,000

Create a file that has the data for each of the locations on a separate worksheet.

Calculate the total sales by month and type of service for each of the locations.

Format the cells appropriately and include subtotal lines as well as double underlines to indicate the end of each worksheet.

Save the worksheets on a file using the name XYZSALES.

Print the four worksheets.

EXERCISE 4 — Adding a Worksheet to an Existing File

INSTRUCTIONS: Retrieve the DIVSALES file.

ABC Company forgot to reveal that it has acquired another company that sells mowers and edgers. The newly acquired organization has been designated as Division 4. The data on sales for the new division follow:

Division 4:	Q1	Q2	Q3	Q4
Mowers	3,000	2,000	9,000	2,000
Edgers	2,000	3,000	6,000	1,000

Add a worksheet to the DIVSALES file and include the data for Division 4. The format of the worksheet for Division 4 should be the same as for the other three divisions.

Print the worksheets.

Save the DIVSALES file.

EXERCISE 5 — Creating a File with Multiple Worksheets

INSTRUCTIONS: Create a file with multiple worksheets that will be helpful to you in some way.

Print the worksheets.

Save the worksheets to a file using a name of your choice.

CHAPTER TWELVE

CONSOLIDATING WORKSHEETS
AND LINKING FILES

OBJECTIVES

In this chapter, you will learn to:

- Use a template to create several worksheets
- Combine several worksheets into a summary worksheet
- Link files to move information between files
- Open a new file

■ CHAPTER OVERVIEW

Sometimes it is necessary to **combine information from several worksheets** into one summary worksheet. An example of such a situation occurs when organizations need to consolidate worksheets for several operating divisions during the budgeting process. In some situations, it is desirable to link worksheets together to facilitate the movement of data between worksheets. When using the linking feature, a change made in one worksheet will automatically update the appropriate cells in the linked worksheets.

In this chapter, you will use the template you constructed for salaries in Chapter 10 to create a worksheet for each of the three divisions in ABC Company. Then you will create a summary worksheet and combine the total salaries data from the three worksheets into the summary worksheet. At this point you will have the total salaries for ABC Company. You will then link the total salary cells in the summary worksheet to the cells associated with salaries on the worksheet in the file BUDGET to copy the salary totals.

■ USE OF A TEMPLATE TO CREATE SEVERAL WORKSHEETS

In the following exercise, you will use the template DIVTEMP you constructed in Chapter 10 to create worksheets for computing total salaries in ABC Company's three operating divisions. Then you will construct a summary worksheet that includes the total salaries for each of the divisions. Finally, the sum of the total salaries for the three divisions will be calculated.

To start the exercise retrieve the DIVTEMP file. Make sure your screen looks like Figure 12-1.

Figure 12-1

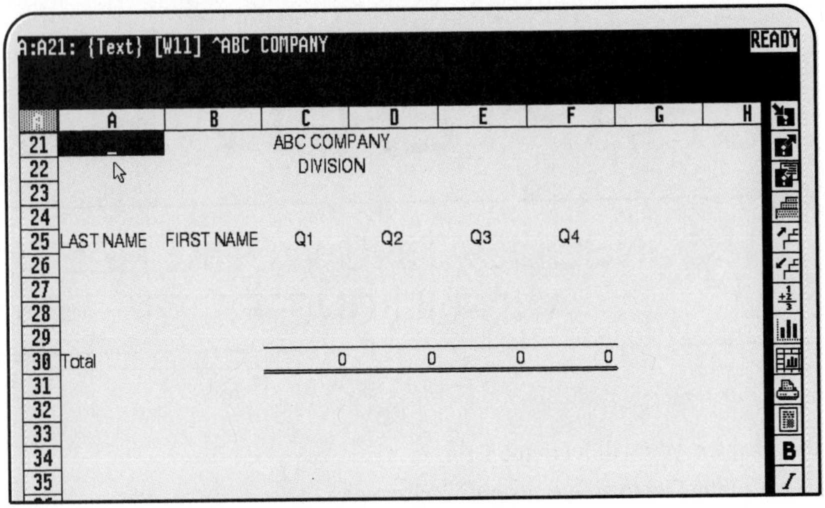

Save the worksheet using the file name DIVISION so you do not risk replacing the template file after you enter data.

You now need to add two worksheets after the current worksheet.

Press	/	**Click**	the Insert Sheet ▓ SmartIcon twice
Select	Worksheet		
Select	Insert		
Select	Sheet		
Select	After		
Type	2		
Press	↵Enter		

You have inserted two additional worksheets in the file.

To see the three worksheets on your screen:

Press	/	**Click**	the Perspective ▓ SmartIcon
Select	Worksheet		
Select	Window		
Select	Perspective		

After moving the cell pointer to cell A:A21, your screen should include three worksheets and look like Figure 12-2.

Figure 12-2

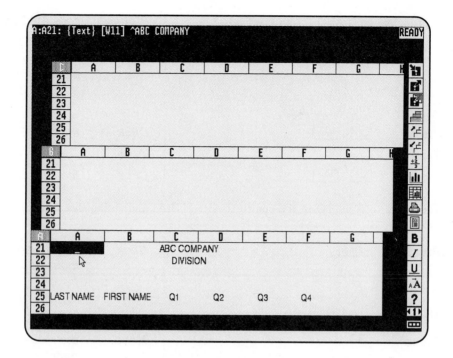

You should be in **GROUP** mode so that when you copy the contents of the spreadsheet model in worksheet A to worksheets B and C, you will also copy the formats.

Press	Ctrl + Home			***Click***	*the worksheet letter A*

The cell pointer is now in cell A:A1. You must be in the worksheet that has the desired formats if you want the formats to be correct after the data are copied to the other worksheets.

Press	/		***Move***	*the mouse pointer to the control panel*
Select	Worksheet		***Choose***	*Worksheet*
Select	Global		***Choose***	*Global*
Select	Group		***Choose***	*Group*
Select	Enable		***Choose***	*Enable*

Notice the **GROUP** indicator at the bottom of your screen is now on.

Copy the information in worksheet A to worksheets B and C:

Press	/		***Move***	*the mouse pointer to the control panel*
Select	Copy		***Choose***	*Copy*

Highlight	cells A:A1 through A:F30		***Highlight***	*cells A:A1 through A:F30*
Press	[←Enter]		***Click***	*the mouse button with the mouse pointer in the control panel*

To finish copying the information and formats:

Press	[Ctrl] + [Page Up]		***Click***	*the Next Sheet* 🔲 *SmartIcon*
Type	.		***Type***	*.*
Press	[Ctrl] + [Page Up]		***Click***	*the Next Sheet* 🔲 *SmartIcon*

The range to copy TO in the control is B:A1..C:A1 indicating that the appropriate range has been specified.

Press	[←Enter]		***Click***	*the mouse button with the mouse pointer in the control panel*

To disable the GROUP mode:

Press	[/]		***Move***	*the mouse pointer to the control panel*
Select	Worksheet		***Choose***	*Worksheet*
Select	Global		***Choose***	*Global*
Select	Group		***Choose***	*Group*
Select	Disable		***Choose***	*Disable*

The GROUP indicator no longer appears on your screen. After moving the cell pointer to cell A:A21, your screen should look like Figure 12-3.

Figure 12-3

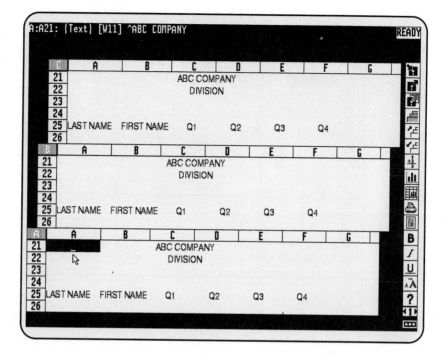

At this point, enter the data for salaries for the three divisions in worksheets A, B, and C. Parts 1 through 3 of Figure 12-4 include the data for the three divisions. Enter the data into the appropriate worksheets. Note the screens illustrate the ability to examine the worksheets in a file when the **Worksheet Window Clear** command or the Perspective SmartIcon is used to eliminate the 3-D perspective.

When the perspective option is not used, you can still move between the worksheets using the combination of the CTRL key with the PAGE UP and PAGE DOWN keys or the Next Sheet ⌐⊏ and Previous Sheet ⊐⌐ SmartIcons.

Figure 12-4
Part 1

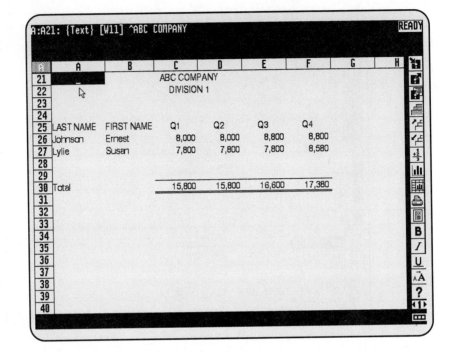

Figure 12-4
Part 2

Figure 12-4
Part 3

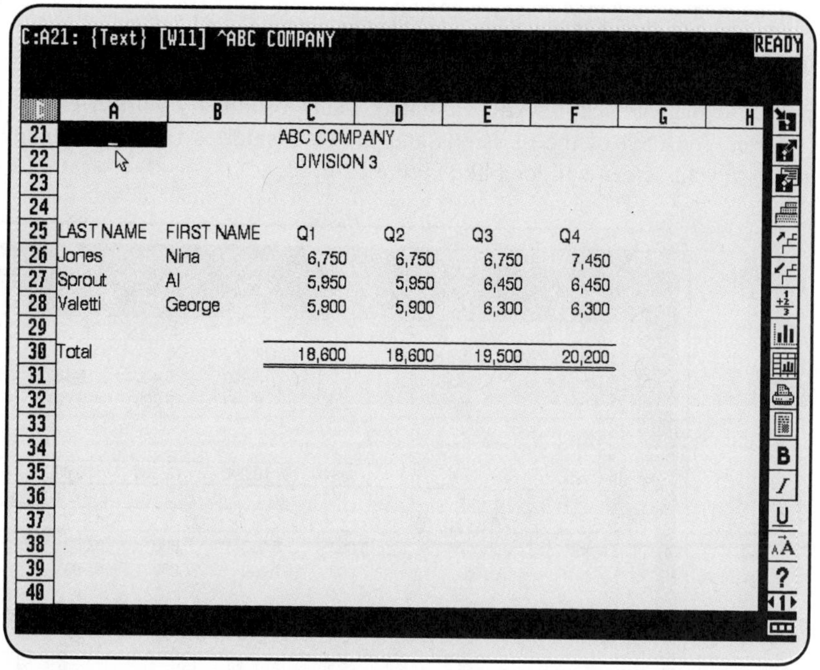

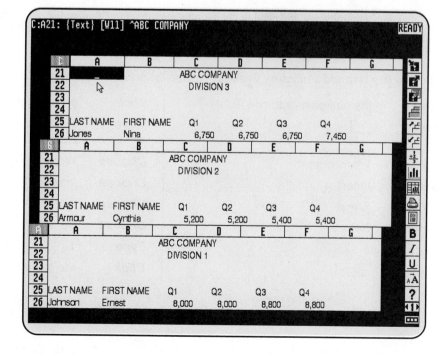

Notice that a total salary value is computed for each quarter for each of the divisions. After you enter the
data and make sure you are using the perspective option, your screen should look similar to Figure 12-5.

Figure 12-5

■ COMBINING SEVERAL WORKSHEETS INTO A SUMMARY WORKSHEET

Suppose the management of ABC Company wants a summary worksheet that includes the salary totals, by quarter, for each of the divisions and the total salaries for the company. When this exercise is completed, your screen will look like Figure 12-6.

Figure 12-6

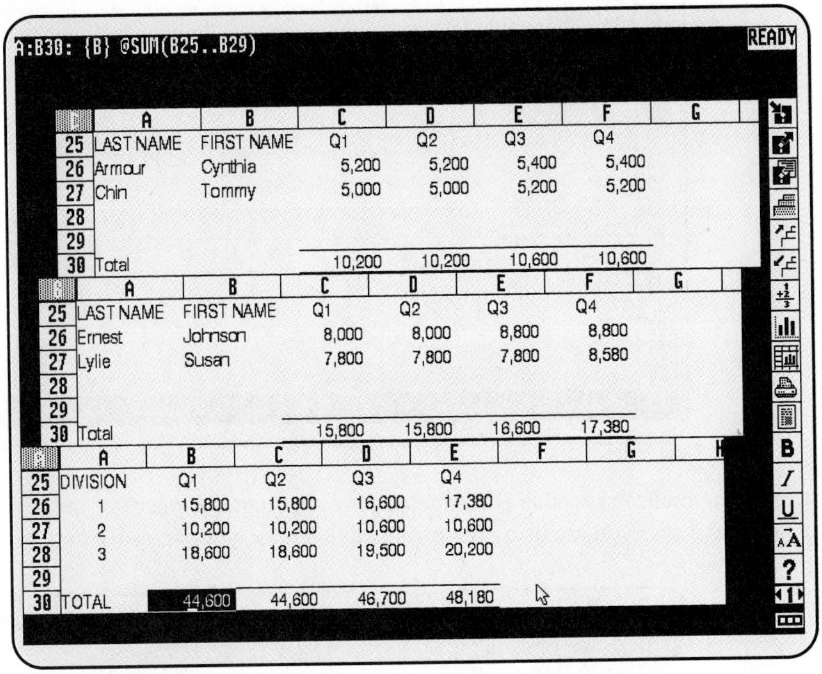

The first step is to add a summary worksheet before the present worksheet A.

Move	the cell pointer to cell A:A21	*Click*	*on cell A:A21*
Press	☐ / ☐	*Move*	*the mouse pointer to the control panel*
Select	Worksheet	*Choose*	*Worksheet*
Select	Insert	*Choose*	*Insert*
Select	Sheet	*Choose*	*Sheet*
Select	Before	*Choose*	*Before*
Type	1	*Type*	*1*
Press	↵Enter	*Click*	*the mouse button*

Notice that a blank worksheet now appears as worksheet A. The information for the three divisions has moved to the next worksheet. That is, the salary data for DIVISIONS 1, 2, and 3 are now in worksheets B, C, and D respectively. Since a maximum of three worksheets can appear on the screen at once, you cannot see worksheet D. After moving the cell pointer to cell A:A21, your screen should look like Figure 12-7.

Figure 12-7

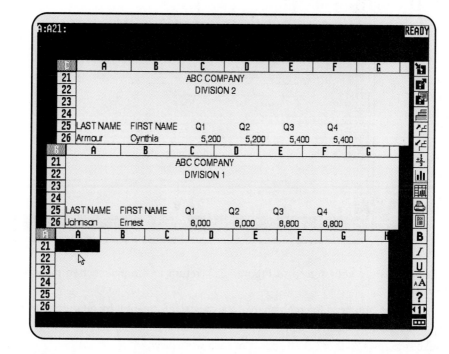

Prior to summarizing the information, you need to enter the titles, column headings, labels, and underlines in worksheet A. When you are finished placing this information on worksheet A and after pressing the ALT+F6 keys, your screen should look like Figure 12-8. This key combination lets you "zoom" on to one worksheet. Notice the ZOOM indicator at the bottom of your screen is now on.

Figure 12-8

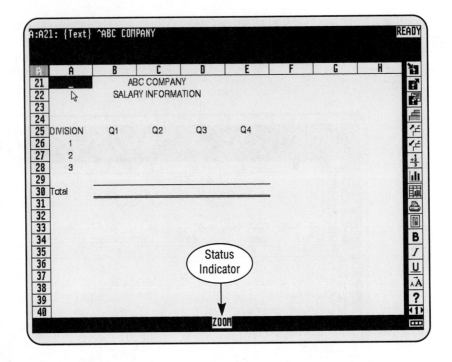

After comparing your screen to Figure 12-8, return to the perspective mode by pressing the ALT+F6 keys again.

At this point, you need to combine the total salary information by quarter from each of the divisions into the summary worksheet as it appears in worksheet A.

Make sure rows 25 through 30 appear in each worksheet.

Move	the cell pointer to cell A:B26	**Click**	*on cell A:B26*
Type	+	**Type**	*+*
Press	Ctrl + Page Up to move the cell pointer to worksheet B	**Click**	*the Next Sheet ⌐ SmartIcon to move the cell pointer to worksheet B*
Move	the cell pointer to cell B:C30	**Click**	*on cell B:C30*
Press	←Enter	**Click**	*the mouse button with the mouse pointer in the control panel*

Your screen should now look like Figure 12-9. If you used the keyboard steps, notice that the formula +B:C30 is stored in cell A:B26 indicating that the total salary for DIVISION 1 in Q1 appears in the cell. If you used the mouse steps, notice that the formula +B:C30..B:C30 is stored in cell A:B26 indicating that the total salary for DIVISION 1 in Q1 appears in the cell.

Figure 12-9

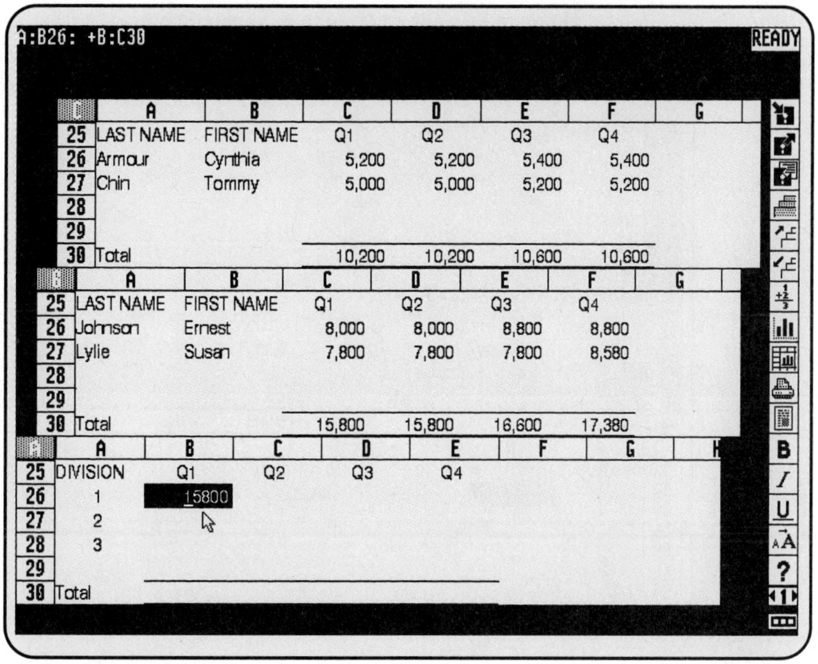

```
A:B26: +B:C30                                                    READY
```

	A	B	C	D	E	F	G
25	LAST NAME	FIRST NAME	Q1	Q2	Q3	Q4	
26	Armour	Cynthia	5,200	5,200	5,400	5,400	
27	Chin	Tommy	5,000	5,000	5,200	5,200	
28							
29							
30	Total		10,200	10,200	10,600	10,600	

	A	B	C	D	E	F	G
25	LAST NAME	FIRST NAME	Q1	Q2	Q3	Q4	
26	Johnson	Ernest	8,000	8,000	8,800	8,800	
27	Lylie	Susan	7,800	7,800	7,800	8,580	
28							
29							
30	Total		15,800	15,800	16,600	17,380	

	A	B	C	D	E	F	G	H
25	DIVISION	Q1	Q2	Q3	Q4			
26	1	15800						
27	2							
28	3							
29								
30	Total							

Now copy the formula in cell A:B26 to the other cells in row 26 of the summary worksheet.

Press	`/`		***Move***	*the mouse pointer to the control panel*
Select	Copy		***Choose***	*Copy*
Press	`←Enter`		***Click***	*the mouse button with the mouse pointer in the control panel*
Highlight	cells A:C26 through A:E26		***Highlight***	*cells A:C26 through A:E26*
Press	`←Enter`		***Click***	*the mouse button with the mouse pointer in the control panel*

Your screen should now look like Figure 12-10.

Figure 12-10

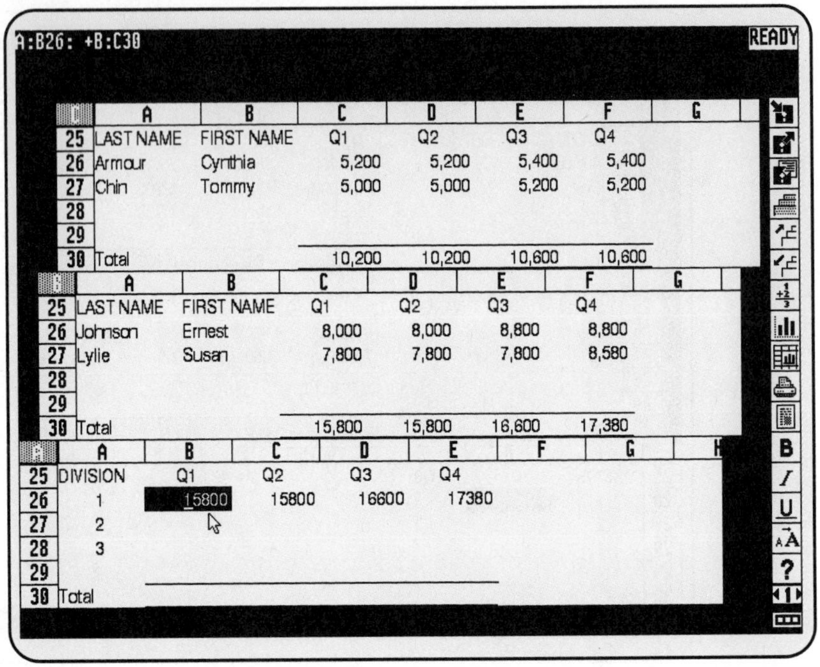

To place the total salary values for DIVISIONS 2 and 3 in the summary worksheet:

Move	the cell pointer to cell A:B27		*Click*	*on cell A:B27*
Type	+		*Type*	*+*
Press	Ctrl + Page Up twice to move the cell pointer to worksheet C		*Click*	*the Next Sheet SmartIcon twice to move the cell pointer to worksheet C*
Move	the cell pointer to cell C:C30		*Click*	*on cell C:C30*
Press	←Enter		*Click*	*the mouse button with the mouse pointer in the control panel*
Move	the cell pointer to cell A:B28		*Click*	*on cell A:B28*
Type	+		*Type*	*+*
Press	Ctrl + Page Up three times to move the cell pointer to worksheet D		*Click*	*the Next Sheet SmartIcon three times to move the cell pointer to worksheet C*
Move	the cell pointer to cell D:C30		*Click*	*on cell D:C30*
Press	←Enter		*Click*	*the mouse button with the mouse pointer in the control panel*

To copy the formulas to cells A:C27 through A:E28 in the summary worksheet:

Move	the cell pointer to cell A:B27		*Click*	*on cell A:B27*
Press	⎡ / ⎤		*Move*	*the mouse pointer to the control panel*
Select	Copy		*Choose*	*Copy*
Highlight	cells A:B27 through A:B28		*Highlight*	*cells A:B27 through A:B28*
Press	⎡←Enter⎤		*Click*	*the mouse button with the mouse pointer in the control panel*
Highlight	cells A:C27 through A:E28		*Highlight*	*cells A:C27 through A:E28*
Press	⎡←Enter⎤		*Click*	*the mouse button with the mouse pointer in the control panel*

The total salary, by quarter, for each division now appears in worksheet A and your screen should look like Figure 12-11.

Figure 12-11

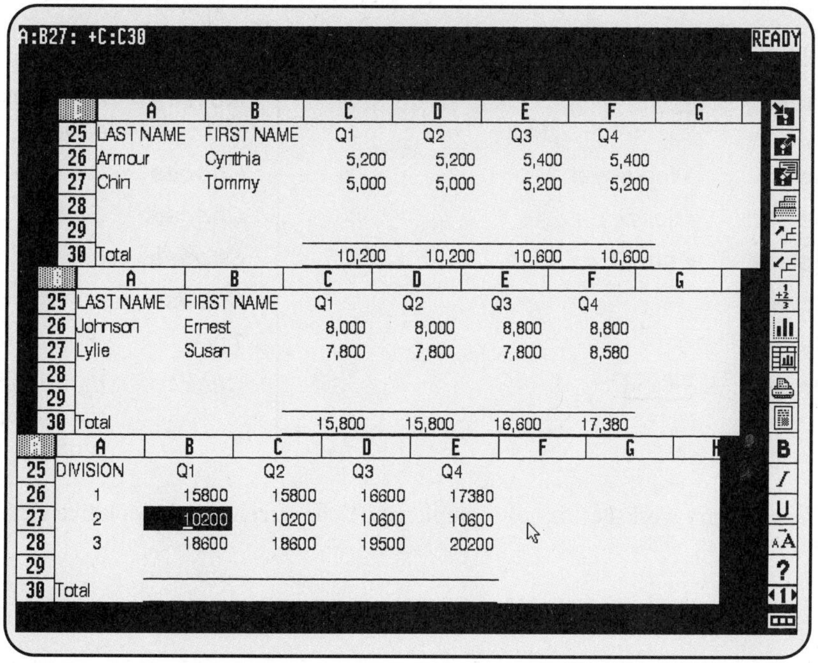

To compute the total salary value for each quarter, you need to complete the following steps:

Move	the cell pointer to cell A:B30		*Click*	*on cell A:B30*

Type	@SUM(		***Click***	*the SUM ⬚ SmartIcon*
Highlight	cells A:B26 through A:B28			
Type	)			
Press	[←Enter]			

To copy the sum formula to cells A:C30 through A:E30:

Press	[/]		***Move***	*the mouse pointer to the control panel*
Select	Copy		***Choose***	*Copy*
Press	[←Enter]		***Click***	*the mouse button with the mouse pointer in the control panel*
Highlight	cells A:C30 through A:E30		***Highlight***	*cells A:C30 through A:E30*
Press	[←Enter]		***Click***	*the mouse button with the mouse pointer in the control panel*

To format the summary worksheet properly:

Press	[/]		***Move***	*the mouse pointer to the control panel*
Select	Worksheet		***Choose***	*Worksheet*
Select	Global		***Choose***	*Global*
Select	Format		***Choose***	*Format*
Select	,		***Choose***	*,*
Type	0		***Type***	*0*
Press	[←Enter]		***Click***	*the mouse button with the mouse pointer in the control panel*

The summary worksheet is now completed. Your screen should look like Figure 12-12.

Figure 12-12

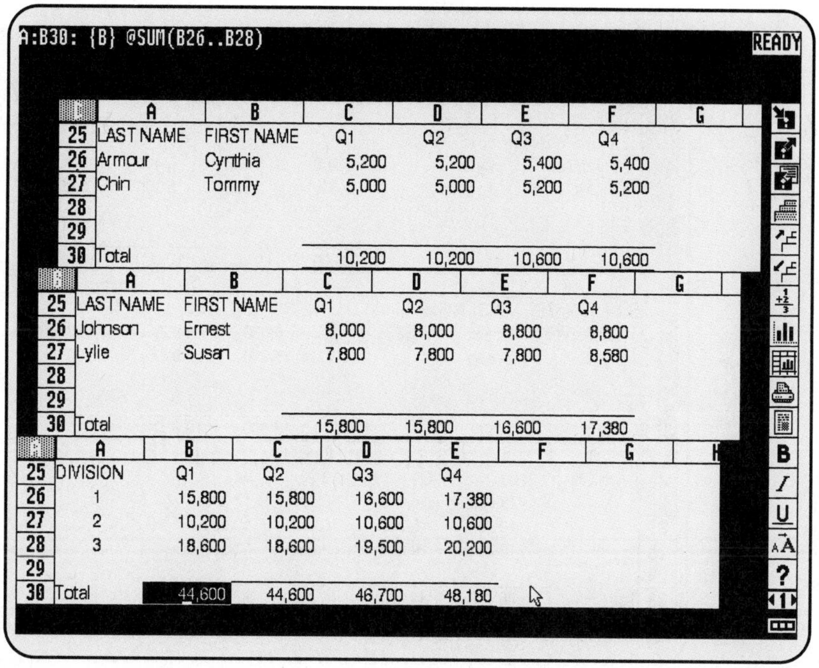

```
A:B30: {B} @SUM(B26..B28)                                    READY
```

	A	B	C	D	E	F	G
25	LAST NAME	FIRST NAME	Q1	Q2	Q3	Q4	
26	Armour	Cynthia	5,200	5,200	5,400	5,400	
27	Chin	Tommy	5,000	5,000	5,200	5,200	
28							
29							
30	Total		10,200	10,200	10,600	10,600	

	A	B	C	D	E	F	G
25	LAST NAME	FIRST NAME	Q1	Q2	Q3	Q4	
26	Johnson	Ernest	8,000	8,000	8,800	8,800	
27	Lylie	Susan	7,800	7,800	7,800	8,580	
28							
29							
30	Total		15,800	15,800	16,600	17,380	

	A	B	C	D	E	F	G	H
25	DIVISION	Q1	Q2	Q3	Q4			
26	1	15,800	15,800	16,600	17,380			
27	2	10,200	10,200	10,600	10,600			
28	3	18,600	18,600	19,500	20,200			
29								
30	Total	44,600	44,600	46,700	48,180			

You essentially linked the worksheets in the file by using formulas. The advantage of such a process is that if you change the salary for an individual, the summary worksheet will be updated automatically. To demonstrate the updating process:

Press   Ctrl + Page Up to move the cell pointer to worksheet B

Move   the cell pointer to cell B:C26

Enter   10000

Click   *the Next Sheet SmartIcon to move the cell pointer to worksheet B*

Click   *on cell B:C26*

Enter   *10000*

Notice that the total salary value for Q1 in the summary worksheet increased by the same amount that you increased the salary for Ernest Johnson. Your screen should now look like Figure 12-13.

Figure 12-13

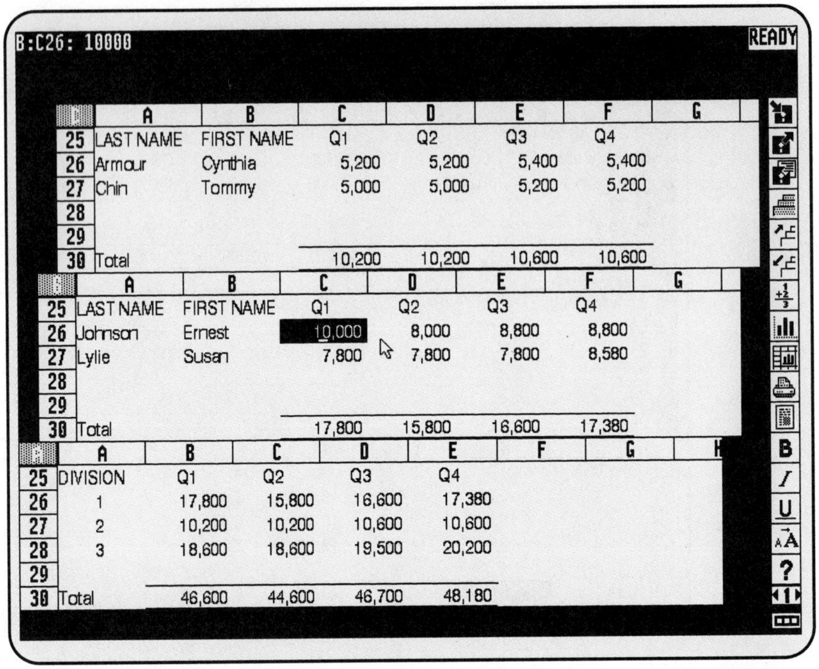

Change the value back to 8,000 and move the cell pointer to cell A1 in worksheet A. Use the information in Figure 12-14 to document the spreadsheet.

Figure 12-14

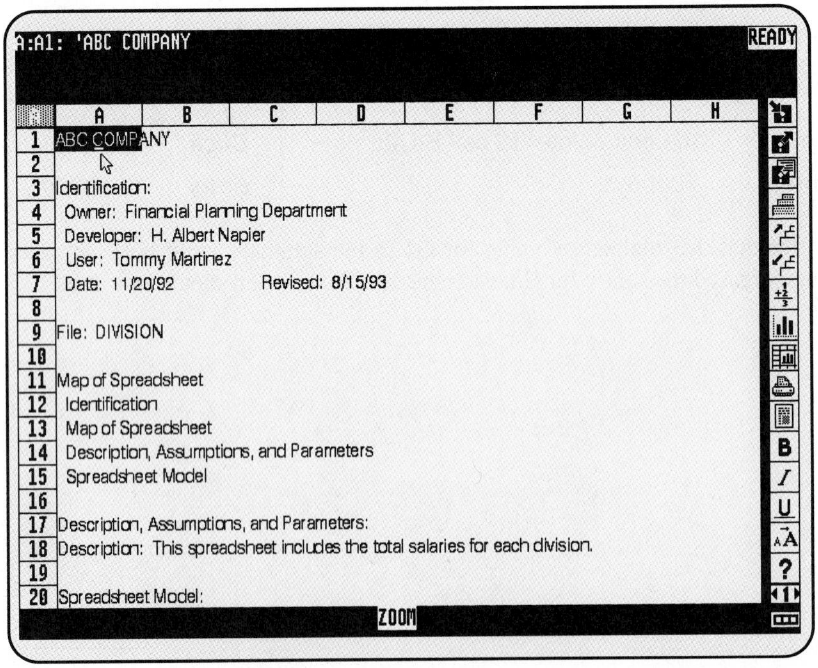

Move the cell pointer to cell A:A21 and then save the DIVISION file using the **F**ile **S**ave **R**eplace command sequence.

■ LINKING FILES TO MOVE INFORMATION BETWEEN FILES

In the previous section, three worksheets were created and some data from the worksheets were consolidated into a summary worksheet by linking the cells in the worksheets of the files together using formulas. Now you will learn how to **link files** together directly.

First, you need to open the BUDGET file and place it before the DIVISION file. Then you will erase the salary values that appear on worksheet A in the BUDGET file. Finally, you will link the two files together and the total salary values will appear on worksheet A in the BUDGET file.

Move	the cell pointer to cell A:A21		*Click*	*on cell A:A21*
Press	⟦ / ⟧		*Move*	*the cell pointer to the control panel*
Select	File		*Choose*	*File*
Select	Open		*Choose*	*Open*
Select	Before		*Choose*	*Before*
Press	⟦F3⟧		*Press*	⟦F3⟧
Move	the cell pointer to the BUDGET file name		*Move*	*the mouse pointer to the BUDGET file name*
Press	⟦←Enter⟧		*Click*	*the mouse button*

The BUDGET worksheet you created in Chapter 4 is shown on your screen. You now have two active files: BUDGET and DIVISION. To get a 3-D look at the files:

Press	⟦ / ⟧		*Click*	*the Perspective* ▦ *SmartIcon*
Select	Worksheet			
Select	Window			
Select	Perspective			

Your screen should now look like Figure 12-15. Notice that the worksheet stored in the BUDGET file appears before the multiple worksheets in the DIVISION file.

Figure 12-15

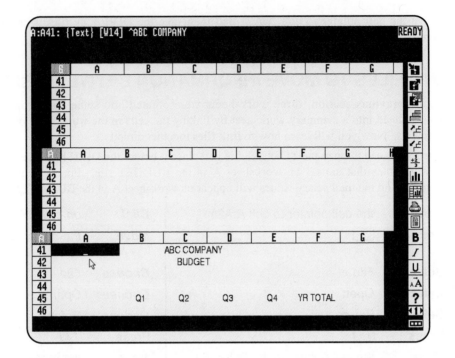

Notice that the cell pointer for worksheets A and B in the DIVISION file is in cells A:A41 and B:A41 respectively. To see the data in these worksheets:

Move	the cell pointer to cell A:A25 in the BUDGET worksheet	*Click*	*on cell A:A25 in the BUDGET worksheet*
Press	`/`	*Move*	*the mouse pointer to the control panel*
Select	Worksheet	*Choose*	*Worksheet*
Select	Window	*Choose*	*Window*
Select	Unsync	*Choose*	*Unsync*

Now the worksheets will not scroll together at the same time. To get the cell pointer in the proper place, move it to cell A:A50 using the pointer-movement keys or by clicking on the cell. Your screen should look like Figure 12-16.

Figure 12-16

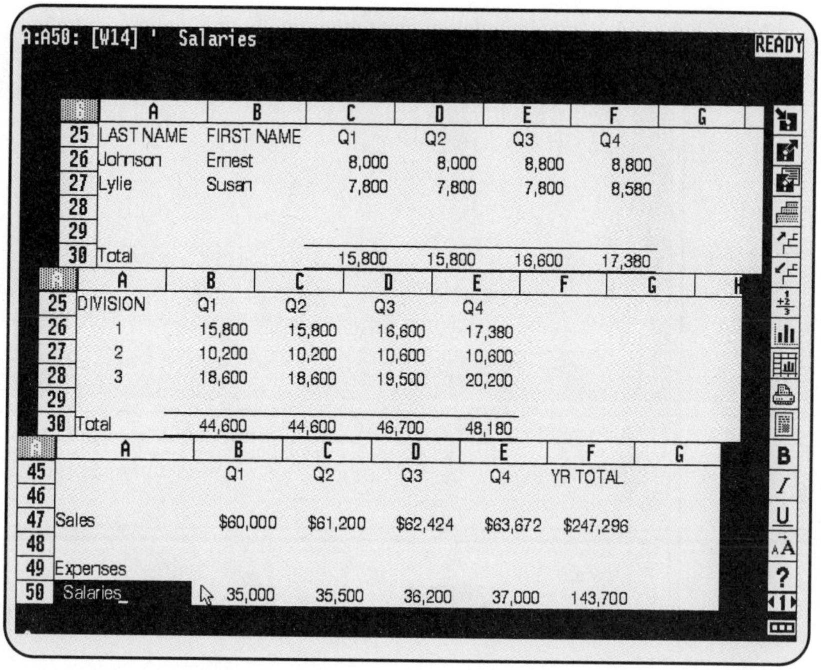

To erase the salary values in the BUDGET file:

Highlight	cells A:B50 through A:E50 in the BUDGET worksheet		*Highlight*	*cells A:B50 through A:E50 in the BUDGET worksheet*
Press	[/]		*Move*	*the mouse pointer to the control panel*
Select	Range		*Choose*	*Range*
Select	Erase		*Choose*	*Erase*

Your screen should now look like Figure 12-17.

Figure 12-17

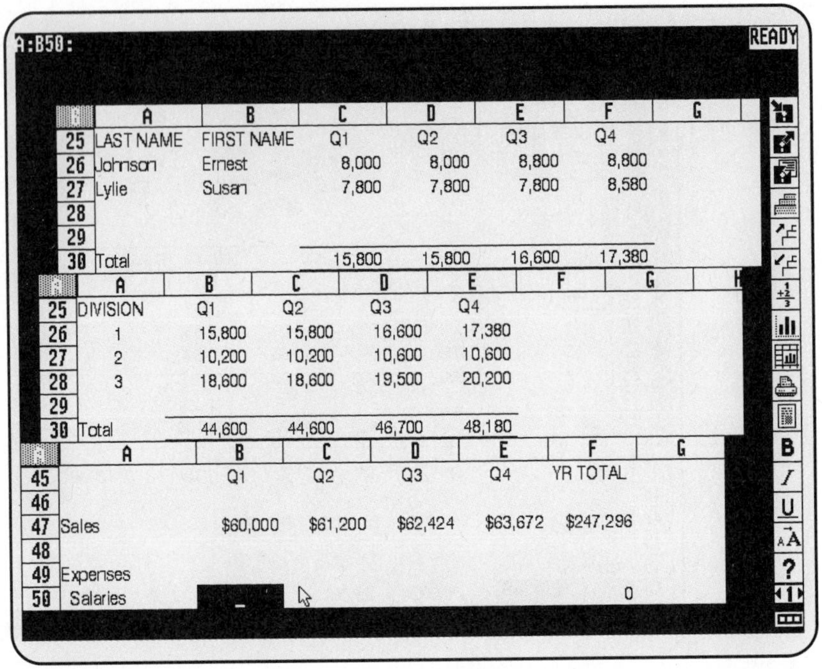

To link the salary values in worksheet A of the DIVISION file to the Salaries cells in the BUDGET file:

Move	the cell pointer to cell A:B50 in the BUDGET worksheet	*Click*	*on cell A:B50 in the BUDGET worksheet*
Type	+	*Type*	*+*
Press	Ctrl + Page Up to move to worksheet A of the DIVISION file	*Click*	*the Next ⯑ Sheet SmartIcon to move to worksheet A of the DIVISION file*
Move	the cell pointer to cell A:B30	*Move*	*the cell pointer to cell A:B30*
Press	←Enter	*Click*	*the mouse button*

To copy the link for the formula appearing in cell A:B50 to cells A:C50 through A:E50:

Press	/	*Move*	*the mouse pointer to the control panel*
Select	Copy	*Choose*	*Copy*
Press	←Enter	*Click*	*the mouse button*
Highlight	cells A:C50 through A:E50	*Highlight*	*cells A:C50 through A:E50*
Press	←Enter	*Click*	*the mouse button*

The cells of the two files are now properly linked and your screen should look like Figure 12-18.

Figure 12-18

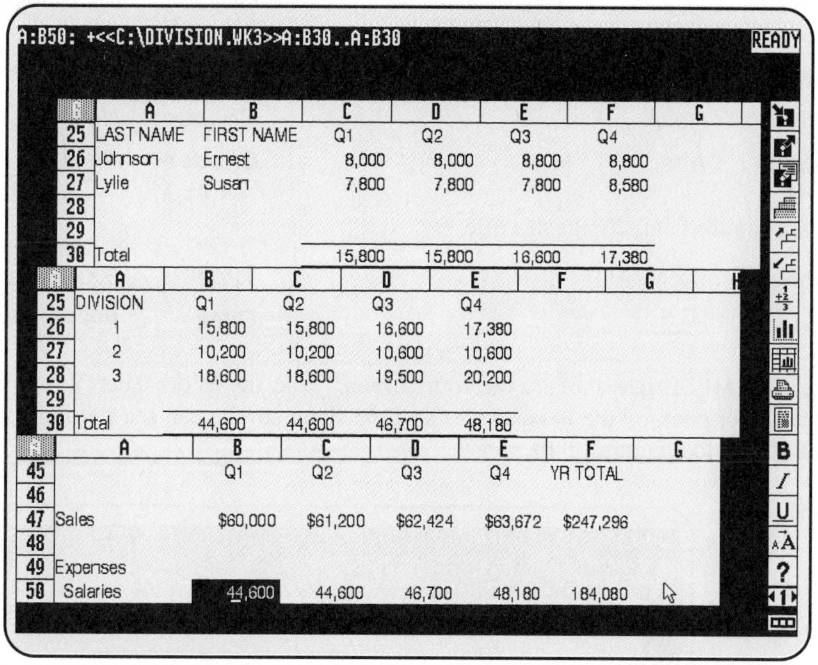

Notice by the cell address in Figure 12-18 the information that appears denotes the directory, file name, and cell that are linked to the cell.

You can link to files that are not currently in memory, but reside on a disk. For example, suppose only the BUDGET file is open. To link to the DIVISION file, you can type the formula +<<C:\DIVISION.WK3>>A:B30..A:B30 in cell A:B50 of the BUDGET worksheet. This formula then can be copied to cells A:C50 through A:E50.

If you change a value in a file that is linked to a formula, you must use the **F**ile Admin Link-Refresh command sequence to recalculate the linked formula.

■ OPENING A NEW FILE

In the last section you opened an additional file that already existed. In some situations, you may need to have a new file in memory along with another file that is currently in memory.

Before illustrating the process for inserting a new file in memory, clear your screen and retrieve the SALES file.

To place a new file in memory after the SALES file:

Press	/	**Move**	the mouse pointer to the control panel
Select	File	**Choose**	File
Select	New	**Choose**	New
Select	After	**Choose**	After

To specify the name for the new file:

Type	EXAMPLE	**Type**	EXAMPLE
Press	←Enter	**Click**	the mouse button

The EXAMPLE file appears on your screen. Use the **W**orksheet **W**indow **P**erspective command sequence or click on the Perspective ⌨ SmartIcon so you can see portions of both files. Your screen should look like Figure 12-19.

Figure 12-19

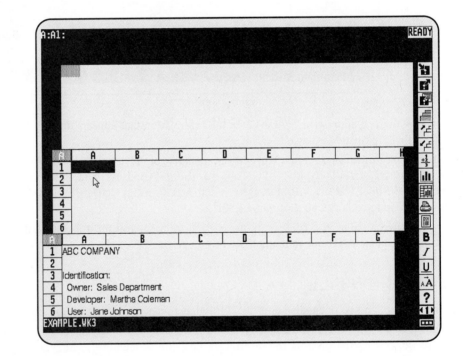

Note that the SALES file appears before the EXAMPLE file.

In some situations, you may need to delete a file from the memory of the computer. Suppose you want to delete the EXAMPLE file.

Press	/	**Move**	the mouse pointer to the control panel

Select	Worksheet		*Choose*	*Worksheet*	
Select	Delete		*Choose*	*Delete*	
Select	File		*Choose*	*File*	
Move	the cell pointer to the EXAMPLE file name		*Move*	*the mouse pointer to the EXAMPLE file name*	
Press	⎸←Enter⎹		*Click*	*the mouse button*	

Only the SALES file appears on your screen.

SUMMARY

You can use a template to create several identical worksheets in a file. Appropriate data can then be entered into the worksheets. A summary worksheet can be used to summarize the data in the individual worksheets in the file. Lotus 1-2-3 also provides the capability to link files to each other through the use of formulas that link cells.

KEY CONCEPTS

Consolidating information between worksheets
File New
File Open
Linking files
Worksheet Delete File

EXERCISE 1

INSTRUCTIONS: Circle T if the statement is true and F if the statement is false.

T   F   1. A template can be used to create several worksheets very rapidly.

T   F   2. Worksheets in a file can be linked together through the use of formulas.

T   F   3. Although worksheets can be linked by formulas, files cannot be linked in the same manner.

T   F   4. Multiple worksheets make it easy to combine information between the worksheets.

T   F   5. Only two files can be open at one time, but many worksheets can be open within one file.

EXERCISE 2

INSTRUCTIONS: Explain a typical situation when the following keystrokes or 1-2-3 commands are used.

Problem 1: [/] **F**ile **O**pen **B**efore

Problem 2: [/] **W**orksheet **I**nsert **S**heet

Problem 3: [/] **W**orksheet **D**elete **F**ile

Problem 4: [Ctrl] + [Home]

Problem 5: [Ctrl] + [Page Up]

Problem 6: [Ctrl] + [Page Down]

EXERCISE 3 — Consolidating Worksheets

INSTRUCTIONS: Retrieve the XYZSALES file that was created as an exercise in Chapter 11.

Add a summary worksheet that contains the total monthly revenues for the New York, Chicago, Houston, and Los Angeles locations.

Include a total line on the summary sheet that computes the total revenues for XYZ Consulting Company.

Print the summary worksheet.

EXERCISE 4 — Linking Files

INSTRUCTIONS: Retrieve the DIVSALES file that was completed as an exercise in Chapter 11.

Rather than include an additional worksheet in the DIVSALES file, open a new file named ABCSUMRY before the DIVSALES file.

Create a summary worksheet in the ABCSUMRY file that includes cells for the quarterly sales of each division and calculates the total revenue by quarter and for the year of ABC Company.

Link the appropriate cells containing the data from the worksheets in the DIVSALES file to the proper cells in the ABCSUMRY file.

Print the ABCSUMRY worksheet.

EXERCISE 5 — Consolidating Multiple Worksheets in a File

INSTRUCTIONS: Create a file with multiple worksheets and include a summary worksheet that will be helpful to you in some way. Link some of the data in the worksheets to the summary worksheet.

Print your worksheets.

EXERCISE 6 — Linking Files

INSTRUCTIONS: Create an application of 1-2-3 that uses the concept of linking files that will be helpful to you in some way.

Print the worksheets associated with the files.

CHAPTER THIRTEEN

INTRODUCTION TO DATABASE CAPABILITIES

OBJECTIVES

In this chapter, you will learn to:

- Identify basic database terms
- Sort data in a spreadsheet
- Query for specific data in a spreadsheet
- Create a computed column in the output range
- Use additional data query options

■ CHAPTER OVERVIEW

1-2-3 can perform **database** capabilities such as sorting data and querying data in a worksheet. Suppose some of the personal information for all employees of an organization is entered into a single worksheet. To sort the names by division within the organization, you can use the **Data Sort** command sequence. To generate a report listing all employees who have been employed by the company for over 10 years, you can use the **Data Query** command sequence. However, 1-2-3 cannot perform database capabilities as extensively as a database management system like dBASE III PLUS or IV, R:BASE System V, or Paradox Release 3.5. or 4.0. This chapter discusses the basic database capabilities of 1-2-3. Chapter 14 contains additional database features available in 1-2-3.

■ IDENTIFYING BASIC DATABASE TERMS

Some of the basic terms used in database management are **field**, **record**, **table**, and **key**.

A **field** is a collection of characters that are grouped together. In 1-2-3, each field is contained in a separate column within the database, or file. An example would be a person's last name. A **field name** is the term used to describe each field. For example, the title LAST NAME might be the field name for the field in which a person's last name is listed. In 1-2-3, each field name is placed in the column containing the field and is located in the cell *immediately* above the first data value in the column.

A **record** is a group of data fields that are combined in some logical pattern. For example, the personnel record for individuals in a company might include the individual's social security number, last name, first name, middle initial, department in which the individual works and so forth. In 1-2-3, each record is listed as a separate row.

A **database table** is a group of records that are placed together on a worksheet in a logical manner. For example, the personnel database table would include all of the personnel records.

A **key** is a specific field that can be used for distinguishing between records. For example, an identification number or the social security number for an employee can be used as a key for a personnel database table. Keys are generally unique to a record.

■ SORTING DATA IN A SPREADSHEET

Sometimes you may need to sort data. For example, it may be necessary to sort transactions by type. The following exercises demonstrate how to sort information in 1-2-3.

Sorting by a Primary Key

Make sure you have a blank worksheet on your screen. Then enter the documentation information in Figure 13-1 on your worksheet.

Figure 13-1

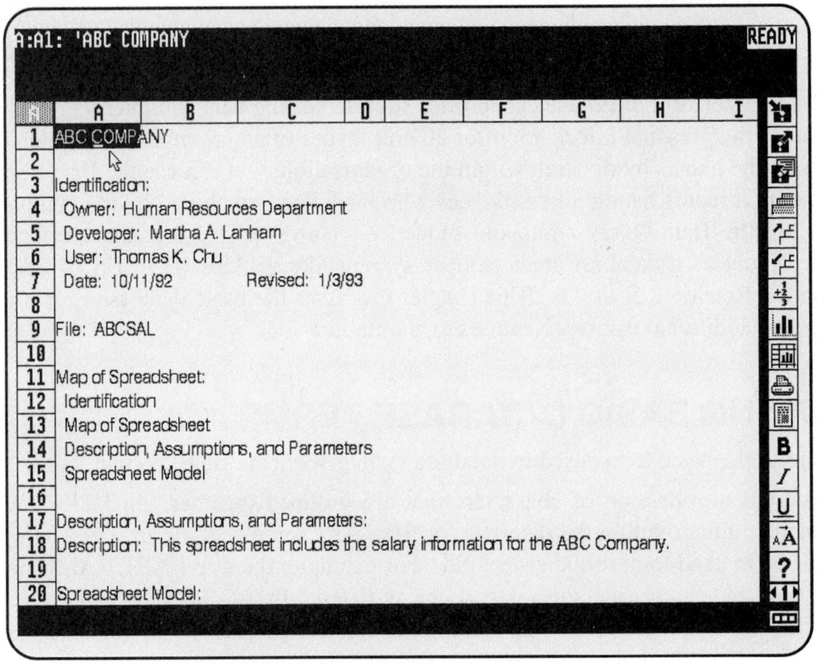

Make sure row 21 is the first row on your worksheet and move the cell pointer to cell A21. Then create the worksheet appearing in Figure 13-2 and save it using the file name ABCSAL.

Figure 13-2

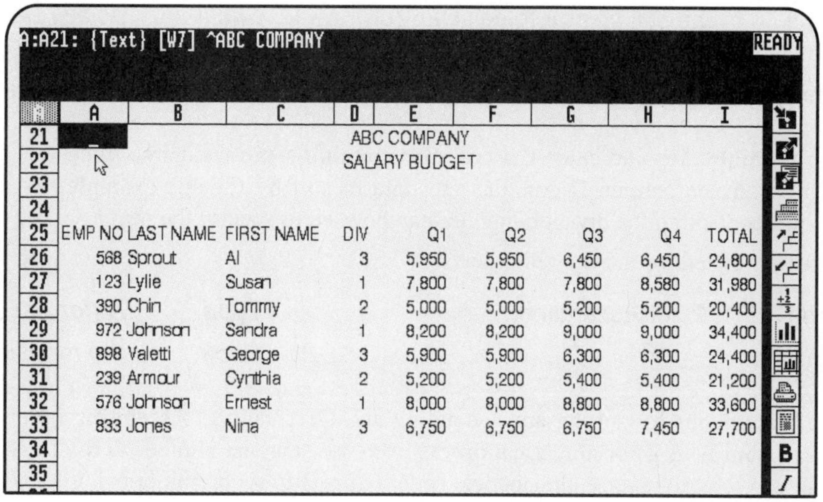

```
A:A21: {Text} [W7] ^ABC COMPANY                                    READY

        A        B          C         D      E       F       G       H       I
  21                                        ABC COMPANY
  22        ▷                              SALARY BUDGET
  23
  24
  25  EMP NO LAST NAME FIRST NAME    DIV     Q1      Q2      Q3      Q4    TOTAL
  26    568 Sprout    Al              3    5,950   5,950   6,450   6,450  24,800
  27    123 Lylie     Susan           1    7,800   7,800   7,800   8,580  31,980
  28    390 Chin      Tommy           2    5,000   5,000   5,200   5,200  20,400
  29    972 Johnson   Sandra          1    8,200   8,200   9,000   9,000  34,400
  30    898 Valetti   George          3    5,900   5,900   6,300   6,300  24,400
  31    239 Armour    Cynthia         2    5,200   5,200   5,400   5,400  21,200
  32    576 Johnson   Ernest          1    8,000   8,000   8,800   8,800  33,600
  33    833 Jones     Nina            3    6,750   6,750   6,750   7,450  27,700
  34
  35
```

Suppose you need to sort the data in the ABCSAL worksheet in order by division number.

Specifying the Data Range

Before sorting the spreadsheet, you need to specify the data range. The **data range** indicates where the database records you want to sort are located on the worksheet. To specify the data range:

Press	/		**Move**	the mouse pointer to the control panel
Select	Data		**Choose**	Data
Select	Sort		**Choose**	Sort
Select	Data-Range		**Choose**	Data-Range

When prompted for the data range:

Highlight	cells A26 through I33		**Highlight**	cells A26 through I33
Press	←Enter		**Click**	the mouse button

All of the records in cells A26 through I33 comprise the data range. Note that only the records and *not* the field names (EMP NO, LAST NAME, FIRST NAME, …) are included in the data range. If the field names are included, they will be sorted. Another common error is to highlight only the column that needs to be sorted when indicating the data range. If this error occurs, only the column specified in the data range will be sorted; none of the data in the adjacent columns (e.g., EMP NO, LAST NAME, FIRST NAME) are sorted with the appropriate division.

Specifying the Primary Key

To specify the primary key:

Select	Primary-Key		**Choose**	Primary-Key

Move	the cell pointer to cell D25 (or any other cell in column D)	**Click**	on cell D25 (or any other cell in column D)
Press	⎵Enter	**Click**	the mouse button

The **primary key** indicates the column containing the field by which the database should sort the records. Since column D contains the data to sort by (in this example, by division), any cell in the column containing the division number can be used to specify the primary key.

When prompted for the desired order:

Type	A (for Ascending)	**Type**	A (for Ascending)
Press	⎵Enter	**Click**	the mouse button

The two options for sorting are Ascending and Descending. **Ascending** order can refer to alphabetical order (from A to Z) or numerical order (from the smallest number to the largest number). **Descending** order can refer to reverse alphabetical order (from Z to A) or numerical order (from the largest number to the smallest number).

Sorting the Data

To begin the sort procedure:

Select	Go	**Choose**	Go

The records should be sorted in Ascending order by division number. Your screen should look like the final illustration in Figure 13-3. Figure 13-3, Parts 1 through 3 display the entire sort procedure.

Step 1 of the Sort Procedure: Specify the Data-Range.

Figure 13-3
Part 1

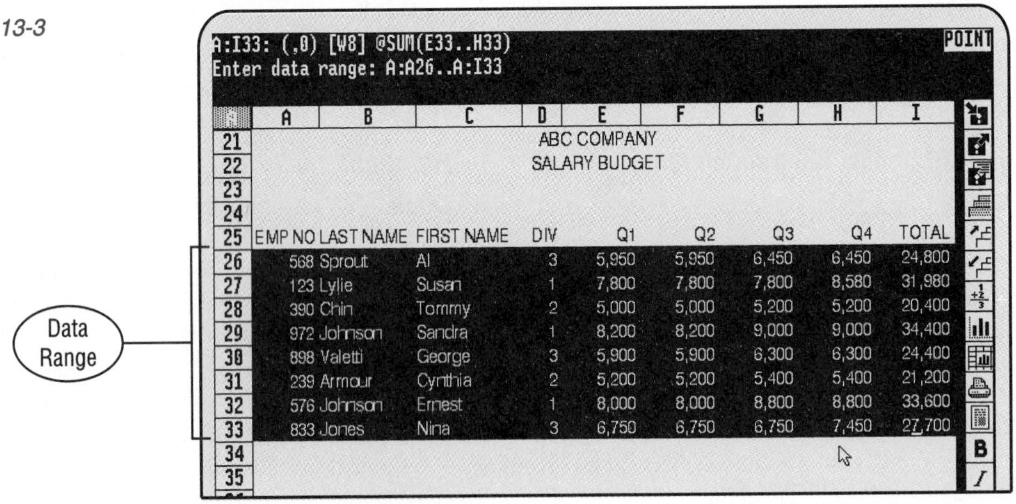

Step 2 of the Sort Procedure: Specify the Sort Column and the Sort Order.

Figure 13-3
Part 2

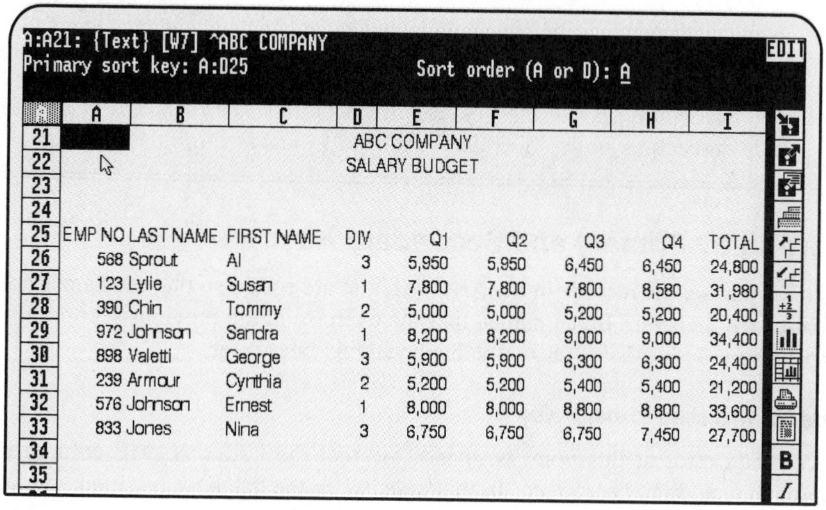

A:A21: {Text} [W7] ^ABC COMPANY
Primary sort key: A:D25 Sort order (A or D): A
EDIT

ABC COMPANY
SALARY BUDGET

EMP NO	LAST NAME	FIRST NAME	DIV	Q1	Q2	Q3	Q4	TOTAL
568	Sprout	Al	3	5,950	5,950	6,450	6,450	24,800
123	Lylie	Susan	1	7,800	7,800	7,800	8,580	31,980
390	Chin	Tommy	2	5,000	5,000	5,200	5,200	20,400
972	Johnson	Sandra	1	8,200	8,200	9,000	9,000	34,400
898	Valetti	George	3	5,900	5,900	6,300	6,300	24,400
239	Armour	Cynthia	2	5,200	5,200	5,400	5,400	21,200
576	Johnson	Ernest	1	8,000	8,000	8,800	8,800	33,600
833	Jones	Nina	3	6,750	6,750	6,750	7,450	27,700

Step 3 of the Sort Procedure: Select **G**o from the Sort Menu to Sort the Database.

Figure 13-3
Part 3

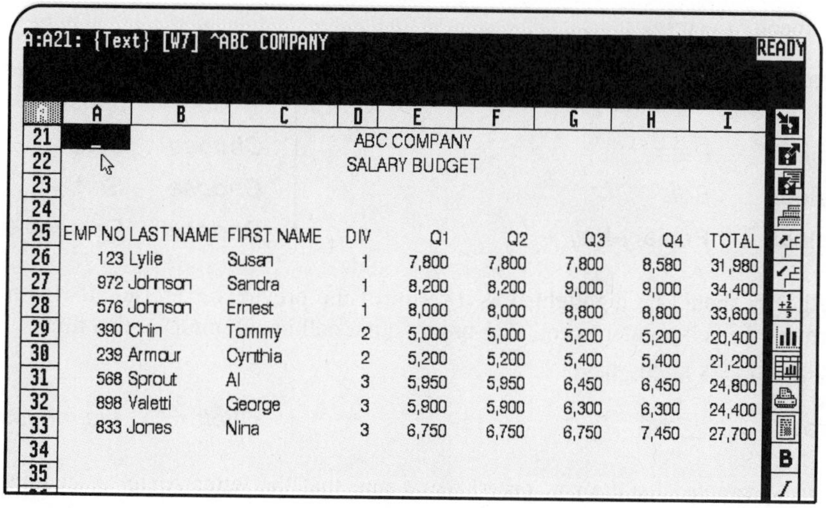

A:A21: {Text} [W7] ^ABC COMPANY
READY

ABC COMPANY
SALARY BUDGET

EMP NO	LAST NAME	FIRST NAME	DIV	Q1	Q2	Q3	Q4	TOTAL
123	Lylie	Susan	1	7,800	7,800	7,800	8,580	31,980
972	Johnson	Sandra	1	8,200	8,200	9,000	9,000	34,400
576	Johnson	Ernest	1	8,000	8,000	8,800	8,800	33,600
390	Chin	Tommy	2	5,000	5,000	5,200	5,200	20,400
239	Armour	Cynthia	2	5,200	5,200	5,400	5,400	21,200
568	Sprout	Al	3	5,950	5,950	6,450	6,450	24,800
898	Valetti	George	3	5,900	5,900	6,300	6,300	24,400
833	Jones	Nina	3	6,750	6,750	6,750	7,450	27,700

User Tip

An alternative method for sorting a primary key is to first highlight the data range. Then move the cell pointer to the column for the primary key and click the A-Z Sort ⬍ SmartIcon. The QuickSort dialog box appears. To begin the sort procedure choose the OK command button. If you want to sort the database in descending order, click the Z-A Sort ⬍ SmartIcon.

Sorting by Primary and Secondary Keys

In this exercise, the records in the ABCSAL file are sorted so that the names appear in alphabetical order within each division. It is assumed that the exercise in the previous section has just been completed and that the sorted records are currently displayed on your screen.

Specifying the Primary Key

A common error at this point is to indicate that the LAST NAME column is the primary key. This approach would not be correct. In this case, when the database is sorted, the last names would be sorted correctly, but the divisions would be out of order. The Division column will be the primary key so that the database is sorted *primarily* by division. The LAST NAME column will be specified as the **secondary key** so that the database is sorted *secondarily* by last name. This will cause the last names to appear in alphabetical order within each division.

To specify the primary key:

Press	/	**Move**	the mouse pointer to the control panel	
Select	Data	**Choose**	Data	
Select	Sort	**Choose**	Sort	
Select	Primary-Key	**Choose**	Primary-Key	

Cell D25 should be highlighted as a result of the previous exercise. If it is not, highlight cell D25 by moving the cell pointer to cell D25 or any other cell in column D at this time.

With cell D25 highlighted:

Press	←Enter	**Click**	the mouse button twice

When prompted for the sort order, make sure that the letter A (for **A**scending order) appears. The A should appear as a result of being selected in the previous exercise. If it does not, type A at this time.

With A specified as the sort order:

Press	←Enter	**Click**	the mouse button

Specifying the Secondary Key

To specify the secondary key:

Select	Secondary-Key		**Choose**	*Secondary-Key*
Move	the cell pointer to cell B25 (or any other cell in column B)		**Click**	*on cell B25 (or any other cell in column B)*
Press	⎡←Enter⎤		**Click**	*the mouse button*

Since column B contains the data to sort by (in this example, by LAST NAME), any cell in column B can be specified as the secondary key.

When prompted for the desired sort order:

Type	A		**Type**	*A*
Press	⎡←Enter⎤		**Click**	*the mouse button*

Sorting the Data

To begin the sort procedure:

Select	Go		**Choose**	*Go*

The database should now be sorted so that the last names are in alphabetical order by division. Your screen should look like Figure 13-4.

Figure 13-4

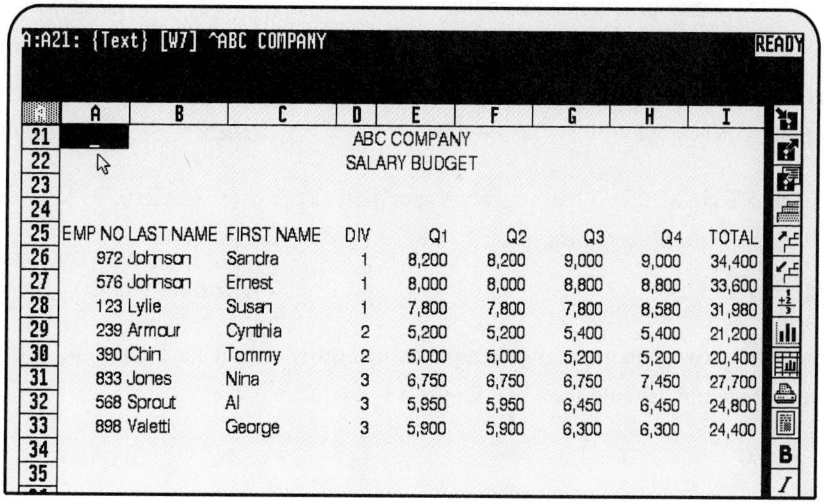

```
A:A21: {Text} [W7] ^ABC COMPANY                                    READY
```

	A	B	C	D	E	F	G	H	I
21					ABC COMPANY				
22					SALARY BUDGET				
23									
24									
25	EMP NO	LAST NAME	FIRST NAME	DIV	Q1	Q2	Q3	Q4	TOTAL
26	972	Johnson	Sandra	1	8,200	8,200	9,000	9,000	34,400
27	576	Johnson	Ernest	1	8,000	8,000	8,800	8,800	33,600
28	123	Lylie	Susan	1	7,800	7,800	7,800	8,580	31,980
29	239	Armour	Cynthia	2	5,200	5,200	5,400	5,400	21,200
30	390	Chin	Tommy	2	5,000	5,000	5,200	5,200	20,400
31	833	Jones	Nina	3	6,750	6,750	6,750	7,450	27,700
32	568	Sprout	Al	3	5,950	5,950	6,450	6,450	24,800
33	898	Valetti	George	3	5,900	5,900	6,300	6,300	24,400
34									
35									

Sorting by More than Two Keys

The example in the previous section sorted the last names in alphabetical order within each division. Notice that the records are not in alphabetical order. Sandra Johnson appears before Ernest Johnson in the list of employees for Division 1. Fortunately, 1-2-3 allows you to add **extra sort keys**. You can use a maximum of 256 sort keys.

Continuing with the example from the previous section, you need to include the FIRST NAME as an extra sort key to sort the employee name in alphabetical order within each division. Since the settings for the **D**ata-Range, **P**rimary-Key, and **S**econdary-Key have already been specified, you only need to complete the command sequence for the extra key.

Press	☐ /		**Move**	*the mouse pointer to the control panel*
Select	Data		**Choose**	*Data*
Select	Sort		**Choose**	*Sort*
Select	Extra-Key		**Choose**	*Extra-Key*

To accept Extra Key 1:

Press	←Enter		**Click**	*the mouse button*

To specify the FIRST NAME field as the additional sort key:

Move	the cell pointer to cell C25 (or any cell in column C)		**Click**	*on cell C25 (or any cell in column C)*
Press	←Enter		**Click**	*the mouse button*
Type	A		**Type**	*A*
Press	←Enter		**Click**	*the mouse button*

The FIRST NAME field has now been specified as the extra sort key.

To complete the sorting process:

Select	Go		**Choose**	*Go*

The data is now properly sorted in alphabetical order within each division.

Your screen now should look like Figure 13-5.

Figure 13-5

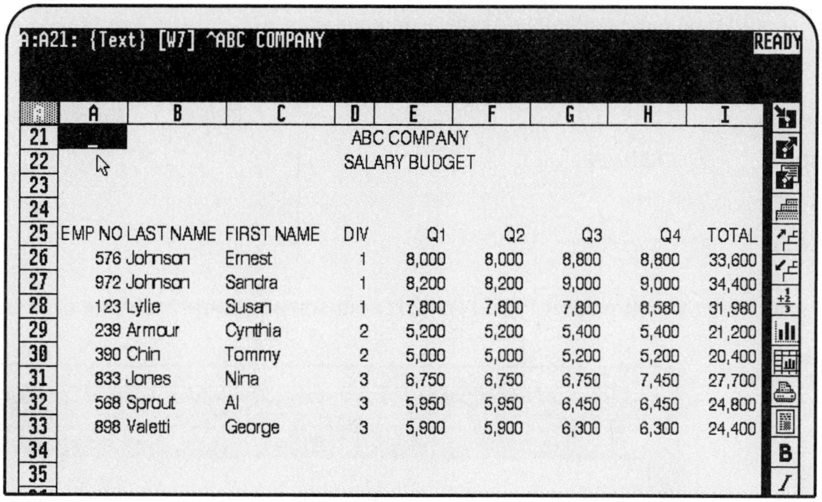

```
a:A21: {Text} [W7] ^ABC COMPANY                                    READY
```

	A	B	C	D	E	F	G	H	I	
21					ABC COMPANY					
22					SALARY BUDGET					
23										
24										
25	EMP NO	LAST NAME	FIRST NAME	DIV	Q1	Q2	Q3	Q4	TOTAL	
26	576	Johnson	Ernest	1	8,000	8,000	8,800	8,800	33,600	
27	972	Johnson	Sandra	1	8,200	8,200	9,000	9,000	34,400	
28	123	Lylie	Susan	1	7,800	7,800	7,800	8,580	31,980	
29	239	Armour	Cynthia	2	5,200	5,200	5,400	5,400	21,200	
30	390	Chin	Tommy	2	5,000	5,000	5,200	5,200	20,400	
31	833	Jones	Nina	3	6,750	6,750	6,750	7,450	27,700	
32	568	Sprout	Al	3	5,950	5,950	6,450	6,450	24,800	
33	898	Valetti	George	3	5,900	5,900	6,300	6,300	24,400	
34										
35										

■ QUERYING FOR DESIRED DATA IN A SPREADSHEET

At times, you may need to perform a **query**, which is the process of searching through a file and selecting items based on specific **criteria**. For example, you may wish to select all stores in a database file that have revenues in excess of $75,000 a year. The following exercises demonstrate how to perform queries in 1-2-3.

Querying with Simple Criteria

In this exercise, the data in the database table ABCSAL will be queried to find individuals in the file that have a total salary greater than $25,000.

Retrieve the original ABCSAL file for use in this exercise.

Placing the Criteria on a Separate Worksheet

Since you have the capability to have multiple worksheets in an individual file, it is useful to place the criteria on a separate worksheet in the file and leave the database table in another worksheet. By using this approach, you do not take as much risk of altering the data.

To add the worksheet for the criteria:

Press	`/`	***Click***	*the Insert Sheet* *SmartIcon*
Select	Worksheet		
Select	Insert		
Select	Sheet		
Select	After		
Type	1		
Press	←Enter		

You should now have a blank worksheet on your screen.

To view the database table along with the new worksheet:

Press	`/`	**Click**	the Perspective 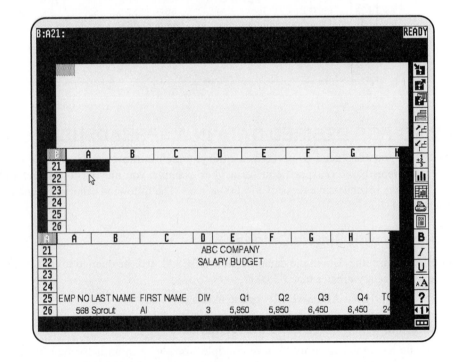 SmartIcon
Select	Worksheet		
Select	Window		
Select	Perspective		

After moving the cell pointer to cell B:A21, your screen should look like Figure 13-6.

Figure 13-6

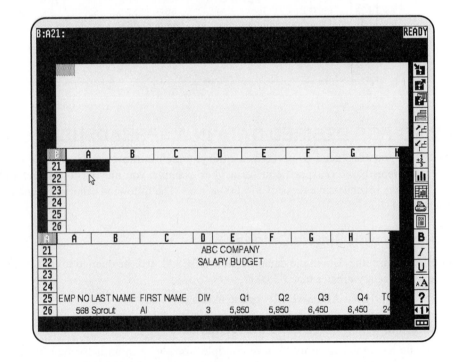

At this point, you need to place the criteria on the worksheet. When you finish placing the criteria on the worksheet, your screen will look like Figure 13-7.

To place the descriptive information on worksheet B:

Move	the cell pointer to cell B:A24	**Click**	on cell B:A24
Enter	CRITERIA RANGES	**Enter**	CRITERIA RANGES

The criteria must consist of at least two cells. The first cell specifies the field name that contains the data relevant to the query (in this case, the relevant data field name is TOTAL). The second line of the criteria must consist of a formula or data that specifies the actual query. The name in the first cell of the criteria range must match the field name in the database table exactly. Therefore, you will copy the field name TOTAL from the database table to the criteria range on worksheet B.

To specify the criteria for the query:

Move	the cell pointer to cell B:B26	***Click***	*on cell B:B26*
Press	⌞ / ⌟	***Move***	*the mouse pointer to the control panel*
Select	Copy	***Select***	*Copy*

When prompted for the range to copy FROM:

Press	⌞Esc⌟	***Click***	*the alternate mouse button*
Move	the cell pointer to cell A:I25	***Click***	*on cell A:I25*
Press	⌞←Enter⌟	***Click***	*the mouse button twice*

When prompted for the range to copy TO:

| **Press** | ⌞←Enter⌟ | ***Click*** | *the mouse button with the mouse pointer in the control panel* |

As indicated earlier, the word TOTAL in the criteria range must be listed exactly the way it is specified in the database table. It does not matter if the label is lowercase or uppercase letters or which label prefix (^, " or ') is used. However, TOTAL must match the field name TOTAL character for character. For example, TOTALS would not render the correct results, because the S in TOTALS is not present in the field name in the database table (cell A:I25).

To define the second line of the criteria:

Move	the cell pointer to cell B:B27	***Click***	*on cell B:B27*
Type	+	***Type***	*+*
Move	the cell pointer to cell A:I26	***Click***	*on cell A:I26*
Type	>	***Type***	*>*

Notice that the cell pointer returns to cell B:B27.

| **Type** | 25000 | ***Type*** | *25000* |
| **Press** | ⌞←Enter⌟ | ***Click*** | *the mouse button* |

The two cells required for the criteria range–the field name TOTAL and the condition (+A:I26>25000) have been entered. In this example, the criteria range indicates that the query is for cells under the field name TOTAL that contain data greater than 25,000.

The number 0 appears in cell B:B27. This is not significant in terms of performing a query; 1-2-3 simply tested the condition +I26>25000 to see if cell I26 is greater than 25,000. Since I26 contains 24,800, the test was false, and a 0 was placed in cell B:B27. If the condition had been true, the number 1 would have appeared in cell B:B27.

An optional step is to format cell B:B27 so that the formula for the criteria is displayed.

To format the cell to show the formula:

Press		***Move***	the mouse pointer to the control panel
Select	Range	***Choose***	Range
Select	Format	***Choose***	Format
Select	Text	***Choose***	Text
Press	←Enter	***Click***	the mouse button with the mouse pointer in the control panel

The formula +A:I26>25000 is now displayed in cell B:B27. Your screen should look like Figure 13-7.

Figure 13-7

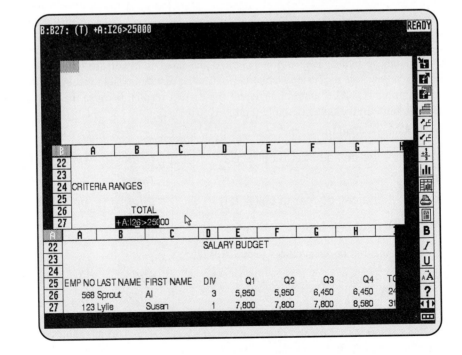

Placing the Output Range on the Worksheet

Once the records matching the criteria have been located, it is possible to copy these records to another part of the worksheet called an **output range**. By specifying an output range, the desired records can be analyzed and manipulated without disturbing the database table in which the records are contained. You will place the output range on worksheet B.

The field names define the output range. The records that match the criteria are copied or output to the cells immediately below the field names in the output range. When the records are copied to the output range and data exists, the data is overwritten.

To specify the output range on worksheet B, the appropriate field names must be copied from worksheet A. The field names in the output range must match the names in the database table character for character. For this reason, you will use the Copy command.

To copy the field names to the output range:

Move	the cell pointer to cell B:A30		*Click*	*on cell B:A30*
Press	⟦ / ⟧		*Move*	*the mouse pointer to the control panel*
Select	Copy		*Choose*	*Copy*

When prompted for the range to copy FROM:

Press	⟦Esc⟧		*Click*	*the alternate mouse button*
Highlight	cells A:A25 through A:I25		*Highlight*	*cells A:A25 through A:I25*
Press	⟦←Enter⟧		*Click*	*the mouse button*

When prompted for the range to copy TO:

Press	⟦←Enter⟧		*Click*	*the mouse button with the mouse pointer in the control panel*

Change the column widths for worksheet B as follows:

Columns	Width
A	7
B	10
C	11
D	4
E - I	8

To document where the output ranges are located (an optional step):

Move	the cell pointer to cell B:A29		*Click*	*on cell B:A29*
Enter	OUTPUT RANGE		*Enter*	*OUTPUT RANGE*

Your screen should look like Figure 13-8.

Figure 13-8

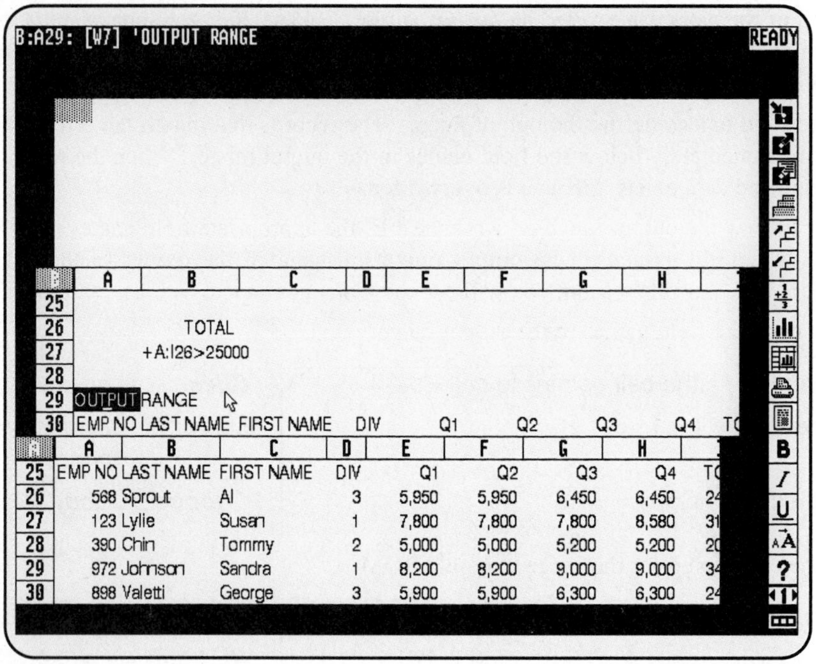

Specifying the Input Range

Now that the criteria and the headings for the output have been entered on the worksheet, you indicate through the Lotus 1-2-3 menu where the records, criteria, and output range are located. After these steps are finished, you complete the actual query operations.

To initiate the query process:

Press	/	**Move**	the mouse pointer to the control panel
Select	Data	**Choose**	Data
Select	Query	**Choose**	Query

First, indicate the input range. The **input range** is the term for the field names and data records located in the database table on worksheet A.

To specify the input range:

Select	Input	**Choose**	Input
Highlight	cells A:A25 through A:I33	**Highlight**	cells A:A25 through A:I33

Your screen should look like Figure 13-9.

Figure 13-9

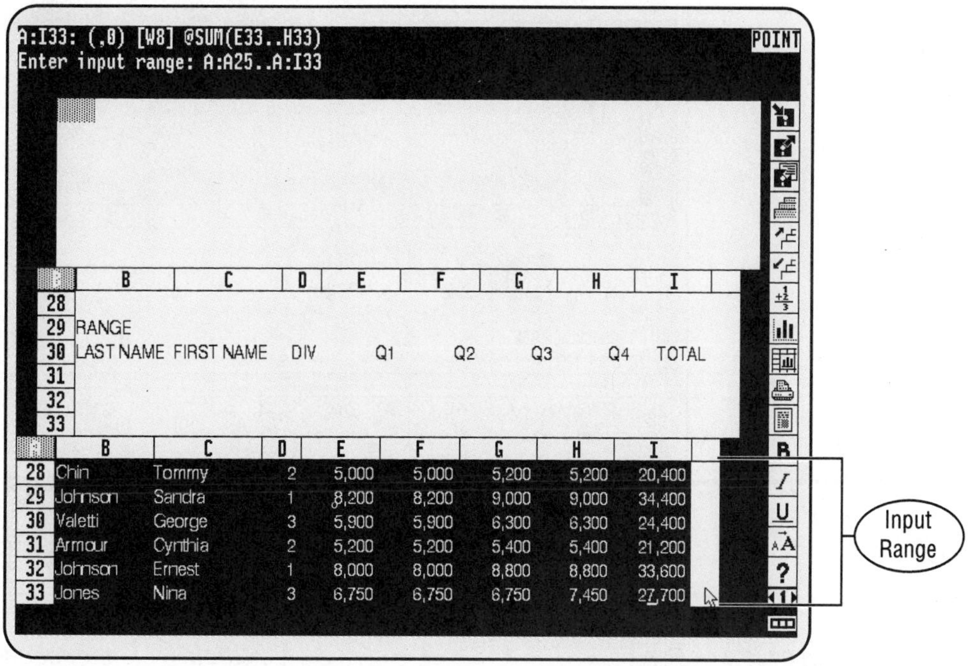

Press   ←Enter | **Click**   the mouse button

Note that the input range includes the field names (EMP NO, LAST NAME, FIRST NAME, . . .). If there are two lines of field titles, include only the bottom row in the input range and use only the words in the bottom line as the field names in your criteria and output ranges. Remember that the first database record must be in the row immediately under the field names without any rows separating the field name from the first record.

Specifying the Criteria Range

To specify where the criteria are located:

Select   Criteria | **Choose**   Criteria

When prompted for the criteria range:

Highlight   cells B:B26 through B:B27 | **Highlight**   cells B:B26 through B:B27

Your screen should now look like Figure 13-10.

Figure 13-10

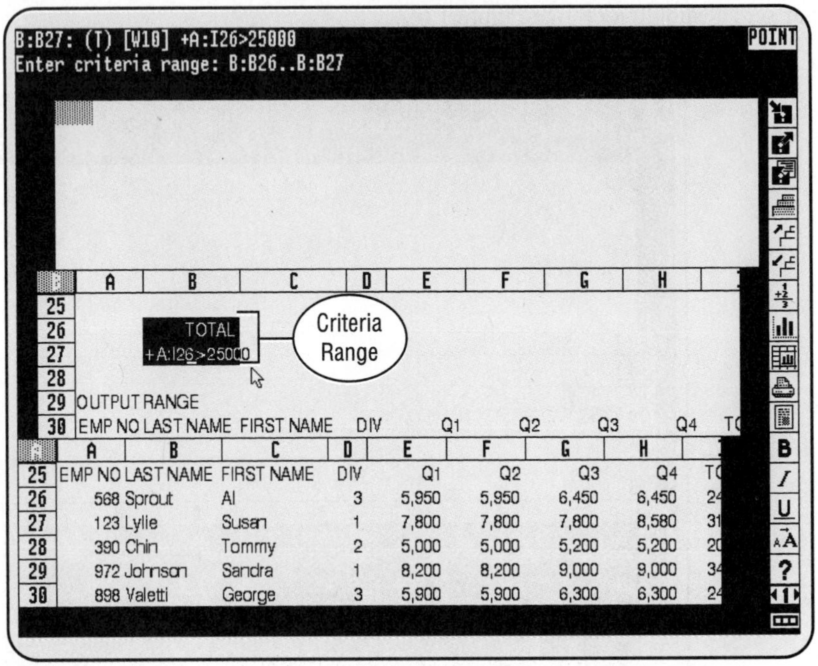

Press `←Enter` | ***Click*** *the mouse button*

Cells B:B26 and B:B27 define the criteria.

Performing a Find

The **Find** command highlights each record that satisfies the criteria. To determine whether the criteria have been specified correctly, you can use the following steps to perform a "Find" that will locate and highlight the records in the database that match the criteria.

To perform the Find procedure:

Select Find | ***Choose*** *Find*

The first record that should be highlighted is that of Susan Lylie on row 27. Since her salary total is $31,980, the criteria are satisfied.

To move to the next record that matches the criteria:

Press `↓` | ***Click*** *the* `↓` *SmartIcon*

The record of Sandra Johnson should be highlighted because the salary total is $34,400 and this amount matches the criteria.

To move to the next record that matches the criteria:

Press ⬛↓⬛ | *Click* *the* ⬇ *SmartIcon*

The record for Ernest Johnson is highlighted.

Press ⬛↓⬛ | *Click* *the* ⬇ *SmartIcon*

The record for Nina Jones is highlighted.

Press ⬛↓⬛ | *Click* *the* ⬇ *SmartIcon*

1-2-3 "beeps" when no more records that satisfy the criteria are in the database (not because Nina Jones is the last record in this database table).

To exit from "FIND" mode:

Press ⬛←Enter⬛ | *Click* *the alternate mouse button*

The Data Query menu should be visible at the top of the screen.

Specifying the Output Range

To specify the Output range:

Select	Output	*Choose*	*Output*
Highlight	cells B:A30 through B:I30	*Highlight*	*cells B:A30 through B:I30*

When the output range is highlighted, your screen should look like Figure 13-11.

Figure 13-11

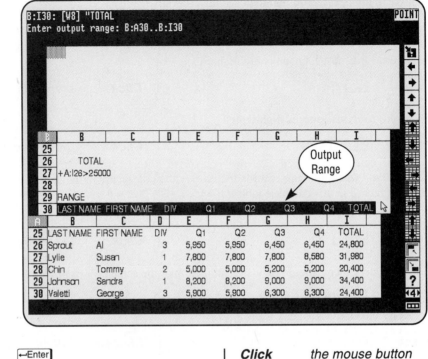

Press	←Enter		*Click*	*the mouse button*

Extracting (Copying) the Desired Data Fields to the Output Range

After the Input range, the Criteria range, and the Output range were specified in the Data Query menu, the Find option verified that the criteria was set correctly. 1-2-3 located only the records in the database table (input range) that matched the criteria. The records that match the criteria can be copied to the area below the specified Output range using the Extract menu option. Only the fields specified in the Output range will be copied. Note that although the menu option you will use is Extract, the records are not really extracted—they are copied; in other words, the records are **not** omitted from the original database table.

To copy the records that satisfy the criteria to the output range:

Select	Extract		*Choose*	*Extract*

To view the extracted data:

Select	Quit		*Choose*	*Quit*
Move	the cell pointer to cell B:A35		*Click*	*on cell B:A35*

Your screen should look like Figure 13-12.

Figure 13-12

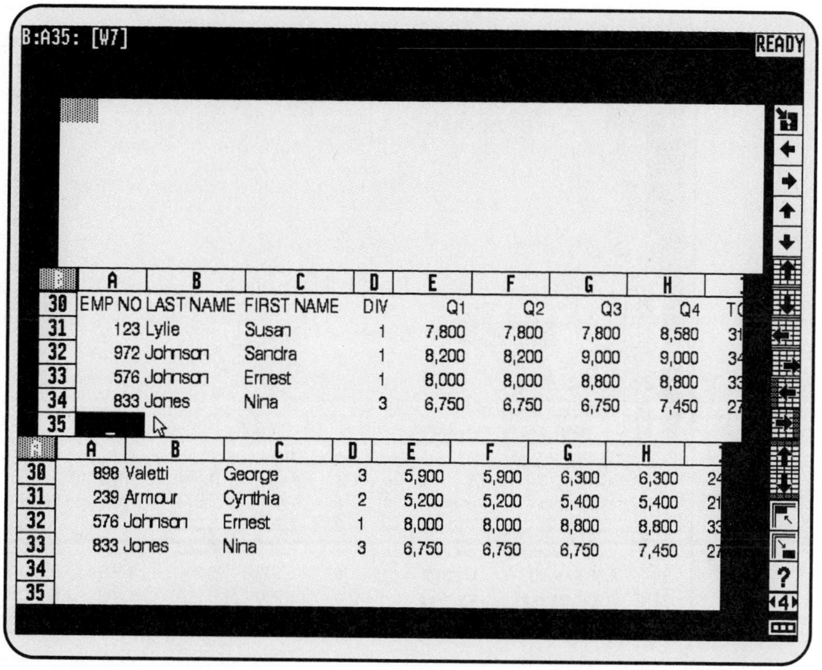

B:A35: [W7]   READY

	A	B	C	D	E	F	G	H	I
30	EMP NO	LAST NAME	FIRST NAME	DIV	Q1	Q2	Q3	Q4	TC
31	123	Lylie	Susan	1	7,800	7,800	7,800	8,580	31
32	972	Johnson	Sandra	1	8,200	8,200	9,000	9,000	34
33	576	Johnson	Ernest	1	8,000	8,000	8,800	8,800	33
34	833	Jones	Nina	3	6,750	6,750	6,750	7,450	27
35									

	A	B	C	D	E	F	G	H	I
30	898	Valetti	George	3	5,900	5,900	6,300	6,300	24
31	239	Armour	Cynthia	2	5,200	5,200	5,400	5,400	21
32	576	Johnson	Ernest	1	8,000	8,000	8,800	8,800	33
33	833	Jones	Nina	3	6,750	6,750	6,750	7,450	27
34									
35									

Querying with Multiple Conditions Using #AND#

In this example, you modify the criteria used in the previous exercise so that the criteria range contains multiple conditions. The database table in the ABCSAL worksheet is then queried to find records for individuals who have a total salary between $20,000 and $22,000, including any salaries that are exactly $20,000 or $22,000. To perform this query, the logical operator **#AND#** is used to combine the two conditions.

Assuming you have just completed the previous exercise and the results are still visible on your screen, complete the following problem.

Changing the Current Criteria to the Desired Criteria

In this exercise, you will change the current criteria to +A:I26>=20000#AND#A:I26<=22000. To change the criteria:

Move	the cell pointer to cell B:B27		***Click***	*on cell B:B27*
Enter	+A:I26>=20000#AND# A:I26<=22000		***Enter***	*+A:I26>=20000#AND# A:I26<=22000 (with no spaces)*

(The first line of the criteria range [cell B:B26–TOTAL] should remain the same.)

Assuming that the cell pointer is in cell B:B27, your screen should look like Figure 13-13.

Figure 13-13

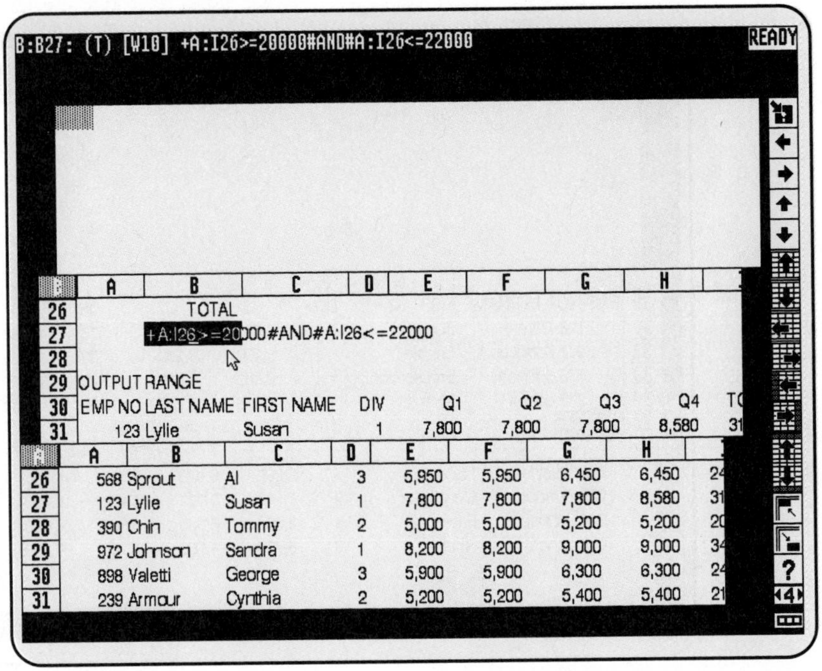

The output range, input range, and criteria range were set and remain the same; although the criteria now being used are different. To perform the query extract with the new criteria:

Press	⌀		*Move*	*the mouse pointer to the control panel*
Select	Data		*Choose*	*Data*
Select	Query		*Choose*	*Query*
Select	Extract		*Choose*	*Extract*

To view the data that have been extracted:

Select	Quit		*Choose*	*Quit*
Move	the cell pointer to cell B:A33		*Click*	*on cell B:A33*

The desired data are now listed. Note that the data in the output range from the previous exercise using **Data Query Extract** were deleted completely and replaced with the data for the current **Data Query Extract**.

Your screen should look like Figure 13-14.

Figure 13-14

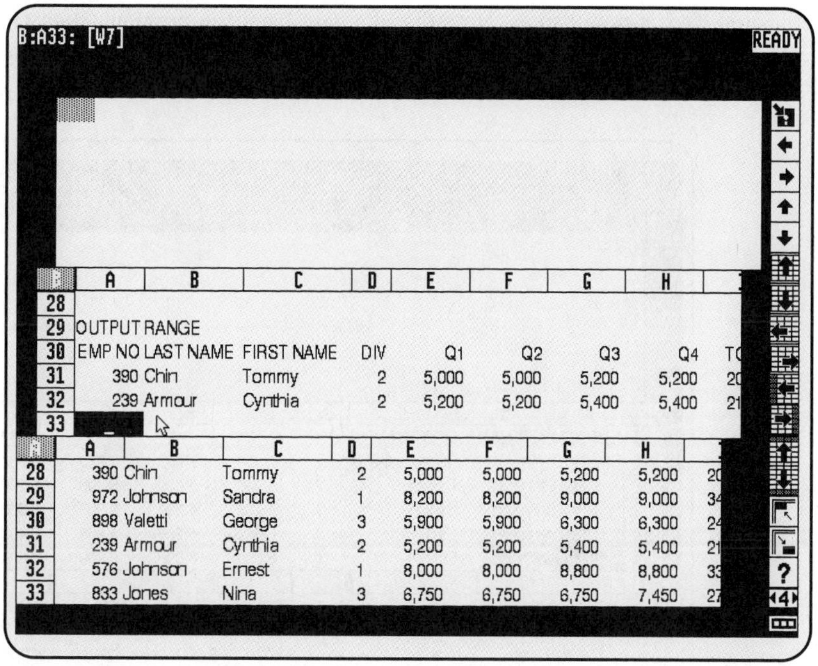

B:A33: [W7]								READY

	A	B	C	D	E	F	G	H	
28									
29	OUTPUT RANGE								
30	EMP NO	LAST NAME	FIRST NAME	DIV	Q1	Q2	Q3	Q4	T
31	390	Chin	Tommy	2	5,000	5,000	5,200	5,200	20
32	239	Armour	Cynthia	2	5,200	5,200	5,400	5,400	21
33									

	A	B	C	D	E	F	G	H	
28	390	Chin	Tommy	2	5,000	5,000	5,200	5,200	20
29	972	Johnson	Sandra	1	8,200	8,200	9,000	9,000	34
30	898	Valetti	George	3	5,900	5,900	6,300	6,300	24
31	239	Armour	Cynthia	2	5,200	5,200	5,400	5,400	21
32	576	Johnson	Ernest	1	8,000	8,000	8,800	8,800	33
33	833	Jones	Nina	3	6,750	6,750	6,750	7,450	27

Querying with Multiple Conditions Using #OR# and Using the Query F7 Key

In this exercise, the database table in the ABCSAL worksheet is queried to find individuals that have a salary less than $22,000 or greater than $30,000 using the logical operator **#OR#**. You will use the QUERY key (the F7 function key) rather than the **D**ata **Q**uery **E**xtract command sequence.

Changing the Current Criteria to the Desired Criteria

In this exercise, the current criteria will be changed from +A:I26>=20000#AND#A:I26<=22000 to +A:I26<22000#OR#A:I26>30000.

To change the criteria:

Move	the cell pointer to cell B:B27		***Click***	*on cell B:B27*
Enter	+A:I26<22000#OR# A:I26>30000		***Enter***	*+A:I26<22000#OR#* *A:I26>30000*

(The first line of the criteria [in cell B26–TOTAL] will remain the same.) Because the same **O**utput range, **I**nput range, and **C**riteria range that were set in a previous exercise will be used, they do not have to be reset, although the criteria being used are different. Instead of executing the **D**ata **Q**uery **E**xtract command sequence, the **QUERY key** (the F7 function key) can be used.

To perform a query extract using the new criteria:

Press	`F7`		***Press***	`F7`

The desired data is now listed. Note that the data from the previous **Data Query Extract** exercise was deleted completely and replaced with the data for the current query. Assuming that the cell pointer is in cell B:A35, your screen should look like Figure 13-15.

Figure 13-15

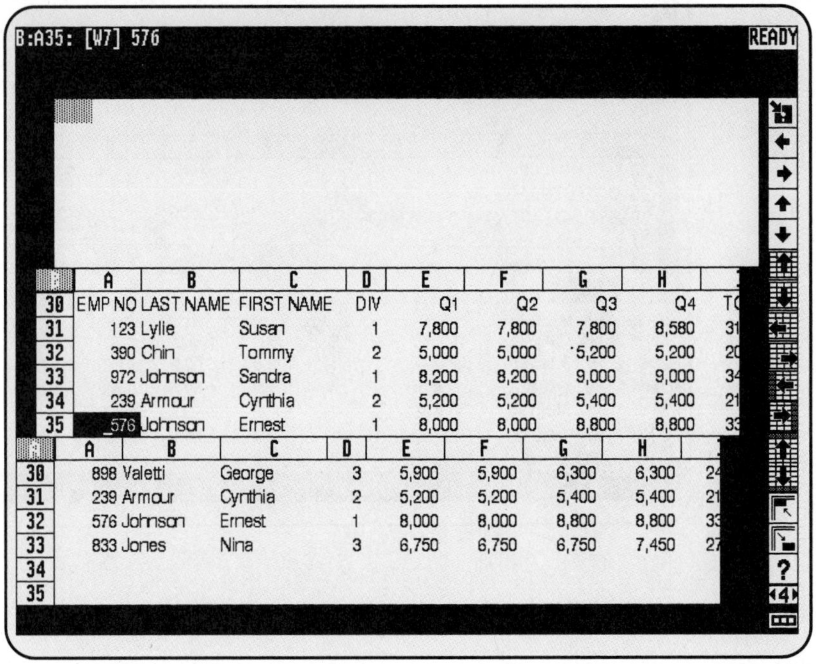

Querying with Multiple Criteria

In this exercise, you will query the ABCSAL database table to find the records for individuals who have a salary less than $25,000 and who are also in DIVISION 3. It is assumed that the results of the previous exercise are still displayed on your screen.

Changing the Current Criteria to the Desired Criteria

In this exercise, the current criteria +A:I26<22000#OR#A:I26>30000 will be changed to +A:I26<25000 and will serve as the first criteria. A second criteria (DIV equal 3) will appear in cells B:C26 and B:C27, respectively.

To change the criteria under TOTAL:

Move	the cell point to cell B:B27		***Click***	*on cell B:B27*
Enter	+A:I26<25000		***Enter***	*+A:I26<25000*

(The first line of the criteria [in cell B:B26–TOTAL] will remain the same.)

To place the new criteria on worksheet B:

Move	the cell pointer to cell B:C26		***Click***	*on cell B:C26*
Press	/		***Move***	*the mouse pointer to the control panel*
Select	Copy		***Choose***	*Copy*

When prompted for the range to copy FROM:

Press	Esc		***Click***	*the alternate mouse button*
Move	the cell pointer to cell A:D25		***Click***	*on cell A:D25*
Press	←Enter		***Click***	*the mouse button*

When prompted for the range to copy TO:

Press	←Enter		***Click***	*the mouse button with the mouse pointer in the control panel*

The field name for division (DIV) now appears in cell B:C26. To enter the specific value to be used:

Move	the cell pointer to cell B:C27		***Click***	*on cell B:C27*
Enter	3		***Enter***	*3*

To specify the proper criteria for the query:

Press	/		***Move***	*the mouse pointer to the control panel*
Select	Data		***Choose***	*Data*
Select	Query		***Choose***	*Query*
Select	Criteria		***Choose***	*Criteria*

Notice that only the criteria in column B (cells B:B26 and B:B27) are highlighted from a previous exercise. Since you placed new criteria in cells B:C26 and B:C27, these cells need to be highlighted before performing the extract.

To include the new criteria in the Criteria Range setting:

Press	→		***Click***	*the* ➡ *SmartIcon*

Cells B:B26 through B:C27 should be highlighted. These cells contain the criteria displayed in Figure 13-16.

Figure 13-16

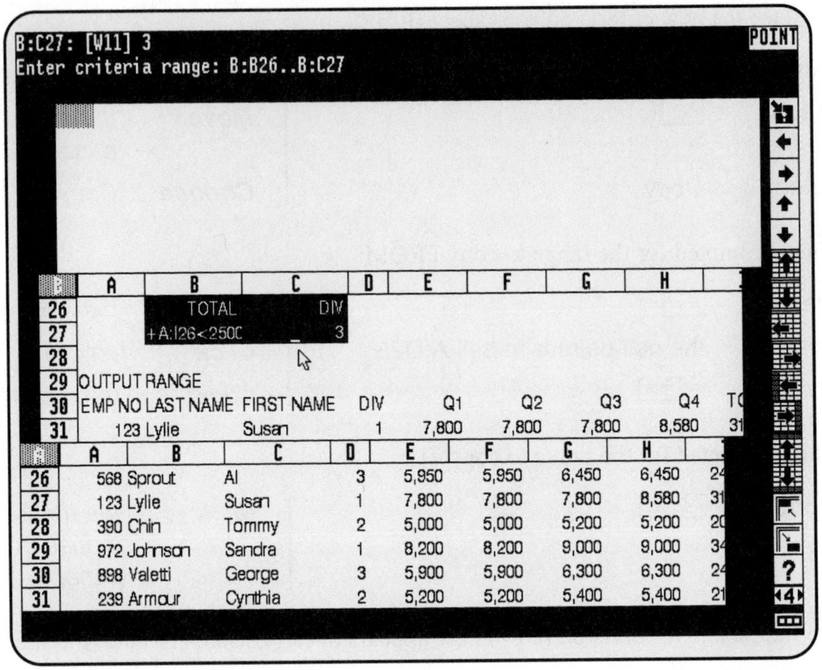

To accept cells B:B26 through B:C27 as the criteria range:

Press	⏎Enter	***Click***	*the mouse button with the mouse pointer in the control panel*

To perform the query extract:

Select	Extract	***Choose***	*Extract*
Select	Quit	***Choose***	*Quit*

The data for the designated criteria now should be listed. Assuming you place the cell pointer in cell B:A33, your screen should look like Figure 13-17.

Figure 13-17

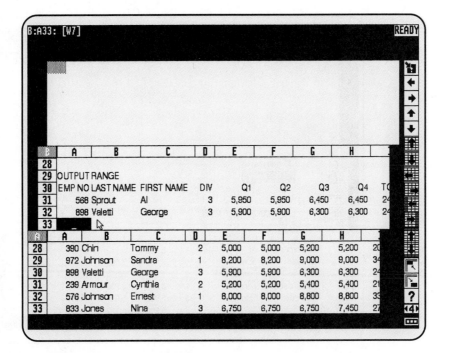

■ CREATING A COMPUTED COLUMN IN THE OUTPUT RANGE

In some situations, you may need to complete a computation on extracted data. You can accomplish such a task using the capability provided by 1-2-3 for placing a computed column in the output range.

Before completing this exercise, you need to erase cells B:A31 through B:I32. Change the criteria in cell B:B27 to +A:I26>25000 and modify the output range in worksheet B so your screen looks like Figure 13-18.

Figure 13-18

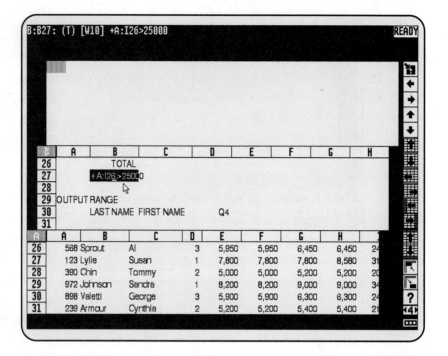

Suppose you want to provide a bonus to those individuals earning more than $25,000 for the year to reward them for their superior performance during the last year. The bonus is equal to 10 percent of the fourth quarter's salary.

To add a column that will calculate the amount of the bonus for those employees:

Move	the cell pointer to cell B:E30	**Click**	on cell B:E30
Enter	+A:H26∗.1	**Enter**	+A:H26∗.1

Use the **R**ange **F**ormat **T**ext command on cell B:E30 so you can see the formula on your screen rather than the computational result. Your screen should look like Figure 13-19.

Figure 13-19

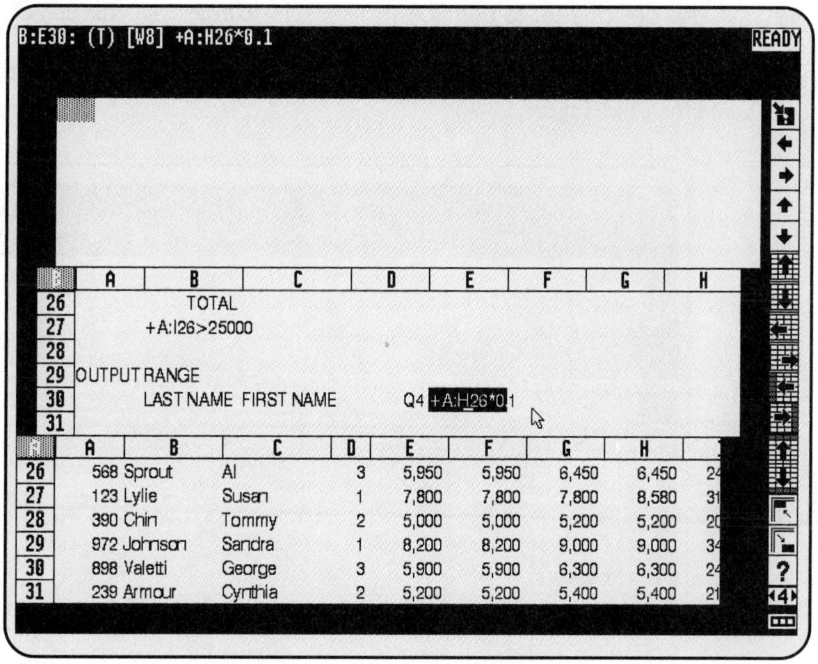

To complete the query using the computed column:

Press	[/]		**Move**	the mouse pointer to the control panel
Select	Data		**Choose**	Data
Select	Query		**Choose**	Query

Define the Input range as cells A:A25 through A:I33 and the Criteria range as cells B:B26 through B:B27.

To include the computed column in the output range:

Select	Output		**Choose**	Output
Press	[Esc]		**Click**	the alternate mouse button
Highlight	cells B:B30 through B:E30		**Highlight**	cells B:B30 through B:E30
Press	[←Enter]		**Click**	the mouse button

To calculate the information for the computed column:

Select	Extract		**Choose**	Extract

To see the results:

Select	Quit		**Choose**	Quit

| **Move** | the cell pointer to cell B:A35 | | ***Click*** | *on cell B:A35* |

Notice that the 745 appearing in cell B:E34 is 10 percent of Nina Jones' fourth quarter salary. Your screen should look like Figure 13-20.

Figure 13-20

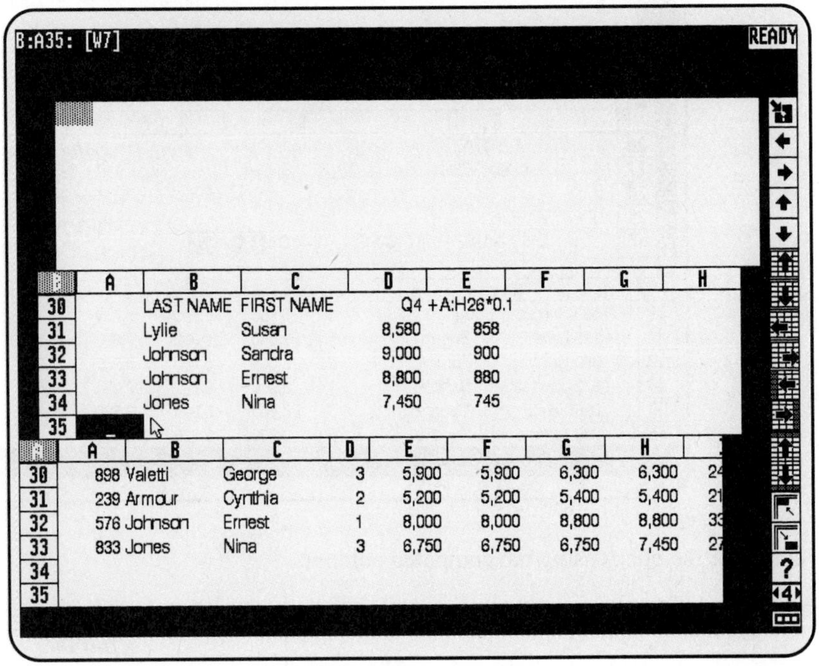

```
B:A35: [W7]                                                    READY

     A     B           C         D      E      F      G      H
 30        LAST NAME  FIRST NAME        Q4 +A:H26*0.1
 31        Lylie      Susan     8,580   858
 32        Johnson    Sandra    9,000   900
 33        Johnson    Ernest    8,800   880
 34        Jones      Nina      7,450   745
 35

     A     B           C         D      E      F      G      H
 30  898 Valetti      George     3     5,900  5,900  6,300  6,300   24
 31  239 Armour       Cynthia    2     5,200  5,200  5,400  5,400   21
 32  576 Johnson      Ernest     1     8,000  8,000  8,800  8,800   33
 33  833 Jones        Nina       3     6,750  6,750  6,750  7,450   27
 34
 35
```

■ USING ADDITIONAL DATA QUERY OPTIONS

In this section, you will use the **Data Query U**nique and the **Data Query D**elete command sequences.

Using the Query Unique Command

You will continue to use the database table in the ABCSAL file with the results of the previous exercise. For the purposes of this exercise, use these instructions to alter the file so that it has a duplicate record.

| **Move** | the cell pointer to cell A:A29 | | ***Click*** | *on A:A29* |

To insert one row:

Press	`/`		***Click***	*the Row Insert ▦ SmartIcon*
Select	Worksheet			
Select	Insert			
Select	Row			
Press	`←Enter`			

To copy Al Sprout's record from row 26 to row 29:

Move	the cell pointer to cell A:A26	*Click*	*on cell A:A26*
Press	⬜ / ⬜	*Move*	*the mouse pointer to the control panel*
Select	Copy	*Select*	*Copy*

When prompted for the range to copy FROM:

| **Highlight** | cells A:A26 through A:I26 | *Highlight* | *cells A:A26 through A:I26* |
| **Press** | ⬜←Enter⬜ | *Click* | *the mouse button with the mouse pointer in the control panel* |

When prompted for the range to copy TO:

| **Move** | the cell pointer to cell A:A29 | *Click* | *on cell A:A29* |
| **Press** | ⬜←Enter⬜ | *Click* | *the mouse button with the mouse pointer in the control panel* |

To modify the current criteria so Sprout will be selected:

| **Move** | the cell pointer to cell B:B27 | *Click* | *on cell B:B27* |
| **Enter** | +A:I26<25000 | *Enter* | *+A:I26<25000* |

To execute a query:

| **Move** | the cell pointer to cell B:A35 | *Click* | *on cell B:A35* |
| **Press** | ⬜ F7 ⬜ | *Press* | *⬜ F7 ⬜* |

Your screen should look like Figure 13-21.

Figure 13-21

	A	B	C	D	E	F	G	H	
30		LAST NAME	FIRST NAME		Q4 +A:H26*0.1				
31		Sprout	Al	6,450	645				
32		Chin	Tommy	5,200	520				
33		Sprout	Al	6,450	645				
34		Valetti	George	6,300	630				
35		Armour	Cynthia	5,400	540				

	A	B	C	D	E	F	G	H	
30	972 Johnson	Sandra		1	8,200	8,200	9,000	9,000	34
31	898 Valetti	George		3	5,900	5,900	6,300	6,300	24
32	239 Armour	Cynthia		2	5,200	5,200	5,400	5,400	21
33	576 Johnson	Ernest		1	8,000	8,000	8,800	8,800	33
34	833 Jones	Nina		3	6,750	6,750	6,750	7,450	27
35									

Because the record for Al Sprout was duplicated in the database, the name Al Sprout appears twice in the output range. By using the following command one of the duplicate records will be deleted from the output range.

Press	/		**Move**	the mouse pointer to the control panel
Select	Data		**Choose**	Data
Select	Query		**Choose**	Query
Select	Unique		**Choose**	Unique

To leave the Data menu:

Select	Quit		**Choose**	Quit

Al Sprout appears only once in the output range. Your screen should look like Figure 13-22.

Figure 13-22

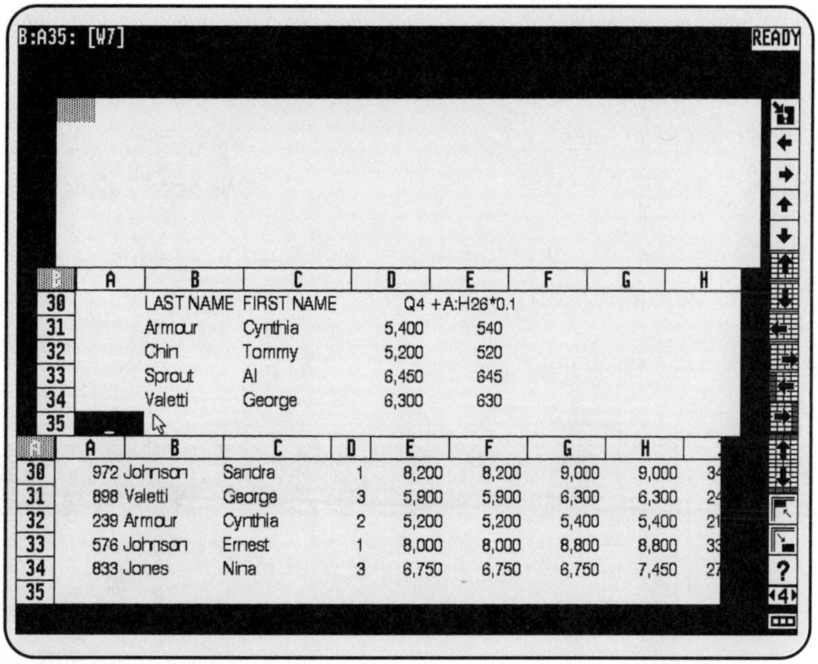

```
B:A35: [W7]                                                           READY

         A        B          C         D      E      F      G      H
   30            LAST NAME FIRST NAME       Q4 +A:H26*0.1
   31            Armour    Cynthia        5,400   540
   32            Chin      Tommy          5,200   520
   33            Sprout    Al             6,450   645
   34            Valetti   George         6,300   630
   35            _

         A        B          C      D    E       F       G       H
   30    972 Johnson   Sandra       1   8,200   8,200   9,000   9,000   34
   31    898 Valetti   George       3   5,900   5,900   6,300   6,300   24
   32    239 Armour    Cynthia      2   5,200   5,200   5,400   5,400   21
   33    576 Johnson   Ernest       1   8,000   8,000   8,800   8,800   33
   34    833 Jones     Nina         3   6,750   6,750   6,750   7,450   27
   35
```

Note that this option does **not** delete duplicate records in the database itself, only in the output range. Al Sprout's record still appears twice in the database.

Using the Query Delete Command

In this exercise, you will use the **D**ata **Q**uery **D**el command. This command is **extremely powerful**, because it **deletes all records in the database that MATCH the criteria**. To make this change permanent on the ABCSAL file, you would use the **F**ile **S**ave command sequence. However, in this case, you will not save the file. In this example, all individuals in the ABCSAL file that earn less than $25,000 will be deleted from the database. It is assumed that you have just completed the previous exercise.

To delete the records that satisfy the criteria:

Press	☐ ∕ ☐		***Move***	*the mouse pointer to the control panel*
Select	Data		***Choose***	*Data*
Select	Query		***Choose***	*Query*
Select	Del		***Choose***	*Del*

The **C**ancel **D**elete menu appears so that you are given a chance to cancel this command or go ahead and delete the records.

To complete the process:

| **Select** | Delete | | ***Choose*** | *Delete* |

To leave the current menu:

| **Select** | Quit | | ***Choose*** | *Quit* |

To see the database table after the records for individuals with salaries less than $25,000 are deleted:

| **Move** | the cell pointer to cell A:A25 | | ***Click*** | *on cell A:A25* |

Your screen should look like Figure 13-23.

Figure 13-23

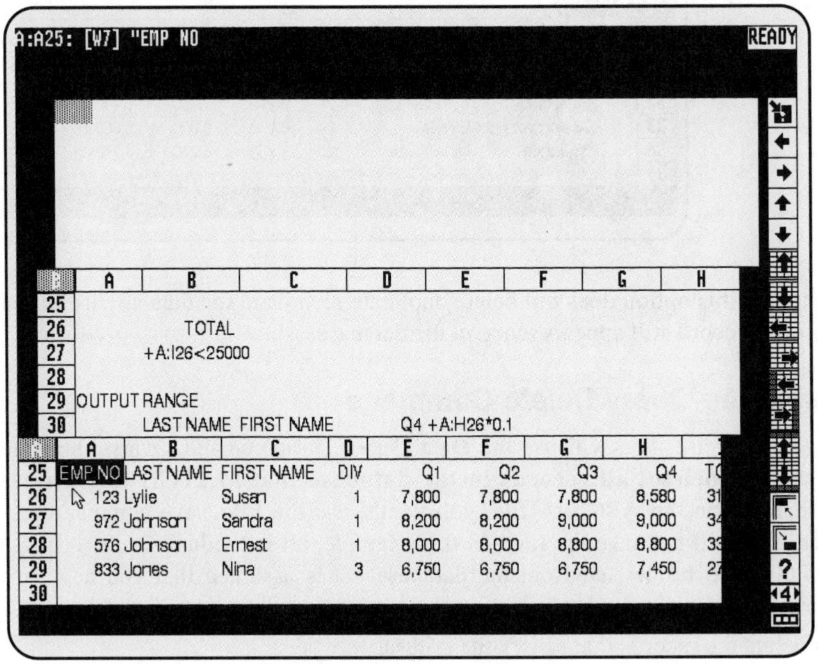

SUMMARY

In Lotus 1-2-3, a spreadsheet may be set up as a database or a collection of related records. The **Data Sort** command sequence can sort records in a database with up to 256 sort keys chosen by the user. The **Data Query** command sequence can perform a query upon a database according to the criteria you specify. You must indicate the database range, the criteria, and an output range for the desired data. You can create a computed column based on specific criteria. Additional Data Query options allow you to delete duplicate records in an output range and delete specified records in a database.

KEY CONCEPTS

#AND#	Extra key
#OR#	Field
Criteria	Field name
Criteria range	Find
Data Query Del	Input range
Data Query Extract	Key
Data Query Find	Output range
Data range	Primary key
Data Sort	Query
Database	QUERY key F7
Database table	Record
Extract	Secondary key

EXERCISE 1

INSTRUCTIONS: Circle T if the statement is true and F if the statement is false.

T   F   1. When sorting a database in Lotus 1-2-3, the data range must include the field names.

T   F   2. The field names must be located in the line directly above the first record of the database for the **Data Query** command sequence to work properly.

T   F   3. It is appropriate to have more than one line consisting of field names designated in the input range.

T   F   4. Each criteria range consists of two cells (a field name and the actual criteria).

T   F   5. The input, criteria, and output ranges must be manually set up on the worksheet and then identified through the menu options.

T   F   6. The output range allows you to copy the desired fields that match the criteria to another area on the worksheet.

T   F   7. When designating the output range, you may highlight only the field names that are desired; the records will appear directly below the field names on the worksheet in the output range when the **Data Query Find** is executed.

T   F   8. The QUERY F7 key allows you to perform a query based upon previously set ranges.

T   F   9. The **Data Query Unique** command deletes multiple records in a database.

EXERCISE 2 — Sorting Records Using the Primary Key

INSTRUCTIONS: Create the PERSON file. Use Figure 13-24 as a guide.

Column A is 18 characters wide.
Column B is 11 characters wide.
Column C is 14 characters wide.
Column D is 7 characters wide.

Figure 13-24

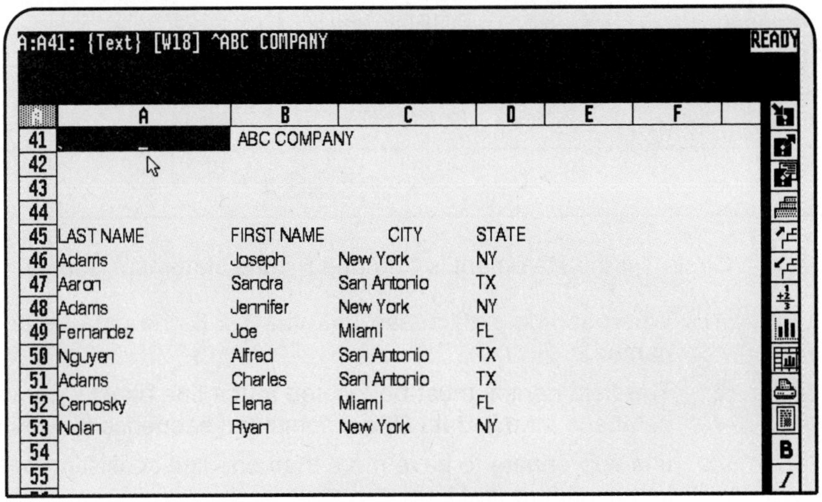

```
A:A41: {Text} [W18] ^ABC COMPANY                                    READY

        A            B            C          D       E       F
   41               ABC COMPANY
   42         ▯
   43
   44
   45  LAST NAME     FIRST NAME      CITY      STATE
   46  Adams         Joseph       New York     NY
   47  Aaron         Sandra       San Antonio  TX
   48  Adams         Jennifer     New York     NY
   49  Fernandez     Joe          Miami        FL
   50  Nguyen        Alfred       San Antonio  TX
   51  Adams         Charles      San Antonio  TX
   52  Cernosky      Elena        Miami        FL
   53  Nolan         Ryan         New York     NY
   54
   55
```

Sort the data in the PERSON file in alphabetical order by city.
Print the worksheet with the properly sorted data.

EXERCISE 3 — Sorting Records Using Primary and Secondary Keys

INSTRUCTIONS: Sort the last names in the PERSON file in alphabetical order by city. (Exercise 4 will place Joseph and Jennifer Adams in the proper order by first name).

Print the worksheet with the properly sorted data.

EXERCISE 4 — Sorting Records Using an Extra Sort Key

INSTRUCTIONS: Assuming that Exercise 3 has just been completed, notice that Joseph Adams and Jennifer Adams from the city of New York are not in the proper order. To place these names in order:

Sort the data using an extra sort key so the names are in proper order.

Print the worksheet with the properly sorted data.

EXERCISE 5 — Querying Records Using One Criterion

INSTRUCTIONS: Retrieve the PERSON file for use in this exercise.

Create the appropriate criteria to extract only individuals living in Miami, FL.

For the output range, extract the person's last name and first name.

Place the criteria and output range on a separate worksheet. Extract the data for the city of Miami.

Print the worksheet with the database table and the worksheet containing the extracted data.

EXERCISE 6 — Querying Records Using Two Criteria

INSTRUCTIONS: Retrieve the PERSON file for use in this exercise.

Create the appropriate criteria to extract only those individuals living in New York, NY or San Antonio, TX.

For the output range, extract the person's last name, first name, city, and state.

Place the criteria and output range on a separate worksheet. Extract the data for those individuals living in New York or San Antonio.

Print the worksheet with the database table and the worksheet containing the extracted data.

EXERCISE 7 — Querying with Multiple Criteria

INSTRUCTIONS: Retrieve the PERSON file for use in this exercise.

Create the appropriate criteria to extract only those individuals having a last name of Adams who live in New York, NY.

For the output range, extract the person's last name and first name.

Place the criteria and the output range on a separate worksheet. Extract the data for the persons with the last name Adams who live in New York.

Print the worksheet with the database table and the worksheet containing the extracted data.

EXERCISE 8 — Using a Computed Column

INSTRUCTIONS: Retrieve the SALES file you created in Chapter 4.

Suppose you want to provide a bonus to those individuals who sold more than $4,000. The bonus is equal to 2% of the sales amount.

Create a "computed column" to calculate the bonus.

For those individuals having sales greater than $4,000, output their name, sales amount, and the computed bonus.

Place the criteria, output range, and computed bonus on a separate worksheet.

Print the worksheet with the database table. Also, print the worksheet containing the extracted data and computed column.

CHAPTER FOURTEEN

ADVANCED DATABASE CAPABILITIES

OBJECTIVES

In this chapter, you will learn to:

- Fill cells with sequential data
- Use data tables
- Use an external database
- Combine information from multiple database tables
- Create a frequency distribution
- Graph a frequency distribution

■ CHAPTER OVERVIEW

In the last chapter, you learned some of the basic database features available in 1-2-3. You will expand your knowledge of the database capabilities in this chapter. You will learn to fill cells with specific sequences of data, create data tables for use in decision-making situations, use data created by an external database management system, combine information using multiple database tables, and create and graph a frequency distribution.

■ FILLING CELLS WITH SEQUENTIAL DATA

In many situations, you may need to enter a sequence of numbers, dates, or times on a worksheet. 1-2-3 facilitates the input of such data using the **Data F**ill command sequence to enter data into various cells on a worksheet.

Entering Sequences of Numbers on a Worksheet

Suppose that you want to enter a sequence of numbers 1 through 10 into cells B6 through B15 of a worksheet. Make sure you have a blank worksheet on your screen.

To enter the sequence of numbers:

Press	☐ /		***Move***	*the mouse pointer to the control panel*
Select	Data		***Choose***	*Data*
Select	Fill		***Choose***	*Fill*

> *User Tip*
> An alternative method for initiating the **Data Fill** command is to click the Data Fill
> ▣ SmartIcon.

When you are prompted for the **fill** range:

Highlight	cells B6 through B15		***Highlight***	*cells B6 through B15*
Press	⏎Enter		***Click***	*the mouse button*

You have designated the set of cells B6 through B15 as the cells in which the sequence of numbers is to be placed.

When prompted for the **start** number:

Type	1		***Type***	*1*
Press	⏎Enter		***Click***	*the mouse button*

To indicate that the **step** value between each number in the sequence is to be the default value of 1:

Press	⏎Enter		***Click***	*the mouse button*

When you are prompted for the **stop** number:

Press	⏎Enter		***Click***	*the mouse button*

You accept the stop number of 8191 because the capacity of the range to be filled will limit the maximum value to less than 8191. Note that only cells B6 through B15 have been filled because that is the range of cells you specified to fill.

Your screen now should have the sequence of numbers 1 through 10 in cells B6 through B15 and look like Figure 14-1.

Figure 14-1

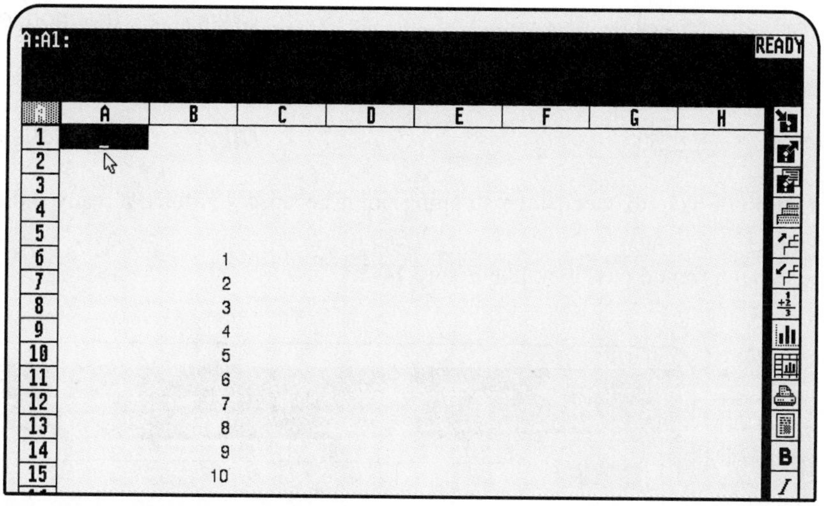

Now, suppose you are asked to enter a sequence of even numbers beginning in cell A3 and ending in cell H3.

To enter this sequence of numbers:

Press	⬚/⬚		*Click*	the Data Fill 🔖 SmartIcon
Select	Data			
Select	Fill			

Note that the fill range from the previous exercise is highlighted. To escape from the previously defined range:

Press	Esc		*Click*	the alternate mouse button

To indicate the fill range for the present problem:

Highlight	cells A3 through H3		*Highlight*	cells A3 through H3
Press	←Enter		*Click*	the mouse button

When prompted for the starting value:

Type	2		*Type*	2
Press	←Enter		*Click*	the mouse button

To specify that the step value is 2:

Type	2		*Type*	2

Press [←Enter]		**Click** *the mouse button*

When you are asked for the stopping point:

Press [←Enter]		**Click** *the mouse button*

You did not have to specify the stopping point because you have already indicated the fill range is A3 through H3.

Your screen should now look like Figure 14-2.

Figure 14-2

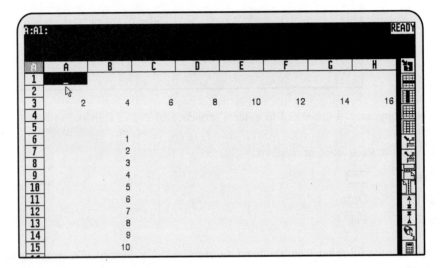

Entering a Sequence of Dates

At times, you may desire to place a series of dates on a worksheet. For example, it may be necessary to place the dates for 10 days in a column, or you may want to enter a series of dates that are a specified amount of time apart such as a week, a month, or quarter.

To illustrate the process of placing a sequence of 10 consecutive days on a worksheet, first make sure that you have a blank worksheet on your screen. Then,

Press [/]		**Click** *the Data Fill* 🔲 *SmartIcon*
Select Data		
Select Fill		

To specify the fill range:

Highlight cells B3 through B12		**Highlight** *cells B3 through B12*
Press [←Enter]		**Click** *the mouse button*

When you are asked for the starting value, you can indicate that the initial date is July 1, 1993 as follows:

Type	7/1/93		*Type*	*7/1/93*
Press	⏎Enter		*Click*	*the mouse button*

To indicate that step value between dates is one:

Press	⏎Enter		*Click*	*the mouse button*

To specify the ending date:

Type	7/10/93		*Type*	*7/10/93*
Press	⏎Enter		*Click*	*the mouse button*

You must enter a stop date and not use the default value of 8191.

Your screen should look like Figure 14-3.

Figure 14-3

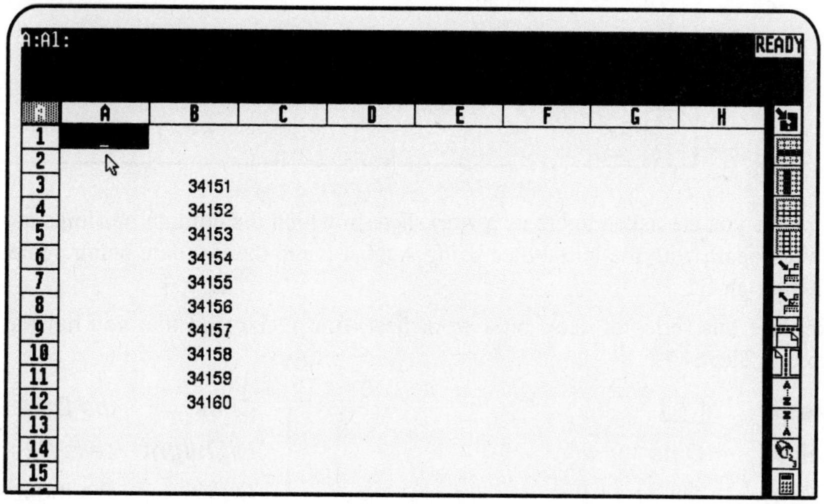

The numbers in cells B3 through B12 are called date serial numbers. Each number represents the number of days that have elapsed since December 31, 1899.

To properly format the dates:

Highlight	cells B3 through B12		*Highlight*	*cells B3 through B12*
Press	/		*Move*	*the mouse pointer to the control panel*
Select	Range		*Choose*	*Range*
Select	Format		*Choose*	*Format*

Select	Date		***Choose***	*Date*
Select	4 (to indicate the long international format to be used)		***Choose***	*4 (to indicate the long international format to be used)*

The dates should now be properly formatted. Your screen should look like Figure 14-4.

Figure 14-4

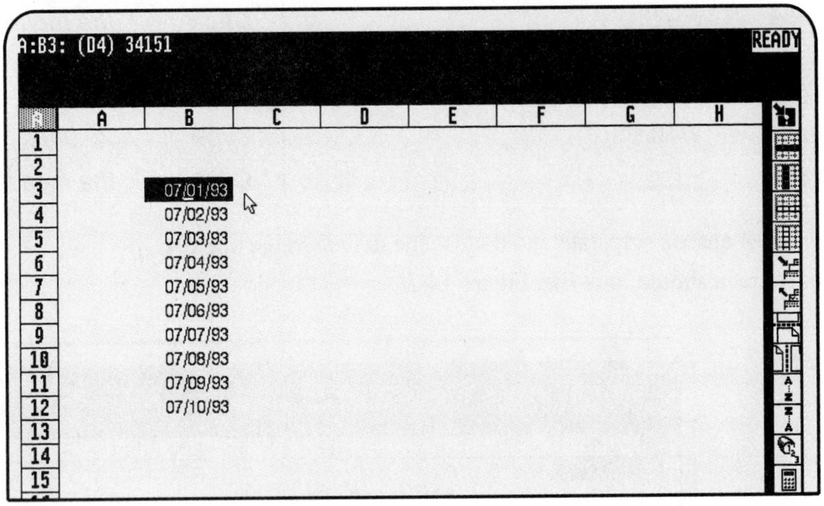

Suppose you are asked to create a worksheet in which the column headings are a series of six dates each a week apart, with the initial date being August 2 and the last date being September 6, appearing in cells B2 through G2.

To place this series of dates on a worksheet, first make sure that you have a blank worksheet on your screen. Then,

Press	/		***Click***	*the Data Fill 🖺 SmartIcon*
Select	Data		***Highlight***	*cells B2 through G2*
Select	Fill		***Click***	*the mouse button*
Highlight	cells B2 through G2			
Press	←Enter			

To indicate that August 2, 1993 is the start date:

Type	8/2/93		***Type***	*8/2/93*
Press	←Enter		***Click***	*the mouse button*

To specify that the step value is 1 week:

Type	1W		***Type***	*1W*

| **Press** | [←Enter] | | *Click* | *the mouse button* |

To enter the stop date:

| **Type** | 9/6/93 | | *Type* | *9/6/93* |
| **Press** | [←Enter] | | *Click* | *the mouse button* |

You have indicated that the last date in the sequence is September 6. Your screen should look like Figure 14-5.

Figure 14-5

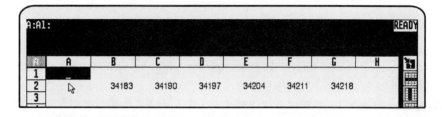

To format the data so only the month and day appear on your screen:

Highlight	cells B2 through G2		*Highlight*	*cells B2 through G2*
Press	[/]		*Move*	*the mouse pointer to the control panel*
Select	Range		*Choose*	*Range*
Select	Format		*Choose*	*Format*
Select	Date		*Choose*	*Date*
Select	5		*Choose*	*5*

Your screen now should be properly formatted and look like Figure 14-6.

Figure 14-6

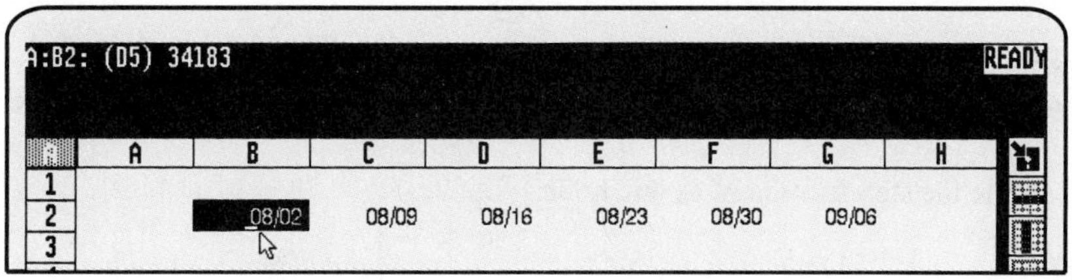

The various step values that you can use for dates are summarized in the following table:

Desired Increment	Step Value
Days	Integer followed by the letter D
Weeks	Integer followed by the letter W
Months	Integer followed by the letter M
Quarters	Integer followed by the letter Q
Years	Integer followed by the letter Y

Entering Sequences of Times

In the last section, you placed sequences of dates on a worksheet. Sometimes you may want to enter specific sequences of times. For example, it might be necessary to prepare a schedule with times separated by a specific time increment.

Suppose you need to prepare a daily calendar that has the sequence of times from 8:00 a.m. to 5:00 p.m. with one hour intervals between each specified time. Before creating this sequence of times, make sure that you have a blank worksheet on your screen.

To place the time sequence in cells A4 through A12:

Press	⌐ / ⌐		*Click*	*the Data Fill* 🖳 *SmartIcon*
Select	Data			
Select	Fill			

To indicate the fill range:

Highlight	cells A4 through A12		*Highlight*	*cells A4 through A12*
Press	⌐←Enter⌐		*Click*	*the mouse button*

To specify the starting time:

Type	8:00 AM		*Type*	*8:00 AM*
Press	⌐←Enter⌐		*Click*	*the mouse button*

To define the step increment as one hour:

Type	1H		*Type*	*1H*
Press	⌐←Enter⌐		*Click*	*the mouse button*

To specify the stopping time:

Press	⌐←Enter⌐		*Click*	*the mouse button*

A series of decimal equivalent times should appear on your screen like those in Figure 14-7. Each time represents the actual time as a percentage of 24 hours.

Figure 14-7

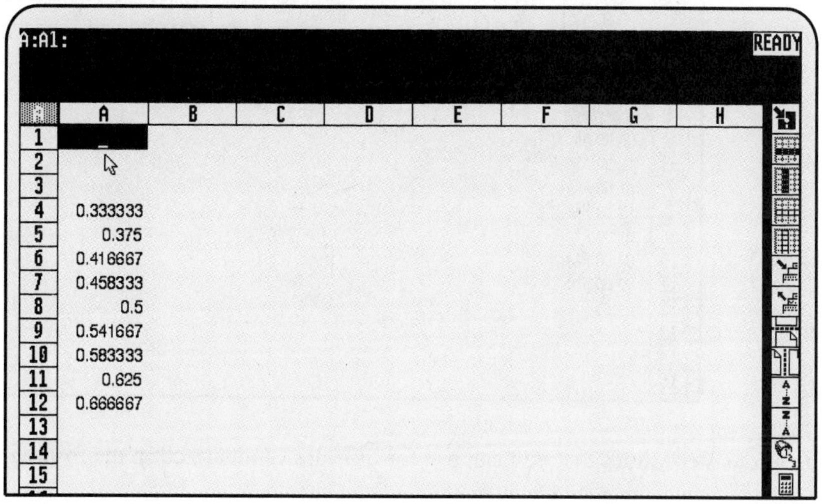

To properly format the times:

Highlight	cells A4 through A12		*Highlight*	*cells A4 through A12*
Press	[/]		*Move*	*the mouse pointer to the control panel*
Select	Range		*Choose*	*Range*
Select	Format		*Choose*	*Format*
Select	Date		*Choose*	*Date*
Select	Time		*Choose*	*Time*

To select the HH:MM AM/PM format option and identify the range of cells to format:

Select	2		*Choose*	*2*

Your screen now should look like Figure 14-8.

Figure 14-8

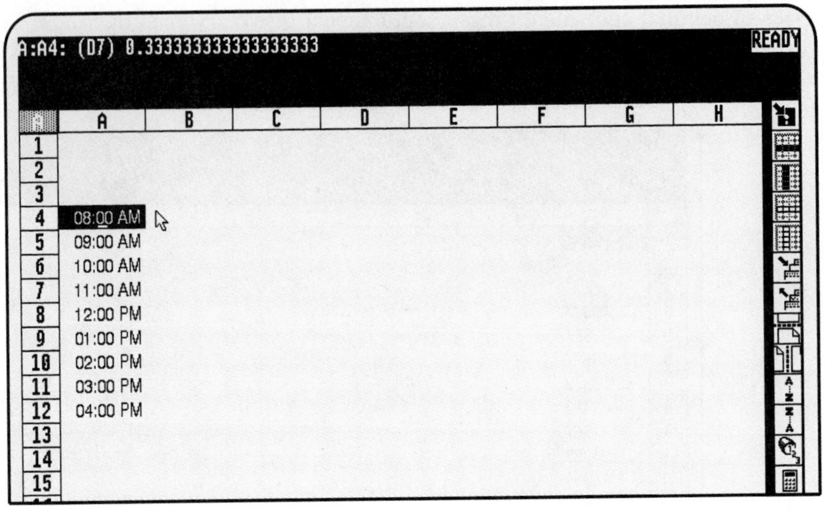

The various step values that you can use for time are summarized in the following table:

Desired Increment	Step Value
Seconds	Integer followed by the letter S
Minutes	Integer followed by the letter MIN
Hours	Integer followed by the letter H

Placing a Sequence of Data on Multiple Worksheets

In some situations, you may need to enter a sequence of data in multiple worksheets. For example, you may want to enter the month and year in a series of worksheets.

Suppose you are working on a budget and desire to use separate worksheets for individual months. Assume you also want to have the month and year appear in cell A1 of a series of worksheets. Before you create the series of worksheets, make sure you have a blank worksheet on your screen.

To place information for January, 1993 through March, 1993 in worksheets A through C, you need to add two worksheets after worksheet A and display the three worksheets using the **W**orksheet **W**indow **P**erspective command sequence or click the Perspective 🗐 SmartIcon.

Your screen now should look like Figure 14-9.

Figure 14-9

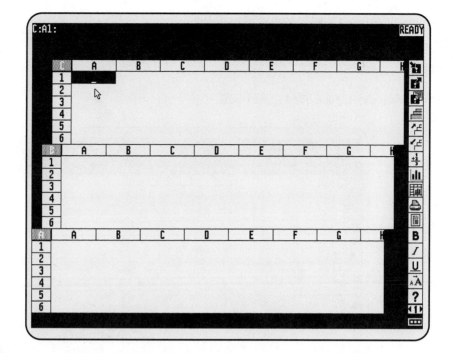

To place the monthly series of data in cell A1 of the worksheets A through C:

Move	the cell pointer to cell A:A1		*Click*	*on cell A:A1*
Press	⬜/		*Click*	*the Data Fill* *SmartIcon*
Select	Data			
Select	Fill			

To specify the fill range:

Highlight	cells A:A1 through C:A1		*Highlight*	*cells A:A1 through C:A1*
Press	↵Enter		*Click*	*the mouse button*

To indicate that the start date is January, 1993:

Type	1/1/93		*Type*	*1/1/93*
Press	↵Enter		*Click*	*the mouse button*

You can define the step amount to be one month as follows:

Type	1M		*Type*	*1M*
Press	↵Enter		*Click*	*the mouse button*

To indicate that you want to stop in March, 1993:

Type	3/1/93		*Type*	*3/1/93*
Press	⟵Enter		*Click*	*the mouse button*

Your screen should look like Figure 14-10.

Figure 14-10

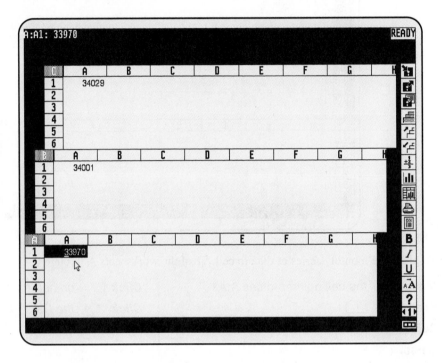

Note that the numbers appearing in the worksheets represent January 1, February 1, and March 1 of 1993. You can then format the dates:

Highlight	cells A:A1 through C:A1		*Highlight*	*cells A:A1 through C:A1*
Press	/		*Move*	*the mouse pointer to the control panel*
Select	Range		*Choose*	*Range*
Select	Format		*Choose*	*Format*
Select	Date		*Choose*	*Date*
Select	3		*Choose*	*3*
Press	⟵Enter		*Click*	*the mouse button with the mouse pointer in the control panel*

The dates are properly formatted and your screen should look like Figure 14-11.

Figure 14-11

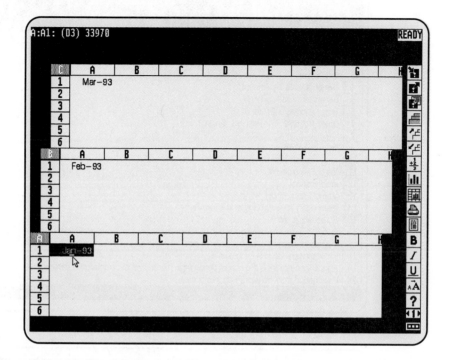

■ USING DATA TABLES

Data tables can illustrate the impact on numbers obtained with formulas when changes in the values of variables occur. A classic example of the need for using a data table occurs when a person tries to evaluate the monthly payment on a loan for various principal amounts, interest rates, and time periods. Another example occurs when a sales manager desires to evaluate the impact on an employee's compensation of proposed changes in quotas and commission rates.

Suppose you are considering the purchase of a new luxury automobile by borrowing the money from a bank. The variables that can change include the principal amount, interest rate, and number of time periods to repay the loan. In this section, you will use the **Data T**able command available in 1-2-3 to evaluate the impact of changes in these loan variables.

Before using the data table options, you need to have a blank worksheet on your screen and then enter the information appearing in Figure 14-12, Parts 1 and 2. Then enter the information in Figure 14-12, Part 3.

The payment amount is computed by using the payment function, @PMT, that is available in 1-2-3. Cell A38 should contain the formula @PMT(A34,A37,A36). The three arguments, A34, A37, and A36, refer to the values used for the principal amount, annual interest rate, and time period respectively. Cell A37, which should have the formula +A35/12, represents the monthly interest rate. Notice that since you want a monthly payment value, the annual interest rate must be converted to a monthly rate by dividing by 12. Each of the entries in the @PMT function is referred to as an argument.

Figure 14-12
Part 1

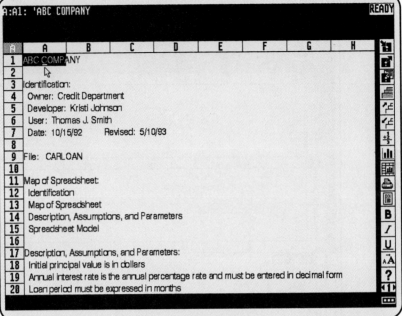

```
A:A1: 'ABC COMPANY                                                    READY

        A      B      C      D      E      F      G      H
 1  ABC COMPANY
 2      ▷
 3  Identification:
 4   Owner:  Credit Department
 5   Developer:  Kristi Johnson
 6   User:  Thomas J. Smith
 7   Date: 10/15/92      Revised:  5/10/93
 8
 9  File:  CARLOAN
10
11  Map of Spreadsheet:
12   Identification
13   Map of Spreadsheet
14   Description, Assumptions, and Parameters
15   Spreadsheet Model
16
17  Description, Assumptions, and Parameters:
18   Initial principal value is in dollars
19   Annual interest rate is the annual percentage rate and must be entered in decimal form
20   Loan period must be expressed in months
```

Figure 14-12
Part 2

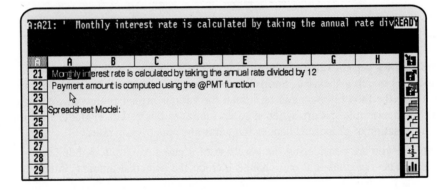

```
A:A21: '  Monthly interest rate is calculated by taking the annual rate div READY

        A      B      C      D      E      F      G      H
21  Monthly interest rate is calculated by taking the annual rate divided by 12
22  Payment amount is computed using the @PMT function
23      ▷
24  Spreadsheet Model:
25
26
27
28
29
```

Figure 14-12
Part 3

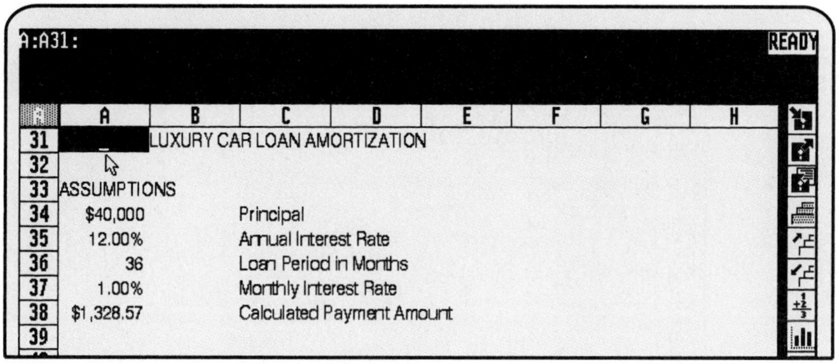

A:A31:   READY

	A	B	C	D	E	F	G	H	
31	_	LUXURY CAR LOAN AMORTIZATION							
32									
33	ASSUMPTIONS								
34	$40,000		Principal						
35	12.00%		Annual Interest Rate						
36	36		Loan Period in Months						
37	1.00%		Monthly Interest Rate						
38	$1,328.57		Calculated Payment Amount						
39									

Changing the Values of One Variable

The **Data Table 1** sequence of commands can be used to change one of the variables used in computing the payment amount. Suppose you want to see the impact of changing the loan period while holding the principal amount and interest rate constant.

To construct a data table for varying the loan period:

Enter	LOAN in cell A41 and PERIOD in cell A42	*Enter*	*LOAN in cell A41 and PERIOD in cell A42*
Enter	the numbers 36, 48, 60, 72, and 84 in cells A45 through A49	*Enter*	*the numbers 36, 48, 60, 72, and 84 in cells A45 through A49*

You may use the **Data F**ill command sequence illustrated earlier in this chapter to expedite the process for entering the loan period values that represent 3 through 7 year loan periods.

Enter	PAYMENT in cell B41 and AMOUNT in cell B42	*Enter*	*PAYMENT in cell B41 and AMOUNT in cell B42*

Data Table operations require the use of input cells. In this case the input cell will be A36 which is the loan period value.

To complete the data table:

Move	the cell pointer to cell B44	*Click*	*on cell B44*
Enter	+A38	*Enter*	*+A38*

The payment amount for a loan period of three years appears in cell B44. This indicates to 1-2-3 that you are using the @PMT function computation that appears in cell A38. Your screen now should look like Figure 14-13.

Figure 14-13

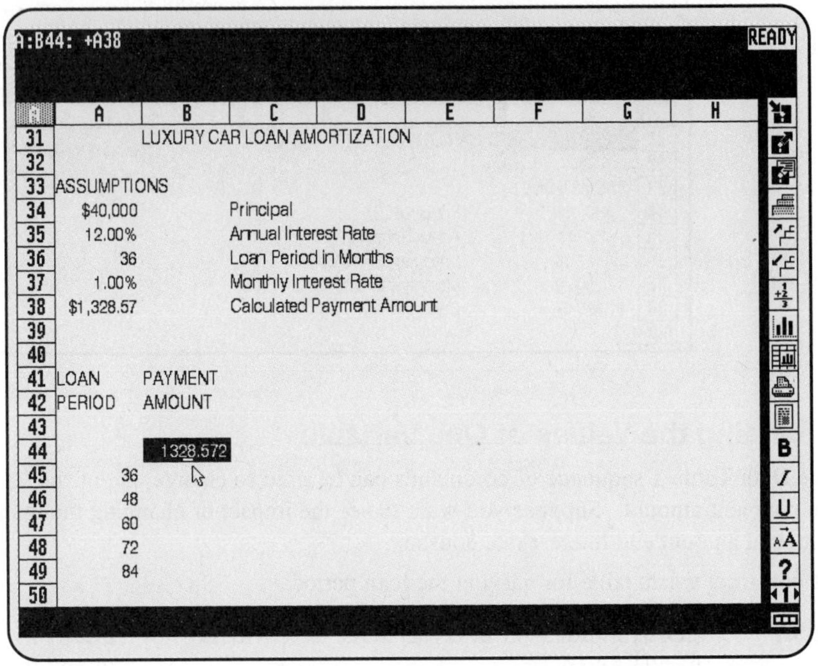

```
A:B44: +A38                                                    READY

        A        B        C        D      E      F      G      H
 31              LUXURY CAR LOAN AMORTIZATION
 32
 33  ASSUMPTIONS
 34    $40,000           Principal
 35    12.00%            Annual Interest Rate
 36      36             Loan Period in Months
 37    1.00%            Monthly Interest Rate
 38  $1,328.57          Calculated Payment Amount
 39
 40
 41  LOAN      PAYMENT
 42  PERIOD    AMOUNT
 43
 44            1328.572
 45      36
 46      48
 47      60
 48      72
 49      84
 50
```

To initiate the **D**ata **T**able command sequence for varying one input variable:

Press	/		***Move***	*the mouse pointer to the control panel*
Select	Data		***Choose***	*Data*
Select	Table		***Choose***	*Table*
Select	1		***Choose***	*1*

To specify the data table range:

Highlight	cells A44 through B49		***Highlight***	*cells A44 through B49*
Press	←Enter		***Click***	*the mouse button*

When prompted for the input cell:

Move	the cell pointer to cell A36		***Click***	*the mouse button on cell A36 twice*
Press	←Enter			

The values for the loan period in cells A45 through A49 are substituted for the loan period parameter in the @PMT function one at a time and a value for the payment amount is determined. In a few seconds, the payment amounts are placed in column B next to the loan period values.

You now can format the values in cell B44 through B49 using the **R**ange **F**ormat , command sequence to make your screen look like Figure 14-14.

Figure 14-14

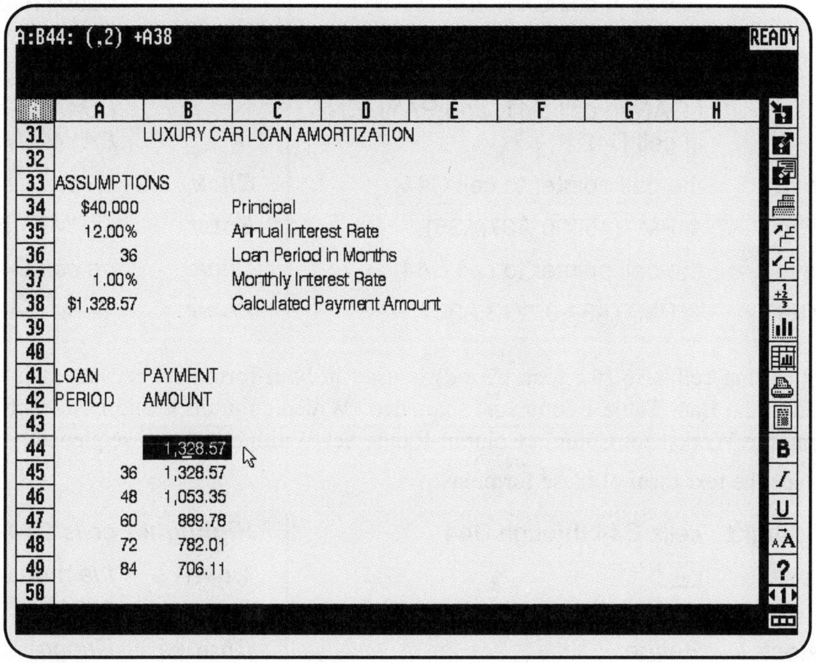

As expected, the payment amount decreases as the loan period increases.

Using the Data Table 1 Command Sequence with Several Formulas

1-2-3 permits you to substitute the value of the input cell in more than one formula. For example, you may want to set up a table that lets you examine simultaneously a change in the principal amount and interest rate for the various loan periods.

Suppose you need to evaluate the following sensitivity cases for the car purchase decision discussed in the last section.

1. What is the payment amount for the various loan period options if the principal is $45,000 instead of $40,000?

2. What is the payment amount for the various loan period options if the annual interest rate is 10% instead of 12%?

Before starting this exercise, make sure that your screen looks like Figure 14-14. Prior to issuing the **D**ata **T**able **1** sequence of commands, complete the following instructions:

To enter the additional @PMT function formulas:

Enter	the labels CASE 1 in cell C40, LOAN in cell C41, and PAYMENT in cell C42		*Enter*	*the labels CASE 1 in cell C40, LOAN in cell C41, and PAYMENT in cell C42*
Enter	the labels CASE 2 in cell D40, LOAN in cell D41, and PAYMENT in cell D42		*Enter*	*the labels CASE 2 in cell D40, LOAN in cell D41, and PAYMENT in cell D42*
Move	the cell pointer to cell C44		*Click*	*on cell C44*
Enter	@PMT(45000,A37,A36)		*Enter*	*@PMT(45000,A37,A36)*
Move	the cell pointer to cell D44		*Click*	*on cell D44*
Enter	@PMT(A34,0.1/12,A36)		*Enter*	*@PMT(A34,0.1/12,A36)*

Notice that cell A36 (the loan period) is used in both formulas, because it is the input cell that will be used in the **Data Table 1** command sequence. Widen columns C and D so each can display 20 characters using the **Worksheet Column Column-Range Set-Width** command sequence.

To see the text form of these formulas:

Highlight	cells C44 through D44		*Highlight*	*cells C44 through D44*
Press	[/]		*Move*	*the mouse pointer to the control panel*
Select	Range		*Choose*	*Range*
Select	Format		*Choose*	*Format*
Select	Text		*Choose*	*Text*

After moving the cell pointer to cell C45, your screen should look like Figure 14-15.

Figure 14-15

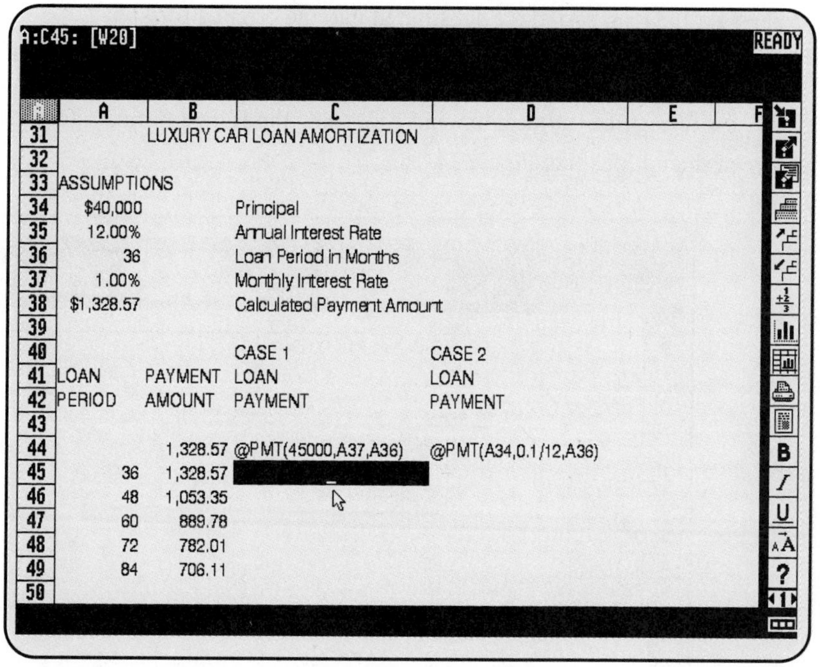

```
A:C45: [W20]                                                              READY

      A          B            C                    D              E       F
31              LUXURY CAR LOAN AMORTIZATION
32
33  ASSUMPTIONS
34   $40,000                  Principal
35   12.00%                   Annual Interest Rate
36        36                  Loan Period in Months
37    1.00%                   Monthly Interest Rate
38  $1,328.57                 Calculated Payment Amount
39
40                           CASE 1               CASE 2
41  LOAN      PAYMENT  LOAN                 LOAN
42  PERIOD    AMOUNT   PAYMENT              PAYMENT
43
44             1,328.57 @PMT(45000,A37,A36)  @PMT(A34,0.1/12,A36)
45        36  1,328.57
46        48  1,053.35
47        60    889.78
48        72    782.01
49        84    706.11
50
```

To initiate the **Data** Table **1** command sequence:

Press	/	**Move**	the mouse pointer to the control panel
Select	Data	**Choose**	Data
Select	Table	**Choose**	Table
Select	1	**Choose**	1

To expand the data table range to include the additional formulas:

Press	Esc	**Click**	the alternate mouse button
Highlight	cells A44 through D49	**Highlight**	cells A44 through D49
Press	←Enter	**Click**	the mouse button

To accept A36 as the input cell:

Press	←Enter	**Click**	the mouse button with the mouse pointer in the control panel

The values for the loan period are substituted into the original formula as well as the new formulas one at a time and a value for the payment amounts is determined. These payment amounts appear in columns B through D next to the loan period values.

You can now format the payment amount data using the **R**ange **F**ormat **,** (comma) command.

Your screen should look like Figure 14-16.

Figure 14-16

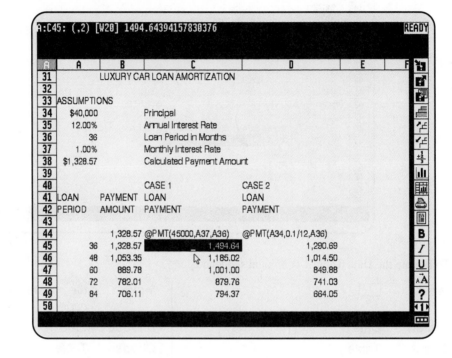

Changing the Values of Two Variables

In some situations, you may want to change two of the variables in a formula. 1-2-3 permits you to simultaneously modify two input cells using the **D**ata **T**able **2** command sequence.

Suppose for the luxury car loan decision introduced in the previous section, you want to vary the loan period and interest rates in the loan payment calculation. You specifically want to determine the loan payment amount for 36, 48, 60, 72, and 84 months using 9%, 10%, 11%, 12%, 13%, and 14% interest rates.

Before initiating the **D**ata **T**able command sequence, create the worksheet in Figure 14-17. Cell A38 contains the function @PMT(A34,A37,A36).

Figure 14-17

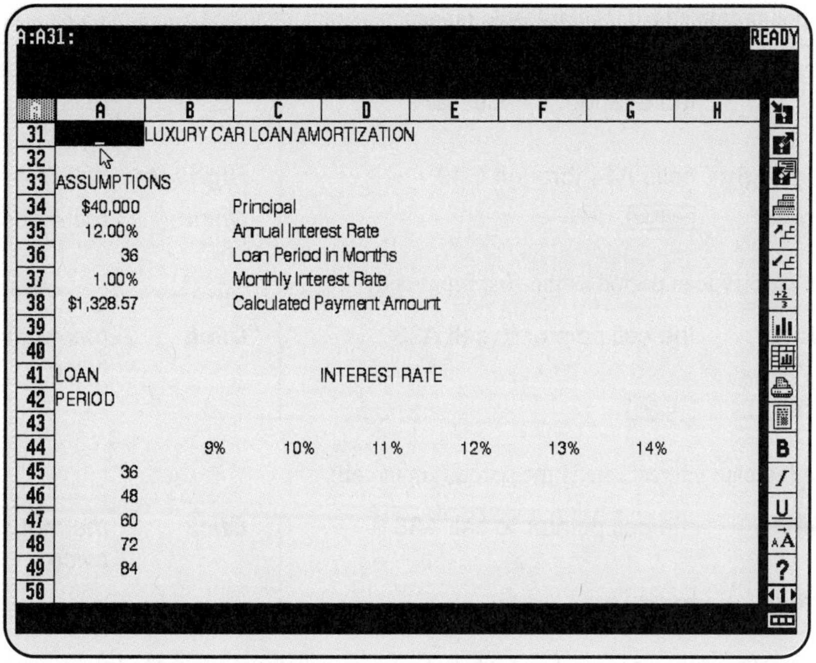

```
A:A31:                                                    READY

        A       B       C       D       E       F       G       H
  31  _       LUXURY CAR LOAN AMORTIZATION
  32
  33  ASSUMPTIONS
  34  $40,000          Principal
  35  12.00%           Annual Interest Rate
  36      36           Loan Period in Months
  37  1.00%            Monthly Interest Rate
  38  $1,328.57        Calculated Payment Amount
  39
  40
  41  LOAN                       INTEREST RATE
  42  PERIOD
  43
  44              9%      10%     11%     12%     13%     14%
  45      36
  46      48
  47      60
  48      72
  49      84
  50
```

When you create a data table that allows you to modify the values of two input cells, the formula that uses the input cells must be placed in the top left corner cell of the data table. In this case you need to place the payment function formula in cell A44.

Move	the cell pointer to cell A44	*Click*	*on cell A44*
Enter	+A38	*Enter*	*+A38*

The payment amount using the initial assumptions now appears in cell A44. If you so desire, you can format the loan payment amount to two decimal places using the **R**ange **F**ormat **,** (comma) command sequence.

To start the **D**ata **T**able command sequence for varying two input cells:

Press		*Move*	*the mouse pointer to the control panel*
Select	Data	*Choose*	*Data*
Select	Table	*Choose*	*Table*
Select	2	*Choose*	*2*

When prompted for the data table range:

Press	Esc to delete the previous data table range, if necessary	*Click*	*the alternate mouse button to delete the previous data table range, if necessary*
Highlight	cells A44 through G49	*Highlight*	*cells A44 through G49*
Press	←Enter	*Click*	*the mouse button*

To specify loan period as the first input cell:

Move	the cell pointer to cell A36	*Click*	*the mouse button on cell A36 twice*
Press	←Enter		

To indicate interest rate is the second input cell:

Move	the cell pointer to cell A35	*Click*	*the mouse button on cell A35 twice*
Press	←Enter		

The values for loan period and interest rate are substituted into the loan payment calculation formula and in a few seconds the values for the various combinations of loan periods and interest rates appear on the worksheet. The values in the left column of the data table (column A) are substituted into input cell 1 (loan period). The values in the top row of the data table (row 44) are substituted into input cell 2 (interest rate). Format the results using the **R**ange **F**ormat **,** (comma) command sequence so your screen looks like Figure 14-18.

Figure 14-18

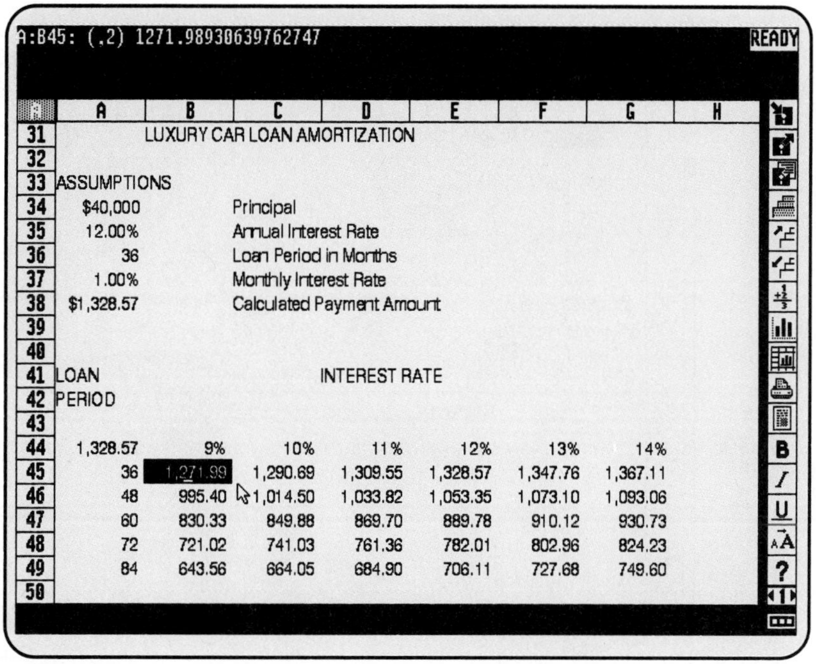

```
A:B45: (.2) 1271.98930639762747                                    READY

        A        B        C        D        E        F        G        H
 31            LUXURY CAR LOAN AMORTIZATION
 32
 33 ASSUMPTIONS
 34   $40,000          Principal
 35   12.00%           Annual Interest Rate
 36     36             Loan Period in Months
 37   1.00%            Monthly Interest Rate
 38  $1,328.57         Calculated Payment Amount
 39
 40
 41 LOAN                        INTEREST RATE
 42 PERIOD
 43
 44  1,328.57      9%      10%      11%      12%      13%      14%
 45      36    1,271.99  1,290.69  1,309.55  1,328.57  1,347.76  1,367.11
 46      48     995.40   1,014.50  1,033.82  1,053.35  1,073.10  1,093.06
 47      60     830.33    849.88    869.70    889.78    910.12    930.73
 48      72     721.02    741.03    761.36    782.01    802.96    824.23
 49      84     643.56    664.05    684.90    706.11    727.68    749.60
 50
```

Changing the Values of Three Variables

In the last section, you used the **Data Table 2** command sequence to simultaneously vary the values for loan period and interest rate for the luxury car loan decision. Now you will create a series of data tables that will let you modify the values of all three of the loan variables at one time.

Suppose you want to vary the values for loan period, interest rate, and principal simultaneously. You also desire to have an individual worksheet for each principal amount that includes the payment amounts for the various loan periods and interest rates that are considered. In this instance, you need to create worksheets for the possible principal amounts of $40,000, $45,000, and $50,000. On each of the worksheets you want to use 36, 48, 60, 72, and 84 for the loan period values and 9%, 10%, 11%, 12%, 13%, and 14% for the interest rates.

Before initiating the **Data Table 3** command sequence, you need to create a worksheet like the one in Figure 14-19.

Figure 14-19

```
A:A31:                                                         READY

        A       B       C       D       E       F       G       H
  31        _    LUXURY CAR LOAN AMORTIZATION
  32        ▷
  33  ASSUMPTIONS
  34   $40,000          Principal
  35   12.00%           Annual Interest Rate
  36        36          Loan Period in Months
  37    1.00%           Monthly Interest Rate
  38  $1,328.57         Calculated Payment Amount
  39
  40
  41  LOAN                      INTEREST RATE
  42  PERIOD
  43
  44                9%     10%     11%     12%     13%     14%
  45        36
  46        48
  47        60
  48        72
  49        84
  50
```

If you have just completed the exercise in the last section, you can prepare the worksheet by erasing cells A44 and cells B45 through G49.

Since you will need to have an individual worksheet for each of the principal amounts, you need to insert two additional worksheets after worksheet A.

To insert the two additional worksheets:

Press	/

Select	Worksheet
Select	Insert
Select	Sheet
Select	After
Type	2
Press	←Enter

Click   the Insert Sheet 🖅 SmartIcon twice

Use the **W**orksheet **W**indow **P**erspective command sequence or click the Perspective 🖳 SmartIcon so you can see portions of the three worksheets on your screen. At this point, copy the contents of worksheet A to worksheets B and C using the **C**opy command sequence. Make sure you use the **W**orksheet **G**lobal **G**roup **E**nable command before you copy the contents of worksheet A so the formats are consistent on the worksheets.

To complete the preparation of the data tables, enter $45,000 and $50,000 in cells B:A34 and C:A34 respectively. Your screen now should look like Figure 14-20.

Figure 14-20

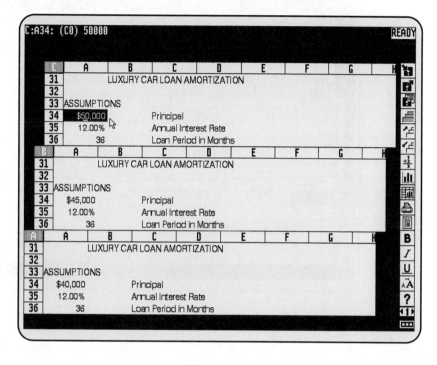

To use the **Data Table 3** command sequence properly, you must place the value for the third input cell in the top left corner of the data table. To enter the principal amount in the appropriate cells:

Move	the cell pointer to cell A:A44		***Click***	*on cell A:A44*
Enter	+A34		***Enter***	*+A34*

Format cell A:A44 using the **R**ange **F**ormat **, 0** command sequence.

You need to copy this formula to cells B:A44 and C:A44 using the Copy command sequence. So that you will be able to see the entire set of loan payment values for all three tables on your screen, move the cell pointer down until row 44 is the first row appearing in each worksheet. Your screen should now look like Figure 14-21.

Figure 14-21

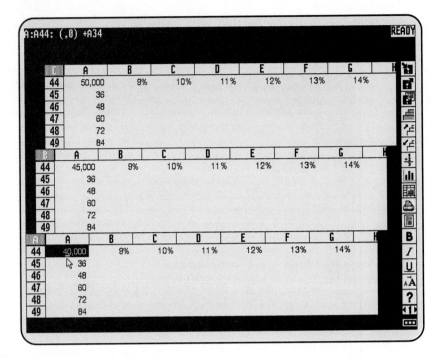

To initiate the **Data Table 3** command sequence:

Move	the cell pointer to cell A:A44		***Click***	*on cell A:A44*
Press	☐ / ☐		***Move***	*the mouse pointer to the control panel*
Select	Data		***Choose***	*Data*
Select	Table		***Choose***	*Table*
Select	3		***Choose***	*3*

To define the table range:

Highlight	cells A:A44 through C:G49		***Highlight***	*cells A:A44 through C:G49*
Press	⏎Enter		***Click***	*the mouse button*

To specify the formula cell is in cell A:A38:

Move	the cell pointer to cell A:A38		***Click***	*on cell A:A38 twice*
Press	⏎Enter			

To indicate loan period is the first input cell:

Move	the cell pointer to cell A:A36		***Click***	*on cell A:A36 twice*

Press   `←Enter`

To specify annual interest rate as the second input cell:

| **Move** | the cell pointer to cell A:A35 | **Click** | on cell A:A35 twice |
| **Press** | `←Enter` | | |

To define principal as the third input cell:

| **Move** | the cell pointer to cell.A:A34 | **Click** | on cell A:A34 twice |
| **Press** | `←Enter` | | |

The various combinations of values for loan period, interest rate, and principal will then be substituted into the @PMT function calculation cell and in a few seconds, the computed loan payment values will appear in the appropriate data tables. Format the results using the **R**ange **F**ormat **,** command sequence so your screen looks like Figure 14-22.

Figure 14-22

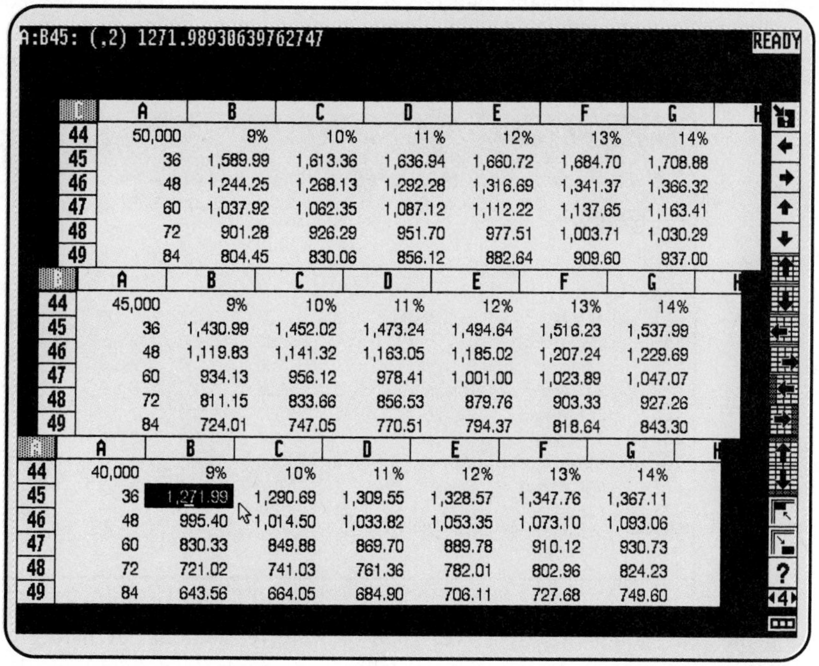

```
A:B45: (.2) 1271.98930639762747                                    READY

          A         B         C         D         E         F         G
    44  50,000       9%        10%       11%       12%       13%       14%
    45      36   1,589.99  1,613.36  1,636.94  1,660.72  1,684.70  1,708.88
    46      48   1,244.25  1,268.13  1,292.28  1,316.69  1,341.37  1,366.32
    47      60   1,037.92  1,062.35  1,087.12  1,112.22  1,137.65  1,163.41
    48      72     901.28    926.29    951.70    977.51  1,003.71  1,030.29
    49      84     804.45    830.06    856.12    882.64    909.60    937.00

          A         B         C         D         E         F         G
    44  45,000       9%        10%       11%       12%       13%       14%
    45      36   1,430.99  1,452.02  1,473.24  1,494.64  1,516.23  1,537.99
    46      48   1,119.83  1,141.32  1,163.05  1,185.02  1,207.24  1,229.69
    47      60     934.13    956.12    978.41  1,001.00  1,023.89  1,047.07
    48      72     811.15    833.66    856.53    879.76    903.33    927.26
    49      84     724.01    747.05    770.51    794.37    818.64    843.30

          A         B         C         D         E         F         G
    44  40,000       9%        10%       11%       12%       13%       14%
    45      36   1,271.99  1,290.69  1,309.55  1,328.57  1,347.76  1,367.11
    46      48     995.40  1,014.50  1,033.82  1,053.35  1,073.10  1,093.06
    47      60     830.33    849.88    869.70    889.78    910.12    930.73
    48      72     721.02    741.03    761.36    782.01    802.96    824.23
    49      84     643.56    664.05    684.90    706.11    727.68    749.60
```

■ USING AN EXTERNAL DATABASE

1-2-3 provides you with the ability of accessing databases that are created using database management system software. Regardless of what database management software is used, these databases are referred to as **external databases**. The database tables contained in an external database are called **external database tables**.

1-2-3 provides the capability to connect to external database tables that have been created by dBASE IV, Paradox, and SQL Server. As more database connections are developed, it will be possible to connect to database tables created by other database management software.

In this section, you will learn to connect to an external database table, to copy data from an external database table to a 1-2-3 worksheet, to query an external database and combine information from an external database table and a 1-2-3 database table.

Connecting to an External Database

In Chapter 13, you used the ABCSAL file that included the employee number, last name, first name, salaries for four quarters, and annual salary total for each employee of ABC COMPANY. Retrieve the ABCSAL file. Assume that the data represented information for individuals currently employed by the company. The data for the current employees appear in Figure 14-23.

Figure 14-23

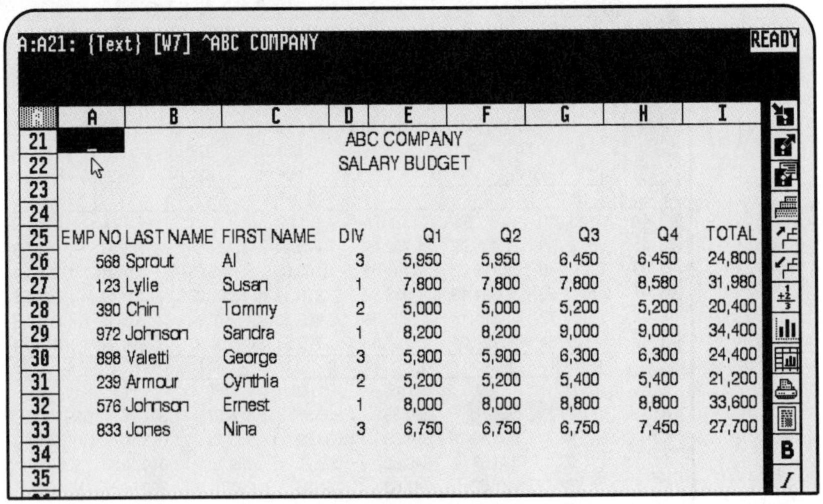
A:A21: {Text} [W7] ^ABC COMPANY READY

	A	B	C	D	E	F	G	H	I
21				ABC COMPANY					
22				SALARY BUDGET					
23									
24									
25	EMP NO	LAST NAME	FIRST NAME	DIV	Q1	Q2	Q3	Q4	TOTAL
26	568	Sprout	Al	3	5,950	5,950	6,450	6,450	24,800
27	123	Lylie	Susan	1	7,800	7,800	7,800	8,580	31,980
28	390	Chin	Tommy	2	5,000	5,000	5,200	5,200	20,400
29	972	Johnson	Sandra	1	8,200	8,200	9,000	9,000	34,400
30	898	Valetti	George	3	5,900	5,900	6,300	6,300	24,400
31	239	Armour	Cynthia	2	5,200	5,200	5,400	5,400	21,200
32	576	Johnson	Ernest	1	8,000	8,000	8,800	8,800	33,600
33	833	Jones	Nina	3	6,750	6,750	6,750	7,450	27,700
34									
35									

During the year, some employees resigned or were terminated. A listing of all personnel employed during the year and their addresses is available in an external database table developed using dBASE IV. A listing of the records in the external database table appears in Figure 14-24. It is placed in 1-2-3 screen format.

Figure 14-24

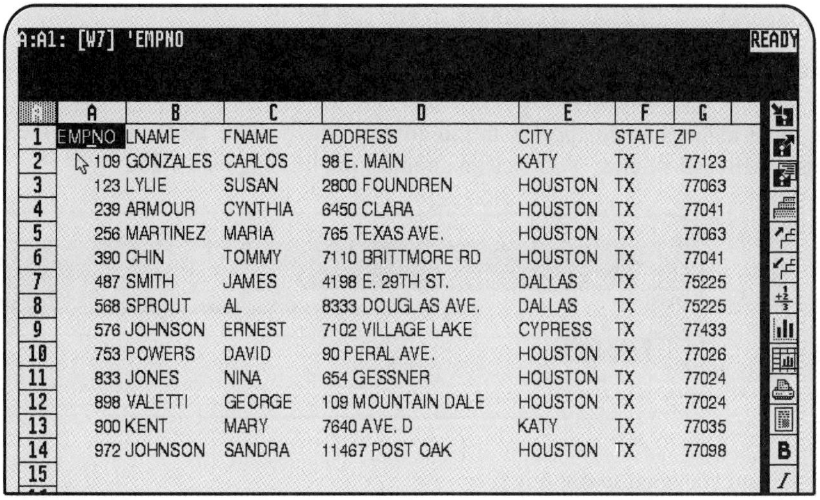

A:A1: [W7] 'EMPNO READY

	A	B	C	D	E	F	G
1	EMPNO	LNAME	FNAME	ADDRESS	CITY	STATE	ZIP
2	109	GONZALES	CARLOS	98 E. MAIN	KATY	TX	77123
3	123	LYLIE	SUSAN	2800 FOUNDREN	HOUSTON	TX	77063
4	239	ARMOUR	CYNTHIA	6450 CLARA	HOUSTON	TX	77041
5	256	MARTINEZ	MARIA	765 TEXAS AVE.	HOUSTON	TX	77063
6	390	CHIN	TOMMY	7110 BRITTMORE RD	HOUSTON	TX	77041
7	487	SMITH	JAMES	4198 E. 29TH ST.	DALLAS	TX	75225
8	568	SPROUT	AL	8333 DOUGLAS AVE.	DALLAS	TX	75225
9	576	JOHNSON	ERNEST	7102 VILLAGE LAKE	CYPRESS	TX	77433
10	753	POWERS	DAVID	90 PERAL AVE.	HOUSTON	TX	77026
11	833	JONES	NINA	654 GESSNER	HOUSTON	TX	77024
12	898	VALETTI	GEORGE	109 MOUNTAIN DALE	HOUSTON	TX	77024
13	900	KENT	MARY	7640 AVE. D	KATY	TX	77035
14	972	JOHNSON	SANDRA	11467 POST OAK	HOUSTON	TX	77098
15							

Suppose you need to connect to the external database table illustrated in Figure 14-24 and have available a dBASE IV file named ABCEMADD (employee addresses for ABC Company). You can also use a dBASE III Plus file. If you have dBASE IV, you can create the file very quickly using the following information on the database structure:

Field Name	**Data Type**	**Field Width**
EMPNO	Numeric	(3,0)
LNAME	Character	10
FNAME	Character	10
ADDRESS	Character	20
CITY	Character	10
STATE	Character	2
ZIP	Numeric	5

The remaining portion of this section assumes you have the database file ABCEMADD available. Make sure you have a blank worksheet on your screen.

To access the external database table:

Press	/	***Move***	*the mouse pointer to the control panel*
Select	Data	***Choose***	*Data*
Select	External	***Choose***	*External*

At this point, a menu appears that contains the options available for working with external databases.

To connect to ABCEMADD database so you can use it:

Select   Use | ***Choose***   *Use*

The table name Sample appears in the control panel. This table contains the driver that allows you to access a dBASE IV file. Your screen should look like Figure 14-25.

Figure 14-25

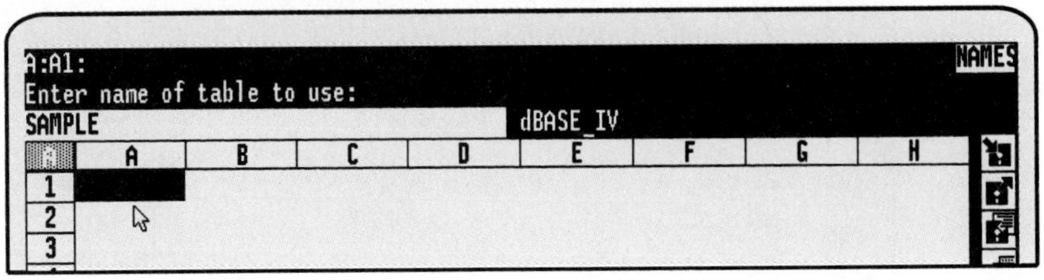

```
A:A1:                                                           NAMES
Enter name of table to use:
SAMPLE                                    dBASE_IV
      A       B       C       D       E       F       G       H
  1
  2    ▷
  3
```

To indicate you want to use this file:

Press   ⮐Enter | ***Click***   *the mouse button with the mouse pointer in the control panel*

The next entry on the control panel requests the directory path for the Sample file. Make sure that you have the proper directory path for your computer. Note that the file containing your external database table must also be in this directory. For this example, it is assumed that the default path that was created when 1-2-3 was installed appears in the control panel.

To select this path:

Press   ⮐Enter | ***Click***   *the mouse button with the mouse pointer in the control panel*

You are then asked to enter the name of the table to use. Your screen should look similar to Figure 14-26.

Figure 14-26

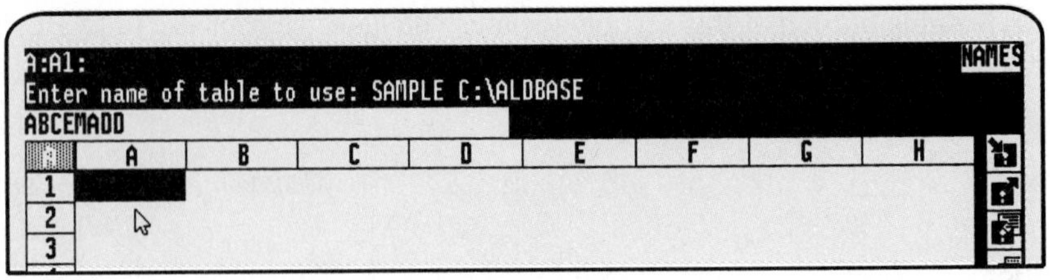

```
A:A1:                                                           NAMES
Enter name of table to use: SAMPLE C:\ALDBASE
ABCEMADD
      A       B       C       D       E       F       G       H
  1
  2    ▷
  3
```

To specify you desire to access ABCEMADD:

Select   the ABCEMADD file | ***Choose***   *the ABCEMADD file*

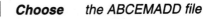

You are requested to enter the range name in 1-2-3 you want to use to refer to the external database. 1-2-3 assumes that you want to use the name of the external database table so ABCEMADD appears in the in the control panel as the suggested range name. You can indicate a different name if you desire. Your screen should look like Figure 14-27.

Figure 14-27

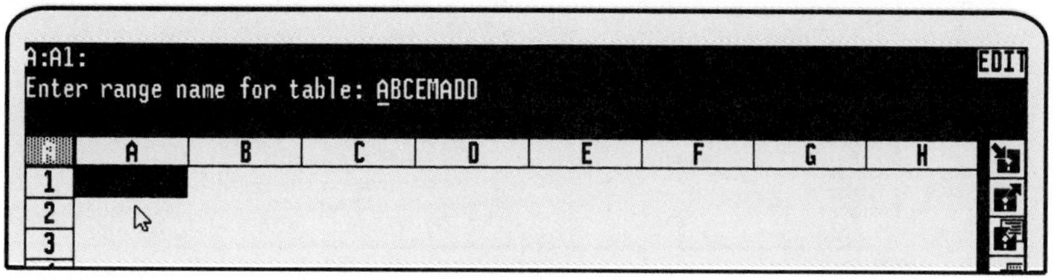

To specify that ABCEMADD is appropriate as the range name:

Press	←Enter		***Click***	*the mouse button*

You are now connected to the external database table.

To exit the external database menu:

Select	Quit		***Choose***	*Quit*

Listing the Fields in an External Database Table

Suppose you want to see a listing of the field names for the external database table.

To create a list of the field names on your screen:

Press	☐ / ☐		***Move***	*the mouse pointer to the control panel*
Select	Data		**Select**	*Data*
Select	External		**Select**	*External*
Select	List		**Select**	*List*
Select	Fields		**Select**	*Fields*

When you are prompted for the range name whose fields are to be listed:

Select	the ABCEMADD file		***Choose***	*the ABCEMADD file*

To indicate you want the field names placed beginning in cell A:A1:

Press	←Enter		***Click***	*the mouse button twice*

Your screen should look like Figure 14-28.

Figure 14-28

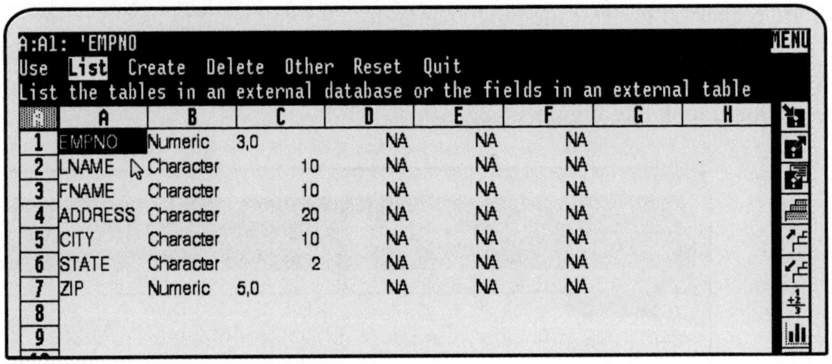

```
A:A1: 'EMPNO                                                    MENU
Use  List  Create  Delete  Other  Reset  Quit
List the tables in an external database or the fields in an external table
     A        B         C      D      E      F      G      H
 1  EMPNO    Numeric   3,0           NA     NA     NA
 2  LNAME    Character        10     NA     NA     NA
 3  FNAME    Character        10     NA     NA     NA
 4  ADDRESS  Character        20     NA     NA     NA
 5  CITY     Character        10     NA     NA     NA
 6  STATE    Character         2     NA     NA     NA
 7  ZIP      Numeric   5,0           NA     NA     NA
 8
 9
```

NA indicates data is not available at this time.

To exit the current menu:

Select	Quit		***Choose***	*Quit*

Copying the External Database Table into a 1-2-3 Worksheet

Since you have access to the external database table, you can copy it into a 1-2-3 worksheet. Before copying the external database table, you need to enter the field names horizontally on your worksheet. You can accomplish the task by transposing the field names in column A to a row below the information appearing on your screen. Make sure the cell pointer is in cell A1, and then:

Press	`/`		***Move***	*the mouse pointer to the control panel*
Select	Range		***Choose***	*Range*
Select	Trans		***Choose***	*Trans*
Highlight	cells A1 through A7		***Highlight***	*cells A1 through A7*
Press	←Enter		***Click***	*the mouse button*

When you are prompted to enter the TO range for transpose:

Move	the cell pointer to cell A10		***Click***	*on cell A10 twice*
Press	←Enter			

The field names appear in cell A10 through F10. You no longer need the data information above the field names. Delete rows 1 through 9 in your worksheet using the **Worksheet Delete Row** command sequence so the horizontal listing of the field names is in row 1. Your screen should look like Figure 14-29.

Figure 14-29

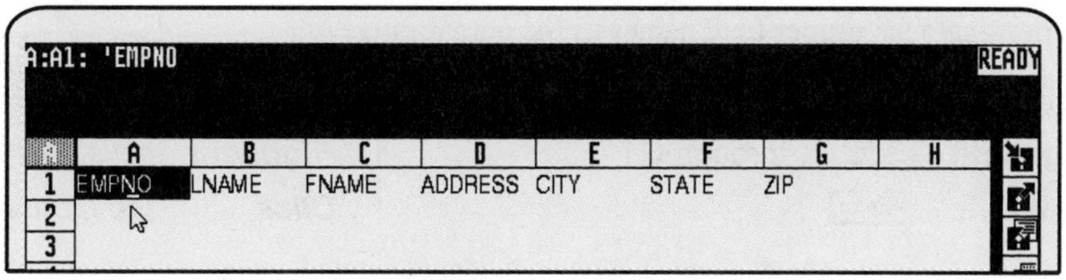

```
A:A1:  'EMPNO                                                    READY

    A         B        C        D       E        F       G       H
1 EMPNO    LNAME    FNAME    ADDRESS CITY     STATE    ZIP
2    ▸
3
```

Prior to copying the external database to your 1-2-3 worksheet:

Copy	cells A1 through G1 to cells A5 through G5	*Copy*	*cells A1 through G1 to cells A5 through G5*

To copy the external database you must complete a data query using the external database.

Press	[/]	*Move*	*the mouse pointer to the control panel*
Select	Data	*Choose*	*Data*
Select	Query	*Choose*	*Query*

To specify the input range:

Select	Input	*Choose*	*Input*
Type	ABCEMADD	*Type*	*ABCEMADD*
Press	[←Enter]	*Click*	*the mouse button*

To exit the current menu:

Select	Quit	*Choose*	*Quit*

To place a criterion on your worksheet that will include all employee records:

Move	the cell pointer to cell A6	*Click*	*on cell A6*
Enter	>0	*Enter*	*>0*

To specify the criteria to use in the query:

Press	[/]	*Move*	*the mouse pointer to the control panel*
Select	Data	*Choose*	*Data*
Select	Query	*Choose*	*Query*
Select	Criteria	*Choose*	*Criteria*
Highlight	cells A5 through A6	*Highlight*	*cells A5 through A6*
Press	[←Enter]	*Click*	*the mouse button*

To designate the proper field names as the output range:

Select	Output		*Choose*	*Output*
Highlight	cells A1 through G1		*Highlight*	*cells A1 through G1*
Press	[←Enter]		*Click*	*the mouse button*

To complete the copying of the external database to your worksheet:

Select	Extract		*Choose*	*Extract*

To exit the current menu:

Select	Quit		*Choose*	*Quit*

The external database table appears on your screen. After moving the cell pointer to cell A1, your screen should look like Figure 14-30.

Figure 14-30

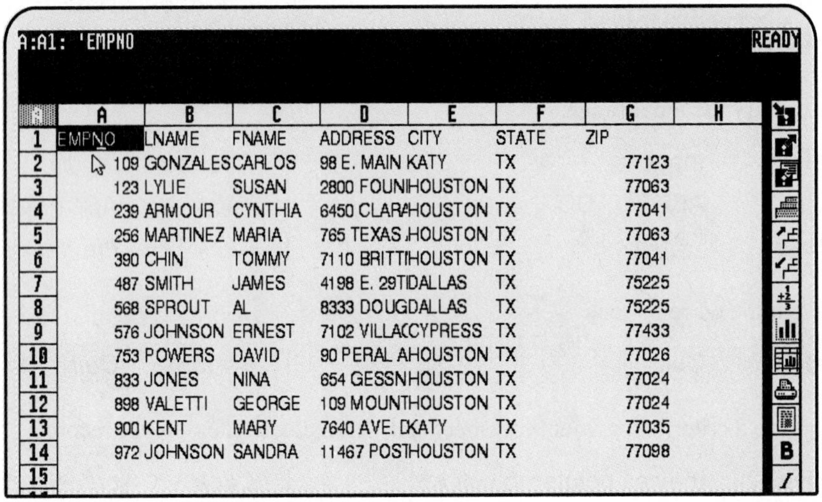

Set up the column widths as follows so you can see the entire external database table that you copied to your worksheet.

Column	Width
A	7
B	10
C	10
D	20
E	10
F	6
G	6

You set columns A, F, and G wider than the actual database field for screen readability purposes only. After moving the cell pointer to cell A1, your screen should look like Figure 14-31. Save the file using the name EMPADDRS.

Figure 14-31

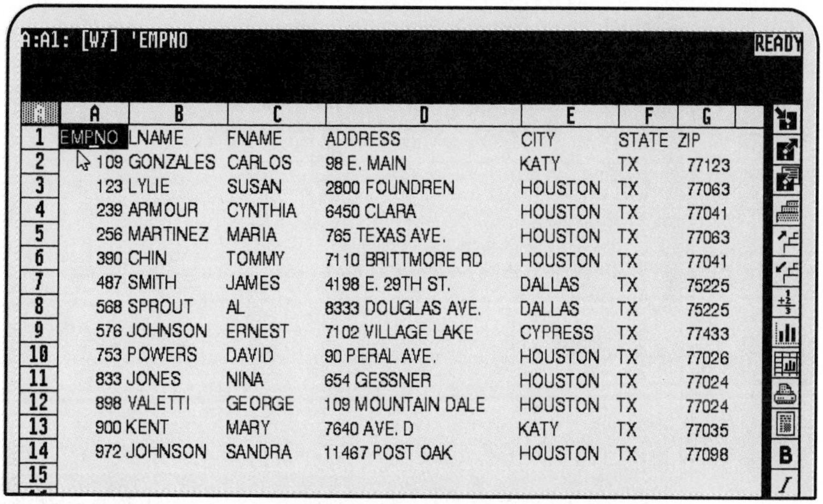

■ COMBINING INFORMATION FROM MULTIPLE DATABASE TABLES

In some situations, you may need to combine information from different database tables based on specific criteria. The process of combining such information is called joining database tables.

To illustrate the joining of information from two database tables into one table, suppose you need a list of the addresses for the current employees at ABC Company. Recall that the ABCSAL file has only the individuals presently employed by the company along with salary information. The EMPADDRS file that you saved earlier in the last section has the addresses for both current and previous employees.

Each of the files has an employee number field that identifies the record. These fields are called key fields or keys. A key field contains unique information that is common across one or more database tables.

To prepare for creating the current employee address database table you need to retrieve the ABCSAL file and then open the EMPADDRS file after the ABCSAL file. Insert a new file named JOIN before the ABCSAL file by using the **File New Before** command sequence. After completing these steps, use the **Worksheet Window Perspective** command sequence or click the Perspective ⊞ SmartIcon to place portions of all the worksheet files on the screen. Your screen should look like Figure 14-32.

Figure 14-32

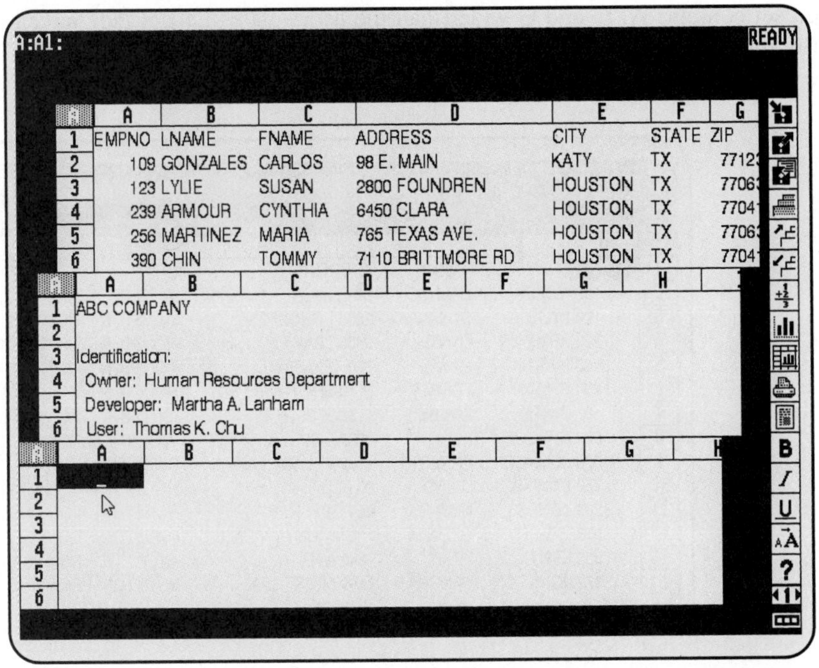

Define the range name ADDRESS that contains cells A:A1 through A:G14 in the EMPADDRS file as its range. Define another range name CURRENT that has cells A:A25 through A:I33 of the ABCSAL file as its range. Save both files.

Entering the JOIN Formula for the Criteria

To combine information from the two database tables, you need to place a criteria range in the JOIN file that contains a formula that joins the database tables in the ABCSAL and EMPADDRS files. For this exercise:

Move	the cell pointer to cell A:B1 in the JOIN file	*Click*	on cell A:B1 in the JOIN file
Enter	CRITERIA	*Enter*	CRITERIA
Move	the cell pointer to cell A:B2	*Click*	on cell A:B2
Enter	+EMP NO=EMPNO	*Enter*	+EMP NO=EMPNO

The characters ERR appear in cell A:B2 because you do not have the range names for EMP NO or EMPNO defined. These are the key fields that include the employee number that is common to salary records in the ABCSAL file and the address records in the EMPADDRS file. The formula indicates that information will be extracted from the database tables when the employee numbers are equal.

To see the text form of the JOIN formula in cell A:B2, format the cell using the **R**ange **F**ormat **T**ext command sequence.

The output range specifies the field names you want to include in the new database table that is formed by joining the database tables in the ABCSAL and EMPADDR files. Use the field names that you want in the new database table in the JOIN file as the output range. Use cells A4 through G4 of the JOIN file in Figure 14-33 as a guide to enter the output range field names.

Figure 14-33

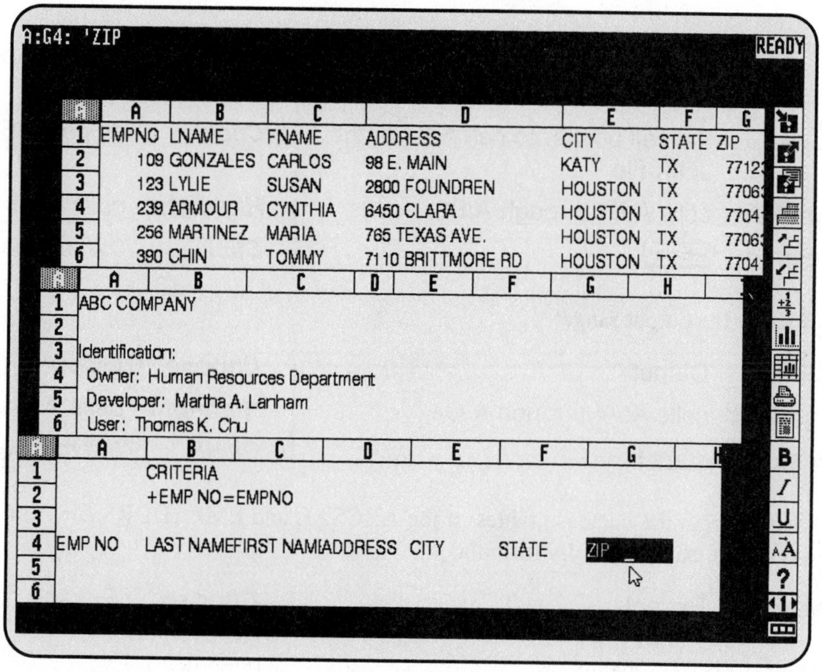

To see the entire field names and eventually the extracted data, set the column width for column A to 7, column B to 11, column C to 11, column D to 20, column E to 10, column F to 6, and column G to 6. Note that the first three field names in the output range are from the ABCSAL database table and the remaining field names are from the EMPADDRS database table.

Extracting the Data for the New Database Table

To create the new "joined" database table:

Press	/	Move	the mouse pointer to the control panel
Select	Data	Choose	Data
Select	Query	Choose	Query

To indicate the input range, you must include the ABCSAL and EMPADDRS database tables.

Select	Input	Choose	Input

When prompted for the input range:

Enter	<<ABCSAL.WK3>>CURRENT, <<EMPADDRS.WK3>> ADDRESS		*Enter*	*<<ABCSAL.WK3>>CURRENT, <<EMPADDRS.WK3>> ADDRESS*

To define the criteria range:

Select	Criteria		*Choose*	*Criteria*
Move	the cell pointer to cell A:B1 in the JOIN file		*Click*	*on cell A:B1 in the JOIN file*
Highlight	cells A:B1 through A:B2		*Highlight*	*cells A:B1 through A:B2*
Press	⎵Enter		*Click*	*the mouse button*

To specify the output range:

Select	Output		*Choose*	*Output*
Highlight	cells A:A4 through A:G4		*Highlight*	*cells A:A4 through A:G4*
Press	⎵Enter		*Click*	*the mouse button*

To extract from the database tables in the ABCSAL and EMPADDRS files and create the database table as a result of using the JOIN formula:

Select	Extract		*Choose*	*Extract*

To quit the current menu:

Select	Quit		*Choose*	*Quit*

Your screen should look like Figure 14-34.

Figure 14-34

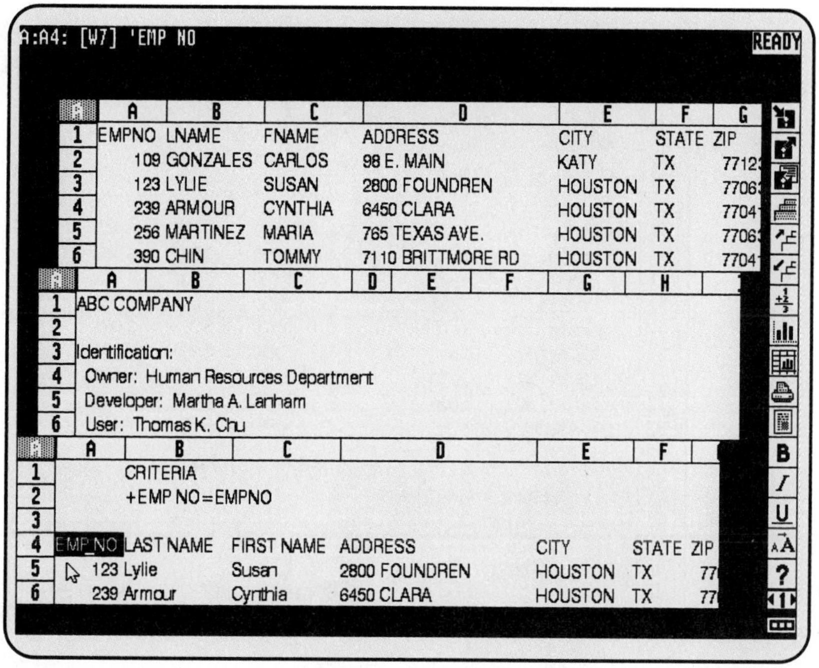

Note that the current employee address database table is in order by employee number, because the process of finding the matches is quicker if both the ABCSAL and EMPADDRS files are sorted in order by the employee number key before the search and matching process begins.

■ CREATING A FREQUENCY DISTRIBUTION

The **Data D**istribution menu option allows you to determine the frequency distribution of any column or row of numbers. A **frequency distribution** counts the number of values that fall within specified intervals. Retrieve the ABCSAL file for use in this exercise.

In this example, you determine the frequency distribution of salaries based on a bin range set up in cells B36 through B39. The **bin range** is a column containing numbers or formulas that specify the intervals for the frequency distribution. The intervals in the bin range are determined by the user and must always be in ascending order. A blank column should exist to the right of this column (with an additional blank row below the last value in the interval range) where the results are placed after the **Data D**istribution procedure is invoked through the menu. First, set up the bin range. Use Figure 14-35 as a guide to enter this information in cells B36 through B39, C36, and D40.

Figure 14-35

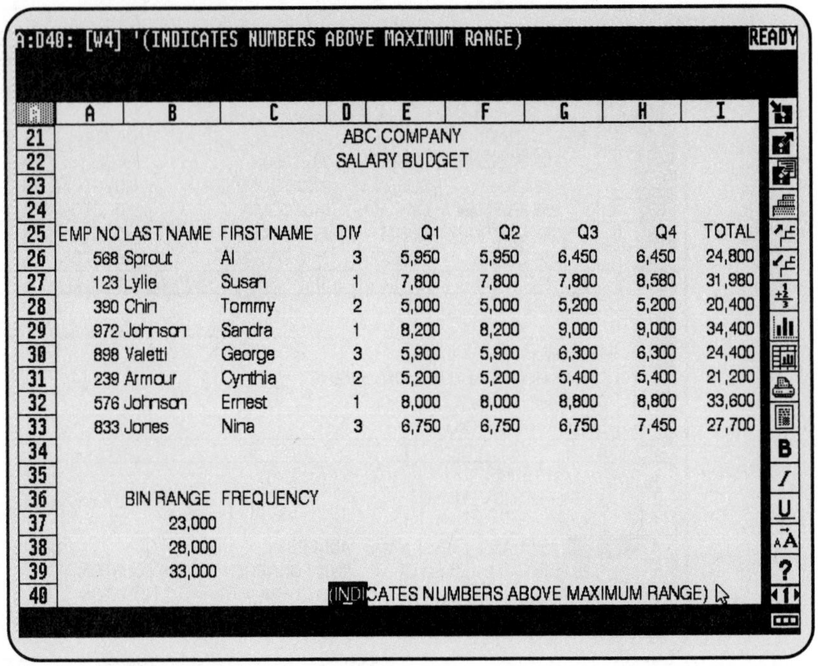

```
A:D40: [W4] '(INDICATES NUMBERS ABOVE MAXIMUM RANGE)          READY
```

	A	B	C	D	E	F	G	H	I
21			ABC COMPANY						
22			SALARY BUDGET						
23									
24									
25	EMP NO	LAST NAME	FIRST NAME	DIV	Q1	Q2	Q3	Q4	TOTAL
26	568	Sprout	Al	3	5,950	5,950	6,450	6,450	24,800
27	123	Lylie	Susan	1	7,800	7,800	7,800	8,580	31,980
28	390	Chin	Tommy	2	5,000	5,000	5,200	5,200	20,400
29	972	Johnson	Sandra	1	8,200	8,200	9,000	9,000	34,400
30	898	Valetti	George	3	5,900	5,900	6,300	6,300	24,400
31	239	Armour	Cynthia	2	5,200	5,200	5,400	5,400	21,200
32	576	Johnson	Ernest	1	8,000	8,000	8,800	8,800	33,600
33	833	Jones	Nina	3	6,750	6,750	6,750	7,450	27,700
34									
35									
36		BIN RANGE	FREQUENCY						
37		23,000							
38		28,000							
39		33,000							
40				(INDICATES NUMBERS ABOVE MAXIMUM RANGE)					

To find the data distribution for the salaries:

Press	/	**Move**	the mouse pointer to the control panel
Select	Data	**Choose**	Data
Select	Distribution	**Choose**	Distribution

The prompt "Enter values range:" appears. Since the distribution for this example is for salaries, highlight the total salary amounts:

Highlight	cells I26 through I33	**Highlight**	cells I26 through I33
Press	←Enter	**Click**	the mouse button

The prompt "Enter bin range:" appears. The bin range chosen for this example is from 23,000 through 33,000.

Highlight	cells B37 through B39	**Highlight**	cells B37 through B39
Press	←Enter	**Click**	the mouse button

The frequency of the salary amounts appears in cells C37 through C40.

The 2 in cell C37 indicates the number of salaries that are less than or equal to $23,000.

The 3 in cell C38 indicates the number of salaries between $23,000 and $28,000 including $28,000.

The 1 in cell C39 indicates the number of salaries between $28,000 and $33,000 including $33,000.

The 2 in cell C40 indicates the number of salaries greater than $33,000.

Your screen should look like the final illustration in Figure 14-36, Part 3. Parts 1 through 3 of Figure 14-36 display the entire **D**ata **D**istribution command sequence.

Step 1 of the Data Distribution Procedure: Specify the Desired Values through the Menu.

Figure 14-36
Part 1

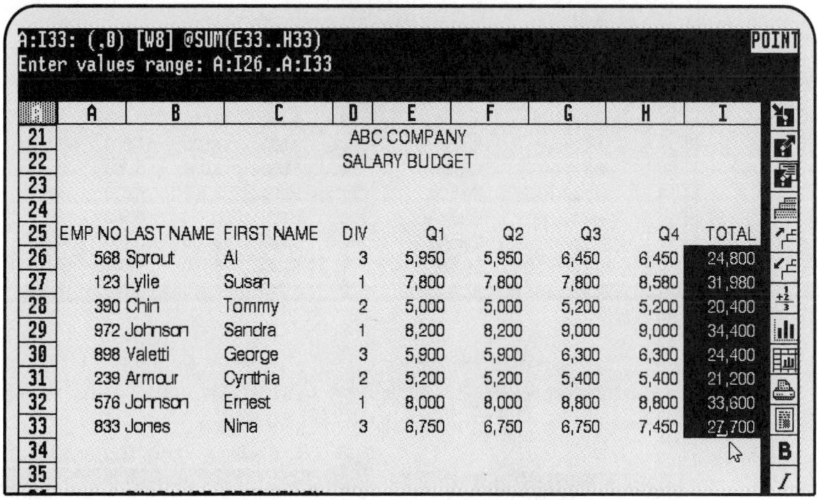

Step 2 of the Data Distribution Procedure: Specify the Desired Bin Range through the Menu.

Figure 14-36
Part 2

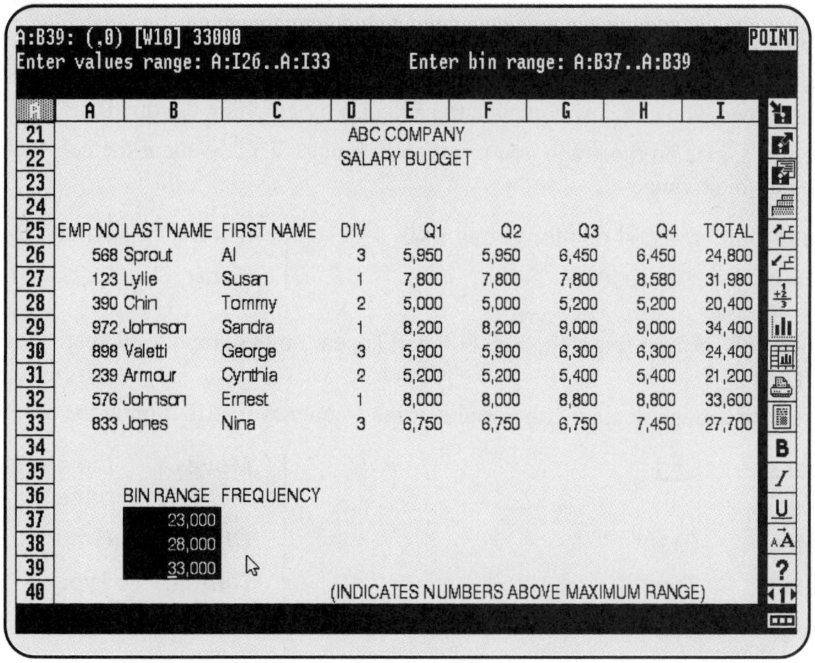

Step 3 of the Data Distribution Procedure: After you press ENTER or click the mouse button, the Frequency Distribution is displayed next to the Specified Bin Range.

Figure 14-36
Part 3

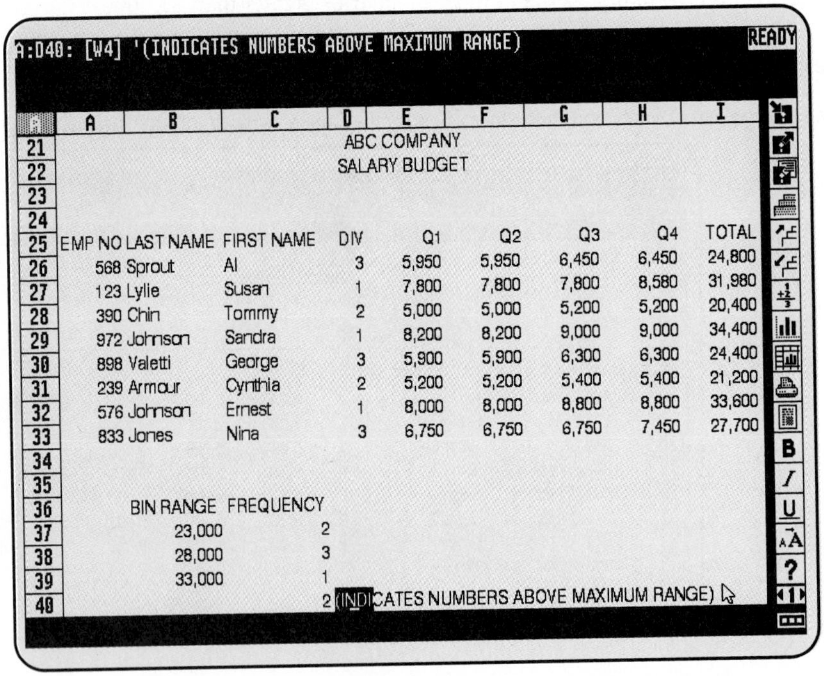

```
A:D40: [W4] '(INDICATES NUMBERS ABOVE MAXIMUM RANGE)                          READY
```

	A	B	C	D	E	F	G	H	I
21				ABC COMPANY					
22				SALARY BUDGET					
23									
24									
25	EMP NO	LAST NAME	FIRST NAME	DIV	Q1	Q2	Q3	Q4	TOTAL
26	568	Sprout	Al	3	5,950	5,950	6,450	6,450	24,800
27	123	Lylie	Susan	1	7,800	7,800	7,800	8,580	31,980
28	390	Chin	Tommy	2	5,000	5,000	5,200	5,200	20,400
29	972	Johnson	Sandra	1	8,200	8,200	9,000	9,000	34,400
30	898	Valetti	George	3	5,900	5,900	6,300	6,300	24,400
31	239	Armour	Cynthia	2	5,200	5,200	5,400	5,400	21,200
32	576	Johnson	Ernest	1	8,000	8,000	8,800	8,800	33,600
33	833	Jones	Nina	3	6,750	6,750	6,750	7,450	27,700
34									
35									
36		BIN RANGE	FREQUENCY						
37		23,000	2						
38		28,000	3						
39		33,000	1						
40			2	(INDICATES NUMBERS ABOVE MAXIMUM RANGE)					

■ GRAPHING A FREQUENCY DISTRIBUTION

Assuming that the previous exercise has just been completed and the data distribution worksheet is on your screen, you can now complete the exercise by graphing the distribution of salaries.

For the X-axis on the graph you use the bin range. To document the cell indicating the numbers above the maximum range:

Move	the cell pointer to cell B40	**Click**	on cell B40
Enter	">33,000	**Enter**	">33,000

When you perform this step, >33,000 will appear on the graph to indicate those numbers beyond the bin range.

To create a graph depicting the results of the frequency distribution in the previous exercise:

Press	/	**Move**	the mouse pointer to the control panel
Select	Graph	**Choose**	Graph
Select	Type	**Choose**	Type
Select	Pie	**Choose**	Pie

For the X-axis on the graph:

Select	X		*Choose*	*X*

For the X-axis, select the numbers in the bin range:

Highlight	cells B37 through B40		*Highlight*	*cells B37 through B40*
Press	←Enter		*Click*	*the mouse button*

To choose the first data range for the frequency data:

Select	A		*Choose*	*A*
Highlight	cells C37 through C40		*Highlight*	*cells C37 through C40*
Press	←Enter		*Click*	*the mouse button*

To enter a title for the graph:

Select	Options		*Choose*	*Options*
Select	Titles		*Choose*	*Titles*
Select	First		*Choose*	*First*

For the graph title:

Type	FREQUENCY DISTRIBUTION OF SALARIES		*Type*	*FREQUENCY DISTRIBUTION OF SALARIES*
Press	←Enter		*Click*	*the mouse button*

To exit the current menu:

Select	Quit		*Choose*	*Quit*

To view the graph:

Select	View		*Choose*	*View*

The graph should look like Figure 14-37.

Figure 14-37

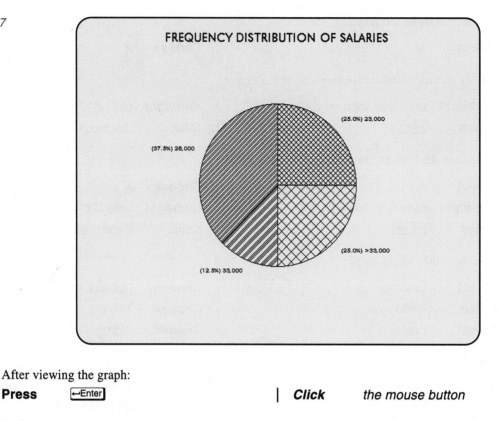

After viewing the graph:

Press   ⎡←Enter⎤ | ***Click***   *the mouse button*

To leave the current menu:

Select   Quit | ***Choose***   *Quit*

You do not need to save or print the graph.

SUMMARY

The **D**ata **F**ill option provides an easy way to place sequences of dates and times on one or more worksheets. The **D**ata **T**able capability allows you to create tables that illustrate the impact of changing values for a variable in a decision-making situation. External database tables created using database management software can be accessed, queried, and copied to a 1-2-3 worksheet. Lotus 1-2-3 also contains a **D**ata **D**istribution command used for determining a frequency distribution for a set of data in a specified range.

KEY CONCEPTS

Bin range	Data table
Data Distribution	External database
Data External	External database table
Data Fill	Frequency distribution

EXERCISE 1

INSTRUCTIONS: Circle T if the statement is true and F if the statement is false.

T   F   1. Database tables created by database management software packages can be accessed using Lotus 1-2-3.

T   F   2. Sequences of numbers or times cannot be placed on multiple worksheets at one time.

T   F   3. The **Data Table** option makes it possible to analyze changes in variables that affect decision-making situations.

T   F   4. A frequency distribution can be created using the **Data Distribution** command sequence.

T   F   5. A graph of a frequency distribution can be prepared by using the **Graph Distribution** command sequence.

EXERCISE 2 — Filling Cells with Numbers

INSTRUCTIONS: Make sure you have a blank worksheet on your screen.

Using the **Data Fill** command sequence, place the sequence of numbers 1, 4, 7, 10, 13, 16, and 19 in cells A2 through G2.

Using the **Data Fill** command sequence, place the sequence of numbers .1, .2, .3, .4, .5, and .6 in cells A6 through A11.

Print the completed worksheet.

EXERCISE 3 — Filling Cells with Dates

INSTRUCTIONS: Make sure you have a blank worksheet on your screen.

Using the **Data Fill** command sequence, place the sequence of dates May 3, May 7, May 11, and May 15 for the year 1993 in cells B2 through E2.

Using the **D**ata **F**ill command sequence, place the dates July 1, August 1, September 1, October 1, November 1, and December 1 for the year 1993 in cells B6 through G6.

Using the **D**ata **F**ill command sequence, place the dates January 15, April 15, July 15, and October 15 for the year 1995 in cells B10 through E10.

Using the **D**ata **F**ill command sequence, place the sequence of dates for January 1 of the years 1993, 1994, 1995, 1996, 1999, and 2000 in cells B15 through G15.

As required, format the date serial numbers so that an appropriate form of the date appears.

Print the worksheet after entering the indicated data.

EXERCISE 4 — Filling Cells with Times

INSTRUCTIONS: Make sure you have a blank worksheet on your screen.

Using the **D**ata **F**ill command sequence, place the times 9:00 a.m., 9:02 a.m., 9:04 a.m., 9:06 a.m., and 9:08 a.m. in cells A1 through A5.

Using the **D**ata **F**ill command sequence, enter the times 8:00 a.m. through 8:00 p.m. where the interval between each time on the worksheet is 2 hours. Place the time 8:00 a.m. in cell A7 and the remaining times should appear in column A below cell A7.

Format the time numbers so they appear properly.

Print the worksheet after placing the times on the worksheet.

EXERCISE 5 — Placing a Sequence of Data on Multiple Worksheets

INSTRUCTIONS: Make sure you have a blank worksheet on your screen.

Using the **D**ata **F**ill command sequence, place the dates for the years January 1 of the years 1993, 1994, and 1995 in cell B2 of the worksheets A, B, and C of a file.

Format the date numbers so that they appear properly.

Print the worksheets after entering and formatting the dates.

EXERCISE 6 — Changing the Value of One Variable in a Data Table

INSTRUCTIONS: Suppose you are considering the purchase of a house. The current interest rate is 11% for a 20-year fixed-rate loan.

Create a data table that contains the monthly payments for a house if the price is $75,000, $80,000, $85,000, $90,000, or $95,000 using the interest rate of 11% and assuming a 20-year loan period.

Print the data table after it is prepared.

EXERCISE 7 — Changing the Values of Two Variables in a Data Table

INSTRUCTIONS: Suppose you are considering the purchase of some property in the $50,000 to $70,000 price range. Assume that you can obtain a 30-year fixed-rate loan from several financial institutions with an interest rate varying between 9% and 11%.

Create a data table that contains the monthly payment amounts after varying the purchase price from $50,000 to $70,000 in increments of $5,000. You also need to use an initial interest rate of 9% and increase it to a maximum of 11% using one-half percent increments.

Use a 30-year loan period for all calculations.

Print the data table after the monthly payment values have been determined.

EXERCISE 8 — Changing the Values of Three Variables in a Data Table

INSTRUCTIONS: Use the worksheet completed in Exercise 7 for this exercise.

Assume that you can finance the purchase of the property for either 20, 25, or 30 years.

Determine the monthly payments for the various loan periods using the purchase price and interest rate assumptions specified in Exercise 7.

Print the worksheets containing the calculated monthly payment values.

EXERCISE 9 — Combining Information from Multiple Database Tables

INSTRUCTIONS: Use the ABCSAL and EMPADDRS files created earlier in this chapter for this exercise.

Create a database table that contains the names and addresses of all present employees of ABC Company that live in Houston.

Print the worksheet containing the database table of the names and addresses of current employees living in Houston.

EXERCISE 10 — Creating a Frequency Distribution

INSTRUCTIONS: Retrieve the ABCSAL file for use in this exercise.

Use the **D**ata **D**istribution menu option to determine the number of people in each division in the ABCSAL data table.

The bin range should encompass the division numbers in the database and be placed on a separate worksheet.

Print the worksheet after calculating the number of people in each division.

EXERCISE 11 — Graphing a Frequency Distribution

INSTRUCTIONS: Use the results of Exercise 10 for this exercise.

Create a pie graph using the data for the distribution of people for the three divisions in ABC Company.

Print the pie graph depicting the data distribution.

CHAPTER FIFTEEN

SPECIAL FUNCTIONS IN LOTUS 1-2-3

OBJECTIVES

In this chapter, you will learn to use and apply the following types of special functions available in 1-2-3:

- Statistical analysis
- Financial analysis
- Date and time
- Logical
- Database
- Mathematical
- Special
- String

■ CHAPTER OVERVIEW

Lotus 1-2-3 has 105 special functions. Suppose you want to compute the monthly payment for a 30-year, $100,000 bank loan with an 11% interest rate. The @PMT function allows you to compute the payment amount. In earlier exercises, you have used some of the other special functions such as @SUM and @ROUND. In this chapter, you will learn to apply many of the special functions used for the following categories: statistical analysis, financial analysis, date and time, logical, database, mathematical, special, and string. Each of the special functions has a specific structure that you must use. The general format of a special function is:

@function name(argument1,argument2,...argumentn)

You must enter the function using the correct syntax or errors will occur. The set of information needed for a function to compute accurately are referred to as arguments. Arguments must be entered in the correct order and must be separated by the correct punctuation. In some cases, an argument may be optional. If an argument is optional, brackets will appear in the text, but are not required when the function is used. Press the ENTER key or click the mouse button after typing the function.

> *In This Chapter*
>
> This chapter includes examples of most of the types of special functions available in 1-2-3. Most of the examples require that you start with a blank worksheet. Rather than specify that you erase your screen, the text simply indicates that you need to have a blank worksheet on your screen or that you need to create a particular worksheet.
>
> For additional information on each function described in this chapter, refer to the Lotus 1-2-3 help feature or Lotus 1-2-3 reference manual.

■ STATISTICAL ANALYSIS FUNCTIONS

Lotus 1-2-3 has 10 **statistical analysis functions**. They include:

@SUM	Computes the sum of a list of cell values
@COUNT	Computes the number of items in a list of cell values
@AVG	Computes the arithmetic mean for a list of cell values
@MIN	Identifies the minimum value for a list of cell values
@MAX	Identifies the maximum value for a list of cell values
@VAR	Computes the population variance for a list of cells
@STD	Computes the population standard deviation for a list of cells
@VARS	Computes the sample variance for a list of cells
@STDS	Computes the sample standard deviation for a list of cells
@SUMPRODUCT	Computes the sum of the products of corresponding items in multiple ranges

The general format for the statistical analysis functions is as follows:

@function name(first cell..last cell)

For example, to compute the sum of the numbers in cells A1 through G1 in a worksheet, the formula @SUM(A1..G1) is used. The function name should be spelled exactly as it is listed above (e.g., the function name for averaging numbers is spelled as AVG). The functions can be entered in upper or lower case.

Using the Statistical Analysis Functions

In this section you will learn to use each of the statistical functions. First, create a worksheet like Figure 15-1.

Figure 15-1

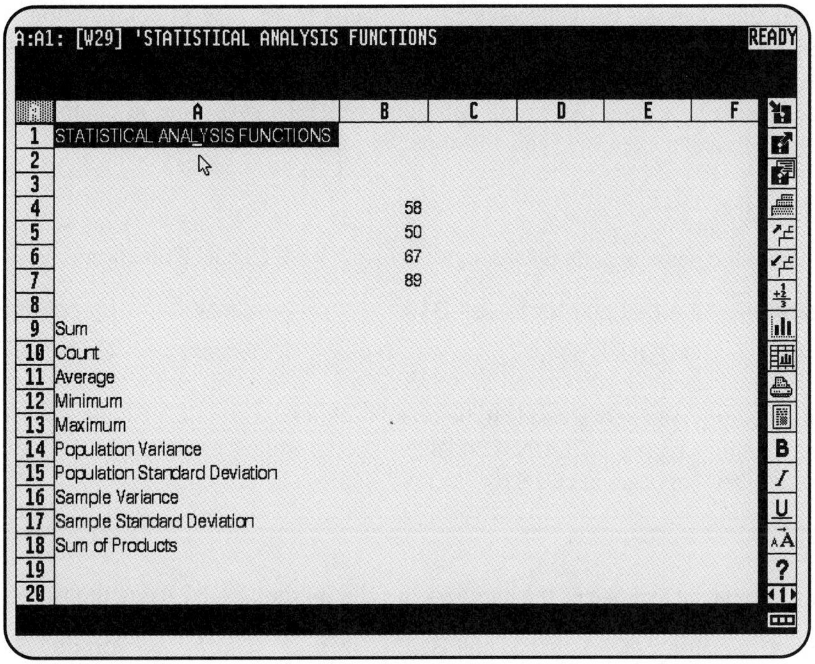

```
A:A1: [W29] 'STATISTICAL ANALYSIS FUNCTIONS                              READY
```

	A	B	C	D	E	F
1	STATISTICAL ANALYSIS FUNCTIONS					
2						
3						
4		58				
5		50				
6		67				
7		89				
8						
9	Sum					
10	Count					
11	Average					
12	Minimum					
13	Maximum					
14	Population Variance					
15	Population Standard Deviation					
16	Sample Variance					
17	Sample Standard Deviation					
18	Sum of Products					
19						
20						

@SUM

To compute the sum of the four numbers in cells B4 through B7 using the @SUM function:

Move	the cell pointer to cell B9		*Click*	*on cell B9*
Type	@SUM(		*Type*	*@SUM(*
Move	the cell pointer to cell B4		*Move*	*the mouse pointer to cell B4*
Type	.		*Drag*	*the mouse pointer to cell B7*
Move	the cell pointer to cell B7		*Type*	*)*
Type	)			

The formula @SUM(B4..B7) now should appear in the control panel.

| **Press** | ⏎Enter | | *Click* | *the mouse button* |

The formula was entered into cell B9; the result is 264.

When using the @SUM formula in worksheets, you may wish to include the cell immediately above and below the range of numbers currently being added. For example, the formula @SUM(B3..B8) could be used instead of @SUM(B4..B7) to total the numbers in this exercise. Then, if rows are inserted (or deleted) at the top or bottom of the range adding (or deleting) more numbers, the @SUM command will correctly adjust the total.

Rather than moving the cell pointer to the cells to be used in computation, you can type the formula @SUM(B4.B7) directly in cell B9 and press ENTER or click the mouse button to obtain the same result. The advantage of highlighting the numbers to be used in the formula is that you will be less likely to make errors by typing the wrong cell addresses. To save time in completing the following statistical analysis function exercises, you will type the formula directly into the cells.

@COUNT

To count the items in cells B4 through B7 using the @COUNT function:

| **Move** | the cell pointer to cell B10 | *Click* | *on cell B10* |
| **Enter** | @COUNT(B4.B7) | *Enter* | *@COUNT(B4.B7)* |

Note that only one period needs to be typed within the formula. Typing @COUNT(B4.B7) produces the same result as typing @COUNT(B4..B7). The formula @COUNT(B4..B7) appears in the control panel. The number 4 appears in cell B10.

@AVG

To compute the average of the numbers in cells B4 through B7 using the @AVG function:

| **Move** | the cell pointer to cell B11 | *Click* | *on cell B11* |
| **Enter** | @AVG(B4.B7) | *Enter* | *@AVG(B4.B7)* |

The formula @AVG(B4..B7) appears in the control panel. The number 66 appears in cell B11.

@MIN

To determine the smallest value of the items in cells B4 through B7 using the @MIN function:

| **Move** | the cell pointer to cell B12 | *Click* | *on cell B12* |
| **Enter** | @MIN(B4.B7) | *Enter* | *@MIN(B4.B7)* |

The formula @MIN(B4..B7) appears in the control panel. The number 50 appears in cell B12.

@MAX

To determine the largest value of the items in cells B4 through B7 using the @MAX function:

| **Move** | the cell pointer to cell B13 | *Click* | *on cell B13* |
| **Enter** | @MAX(B4.B7) | *Enter* | *@MAX(B4.B7)* |

The formula @MAX(B4..B7) appears in the control panel. The number 89 appears in cell B13.

@VAR for a Population

To determine the population variance of the numbers in cells B4 through B7 using the @VAR function:

| **Move** | the cell pointer cell B14 | *Click* | *on cell B14* |

Enter   @VAR(B4.B7) | **Enter**   @VAR(B4.B7)

The formula @VAR(B4..B7) appears in the control panel. The number 212.5 appears in cell B14. It is assumed you have all the values that need to be considered, and the data are not a sample of values from a larger set of data.

@STD for a Population

To determine the standard deviation of the numbers in cells B4 through B7 using the @STD function:

Move   the cell pointer to cell B15 | **Click**   on cell B15
Enter   @STD(B4.B7) | **Enter**   @STD(B4.B7)

The formula @STD(B4..B7) appears in the control panel. The number 14.57738 appears in cell B15. It is assumed you have all the values that need to be considered, and the data are not a sample of values from a larger set of data.

@VARS

When you computed the population variance, you assumed that you had all of the data that you were considering. If instead, the data are only a sample of all the data that you want to consider, then the formula for computing the variance is:

$$\sum_{i=1}^{n} (x_i - \bar{x})^2/(n-1) \quad \text{rather than} \quad \sum_{i=1}^{n} (x_i - \mu)^2/n.$$

Assuming the data in B4 through B7 are a sample, calculate the sample variance.

Move   the cell pointer to cell B16 | **Click**   on cell B16
Enter   @VARS(B4.B7) | **Enter**   @VARS(B4.B7)

The value 283.3333 appears in cell B16.

@STDS

When you computed the population standard deviation, you assumed that you had all of the data that you want to examine. If, instead, the data are only a sample, then the formula for computing the standard deviation is:

$$\sqrt{\frac{\sum_{i=1}^{n} (x_i - \bar{x})^2}{n-1}} \quad \text{rather than} \quad \sqrt{\frac{\sum_{i=1}^{n} (x_i - \mu)^2}{n}}.$$

If the data in cells B4 through B7 are a sample, then you can compute the sample standard deviation as follows.

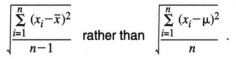

| **Move** | the cell pointer to cell B17 | **Click** | on cell B17 |
| **Enter** | @STDS(B4.B7) | **Enter** | @STDS(B4.B7) |

The value 16.83251 appears in cell B17.

Your screen should look like Figure 15-2.

Figure 15-2

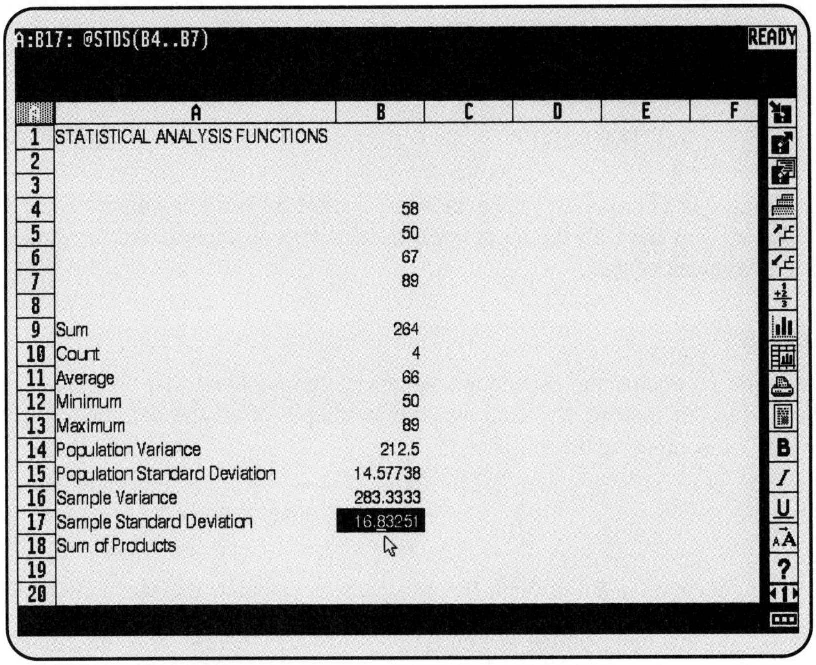

```
A:B17: @STDS(B4..B7)                                              READY

             A                    B      C      D      E      F
  1  STATISTICAL ANALYSIS FUNCTIONS
  2
  3
  4                                58
  5                                50
  6                                67
  7                                89
  8
  9  Sum                          264
 10  Count                          4
 11  Average                       66
 12  Minimum                       50
 13  Maximum                       89
 14  Population Variance        212.5
 15  Population Standard Deviation 14.57738
 16  Sample Variance          283.3333
 17  Sample Standard Deviation 16.83251
 18  Sum of Products
 19
 20
```

@SUMPRODUCT

In some situations, you may need to multiply one set of numbers by another set of numbers and then sum the results. Refer to Figure 15-3 and notice that two additional sets of values have been placed on the worksheet in cells D9..D11 and E9..E11. Suppose you want to multiply the corresponding values in column D by the values in column E and place the results in cell B18. Enter the values appearing in cells D9 through E11 in Figure 15-3.

| **Move** | the cell pointer to cell B18 | **Click** | on cell B18 |
| **Enter** | @SUMPRODUCT(D9.D11, E9.E11) | **Enter** | @SUMPRODUCT(D9.D11, E9.E11) |

The result is 275 which is computed by summing the products of the corresponding elements in columns D and E. The products that are included in the sum are 50, 120, and 105.

When you finish the statistical functions exercise, your screen should look like Figure 15-3.

Figure 15-3

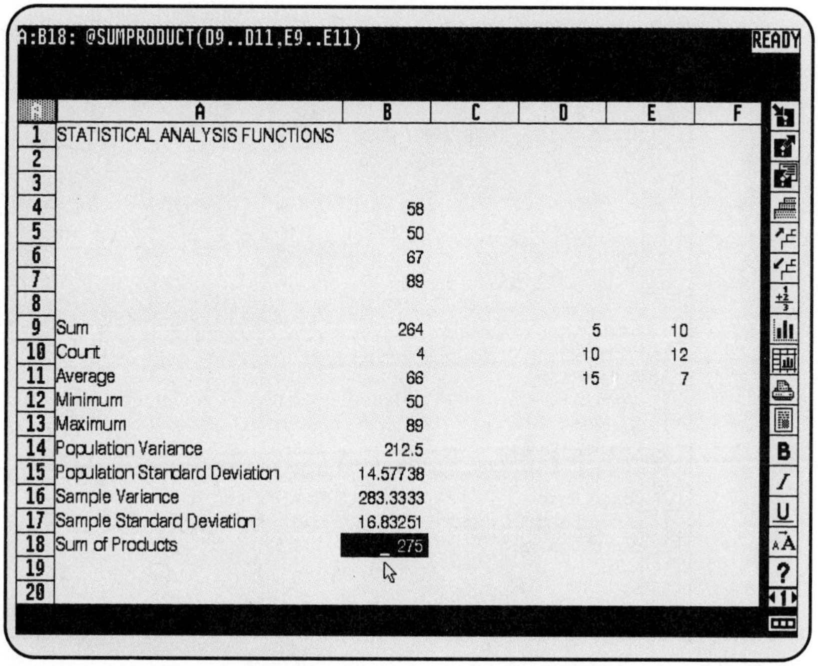

When using the statistical analysis functions, it is important to note that labels have a value of zero and can distort the desired computations. In the following exercise, you will erase one of the numbers in the range B4..B7 by pressing the space bar. The results are then discussed.

Move	the cell pointer to cell B6	**Click**	on cell B6
Press	the space bar	**Press**	the space bar
Press	←Enter	**Click**	the mouse button

Although cell B6 appears to be blank, it actually contains a label. In the control panel, an apostrophe appears. Whenever a label is typed, the default label prefix is the apostrophe. The cell is not really blank; it contains a space. A space is treated as a label and therefore is given a value of 0 when used in a computation. For example, the minimum value computed by the @MIN function is now zero. The count computed by the @COUNT function still shows four items since the @COUNT function counts both numeric and non-numeric items. Refer to Figure 15-4 to see how the label distorts the results of the computations.

A label counts as the value 0 in computations.

Figure 15-4

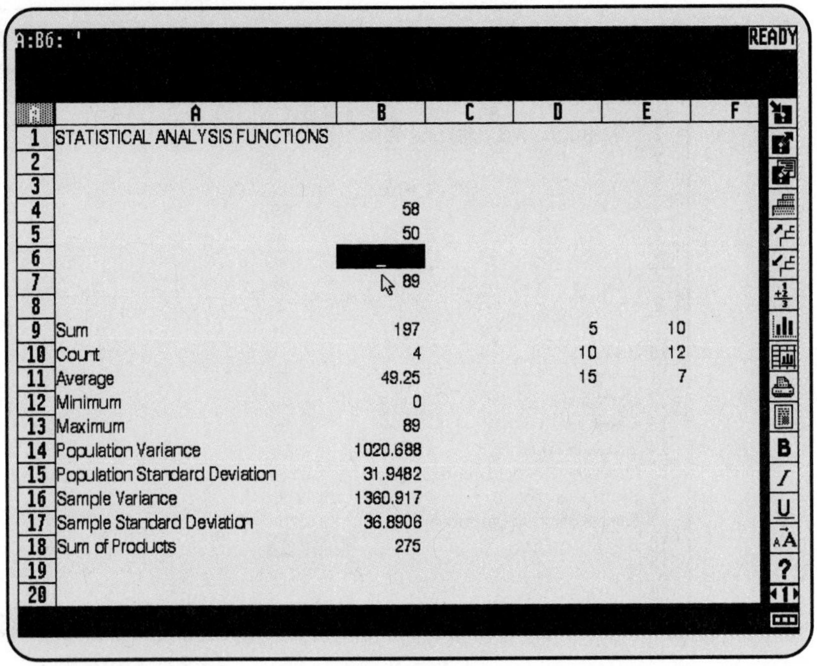

	A	B	C	D	E	F
1	STATISTICAL ANALYSIS FUNCTIONS					
2						
3						
4		58				
5		50				
6						
7		89				
8						
9	Sum	197		5	10	
10	Count	4		10	12	
11	Average	49.25		15	7	
12	Minimum	0				
13	Maximum	89				
14	Population Variance	1020.688				
15	Population Standard Deviation	31.9482				
16	Sample Variance	1360.917				
17	Sample Standard Deviation	36.8906				
18	Sum of Products	275				
19						
20						

You can correct this problem by erasing the contents of cell B6. To truly erase cell B6, use the **Range Erase** command sequence. Notice that the formulas have accurately calculated the desired results. Your screen should look like Figure 15-5.

A blank cell will not be used as a value in computations.

Figure 15-5

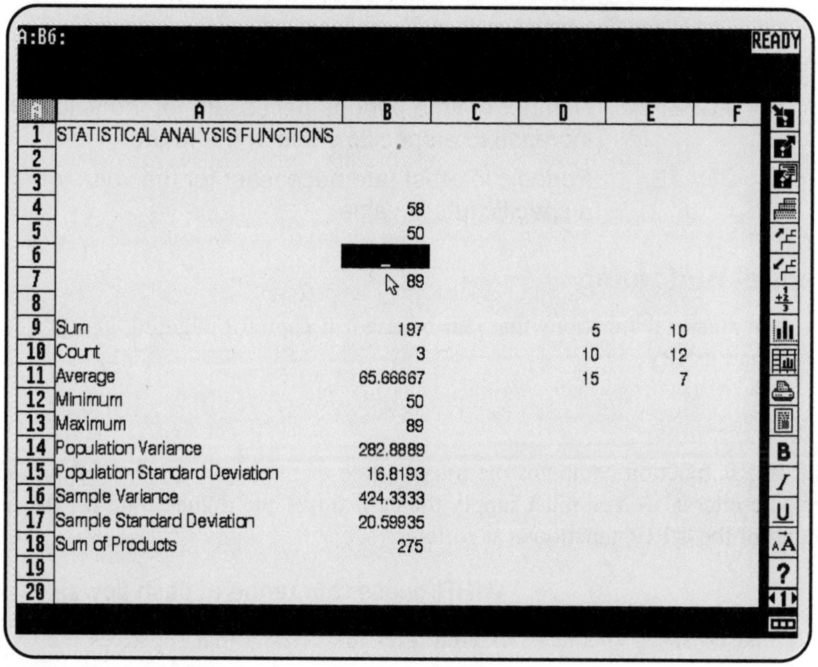

```
A:B6:                                                          READY

        A                        B      C      D      E      F
 1  STATISTICAL ANALYSIS FUNCTIONS
 2
 3
 4                              58
 5                              50
 6
 7                              89
 8
 9  Sum                        197             5     10
10  Count                        3            10     12
11  Average                65.66667          15      7
12  Minimum                     50
13  Maximum                     89
14  Population Variance    282.8889
15  Population Standard Deviation  16.8193
16  Sample Variance        424.3333
17  Sample Standard Deviation  20.59935
18  Sum of Products            275
19
20
```

■ FINANCIAL ANALYSIS FUNCTIONS

The 12 **financial analysis functions** available in Lotus 1-2-3 include:

CAPITAL BUDGETING:

@IRR	Internal rate of return
@NPV	Net present value

ANNUITIES:

@FV	Future value
@PV	Present value
@TERM	Number of time periods needed in the term of an ordinary annuity to accumulate a future value earning a specific periodic interest rate
@PMT	Payment amount

DEPRECIATION:

@SLN	Straight-line depreciation
@DDB	Double-declining balance depreciation

@SYD	Sum-of-the-years' digits depreciation
@VDB	Variable declining balance depreciation

SINGLE-SUM COMPOUNDING:

@CTERM	Number of time periods necessary for the value of an investment to increase to a specific value in the future
@RATE	Periodic interest rate necessary for the value of an investment to grow to a specific future value

Capital Budgeting

The two financial functions that can be used in capital budgeting and project evaluation activities are @IRR and @NPV.

@IRR

The @IRR function computes the internal rate of return for a series of cash flows that occur at regular periodic intervals. You must supply the cash flows and a guess rate for the internal rate of return. The format of the @IRR function is as follows:

@IRR(guess rate,range of cash flows)

Note that no space should be entered after the comma that separates the two arguments in the @IRR function.

In this exercise, suppose that an investment is being considered that requires a cash investment of $2,100 the first year and the anticipated cash flows in years 2 through 5 are respectively $1,300, $700, $500, and $300.

Make sure a blank worksheet appears on your screen. Create a worksheet like the one appearing in Figure 15-6.

Figure 15-6

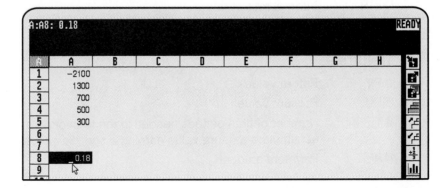

The initial investment, actually a cash outflow, is in cell A1. The negative number indicates the initial cash investment made by the investor. The range of anticipated cash flows from the investment appear in cells A2 through A5. The guess at the internal rate of return of 18 percent appears in cell A8.

To find the internal rate of return for the investment on which you entered data:

Move	the cell pointer to cell A11		**Click**	*on cell A11*
Enter	@IRR(A8,A1.A5)		**Enter**	*@IRR(A8,A1.A5)*

The first argument in the @IRR formula identifies A8 as the cell with the guess rate of 18 percent. The second argument identifies A1..A5 as the cash flows beginning with the initial investment of $2,100 and ending with the cash flow in YEAR 5 of $300.

The special function appears in the control panel. The result, .168349 or about 16.83 percent, is displayed. Your screen should look like Figure 15-7.

Figure 15-7

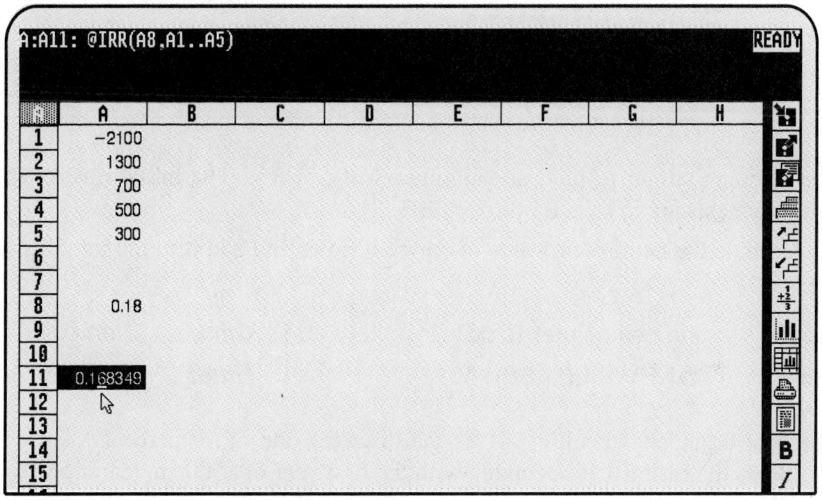

Note that the guess rate could have been entered directly into the function as @IRR(.18,A1..A5). The advantage of the guess rate being entered outside of the function is that it can be changed more readily. The cash flows must be entered as a range of cells or a range name that is located elsewhere on the worksheet. A single-cell item, however, can be either entered directly into the formula or referenced with a cell address (e.g., .18 or A8 is acceptable in the @IRR function in the previous exercise).

ERR may appear as a result of using the @IRR function if convergence to within .0000001 does not occur within 30 iterations. Change the guess rate to a higher or lower value until a value appears for the internal rate of return.

@NPV

The net present value computes the present value for a set of cash flows using a specified discount rate. All cash flows are assumed to occur at the end of each year. The format of the @NPV function is:

@NPV(rate,range of cash flows)

In this exercise, consider an investment project that requires you to invest $2,000 initially and you receive payments of $900, $850, $600, $350, $200, and $50 at the end of the first through the sixth years. Assume that 10 percent is an appropriate discount rate.

To solve this problem, create the worksheet in Figure 15-8.

Figure 15-8

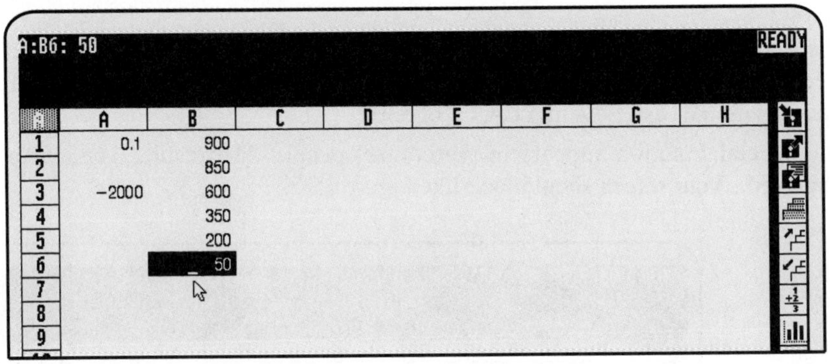

The discount rate is 10 percent and appears in cell A1. The initial investment is in cell A3. The cash flow payments are in cells B1 through B6.

To compute the net present value of the cash flows and add it to the initial investment of $2,000 (in cell A3):

| **Move** | the cell pointer to cell C1 | | *Click* | *on cell C1* |
| **Enter** | @NPV(A1,B1.B6)+A3 | | *Enter* | *@NPV(A1,B1.B6)+A3* |

The first argument identifies A1 as the discount rate of 10 percent. The second argument identifies B1..B6 as the cash flows beginning with the first year of $900 and ending with the last year at $50. Note that A3 (the initial investment) must be added to the net present value of the cash flows because, if it is included in the formula, it will be discounted.

The formula appears in the control panel. The result, 362.9127 or about $362.91, is displayed. Your screen should look like Figure 15-9.

Figure 15-9

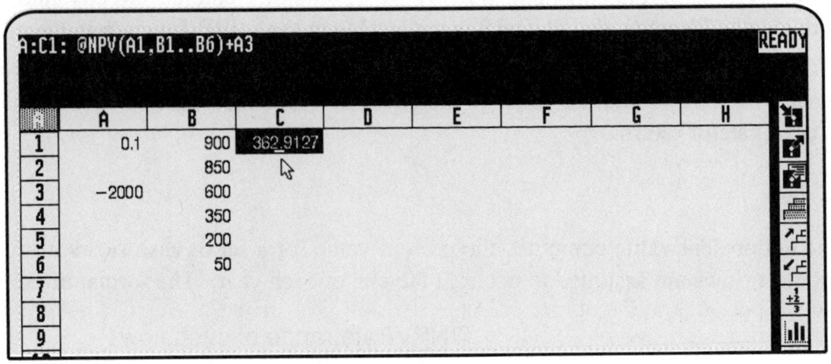

If desired, you can format the results with a dollar sign and two decimal places using the **R**ange **F**ormat **C**urrency command sequence.

Annuities

The four functions available in 1-2-3 related to ordinary annuities include: @FV, @PV, @TERM, and @PMT.

@FV

The future value function computes the future value of an annuity given the payment per period, an interest rate per period, and the number of periods. The general format of the @FV function is as follows:

@FV(payment,interest rate,term)

Assume you want to compute the future value of an annuity when the payment amount is $1,500, the interest rate is 13 percent, and the term is 10 years.

In the previous exercises in this chapter, single-cell items used in the financial analysis functions were not placed directly into the function, but were referenced by cell address. In this example, all three arguments are single-cell items. Instead of entering a formula in a format such as the following–@FV(C1,C2,C3)–all of the arguments in this formula can be placed directly into the formula–@FV(1500,.13,10).

To find the future value of the given data, make sure there is a blank worksheet on your screen. Then,

| **Move** | the cell pointer to cell A1 | **Click** | on cell A1 |
| **Enter** | @FV(1500,.13,10) | **Enter** | @FV(1500,.13,10) |

The first argument specifies the payment per year as $1,500. The second argument specifies the interest rate as 13 percent. The third argument specifies the term as 10 years.

The special function appears in the control panel. The result, 27629.62 or about $27,629.62, is displayed on the worksheet. Your screen should look like Figure 15-10.

Figure 15-10

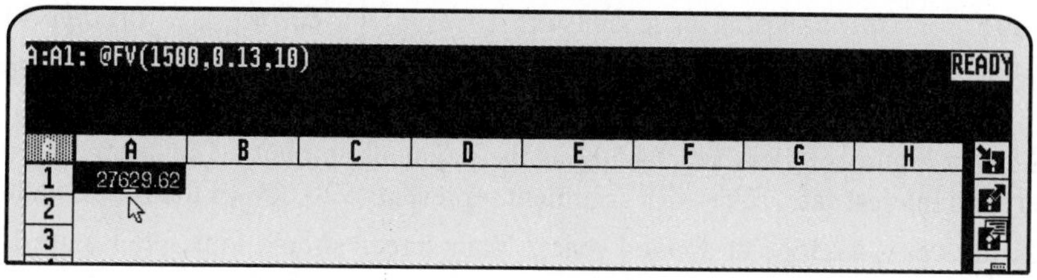

@PV

The present value function computes the present value of an annuity given a payment per period, interest rate per period, and the number of time periods. The general format of the @PV function is as follows:

@PV(payment,rate,number of periods)

In this exercise, you will determine the present value of an annuity where payments are $1,500 per year, the interest rate is 13 percent, and the term is 10 years.

To find the present value of the given data:

Move	the cell pointer to cell A1		*Click*	*on cell A1*
Enter	@PV(1500,.13,10)		*Enter*	*@PV(1500,.13,10)*

The first argument identifies the payment amount of $1,500. The second argument identifies the interest rate of 13 percent. The third argument identifies the term as 10 years.

The special function appears in the control panel. The result is 8139.365 or about $8,139.37. Your screen should look like Figure 15-11.

Figure 15-11

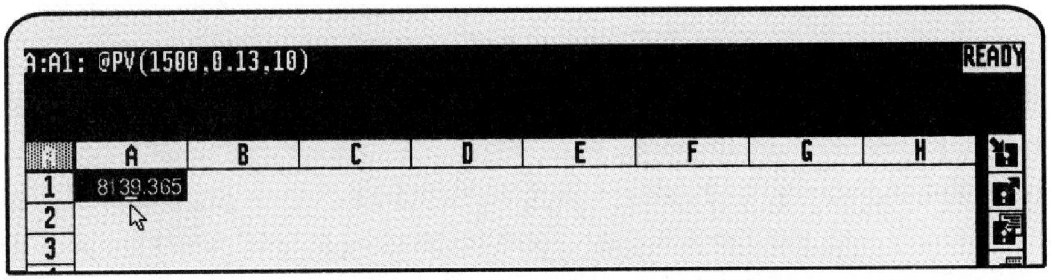

A:A1: @PV(1500,0.13,10)   READY

	A	B	C	D	E	F	G	H
1	8139.365							
2								
3								

@TERM

@TERM calculates the number of payment periods in a term of an ordinary annuity necessary to accumulate a future value earning a periodic interest rate. Each payment is equal to the given payment amount in the formula. The general format for the @TERM function is as follows:

$$@TERM(payment,periodic\ interest\ rate,future\ value)$$

In this exercise, assume that $4,500 has been deposited each year on the same date into an account that pays an interest rate of 6 percent, compounded annually. The @TERM function will be used to determine how long it will take for you to have $20,000 in the account.

Using the given data:

Move	the cell pointer to cell A1		*Click*	*on cell A1*
Enter	@TERM(4500,.06,20000)		*Enter*	*@TERM(4500,.06,20000)*

The first argument identifies $4,500 as the payment amount. The second argument identifies .06 as the periodic interest rate. The third argument represents $20,000 as the future value.

The answer is 4.05686 or about 4 years. Your screen should look like Figure 15-12.

Figure 15-12

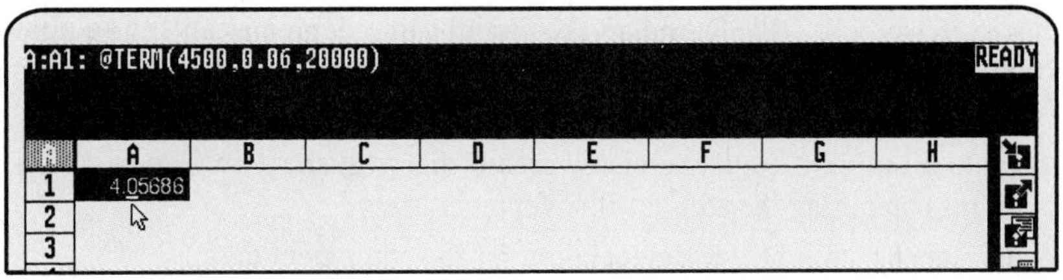

@PMT

You can compute the payment per period if you are given the principal amount, the interest rate per period, and the number of periods. The general format for the @PMT function is as follows:

@PMT(principal, interest rate, term)

Suppose the principal of a loan is $1,200, the interest rate is 15 percent, and there are annual payments for 10 years.

To determine the payment per year of the given data:

Move	the cell pointer to cell A1		***Click***	*on cell A1*
Enter	@PMT(1200,.15,10)		***Enter***	*@PMT(1200,.15,10)*

The first argument identifies the principal of $1,200. The second argument identifies the interest rate of 15 percent. The third argument identifies the term as 10 years.

The special function appears in the control panel. The result is 239.1025 or about $239.10 per year. Your screen should look like Figure 15-13.

Figure 15-13

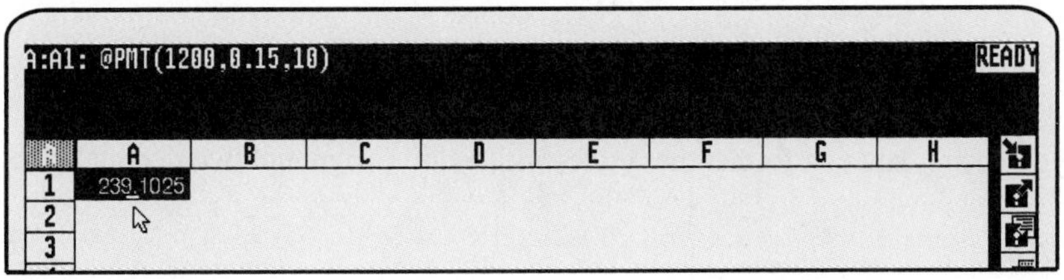

Depreciation

The four depreciation functions included in Lotus 1-2-3 are: @SLN, @DDB, @SYD, and @VDB.

Make sure you have a blank worksheet on your screen.

@SLN

The **straight-line depreciation** of an asset can be computed for one period given the cost, salvage value, and estimated useful life of the asset. The general format for the @SLN function is as follows:

@SLN(cost,salvage value,estimated useful life)

In this exercise, you will determine the straight-line depreciation for equipment that is purchased for $13,000. The estimated useful life of the equipment is 6 years and the salvage value is estimated at $1,000.

To complete the next four exercises, create the worksheet in Figure 15-14, but do not include the function for computing the straight-line depreciation.

To determine the straight-line depreciation for the equipment data:

Move	the cell pointer to cell B5	*Click*	*on cell B5*
Enter	@SLN(B1,B2,B3)	*Enter*	*@SLN(B1,B2,B3)*

The first argument identifies B1 as the cell containing the cost of $13,000. The second argument identifies B2 as the cell containing the salvage value of $1,000. The third argument identifies B3 as the cell containing the useful life of 6 years. The formula @SLN(13000,1000,6) could have been entered as an alternative to using cell addresses for the various arguments.

The special function appears in the control panel. The result, 2000 or $2,000, is displayed on the worksheet. Your screen should look like Figure 15-14.

Figure 15-14

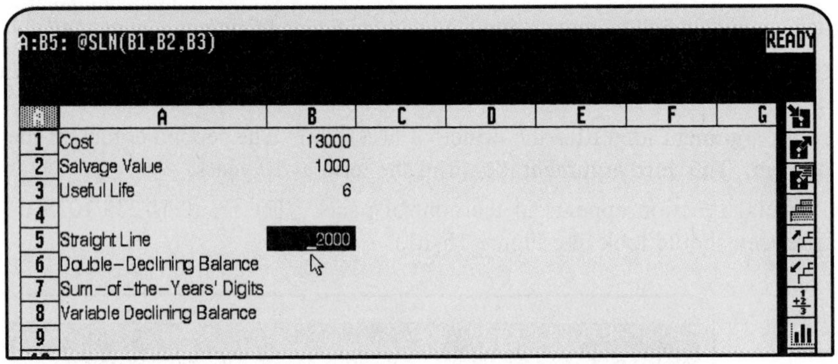

If you desire, you can format the results with a dollar sign and two decimal places.

@DDB

This exercise assumes you have just finished the previous exercise and the results are still displayed on your screen.

The depreciation of an asset using the **double-declining balance** method can be computed for a specified period given the cost, salvage value, estimated useful life, and the desired time period. The general format for the @DDB function is as follows:

@DDB(cost,salvage value,estimated useful life,period)

In this exercise, you will use the data given in the previous exercise to compute the depreciation for the equipment for the first year using the double-declining balance method.

To document that the depreciation will be computed only for Year 1 in this example (an optional step):

Move	the cell pointer to cell C6	**Click**	on cell C6
Enter	Year 1	**Enter**	Year 1

To compute the depreciation using the double-declining balance method:

Move	the cell pointer to cell B6	**Click**	on cell B6
Enter	@DDB(B1,B2,B3,1)	**Enter**	@DDB(B1,B2,B3,1)

The first argument identifies B1 as the cell containing the cost at $13,000. The second argument identifies B2 as the cell containing the salvage value at $1,000. The third argument identifies B3 as the cell containing the useful life of the equipment at 6 years. The fourth argument indicates that this computation represents the depreciation for Year 1.

The special function appears in the control panel. The result, 4333.333 or about $4,333.33, is displayed. Your screen should look like Figure 15-15.

Figure 15-15

To compute the depreciation for the other time periods, you would have to enter the function again for each of the desired time periods.

@SYD

This exercise assumes you have just finished the previous exercise and the results are still displayed on the screen.

The depreciation of an asset using the **sum-of-the-years' digits** method can be computed for a specified period given the cost, salvage value, estimated useful life, and the desired time period. The general format for the @SYD function is as follows:

@SYD(cost,salvage value,estimated useful life,period)

In this exercise, you will use the data given in the previous exercise to calculate the depreciation for the equipment for the third year using the sum-of-the-years' digits method.

To indicate that the depreciation will be computed only for Year 3 in this example:

| **Move** | the cell pointer to cell C7 | **Click** | on cell C7 |
| **Enter** | Year 3 | **Enter** | Year 3 |

To compute the depreciation using the sum-of-the-years' digits method:

| **Move** | the cell pointer to cell B7 | **Click** | on cell B7 |
| **Enter** | @SYD(B1,B2,B3,3) | **Enter** | @SYD(B1,B2,B3,3) |

The first argument identifies B1 as the cell containing the cost at $13,000. The second argument identifies B2 as the cell containing the salvage value of $1,000. The third argument identifies B3 as the cell containing the useful life of 6 years. The fourth argument indicates that this computation is for Year 3.

The special function appears in the control panel. The result, 2285.714 or about $2,285.71, is displayed on the worksheet. Your screen should look like Figure 15-16.

Figure 15-16

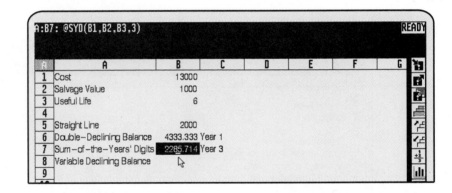

If you desire, the results could be formatted with a dollar sign and two decimal places. To compute the depreciation values for the other time periods, you would have to enter the function again for each of the desired time periods.

@VDB

This exercise assumes that you have just completed the exercise in the previous section and the results are still displayed on your screen. The general formula for the @VDB (**variable declining balance**) function is:

$$@VDB(cost,salvage,life,start\text{-}period,end\text{-}period,depreciation\text{-}factor),(switch))$$

This function calculates the depreciation allowance of an asset for a length of time specified by the start-period and the end-period using the double-declining balance method. You can use the optional depreciation-factor to allow the percentage of straight-line depreciation to vary so you calculate depreciation values other than those determined using the double-declining balance method. The optional switch allows you to change the depreciation values in periods when the straight-line depreciation value is greater than that determined using the double-declining balance calculation.

The depreciation-factor can be any value greater than 0. If you do not specify a value for depreciation-factor, the @VDB function will compute depreciation using the double-declining balance method.

You should only include a value for the switch option if you do not want @VDB to automatically switch from declining balance to straight-line when the straight-line depreciation is greater than declining-balance. The values that can be used for the switch are 0 and 1. If the value for the switch is 0, which is the default value, @VDB automatically changes from declining-balance to straight-line when straight-line values are greater. If the value assigned to the switch is 1, then @VDB never switches from the declining-balance method.

In this exercise you will use the data given in the previous exercise to compute the depreciation for YEAR 1 using 150 percent instead of 200 percent for the depreciation factor. You will also assume that you want to automatically switch to straight-line depreciation when the values for straight-line depreciation are greater than the values for 150 percent declining balance.

To document that the depreciation value will be computed only for YEAR 1 (an optional step):

| **Move** | the cell pointer to cell C8 | *Click* | *on cell C8* |
| **Enter** | YEAR 1 | *Enter* | *YEAR 1* |

To calculate the depreciation for the first year, assuming you purchased the equipment on the first day of the year, using the variable-rate depreciation function:

| **Move** | the cell pointer to cell B8 | *Click* | *on cell B8* |
| **Type** | @VDB(B1,B2,B3,0,1,1.5,0) | *Type* | *@VDB(B1,B2,B3,0,1,1.5,0)* |

The first three arguments indicate the cost is $13,000, the salvage value is $1,000 and the estimated useful life is 6 years. The fourth and fifth arguments specify that the depreciation is to be computed for the first year. The sixth argument designates the depreciation factor at 150 percent. The seventh argument indicates that the @VDB function is to automatically switch to straight-line depreciation when it is greater than the declining-balance depreciation.

Note the 0 value did not actually need to be included, because the switch is optional and the default value is 0.

To enter the function:

| **Press** | [←Enter] | *Click* | *the mouse button* |

The special function appears in the control panel. The result, 3250 or $3,250.00, is displayed in cell B8. Your screen should look like Figure 15-17.

Figure 15-17

```
A:B8: @VDB(B1,B2,B3,0,1,1.5,0)                              READY

              A                 B       C      D      E      F      G
  1  Cost                     13000
  2  Salvage Value             1000
  3  Useful Life                  6
  4
  5  Straight Line             2000
  6  Double-Declining Balance  4333.333 Year 1
  7  Sum-of-the-Years' Digits  2285.714 Year 3
  8  Variable Declining Balance     3250 Year 1
  9
```

To compute the depreciation values for the other time periods, you would have to enter the function again for each of the desired time periods.

Compounding

The two single-sum compounding functions available in 1-2-3 are @CTERM and @RATE.

@CTERM

The @CTERM function calculates the number of compounding periods for an investment with a specified initial value to increase to a future value. A fixed interest rate per compounding period is used. The general format for the @CTERM function is as follows:

@CTERM(periodic interest rate, future value, present value)

In this exercise, assume that $4,500 was deposited in an account that pays an annual interest rate of 6 percent, compounded monthly. The @CTERM function can be used to determine how long it will be before you have $20,000 in the account.

Make sure you have a blank worksheet on your screen. Using the given data:

Move	the cell pointer to cell A1	**Click**	on cell A1
Enter	@CTERM(.06/12,20000,4500)	**Enter**	@CTERM(.06/12,20000,4500)

The first argument identifies the periodic interest rate compounded monthly as .06/12. The second argument specifies the future value at $20,000. The third argument indicates the present value of $4,500.

The special function appears in the control panel. The answer is 299.0762 (represented in months) or about 25 years. Your screen should look like Figure 15-18.

Figure 15-18

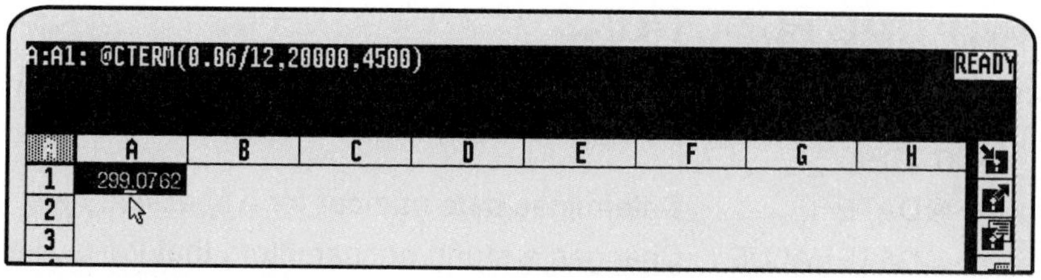

If you desire, you can format the number 299.0762 to 2 decimal places and place Months in cell B1.

@RATE

@RATE calculates the periodic interest rate necessary for a specific initial value to increase to a particular future value over the number of compounding periods in the term. If the investment is compounded monthly, you must multiply the @RATE by 12 to determine the annual rate. The general format for the @RATE function is as follows:

$$@RATE(future\ value, present\ value, term)$$

Suppose $4,500 has been invested in a bond that matures in 14 years to $20,000. Interest is compounded monthly. You can use the @RATE function to determine the periodic interest rate.

Make sure you have a blank worksheet on your screen. Using the given data:

Move	the cell pointer to cell A1	**Click**	on cell A1
Enter	@RATE(20000,4500,14*12)	**Enter**	@RATE(20000,4500,14*12)

The first argument identifies $20,000 as the future value. The second argument identifies $4,500 as the present value. The third argument specifies the terms in 168 months (14 years times 12 months).

The special function appears in the control panel. The answer is 0.008918 per month. You must multiply the value in cell A1 by 12 and place the results in A2 to calculate an annual rate. Your screen should look like Figure 15-19.

Figure 15-19

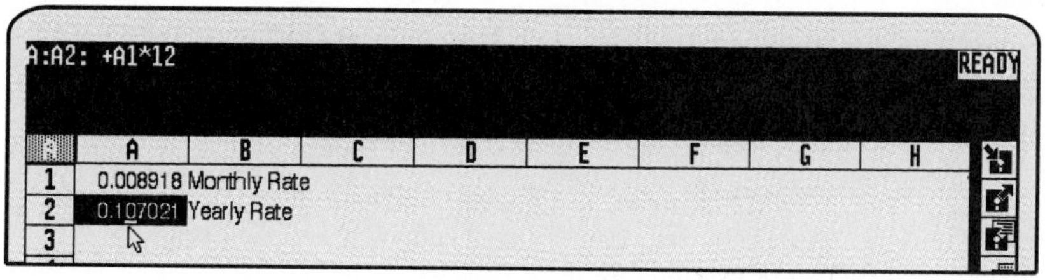

If you desire, you can format the rates as you deem appropriate. You may also place the Monthly Rate and Yearly Rate labels on your worksheet.

■ DATE AND TIME FUNCTIONS

There are 13 **date and time functions** available in 1-2-3. They can be grouped as follows:

DATE:

@DATE	Determines date number for a specified date
@DATEVALUE	Changes a string of characters that looks like a date into a date number
@DAY	Calculates the day of the month from a date number
@MONTH	Computes the month from a date number
@YEAR	Determines the year from a date number
@D360	Calculates the number of days between two dates assuming there are 360 days in a year

TIME:

@TIME	Computes a time number for a specific time consisting of an hour, minute, and second
@TIMEVALUE	Changes a string of characters that looks like a time into a time number
@HOUR	Calculates the hour from a time number
@MINUTE	Computes the minute from a time number
@SECOND	Determines the second from a time number

CURRENT DATE AND TIME:

@TODAY	Computes the date number for the current date
@NOW	Calculates a value that corresponds to the current date and time

Date

The six date functions available in 1-2-3 include @DATE, @DATEVALUE, @DAY, @MONTH, @YEAR, and @D360.

Make sure you have a blank worksheet on your screen.

@DATE

The format of the @DATE function is:

@DATE(year,month,day)

where year is any two-digit number between 00 and 99, month is any integer between 1 and 12 and day is any integer between 1 and 31. If the year number used is 100, 101, and so forth, a date for the year 2000, 2001, and so forth will be returned.

To enter the date June 24, 1993 with the @DATE function in cell A1:

| **Move** | the cell pointer to cell A1 | *Click* | *on cell A1* |
| **Enter** | @DATE(93,6,24) | *Enter* | *@DATE(93,6,24)* |

The number 34144 appears in cell A1. This number indicates that 34,144 days have passed since December 31, 1899.

To format the date appropriately:

Press	/	*Move*	*the mouse pointer to the control panel*
Select	Range	*Choose*	*Range*
Select	Format	*Choose*	*Format*
Select	Date	*Choose*	*Date*

Five different options for ways to display the date appear on the menu. The sixth option for displaying the time is discussed later in this chapter. Your screen should look like Figure 15-20.

Figure 15-20

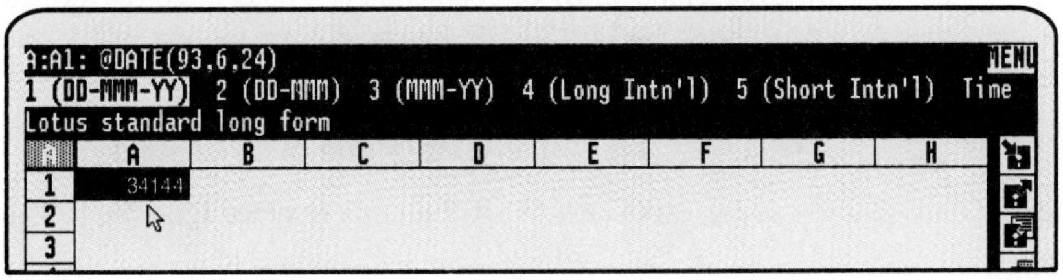

```
A:A1: @DATE(93,6,24)                                              MENU
1 (DD-MMM-YY)  2 (DD-MMM)  3 (MMM-YY)  4 (Long Intn'l)  5 (Short Intn'l)  Time
Lotus standard long form
     A        B        C        D        E        F        G        H
 1   34144
 2      ▷
 3
```

Depending on which option is chosen, the date in cell A1 can be displayed in one of the following five formats:

24-Jun-93

24-Jun

Jun-93

06/24/93

06/24

Other formats for options 4 and 5 can be accessed through the **W**orksheet **G**lobal **D**efault **O**ther **I**nternational **D**ate command sequence.

To select option 4 from the Date Format menu:

| **Select** | 4 | *Choose* | *4* |

When prompted for the range to format:

| **Press** | ←Enter | | **Click** | *the mouse button with the mouse pointer in the control panel* |

The date format 06/24/93 is now displayed. Your screen should look like Figure 15-21.

Figure 15-21

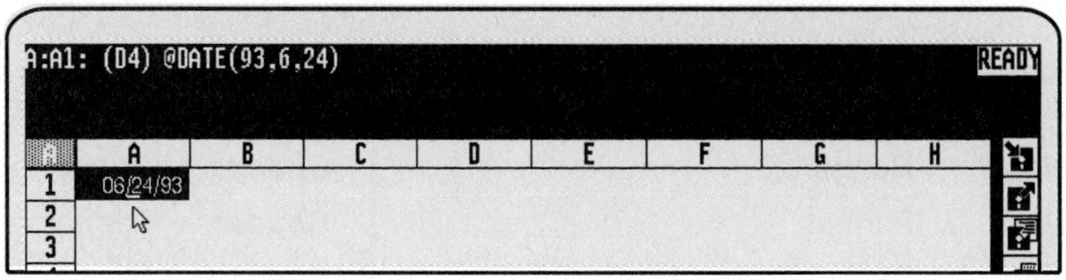

```
A:A1: (D4) @DATE(93,6,24)                                    READY

          A       B       C       D       E       F       G       H
   1   06/24/93
   2      ▷
   3
```

@DATEVALUE

This function returns the number of days that have elapsed since December 31, 1899 just as the @DATE function does. However, a single string of characters can be entered for the argument in the parentheses. The date string used in the @DATEVALUE function must be one of the acceptable Lotus 1-2-3 date formats. The format of the @DATEVALUE function is:

@DATEVALUE(string of characters)

Suppose you want to use the @DATEVALUE function to place June 24, 1993 on your worksheet.

| **Move** | the cell pointer to cell A1 | | **Click** | *on cell A1* |
| **Enter** | @DATEVALUE("24-Jun-93") | | **Enter** | *@DATEVALUE("24-Jun-93")* |

Then you decide to determine the number of days between December 31, 1993 and June 24, 1993. To calculate the number of days between the two dates:

| **Move** | the cell pointer to cell A2 | | **Click** | *on cell A2* |
| **Enter** | @DATEVALUE("31-Dec-93")-@DATEVALUE("24-Jun-93") | | **Enter** | *@DATEVALUE("31-Dec-93")-@DATEVALUE("24-Jun-93")* |

An alternative way to determine the number of days between June 24, 1993 and December 31, 1993 is:

| **Move** | the cell pointer to cell A3 | | **Click** | *on cell A3* |
| **Enter** | @DATEVALUE("31-Dec-93")-A1 | | **Enter** | *@DATEVALUE("31-Dec-93")-A1* |

Your screen should look like Figure 15-22.

Figure 15-22

```
A:A3: @DATEVALUE("31-Dec-93")-A1                                    READY

        A        B        C        D        E        F        G        H
  1    34144
  2     190
  3     190
```

Note that the values in cells A2 and A3 are the same. You simply used two different approaches for entering the formulas.

@MONTH

At times, you may be given a date number for which you need to determine the month, day or year corresponding to the date number. For example, suppose you need to determine the month, day, and year represented by the date number 34144.

The @MONTH function determines the month in which a particular date number occurs. The value computed using the @MONTH function will be an integer between 1 and 12 for the months January through December respectively. The format of the @MONTH function is:

@MONTH(date number)

Make sure you have a blank worksheet on your screen.

To determine the month in which the date number 34144 occurs:

Move	the cell pointer to cell A1		*Click*	*on cell A1*
Enter	Month		*Enter*	*Month*
Move	the cell pointer to cell B1		*Click*	*on cell B1*
Enter	@MONTH(34144)		*Enter*	*@MONTH(34144)*

Your screen should look like Figure 15-23. The value of 6 appearing in cell B1 indicates the date number occurs in the month of June.

Figure 15-23

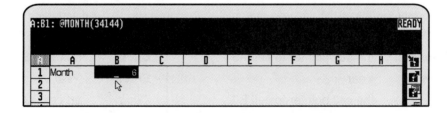

```
A:B1: @MONTH(34144)                                                READY

        A        B        C        D        E        F        G        H
  1   Month      6
  2
  3
```

@DAY

The @DAY function determines on what day of the month a date occurs for a date number. An integer between 1 and 31 is entered into the cell in which the @DAY function is used. The format of the @DAY function is:

@DAY(date number)

For example, suppose you want to know the day of the month on which the date number 34144 occurred. To calculate the day of the month while leaving the results of the previous example in your worksheet:

Move	the cell pointer to cell A2	***Click***	*on cell A2*
Enter	Day	***Enter***	*Day*
Move	the cell pointer to cell B2	***Click***	*on cell B2*
Enter	@DAY(34144)	***Enter***	*@DAY(34144)*

Your screen should look like Figure 15-24.

Figure 15-24

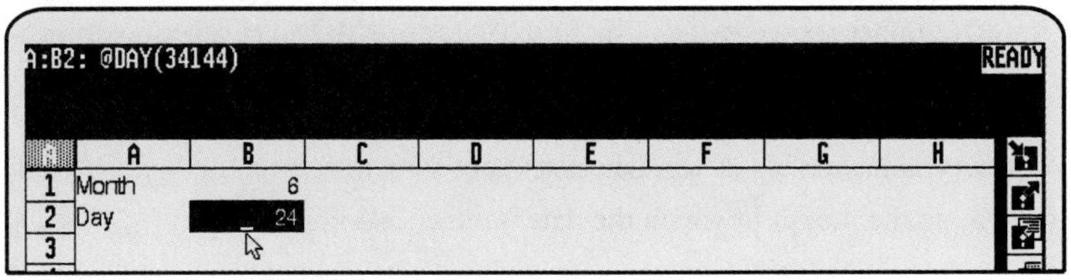

@YEAR

The @YEAR function determines the year in which a date number occurs. The value that appears in a cell in which the function is used will be a number between 0 and 99 representing the last two digits in the year. The number sequence 100, 101, and so on indicates years 2000, 2001, and so on. The format of the @YEAR function is:

@YEAR(date number)

Keep the results of the previous example in your worksheet. To determine the year in which the date number 34144 occurs:

Move	the cell pointer to cell A3	***Click***	*on cell A3*
Enter	Year	***Enter***	*Year*
Move	the cell pointer to cell B3	***Click***	*on cell B3*
Enter	@YEAR(34144)	***Enter***	*@YEAR(34144)*

Your screen should look like Figure 15-25.

Figure 15-25

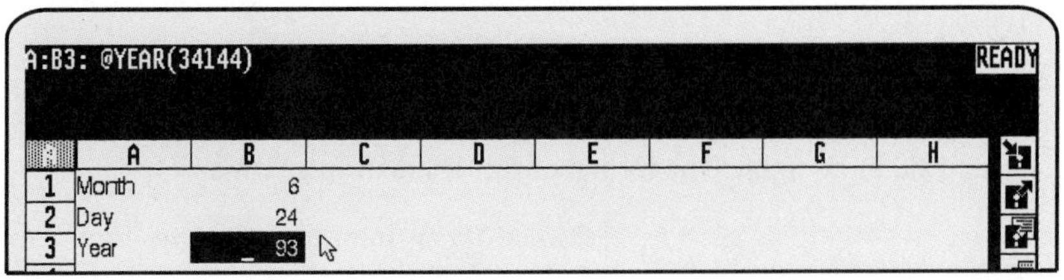

The value of 93 in cell B3 indicates that the date number 34144 occurs in the year 1993. Combining the information appearing in Figure 15-25, the date number represents June 24, 1993. This result is consistent with the date number you computed using the @DATE function for June 24, 1993, earlier in this chapter.

@D360

The @D360 function computes the number of days between two dates. This function uses a 360-day year and assumes there are 30 days in each month.

Make sure you have a blank worksheet window on your screen.

The format of the @D360 function is:

$$@D360(start\text{-}date,end\text{-}date)$$

Suppose you want to determine the number of days between July 1, 1993 and January 1, 1993. Begin this example with a blank worksheet. To calculate the number of days:

Move	the cell point to cell A1	***Click***	*on cell A1*
Enter	@D360(@DATE(93,1,1),@DATE (93,7,1))	***Enter***	*@D360(@DATE(93,1,1),@DATE (93,7,1))*

Your screen should look like Figure 15-26.

Figure 15-26

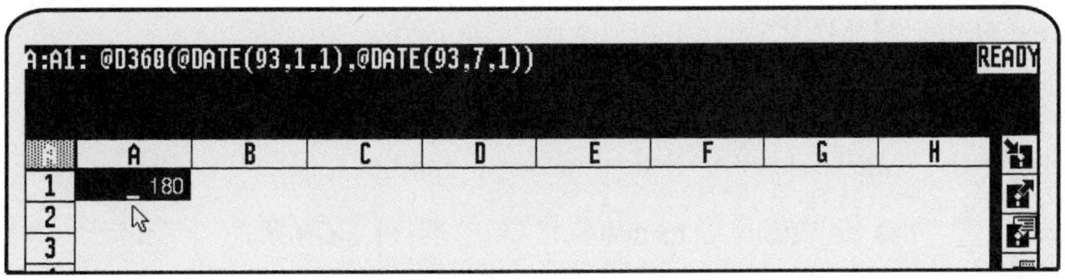

Notice that the time period represents six months and the calculated number of days is 180 indicating that the function in fact does assume there are 30 days per month.

Time

The five time functions available in 1-2-3 include @TIME, @TIMEVALUE, @HOUR, @MINUTE, and @SECOND.

@TIME

This function is used to calculate a time serial number that represents the percentage of the day for the time specified. The function returns a value between 0 and .99999. For example, the number 0 represents 12:00 midnight. The format of the @TIME function is:

@TIME(hour,minute,second)

Suppose you want to know the time serial number for the time 7:10:59 p.m. To obtain the time serial number:

Move	the cell pointer to cell A1	**Click**	on cell A1
Enter	@TIME(19,10,59)	**Enter**	@TIME(19,10,59)

Since a 24 hour clock is used, 19 is used for the hour instead of 7 to indicate time after noon. The number .799294 now appears in cell A1. This time serial number indicates that 7:10:59 is about 80 percent through the day.

Your screen should look like Figure 15-27.

Figure 15-27

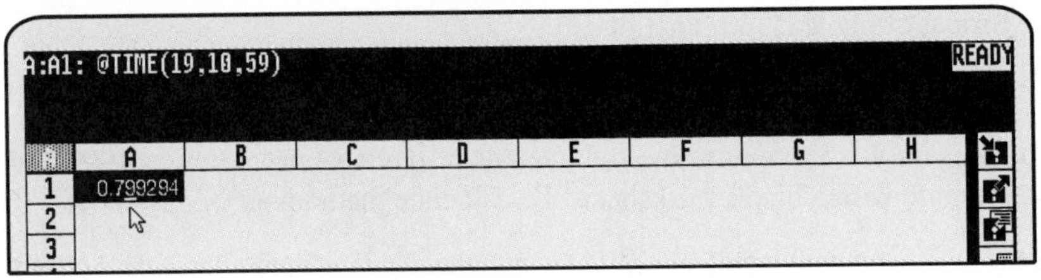

@TIMEVALUE

This function returns the time serial number just as the @TIME function does. However, a single string of characters can be entered for the arguments instead of the hour, minute, and second. The time string used in the @TIMEVALUE function must be one of the acceptable time formats available in Lotus 1-2-3. The format of the @TIMEVALUE function is:

@TIMEVALUE(string of characters)

Suppose you want to determine the time serial number for the time 7:10:59 p.m.

Move	the cell pointer to cell A1	**Click**	on cell A1
Enter	@TIMEVALUE("7:10:59 pm")	**Enter**	@TIMEVALUE("7:10:59 pm")

Your screen should look like Figure 15-28.

Figure 15-28

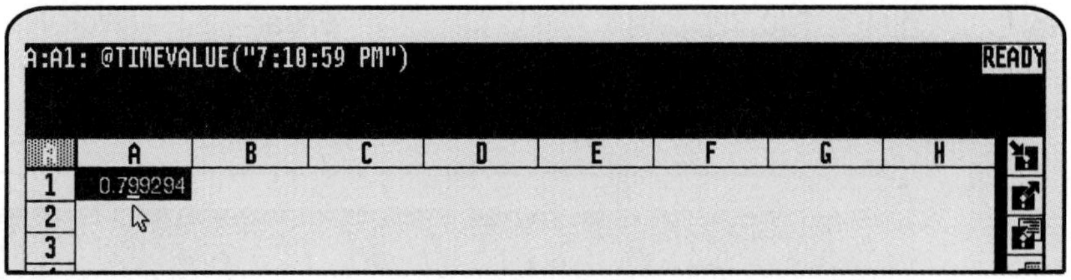

```
A:A1: @TIMEVALUE("7:10:59 PM")                                    READY

         A         B       C        D       E       F       G       H
1    0.799294
2        ▷
3
```

Notice that the time serial number 0.799294 is the same value that you obtained when you used the @TIME function.

To format your screen so you can see the time:

Press	⬚/⬚		***Move***	*the mouse pointer to the control panel*
Select	Range		***Choose***	*Range*
Select	Format		***Choose***	*Format*
Select	Date		***Choose***	*Date*
Select	Time		***Choose***	*Time*
Select	1		***Choose***	*1*
Press	⬚←Enter⬚		***Click***	*the mouse button with the mouse pointer in the control panel*

You will need to widen column A to 10 characters using the **W**orksheet **C**olumn **S**et-**W**idth command sequence to see the time.

@HOUR

In some situations, you may be given a time serial number for which you need to determine the hour, minute, and second corresponding to the time serial number. The @HOUR function determines the hour associated with a given time serial number.

Make sure you have a blank worksheet on your screen.

The format for the @HOUR function is:

@HOUR(time serial number)

Suppose you are given the time serial number 0.799294. To determine the hour of the day represented by this time serial number:

Move	the cell pointer to cell A1		***Click***	*on cell A1*
Enter	Hour		***Enter***	*Hour*
Move	the cell pointer to cell B1		***Click***	*on cell B1*

| **Enter** | @HOUR(0.799294) | | ***Enter*** | *@HOUR(0.799294)* |

Your screen should look like Figure 15-29.

Figure 15-29

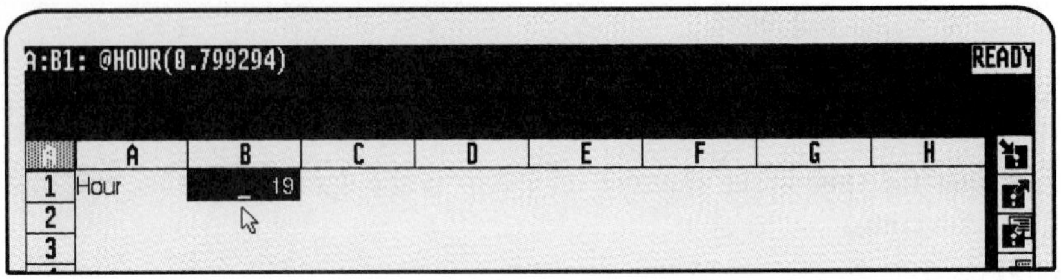

```
A:B1: @HOUR(0.799294)                                    READY

      A         B        C       D       E       F       G       H
  1 Hour          19
  2
  3
```

The value 19 appearing in cell B1 indicates that the time serial number represents a time between 7:00 p.m. and 8:00 p.m.

@MINUTE

The @MINUTE function calculates the minute of the hour represented by a time serial number. The format of the @MINUTE function is:

@MINUTE(time serial number)

Using the example time serial number 0.799294 again, you can compute the minute indicated by the time serial number using this function.

To compute the minute number while leaving the results of the previous example in your worksheet:

Move	the cell pointer to cell A2		***Click***	*on cell A2*
Enter	Minute		***Enter***	*Minute*
Move	the cell pointer to cell B2		***Click***	*on cell B2*
Enter	@MINUTE(0.799294)		***Enter***	*@MINUTE(0.799294)*

Your screen should look like Figure 15-30.

Figure 15-30

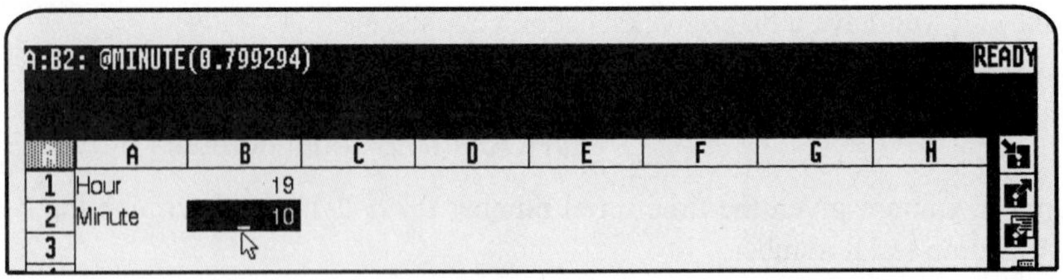

```
A:B2: @MINUTE(0.799294)                                  READY

      A         B        C       D       E       F       G       H
  1 Hour          19
  2 Minute        10
  3
```

The value of 10 appearing in cell B2 specifies that the tenth minute is represented by the time serial number.

@SECOND

This function computes the second associated with a specific time serial number. The format for the @SECOND function is:

@SECOND(time serial number)

To determine the second associated with the time serial number 0.799294 that was used in the last two examples:

Move	the cell pointer to cell A3		***Click***	*on cell A3*
Enter	Second		***Enter***	*Second*
Move	the cell pointer to cell B3		***Click***	*on cell B3*
Enter	@SECOND(0.799294)		***Enter***	*@SECOND(0.799294)*

Your screen should look like Figure 15-31.

Figure 15-31

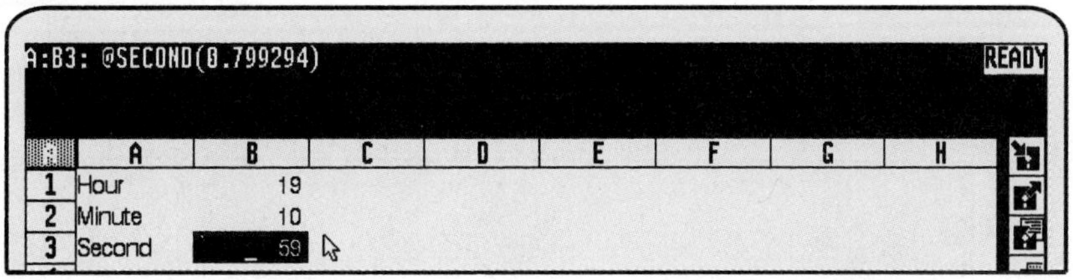

The value of 59 in cell B3 indicates the second represented by the time serial number is 59. Combining the information appearing in Figure 15-31, the time serial number 0.799294 represents the time 7:10:59 p.m. This result is consistent with the time serial number you calculated using the @TIME function for 7:10:59 p.m.

Current Date and Time

The two functions available in 1-2-3 to specify the current date and time are @TODAY and @NOW. These functions are very useful in documenting when a worksheet was last calculated. It is a good idea to use one of these functions on all of your worksheets.

@TODAY

The @TODAY function determines the date based on the current system date used by your computer. The format for the @TODAY function is:

@TODAY

To illustrate the use of the @TODAY function:

Move	the cell pointer to cell A1		***Click***	*on cell A1*

Enter	Today		*Enter*	*Today*	
Move	the cell pointer to cell B1		*Click*	*on cell B1*	
Enter	@TODAY		*Enter*	*@TODAY*	

The date number for the current date now appears in cell B1. To format the date so you can determine the date, use the **Range Format Date** command sequence and select the first format option. You will need to set the column width to at least 10 using the **Worksheet Column Set-Width** command sequence.

Your screen should look similar to Figure 15-32.

Figure 15-32

You can use this function when you need to place the current date on your worksheet.

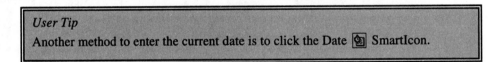

User Tip
Another method to enter the current date is to click the Date ▣ SmartIcon.

@NOW

The @NOW function returns the current date and time. You can format the resulting value using any of the date or time formats available in 1-2-3. The format for the @NOW function is:

$$@NOW$$

Suppose you want to place the current time on your worksheet with today's date from the last example:

Move	the cell pointer to cell A2		*Click*	*on cell A2*	
Enter	Now		*Enter*	*Now*	
Move	the cell pointer to cell B2		*Click*	*on cell B2*	
Enter	@NOW		*Enter*	*@NOW*	

The value on your screen includes the current date number and the time serial number. The integer portion of the value is the date number, and the decimal portion is the time serial number.

Use the **Range Format Date Time** command sequence, and select the second format option to format cell B2 so you can see a time.

Your screen should look similar to Figure 15-33.

Figure 15-33

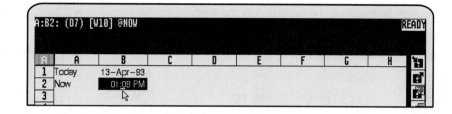

The current time now should appear on your screen. Note that if you enter anything in the worksheet, the time will also be updated on the screen. The @NOW function is particularly useful if you make changes to a worksheet several times in one day for "what-if" analysis purposes.

■ LOGICAL FUNCTIONS

There are eight **logical functions** available in 1-2-3. The logical functions are:

@IF	Used to test a condition to determine if it is true or false
@FALSE	Returns a value of 0 (false)
@TRUE	Returns a value of 1 (true)
@ISERR	Returns a value of 1 (true) if the cell contains an error (ERR); otherwise the value returned is 0
@ISNA	Returns a value of 1 if not available (NA) appears in a cell; otherwise the value is 0
@ISNUMBER	Returns a value of 1 if a value or blank cell is present; otherwise the value is 0
@ISRANGE	Returns a value of 1 if a range is defined; otherwise the value is 0
@ISSTRING	Returns a value of 1 if a string of characters is present; otherwise the value is 0

@IF

The @IF function allows you to test a condition and select one of two options depending on the results of the test. The general format of the @IF function is:

@IF(condition,result if condition is true,result if condition is false)

Make sure you have a blank worksheet on your screen.

To illustrate the use of the @IF function, suppose the income before taxes for a company is $250,000 and the tax rate is 40 percent. Assume you enter 250000 in cell A1 of a worksheet and .40 in A2. To compute the taxes due, you could create the formula +A1∗A2 and place it in cell A3.

However, in some situations, an organization may lose money. Therefore, the formula will not work properly, because the company cannot pay a negative amount of taxes. In fact, the tax amount should be zero.

The @IF function can be used so that the formula can work properly. To illustrate the use of the @IF function:

Move	the cell pointer to cell A1		*Click*	*on cell A1*
Enter	250000		*Enter*	*250000*
Move	the cell pointer to cell A2		*Click*	*on cell A2*
Enter	.40		*Enter*	*.40*
Move	the cell pointer to cell A3		*Click*	*on cell A3*
Enter	@IF(A1>0,A1*A2,0)		*Enter*	*@IF(A1>0,A1*A2,0)*

The first argument, A1>0, is the condition. This condition is used to determine if the value in A1 is greater than 0. The second argument, A1*A2, is the formula that will be used to place a value in cell A3 if the condition is true. The third argument, 0, indicates that a 0 will be entered in cell A3 if the condition is false.

The formula appears in the control panel, and the number 100000 is in cell A3. Since the condition, A1>0, is true, the formula A1*A2 is calculated and the value of 100000 is placed in the cell.

Your screen should look like Figure 15-34.

Figure 15-34

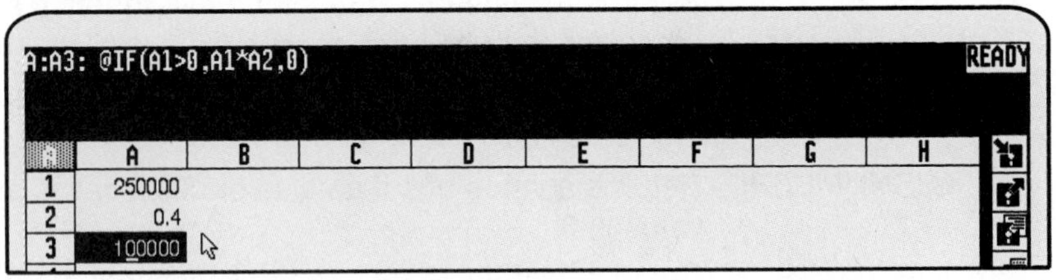

To test the false argument in the @IF function:

Move	the cell pointer to cell A1		*Click*	*on cell A1*
Enter	-250000		*Enter*	*-250000*

Notice that the value in cell A3 changes to 0.

The remaining portion of the @IF function section includes illustrations of logical operators that can be used in an @IF function and nested @IF functions.

Logical Operators

Logical operators combine the numbers within conditional statements or formulas. The logical operators for simple logical statements are as follows:

Operator	Definition
=	equal
<	less than

Operator	Definition
<=	less than or equal
>	greater than
>=	greater than or equal
<>	not equal

Logical Operators for Compound Statements

Logical operators can be used to combine multiple conditions. The #AND#, #OR#, and #NOT# logical operators for Lotus 1-2-3 are now discussed.

#AND#

#AND# can be used to combine multiple statements. For example, @IF(A5=0#AND#B5=0,Z5,C5) tests two conditions. More than one #AND# may be used in a formula. When the #AND# statement is used to link multiple conditions, *all* conditions must be true before the true result (Z5) can be executed.

#OR#

#OR# can be used to test if one argument *or* the other is true. For example, @IF(A5=0#OR#B5=0,Z5,C5) would result in the *true* result (Z5) if *either* A5=0 or B5=0. When the #OR# statement is used to link multiple conditions, *all* conditions must be false for the false result (C5) to be executed.

#NOT#

#NOT# can be used to indicate that a condition is not true. For example, @IF(#NOT#A5=0#OR#B5=0,Z5,C5) tests whether A5 is *not* equal to zero or if B5=0. Unlike the logical operators #OR# and #AND#, the #NOT# logical operator is used *before* a condition.

Nested IF

One @IF function may be nested inside another, as illustrated by the following example:

@IF(B1=25,B2B1,@IF(B1=35,B3B1,@IF(B1=45,B4B1,0)))

The @IF function is read from left to right. The first two @IF functions have @IF functions for the false response. The parentheses used to end the @IF functions are at the end of the formula.

@FALSE

When the @FALSE function is used, it returns a value of 0. The format of the @FALSE function is:

@FALSE

Make sure you have a blank worksheet on your screen.

Suppose you want to pay someone a commission of 10 percent of the sales amount if his or her sales are at least $1,000 and nothing if sales are less than $1,000.

To illustrate the use of the @FALSE function to solve this problem:

Move	the cell pointer to cell A1	*Click*	*on cell A1*
Enter	Sales	*Enter*	*Sales*
Move	the cell pointer to cell A2	*Click*	*on cell A2*
Enter	Commission	*Enter*	*Commission*
Move	the cell pointer to cell C1	*Click*	*on cell C1*
Enter	900	*Enter*	*900*
Move	the cell pointer to cell C2	*Click*	*on cell C2*
Enter	@IF(C1>=1000,C1*.10, @FALSE)	*Enter*	*@IF(C1>=1000,C1*.10, @FALSE)*

In this @IF function, the @FALSE function will place a value of 0 in cell C2 whenever the sales amount is less than $1,000.

Your screen should look like Figure 15-35.

Figure 15-35

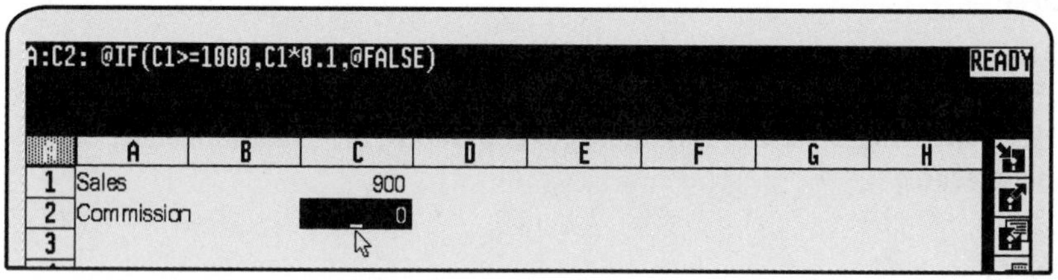

```
A:C2: @IF(C1>=1000,C1*0.1,@FALSE)                                    READY

        A       B       C       D       E       F       G       H
   1  Sales            900
   2  Commission         0
   3
```

Notice that since the sales amount is less than $1,000, a value of 0 appears in cell C2. Change the value of sales to $1,000 and then $1,500 to make sure the @FALSE function works properly.

@TRUE

The @TRUE function returns a value of 1 when it is used. The format of the @TRUE function is:

$$@TRUE$$

Assume that you need to determine whether the value in a cell is less than 500. You can use the @TRUE and @FALSE functions together with an @IF function to indicate whether the value is less than 500.

Make sure you have a blank worksheet on your screen.

To illustrate the use of the @TRUE function:

Move	the cell pointer to cell A1	*Click*	*on cell A1*
Enter	450	*Enter*	*450*
Move	the cell pointer to cell A2	*Click*	*on cell A2*
Enter	@IF(A1<500,@TRUE,@FALSE)	*Enter*	*@IF(A1<500,@TRUE,@FALSE)*

Your screen should look like Figure 15-36.

Figure 15-36

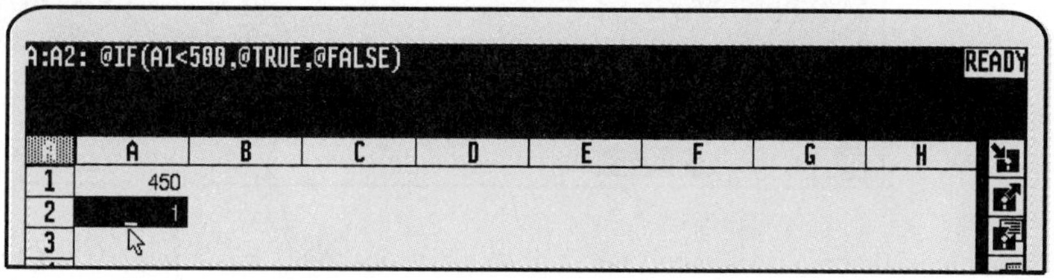

The value of 1 in cell A2 indicates that the @TRUE function was used. Change the value in cell A1 to 500 and then 750 to make sure the functions work properly.

@ISERR

The @ISERR function determines whether the contents of a cell contain ERR. For example, the characters are placed in a cell by 1-2-3 whenever you try to divide by zero. If ERR is present when the @ISERR function is used, the value of 1 (true) is returned, otherwise a value of 0 (false) is returned.

The format of the @ISERR function is:

$$@ISERR(x)$$

where x can be a cell location, string of characters, condition, or value.

Make sure you have a blank worksheet on your screen.

Suppose that you need to divide the value in one cell by the value in another cell. In some cases the denominator may be zero, but you do not want ERR to appear in the cell where the division occurs. The @ISERR function can be used in such a situation.

To illustrate the use of the @ISERR:

Move	the cell pointer to cell B1		*Click*	*on cell B1*
Enter	50		*Enter*	*50*
Move	the cell pointer to cell B2		*Click*	*on cell B2*
Enter	0		*Enter*	*0*
Move	the cell pointer to cell B3		*Click*	*on cell B3*
Enter	+B1/B2		*Enter*	*+B1/B2*

You now have the characters ERR in cell B3. Suppose you want the number 0 to appear in cell B3 if an attempt to divide by 0 occurs. Make sure the cell pointer is in cell B3.

Enter   @IF(@ISERR(B1/B2),0,B1/B2) | *Enter*   *@IF(@ISERR(B1/B2),0,B1/B2)*

If division by 0 is attempted, then a 0 is placed in cell B3, otherwise cell B1 is divided by B2.

Your screen should look like Figure 15-37.

Figure 15-37

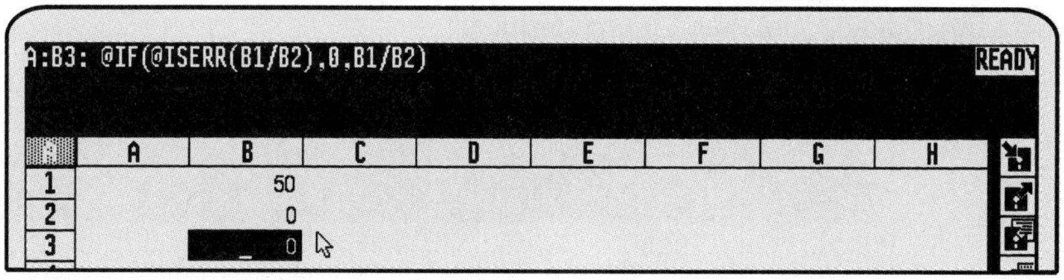

The value of 0 appearing in cell B3 indicates division by 0 was attempted. Change the value in B2 to 10 to verify the @ISERR function works properly.

@ISNA

The @ISNA function is used to verify whether NA appears in a cell. The format of the @ISNA function is:

$$@ISNA(x)$$

where *x* can be a cell location, string of characters, condition, or value.

Make sure you have a blank worksheet on your screen.

To illustrate the use of the @ISNA function:

Move	the cell pointer to cell A1	*Click*	on cell A1
Enter	@NA	*Enter*	@NA

Note that the characters NA, meaning not available, appear in cell A1. Assume that you would like to place a 1 in cell B1 if NA is present and a 0 if NA does not appear.

Move	the cell pointer to cell B1	*Click*	on cell B1
Enter	@IF(@ISNA(A1),1,0)	*Enter*	@IF(@ISNA(A1),1,0)

Your screen should look like Figure 15-38.

Figure 15-38

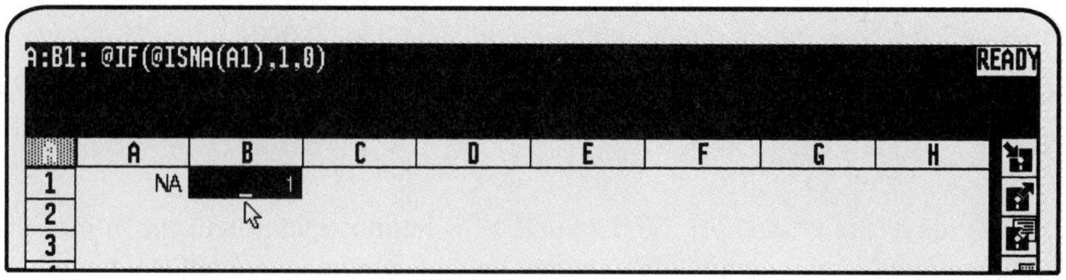

The value 1 in the cell indicates NA appears in cell A1. To illustrate another approach to the problem, enter @IF(@ISNA(A1),@TRUE,@FALSE) in cell B1. The value of 1 should also appear in cell B1. Change the contents of cell A1 to 100 and verify that the @ISNA function works properly when A1 does not contain NA.

@ISNUMBER

The @ISNUMBER function determines if a value or a blank is present. The format of the @ISNUMBER function is:

@ISNUMBER(x)

where *x* can be any cell location, string of characters, condition, or value. If a value or a blank cell is present, a 1 is returned, otherwise a 0 is returned.

Make sure you have a blank worksheet on your screen.

Suppose you need to check a cell to determine what type of data is included in the cell. To ascertain whether a value or blank cell is present:

Move	the cell pointer to cell B1		***Click***	*on cell B1*
Enter	100		***Enter***	*100*
Move	the cell pointer to cell A3		***Click***	*on cell A3*
Enter	@ISNUMBER(B1)		***Enter***	*@ISNUMBER(B1)*

Your screen should look like Figure 15-39.

Figure 15-39

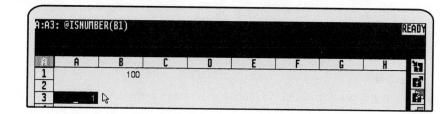

The number 1 appears in cell A3 indicating that a value appears in cell B1. Use the **Range Erase** command sequence to erase cell B1. The value 1 remains in cell A3, because the B1 is now a blank cell. If you press the space bar and press the ENTER key, a 0 will appear in cell A3 specifying that B1 does not contain a value or it is not a blank cell.

@ISRANGE

The @ISRANGE function is used to determine whether a string of characters is a range name that has been defined for the worksheet. The format of the @ISRANGE function is:

@ISRANGE(string of characters)

Before you use the @ISRANGE function, you need to create the worksheet appearing in Figure 15-40.

Figure 15-40

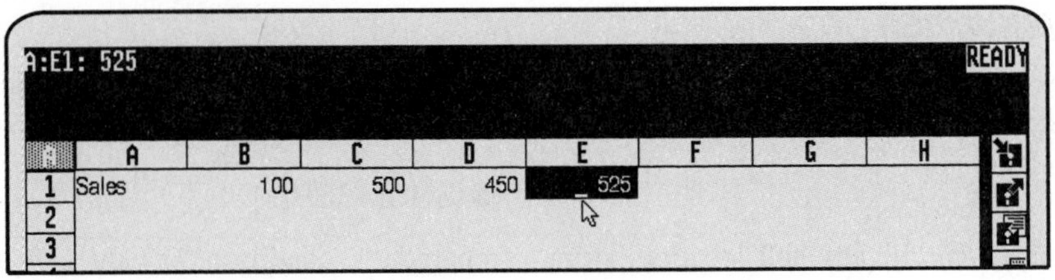

Use the **R**ange **N**ame **C**reate command sequence to create the name SALES for the range of cells that includes the sales values in cells B1 through E1.

To illustrate the use of the @ISRANGE function:

Move	the cell pointer to cell A3	**Click**	on cell A3
Enter	@ISRANGE(SALES)	**Enter**	@ISRANGE(SALES)

Your screen should now look like Figure 15-41.

Figure 15-41

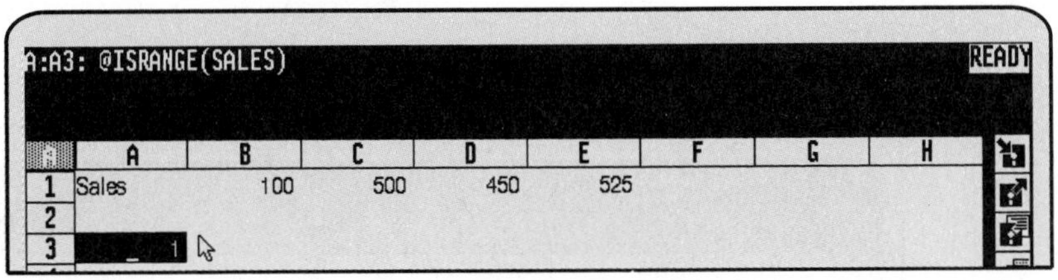

The value of 1 appearing in cell A3 indicates the range name SALES has been defined for the worksheet. If the range name had not been defined, a 0 would have appeared in cell A3.

@ISSTRING

The @ISSTRING function is used to determine whether a string of characters is present. The format for the @ISSTRING function is:

$$@ISSTRING(x)$$

where *x* can be a cell location, string of characters, condition, or value. If a string of characters is present, a 1 is returned. When a value or a blank cell is present, a value of 0 is returned.

Make sure you have a blank worksheet on your screen.

Suppose you have a set of characters in a cell and you need to determine whether the cell contains a set of alphanumeric characters.

To illustrate how you can use the @ISSTRING function to determine what type of characters are present in the cell:

Move	the cell pointer to cell C1	**Click**	on cell C1
Enter	Lotus 1-2-3 Release 3.4	**Enter**	*Lotus 1-2-3 Release 3.4*

Move	the cell pointer to cell C3	**Click**	on cell C3
Enter	@ISSTRING(C1)	**Enter**	@ISSTRING(C1)

Your screen should look like Figure 15-42.

Figure 15-42

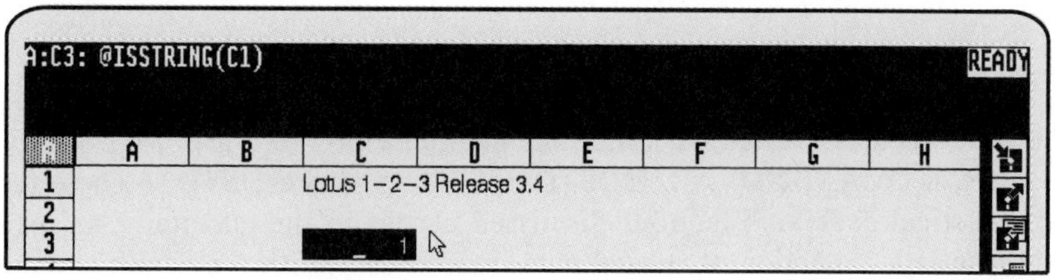

The value 1 appears in cell C3 indicating that the contents of C1 are a string of alphanumeric characters or a space. Use the **R**ange **E**rase command sequence to erase cell C1. A zero then appears in cell C3 indicating C1 is a blank cell. Enter the value 200 in cell C1. The zero value remains in cell C3, because a value is present in cell C1.

■ DATABASE STATISTICAL FUNCTIONS

There are 11 **database statistical functions** available in 1-2-3. They are grouped into two categories:

DATABASE STATISTICAL FUNCTIONS:

@DSUM	Calculates the sum of values for a field in a database table satisfying a criteria range
@DCOUNT	Determines the number of non-blank cells for a field in a database table satisfying a criteria range
@DAVG	Computes the arithmetic mean of values for a field in a database table satisfying a criteria range
@DMIN	Determines the minimum value for a field in a database table satisfying a criteria range
@DMAX	Determines the maximum value for a field in a database table satisfying a criteria range
@DVAR	Calculates the population variance for a field in a database table satisfying a criteria range
@DSTD	Computes the population standard deviation for a field in a database table satisfying a criteria range
@DVARS	Calculates the sample variance for a field in a database table satisfying a criteria range
@DSTDS	Computes the sample standard deviation for a field in a database table satisfying a criteria range

DATABASE QUERY FUNCTIONS:

@DGET   Finds a value in a database table or field satisfying a criteria range

@DQUERY   Sends a command to an external database management software package

Database Statistical Functions

The nine database statistical functions available in 1-2-3 are: @DSUM, @DCOUNT, @DAVG, @DMIN, @DMAX, @DVAR, @DSTD, @DVARS, and @DSTDS. These functions are very similar to the statistical analysis functions discussed earlier in this chapter. As mentioned in Chapter 13, a **database** is a collection of related data or records. With the database statistical functions, you can complete a statistical analysis on a set of cells that satisfy a particular criteria.

For example, you may have a database of all employees located in California, but you only want to know how many of the people live in Los Angeles. @COUNT can determine how many employees are in the entire database. @DCOUNT can be used to obtain a count for only those individuals living in Los Angeles. The database statistical functions are designed for use on database tables. The D in front of each function indicates that it is a database statistical function.

The format for all of the database statistical functions is:

$$\text{@function name(input range,field location,criteria)}$$

The **input range** is the database area that includes the field names and records in the database. The **field location** is used to indicate which column should be used for the calculations. When specifying the column in the database, start counting with the number zero. Therefore, if the third column in a database is the desired field location, it is referred to as field number two in the function. The **criteria** range specifies the criteria that must be satisfied.

Before you use the database statistical functions, you need to create the database table in Figure 15-43.

Figure 15-43

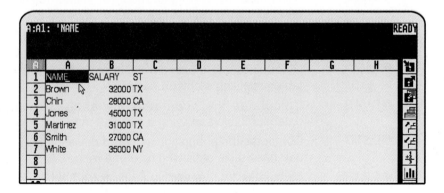

The database table includes the last name, salary, and state location of employees working for an organization. Save the worksheet on a file using the name SALS.

Assume that you want to apply the database statistical functions to those individuals earning more than $30,000. The individuals satisfying this criterion are Brown, Jones, Martinez, and White.

To place the criterion on your worksheet:

Move	the cell pointer to cell D2	**Click**	*on cell D2*
Enter	SALARY	**Enter**	*SALARY*
Move	the cell pointer to cell D3	**Click**	*on cell D3*
Enter	+B2>30000	**Enter**	*+B2>30000*

Because the salary figure in B2 is greater than 30000, the number 1 should appear in cell D3, showing it to be a true example of the formula. Use the **R**ange **F**ormat **T**ext command sequence to place the text version of the criterion on your screen.

Create the range name CRITERIA and include the cells D2 through D3 as the range. Place the word CRITERIA in cell D1 and names of the database statistical functions in cells D6 through D14. Your screen should look like Figure 15-44.

Figure 15-44

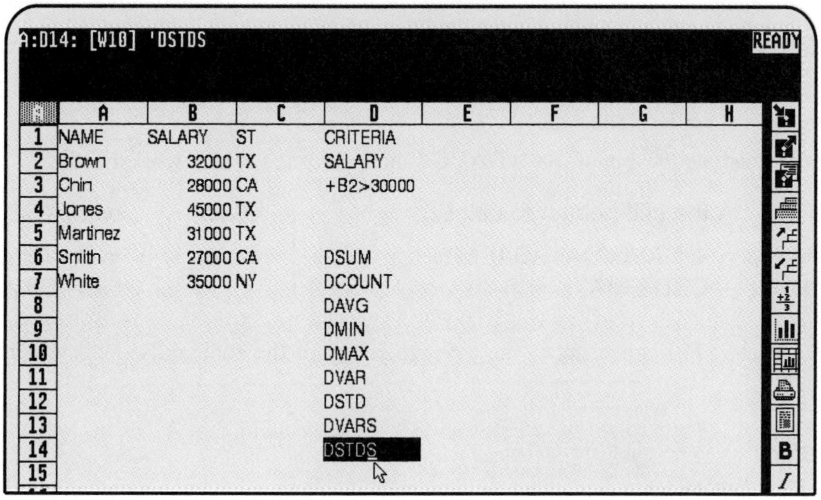

Create the range name DATABASE and include cells A1 through C7 as the range.

@DSUM

The @DSUM function computes the sum of values for a field that satisfies a criterion.

To compute the sum for the cells satisfying the criteria in the SALS worksheet:

Move	the cell pointer to cell E6	**Click**	*on cell E6*
Enter	@DSUM(DATABASE,1, CRITERIA)	**Enter**	*@DSUM(DATABASE,1, CRITERIA)*

DATABASE identifies cells A1 through C7 as the input range, the 1 indicates SALARY as the field location, and CRITERIA specifies D2 through D3 as the criteria range. The value 143000 appears in cell E6. This is the sum of the salaries for Brown, Chin, Martinez, and White who each earn more than $30,000.

@DCOUNT

This function counts the number of non-blank cells for a field in a database table that satisfies a specified criterion.

To illustrate the use of the @DCOUNT function for the SALS worksheet:

Move	the cell pointer to cell E7		*Click*	*on cell E7*
Enter	@DCOUNT(DATABASE,1, CRITERIA)		*Enter*	*@DCOUNT(DATABASE,1, `CRITERIA)*

The value 4 appears in cell E7 indicating there are four individuals in the database who have a salary greater than $30,000.

@DAVG

The @DAVG function calculates the arithmetic mean of the values for a field in a database table that satisfies a specified criterion.

To demonstrate the use of the @DAVG function for the SALS worksheet:

Move	the cell pointer to cell E8		*Click*	*on cell E8*
Enter	@DAVG(DATABASE,1, CRITERIA)		*Enter*	*@DAVG(DATABASE,1, CRITERIA)*

The value 35750 appearing is the average salary of the four individuals that have a salary greater than $30,000.

@DMIN

The @DMIN function determines the minimum value for a field in a database table that satisfies a specified criterion.

To illustrate the use of the @DMIN function for the SALS worksheet:

Move	the cell pointer to cell E9		*Click*	*on cell E9*
Enter	@DMIN(DATABASE,1, CRITERIA)		*Enter*	*@DMIN(DATABASE,1, CRITERIA)*

The value 31000 that appears in cell E9 indicates that the lowest salary among the individuals having a salary greater than $30,000 is $31,000.

@DMAX

The @DMAX function determines the maximum value for a field in a database table that satisfies a specified criterion.

To demonstrate the use of the @DMAX function for the SALS worksheet:

Move	the cell pointer to cell E10		***Click***	*on cell E10*
Enter	@DMAX(DATABASE,1, CRITERIA)		***Enter***	*@DMAX(DATABASE,1, CRITERIA)*

The value 45000 that appears in cell E9 specifies that the highest salary among the employees having a salary greater than $30,000 is $45,000.

@DVAR

The @DVAR function computes the population variance for the values in a field of a database table that satisfies a specified criterion.

To illustrate the use of the @DVAR function for the SALS worksheet:

Move	the cell pointer to cell E11		***Click***	*on cell E11*
Enter	@DVAR(DATABASE,1, CRITERIA)		***Enter***	*@DVAR(DATABASE,1, CRITERIA)*

The value 30687500 that appears in cell E10 is the population variance for the salaries for the persons having a salary greater than $30,000.

@DSTD

The @DSTD function computes the population standard deviation for the values in a field of a database table that satisfies a specified criterion.

To demonstrate the use of the @DSTD function for the SALS worksheet:

Move	the cell pointer to cell E12		***Click***	*on cell E12*
Enter	@DSTD(DATABASE,1, CRITERIA)		***Enter***	*@DSTD(DATABASE,1, CRITERIA)*

The value 5539.63 is the standard deviation for the salaries of the employees that have a salary greater than $30,000.

@DVARS

The @DVARS function computes the population sample variance for the values in a field of a database table that satisfy a specified criterion. It is assumed that the database table includes only a sample or portion of the data that can be considered.

To illustrate the use of the @DVARS function for the SALS worksheet:

| **Move** | the cell pointer to cell E13 | **Click** | on cell E13 |
| **Enter** | @DVARS(DATABASE,1, CRITERIA) | **Enter** | @DVARS(DATABASE,1, CRITERIA) |

The value 40916667 appearing in cell E13 is the sample variance for the salaries of the personnel earning more than $30,000.

@DSTDS

The @DSTDS function calculates the sample standard deviation for the values in a field of a database table that satisfy a specified criterion. It is assumed that the database table includes only a sample or a portion of the data that can be considered.

To demonstrate the use of the @DSTDS function for the SALS worksheet:

| **Move** | the cell pointer to cell E14 | **Click** | on cell E14 |
| **Enter** | @DSTDS(DATABASE,1, CRITERIA) | **Enter** | @DSTDS(DATABASE,1, CRITERIA) |

The value 6396.614 appearing in cell E14 is the sample standard deviation for the salaries of the employees having a salary greater than $30,000. After you enter all the database statistical functions, your screen should look like Figure 15-45.

Figure 15-45

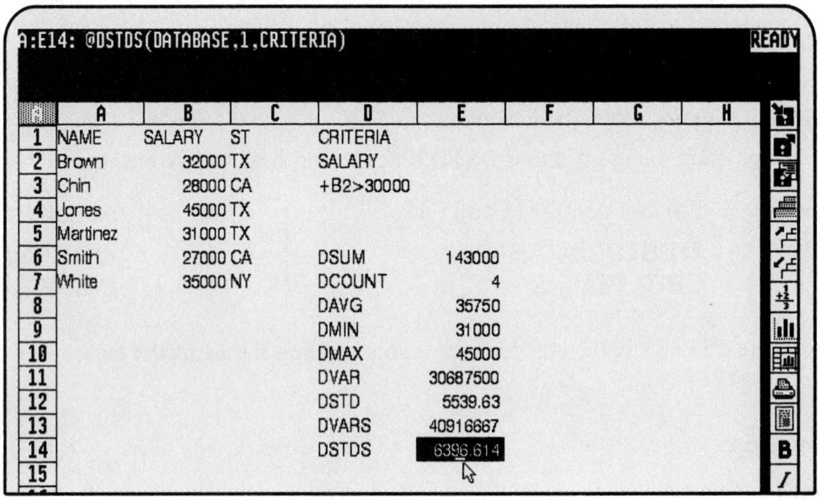

```
A:E14: @DSTDS(DATABASE,1,CRITERIA)                          READY

      A        B       C        D         E       F      G      H
 1  NAME    SALARY    ST     CRITERIA
 2  Brown    32000 TX         SALARY
 3  Chin     28000 CA         +B2>30000
 4  Jones    45000 TX
 5  Martinez 31000 TX
 6  Smith    27000 CA         DSUM       143000
 7  White    35000 NY         DCOUNT          4
 8                            DAVG        35750
 9                            DMIN        31000
10                            DMAX        45000
11                            DVAR     30687500
12                            DSTD      5539.63
13                            DVARS    40916667
14                            DSTDS    6396.614
15
```

Database Query Functions

The two database query functions available in 1-2-3 are @DGET and @DQUERY.

@DGET

The @DGET function allows you to search a database table and find a value or a label. The format of the @DGET function is:

$$@DGET(input,field,criteria)$$

where input is the range of fields to search, field is the name of the field within the input range to be searched, and criteria is the criteria range. Before illustrating the use of the @DGET function, you need to retrieve the ABCSAL file you created in Chapter 13 and define the range name DATABASE that has cells A25 through I33 as its range.

Suppose you would like to know the total salary for the employee with the last name ARMOUR. The @DGET function can be used to search the TOTAL column in the ABCSAL data table to find the salary.

Move	the cell pointer to cell B37		*Click*	*on cell B37*
Enter	CRITERIA		*Enter*	*CRITERIA*
Move	the cell pointer to cell B38		*Click*	*on cell B38*
Enter	LAST NAME		*Enter*	*LAST NAME*
Move	the cell pointer to cell B39		*Click*	*on cell B39*
Enter	ARMOUR		*Enter*	*ARMOUR*

Define the range name CRITERIA that has cells B38 and B39 as its range.

To use the @DGET function to determine ARMOUR's total salary:

Move	the cell pointer to cell E39		*Click*	*on cell E39*
Enter	@DGET(DATABASE,"TOTAL", CRITERIA)		*Enter*	*@DGET(DATABASE,"TOTAL", CRITERIA)*

The bottom part of your screen should look like Figure 15-46.

Figure 15-46

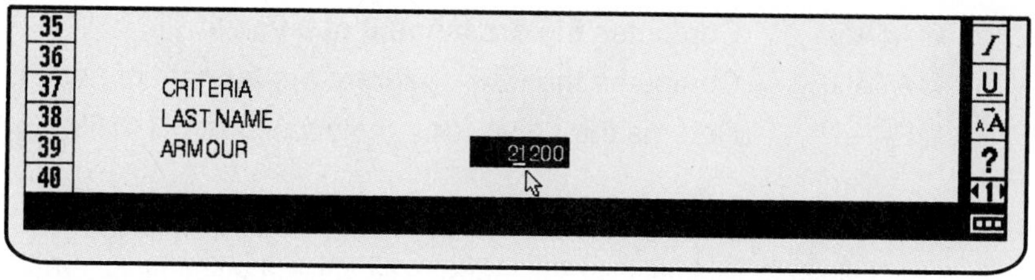

@DQUERY

The @DQUERY allows you to send a command to an external database management software program. The general format of the @DQUERY function is:

@DQUERY(function,external-argument)

where function is the name of a command available in the database management program and external-argument is the series of arguments that the external command requires. See the 1-2-3 help feature for more information on this function.

■ MATHEMATICAL FUNCTIONS

The 17 **mathematical functions** available in Lotus 1-2-3 include:

GENERAL:

@ABS	Computes the absolute value of a number in a cell
@EXP	Computes the number e raised to a specific power
@INT	Determines the integer portion of a value
@LN	Computes the natural logarithm (base e) of a value
@LOG	Computes the common logarithm (base 10) of a value
@MOD	Computes the remainder (modulus) of two values
@RAND	Generates a random number value between 0 and 1
@ROUND	Rounds a value to a specific number of decimal places
@SQRT	Computes the positive square root of a number

TRIGONOMETRIC:

@COS	Computes the cosine of an angle
@ACOS	Computes the arc cosine of a value
@SIN	Computes the sine of an angle
@ASIN	Computes the arc sine of a value
@TAN	Computes the tangent of an angle
@ATAN	Computes the arc tangent of a value
@ATAN2	Computes the four-quadrant arc tangent of two values
@PI	Returns the value for π (calculated at 3.14159265358979324)

General Functions

There are nine general mathematical functions. The general mathematical functions are @ABS, @EXP, @INT, @LN, @LOG, @MOD, @RAND, @ROUND, and @SQRT.

@ABS

The @ABS function determines the absolute value. The number returned will always be positive. The format of the @ABS function is:

$$@ABS(x)$$

where x is any value.

Make sure you have a blank worksheet on your screen.

To illustrate the use of the @ABS function:

Move	the cell pointer to cell A1	*Click*	*on cell A1*
Enter	25	*Enter*	*25*
Move	the cell pointer to cell A2	*Click*	*on cell A2*
Enter	-50	*Enter*	*-50*
Move	the cell pointer to cell B1	*Click*	*on cell B1*
Enter	@ABS(A1)	*Enter*	*@ABS(A1)*
Move	the cell pointer to cell B2	*Click*	*on cell B2*
Enter	@ABS(A2)	*Enter*	*@ABS(A2)*

Your screen should look like Figure 15-47.

Figure 15-47

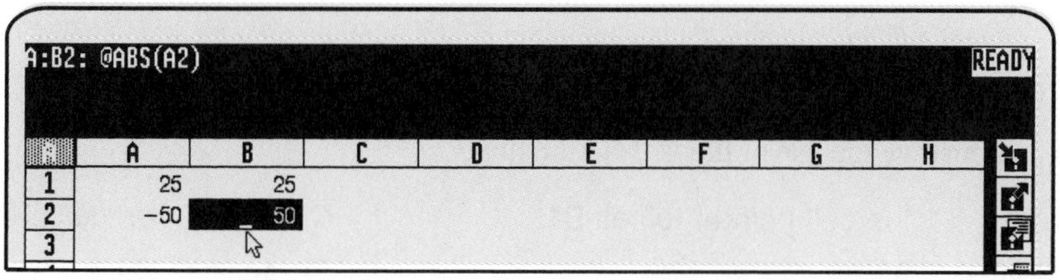

Notice that the absolute value of a positive number is the same positive number while the absolute value of a negative number is a positive number.

@EXP

The @EXP function computes the value of the number e raised to a specific power. The number e used in 1-2-3 has the approximate value of 2.718282.

The format of the @EXP function is:

$$@EXP(x)$$

where x is any value within the limits specified by the Lotus 1-2-3 reference manual. These limits are approximately from -11356 to 11356.

Make sure you have a blank worksheet on your screen.

To demonstrate the use of the @EXP function:

Move	the cell pointer to cell A1	*Click*	*on cell A1*
Enter	@EXP(3)	*Enter*	*@EXP(3)*

Your screen should look like Figure 15-48.

Figure 15-48

```
A:A1: @EXP(3)                                              READY

        A       B      C      D      E      F      G      H
  1  20.08554
  2        ▷
  3
```

The value 20.08554 appearing in cell A1 is *e* (2.718282) raised to the power of 3.

@INT

The @INT function determines the integer portion of a value in a cell. The format for the @INT function is:

$$@INT(x)$$

where *x* is any value.

Make sure you have a blank worksheet on your screen.

To demonstrate the use of the @INT function:

Move	the cell pointer to cell B1	*Click*	*on cell B1*
Enter	33.1	*Enter*	*33.1*
Move	the cell pointer to cell B2	*Click*	*on cell B2*
Enter	@INT(B1)	*Enter*	*@INT(B1)*

Your screen should look like Figure 15-49.

Figure 15-49

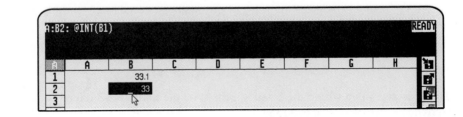

```
A:B2: @INT(B1)                                            READY

        A       B      C      D      E      F      G      H
  1             33.1
  2             33
  3        ▷
```

Notice that the value in cell B2 is 33 and the decimal portion of the number appearing in B1 has been omitted.

@LN

This function calculates the natural logarithm (base *e*) of a value. The format of the @LN function is:

$$@LN(x)$$

where *x* is any value greater than 0.

Make sure you have a blank worksheet on your screen.

To illustrate the use of the @LN function:

Move	the cell pointer to cell A1	*Click*	*on cell A1*
Enter	2	*Enter*	*2*
Move	the cell pointer to cell A2	*Click*	*on cell A2*
Enter	@LN(A1)	*Enter*	*@LN(A1)*

Your screen should look like Figure 15-50.

Figure 15-50

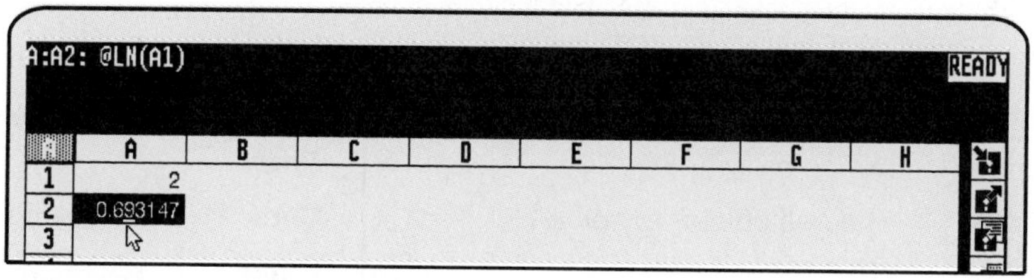

The value 0.693147 in A2 is the natural logarithm of the number 2.

@LOG

The @LOG function computes the common logarithm (base 10) for a value. The format for the @LOG function is:

$$@LOG(x)$$

where *x* is any value greater than 0.

Make sure you have a blank worksheet on your screen.

To demonstrate the use of the @LOG function:

Move	the cell pointer to cell B1	*Click*	*on cell B1*
Enter	20	*Enter*	*20*
Move	the cell pointer to cell B2	*Click*	*on cell B2*
Enter	@LOG(B1)	*Enter*	*@LOG(B1)*

Your screen should look like Figure 15-51.

Figure 15-51

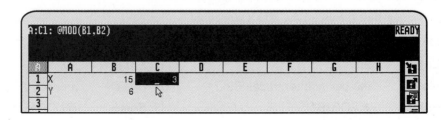

The value 1.30103 in cell B2 is the common logarithm for the number 20.

@MOD

The @MOD function computes the remainder (modulus) when you divide one number by another. The format for the @MOD function is:

$$@MOD(x,y)$$

where *x* is any value and *y* is any value other than 0. The sign (+ or -) of the value *x* specifies the sign of the result.

Make sure you have a blank worksheet on your screen.

To illustrate the use of the @MOD function:

Move	the cell pointer to cell A1	*Click*	*on cell A1*
Enter	X	*Enter*	*X*
Move	the cell pointer to cell B1	*Click*	*on cell B1*
Enter	15	*Enter*	*15*
Move	the cell pointer to cell A2	*Click*	*on cell A2*
Enter	Y	*Enter*	*Y*
Move	the cell pointer to cell B2	*Click*	*on cell B2*
Enter	6	*Enter*	*6*
Move	the cell pointer to cell C1	*Click*	*on cell C1*
Enter	@MOD(B1,B2)	*Enter*	*@MOD(B1,B2)*

Your screen should look like Figure 15-52.

Figure 15-52

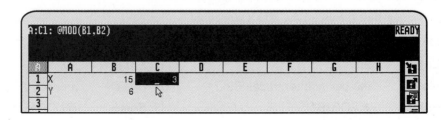

The value 3 is computed by dividing 15 by 6 and determining that the answer is 2 plus a remainder (modulus) of 3.

@RAND

The @RAND function calculates a random number between 0 and 1. The format of the @RAND function is:

@RAND

If you need to have a random number within a particular interval you must multiply the @RAND function by an appropriate value.

Make sure you have a blank worksheet on your screen.

To illustrate the use of the @RAND function:

Move	the cell pointer to cell A1	**Click**	*on cell A1*
Enter	@RAND	**Enter**	*@RAND*
Move	the cell pointer to cell A2	**Click**	*on cell A2*
Enter	100@RAND	**Enter**	*100@RAND*

Your screen should look similar to Figure 15-53.

Figure 15-53

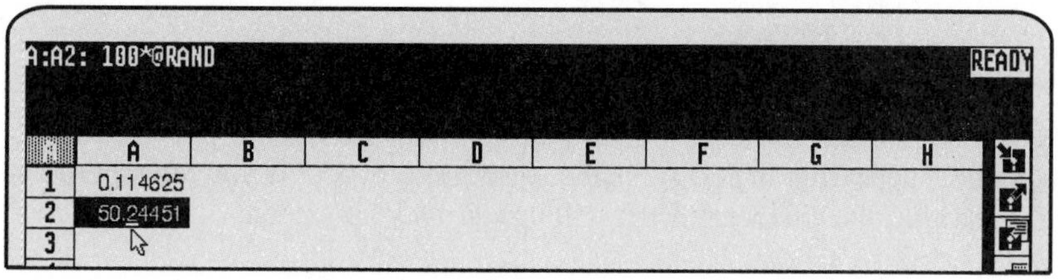

The value appearing in cell A1 is a random number between 0 and 1. The value in cell A2 is a random number between the interval 0 and 100. It was computed by multiplying a value determined using the @RAND function by 100.

@ROUND

The @ROUND function is used to round a value to a specific number of decimal places. The format for the @ROUND function is:

@ROUND(x,y)

where x is any value or formula and y is the number of decimal places you desire to the right of the decimal place. Chapter 4 includes an extensive discussion of the @ROUND function and several illustrations of its use.

@SQRT

The @SQRT function determines the positive square root for a value. The format of the @SQRT function is:

$$@SQRT(x)$$

where *x* is any positive value or formula that results in a positive number.

Make sure you have a blank worksheet on your screen.

To demonstrate the use of the @SQRT function:

Move	the cell pointer to cell A1	*Click*	*on cell A1*
Enter	25	*Enter*	*25*
Move	the cell pointer to cell A2	*Click*	*on cell A2*
Enter	@SQRT(A1)	*Enter*	*@SQRT(A1)*

Your screen should look like Figure 15-54.

Figure 15-54

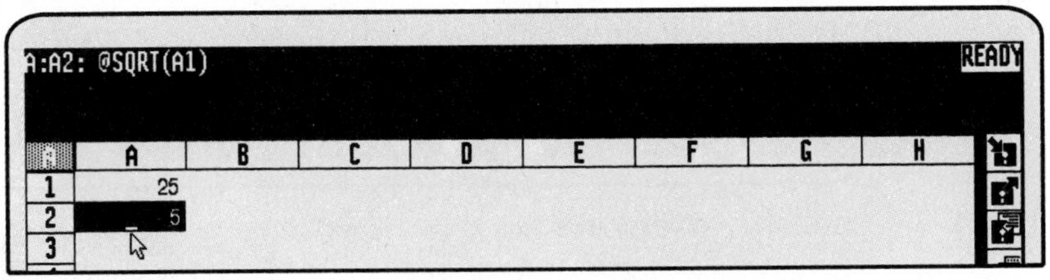

The value 5 appearing in cell A2 is the square root of 25. If you attempt to compute the square root of a negative value, the characters ERR will appear on your screen.

Trigonometric Functions

The trigonometric-related functions available in 1-2-3 are @COS, @ACOS, @SIN, @ASIN, @TAN, @ATAN, @ATAN2, and @PI. These functions are used primarily by engineers and scientists. If you need to use these functions, please see the Lotus 1-2-3 reference manual.

■ SPECIAL FUNCTIONS

There are 16 **special functions** available in 1-2-3. They can be categorized as follows:

CELL AND RANGE INFORMATION:

@@	Returns the contents of the cell whose name or address is in another cell
@CELL	Returns information about a cell or its contents
@CELLPOINTER	Returns information about the current cell or its contents

@COLS	Determines the number of columns that are in a range
@COORD	Creates an absolute, mixed, or relative cell address from values specified as arguments
@ROWS	Determines the number of rows in a range
@SHEETS	Determines the number of worksheets in a range

ERROR TRAPPING:

@ERR	Returns the characters ERR for error
@NA	Returns the characters NA for not available
@?	Returns the characters NA if an add-in is not attached

LOOKUP CALCULATIONS:

@CHOOSE	Finds a specific value or string in a list
@HLOOKUP	Finds the contents of a cell in a specified row in a horizontal lookup table
@VLOOKUP	Finds the contents of a cell in a specified column of a vertical lookup table
@INDEX	Finds the contents of the cell in a specified row and column in a range

SYSTEM AND SESSION INFORMATION

| @INFO | Provides information on the current session |
| @SOLVER | Provides information on the status of the solver |

Cell and Range Information

The seven cell and range information functions available in 1-2-3 are @@, @CELL, @CELLPOINTER, @COLS, @COORD, @ROWS, and @SHEETS.

@@

The @@ function returns the contents of the cell whose name or address is in another cell. The format of the @@ function is:

$$@@(location)$$

where location is the name or address of a single-cell range.

Make sure you have a blank worksheet on your screen.

To illustrate the use of the @@ function:

| **Move** | the cell pointer to cell A1 | *Click* | *on cell A1* |
| **Enter** | 15 | *Enter* | *15* |

Move	the cell pointer to cell C1		*Click*	*on cell C1*
Enter	A1		*Enter*	*A1*
Move	the cell pointer to cell C3		*Click*	*on cell C3*
Enter	@ @(C1)		*Enter*	*@ @(C1)*

C1 has as its contents the label A1. The @function directs 1-2-3 to go to the cell referenced in cell A1 and place the contents of cell A1 in C3.

Your screen should look like Figure 15-55.

Figure 15-55

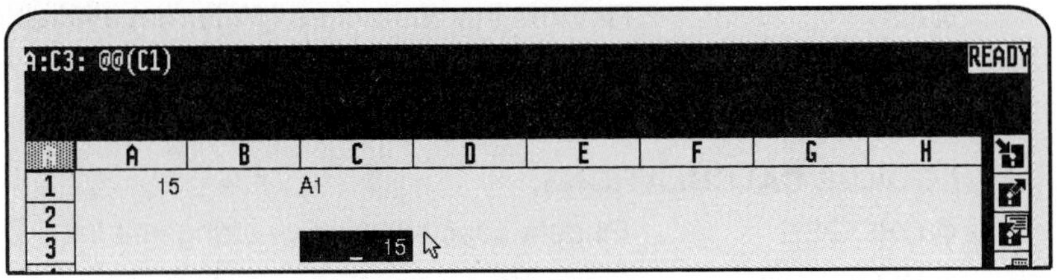

If the location you use refers to more than one cell, ERR will be returned.

@CELL

The @CELL function returns information about a cell or its contents. The format of the @CELL function is:

@CELL(attribute,location)

The attribute can be any of 10 strings allowed by 1-2-3. The location can be any cell address or range name. The Lotus 1-2-3 reference manual contains a list of the 10 strings that can be used for the attribute argument and the value returned for each of the possible attributes.

@CELLPOINTER

The @CELLPOINTER function returns information about the current cell. The format of the @CELLPOINTER function is:

@CELLPOINTER(attribute)

The attribute can be any of 10 strings allowed by 1-2-3 for the @CELL function. Refer to the Lotus 1-2-3 reference manual for the possible attributes and the value returned for each of the possible attributes.

@COLS

The @COLS function counts the number of columns in a specified range. The format of the @COLS function is:

@COLS(range)

where the range can be specified or a range name can be used.

Make sure you have a blank worksheet on your screen.

To demonstrate the use of the @COLS function:

| **Move** | the cell pointer to cell A1 | **Click** | on cell A1 |
| **Enter** | @COLS(B1.M1) | **Enter** | @COLS(B1.M1) |

Your screen should look like Figure 15-56.

Figure 15-56

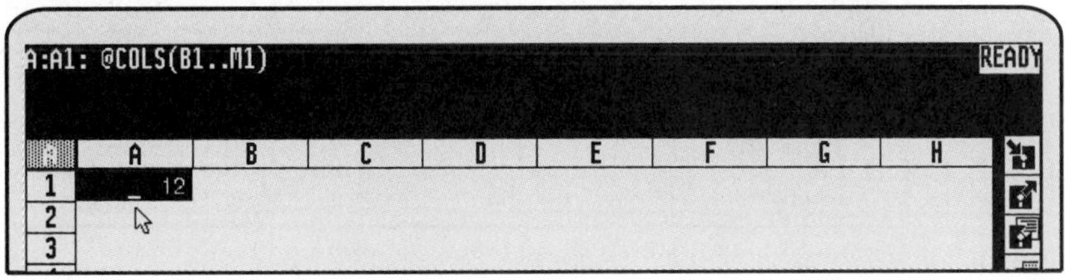

```
A:A1: @COLS(B1..M1)                                                    READY

     A        B       C       D       E       F       G       H
1        12
2      ▷
3
```

The value 12 appearing in cell A1 indicates there are 12 columns in the specified range B1 through M1.

@COORD

The @COORD function creates an absolute, mixed, or relative cell address from values you provide as arguments. The format of the @COORD function is:

$$@COORD(worksheet,column,row,absolute)$$

where worksheet and column can be any integer between 1 and 256. Row can be any value between 1 and 8,192. Absolute can be an integer between 1 and 8. This function uses the value for absolute to determine the reference type as relative, absolute, or mixed. The following table, taken from the Lotus 1-2-3 reference manual, includes the possible values of absolute and the effect on the cell address that is created.

Value	Worksheet	Column	Row	Example
1	Absolute	Absolute	Absolute	$A:$A$1
2	Absolute	Relative	Absolute	$A:A$1
3	Absolute	Absolute	Relative	$A:$A1
4	Absolute	Relative	Relative	$A:A1
5	Relative	Absolute	Absolute	A:$A$1
6	Relative	Relative	Absolute	A:A$1
7	Relative	Absolute	Relative	A:$A1
8	Relative	Relative	Relative	A:A1

Make sure you have a blank worksheet window on your screen.

To illustrate the use of the @COORD function:

Move	the cell pointer to cell A1		***Click***	*on cell A1*
Enter	@COORD(2,3,5,7)		***Enter***	*@COORD(2,3,5,7)*

Your screen should look like Figure 15-57.

Figure 15-57

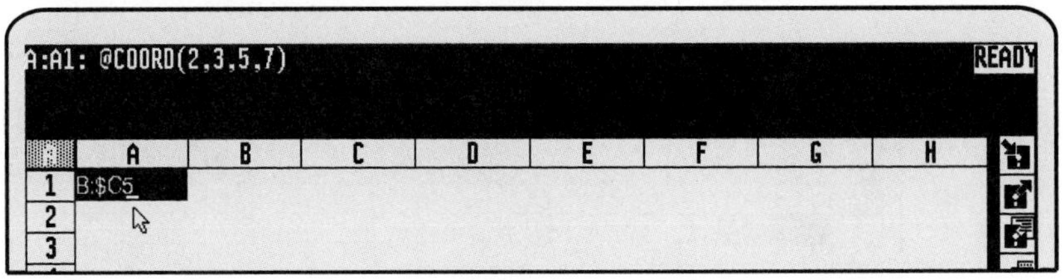

```
A:A1: @COORD(2,3,5,7)                                                    READY

        A        B        C        D        E        F        G        H
    1  B:$C5
    2        ▷
    3
```

The cell address B:$C5, created by the @COORD function, appears in cell A1.

@ROWS

The @ROWS function counts the number of rows in a range. The format of the @ROWS function is:

$$@ROWS(range)$$

where range can be a specified range or a range name.

Make sure you have a blank worksheet on your screen.

To illustrate the use of the @ROWS function:

Move	the cell pointer to cell A1		***Click***	*on cell A1*
Enter	@ROWS(B32.B297)		***Enter***	*@ROWS(B32.B297)*

Your screen should look like Figure 15-58.

Figure 15-58

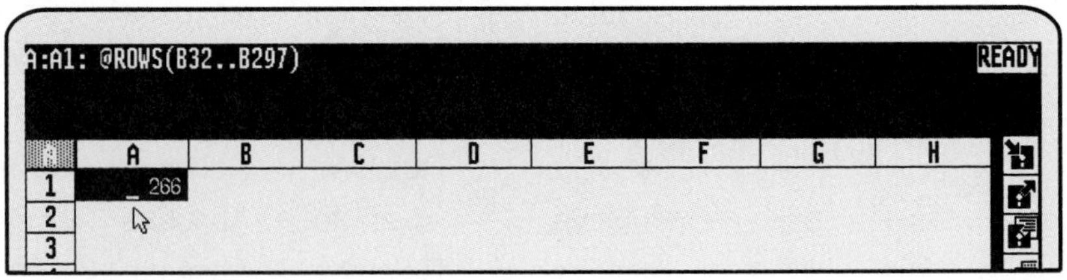

```
A:A1: @ROWS(B32..B297)                                                   READY

        A        B        C        D        E        F        G        H
    1     266
    2        ▷
    3
```

The value 266 appearing in cell A1 indicates that there are 266 rows in the range B32 through B297.

@SHEETS

The @SHEETS function determines how many worksheets there are in a specified range. The format of the @SHEETS function is:

@SHEETS(range)

where range can be a specified range or a range name.

Make sure you have a blank worksheet window on your screen.

To demonstrate the use of the @SHEETS function, insert 5 worksheets after worksheet A, then:

| **Move** | the cell pointer to cell A:B1 | *Click* | *on cell A:B1* |
| **Enter** | @SHEETS(B:A1.F:A1) | *Enter* | *@SHEETS(B:A1.F:A1)* |

Your screen should look like Figure 15-59.

Figure 15-59

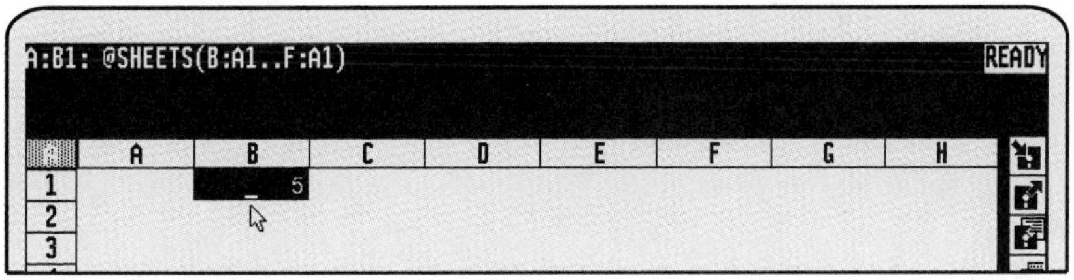

The number 5 in cell A:B1 indicates there are five worksheets in the indicated range.

Error Trapping

The three error trapping functions available in 1-2-3 are @ERR, @NA, and @?.

@ERR

The @ERR function returns the characters ERR (Error). The format for the @ERR is:

@ERR

Make sure you have a blank worksheet on your screen.

To illustrate the use of the @ERR function:

Move	the cell pointer to cell A1	*Click*	*on cell A1*
Enter	25	*Enter*	*25*
Move	the cell pointer to cell A2	*Click*	*on cell A2*
Enter	5	*Enter*	*5*

Suppose you want to place a formula in cell A3 that will divide the value in cell A1 by the value in cell A2 only if the value in A2 is greater than 10. If the value is less than or equal to 10, you want to place the ERR characters in cell A3. To accomplish this task:

Move	the cell pointer to cell A3	**Click**	on cell A3
Enter	@IF(A2>10,A1/A2,@ERR)	**Enter**	@IF(A2>10,A1/A2,@ERR)

Your screen should look like Figure 15-60.

Figure 15-60

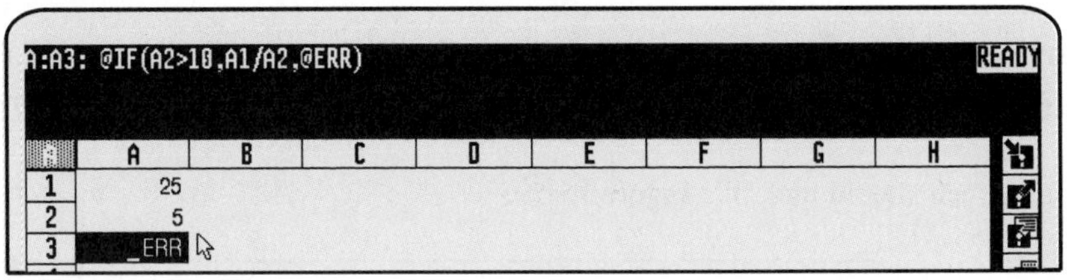

The characters ERR appear in cell A3, because the value in cell A2 is not greater than 10. Change the value in A2 to a value greater than 10 to verify that the function works properly.

@NA

The @NA function returns the characters NA (not available). The format for the @NA function is:

$$@NA$$

Make sure you have a blank worksheet on your screen.

To demonstrate the use of the @NA function:

Move	the cell pointer to cell B1	**Click**	on cell B1
Enter	0	**Enter**	0

Suppose you want to place the characters NA in cell A4 if the value in cell B1 is 0, meaning the data is not available yet. Otherwise you want to place the value appearing in cell B1 in cell A4.

Move	the cell pointer to cell A4	**Click**	on cell A4
Enter	@IF(B1=0,@NA,B1)	**Enter**	@IF(B1=0,@NA,B1)

Your screen should look like Figure 15-61.

Figure 15-61

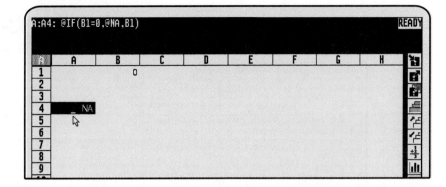

The NA appearing in cell A4 indicates that the present value in cell B1 is 0. Change the value in cell B1 to some other number and the value will appear in cells B1 and A4.

@?

The @? function returns the characters NA if an @function from an add-in is encountered and the add-in has not been attached.

Lookup Calculations

The four lookup calculation functions available in 1-2-3 include: @CHOOSE, @HLOOKUP, @VLOOKUP, and @INDEX.

@CHOOSE

The @CHOOSE function finds a value or a string in a specified list. The format of the @CHOOSE function is:

@CHOOSE(offset number,list)

The offset number is the position of an item in a list. The initial item in the list has an offset number of 0. The second item has an offset number of 1, and so on.   The final offset number is the total number of items minus 1. The offset number must be a positive integer and have a value less than or equal to 49. The list can contain any set of values, strings, and range references, or any combination of them. Before using the @CHOOSE function, you need to create the worksheet appearing in Figure 15-62.

Figure 15-62

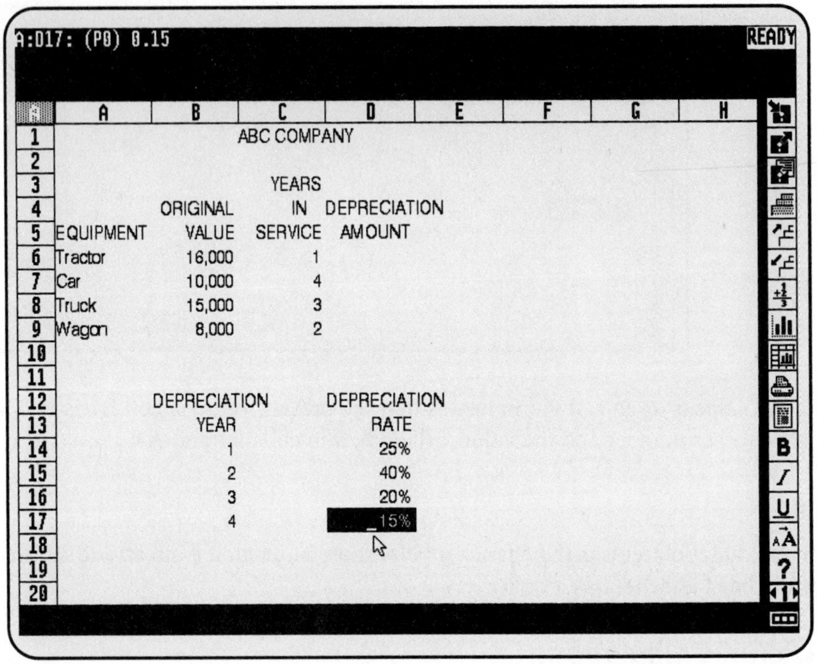

You need to compute the annual depreciation for the four pieces of equipment listed in cells A6 through A9. Suppose that each of the properties has an economic useful life of four years. The depreciation rate used for the properties depends on how long the property has been in service. For example, the depreciation rate for the tractor is 25 percent, because it has been in service for only one year. The depreciation amount for the tractor is $4,000 (.25 times 16,000).

To demonstrate the use of the @CHOOSE function to compute the depreciation amount for the tractor:

Move	the cell pointer to cell D6		***Click***	*on cell D6*
Enter	+B6@CHOOSE(C6,@ERR, $D$14,$D$15,$D$16,$D$17, @ERR)		***Enter***	*+B6@CHOOSE(C6,@ERR, $D$14,$D$15,$D$16,$D$17, @ERR)*

The value 4,000 appearing in cell D6 is the depreciation amount based on the depreciation rate of 25 percent. Cell C6 is the cell having the offset number and has the value 1 in it. Since the YEARS IN SERVICE value in cell C6 is 1, the second item in the list is used. Note that @ERR is used for the items in the list if the offset number is 0 and greater than 4. In this manner, if YEARS IN SERVICE is entered incorrectly, then ERR will appear for the depreciation amount.

Verify that the @CHOOSE function works for the other equipment by copying the formula in cell D6 to cells D7 through D9.

The top part of your screen should look like Figure 15-63.

Figure 15-63

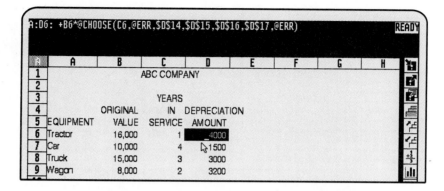

Change the value for the YEARS OF SERVICE to 0 and 5 for one of the equipment types. ERR will appear in the cell in both cases.

@HLOOKUP

The @HLOOKUP function determines the contents of a cell for a specified row in a horizontal lookup table. A horizontal lookup table is a range of cells that has value or label information in ascending order in the first row. The format of the @HLOOKUP function is:

$$@HLOOKUP(x,range,row\text{-}offset)$$

where x is a value or label and range is the set of cells contained in the horizontal lookup table. Row-offset is the position number of the row within the horizontal lookup table where the cell being referenced resides.

1-2-3 locates the cell in the first row having a label that matches x or contains a value that is greater than or equal to x but less than the value of the next cell to the right. It then moves down the column based on the row-offset number and returns the contents of the cell. If labels appear in the first row instead of values, 1-2-3 checks for exact matches.

The row-offset number is the position a row occupies in the range. The first row has an offset number of zero, the second row has an offset number of 1 and so on. For example, in Figure 15-64, the row-offset number for cell B7 is 3 because the horizontal lookup table begins in cell B4 or row 0. The row-offset number can be 0 or any positive integer between 1 and 19. The maximum value that row-offset can have is 19.

Before illustrating the use of the @HLOOKUP function, you need to create the worksheet in Figure 15-64.

Figure 15-64

```
A:C18: [W13] 1                                                    READY

      A            B            C            D            E        F
 1  HORIZONTAL LOOKUP TABLE FOR TAX WITHHOLDING
 2
 3   ALLOWANCES                          SALARY
 4                    1,760        1,800        1,840        1,880
 5          0          248          257          266          275
 6          1          229          238          247          256
 7          2          211          220          228          238
 8          3          196          203          210          220
 9          4          182          189          196          202
10
11
12                              WITHHOLDING    AMOUNT
13   EMPLOYEE       SALARY      ALLOWANCES     WITHHELD
14  Avery           1,850            2
15  Chen            1,875            0
16  Gonzalez        1,825            3
17  Smith           1,800            4
18  Woods           1,775            1
19
20
```

The horizontal lookup table contains the cells B4 through E9. The information in cells A5 through A9 is for documentation purposes only. The table is used to determine the amount of withholding tax an employee must pay depending on the salary and number of exemptions declared. For example, an individual earning more than $1,840 and less than or equal to $1,880 who has 2 exemptions must have $228 withheld from his or her paycheck.

To demonstrate the use of the @HLOOKUP function for this situation:

Move	the cell pointer to cell D14		*Click*	*on cell D14*
Enter	@HLOOKUP(B14,$B$4:$E$9, C14+1)		*Enter*	*@HLOOKUP(B14,$B$4:$E$9, C14+1)*

Make sure you include the $ signs to specify the absolute references. The value 228 appearing in cell D14 is the amount of withholding for an individual who has 2 withholding allowances, earning more than $1,840 and less than $1,880. Note that the value 1,850 is greater than or equal to 1,840 and less than 1,880. The offset number is the value of cell C14 plus one because the row offset is one more than the corresponding number of allowances.

To verify that the @HLOOKUP function works properly for the remaining employees, copy the formula in cell D14 to cells D15 through D18. When you are finished, the bottom part of your screen should look like Figure 15-65.

Figure 15-65

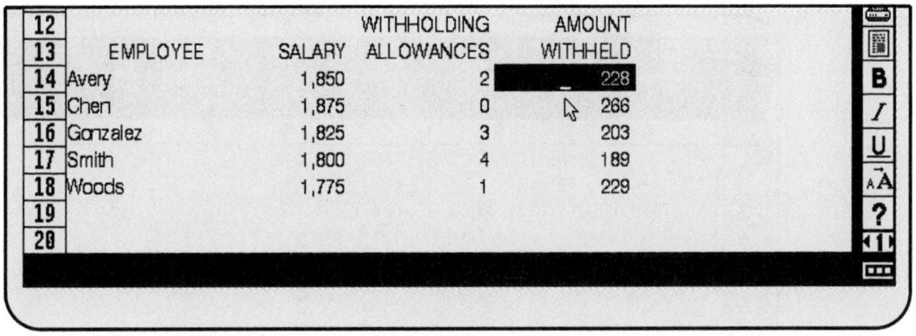

12			WITHHOLDING	AMOUNT
13	EMPLOYEE	SALARY	ALLOWANCES	WITHHELD
14	Avery	1,850	2	228
15	Chen	1,875	0	266
16	Gonzalez	1,825	3	203
17	Smith	1,800	4	189
18	Woods	1,775	1	229
19				
20				

@VLOOKUP

The @VLOOKUP function determines the contents of a cell for a specified column in a vertical lookup table. A vertical lookup table is a range of cells that has label or value information in ascending order in the first column. The format of the @VLOOKUP function is:

$$@VLOOKUP(x, range, column\text{-}offset)$$

where x is a label or value and range is the set of cells contained in the vertical lookup table. Column-offset is the position number of the column within the vertical lookup table where the cell being referenced resides.

1-2-3 locates the cell in the first column having a label that matches x or a value that is greater than or equal to x but less than the value of the next cell below. It then moves across the row based on the column-offset number and returns the contents of the cell. If labels are used in the first column instead of values, 1-2-3 checks for exact matches.

The column-offset number is the position a column occupies in the range. The first column can have a value of 0; the second column has an offset number of 1 and so on. For example, in Figure 15-66, the column-offset number for cell B7, is 1 because the vertical lookup table begins in cell A6 or column 0. The column-offset number can be 0 or any positive integer between 1 and 19. The maximum value that the column-offset can have is 19.

Before illustrating the use of the @VLOOKUP function, you need to create the worksheet in Figure 15-66. The AMOUNT cells are calculated by multiplying QUANTITY times PRICE, and the total AMOUNT is determined by summing the individual item sales amounts.

Figure 15-66

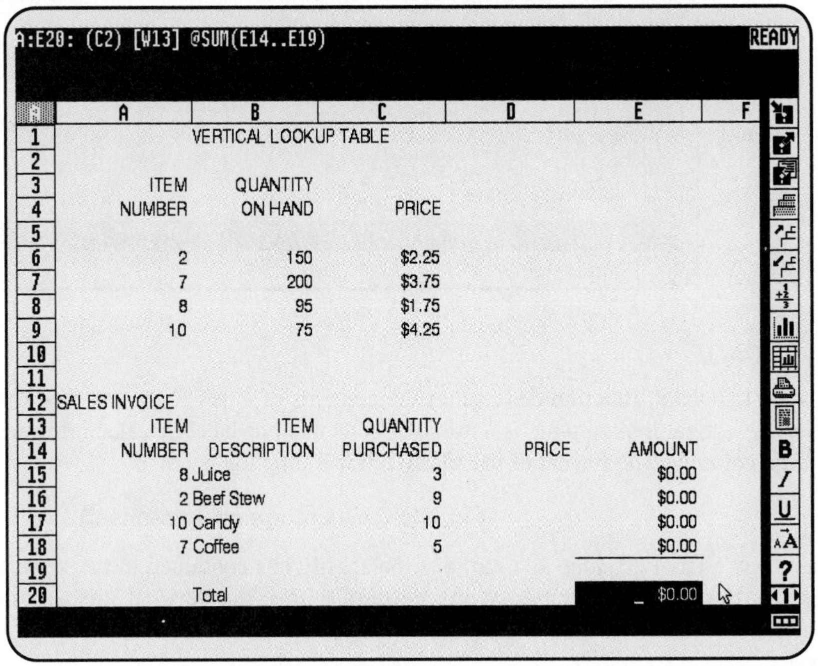

```
A:E20: (C2) [W13] @SUM(E14..E19)                                    READY

        A              B            C         D         E        F
1                  VERTICAL LOOKUP TABLE
2
3              ITEM        QUANTITY
4             NUMBER       ON HAND        PRICE
5
6                2           150         $2.25
7                7           200         $3.75
8                8            95         $1.75
9               10            75         $4.25
10
11
12 SALES INVOICE
13              ITEM         ITEM      QUANTITY
14            NUMBER     DESCRIPTION   PURCHASED    PRICE    AMOUNT
15              8 Juice                   3                 $0.00
16              2 Beef Stew               9                 $0.00
17             10 Candy                  10                 $0.00
18              7 Coffee                  5                 $0.00
19
20                 Total                                  _ $0.00
```

The vertical lookup table is in cells A6 through C9. This table includes information on the prices for four items sold by a distributor. The table is used to specify the proper sales price for items on a sales invoice.

To demonstrate the use of the @VLOOKUP function for this situation:

Move	the cell pointer to cell D15	*Click*	*on cell D15*
Enter	@VLOOKUP(A15,$A$6.$C$9,2)	*Enter*	*@VLOOKUP(A15,$A$6.$C$9,2)*

Make sure you include the $ signs to specify the absolute references. The value of $1.75 in cell D15 is the price for juice (item number 8). Note that the column-offset number is 2, because the prices for the items are in the third column of the vertical lookup table.

To verify that the @VLOOKUP function works properly for the other sales items, copy the contents of cell D15 to cells D16 through D18.

When you are finished, the bottom part of your screen should look like Figure 15-67.

Figure 15-67

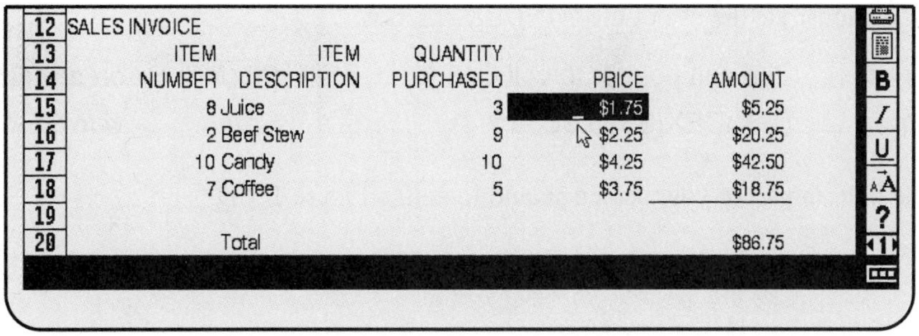

@INDEX

The @INDEX function determines the contents of a cell in a range of cells for a specific set of column-offset and row-offset numbers. The format of the @INDEX function is:

$$@INDEX(range,column\text{-}offset,row\text{-}offset)$$

The range can be any specified range of cells or range name.

Column-offset and row-offset are offset numbers. These numbers correspond to the column, row, or worksheet position of the desired cell in the range. The first column and row in the range have an offset of 0. Subsequent columns and rows are numbered as positive integers to a maximum value of 19.

Before illustrating the use of the @INDEX function, you need to create the worksheet in Figure 15-68.

Figure 15-68

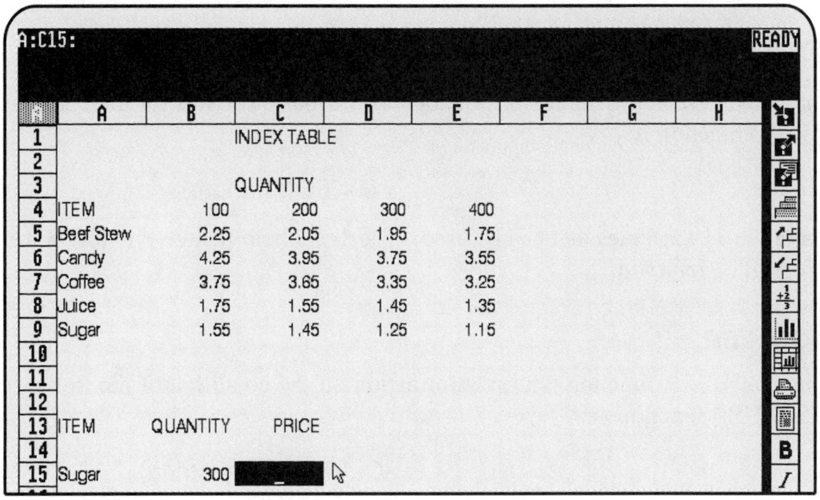

This worksheet includes an index table containing the price for some items based on the quantity purchased. You also need to create the range name PRICE_TABLE and include cell B5 through E9 as its range.

To demonstrate the use of the @INDEX function:

Move	the cell pointer to cell C15		*Click*	*on cell C15*
Enter	@INDEX($B$5.$E$9,2,4)		*Enter*	*@INDEX($B$5.$E$9,2,4)*

The bottom part of your screen should look like Figure 15-69.

Figure 15-69

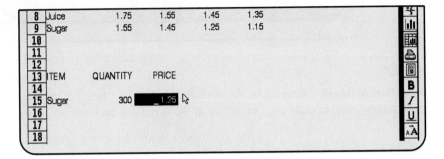

The value 1.25 appears in cell C15 indicating the price for SUGAR when the purchase QUANTITY is 300 units.

System and Session Information

The @INFO and the @SOLVER functions are the two system and session information functions.

@INFO

The @INFO function returns information on various attributes for the current session. The format of the @INFO function is:

@INFO(attribute)

There are 11 attributes that can be used. The 1-2-3 help feature contains a list of these attributes and the information returned.

@SOLVER

The @SOLVER function returns information on the condition of the Solver feature. The format of the @SOLVER function is:

@SOLVER(query-string)

There are 8 attributes that can be used. The 1-2-3 help feature contains a list of these query-strings and the information returned.

■ STRING FUNCTIONS

There are 18 **string functions** available in 1-2-3. The term *string* refers to any set of characters. The string functions can be categorized as follows:

SPECIAL CHARACTERS AND CREATING CHARACTERS:

@CHAR	Returns the character provided by the Lotus Multibyte Character Set (LMBCS) code
@CODE	Returns the LMBCS code corresponding to the first character in a string
@REPEAT	Duplicates a string of characters a specified number of times

EXTRACTING PORTIONS OF A STRING FROM A LABEL OR PROVIDING INFORMATION ON A LABEL:

@FIND	Determines the position of the first character of a string within another string
@LEFT	Returns a specified number of characters beginning with the first character in the string
@LENGTH	Determines the number of characters in a string
@MID	Returns an indicated number of characters beginning with a specific character
@REPLACE	Replaces the characters in one string with another specified string of characters
@RIGHT	Returns a specified number of characters at the end of a string

CHANGING THE CASE OF A STRING:

@LOWER	Changes all letters in a string to lowercase
@PROPER	Changes the first letter of each word in a string to uppercase; all other letters in the string are lowercase
@UPPER	Changes all letters in a string to uppercase

CONVERTING VALUES TO STRINGS AND STRINGS TO VALUES:

@STRING	Changes a value into a label with a specified number of decimal places
@TRIM	Deletes all leading, trailing, and consecutive spaces from a string
@VALUE	Changes a string of characters from a label to a number

DETERMINING THE CHARACTERISTICS OF A STRING:

@EXACT	Determines whether two strings of characters are the same

@N	Returns the value (number) in the first cell in a range if it contains a number; otherwise a zero is returned
@S	Returns the label in the first cell in a range if it contains a label; otherwise a blank cell is returned

Special Characters and Creating Characters

The three functions for manipulating special characters in 1-2-3 are @CHAR, @CODE, and @REPEAT.

@CHAR

The @CHAR function returns the character that the Lotus Multibyte Character Set (LMBCS) code provides. The format of the @CHAR function is:

$$@CHAR(x)$$

where x is an integer. See the Lotus 1-2-3 reference manual for further information.

@CODE

The @CODE function returns the Lotus Multibyte Character Set (LMBCS) code for the first character in a string. The format of the @CODE function is:

$$@CODE(x)$$

where x is a string. See the Lotus 1-2-3 reference manual for further information.

@REPEAT

The @REPEAT function is used to duplicate a string of characters a specific number of times. The format of the @REPEAT function is:

$$@REPEAT(string,n)$$

where string is a set of characters and n is the number of times the string is to be repeated. The value of n can be any positive integer.

Make sure you have a blank worksheet on your screen.

To illustrate the use of the @REPEAT function:

Move	the cell pointer to cell A1	**Click**	on cell A1
Enter	@REPEAT("Worksheet ",3)	**Enter**	@REPEAT("Worksheet ",3)

Your screen should look like Figure 15-70.

Figure 15-70

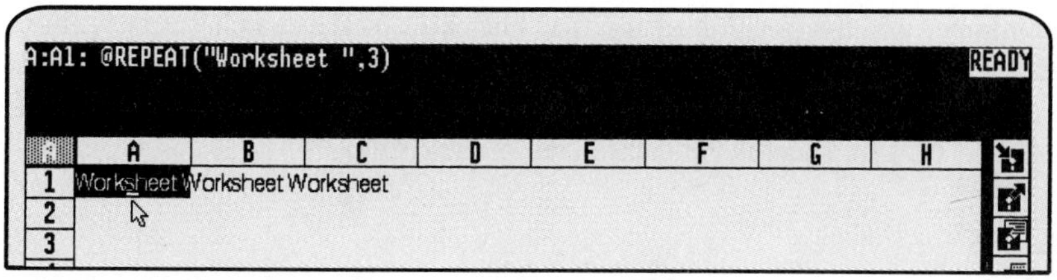

The set of characters "Worksheet " is repeated three times in cell A1. Note that a space occurs between the words because you placed a space before the second " in the string definition.

Extracting Portions of a String from a Label or Providing Information on a Label

The six string functions in 1-2-3 used to extract portions of a string from a label or provide information about the label are @FIND, @LEFT, @LENGTH, @MID, @REPLACE, and @RIGHT.

@FIND

The @FIND function determines the position within a string where another string starts. The format of the @FIND function is:

$$@FIND(search\text{-}string,string,start\text{-}number)$$

where search-string is the set of characters being sought in the string. The search-string and string can be any string of characters, a reference to a cell, or a formula that calculates a string. Start-number is an offset number of a character in a string. It can have a value of 0 or any positive integer. The first character in string is the number zero, the second is number one, and so on.

Make sure you have a blank worksheet on your screen.

To illustrate the use of the @FIND function:

Move	the cell pointer to cell A1	*Click*	on cell A1
Enter	Spreadsheet Analysis	*Enter*	*Spreadsheet Analysis*
Move	the cell pointer to cell A3	*Click*	on cell A3
Enter	@FIND("sheet",A1,0)	*Enter*	*@FIND("sheet",A1,0)*

Your screen should look like Figure 15-71.

Figure 15-71

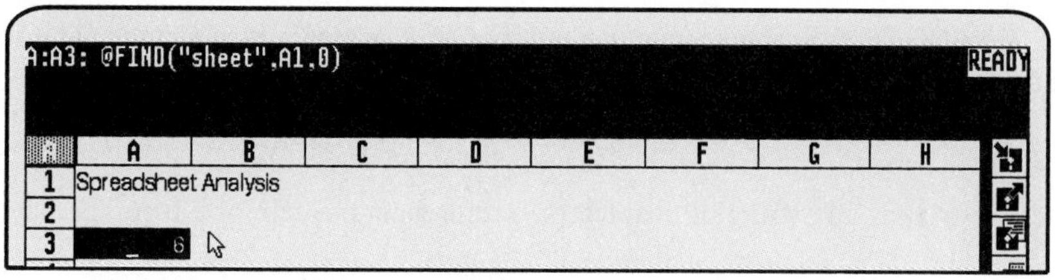

The number 6 is the position of the first character of the search-string within the string being searched. If the @FIND function cannot locate the search string in the string, ERR will appear in cell A3. @FIND is case sensitive. For example, if "Sheet" had been specified in the example, ERR would have appeared in cell A3 because sheet is not capitalized in the string.

@LEFT

The @LEFT function returns a specified number of characters from a string beginning with the first character in the string. The format of the @LEFT function is:

$$@LEFT(string,n)$$

String can be any string of characters, a reference to a cell, or a formula that calculates a label. The n is the number of characters to be returned from the string.

Make sure you have a blank worksheet on your screen.

To demonstrate the use of the @LEFT function:

| **Move** | the cell pointer to cell B1 | **Click** | on cell B1 |
| **Enter** | Mastering and Using Lotus 1-2-3 | **Enter** | *Mastering and Using Lotus 1-2-3* |

Suppose you want to return the characters *Mastering* and place them in cell B3.

| **Move** | the cell pointer to cell B3 | **Click** | on cell B3 |
| **Enter** | @LEFT(B1,9) | **Enter** | *@LEFT(B1,9)* |

Your screen should look like Figure 15-72.

Figure 15-72

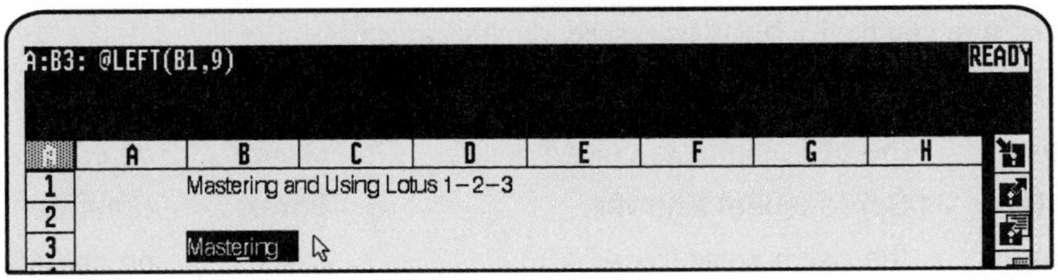

The string of characters *Mastering* now appears in cell B3.

@LENGTH

The @LENGTH function counts the number of characters in a string. The format of the @LENGTH function is:

$$@LENGTH(string)$$

where a string is any string of characters, a reference to a cell, or a formula that calculates a string.

Make sure you have a blank worksheet on your screen.

To illustrate the use of the @LENGTH function:

Move	the cell pointer to cell A1	*Click*	*on cell A1*
Enter	Boyd & Fraser Publishing Company	*Enter*	*Boyd & Fraser Publishing Company*
Move	the cell pointer to cell A4	*Click*	*on cell A4*
Enter	@LENGTH(A1)	*Enter*	*@LENGTH(A1)*

Your screen should look like Figure 15-73.

Figure 15-73

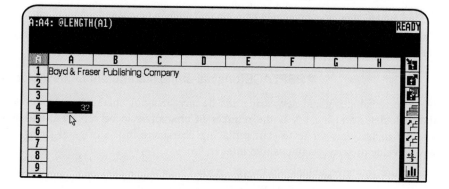

The number 32 appears in cell A4 indicating there are 32 characters in the string that is contained in cell A1.

@MID

The @MID function is used to return a specific number of characters beginning at a particular point in a string. The format of the @MID function is:

$$@MID(string,start\text{-}number,n)$$

where string is any string of characters, a reference to a cell, or a formula that calculates a string, and *n* is the number of characters to return. Start-number can be zero or any positive integer.

Make sure you have a blank worksheet on your screen.

To demonstrate the use of the @MID function:

Move	the cell pointer to cell B1	*Click*	*on cell B1*
Enter	Mastering and Using Lotus 1-2-3 Release 3.4	*Enter*	*Mastering and Using Lotus 1-2-3 Release 3.4*
Move	the cell pointer to cell B3	*Click*	*on cell B3*
Enter	@MID(B1,20,11)	*Enter*	*@MID(B1,20,11)*

Your screen should look like Figure 15-74.

Figure 15-74

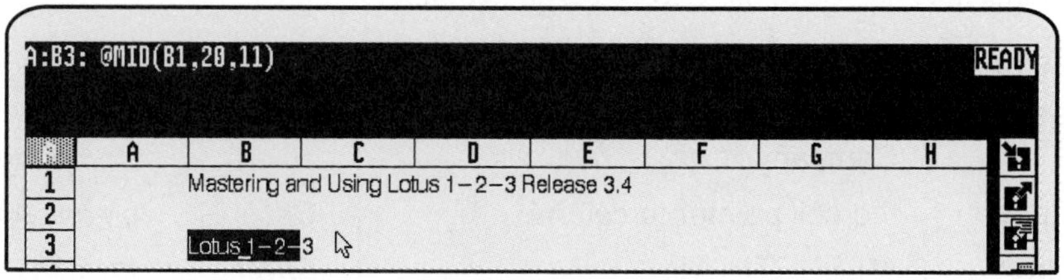

```
A:B3: @MID(B1,20,11)                                                    READY
```

	A	B	C	D	E	F	G	H	
1		Mastering and Using Lotus 1−2−3 Release 3.4							
2									
3		Lotus 1−2−3							

The set of characters Lotus 1-2-3 appears in cell B3 as a result of using the @MID function.

@REPLACE

The @REPLACE function finds a set of characters in a string and replaces the characters with another set of characters. The format of the @REPLACE function is:

@REPLACE(original-string,start-number,n,new-string)

where original-string and new-string can be any string of characters, a reference to a cell, or a formula that calculates a string. *N* is the number of characters to be replaced, and start-number is an offset-number identifying where to start replacing characters in the original-string. Start-number and *n* can have a value of zero or any positive integer.

Make sure you have a blank worksheet on your screen.

To illustrate the use of the @REPLACE function:

Move	the cell pointer to cell A1	**Click**	on cell A1
Enter	Softball and Feetball are popular sports	**Enter**	Softball and Feetball are popular sports

To replace the ee in Feetball with oo:

Move	the cell pointer to cell A3	**Click**	on cell A3
Enter	@REPLACE(A1,14,2,"oo")	**Enter**	@REPLACE(A1,14,2,"oo")

Your screen should look like Figure 15-75.

Figure 15-75

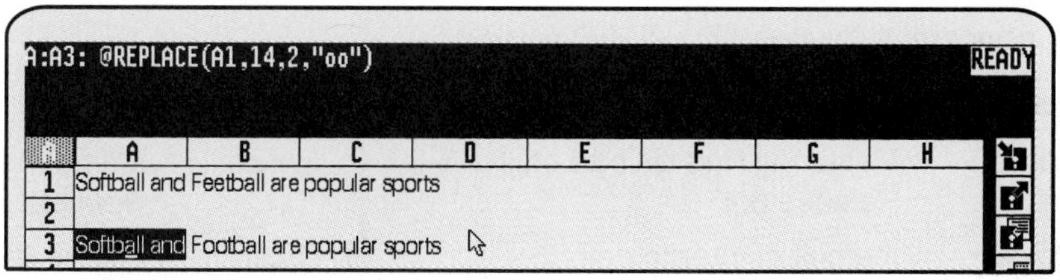

```
A:A3: @REPLACE(A1,14,2,"oo")                                           READY
```

	A	B	C	D	E	F	G	H	
1	Softball and Feetball are popular sports								
2									
3	Softball and Football are popular sports								

The spelling error appearing in cell A1 is now corrected in cell A3.

@RIGHT

The @RIGHT function returns characters from the end of a string. The format of the @RIGHT function is:

$$@RIGHT(string,n)$$

where string is any string of characters, a reference to a cell, or a formula that calculates a string. The n is the number of characters to return and can be any positive integer.

Make sure you have a blank worksheet on your screen.

To demonstrate the use of the @RIGHT function:

Move	the cell pointer to cell B1	**Click**	*on cell B1*
Enter	Software Package	**Enter**	*Software Package*
Move	the cell pointer to cell B3	**Click**	*on cell B3*
Enter	@RIGHT(B1,7)	**Enter**	*@RIGHT(B1,7)*

Your screen should look like Figure 15-76.

Figure 15-76

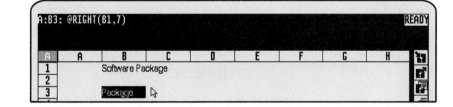

The word Package now appears in cell B3 because it represents the last seven characters of the string in B1.

Changing the Case of a String

The three functions available in 1-2-3 to change the case of a string are @LOWER, @PROPER, and @UPPER.

@LOWER

The @LOWER function changes all letters in a string to lowercase. The format of the @LOWER function is:

$$@LOWER(string)$$

where string is any string of characters, a reference to a cell, or a formula that calculates a string.

Make sure you have a blank worksheet on your screen.

To illustrate the use of the @LOWER function:

Move	the cell pointer to cell A1	*Click*	*on cell A1*
Enter	SOUTHWEST	*Enter*	*SOUTHWEST*
Move	the cell pointer to cell A3	*Click*	*on cell A3*
Enter	@LOWER(A1)	*Enter*	*@LOWER(A1)*

Your screen should look like Figure 15-77.

Figure 15-77

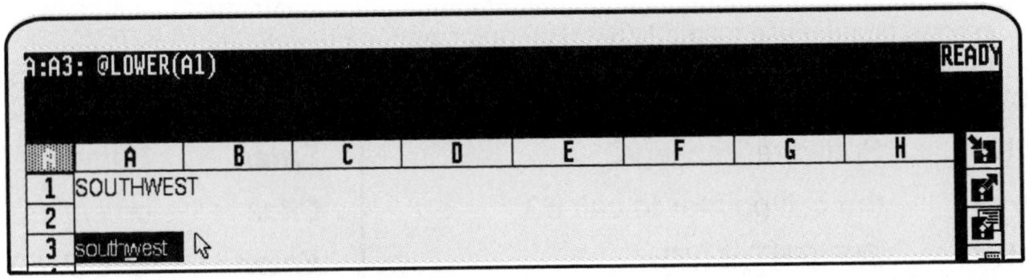

The letters appearing in cell A3 are all lowercase.

@PROPER

The @PROPER function makes the first letter of each word in a string uppercase. The remaining letters are lowercase. The format of the @PROPER function is:

$$@PROPER(string)$$

where string is any string of characters, a reference to a cell, or a formula that calculates a string.

Make sure you have a blank worksheet on your screen.

To demonstrate the use of the @PROPER function:

Move	the cell pointer to cell B1	*Click*	*on cell B1*
Enter	mastering and using lotus 1-2-3 release 3.4	*Enter*	*mastering and using lotus 1-2-3 release 3.4*
Move	the cell pointer to cell B3	*Click*	*on cell B3*
Enter	@PROPER(B1)	*Enter*	*@PROPER(B1)*

Your screen should look like Figure 15-78.

Figure 15-78

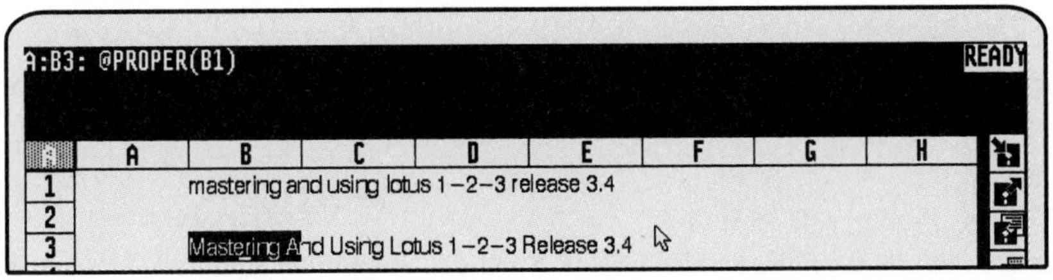

The first letter of each word in row 3 is uppercase and the other letters are lowercase.

@UPPER

The @UPPER function converts all lowercase letters in a string to uppercase letters. The format of the @UPPER function is:

@UPPER(string)

where string is any string of characters, a reference to a cell, or a formula that calculates a string.

Make sure you have a blank worksheet on your screen.

To illustrate the use of the @UPPER function:

Move	the cell pointer to cell A1	*Click*	*on cell A1*
Enter	California	*Enter*	*California*
Move	the cell pointer to cell A3	*Click*	*on cell A3*
Enter	@UPPER(A1)	*Enter*	*@UPPER(A1)*

Your screen should look like Figure 15-79.

Figure 15-79

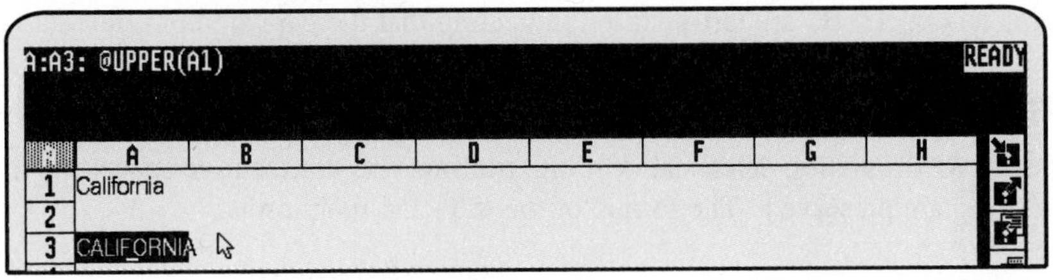

All letters in California are now uppercase in cell A3.

Converting Values to Strings and Strings to Values

The three functions available in 1-2-3 related to converting values to strings and strings to values are: @STRING, @TRIM, and @VALUE.

@STRING

The @STRING function changes a value into a label with a specified number of decimal places. The format of the @STRING function is:

$$@STRING(x,n)$$

where *x* can be a value, a reference to a cell, or a formula that calculates a string. The *n* refers to the number of decimal places you want in the string, and can be 0 or any positive integer between 1 and 15.

Make sure you have a blank worksheet on your screen.

To demonstrate the use of the @STRING function:

Move	the cell pointer to cell B1	**Click**	on cell B1
Enter	123.45	**Enter**	123.45
Move	the cell pointer to cell B3	**Click**	on cell B3
Enter	@STRING(B1,0)	**Enter**	@STRING(B1,0)

Your screen should look like Figure 15-80.

Figure 15-80

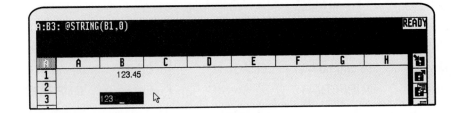

The value in cell B1 has been converted to the string 123 that appears in cell B3. Note that the characters in cell B3 are left-justified indicating that the data are considered a label and not a value.

@TRIM

The @TRIM function deletes all leading, trailing, and consecutive spaces from a string. Single spaces in the string are preserved. The format of the @TRIM function is:

$$@TRIM(string)$$

where string is any string of characters, a reference to a cell, or a formula that calculates a string.

Make sure you have a blank worksheet on your screen.

To illustrate the use of the @TRIM function:

Move	the cell pointer to cell A1	**Click**	on cell A1
Enter	Worksheets are fun to create	**Enter**	Worksheets are fun to create

Note that there are two spaces before Worksheets and between the words Worksheets, are, fun, and to.

Move	the cell pointer to cell A3	**Click**	on cell A3
Enter	@TRIM(A1)	**Enter**	@TRIM(A1)

Your screen should look like Figure 15-81.

Figure 15-81

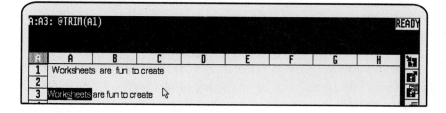

The leading spaces and extra spaces in the string have been deleted. Note that the space between to and create remains because there was only one space originally.

@VALUE

The @VALUE function changes a string of characters that looks like a number into a value. The format of the @VALUE function is:

$$@VALUE(string)$$

where string can only include numbers or numeric symbols.

Make sure you have a blank worksheet on your screen.

To demonstrate the use of the @VALUE function:

Move	the cell pointer to cell B1	**Click**	on cell B1
Enter	'97.5%	**Enter**	'97.5%
Move	the cell pointer to cell B3	**Click**	on cell B3
Enter	@VALUE(B1)	**Enter**	@VALUE(B1)

Your screen should look like Figure 15-82.

Figure 15-82

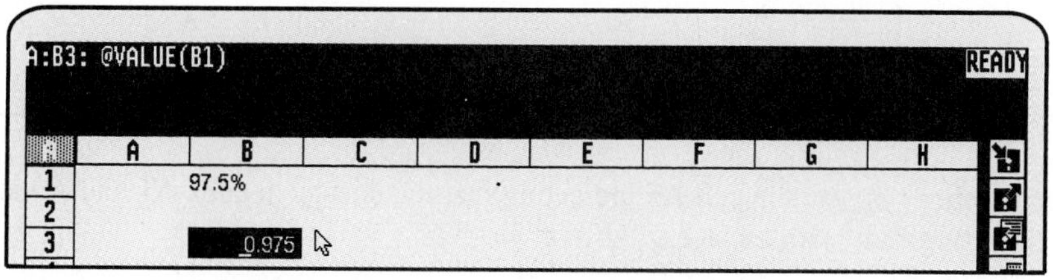

The string in cell B1 has been converted into the numeric value appearing in cell B3.

Determining the Characteristics of a String

The three functions available in 1-2-3 for determining the characteristics of a string are: @EXACT, @N, and @S.

@EXACT

The @EXACT function determines whether two strings of characters are the same. The format of the @EXACT function is:

$$@EXACT(string1,string2)$$

where string1 and string2 can be any string of characters, a reference to a cell, or a formula that calculates a string.

If string1 and string2 are exactly the same, a value of one is returned; otherwise a zero is returned.

Make sure you have a blank worksheet on your screen.

To illustrate the use of the @EXACT function:

Move	the cell pointer to cell A1	**Click**	on cell A1
Enter	Southwestern states	**Enter**	*Southwestern states*
Copy	cell A1 to cell A3	**Copy**	*cell A1 to cell A3*
Move	the cell pointer to cell A5	**Click**	on cell A5
Enter	@EXACT(A1,A3)	**Enter**	*@EXACT(A1,A3)*

Your screen should look like Figure 15-83.

Figure 15-83

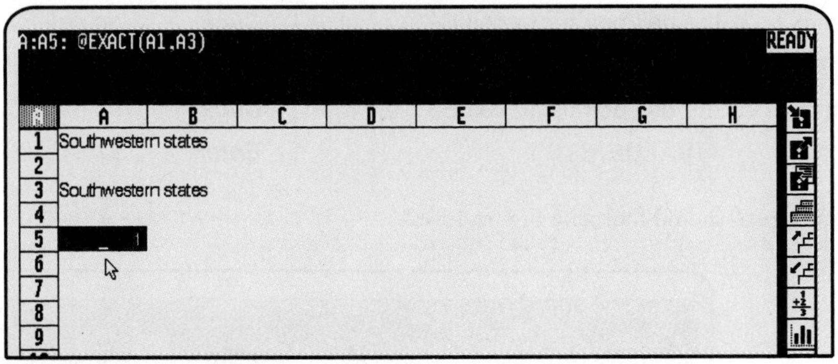

The number 1 appears in cell A5 indicating that the strings in cells A1 and A3 are the same. Edit cell A3 so the string ends with a space.

Move	the cell pointer to cell A3	**Click**	on cell A3
Press	F2	**Press**	F2

Press	the space bar		*Press*	*the space bar*
Press	←Enter		*Click*	*the mouse button*

The number 0 appears in cell A5 because the strings in cells A1 and A3 are not exactly alike. Any differences in case between the two strings would also result in a 0 in cell A5.

@N

The @N function returns the value appearing in the first cell of a range if the content of the cell is a numeric value, otherwise a zero is returned. The format of the @N function is:

$$@N(range)$$

where range is any specified set of cells or a range name.

Make sure you have a blank worksheet on your screen.

To demonstrate the use of the @N function:

Move	the cell pointer to cell B1		*Click*	*on cell B1*
Enter	125		*Enter*	*125*
Move	the cell pointer to cell C1		*Click*	*on cell C1*
Enter	150		*Enter*	*150*

Create the range name NUM_TEST that has cells B1 and C1 as its range.

Move	the cell pointer to cell B3		*Click*	*on cell B3*
Enter	@N(NUM_TEST)		*Enter*	*@N(NUM_TEST)*

Your screen should look like Figure 15-84.

Figure 15-84

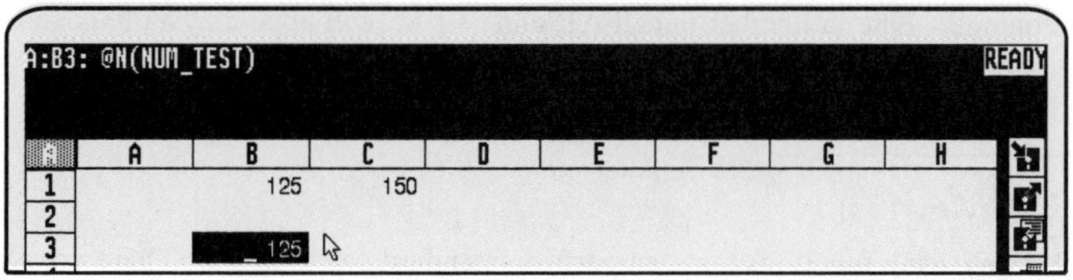

The number 125 appearing in cell B3 indicates that the first cell in the range NUM_TEST is a value. Change the contents of B1 to a label and a value of zero will appear in cell B3, indicating that the content of the first cell of the range NUM_TEST is not a number.

@S

The @S function returns a label for the entry in the upper left corner of a specified range. If the cell already contains a label, nothing is changed. If the cell contains a value or is blank, @S returns an empty string.

The format of the @S function is:

$$@S(range)$$

where range is any specified set of cells or a range name.

Make sure you have a blank worksheet on your screen.

To illustrate the use of the @S function:

Move	the cell pointer to cell A1	**Click**	on cell A1
Enter	June	**Enter**	June
Move	the cell pointer to cell B1	**Click**	on cell B1
Enter	July	**Enter**	July

Create the range name LABEL_TEST that has cells A1 and B1 as its range.

| **Move** | the cell pointer to cell A3 | **Click** | on cell A3 |
| **Enter** | @S(LABEL_TEST) | **Enter** | @S(LABEL_TEST) |

Your screen should look like Figure 15-85.

Figure 15-85

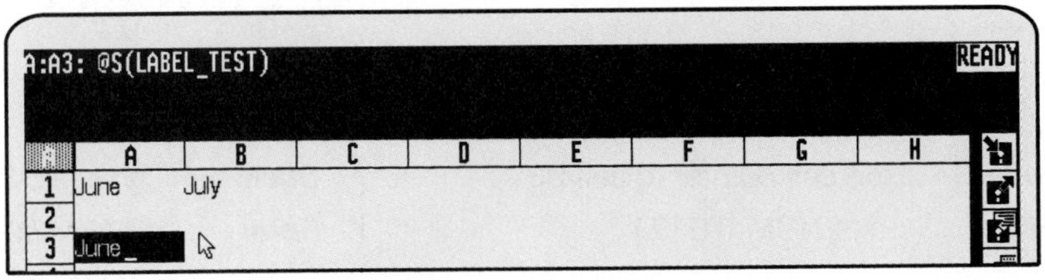

The month June appears in cell A3 indicating that the first cell in the range LABEL_TEST has a label as its contents. Enter a number in cell A1, and cell A3 will appear as a blank cell. If you erase cell A1, cell A3 will also appear as a blank cell.

SUMMARY

1-2-3 has many functions that can perform standard calculations. There are eight different categories of functions: statistical analysis, financial analysis, date and time, logical, database statistical, mathematical, special, and string.

KEY CONCEPTS

Database statistical functions
Date and time functions
Financial analysis functions
Logical functions

Mathematical functions
Special functions
Statistical analysis functions
String functions

EXERCISE 1

INSTRUCTIONS: Circle T if the statement is true and F if the statement is false.

T   F   1.   @MIN determines the minute for a given serial number.

T   F   2.   Multiple items in a range may be listed individually (e.g., the syntax in the formula @COUNT(B1,B3,B4) is correct).

T   F   3.   Arguments within an @function may be placed in any order desired by the user.

T   F   4.   Extra spaces are not acceptable within @functions.

T   F   5.   A label has a value of 0 and will be counted as such if included in a range for an @function.

T   F   6.   It is possible to alter an @function with arithmetic operations to get the desired result (e.g., the formula @PMT(B1,B2/12,B3*12) is syntactically correct).

T   F   7.   If a worksheet file containing the @NOW function (formatted to show the date) is retrieved and automatically recalculates, the @NOW function will display the *current* system date.

T   F   8.   A single-cell item in an argument may not be entered directly into the formula, e.g., the formula @NPV(A1,B1..B6) cannot be entered as @NPV(.1,B1..B6).

T   F   9.   More than one @function may be used in a formula.

T   F   10.   The @IF statement allows you to test one or more conditions in a worksheet and provide appropriate responses, either a true result or a false result.

T   F   11.   Date and time special functions are available in 1-2-3.

T   F   12.   XLOOKUP allows you to look up values in a row or a table.

T   F   13.   You can modify the appearance of a series of characters using the string functions.

T   F   14.   Data queries cannot be accomplished using special functions.

EXERCISE 2 — Using the Statistical Analysis Functions

INSTRUCTIONS: Using the data 111, 125, 116, 130, and 127, apply the statistical analysis functions available in 1-2-3 to:

1. Determine the sum of the numbers.

2. Count the number of values.

3. Compute the arithmetic mean of the values.

4. Determine the minimum value.

5. Calculate the maximum value.

6. Compute the population variance.

7. Determine the population standard deviation.

8. Compute the sample variance.

9. Calculate the sample standard deviation.

Print the worksheet after completing the calculations.

EXERCISE 3 — Using the SUMPRODUCT Function

INSTRUCTIONS: Make sure you have a blank worksheet on your screen.

Place the numbers 10, 25, and 15 in cells A3 through A5. Enter the numbers 5, 10, and 20 in cells D3 through D5.

Compute the sum of the products of the numbers and place the answer in cell A10.

Print the worksheet.

EXERCISE 4 — Using the Financial Analysis Functions

INSTRUCTIONS: Use the financial analysis functions available in 1-2-3 to solve the following exercises.

1. Compute the internal rate of return for the following cash flow stream, using .15 as the guess rate: -1000, -500, 900, 800, 700, 600, 400, 200, 100.

2. Compute the net present value for the following cash flow stream, using .10 as the discount rate: -1500, 900, 800, 700, 600, 400, 200, 100.

3. Compute the future value if the payment per period is 500, the interest rate is 10%, and the term is 15 years.

4. Compute the present value, using the arguments previously given in problem 3.

5. Compute the payment amount for a $100,000 loan that has an interest rate of 10 percent and is to be paid on an annual basis for a period of 12 years.

6. Compute the *monthly* payment amount assuming all arguments in problem 5 stay the same except the time period is 30 years.

7. Compute the straight-line depreciation for an office machine having an initial cost of $13,000, an estimated useful life of 8 years, and a salvage value of $200.

8. Using the data given in problem 7, compute the depreciation of the office machine for the sixth year using the double-declining balance method.

9. Using the data given in problem 7, compute the depreciation of the office machine for the sixth year using the sum-of-the-years'-digits method.

10. Using the data given in problem 7, compute the depreciation of the office machine for the fourth year using the variable declining balance method. You should use 150% as the depreciation factor.

11. Suppose $10,000 has been invested in an account that pays an annual interest rate of 10%, compounded monthly. Determine how long it will take to get $30,000 in the account.

12. Suppose that $5,000 is deposited at the end of each year into a bank account. If 8% interest is earned per year, compute how long it will take to earn $20,000.

13. Suppose $15,000 has been invested in a bond that matures in 9 years to $25,000. Interest is compounded monthly. Determine the monthly interest rate.

Print the worksheet(s) showing your answers.

EXERCISE 5 — Using the Date and Time Functions

INSTRUCTIONS: Use the date and time functions available in 1-2-3 to solve the following exercises.

1. Using the @DATE function, enter the date January 19, 1993, into cell A1. Format the date using option 1 from the Date format menu. Notice that the cell fills with asterisks; widen column A appropriately.

2. Using the @TIME function, enter the time 9:49 PM in cell A2.

3. Calculate the number of days between January 3, 1994, and June 27, 1991.

4. Determine the number of days between January 3, 1994, and June 27, 1991, assuming there are 360 days in a year.

5. Use the @NOW function to place the current date on your screen.

6. For the time 8:14:10 a.m., place the hour in cell B1, the minute in cell B2, and the second in cell B3.

7. Determine the time of day represented by the time serial number .481234.

Print the worksheet after completing all parts of the exercise.

EXERCISE 6 — Using the Logical Functions

INSTRUCTIONS: Make sure you have a blank worksheet on your screen. Then enter the following data on the worksheet.

Cell	Data
A1	20
A2	30
A3	50
A10	@NA
A11	10
A12	Worksheet

1. In cell B1, determine whether the value in A1 is within the range from 30 to 40. If the value is in the range, place the word **True** in cell B1; otherwise, place the word **False** in cell B1.

2. In cell B2, determine whether the value in A2 is greater than 25. If the value in cell A2 is greater than 25, use the @TRUE function to enter a value of 1 in cell B2. If the value is less than or equal to 25, use the @FALSE function to place the value 0 in cell B2.

3. In cell B3, determine whether the value in A3 is greater than 60. If the value in cell A3 is greater than 60, use the @TRUE function to enter a value of 1 in cell B3. If the value is less than or equal to 60, use the @FALSE function to place the value 0 in cell B3.

Print the worksheet with the results of the first three questions.

4. Change the values entered in cells A1, A2, A3 to:

Cell	Data
A1	35
A2	10
A3	75

Print the worksheet with the results after entering the new values. Print a list of the cell formulas for cells A1 through B3.

Define the range name ABC and include cells A10 through A12 as its range.

5. In cell B10, determine if the content of cell A10 contains @NA; if so, place a 1 in cell B10; otherwise place a 0 in cell B10.

6. In cell B11, determine if the content of cell A11 is a value. If cell A11 contains a value, place a 1 in cell B11; otherwise enter a 0 in cell B11.

7. In cell B12, determine if cell A12 contains a string of characters. If a string of characters appears in cell A12, place a 1 in cell B12; otherwise, place a 0 in cell B12.

8. In cell B14, determine if the range ABC is defined for the worksheet. If the range is present, place a 1 in cell B14; otherwise, enter a 0 in cell B14.

Print the results for questions 5 through 8. Include a list of cell formulas for cells A10 through B14.

EXERCISE 7 — Using the Database Statistical Functions

INSTRUCTIONS: Create the database table in Figure 15-86.

Figure 15-86

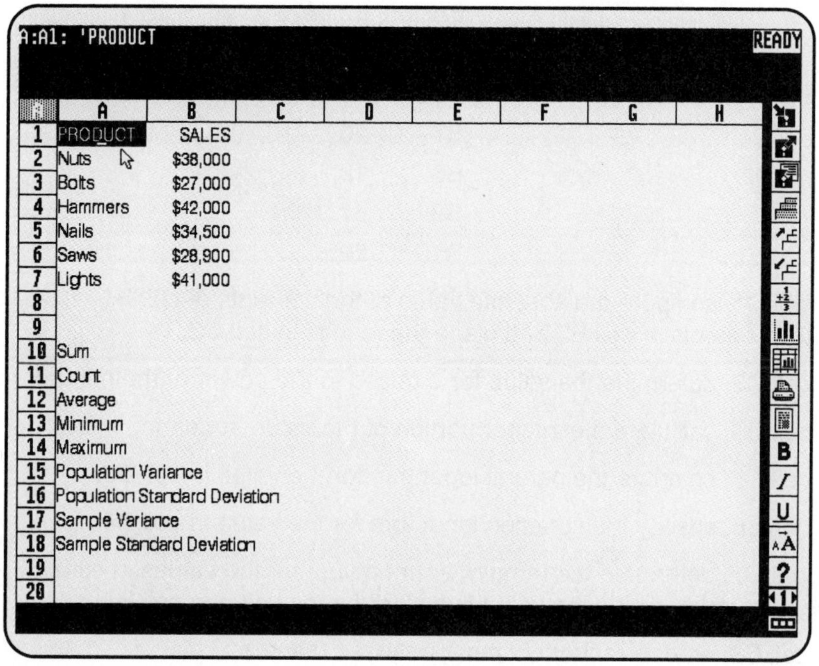

```
A:A1: 'PRODUCT                                                          READY

     A          B          C      D      E      F      G      H
 1  PRODUCT    SALES
 2  Nuts       $38,000
 3  Bolts      $27,000
 4  Hammers    $42,000
 5  Nails      $34,500
 6  Saws       $28,900
 7  Lights     $41,000
 8
 9
10  Sum
11  Count
12  Average
13  Minimum
14  Maximum
15  Population Variance
16  Population Standard Deviation
17  Sample Variance
18  Sample Standard Deviation
19
20
```

1. Construct criteria that will determine if a product included in the database table has sales of more than $35,000.

2. Place the appropriate database statistical functions in cells E10 through E18 to compute the indicated items.

Print the worksheet after answering questions 1 and 2.

EXERCISE 8 — Using the Mathematical Functions

INSTRUCTIONS: Make sure you have a blank worksheet on your screen. Then enter the following data on the worksheet.

Cell	Data
B1	-45
B2	45
B3	2
B4	52.9876
B5	1.5
B6	10
B7	20
B8	12
B9	67.3468
B10	225

1. In cell C1, compute the absolute value of the contents of cell B1. Calculate the absolute value of the contents of cell B2 and place the results in cell C2.

2. In cell C3, determine the value for *e* raised to the power of the number included in cell B3.

3. In cell C4, calculate the integer portion of the value appearing in cell B4.

4. In cell C5, compute the natural logarithm for the value in cell B5.

5. In cell B6, specify the common logarithm for the value in cell B6.

6. In cell C7, determine the remainder (modulus) for the values in cells B7 and B8. In computing the remainder, divide the value in cell B7 by the value in cell B8.

7. In cell C8, enter a random number between 0 and 1.

8. In cell C9, round the value appearing in cell B9 to three decimal places.

9. In cell C10, compute the square root of the value in cell B10.

Print the worksheet with the answers to questions 1 through 9. Also print the cell formulas.

EXERCISE 9 — Using the Cell, Range, and Error Trapping Functions

---

INSTRUCTIONS: Make sure you have a blank worksheet on your screen.

1. Enter the number 25 in cell A2. Place A2 in cell D1. Use the @@ function to place 25 in cell B3.

2. Define the range name COLUMNS that includes cells A1 through K1. In cell A5, specify the number of columns in the range named COLUMNS.

3. In cell A7, specify the worksheet coordinate C:$D$1 using the @COORD function.

4. Define the range named ROWS that includes cells B2 through B233. In cell A9, specify the number of rows in the range named ROWS.

5. Insert 5 worksheets after the current worksheet. Define the range name SHTS that includes cells B:A1 through F:A1 as its range. In cell A:A11 specify the number of sheets in the range SHTS.

6. Enter a 10 in cell B14 and a 0 in cell C14. In cell A14, place a formula that enters ERR in cell A14 when the value in cell C14 is zero; otherwise, compute the product of the values in cells B14 and C14.

7. Enter the number 100 in cell B16. Place the characters @NA (meaning not available) in cell A16 if the value in cell B16 is less than 500; otherwise, place the contents of cell B16 in cell A16.

Print the worksheet after solving questions 1 through 7. Also print the cell formulas.

EXERCISE 10 — Using the Lookup Functions

INSTRUCTIONS: Create the worksheet appearing in Figure 15-87.

Figure 15-87

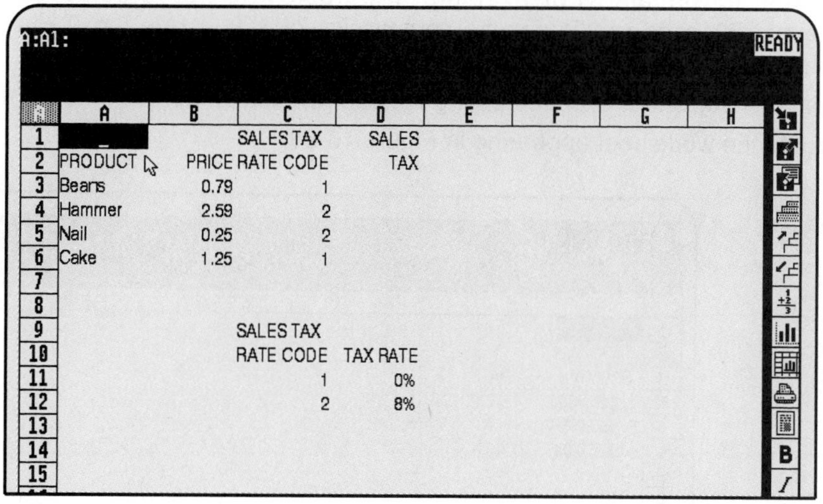

You need to compute the sales tax amount for the four products based on the sales tax rate code. Use the @CHOOSE function to assist you in computing the proper sales tax amount for the four items.

Print the worksheet after completing the calculation of the sales tax amounts. Also print the cell formulas.

Create the worksheet appearing in Figure 15-88.

Figure 15-88

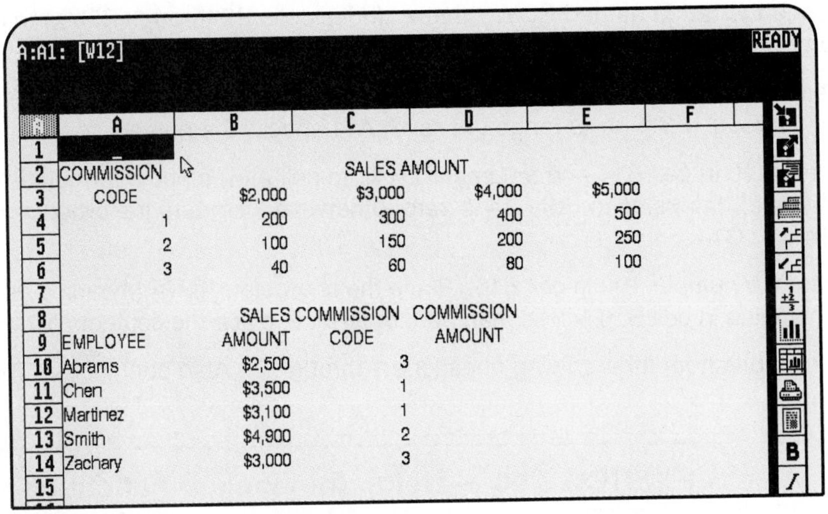

```
A:A1: [W12]                                                    READY

         A          B          C          D          E      F
1   ___
2   COMMISSION                    SALES AMOUNT
3       CODE       $2,000     $3,000     $4,000     $5,000
4           1         200        300        400        500
5           2         100        150        200        250
6           3          40         60         80        100
7
8                   SALES   COMMISSION  COMMISSION
9   EMPLOYEE        AMOUNT     CODE       AMOUNT
10  Abrams         $2,500        3
11  Chen           $3,500        1
12  Martinez       $3,100        1
13  Smith          $4,900        2
14  Zachary        $3,000        3
15
```

You need to calculate the commission owed each of the salespersons. The amount of commission is based on a commission code assigned to each individual and the sales amount for the individuals. For example, a person who has a sales amount of $2,800 and a commission code of 2 is owed a commission of $100. Use the @HLOOKUP function to help calculate the proper commission amounts.

Print the worksheet after computing the commission amounts. Also print the cell formulas.

Create the worksheet appearing in Figure 15-89.

Figure 15-89

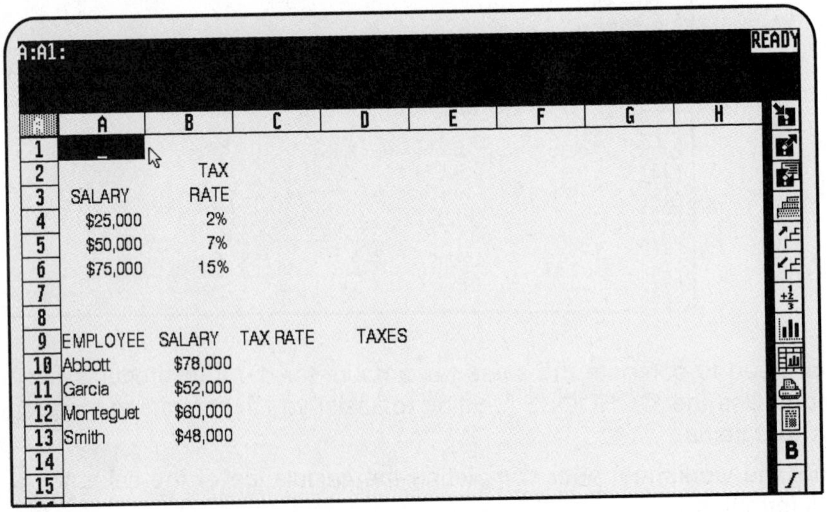

```
A:A1:                                                          READY

         A        B        C        D        E      F      G      H
1   ___
2                 TAX
3   SALARY       RATE
4   $25,000       2%
5   $50,000       7%
6   $75,000      15%
7
8
9   EMPLOYEE  SALARY   TAX RATE      TAXES
10  Abbott    $78,000
11  Garcia    $52,000
12  Monteguet $60,000
13  Smith     $48,000
14
15
```

You must compute the state income taxes owed by the individuals. The tax amount owed by each employee is computed by multiplying the salary amount times the appropriate tax rate. For example, if a person has a salary equal to $50,000, then the amount of state income tax due is $3,500. Use the @VLOOKUP function to determine the proper tax rate for each employee.

Print the worksheet after calculating the tax amount due for each of the employees. Also print the cell formulas.

EXERCISE 11 — Using the String Functions

INSTRUCTIONS: Make sure you have a blank worksheet on your screen.

1. Repeat the string of characters "Graph" six times in cell A1. Do not include the quotes.

2. Enter the label: "1-2-3 is a great software package" in cell A3. Do not include the quotes. Find the position of the word *great* in the label and place the answer in cell B4.

3. Using the label in cell A3, place the characters 1-2-3 in cell D4.

4. Using the label in cell A3, determine the number of characters in the label and place the answer in cell F4.

5. Using the label in cell A3, place the word *software* in cell B6.

6. Copy the label in cell A3 to cell A8. Using the label in cell A8, replace the word *great* with *wonderful*.

7. Using the label in cell A8, place the words *software package* in cell B9.

8. Enter the words "Fall is a beautiful time of year" in cell A11. Do not include the quotes.

9. Using the label in cell A11, change all of the letters to lowercase and place the results in cell A12.

10. Using the label in cell A11, change all of the letters to uppercase and place the results in cell A13.

11. Using the label in cell A11, capitalize the first letter in each word and make all other letters lowercase and place the results in cell A14.

Print the worksheet with the answers to questions 1 through 11. Also print the cell formulas.

EXERCISE 12 — Using the String Functions

INSTRUCTIONS: Make sure you have a blank worksheet on your screen.

1. Enter the number 592.783 in cell A1. Using the value in cell A1, change the value to a label with three decimal places and place the results in cell B1.

2. Enter the label "Lotus 1-2-3   is   fun to   use" in cell A3. Do not include the quotes. Remove the leading spaces and extra spaces between the words. Place the results in cell A4.

3. Enter 123.456 as a label in cell A6. Change the label in cell A6 to a number and place the results in cell B6.

4. Enter the string of characters "Northeast" in cell A8. Do not include the quotes. Place the same characters in cell A9 except omit the letter s. In cell A10, determine whether the contents of cells A8 and A9 are exactly the same. If they are not exactly the same, place a 0 in cell A10; otherwise, a 1 should appear in cell A10.

5. Place the values 1, 2 and 3 in cells A12, B12, and C12 respectively, and create the range name NUM that includes these cells as the range. In cell A13, place the contents of the first cell in the range if the first cell in the range is a value.

Print the worksheet after completing questions 1 through 5.

CHAPTER SIXTEEN

INTRODUCTION TO MACROS

OBJECTIVES

In this chapter, you will learn to:

- ■ Define range names for use in macros
- ■ Use a standard procedure for creating a macro
- ■ Place macros in a suitable location on a worksheet
- ■ Create and execute a macro
- ■ Debug a macro
- ■ Create a print macro
- ■ Create a macro using the record feature
- ■ Create and use a macro library
- ■ Add a macro to the User SmartIcon palette
- ■ Utilize a macro on the User SmartIcon palette
- ■ Remove a macro from the User SmartIcon palette

■ CHAPTER OVERVIEW

A **macro** is a set of written instructions representing keystrokes in Lotus 1-2-3. The macro keystrokes represent the keystrokes exactly as they are typed when you select them from various worksheet menus, enter data, or move the cell pointer.

Macros are especially useful when performing detailed, repetitive routines. You can write macros that consolidate worksheets, perform special edit routines, or print reports and graphs. Advanced uses of macros can involve using macro commands that perform loops, subroutines, *IF* statements, and many other features common to programming languages. A macro enables users of 1-2-3 to complete intricate spreadsheet analysis. In this chapter, you will learn the basics of macros. The next chapter contains more advanced macro topics.

■ DEFINING RANGE NAMES

A **range name** is a name that is assigned to a specific cell or group of cells. Range names are used to specify the location of a macro. They are also used to identify ranges of cells within macros. By using

551

range names, you can create macro programs that are more self-sufficient and require less editing and maintenance.

To illustrate the use of a range name, retrieve the BUDGET file you created in Chapter 4. Your screen should now look like Figure 16-1.

Figure 16-1

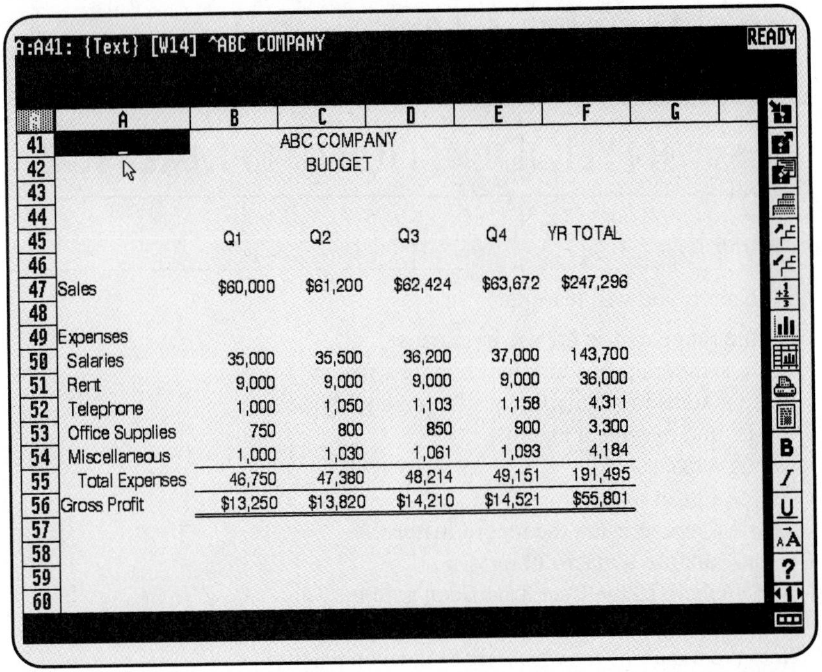

A:A41: {Text} [W14] ^ABC COMPANY READY

	A	B	C	D	E	F	G
41			ABC COMPANY				
42			BUDGET				
43							
44							
45		Q1	Q2	Q3	Q4	YR TOTAL	
46							
47	Sales	$60,000	$61,200	$62,424	$63,672	$247,296	
48							
49	Expenses						
50	Salaries	35,000	35,500	36,200	37,000	143,700	
51	Rent	9,000	9,000	9,000	9,000	36,000	
52	Telephone	1,000	1,050	1,103	1,158	4,311	
53	Office Supplies	750	800	850	900	3,300	
54	Miscellaneous	1,000	1,030	1,061	1,093	4,184	
55	Total Expenses	46,750	47,380	48,214	49,151	191,495	
56	Gross Profit	$13,250	$13,820	$14,210	$14,521	$55,801	
57							
58							
59							
60							

Suppose you want to use a range name to represent the Salaries values in cells B50 through E50.

To specify the range name SALARIES for these cells:

Highlight	cells B50 through E50
Press	[/]
Select	Range
Select	Name
Select	Create

Highlight	*cells B50 through E50*
Move	*the mouse pointer to the control panel*
Choose	*Range*
Choose	*Name*
Choose	*Create*

When prompted for a range name:

Type	SALARIES
Press	[←Enter]

Type	*SALARIES*
Click	*the mouse button*

Move the cell pointer to cell F50 and note that the @SUM formula now has SALARIES inside the parentheses rather than B50..E50. The range of cells associated with the named range SALARIES was substituted in the @SUM formula for the word SALARIES and the proper total was computed.

You can use the F5 key to move the cell pointer to the first cell in a range. For example:

Press   F5 | **_Click_**   _the GoTo_ 🔲 _SmartIcon_

When prompted for the address to go to:

Type   SALARIES | **_Type_**   _SALARIES_

Press   ←Enter | **_Click_**   _the mouse button_

The cell pointer is in cell B50.

■ PROCESS FOR CREATING A MACRO

The steps used to create a macro are:

1. *Practice the procedure* the macro is to perform. Manually press the keystrokes necessary to accomplish what the macro will do.

2. When you are sure of the keystrokes, perform them again and *write down each keystroke* exactly as it is to be typed.

3. With a written list of the macro keystrokes, type the keystrokes in an empty area of the worksheet in which the macro will be executed. It is a good idea to type in an area to the right of the Identification area.

   The macro instructions must be in the order of performance, must appear as labels, and must be contained in one column. If an instruction begins with any symbol other than an alphabet letter, you should start the command with an apostrophe (the ' symbol located below the " double quote). This procedure of manually inserting the apostrophe (') will prevent executing some commands as they are being typed (such as intending to type the / symbol and bringing up the command menu instead).

4. After entering the complete set of steps for the macro, *name the macro as a named range*. There are two ways to name a macro. You can use the \ key and a single letter, or a range name consisting of any combination of 15 allowable letters, such as PRINT_MACRO. Only the first cell in the column of macro steps is needed for the range name; however, the entire set of steps can be specified in the range. The macro will stop executing when it encounters a blank cell in the column containing the macro commands.

5. Before running and testing the macro, *save the file containing the worksheet and macro steps*. Then, if the macro does not work properly, you can retrieve the worksheet as it was before any changes were made by the macro.

6. *Execute the macro*. If you named your macro using the \ key and a single letter, you can run the macro by holding down the ALT key and then typing the letter. If the macro name consists of any other combination of characters, hold down the ALT key and press the F3 key. Then move the pointer to the desired macro name and press the ENTER key or type the name of the macro and press the ENTER key.

7. The macro should perform automatically. If it does not, the macro instructions are incorrect and you will need to *edit and revise the macro*. You may need to press the ESC key to exit a macro that has stopped because it encountered an error. Another way to stop a macro once it has begun execution is to hold down the CTRL key and press the BREAK key. The BREAK key is located on the PAUSE key on most keyboards.

   After determining the error, retrieve the original copy of the file with the macro. Edit the macro on the retrieved worksheet, then save and replace it before testing the macro again. If the original worksheet and macro are not retrieved from the disk after it has incorrectly run, the worksheet may contain unwanted changes that were made to the worksheet during macro execution.

8. After a macro has executed correctly, you should *document (write an explanation of what the macro instructions do)* the macro in a column to the right of the macro steps and then write the macro's name either above or to the left of the macro steps. The documentation process is optional. However, a written explanation of a macro's purpose will prove valuable to a user who did not create the macro, but needs to know what the macro does without spending extra time to analyze it. Documentation is also useful for the macro's author, saving time from having to decipher the macro at a later date when the macro may need to be altered or used in another application.

■ LOCATION OF A MACRO

Macros can be placed on separate files, separate worksheets, or on the same worksheet on which the macro is to be used. It is recommended that the macro be saved on a separate worksheet or on a separate file. By using either of these approaches for storing your macro, you are less likely to modify by accident the cells containing the macro keystrokes when you are working in the worksheet file.

If you must place the macro on the worksheet on which it will be used, place it to the right of the Identification area on the worksheet.

■ CREATING AND EXECUTING A MACRO

In Chapter 12, you consolidated salary information for three divisions of ABC Company into a summary worksheet. You then linked the total salary data appearing in the DIVISION file to the SALARIES row in the BUDGET file. 1-2-3 also allows you to combine information between files rather than linking them. In this section, you will build a macro to combine the total salary data from the summary worksheet in the DIVISION file into the BUDGET file.

In this example, you will place the macro instructions on worksheet B of the BUDGET file. By placing the macro instructions on a separate worksheet from the BUDGET worksheet, you are less likely to accidentally modify the cells containing the macro keystrokes.

Insert a worksheet after the BUDGET worksheet and place both worksheets on your screen. Make sure row 41 is the first visible row in worksheet A. Use the **W**orksheet **W**indow **U**nsync command sequence and have row 1 be the first visible row in worksheet B. After completing these steps, your screen should look like Figure 16-2.

Figure 16-2

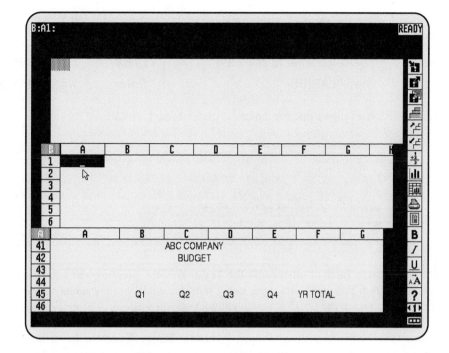

Manually Practicing the Macro Keystrokes and Recording Every Keystroke on Paper

For the purposes of this exercise, it is assumed that you have gone through the process for combining files and written the required keystrokes on a sheet of paper.

Entering the Keystrokes on the Worksheet

Begin entering the keystrokes by placing the name of the macro as a title on worksheet B.

Move	the cell pointer to cell B:A1	*Click*	*on cell B:A1*
Enter	Macro \C	*Enter*	*Macro \C*
Move	the cell pointer to cell B:B1	*Click*	*on cell B:B1*
Enter	Macro for combining data from the DIVISION file	*Enter*	*Macro for combining data from the DIVISION file*
Move	the cell pointer to B:B2	*Click*	*on cell B:B2*
Enter	into the BUDGET file	*Enter*	*into the BUDGET file*

When you name the macro later using the **R**ange **N**ame **C**reate command sequence, you will give it the name \C.

You will place the macro instructions as labels beginning in cell B:B4. To enter the first macro instruction:

Move	the cell pointer to cell B:B4		*Click*	*on cell B:B4*
Enter	'/reSALARIES~		*Enter*	*'/reSALARIES~*

SALARIES is a range name for the cells A:B50 through A:E50.

> *Design Tip*
>
> The use of range names in macros is very advantageous. For example, you may insert or delete rows in your worksheet. By using range names, the various ranges of cells you include in your macro are automatically updated. If range names are not used, you must revise the ranges manually.

The first macro instruction records the keystrokes for pressing the / key, selecting the **R**ange **E**rase command from the menu structure, using the SALARIES range name to specify the range of cells to erase, and pressing the ENTER key to complete the procedure. The entry must begin with an apostrophe to enter the keystrokes as a label. The ~ (**tilde**) character represents the ENTER key in a macro instruction. Notice that the command letters for **R**ange **E**rase are lowercase letters and that the range name SALARIES is in uppercase letters. This procedure is optional. Many macro authors use this convention so that the macro can be read more easily; the uppercase characters represent what you input, such as range names, cell addresses, or file names. The lowercase characters represent menu commands.

To enter the second macro instructions:

Move	the cell pointer to cell B:B5		*Click*	*on cell B:B5*
Enter	{goto}SALARIES~		*Enter*	*{goto}SALARIES~*

This second instruction records pressing the F5 key or clicking the GoTo 🔲 SmartIcon, typing the named range SALARIES, and pressing the ENTER key or clicking the mouse button with the mouse pointer in the control panel. As a result of executing this macro instruction, the cell pointer is moved to the initial cell in the range name SALARIES, which is cell A:B50 in this example.

To enter the third macro instruction:

Move	the cell pointer to cell B:B6		*Click*	*on cell B:B6*
Enter	'/fcanTOTAL~		*Enter*	*'/fcanTOTAL~*

In this third macro instruction, you have indicated that you want to execute the **F**ile **C**ombine **A**dd **N**amed/Specified-Range command sequence. TOTAL is the range name for the total salary cells in the DIVISION file that will be added to the SALARIES cells in the BUDGET file.

To specify the fourth macro instruction:

Move	the cell pointer to cell B:B7		*Click*	*on cell B:B7*
Enter	DIVISION~		*Enter*	*DIVISION~*

This fourth instruction indicates that the range name TOTAL is in the DIVISION file. Before executing the macro, you will need to define TOTAL as the range name for cells A:B30 through A:E30 in the DIVISION file that contains the total of the salaries for the three divisions. When this macro instruction is executed, the values from the range name TOTAL in the DIVISION file are added to the respective cells of the range name SALARIES in the BUDGET file.

To enter the final macro instruction:

Move	the cell pointer to cell B:B8		***Click***	*on cell B:B8*
Enter	{goto}BEGIN~		***Enter***	*{goto}BEGIN~*

This last instruction is optional. It was included so that the cell pointer is moved to the beginning of the spreadsheet model after the macro is executed. In this case, you need to create the range name BEGIN that has the cell A:A41 as its range. If the cell pointer is not in cell A:A41 after the macro is executed, you will know that the macro has not executed correctly. When all of the macro instructions are entered, your screen should look like Figure 16-3.

Figure 16-3

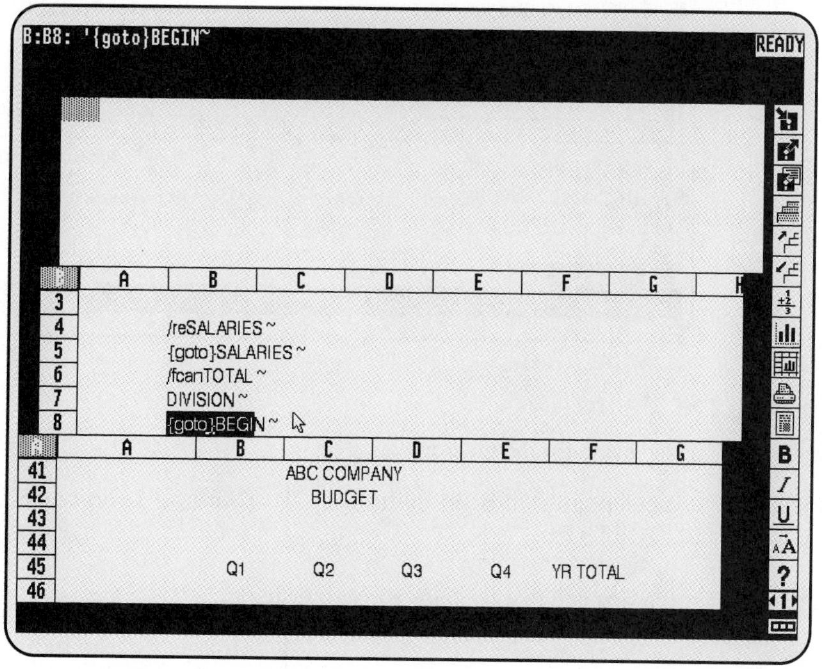

The range name SALARIES which includes the range of cells A:B50 through A:E50 was created earlier in this chapter. Create the range name BEGIN that includes cell A:A41 as its range.

To save the range names and the macro worksheet, save the file with the name BUDGET3 using the **File Save** command sequence.

Before you can define the range name TOTAL, you must open the DIVISION file and place it after the BUDGET file. Use the **File O**pen **A**fter command sequence or click the Open [icon] SmartIcon to open the DIVISION file. Define the range name TOTAL with cells A:B30 through A:E30 as its range.

Use the **W**orksheet **W**indow **U**nsync command sequence and adjust the location of the rows in the worksheets so your screen looks like Figure 16-4.

Figure 16-4

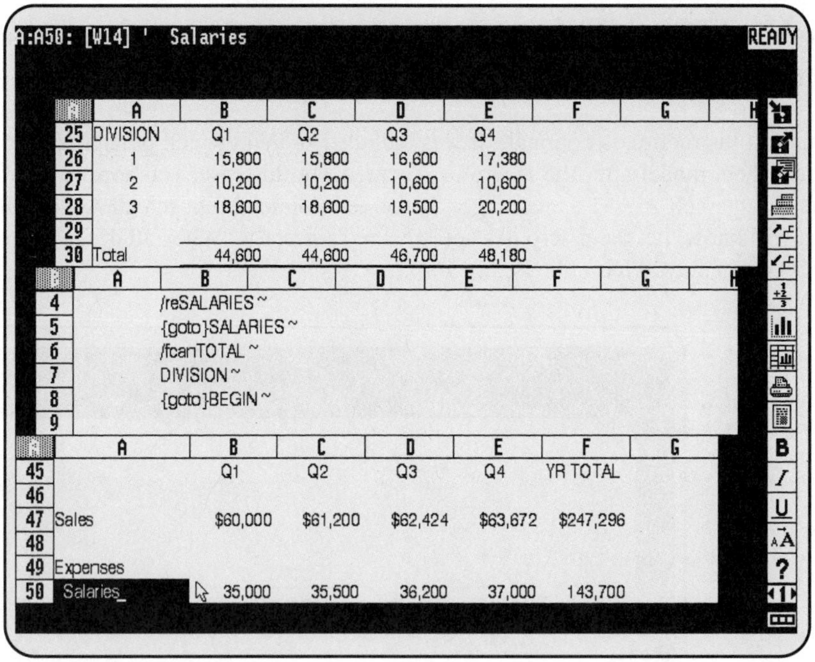

Naming the Macro

To define \C as the name for the macro:

Move	the cell pointer to B:B4 in the BUDGET3 file	**Click**	on cell B:B4 in the BUDGET3 file

Note that B4 is the first cell that contains a macro instruction.

Press	[/]	**Move**	the mouse pointer to the control panel
Select	Range	**Choose**	Range
Select	Name	**Choose**	Name
Select	Create	**Choose**	Create

When prompted to enter the macro name:

Type	\C		*Type*	*\C*
Press	←Enter		*Click*	*the mouse button*

To indicate the first cell of the macro as the range:

Press	←Enter		*Click*	*the mouse button with the mouse pointer in the control panel*

The macro now is named \C. The macro will execute the instructions in cell A:B4 and continue executing macro instructions in column B below cell A:B4 until it encounters a blank cell. When a blank cell is found, the macro stops executing. If you so desire, you can include all cells with the macro instructions in the range name \C.

Saving the File Containing the Macro Keystrokes

Before executing or testing the macro, you should save the file containing the macro and any worksheets that were modified. In this case, you need to save the BUDGET3 and the DIVISION files.

To save all modified files:

Press	/		*Click*	*the File Save* 🔳 *SmartIcon*
Select	File			
Select	Save			
Press	←Enter			

By pressing the ENTER key or clicking the File Save 🔳 SmartIcon, you indicated that all modified files are to be saved.

When prompted whether to **C**ancel, **R**eplace, or **B**ackup:

Select	Replace		*Choose*	*Replace*

Executing the Macro

To execute the macro:

Press	Alt + C		*Press*	*Alt + C*

The macro then executes. If the macro has executed properly, your screen should look like Figure 16-5.

Figure 16-5

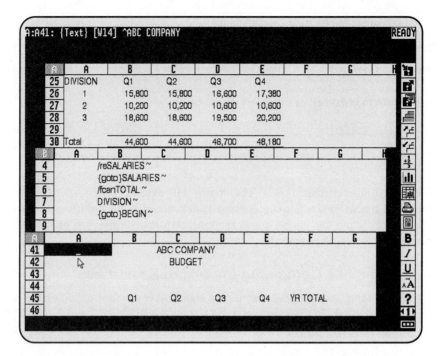

To see the results of the macro on the SALARIES row, move the cell pointer to cell A:A50 in the BUDGET3 worksheet. Notice that the cells in the range name TOTAL (cells A:B30 through A:E30 in the DIVISION file) have been added to the cells in the range name SALARIES of the BUDGET3 file. Your screen should look like Figure 16-6.

Figure 16-6

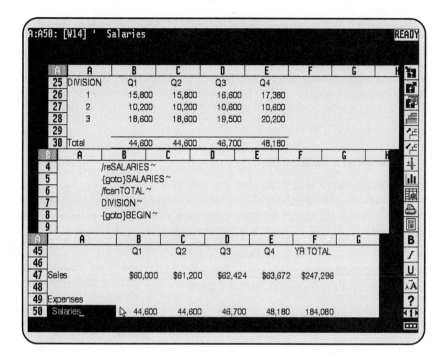

Editing and Correcting a Macro

If the macro stops and *beeps*, look carefully at the screen to determine at what point the macro seemed to have trouble executing. To exit the macro, press the CTRL+BREAK keys simultaneously. (The BREAK key is located on the PAUSE key.) Depending on the macro, you may need to press the ESC key after pressing CTRL+BREAK. Move to the area where the macro instructions are written to see if the error can be determined. Compare your screen with Figure 16-3. Typical errors include:

- Macro steps were preceded with an incorrect symbol (use the apostrophe on the double quote key).

- Another character was entered instead of the tilde (~) or a tilde was omitted in an instruction.

- Parentheses (the ( ) symbols) or brackets (the [ ] symbols) were entered instead of braces (the { } symbols).

- The backward slash (the \ symbol) was used instead of the slash (the / symbol). Recall that the backward slash is a repeating prefix that repeats any characters following it or is used for naming the macro.

- A space was inserted in an inappropriate place.

- The letter O was typed instead of a zero; the lowercase letter l was typed instead of the number one.

If the macro doesn't execute at all or attempts to enter a label and stops, consider these two typical errors:

- The forward slash was used for the range name instead of the backward slash (use **R**ange **N**ame **C**reate to see if the range was named /C instead of \C), or no range name was given to the macro.

■ The range name was correct, but the first line of the macro is not a macro step (for example, if the top cell of the macro is a blank cell, the macro will never start executing).

Once the error is determined, **retrieve** the original copy of the BUDGET3 file without saving any changes to the previous worksheet and correct the appropriate macro steps(s). Then **save** the file before trying to execute the macro again. If the original file is not retrieved, the results of the incorrect macro will remain on the spreadsheet. Save the file after the macro executes properly using the **F**ile **S**ave **R**eplace command sequence.

Documenting the Macro

Documenting a macro is optional, but you can save valuable time later when you are trying to edit or execute the macro. The documentation in this example explains every cell of the macro. Sometimes it is more appropriate to document a macro by writing a paragraph to explain a macro's overall purpose and then write additional paragraphs to explain sections.

To enter the corresponding explanations of the macro commands in column C to document what the macro does, retrieve the BUDGET3 file using the **F**ile **R**etrieve command sequence.

To create a title for the macro (an optional step):

Move	the cell pointer to cell B:A4	*Click*	*on cell B:A4*
Enter	'\C	*Enter*	*'\C*

Recall that you placed Macro \C in cell B:A1.

Creating a title is optional, because it is not required to make the macro execute; however, the macro title is useful as documentation. A common convention is to put the macro name in the column to the left of the macro keystrokes. In this way, if several macros are on a single worksheet, the names will be clearly visible in the column to the left of the macro steps.

To document the macro steps:

Move	the cell pointer to cell B:D4	*Click*	*on cell B:D4*

Refer to Figure 16-7 to enter the documentation for the macro in cells B:D4 through B:D8.

Figure 16-7

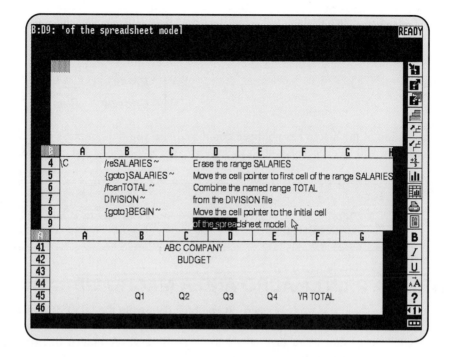

After entering the documentation:

Move   the cell pointer to cell A:A41 | ***Click***   *on cell A:A41*

Save the BUDGET3 file using the **F**ile **S**ave **R**eplace command sequence.

■ PROCESS FOR DEBUGGING A MACRO

Whenever a macro contains many instructions, it may be difficult to determine which macro entry may be causing an error. Fortunately, Lotus 1-2-3 has a feature that permits executing the macro one keystroke at a time. This process can be used to help eliminate errors, sometimes referred to as "bugs," and is therefore often called "debugging."

To use the single-step mode of execution:

Press   [Alt]+[F2] | ***Press***   [Alt]+[F2]
Select   Step | ***Choose***   *Step*

The word STEP now appears at the bottom of your screen. When you execute the macro you are examining, it will be executed one keystroke at a time. You will press ENTER each time you want to move to the next keystroke in the macro. As you start executing the macro, the macro commands replace the date and time indicator in the status line. If you execute the \C macro created in the last section, the cell address and characters for the macro keystrokes in cell B:B4 should appear in the status line. As you press the ENTER key, the next character is highlighted.

When an error is determined, press CTRL+BREAK to stop the execution of the macro. You can then edit the appropriate cell contents in the macro so the macro will execute properly.

To leave the STEP mode:

Press	Alt + F2		**Press**	Alt + F2
Select	Step		**Choose**	Step

If execution of the macro has not been completed and you did not press CTRL+BREAK, the remaining macro steps will be executed as soon as you leave the STEP mode and press the ENTER key.

User Tip

An alternative method for initiating the STEP mode is to click the Step 🏃 SmartIcon. To stop using the STEP mode, click the Step 🏃 SmartIcon.

■ CREATING A PRINT MACRO AND A MACRO LIBRARY

In the last section, you wrote a macro to combine data from the DIVISION file into the BUDGET file. Macros can also be used to print worksheets. In this section, you will write a macro to print the BUDGET3 worksheet, and then create a macro library. A **macro library** is a convenient way to organize macros that can be used with many worksheet files.

You developed the macro called \C to combine salary information from the DIVISION file into the BUDGET3 file. It is logical to include such a macro on a separate worksheet in the BUDGET3 file, because you are not very likely to use it for other files.

However, when you do need to use the same macro in more than one file, it is a good idea to save it on a separate file. The macro file can then be opened when necessary and used with a specific worksheet in another file. When you have several such macros, you may want to combine them on one file and create a macro library.

An example of a macro that might be included in a macro library is one that can be used to print worksheets. To illustrate the process of creating a macro library, you will first add a new file for the library, then create a macro to print the BUDGET3 worksheet, and then save the macro in a file you will use as a macro library.

Before creating the print macro, erase whatever you presently have on your screen and retrieve the BUDGET3 file.

The first step in creating the print macro and a macro library is to add a new file after the BUDGET3 file.

Press	/		**Move**	the mouse pointer to the control panel
Select	File		**Choose**	File
Select	New		**Choose**	New

Select	After		*Choose*	*After*

When you are prompted for the name of the file:

Type	MACROLIB		*Type*	*MACROLIB*
Press	⌷←Enter⌷		*Click*	*the mouse button*

You have indicated that the file MACROLIB is to be placed after the BUDGET3 file.

To give the macro a title and a description:

Move	the cell pointer to cell A:A1 in the MACROLIB file		*Click*	*on cell A:A1 in the MACROLIB file*
Enter	PRINT_MACRO		*Enter*	*PRINT_MACRO*
Move	the cell pointer to cell A:B1		*Click*	*on cell A:B1*
Enter	Macro for printing a spreadsheet		*Enter*	*Macro for printing a spreadsheet*

The macro name will be created later. Widen column A to 12 so it contains the entire macro title.

To enter the first instruction of the macro:

Move	the cell pointer to cell A:B3		*Click*	*on cell A:B3*
Enter	{goto}BEGIN~		*Enter*	*{goto}BEGIN~*

This instruction makes sure that the cell pointer is in the cell at the top left corner of the spreadsheet model before you print the spreadsheet.

To place the second instruction of the macro on the worksheet:

Move	the cell pointer to cell A:B4		*Click*	*on cell A:B4*
Enter	':prsPRINT_RANGE~g		*Enter*	*':prsPRINT_RANGE~g*

This instruction specifies that the range of cells defined by the range name PRINT_RANGE is to be printed and to print the worksheet range.

Your screen should now look like Figure 16-8.

Figure 16-8

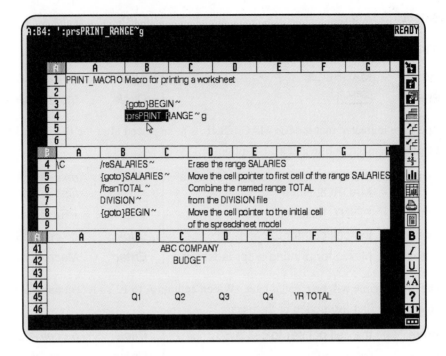

To name the macro:

Move	the cell pointer to cell A:B3 in the MACROLIB file		*Click*	on cell A:B3 in the MACROLIB file
Press	[/]		*Move*	the mouse pointer to the control panel
Select	Range		*Choose*	Range
Select	Name		*Choose*	Name
Select	Create		*Choose*	Create

To enter the name to create:

Type	PRINT_MACRO		*Type*	PRINT_MACRO
Press	[←Enter]		*Click*	the mouse button

Notice that you used a different naming mechanism. This approach was taken so you can learn to execute a macro using a different method from the one described in the last section.

To specify the initial cell of the macro as the range:

Press	[←Enter]		*Click*	the mouse button with the mouse pointer in the control panel

Before executing the macro, you need to specify the range of cells to be printed by creating the named range of cells, PRINT_RANGE, and save all modified files.

Highlight	cells A:A41 through A:F66 in the BUDGET3 file		*Highlight*	*cells A:A41 through A:F66 in the BUDGET3 file*
Press	⟋		*Move*	*the mouse pointer to the control panel*
Select	Range		*Choose*	*Range*
Select	Name		*Choose*	*Name*
Select	Create		*Choose*	*Create*

When prompted for the name of the range to create:

Type	PRINT_RANGE		*Type*	*PRINT_RANGE*
Press	←Enter		*Click*	*the mouse button*

Save all modified files using the **F**ile **S**ave **R**eplace command sequence.

To execute PRINT_MACRO:

Move	the cell pointer to cell A:A41 in the BUDGET3 file		*Click*	*on cell A:A41 in the BUDGET3 file*
Press	Alt + F3		*Press*	*Alt + F3*

To select the PRINT_MACRO from the macro library file MACROLIB:

Press	F3		*Press*	*F3*
Select	<<MACROLIB.WK3>>		*Choose*	*<<MACROLIB.WK3>>*

You have indicated that the macro you need to use is in the MACROLIB file.

To specify PRINT_MACRO is the appropriate macro to use:

Press	F3		*Press*	*F3*
Select	PRINT_MACRO		*Choose*	*PRINT_MACRO*

The BUDGET3 worksheet will then be printed.

User Tip

An alternative method to using the ALT+F3 key combination for selecting a macro to run is to click the Run 📶 SmartIcon.

Document your print macro using the information in Figure 16-9.

Figure 16-9

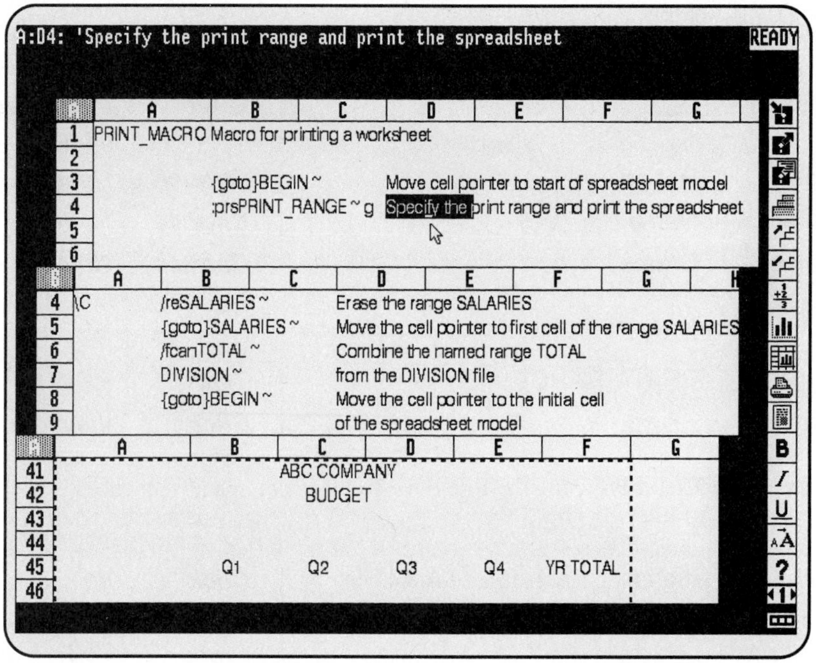

A:D4: 'Specify the print range and print the spreadsheet   READY

	A	B	C	D	E	F	G
1	PRINT_MACRO Macro for printing a worksheet						
2							
3		{goto}BEGIN ~		Move cell pointer to start of spreadsheet model			
4		:prsPRINT_RANGE ~ g		Specify the print range and print the spreadsheet			
5							
6							

	A	B	C	D	E	F	G	H
4	\C	/reSALARIES ~		Erase the range SALARIES				
5		{goto}SALARIES ~		Move the cell pointer to first cell of the range SALARIES				
6		/fcanTOTAL ~		Combine the named range TOTAL				
7		DIVISION ~		from the DIVISION file				
8		{goto}BEGIN ~		Move the cell pointer to the initial cell				
9				of the spreadsheet model				

	A	B	C	D	E	F	G
41			ABC COMPANY				
42			BUDGET				
43							
44							
45		Q1	Q2	Q3	Q4	YR TOTAL	
46							

Save the MACROLIB file so the documentation will be permanently attached to the macro instructions.

■ CREATING A MACRO USING THE RECORD FEATURE

In the first part of this chapter, you created a macro by entering the macro keystrokes that comprise the macro instructions one keystroke at a time. As you work through the remaining portion of this chapter, you will learn an easier way to create a macro.

You will recreate the macro which was completed earlier using the **record** capability of 1-2-3. Prior to recording the macro, make sure the worksheet from the original BUDGET file is on your screen. Create the range name SALARIES that include the range of cells B50 through E50. Create the range name BEGIN that includes cell A41 as its range.

In this exercise, you will place the macro on a worksheet within the BUDGET file. However, you could also use a separate file or include the macro in the macro library file you created in the last section.

Insert another worksheet after worksheet A in the BUDGET file, and use the **W**orksheet **W**indow **P**erspective command sequence or click the Perspective SmartIcon to display both worksheets. Use the **W**orksheet **W**indow **U**nSync command sequence and have row 41 be the first row in worksheet A.

To place a title for the macro on the worksheet:

| **Move** | the cell pointer to cell B:A3 | **Click** | on cell B:A3 |
| **Enter** | '\C | **Enter** | '\C |

Rather than recording the macro keystrokes on paper as you go through the process of combining the data from the DIVISION file into the worksheet in the BUDGET file, you can have 1-2-3 record the keystrokes for you. There are four steps you need to complete:

1. Enter the record mode.
2. Erase the record buffer.
3. Complete the task you want to include in the macro.
4. Place the recorded keystrokes on the appropriate worksheet.

Recording the Macro Keystrokes

To enter the record mode:

Press	Alt + F2		***Press***	*Alt + F2*
Select	Copy		***Choose***	*Copy*

There may already be some characters in the record buffer that you do not want to include in your macro. To erase the characters:

Press	Esc twice		***Click***	*the alternate mouse button twice*
Select	Erase		***Choose***	*Erase*

Now you are ready to go through the process you used earlier in this chapter to combine the salary information from the DIVISION file into worksheet A of the BUDGET3 file. You need not be concerned about typing errors, because you can correct them at a later point.

Record the following keystrokes:

Press	F5		***Click***	*the GoTo ⊶ SmartIcon*
Type	BEGIN		***Type***	*BEGIN*
Press	←Enter		***Click***	*the mouse button*
Press	/		***Move***	*the mouse pointer to the control panel*
Select	Range		***Choose***	*Range*
Select	Erase		***Choose***	*Erase*
Type	SALARIES		***Type***	*SALARIES*
Press	←Enter		***Click***	*the mouse button*
Press	F5		***Click***	*the GoTo ⊶ SmartIcon*
Type	SALARIES		***Type***	*SALARIES*
Press	←Enter		***Click***	*the mouse button*
Press	/		***Move***	*the mouse pointer to the control panel*

Select	File		***Choose***	*File*
Select	Combine		***Choose***	*Combine*
Select	Add		***Choose***	*Add*
Select	Named/Specified-Range		***Choose***	*Named/Specified-Range*
Type	TOTAL		***Type***	*TOTAL*
Press	⏎Enter		***Click***	*the mouse button*
Type	DIVISION		***Type***	*DIVISION*
Press	⏎Enter		***Click***	*the mouse button*
Press	F5		***Click***	*the GoTo* 🚌 *SmartIcon*
Type	BEGIN		***Type***	*BEGIN*
Press	⏎Enter		***Click***	*the mouse button*

To see the recorded keystrokes:

Press	Alt + F2		***Press***	*Alt + F2*
Select	Copy		***Choose***	*Copy*

You can see the keystrokes that have been recorded at the top of the screen. Your screen should look similar to Figure 16-10. If you made typing errors while entering the keystrokes, you screen will not look like Figure 16-10, but you can correct the errors shortly.

Figure 16-10

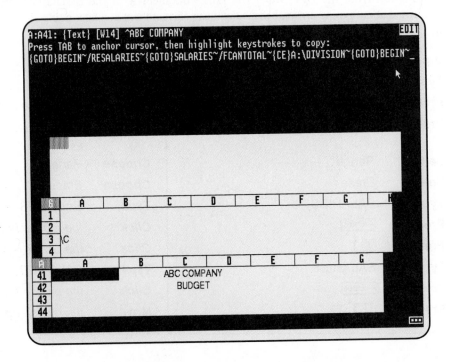

When you are finished comparing your screen with Figure 16-10:

Press	Esc three times		***Click***	*the alternate mouse button three times*

Placing the Macro Keystrokes on the Appropriate Worksheet

To copy the macro keystrokes on worksheet B and place the keystrokes in cells based on logical break points in the macro:

Move	the cell pointer to cell B:B3		***Click***	*on cell B:B3*
Widen	column B so it contains 15 characters		***Widen***	*column B so it contains 15 characters*

You need to widen column B so the longest macro instruction can fit in a cell. Otherwise, 1-2-3 will place some of the characters in the cell below.

To enter the first macro instruction in cell B:B3:

Press	Alt + F2		***Press***	*Alt + F2*
Select	Copy		***Choose***	*Copy*

To move to the initial character in the macro keystroke string:

Press	Home		***Press***	*Home*

To specify the cells to copy:

Press	Tab⇆		***Press***	*Tab⇆*

The TAB key is used rather than the period to identify the initial character to highlight.

Press	→		***Press***	*→*

until the first ~ (tilde) keystroke is highlighted. Your screen should look like Figure 16-11.

Figure 16-11

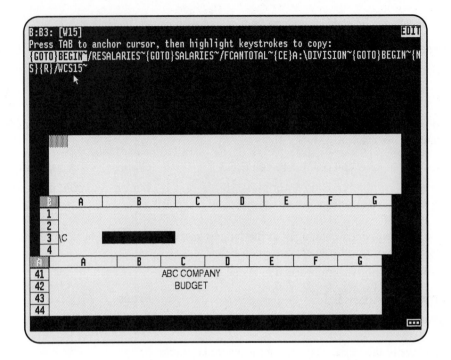

To place the highlighted keystrokes in cell B:B3:

| **Press** | ⟨←Enter⟩ twice | | **Press** | ⟨←Enter⟩ twice |

The first ENTER key indicates that the highlighted keystrokes are to be copied. The second ENTER key confirms that you want the keystrokes copied to cell B:B3. This set of keystrokes specifies the cell pointer is to be moved to the beginning of the spreadsheet model in cell A:A41.

To place the second macro instruction in cell B:B4:

Move	the cell pointer to cell B:B4	**Click**	on cell B:B4
Press	⟨Alt⟩ + ⟨F2⟩	**Press**	⟨Alt⟩ + ⟨F2⟩
Select	Copy	**Choose**	Copy
Move	the cursor to the first /	**Move**	the cursor to the first /
Press	⟨Tab⟩	**Press**	⟨Tab⟩
Press	⟨→⟩ until the ~ (tilde) after the first occurrence of SALARIES is highlighted	**Press**	⟨→⟩ until the ~ (tilde) after the first occurrence of SALARIES is highlighted
Press	⟨←Enter⟩ twice	**Press**	⟨←Enter⟩ twice

This set of keystrokes indicates that the cells in the range name SALARIES are to be erased.

To place the third macro instruction in cell B:B5:

Move	the cell pointer to cell B:B5		*Click*	*on cell B:B5*
Press	Alt + F2		*Press*	*Alt + F2*
Select	Copy		*Choose*	*Copy*
Move	the cursor to the second {		*Move*	*the cursor to the second {*
Press	Tab⇆		*Press*	*Tab⇆*
Press	→ until the ~ (tilde) after {GOTO}SALARIES is highlighted		*Press*	*→ until the ~ (tilde) after {GOTO}SALARIES is highlighted*
Press	←Enter twice		*Press*	*←Enter twice*

This set of keystrokes indicates that the cell pointer is to be moved to the initial cell in the range name SALARIES. In this example, the cell pointer will be moved to cell A:B50 when the macro is executed.

Enter the fourth macro instruction in cell B:B6:

Move	the cell pointer to cell B:B6		*Click*	*on cell B:B6*
Press	Alt + F2		*Press*	*Alt + F2*
Select	Copy		*Choose*	*Copy*
Highlight	/FCANTOTAL~		*Highlight*	*/FCANTOTAL~*
Press	←Enter twice		*Press*	*←Enter twice*

With this macro instruction, you have specified that you want 1-2-3 to complete a **F**ile **C**ombine **A**dd command sequence using the cells in range name TOTAL.

Enter the fifth macro instruction in cell B:B7:

Move	the cell pointer to cell B:B7		*Click*	*on cell B:B7*
Press	Alt + F2		*Press*	*Alt + F2*
Select	Copy		*Choose*	*Copy*
Highlight	{CE}A:\DIVISION~		*Highlight*	*{CE}A:\DIVISION~*
Press	←Enter twice		*Press*	*←Enter twice*

This set of macro keystrokes indicates that the named range TOTAL is in the DIVISION file. The {CE} command clears the default entry that appears in the control panel. It has the same effect as pressing the ESC key.

To enter the sixth and final macro instruction:

Move	the cell pointer to cell B:B8		*Click*	*on cell B:B8*
Press	Alt + F2		*Press*	*Alt + F2*

Select	Copy		***Choose***	*Copy*
Highlight	{GOTO}BEGIN~		***Highlight***	*{GOTO}BEGIN~*
Press	⟵Enter twice		***Press***	*⟵Enter twice*

This set of macro keystrokes moves the cell pointer to the beginning of the spreadsheet model. Your screen should look like Figure 16-12.

Figure 16-12

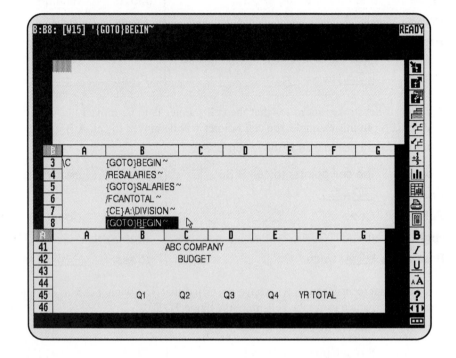

If you have errors in any of the cells, correct them using Figure 16-12 as a guide.

To name the macro:

Move	the cell pointer to cell B:B3		***Click***	*on cell B:B3*
Press	/		***Move***	*the mouse pointer to the control panel*
Select	Range		***Choose***	*Range*
Select	Name		***Choose***	*Name*
Select	Create		***Choose***	*Create*

When prompted for a range name:

Type	\C		***Type***	*\C*
Press	⟵Enter		***Click***	*the mouse button*

To specify the first cell in the macro as the range:

Press	←Enter		**Click**	the mouse button with the mouse pointer in the control panel

Executing the Macro

Before executing the macro, save the file using the name BUDGET4.

To execute the macro:

Press	Alt + C		**Press**	Alt + C

The macro will then execute. Move the cell pointer to cell A:B50 to see that the macro did in fact execute properly. Your screen should look like Figure 16-13.

Figure 16-13

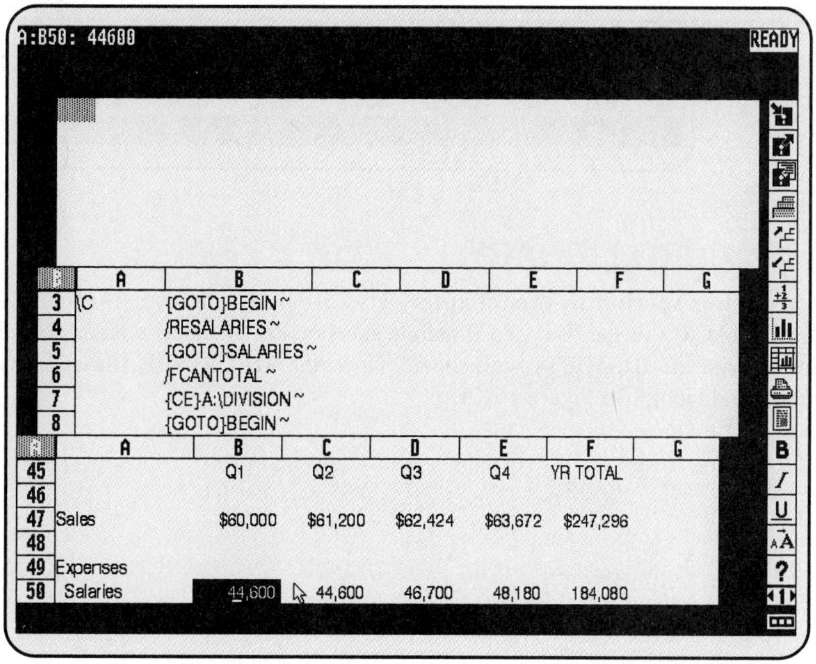

Document your macro using the comments in Figure 16-14 to specify the macro title and what the individual instructions do.

Figure 16-14

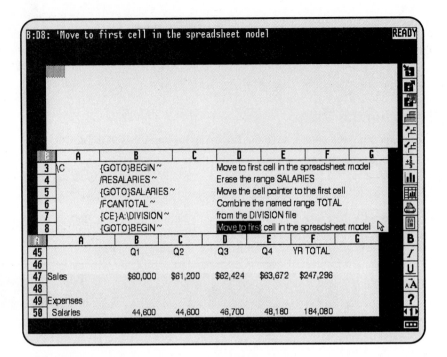

■ USING A MACRO LIBRARY

In an earlier section in this chapter, you created a macro library file and saved the macro PRINT_MACRO in the file. To illustrate the process of using a macro library, assume that you now want to print the BUDGET4 worksheet. Open the MACROLIB file after the BUDGET4 file. Your screen should look like Figure 16-15.

Figure 16-15

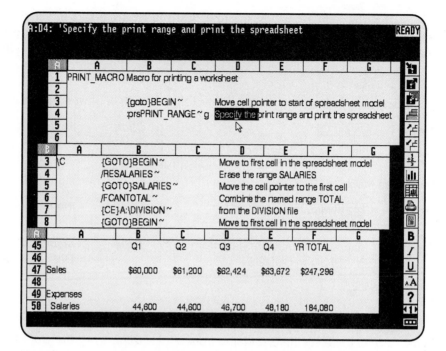

Before executing the macro PRINT_MACRO, create the range name PRINT_RANGE that includes the range of cells A:A41 through A:F66 in the BUDGET4 file.

To execute the macro and print the worksheet:

Move	the cell pointer to any cell in worksheet A of the BUDGET4 file	*Click*	*on any cell in worksheet A of the BUDGET4 file*
Press	Alt + F3	*Press*	*Alt + F3*
Press	F3	*Press*	*F3*
Select	<<MACROLIB.WK3>>	*Choose*	*<<MACROLIB.WK3>>*
Select	PRINT_MACRO	*Choose*	*PRINT_MACRO*

The macro will then execute and print the specified range.

■ ADDING A MACRO TO THE USER SMARTICON PALETTE

Macros can be assigned to the **User SmartIcon palette**. This palette has the user SmartIcons U1 through U12 on it and is the last SmartIcon palette.

You can either create a macro for the specific user SmartIcon or copy a macro that already exists on a worksheet to the user SmartIcon.

Suppose that you want to copy the macro \C that you created earlier in this chapter and place it on the user SmartIcon U1. Then, whenever you want to combine the information from the DIVISION worksheet into the BUDGET worksheet, you can select the U1 user SmartIcon rather than use the macro \C. This approach is very useful when you repeat the use of the macro and do not wish to remember the name of the macro.

Before beginning this example, make sure the original BUDGET4 worksheet is on your screen.

Press	Ctrl + F10	**Click**	the User U SmartIcon
Select	the User U SmartIcon		

The Assign Macro to U1 dialog box appears. To complete the information in the dialog box:

Press	Tab⇆ twice to select the Icon Description text box	**Click**	the Icon Description text box
Type	Macro for combining data from DIVISION to BUDGET	**Type**	*Macro for combining data from DIVISION to BUDGET*
Press	←Enter		

The description of the macro appears on the dialog box.

Type	G to select the Get Macro from Sheet command button	**Click**	the Get Macro from Sheet command button
Highlight	cells B:B3 through B:B8	**Highlight**	*cells B:B3 through B:B8*
Press	←Enter	**Click**	*the mouse button*

The macro commands in cells B:B3 through B:B8 have been copied to the Macro Text area. Your screen should look like Figure 16-16.

Figure 16-16

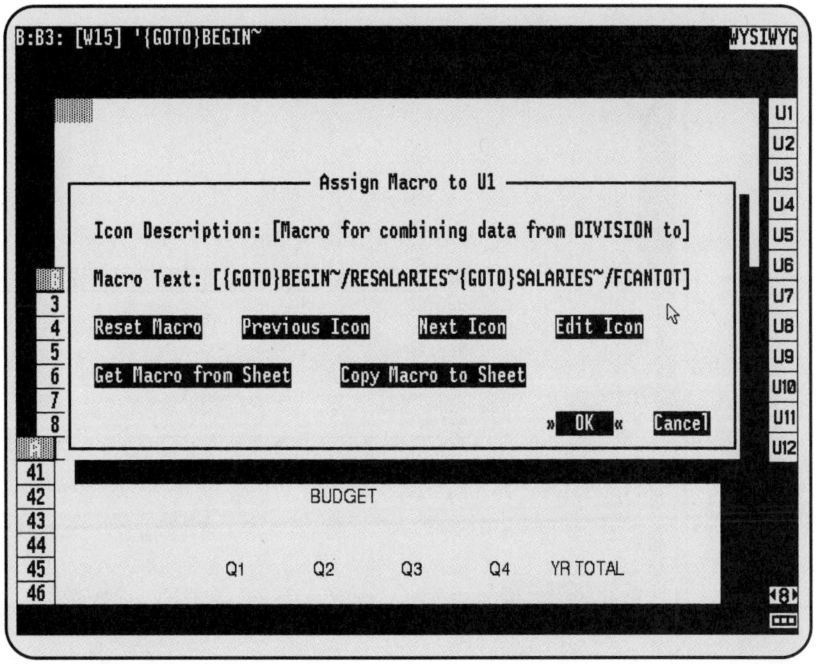

```
B:B3: [W15] '{GOTO}BEGIN~                                              WYSIWYG

                                                                          U1
                                                                          U2
                          ─── Assign Macro to U1 ───                      U3
                                                                          U4
        Icon Description: [Macro for combining data from DIVISION to]     U5
                                                                          U6
        Macro Text: [{GOTO}BEGIN~/RESALARIES~{GOTO}SALARIES~/FCANTOT]     U7
     3
     4   Reset Macro    Previous Icon     Next Icon      Edit Icon        U8
     5                                                                    U9
     6   Get Macro from Sheet      Copy Macro to Sheet                    U10
     7
     8                                   »  OK  «     Cancel              U11
                                                                          U12
    41
    42                          BUDGET
    43
    44
    45           Q1      Q2       Q3      Q4     YR TOTAL
    46
```

To complete the process:

Press   ⏎Enter | *Click*   *the OK command button*

Save the worksheet using the name BUDGET5.

■ UTILIZING A USER SMARTICON

After a macro is assigned to a user SmartIcon, it can be executed by pressing the CTRL+F10 key combination and selecting the user SmartIcon with the pointer-movement keys or by using the mouse to click the user SmartIcon.

For example, suppose you want to execute the macro you assigned to the U1 user SmartIcon in the BUDGET5 worksheet. Make sure the BUDGET5 worksheet and the desired User SmartIcon palette appear on your screen.

To execute the macro \C using the U1 user SmartIcon:

Press   Ctrl + F10 | *Click*   *the U1 user* *SmartIcon*
Select   the U1 user SmartIcon |

The macro is executed. After moving the cell pointer to cell A:A50, your screen should look like Figure 16-17.

Figure 16-17

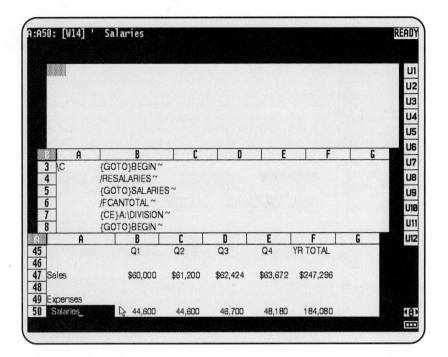

■ REMOVING A MACRO FROM THE USER SMARTICON PALETTE

A macro can be removed from the User SmartIcon palette. Make sure the BUDGET5 worksheet is on your screen.

To remove the macro you assigned to the ⎡U1⎤ user SmartIcon:

Press	⎡Ctrl⎤ + ⎡F10⎤	***Click***	*the User* **U** *SmartIcon*
Select	the User **U** SmartIcon	***Click***	*the Reset Macro command button*
Type	R to select the Reset Macro command button	***Click***	*the OK command*
Press	⎡←Enter⎤		

The macro \C has been removed from the User SmartIcon palette.

SUMMARY

A macro is a way to automate Lotus 1-2-3 keystrokes. Macros provide an efficient way to automate repetitive procedures. Macros permit users who are unfamiliar with 1-2-3 to perform spreadsheet operations such as printing a worksheet. It is important to define range names for specific cells and use the range names in macro instructions. Macros can be as simple or as complex as you desire. The use of a macro library file to store frequently used macros can save time.

KEY CONCEPTS

Alt + F2	Macro library
Alt + F3	Macro name
Ctrl + Break	Range name
Ctrl + F10	Record
Debugging	Step
Documentation	Tilde (~)
Location of a macro	User SmartIcon palette
Macro	

EXERCISE 1

INSTRUCTIONS: Circle T if the statement is true and F if the statement is false.

T   F   1. The range name for a macro must be taken from a label already existing on the worksheet.

T   F   2. The range name for a macro must begin with a forward slash (/) and a letter of the alphabet.

T   F   3. A macro is a way to automate a repetitive procedure.

T   F   4. Certain keystrokes in a macro must be enclosed in braces (the { and } characters).

T   F   5. In a macro, the tilde (the ~ symbol) represents pressing the forward slash (the command key /).

T   F   6. To execute the macro named \Z, the user must hold down the CTRL key and press the letter Z.

T   F   7. A range name for a macro must contain the first macro step as the first line in the range.

T   F   8. When you enter data on a worksheet manually, you can use the tilde instead of pressing ENTER.

T   F   9. Either apostrophe (the ' or the `) can be used to preface a macro step.

T   F   10. Documentation must be included in a macro.

T   F   11. You can automatically record macro keystrokes.

T   F   12. Macro libraries can be used to store macros that are applicable to more than one worksheet.

T   F   13. Macro instructions can be executed one step at a time by using ALT+F1.

T   F   14. It does not matter where you place macros on a worksheet.

EXERCISE 2 — Creating a Macro

INSTRUCTIONS: Retrieve the DIVSALES file you created in Chapter 11. The file contained data on sales of mowers and edgers for the three divisions in ABC Company.

Write a macro that:

Inserts a new worksheet at the beginning of the file.

Creates a summary worksheet on the inserted worksheet that contains the total sales for each quarter of each division.

Computes the total annual sales for each division and the annual sales for the company.

For the purposes of this exercise, use the **F**ile **C**ombine **A**dd or **F**ile **C**ombine **C**opy command sequence to place the information on the summary worksheet.

The macro should be placed on a separate worksheet. The macro should be properly documented.

Print the summary worksheet, the sales worksheets, and the worksheet on which the macro appears.

Save the worksheets, including the macro worksheet, on a file named ABCMAC.

EXERCISE 3 — Creating a Print Macro

INSTRUCTIONS: Retrieve the ABCMAC file you created in the previous exercise.

Create a macro that prints the summary worksheet and the division sales worksheets.

Place the print macro on the worksheet on which the macro you completed in the previous exercise appears. Document the print macro properly.

Print the worksheet that has the print macro on it.

EXERCISE 4 — Using a Macro to Sort Data

INSTRUCTIONS: Retrieve the PERSON file you created as an exercise in Chapter 13.

Write a macro that sorts the database in order by state, last name, and first name.

Place the macro on a separate worksheet after the worksheet containing the database table.

Create a macro that prints the sorted database table. Document both macros properly.

Print the sorted database table and the worksheet containing the macros for sorting and printing the database table.

EXERCISE 5 — Using Macros to Create and Print a Graph

INSTRUCTIONS: Retrieve the PRACTICE file you created as an exercise in Chapter 4.

Reset all graph settings associated with the file and delete any graph files present.

Write a macro to create a bar graph that includes the data of the variables Revenue, Profit before Tax, and Profit after Tax for the five years. Include appropriate graph title and legend information.

Create a macro that prints the bar graph.

Place the macros for creating and printing the bar graph on a separate worksheet.

Document both macros properly.

Print the worksheet that contains the macros.

EXERCISE 6 — Using Macros Assigned to a User Icon

INSTRUCTIONS: Retrieve the ABCMAC file you created in Exercise 2.

Assign the macro to the ⌊U3⌋ User SmartIcon.

Execute the macro using the ⌊U3⌋ User SmartIcon.

Remove the macro from the ⌊U3⌋ User SmartIcon.

CHAPTER SEVENTEEN

ADVANCED MACRO COMMANDS
AND EXAMPLES

OBJECTIVES

In this chapter, you will learn to:

- ■ Use macro key names
- ■ Create macros for various types of worksheet operations such as sorting data, restricting input to specific cells, and automatically executing a macro
- ■ Use advanced macro commands to:
    - Create interactive macros
    - Change program flow and loop through a series of instructions
    - Develop subroutines
    - Create user-designed menus

■ CHAPTER OVERVIEW

Chapter 16 introduced the use of macros in Lotus 1-2-3 and defined the process for creating a macro. In the first part of this chapter, some additional macro examples are illustrated. The command language available in Lotus 1-2-3 is then introduced. Finally, you learn to use the command language by creating several macros.

■ MACRO KEY NAMES

In the process of creating a macro, many **key names** are used to represent operations that are available in Lotus 1-2-3. For example, the down pointer-movement key is designated by the symbol {down} or {d}. The following is a list of the macro key names used to designate keystrokes including key names for function keys and directional keys.

The key names have been placed in alphabetical order. Key names that incorporate special characters appear at the end of the list.

Keys	Macro Key Name
Abs `F4`	{abs}
Addin `Alt`+`F10`	{addin} or {app4}
App1 `Alt`+`F7`	{app1}
App2 `Alt`+`F8`	{app2}
App3 `Alt`+`F9`	{app3}
Backspace	{backspace} or {bs}
`Ctrl`+`←`	{bigleft}
`Ctrl`+`→`	{bigright}
Calc `F9`	{calc}
`Ctrl`+`Break`	{break}
Del `Delete`	{delete} or {del}
Down `↓`	{down} or {d}
Edit `F2`	{edit}
End `End`	{end}
Enter `←Enter`	~
Escape `Esc`	{esc}
`F4`	{anchor}
File `Ctrl`+`End`	{file}
First Cell `Ctrl`+`Home`	{firstcell} or {fc}
First File `Ctrl`+`End` `Home`	{firstfile}, {ff}, or {file}{home}
GoTo `F5`	{goto}
Graph `F10`	{graph}
Help `F1`	{help}
Home `Home`	{home}
Insert `Insert`	{insert} or {ins}
Last Cell `End`+`Home`	{lastcell} or {lc}
Last File `Ctrl`+`End` `End`	{lastfile}, {lf}, or {file}{end}
Left `←`	{left} or {l}
Name `F3`	{name}
Next File `Ctrl`+`End` `Ctrl`+`Page Up`	{nextfile}, {nf}, or {file}{ns}
Next Sheet `Ctrl`+`Page Down`	{nextsheet} or {ns}
PgDn `Page Down`	{pgdn}
PgUp `Page Up`	{pgup}
Prev File `Ctrl`+`End` `Ctrl`+`Page Down`	{prevfile}, {pf}, or {file}{ps}
Prev Sheet `Ctrl`+`Page Down`	{prevsheet} or {ps}
Query `F7`	{query}
Right `→`	{right} or {r}
Table `F8`	{table}
Tab `Tab⇆`	{tab}
Up `↑`	{up} or {u}
Window `F6`	{window}
Zoom `Alt`+`F6`	{zoom}
/ (slash) or < (less than)	/, <, or {menu}
{~} to have tilde appear as ~	{~}
{{} and {}} to have braces appear as { and }	{{} and {}}

Sometimes you may want to specify two or more repetitions of the same key. This repeating can be accomplished by including a repetition factor within the braces. For example, to move the cell pointer down four cells you can use either of the following macro instructions:

{down 4} or {d 4}

■ SOME ADDITIONAL MACRO EXAMPLES

To help you learn more about using macros, in this section you will create and execute additional macros for sorting data, completing a data query, inputting values for a worksheet, restricting the entry of data to specific cells in a worksheet, and automatically executing a macro.

Sorting Data

In Chapter 13 you created a worksheet that had salary information about the employees of ABC Company and saved it on a file named ABCSAL. Suppose that you want to sort the data in ascending order by division and alphabetically within each division. To complete this example problem, you need to retrieve the ABCSAL file.

Insert a worksheet after the ABCSAL worksheet. After inserting the worksheet, use the **Worksheet Window Perspective** command sequence or click the Perspective SmartIcon to display both worksheets. Use the **Worksheet Window Unsync** command sequence to make row 21 the first row in worksheet A and row 1 the first row of worksheet B. Move the cell pointer to cell B:A1. Your screen should look like Figure 17-1.

Figure 17-1

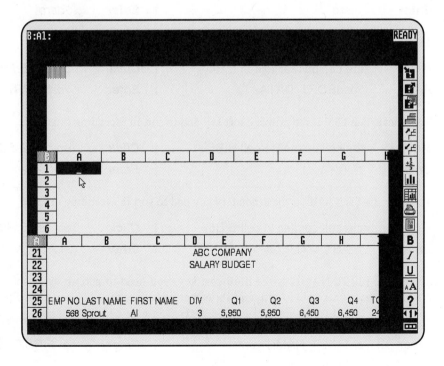

A macro will be created to accomplish the sort. You must:

1. Erase any previously set sort ranges.
2. Specify the data range to sort.
3. Define sort keys for the division number, last name, and first name.
4. Indicate that the data is to be sorted.

To enter the macro title:

Move	the cell pointer to cell B:A1		*Click*	*on cell B:A1*
Enter	Macro Sort		*Enter*	*Macro Sort*
Move	the cell pointer to cell B:C1		*Click*	*on cell B:C1*
Enter	Macro for Sorting Data		*Enter*	*Macro for Sorting Data*

To enter the macro name:

Move	the cell pointer to cell B:A3		*Click*	*on cell B:A3*
Enter	SORT		*Enter*	*SORT*

To make sure no sort settings are on the file:

Move	the cell pointer to cell B:B3		*Click*	*on cell B:B3*
Enter	'/dsrq		*Enter*	*'/dsrq*

To specify the data range to sort:

Move	the cell pointer to cell B:B4		*Click*	*on cell B:B4*
Enter	'/dsdSORT_DATA~		*Enter*	*'/dsdSORT_DATA~*

To indicate that DIV is the primary sort key and to sort in ascending order:

Move	the cell pointer to cell B:B5		*Click*	*on cell B:B5*
Enter	pDIV~a~		*Enter*	*pDIV~a~*

To define LAST NAME as the secondary key and to sort in ascending order:

Move	the cell pointer to cell B:B6		*Click*	*on cell B:B6*
Enter	sLAST_NAME~a~		*Enter*	*sLAST_NAME~a~*

To include FIRST NAME as the third sort key, you need to add an extra sort key, specify the FIRST NAME as the proper field to sort, and show that the names are to be sorted in alphabetical order.

Move	the cell pointer to cell B:B7		*Click*	*on cell B:B7*
Enter	e~FIRST_NAME~a~		*Enter*	*e~FIRST_NAME~a~*

To indicate it is appropriate to execute the sort and then exit the sort menu:

Move	the cell pointer to cell B:B8	**Click**	on cell B:B8
Enter	g	**Enter**	g

Except for the documentation that appears on the worksheet, your screen now should look like Figure 17-2.

Figure 17-2

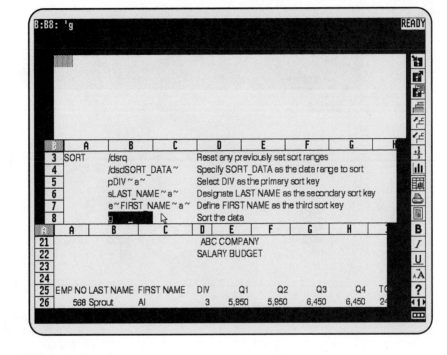

Before you can execute the macro, you need to create the following range names and include the indicated cells for each range name.

Range Name	Cell(s) to Include in the Range
SORT_DATA	A:A26..A:I33
DIV	A:D25
LAST_NAME	A:B25
FIRST_NAME	A:C25
SORT	B:B3

After checking your macro with the one in Figure 17-2 and making any necessary corrections, save the file using the file name ABCSAL2.

To execute the macro SORT:

Press	Alt + F3	**Press**	Alt + F3
Select	SORT	**Choose**	SORT

After the macro is executed and you use the **Worksheet Window Clear** command sequence or click the Perspective [icon] SmartIcon to display the SALARY BUDGET worksheet, your screen should look like Figure 17-3. Notice that the data have been sorted alphabetically by division.

Figure 17-3

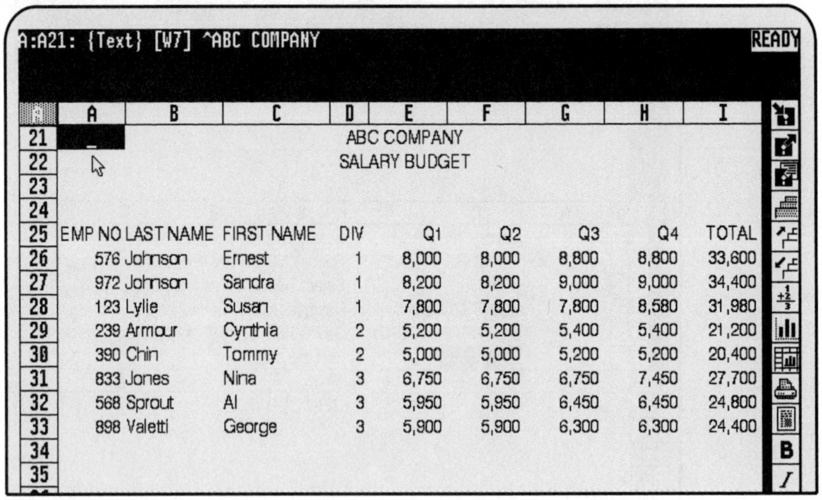

Retrieve the original ABCSAL2 file. Move to worksheet B and document your macro using the comments in Figure 17-2. After completing the documentation, save and replace the ABCSAL2 file.

Restricting Data Entry to Specific Cells in a Worksheet

To complete this exercise, you will need to create a loan amortization worksheet. This loan amortization worksheet will also be used in later sections of this chapter.

Make sure you have a blank worksheet on your screen. Enter the documentation information in Figure 17-4, Parts 1 and 2.

Figure 17-4
Part 1

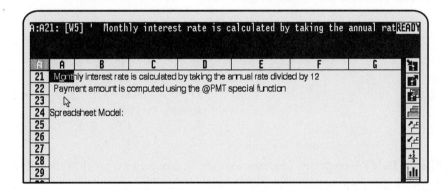

Figure 17-4
Part 2

Enter the labels and values for the worksheet by referring to Figure 17-4, Part 3.

Figure 17-4
Part 3

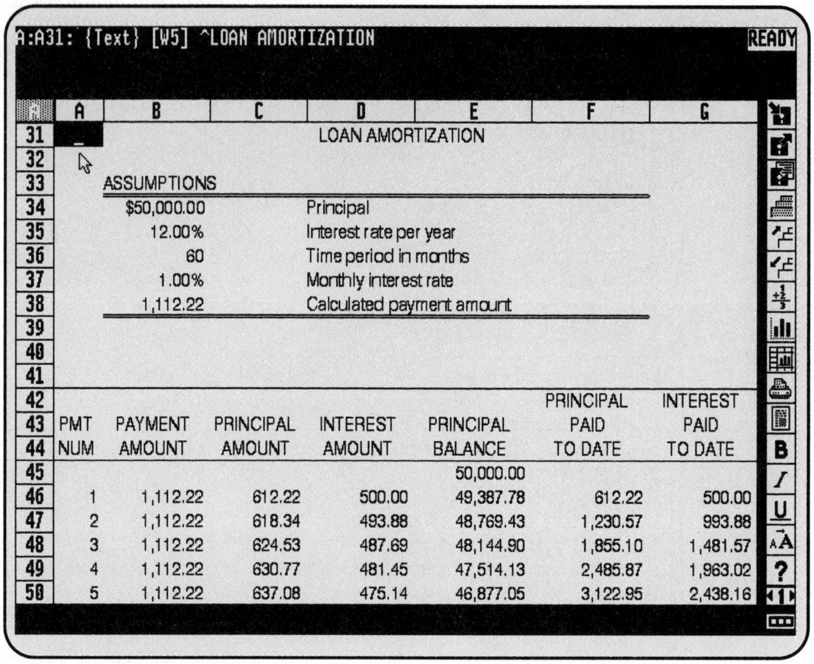

```
A:A31: {Text} [W5] ^LOAN AMORTIZATION                              READY
```

	A	B	C	D	E	F	G	
31				LOAN AMORTIZATION				
32								
33		ASSUMPTIONS						
34		$50,000.00		Principal				
35		12.00%		Interest rate per year				
36		60		Time period in months				
37		1.00%		Monthly interest rate				
38		1,112.22		Calculated payment amount				
39								
40								
41								
42						PRINCIPAL	INTEREST	
43	PMT	PAYMENT	PRINCIPAL	INTEREST	PRINCIPAL	PAID	PAID	
44	NUM	AMOUNT	AMOUNT	AMOUNT	BALANCE	TO DATE	TO DATE	
45					50,000.00			
46	1	1,112.22	612.22	500.00	49,387.78	612.22	500.00	
47	2	1,112.22	618.34	493.88	48,769.43	1,230.57	993.88	
48	3	1,112.22	624.53	487.69	48,144.90	1,855.10	1,481.57	
49	4	1,112.22	630.77	481.45	47,514.13	2,485.87	1,963.02	
50	5	1,112.22	637.08	475.14	46,877.05	3,122.95	2,438.16	

To assist you in the preparation of the worksheet, the column widths are:

Column	Width
A	5
B	11
C	10
D	11
E	12
F	12
G	11

Use the **D**ata **F**ill command sequence to enter the numbers 1 through 60 in cells A46 through A105. Enter formulas into cells as described below.

Cell	Formula
B37	+B35/12
B38	@PMT(B34,B37,B36)
E45	+B34
B46	+B38
C46	+B46-D46
D46	+B34*B37
E46	+E45-C46

F46	+C46
G46	+D46
B47	@IF($B$38>E46,$B$37*E46+E46,$B$38)
C47	+B47-D47
D47	+$B$37*E46
E47	+E46-C47
F47	+F46+C47
G47	+G46+D47

After you have entered the formulas for cells B47 through G47, copy these cell formulas to cells B48 through G105. You have created an amortization schedule worksheet that can be used for loan repayment periods from one to 60 months. Use the **R**ange **F**ormat **, 2** command sequence to properly format cells B45 through G105. Your screen should now look like Figure 17-4, Part 3.

Save the worksheet using the file name AMORT.

Sometimes it may be useful to limit an individual's ability to enter data in only a certain set of cells. For example, in the loan amortization schedule worksheet, suppose you want an individual to be allowed only to change the principal, interest rate, and time period. Such an approach prohibits users of the amortization worksheet from accidentally changing any of the formulas on the worksheet.

The steps that you need to have in a macro for restricting the data entry to the principal, interest rate, and time period cells are as follows:

1. Change the calculation mode to manual so you do not have to wait for the worksheet to be recalculated before you enter the next data item.

2. Protect all of the cells in the worksheet.

3. Unprotect only those cells that may be modified.

4. Calculate the worksheet after all data entry is completed.

Before you enter the macro instructions, insert a worksheet after the loan amortization schedule on which you will save the macro. Display both worksheets by executing the **W**orksheet **W**indow **P**erspective command sequence or clicking the Perspective ▦ SmartIcon. Make sure row 31 is the first row displayed in worksheet A and row 1 is the first row displayed in worksheet B.

To place a title for the macro on the worksheet:

Move	the cell pointer to cell B:A1		*Click*	*on cell B:A1*
Enter	Macro Data Entry		*Enter*	*Macro Data Entry*
Move	the cell pointer to cell B:C1		*Click*	*on cell B:C1*
Enter	Macro for Restricting Data Entry to the Cells		*Enter*	*Macro for Restricting Data Entry to the Cells*
Move	the cell pointer to cell B:C2		*Click*	*on cell B:C2*
Enter	for Principal, Interest Rate, and Time Period		*Enter*	*for Principal, Interest Rate, and Time Period*

To place the name of the macro on the worksheet:

Move	the cell pointer to cell B:A4	**Click**	on cell B:A4
Enter	\D	**Enter**	\D

To make sure the macro executes at the beginning of the spreadsheet model on worksheet A:

Move	the cell pointer to cell B:B4	**Click**	on cell B:B4
Enter	{goto}BEGIN~	**Enter**	{goto}BEGIN~

BEGIN is a range name that will have the initial cell of the spreadsheet model as its range. In this example, BEGIN will have the cell A:A31 as its range. Establishing a beginning cell is optional for this macro.

To specify that manual calculation mode is to be used:

Move	the cell pointer to cell B:B5	**Click**	on cell B:B5
Enter	'/wgrm	**Enter**	'/wgrm

You can protect all cells in the worksheet as follows:

Move	the cell pointer to cell B:B6	**Click**	on cell B:B6
Enter	'/wgpe	**Enter**	'/wgpe

To allow data entry for the principal, interest rate, and time period, you must unprotect the range of cells A:B34 through A:B36:

Move	the cell pointer to cell B:B7	**Click**	on cell B:B7
Enter	'/ruPRIN_INT_TIME~	**Enter**	'/ruPRIN_INT_TIME~

PRIN_INT_TIME is a range name that will have the data entry cells for the principal, interest rate, and time period. For this example, the cells A:B34 through A:B36 will be included in the range.

The **Range Input** command in 1-2-3 is used to restrict the cells in which you can enter data on the worksheet. Since you have protected all cells on the worksheet and unprotected the cells in which data entry is allowed, you can specify the entire spreadsheet model (cells A:A31..A:G105) in the **Range Input** command.

Move	the cell pointer to cell B:B8	**Click**	on cell B:B8
Enter	'/riINPUT_RANGE~	**Enter**	'/riINPUT_RANGE~

To specify that the worksheet is to be recalculated after the data entry is completed and to return the cell pointer to cell A:A31:

Move	the cell pointer to cell B:B9	**Click**	on cell B:B9
Enter	{calc}	**Enter**	{calc}

Move	the cell pointer to cell B:B10		**Click**	*on cell B:B10*
Enter	{goto}BEGIN~		**Enter**	*{goto}BEGIN~*

Except for the documentation on the macro worksheet, your screen should look like Figure 17-5.

Figure 17-5

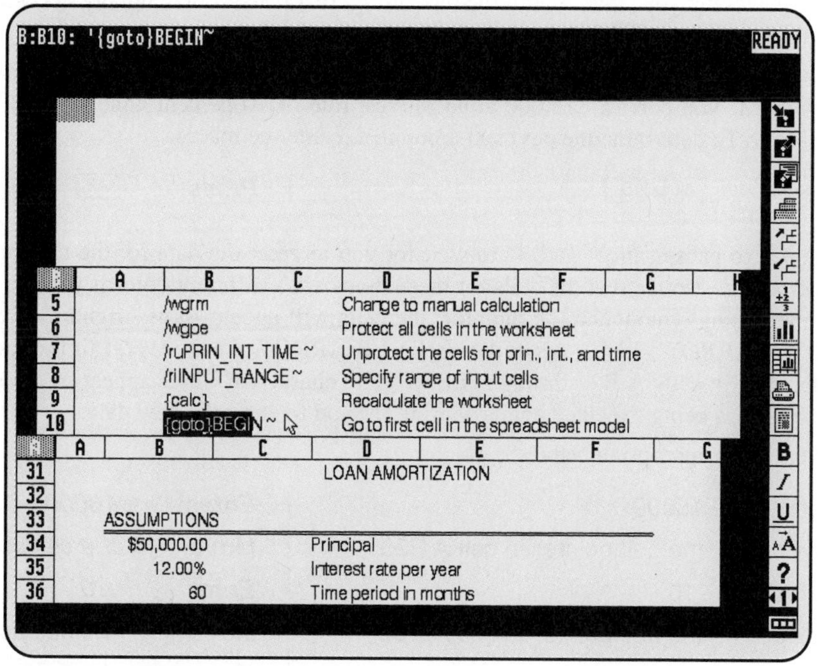

Create the following range names and include the indicated cells for each range name.

Range Name	Cell(s) to Include in the Range
BEGIN	A:A31
PRIN_INT_TIME	A:B34..A:B36
INPUT_RANGE	A:A31..A:G105

Before you execute the macro, name it \D.

Move	the cell pointer to cell B:B4		**Click**	*on cell B:B4*
Press	⎡ / ⎤		**Move**	*the mouse pointer to the control panel*
Select	Range		**Choose**	*Range*
Select	Name		**Choose**	*Name*
Select	Create		**Choose**	*Create*

Type	\D		**Type**	*\D*
Press	⟵Enter twice		***Click***	*the mouse button with the mouse pointer in the control panel*

After checking your macro with the one in Figure 17-5 and making any necessary changes, save the file using the name AMORTRI.

Suppose that you want to use the loan amortization schedule worksheet to determine the monthly payment if you borrow $15,000 at an interest rate of 10 percent annually and have 48 months to repay the loan. To determine the payment amount, execute the macro:

Press	Alt + D		***Press***	*Alt + D*

The macro pauses at cell A:B34 to wait for you to enter the data for the new principal, interest rate, and time period. Notice that the cells for these items are a different color if you are using a color monitor. If you are using a monochrome monitor, the cells will appear to be brighter. Press the RIGHT ARROW, DOWN ARROW, LEFT ARROW, AND UP ARROW keys several times and note that you can only enter data in cells A:B34 through A:B36. The characters CMD appear in the status line indicating that the macro is being executed and is waiting for you to enter the new data.

To enter the appropriate values:

Enter	15000		***Enter***	*15000*
Move	the cell pointer to cell A:B35		***Move***	*the cell pointer to cell A:B35*
Enter	.10		***Enter***	*.10*
Move	the cell pointer to cell A:B36		***Move***	*the cell pointer to cell A:B36*
Enter	48		***Enter***	*48*
Press	⟵Enter		***Click***	*the mouse button*

To finish execution of the macro:

Press	⟵Enter		***Press***	⟵Enter

Use the **Worksheet Window Clear** command sequence or click the Perspective 🖥 SmartIcon to display more of the loan amortization schedule on your screen. Your screen should look like Figure 17-6.

Figure 17-6

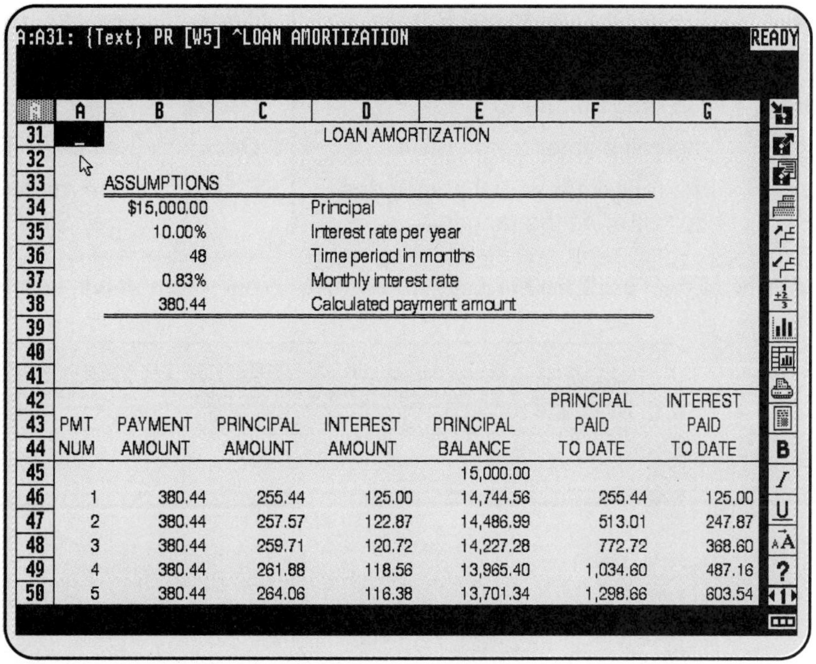

```
A:A31: {Text} PR [W5] ^LOAN AMORTIZATION                              READY
```

	A	B	C	D	E	F	G
31					LOAN AMORTIZATION		
32							
33		ASSUMPTIONS					
34		$15,000.00		Principal			
35		10.00%		Interest rate per year			
36		48		Time period in months			
37		0.83%		Monthly interest rate			
38		380.44		Calculated payment amount			
39							
40							
41							
42						PRINCIPAL	INTEREST
43	PMT	PAYMENT	PRINCIPAL	INTEREST	PRINCIPAL	PAID	PAID
44	NUM	AMOUNT	AMOUNT	AMOUNT	BALANCE	TO DATE	TO DATE
45					15,000.00		
46	1	380.44	255.44	125.00	14,744.56	255.44	125.00
47	2	380.44	257.57	122.87	14,486.99	513.01	247.87
48	3	380.44	259.71	120.72	14,227.28	772.72	368.60
49	4	380.44	261.88	118.56	13,965.40	1,034.60	487.16
50	5	380.44	264.06	116.38	13,701.34	1,298.66	603.54

Retrieve the AMORTRI file and disable worksheet protection by using the **W**orksheet **G**lobal **P**rotection **D**isable command. Document your macro using the information in Figure 17-5. After placing the documentation on the worksheet, save and replace the AMORTRI file.

In this macro, you may use the {form} command rather than the **R**ange **I**nput command to restrict the cells for data entry. To use the {form} command with the above macro, replace /riINPUT_RANGE~ with {form INPUT_RANGE}. The macro will execute the same way as with the **R**ange **I**nput command.

By using the {form} command, you can limit user input more specifically than with the **R**ange **I**nput command. To learn more about the {form} command, refer to the Advanced Macro Commands section later in this chapter.

Executing a Macro Automatically

In some situations, you may want to execute a macro automatically when a file is retrieved. For example, you may want the macro containing the loan amortization schedule to execute immediately so the individual using the loan amortization schedule only has to enter the new values for the principal, interest rate, and time period.

When a macro is named \0 (zero), it is executed when the file on which it resides is retrieved or opened. Before you can automatically execute the loan amortization schedule macro, you must retrieve the file containing the macro, change the name of the macro to \0, and resave the file.

To accomplish these steps:

Retrieve   the AMORTRI file | Retrieve   *the AMORTRI file*

Move	the cell pointer to cell B:A4		***Click***	*on cell B:A4*
Enter	'\0		***Enter***	*'\0*
Delete	the range name \D		***Delete***	*the range name \D*
Move	the cell pointer to cell B:B4		***Click***	*on cell B:B4*
Create	the range name \0 that includes cell B:B4 as the range		***Create***	*the range name \0 that includes cell B:B4 as the range*

Save the worksheet using the file name AUTOMAC. Your screen should look like Figure 17-7.

Figure 17-7

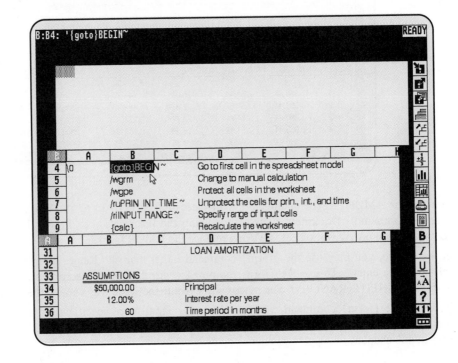

Suppose that you want to determine the monthly payment amount for a loan of $10,000 at an interest rate of 11 percent and time period of 36 months to pay the loan.

To illustrate the use of the automatic execution of a macro for this situation:

Erase	the worksheet from your screen		***Erase***	*the worksheet from your screen*
Retrieve	the AUTOMAC file		***Retrieve***	*the AUTOMAC file*

Notice that the macro has been initiated and the cell pointer is in cell A:B34. You now need to enter the data for the principal amount, interest rate, and time period.

Enter	10000 in cell A:B34		***Enter***	*10000 in cell A:B34*

Enter	.11 in cell A:B35		*Enter*	*.11 in cell A:B35*
Enter	36 in cell A:B36		*Enter*	*36 in cell A:B36*
Press			*Press*	

The macro has finished executing. After moving the cell pointer to cell A:A38 so you can see the payment amount, your screen should look like Figure 17-8.

Figure 17-8

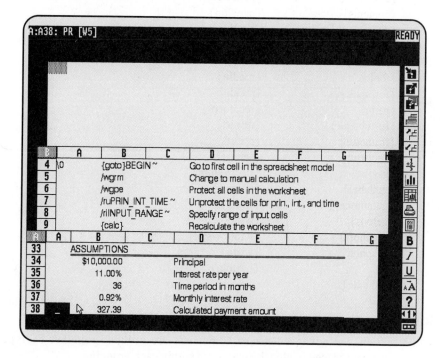

You do not need to save the new loan amortization schedule.

■ ADVANCED MACRO COMMANDS

Lotus 1-2-3 Release 3.4 has 55 **advanced macro commands**. In this section, a list of the commands is introduced, groupings of the commands by typical use are presented, and a brief explanation of each command is provided. For additional information on each advanced macro command, refer to the Lotus 1-2-3 reference manual.

Listing of Advanced Macro Commands

The advanced macro commands available in Release 3.4 are:

{?}	{beep}
{appendbelow}	{blank}
{appendright}	{bordersoff}

{borderson}   {let}
{branch}   {look}
{break}   {menubranch}
{breakoff}   {menucall}
{breakon}   {onerror}
{clearentry} or {ce}   {open}
{close}   {paneloff}
{contents}   {panelon}
{define}   {put}
{dispatch}   {quit}
{filesize}   {read}
{for}   {readln}
{forbreak}   {recalc}
{form}   {recalccol}
{formbreak}   {restart}
{frameoff}   {return}
{frameon}   {setpos}
{get}   {subroutine}
{getlabel}   {system}
{getnumber}   {wait}
{getpos}   {windowsoff}
{graphoff}   {windowson}
{graphon}   {write}
{if}   {writeln}
{indicate}

Summary of Advanced Macro Commands by Type of Use

In this section, the advanced macro commands are grouped together by typical use. For ease of reference they are placed in alphabetical order within each grouping.

Controlling the Appearance of the Screen

In some situations, you may want to change the appearance of the screen. The following macro commands can be used to alter the appearance of the screen:

{beep}   {graphon}
{bordersoff}   {indicate}
{borderson}   {paneloff}
{frameoff}   {panelon}
{frameon}   {windowsoff}
{graphoff}   {windowson}

Interaction Between User and Keyboard

The following commands can be employed to create macros that provide **interactive** capability:

{?}	{getlabel}
{break}	{getnumber}
{breakoff}	{look}
{breakon}	{menubranch}
{form}	{menucall}
{formbreak}	{wait}
{get}	

Changing the Flow of Instructions in a Macro

In some cases, it may be desirable to modify the exact sequence of commands in a macro. The following commands permit you to control the sequence of command execution.

{branch}	{onerror}
{define}	{quit}
{dispatch}	{restart}
{for}	{return}
{forbreak}	{*subroutine*}
{if}	{system}

Manipulating the Format and Location of Data

These commands can be used to manipulate the format and location of data in a worksheet:

{appendbelow}	{let}
{appendright}	{put}
{blank}	{recalc}
{clearentry} or {ce}	{recalccol}
{contents}	

File Operations

In some cases, it may be useful to execute tasks related to files. These commands permit you to manipulate files during the execution of a macro.

{close}	{readln}
{filesize}	{setpos}
{getpos}	{write}
{open}	{writeln}
{read}	

Specific Advanced Macro Commands

Explanations of the various advanced macro commands are contained in this section. For additional details on the many commands, see the Lotus 1-2-3 reference manual.

The following format is used in the descriptions of the commands:

$$\{Keyword\ arg1,arg2,...,argn\}$$

Arguments that are shown within angle brackets (< >) are optional.

{?}

The {?} command halts the execution of a macro to permit moving the cell pointer to enter data in a cell or to move the menu pointer to complete part of a command. When you press the ENTER key, the macro continues execution.

The {?} has the following format:

$$\{?\}$$

{appendbelow}

The {appendbelow} command permits you to copy data in a worksheet from a source location to the rows below the target location.

The {appendbelow} command has the following format:

$$\{appendbelow\ target\text{-}location,source\text{-}location\}$$

{appendright}

The {appendright} command allows you to copy data in a worksheet from a source location immediately to the right of the target location.

The {appendright} command has the following format:

$$\{appendright\ target\text{-}location,source\text{-}location\}$$

{beep}

The {beep} command causes the computer bell to sound. The number is optional. There are four tones to the "beep." Therefore, the number 1, 2, 3, or 4 can appear within the {beep} command. If no number is specified, the default is the first tone.

The {beep} command has the following format:

$$\{beep\ <number>\}$$

The {beep} command does not produce a tone if you turn off the bell by using the **Worksheet Global Default Other Beep No** command sequence.

{blank}

The {blank} command erases the contents of the designated cell. The cell pointer does not move to the designated cell location and does not change the cell formats.

The {blank} command has the following format:

{blank cell-location}

{bordersoff}

The {bordersoff} command suppresses the display of the worksheet frame that includes the column letters and row numbers. It works the same as {frameoff}.

The {bordersoff} command has the following format:

{bordersoff}

{borderson}

The {borderson} command restores the display of the worksheet frame that includes the column letters and row numbers. It works the same as {frameon}.

The {borderson} command has the following format:

{borderson}

{branch}

The {branch} command directs control to the designated cell and continues the execution of the macro using the instructions in the designated cell. The branch command does not return the user to the original macro.

The {branch} command has the following format:

{branch cell-location}

{break}

The {break} command stops the execution of a macro. It has the effect of pressing the CTRL+BREAK keys.

The {break} command has the following format:

{break}

{breakoff} and {breakon}

The {breakoff} command disables the CTRL+BREAK functionality that interrupts a macro. The {breakon} command reverses the {breakoff} command.

The {breakoff} and {breakon} commands have the following format:

{breakoff}

{breakon}

{clearentry} or {ce}

The {clearentry} or {ce} command clears the default entry that appears in the control panel. It has the same effect as pressing the ESC key.

The {clearentry} or {ce} command has the following format:

{clearentry} or {ce}

{close}

The {close} command closes a file that was previously opened using the {open} command and saves any changes that were made while the file was open.

The {close} command has the following format:

{close}

{contents}

The {contents} command stores the data from one cell in another cell as a label. The width of the label as well as the type of format desired can be specified for the target location. Refer to the Lotus 1-2-3 reference manual for the codes of the format numbers.

The {contents} command has the following format:

{contents target-location,source-location,<width-number>,<format-number>}

{define}

The {define} command allocates where variables that are passed to a subroutine are stored. If used, it is the first command in the subroutine.

The {define} command has the following format:

{define cell-location1:type1,cell-location2:type 2...}

{dispatch}

The {dispatch} command directs control to another cell for instructions on where the macro should branch.

The {dispatch} command has the following format:

{dispatch cell-location}

{filesize}

The {filesize} command records the number of bytes in the currently retrieved file. The number is recorded in the specified cell-location. The {filesize} command can only be used after the {open} command.

The {filesize} command has the following format:

{filesize cell-location}

{for}

The {for} command allows a set of commands to be repeated a specified number of times. The process of repeating a set of commands is often referred to as looping.

The {for} command has the following format:

{for counter-location,begin-number,end-number,step,starting-location}

The counter-location is used to keep track of the number of times the loop of instructions is to be executed. The begin-number specifies the initial number with which the loop should begin its count, and the end-number specifies the number at which the loop should stop executing. The step tells what increment the loop count should use. The starting-location indicates the first cell or range name of the subroutine to be executed.

{forbreak}

The {forbreak} command breaks or interrupts the current {for} loop.

The {forbreak} command has the following format:

{forbreak}

{form}

The {form} command temporarily halts the execution of a macro to allow the entry and editing of data in the unprotected cells in the input-location.

The {form} command has the following format:

{form input-location,<call-table>,<include-list>,<exclude-list>}

The call-table, include-list, and exclude-list are optional items.

{formbreak}

The {formbreak} command breaks or interrupts the {form} command.

The {formbreak} command has the following format:

{formbreak}

{frameoff}

The {frameoff} command suppresses the display of the worksheet frame that includes the worksheet letter, column letters, and row numbers.

The {frameoff} command has the following format:

{frameoff}

{frameon}

The {frameon} command restores the display of the worksheet frame that includes the worksheet letter, column letters, and row numbers.

The {frameon} command has the following format:

{frameon}

{get}

The {get} command stops the macro and allows an individual to enter a single character in the designated cell-location.

The {get} command has the following format:

{get cell-location}

{getlabel}

The {getlabel} command stops the macro and prompts a person to enter a label that will be placed in the specified cell-location.

The {getlabel} command has the following format:

{getlabel prompt-string,cell-location}

{getnumber}

The {getnumber} command stops the macro and prompts an individual to enter a value that will be placed in the specified cell-location.

The {getnumber} command has the following format:

{getnumber prompt-string,cell-location}

{getpos}

The {getpos} command determines the position of the cell pointer in the open file and stores the position in the designated cell-location.

The {getpos} command has the following format:

{getpos cell-location}

{graphoff}

The {graphoff} command erases a graph displayed by the {graphon} command and displays the current worksheet on the screen.

The {graphoff} command has the following format:

{graphoff}

{graphon}

The {graphon} command has the following format:

{graphon <named-graph>,<nodisplay>}

The named-graph and nodisplay arguments are optional.

Depending on the options selected, three things can happen when the {graphon} command is used. If {graphon} is used with no arguments, then a full-screen view of the current graph will be displayed on your screen as the macro continues to execute. If {graphon named-graph} is used, then the named-graph will appear on your screen while the macro continues to execute. If {graphon named-graph, nodisplay} is executed, the named-graph will become the current graph and no graph will be displayed on your screen.

{if}

The {if} command tests the condition following the word *if*. When the *if* condition is true, the commands that immediately follow the {if} command in the same cell are executed. If the condition is false, the command in the cell immediately below the {if} command is executed.

The {if} command has the following format:

{if condition}

{indicate}

The {indicate} command allows you to change the mode indicator, located at the top right corner of the screen.

The {indicate} command has the following format:

{indicate <string>}

If this command is used, Lotus 1-2-3 replaces the mode indicator with the specified string of characters.

{let}

The {let} command stores the specified entry (a number or string) in the designated cell-location.

The {let} command has the following format:

{let cell-location,entry}

{look}

The {look} command keeps track of whether or not you typed a keystroke while a macro was running. The keystroke (if any) is stored in the designated cell-location.

The {look} command has the following format:

{look cell-location}

{menubranch}

The {menubranch} command allows you to select a menu item and then execute the corresponding macro commands for the menu item. Menu items begin in the designated cell-location.

The {menubranch} command has the following format:

{menubranch cell-location}

{menucall}

The {menucall} command allows a user to select a menu item and then execute the corresponding subroutine for the menu item. Menu items begin in the designated cell-location.

The {menucall} command has the following format:

$$\{menucall\ cell\text{-}location\}$$

{onerror}

If an error occurs during execution of a macro, then the macro will continue at the designated branch-location. If desired, an error message can be included in the cell designated for the message-location.

The {onerror} command has the following format:

$$\{onerror\ branch\text{-}location, <message\text{-}location>\}$$

{open}

The {open} command allows you to open an ASCII or print file for the purposes of reading or writing.

The {open} command has the following format:

$$\{open\ filename, access\text{-}mode\}$$

The access-mode indicates R(Read), W(Write), or M(Modify) the file.

{paneloff} and {panelon}

The {paneloff} command prevents the appearance of information in the control panel during macro execution. The {panelon} command reverses the {paneloff} command.

The {paneloff} and {panelon} commands have the following format:

$$\{paneloff\}$$
$$\{panelon\}$$

{put}

The {put} command places an entry (number or string of characters) in the designated column and row within the designated two-dimensional range.

The {put} command has the following format:

$$\{put\ range, column\text{-}number, row\text{-}number, entry\}$$

For example, if the range was A1..B3, the column number was 0, and the row number was 1, the number or string would be placed in cell A2.

{quit}

The {quit} command stops the execution of the macro.

The {quit} command has the following format:

$$\{quit\}$$

{read}

The {read} command reads a specified number of characters or bytes (0 to 240 characters can be used) from a file and places the characters at the designated cell-location. The {read} command can only be used after the {open} command.

The {read} command has the following format:

{read byte-number,cell-location}

{readln}

The {readln} command reads and copies one line of information from the open file to the designated cell location. The {readln} command can only be used after the {open} command.

The {readln} command has the following format:

{readln cell-location}

{recalc}

The {recalc} command recalculates the cells in the designated cell-location row by row.

The {recalc} command has the following format:

{recalc cell-location,<condition>,<iterations>}

{recalccol}

The {recalccol} command recalculates the cells in designated cell-location column by column.

The {recalccol} command has the following format:

{recalccol cell-location,<condition>,<iterations>}

{restart}

The {restart} command clears the subroutine stack. When {restart} is encountered, 1-2-3 continues to the end of the current subroutine. Instead of returning to the original macro location, the macro then stops executing.

The {restart} command has the following format:

{restart}

{return}

The {return} command transfers control from a subroutine to the next instruction in the macro from which the subroutine was called.

The {return} command has the following format:

{return}

{setpos}

The {setpos} command sets the new position for the byte pointer in the currently retrieved file to the indicated position. The {setpos} command can only be used after the {open} command.

The {setpos} command has the following format:

{setpos byte-position}

{subroutine}

The {subroutine} command calls a subroutine. The command name is actually the range name or cell address where the first subroutine command is located in your worksheet. The optional arguments can be utilized to pass information to a subroutine.

The {subroutine} command has the following format:

{subroutine <argument>,<argument>...}

{system}

The {system} command temporarily halts execution of 1-2-3 and the specified operating system command is processed.

The {system} command has the following format:

{system command}

The command is any legal operating system command that needs to be executed.

{wait}

The {wait} command suspends macro execution until the designated time.

The {wait} command has the following format:

{wait time-number}

{windowsoff} and {windowson}

The {windowsoff} command prevents redrawing the screen (except for the control panel) during macro execution. The {windowson} command reverses the {windowsoff} command.

The {windowsoff} and {windowson} commands have the following format:

{windowsoff}
{windowson}

{write}

The {write} command writes characters into the currently open file. The {write} command can only be used after the {open} command.

The {write} command has the following format:

{write string}

{writeln}

The {writeln} command writes the specified string of characters to the currently open file and adds a carriage-return line-feed sequence to the end of the string. The {writeln} command can only be used after the {open} command.

The {writeln} command has the following format:

{writeln string}

■ SOME EXAMPLES OF USING ADVANCED MACRO COMMANDS

In this section, you will create several macros that illustrate some typical applications of advanced macro commands.

Interactive Macros

In many situations, you may want to allow users of a macro to enter data while a macro is executing. For example, you may want to prompt an individual to enter values or labels into some specific cells.

Entering a Sequence of Numbers

Sometimes you may need to enter rows or columns of numbers on a worksheet. Suppose you wanted to enter the set of numbers 10, 25, 15, and 32 in cells B25 through B28 in worksheet A of a worksheet file. You will create a macro that moves the cell pointer down one cell after entering each of the numbers to expedite the process of entering the data.

Before creating the macro, make sure you have a blank worksheet on your screen and then enter the information in Figure 17-9, Parts 1 and 2.

Figure 17-9
Part 1

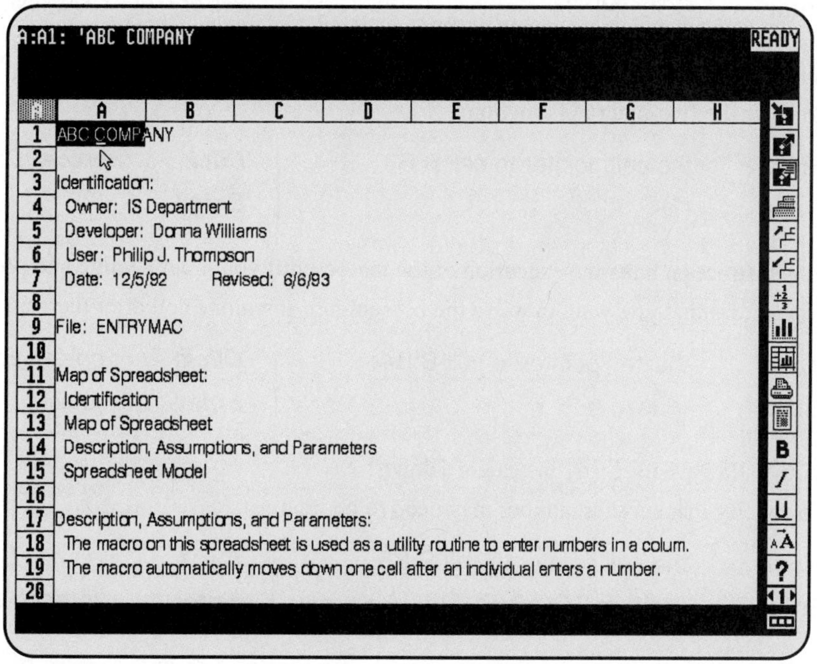

Figure 17-9
Part 2

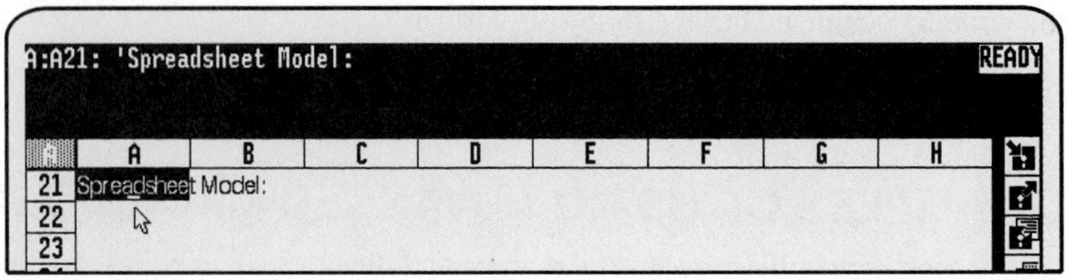

```
A:A21: 'Spreadsheet Model:                                      READY
┌────┬──────┬──────┬──────┬──────┬──────┬──────┬──────┬──────┐
│    │  A   │  B   │  C   │  D   │  E   │  F   │  G   │  H   │
├────┼──────┴──────┴──────┴──────┴──────┴──────┴──────┴──────┤
│ 21 │Spreadsheet Model:                                      │
│ 22 │  ░                                                     │
│ 23 │                                                        │
└────┴────────────────────────────────────────────────────────┘
```

Insert a worksheet after worksheet A. Display both worksheets on your screen. Make sure the first row displayed in worksheet A is row 25. The first row displayed in worksheet B should be row 1.

To place a title for the macro that will be used for entering the set of numbers:

Move	the cell pointer to cell B:A1	**Click**	on cell B:A1
Enter	Macro Input	**Enter**	Macro Input
Move	the cell pointer to cell B:C1	**Click**	on cell B:C1
Enter	Macro for entering numbers in a column	**Enter**	Macro for entering numbers in a column

To place the name of the macro on the macro worksheet:

Move	the cell pointer to cell B:A3	**Click**	on cell B:A3
Enter	COL_INPUT	**Enter**	COL_INPUT

Widen column A so it displays 12 characters.

To enter the first macro instruction:

Move	the cell pointer to cell B:B3	**Click**	on cell B:B3
Enter	{?}	**Enter**	{?}

This instruction halts the execution of the macro until you input a value and press the ENTER key.

To indicate that you want to move the cell pointer down one cell after the value is entered.

Move	the cell pointer to cell B:B4	**Click**	on cell B:B4
Enter	{down}	**Enter**	{down}

You could have used {d} instead of {down}.

To specify that another number may need to be input:

Move	the cell pointer to cell B:B5	**Click**	on cell B:B5
Enter	{branch COL_INPUT}	**Enter**	{branch COL_INPUT}

This instruction directs 1-2-3 to move to the first instruction in the macro so that you may enter another number if you desire.

Before you execute the macro:

Name	the macro COL_INPUT and include cell B:B3 as the cell in the range		*Name*	*the macro COL_INPUT and include cell B:B3 as the cell in the range*
Enter	the documentation in cell B:E3 through B:E5 as shown in Figure 17-10		*Enter*	*the documentation in cell B:E3 through B:E5 as shown in Figure 17-10*

After moving the cell pointer to cell B:A1, your screen should look like Figure 17-10.

Figure 17-10

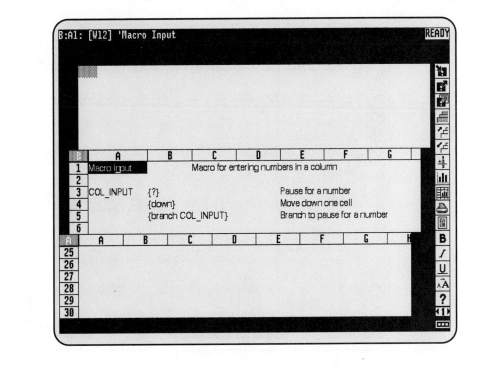

After comparing your macro with Figure 17-10 and making any necessary modifications, save the macro using the name ENTRYMAC.

Before executing the macro, move the cell pointer to the cell in which you want to enter the first number.

Move	the cell pointer to cell A:B25		*Click*	*on cell A:B25*

Execute the macro. Note that as soon as you start executing the macro, CMD appears in the status line indicating that the macro is executing and is waiting for you to enter a number.

Enter	10		*Enter*	*10*

After you press the ENTER key, the cell pointer moves down one cell. The macro pauses again for you to enter another number in cell A:B26. Continue to enter the numbers until 25, 15, and 32 appear in cells B26 through B29.

To terminate the execution of the macro:

Press	Ctrl + Break		**Press**	Ctrl + Break
Press	Esc		**Click**	*the alternate mouse button*

A beep will be sounded to indicate the macro has been terminated. Your screen should look like Figure 17-11. Do not save the results that appear on your screen.

Figure 17-11

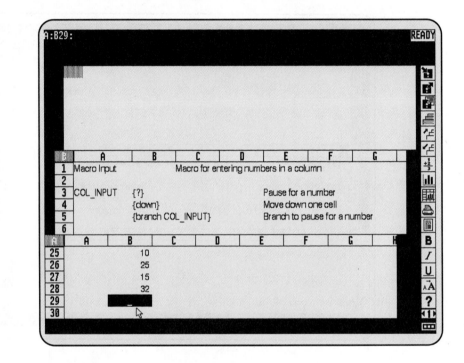

Prompting Users to Enter Labels and Numeric Data

At times it is helpful to place a message at the top of the screen to prompt a user to enter a specific label or a value. In this section, you use the {getlabel} and {getnumber} commands to display prompts requesting the entry of labels and numbers.

Suppose that you want to create a macro that prompts a person using the loan amortization schedule worksheet to enter the purpose for obtaining the loan, the principal amount, interest rate, and time period.

You need to retrieve the AMORT file, insert worksheet B for the macro, and display the two worksheets. Make sure row 31 is the first row displayed in worksheet A and row 1 is the first row displayed in worksheet B. Move to cell B:A1 and enter the macro title and name as it appears in Figure 17-12.

Figure 17-12

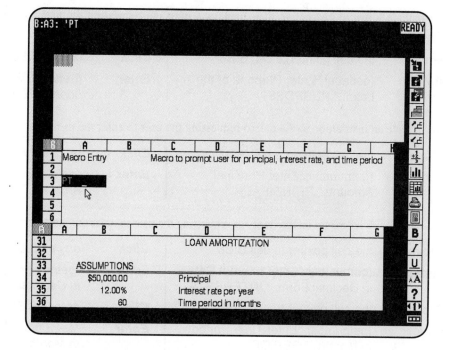

The set of steps that must be included in your macro are:

1. Erase the old values in cells A:B34 through A:B36.
2. Set the calculation mode to manual.
3. Use the {getlabel} and {getnumber} commands to prompt the user to enter the information for loan purpose, principal amount, interest rate, and time period.
4. Calculate the monthly payment amount after all necessary information has been input.

To include an instruction in the macro that erases the current entries for principal amount, interest rate, and time period:

Move	the cell pointer to cell B:B3	*Click*	on cell B:B3
Enter	{blank DATA_AREA}	*Enter*	{blank DATA_AREA}

To specify that manual recalculation mode is to be used:

Move	the cell pointer to cell B:B4	*Click*	on cell B:B4
Enter	'/wgrm	*Enter*	'/wgrm

To move the cell pointer to the initial cell in the spreadsheet model:

Move	the cell pointer to cell B:B5	*Click*	on cell B:B5
Enter	{goto}BEGIN~	*Enter*	{goto}BEGIN~

To include a macro instruction that displays a message requesting the user to input the purpose of the loan and place the entry in cell A:D32:

Move	the cell pointer to cell B:B6		*Click*	*on cell B:B6*
Enter	{getlabel "Enter Purpose of the Loan: ",PURPOSE}~		*Enter*	*{getlabel "Enter Purpose of the Loan: ",PURPOSE}~*

To include an instruction in the macro requesting the user to enter the principal amount:

Move	the cell pointer to cell B:B7		*Click*	*on cell B:B7*
Enter	{getnumber "Enter Principal Amount: ",PRINCIPAL}~		*Enter*	*{getnumber "Enter Principal Amount: ",PRINCIPAL}~*

To specify similar macro instructions for requesting the user to enter the interest rate and time period data:

Move	the cell pointer to cell B:B8		*Click*	*on cell B:B8*
Enter	{getnumber "Enter Interest Rate in Decimal Form: ",INTEREST}~		*Enter*	*{getnumber "Enter Interest Rate in Decimal Form: ",INTEREST}~*
Move	the cell pointer to cell B:B9		*Click*	*on cell B:B9*
Enter	{getnumber "Enter Time Period in Months: ",PERIOD}~		*Enter*	*{getnumber "Enter Time Period in Months: ",PERIOD}~*

To include an instruction that indicates the worksheet needs recalculation:

Move	the cell pointer to cell B:B10		*Click*	*on cell B:B10*
Enter	{calc}		*Enter*	*{calc}*

After you enter the macro instructions, your screen should look like Figure 17-13.

Figure 17-13

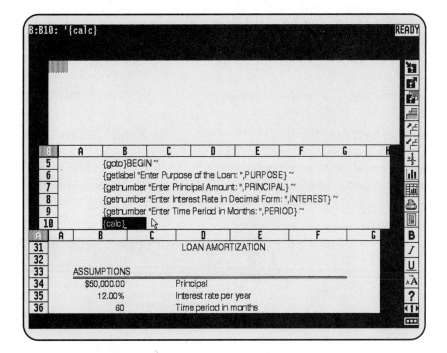

Create the following range names:

Range Name	Cell(s) to Include in the Range
DATA_AREA	A:B34..A:B36
BEGIN	A:A31
PURPOSE	A:D32
PRINCIPAL	A:B34
INTEREST	A:B35
PERIOD	A:B36

Create the macro name PT and include B:B3 as the cell in its range. Before executing the macro PT, save the current worksheet on file PROMPTMC.

So that you can see the use of the macro, use the **W**orksheet **W**indow **C**lear command sequence or click the Perspective SmartIcon to display worksheet A on your screen. Execute the macro PT. Notice that the cell pointer is moved to cell A:A31 and cells A:B34 through A:B36 are *blank*. A message appears at the top of the screen requesting you to "Enter Purpose of the Loan:"

Enter   Furniture Purchases | *Enter*   *Furniture Purchases*

The label now appears in cell A:D32, and a new prompt requesting you to enter the principal amount of the loan appears at the top of the screen.

Enter   20000 | *Enter*   *20000*

The number $20,000 now appears in the worksheet in cell A:B34. A prompt indicating that you need to enter the interest rate in decimal form now appears at the top of the screen.

Enter .12 | *Enter* *.12*

The interest rate 12 percent now appears in cell A:B35. You are requested to enter the time period in months for repaying the loan.

Enter 60 | *Enter* 60

The time period for 60 months now appears in cell A:B36. The macro completes the calculation of the monthly payment amount. Your screen should look like Figure 17-14. Do not save the results of this exercise.

Figure 17-14

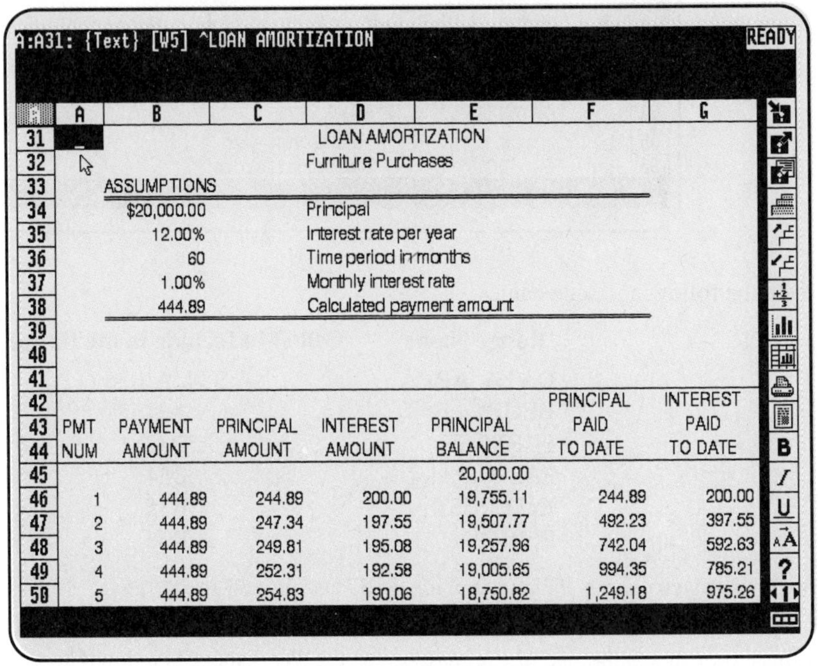

Changing Program Flow and Looping

Sometimes you may want to change the flow of instructions when a macro is used. For example, you may want to repeat a set of instructions a specific number of times or until a particular condition occurs. In this section, you create macros that **loop** through a sequence of instructions when the number of iterations that needs to be completed is either known or unknown.

Executing a Loop of Instructions When the Number of Iterations Is Known

The macro you will create in this section illustrates the use of the {for} command to loop through a set of instructions a specific number of times. For this exercise, you need to have two blank worksheets on your screen in perspective windows. Enter the numbers on worksheet A so that your screen looks like Figure 17-15.

Figure 17-15

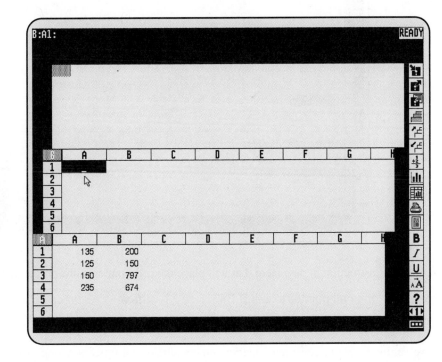

Suppose you want to add the numbers in column A and column B for each row and place the sum in column C. You will now create a macro to accomplish this objective. Before entering the macro, enter the title and macro name information that appear in Figure 17-16.

Figure 17-16

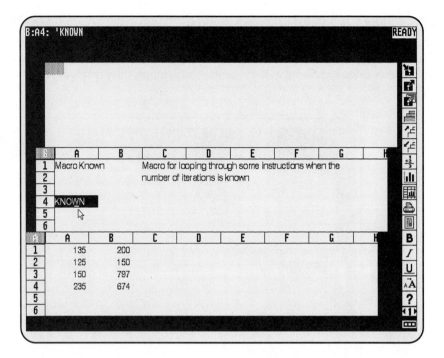

To place an instruction in the macro that will place the cell pointer in the proper starting cell position:

Move	the cell pointer to cell B:B4		***Click***	*on cell B:B4*
Enter	{goto}BEGIN~		***Enter***	*{goto}BEGIN~*

To solve this problem, you need a macro command that will process a loop of instructions that adds the numbers in columns A and B for each row and then places the cell pointer in the proper starting cell position for the next summation operation:

Move	the cell pointer to cell B:B5		***Click***	*on cell B:B5*
Enter	{for COUNT,1,4, 1,LOOP}		***Enter***	*{for COUNT,1,4, 1,LOOP}*

This macro command indicates that the set of macro instructions which starts with the initial cell in the range name LOOP is to be executed four times. The cell which has the range name COUNT is initialized with a value of 1 and incremented by 1 each time the LOOP routine is executed. The first number after COUNT is the initialization value, the second number is the termination value, and the third number is the value by which COUNT is to be incremented each time the set of instructions is executed. When the value of COUNT exceeds the termination value, the looping process is ended.

To specify that the cell pointer is to be moved to cell A1 after the macro is executed:

Move	the cell pointer to cell B:B6		***Click***	*on cell B:B6*
Enter	{goto}FIRST~		***Enter***	*{goto}FIRST~*

To place the name of the LOOP routine on the worksheet:

Move	the cell pointer to cell B:A8		*Click*	*on cell B:A8*
Enter	LOOP		*Enter*	*LOOP*

To include a macro instruction that adds the numbers in column A and B for a row and enters the sum in column C for the row:

Move	the cell pointer to cell B:B8		*Click*	*on cell B:B8*
Enter	'+{left}{left}+{left}~		*Enter*	*'+{left}{left}+{left}~*

Assuming that the cell pointer is in A:C1 when the macro is executed, this macro instruction specifies that a formula is used that sums the value two columns to the left of C1 and the value one column to the left of C1. The ~ symbol represents the ENTER key. When the macro processes this keystroke, the formula (+A1+B1) is placed in C1.

To indicate that the cell pointer needs to be moved down one cell in column C before the routine is executed again:

Move	the cell pointer to cell B:B9		*Click*	*on cell B:B9*
Enter	{down}		*Enter*	*{down}*

To include the COUNT variable name on the worksheet:

Move	the cell pointer to cell B:A12		*Click*	*on cell B:A12*
Enter	COUNT		*Enter*	*COUNT*

Create the following range names:

Range Name	**Cell to Include in the Range**
BEGIN	A:C1
COUNT	B:B12
LOOP	B:B8
FIRST	A:A1

Use the **Worksheet Window Clear** command sequence or click the Perspective ⌨ SmartIcon to display only worksheet B. Your screen should look like Figure 17-17.

Figure 17-17

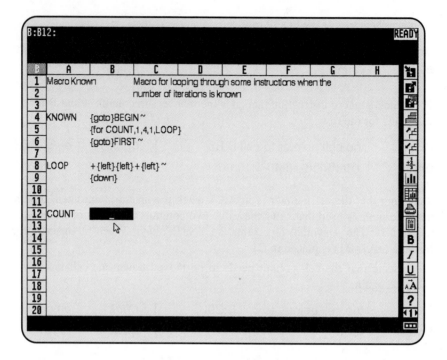

After you compare your macro instructions with those in Figure 17-17 and make any necessary modifications, create the range name KNOWN for the macro name and include cell B:B4 as its range. Save the worksheet file using the name KNOWNMAC.

After you execute the macro and issue the **W**orksheet **W**indow **P**erspective command sequence or click the Perspective SmartIcon, your screen should look like Figure 17-18. Notice that the values for columns A and B for each row have been added and the resulting total placed in column C.

Figure 17-18

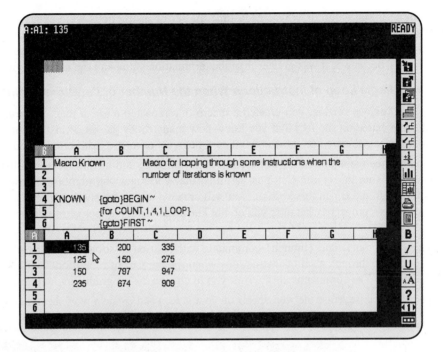

To see what happened on the macro worksheet, display only worksheet B on your screen. Refer to Figure 17-19.

Figure 17-19

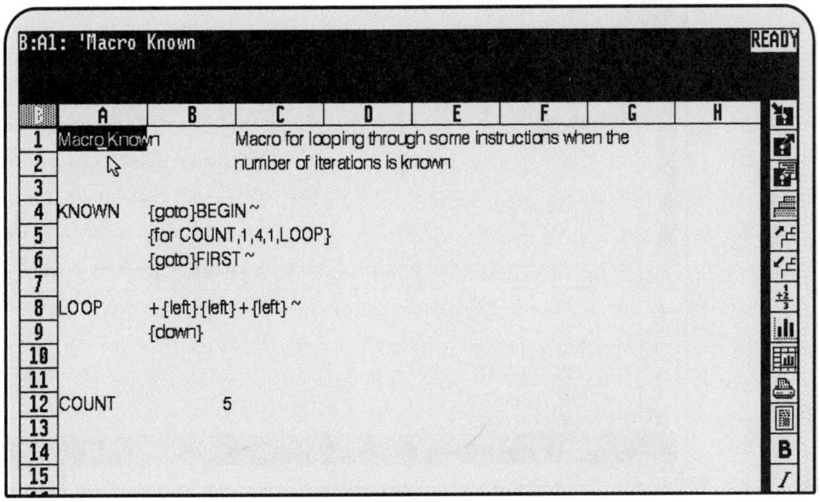

To see what happened on the macro worksheet, display only worksheet B on your screen. Refer to Figure 17-19.

Notice that the number 5 appears in cell B:B12. The number 5 indicates that as the set of macro instructions associated with the range name LOOP was executed, the value of COUNT was incremented from an initial value of 1 by 1 each time the set of instructions were executed. The value of COUNT was compared to the termination value of 4. When the value of COUNT was less than or equal to 4, the set of instructions associated with the range name LOOP was again executed. When the value of COUNT became 5, it was greater than the termination value and the macro stopped executing.

Executing a Loop of Instructions When the Number of Iterations is Unknown

In the previous section, you created a macro that repeated a set of macro instructions a specific number of times based on the fact that you knew how many times the set of instructions needed to be executed. Sometimes you may not know how many times a set of macro instructions should to be repeated.

You created the macro in the last section to horizontally add the numbers in column A and column B and enter the sum in column C. You assumed that you knew the number of rows containing numbers in columns A and B. In this section, you will create a macro for solving a problem general enough so that it will work properly whenever you do not know the exact number of rows that have values in columns A and B.

The {if}, {quit}, and {branch} commands will be used to solve the problem. These commands allow you to loop through a set of instructions when the number of repetitions is not known prior to executing the macro. The commands also permit you to change the program flow within a macro.

For this exercise, erase the worksheets on your screen and create a worksheet that looks like Figure 17-20.

Figure 17-20

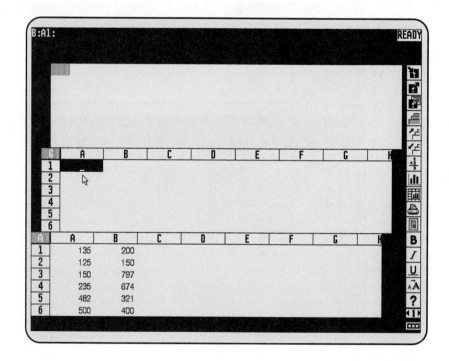

The steps necessary to solve this problem are:

1. Move the cell pointer to the proper starting position.
2. Add the two horizontal numbers in column A and B and enter the sum in column C.
3. Move the cell pointer down one cell in column C and then to the left once so the cell pointer is in column B.
4. Create a test range consisting of the cell in column B and the cell immediately above it. Recall that the cell above the one in column B has a number in it.
5. Move the cell pointer to the right once so the cell pointer is in column C. Note that this cell is the cell in which you will place a sum if the cell immediately to the left of column B has a number in it.
6. Use the @COUNT function to determine the number of nonblank cells in the test range. If the count equals one, then the cell in column B is blank and, therefore, does not have a number in it. The macro then needs to stop executing. If the count is two, the instructions for adding the cells in column A and B need to be repeated.

Before entering the macro instructions, enter the title of the macro and macro name information that appear in Figure 17-21.

Figure 17-21

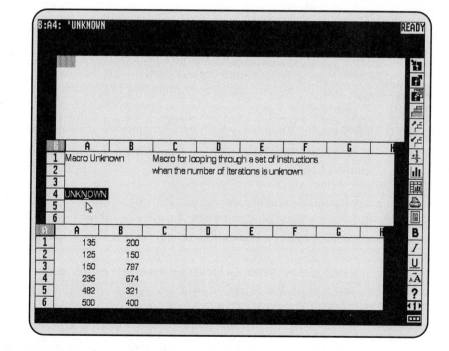

Assume that the values in columns A and B always begin with row 1 in the worksheet on which the macro is used. To specify C1 as the location for the first sum:

Move	the cell pointer to cell B:B4	**Click**	on cell B:B4
Enter	{goto}BEGIN~	**Enter**	{goto}BEGIN~

To include a macro instruction for adding the numbers for the present row in columns A and B and entering the sum in column C:

| **Move** | the cell pointer to cell B:B5 | **Click** | on cell B:B5 |
| **Enter** | '+{left}{left}+{left}~ | **Enter** | '+{left}{left}+{left}~ |

To define a macro instruction that moves the cell pointer down one row and to the left one cell so the cell pointer will be in column B:

| **Move** | the cell pointer to cell B:B6 | **Click** | on cell B:B6 |
| **Enter** | {down}{left} | **Enter** | {down}{left} |

To enter a macro instruction that creates a test range consisting of the cell in column B and the one immediately above it:

| **Move** | the cell pointer to cell B:B7 | **Click** | on cell B:B7 |
| **Enter** | '/rncTEST~{up}~ | **Enter** | '/rncTEST~{up}~ |

To include a macro instruction for moving the cell pointer to the right one cell so it will be in column C again:

| **Move** | the cell pointer to cell B:B8 | **Click** | on cell B:B8 |
| **Enter** | {right} | **Enter** | {right} |

At this point you need to specify a macro instruction that determines if the range name TEST has a count = 1.

| **Move** | the cell pointer to cell B:B9 | **Click** | on cell B:B9 |
| **Enter** | {if @COUNT(TEST)=1} {branch END} | **Enter** | {if @COUNT(TEST)=1} {branch END} |

The above macro instruction should appear on one line with no spaces between the braces.

Note that if the count for the range name TEST equals 1, control will be transferred to the initial cell in the range name END. In this situation, the cell in column B is blank, and the macro needs to be terminated.

If the count for the range name TEST equals 2, then there are numbers in column A and B that need to be summed. You also will need to delete the range name TEST so it can be created again to determine whether the macro needs to stop executing.

To include a macro instruction for deleting the range name TEST:

| **Move** | the cell pointer to cell B:B10 | **Click** | on cell B:B10 |
| **Enter** | '/rndTEST~ | **Enter** | '/rndTEST~ |

To specify a macro instruction that transfers control to the macro instruction that sums the numbers in columns A and B:

Move	the cell pointer to cell B:B11	**Click**	on cell B:B11
Enter	{branch ADD}	**Enter**	{branch ADD}

At this point, you need to:

Move	the cell pointer to cell B:A5	**Click**	on cell B:A5
Enter	ADD	**Enter**	ADD

You will create the range name ADD and specify its range to be cell B:B5. Note that cell B:B5 includes the macro instruction for summing the numbers in columns A and B and then entering the total in column C.

Now, you need to place the macro instructions for ending the macro on the macro worksheet. You must define the location of the range name END so the {branch END} command named earlier will execute properly, delete the range name TEST, move the cell pointer to cell A1 and quit. To define the location of the range name END and to delete the range name TEST:

Move	the cell pointer to cell B:A13	**Click**	on cell B:A13
Enter	END	**Enter**	END
Move	the cell pointer to cell B:B13	**Click**	on cell B:B13
Enter	'/rndTEST~	**Enter**	'/rndTEST~

You will create the range name END and define its range as cell B:B13. Note that the identifiers ADD and END are not actually required, but the use of such labels clarifies flow of the macro execution.

To include the macro instruction that moves the cell pointer to cell A1 after all of the sets of numbers in columns A and B have been summed:

Move	the cell pointer to cell B:B14	**Click**	on cell B:B14
Enter	{goto}START~	**Enter**	{goto}START~

To define the macro instruction that stops the execution of the macro:

Move	the cell pointer to cell B:B15	**Click**	on cell B:B15
Enter	{quit}	**Enter**	{quit}

The {quit} command in this macro is not essential, because the macro would end when a blank cell was encountered. However, the {quit} command clarifies the ending point for the macro.

Create the following range names:

Range Name	Cell to Include in the Range
ADD	B:B5
END	B:B13
BEGIN	A:C1
START	A:A1

So you can see the complete macro, use the **W**orksheet **W**indow **C**lear command sequence or click the Perspective ▦ SmartIcon to display only worksheet B. Your screen should look like Figure 17-22.

Figure 17-22

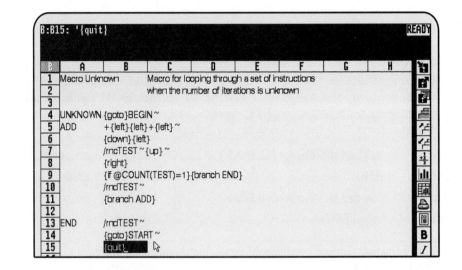

After you compare your macro with Figure 17-22 and make any necessary modifications, name your macro using the name UNKNOWN. Include cell B:B4 as the range. Save the worksheet using the file name UNKNOMAC.

Execute the macro UNKNOWN. The top part of your screen should look like Figure 17-23. You do not need to save the results after the macro is executed.

Figure 17-23

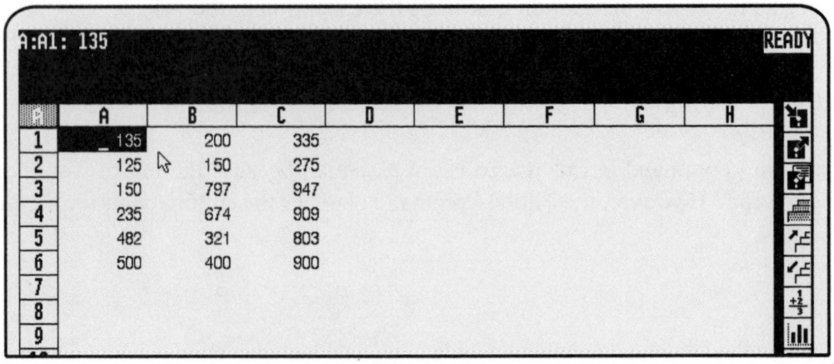

	A	B	C	D	E	F	G	H
1	135	200	335					
2	125	150	275					
3	150	797	947					
4	235	674	909					
5	482	321	803					
6	500	400	900					
7								
8								
9								

A:A1: 135   READY

Using Subroutines

Subroutines are independent sets of instructions that can be called at any point in a macro. One advantage of using a subroutine is that the set of instructions can be easily called from any place in the macro so that the set of commands do not have to be duplicated in the macro. Another advantage of using a subroutine is that it can be called from several different locations within a macro.

For this example, you want to create a macro that permits you to input a code that designates whether or not you want to print the loan amortization schedule after the monthly payment amount is calculated.

Before you complete this example, retrieve the AMORT file, insert an additional worksheet after the AMORT worksheet and display both worksheets on your screen. Make sure row 31 is the first row displayed in worksheet A and row 1 is the first row displayed in worksheet B. After you place the macro title and name information on worksheet B, your screen should look like Figure 17-24.

Figure 17-24

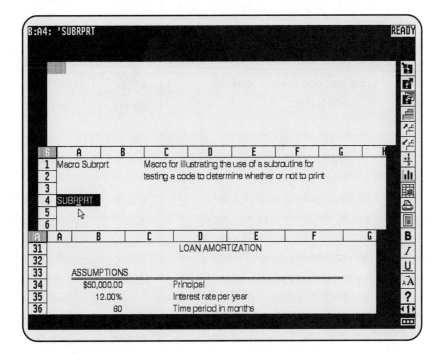

The steps that must be included in the macro to solve this problem are:

1. Set the worksheet to manual recalculation mode.
2. Prompt the user to enter the data for principal, interest rate, and time period.
3. Calculate the loan payment using the data input for principal, interest rate, and time period.
4. Prompt the user to enter a code to indicate whether the person wants to print the loan amortization schedule.
5. Test the code and, if appropriate, print the loan amortization schedule.

So you can see all of the macro instructions on your screen, display only worksheet B.

To make sure the macro executes on the loan amortization schedule, you need to place an instruction in the macro to move the cell pointer to cell A:A31.

| **Move** | the cell pointer to cell B:B4 | *Click* | *on cell B:B4* |
| **Enter** | {goto}BEGIN~ | *Enter* | *{goto}BEGIN~* |

You will create the range name BEGIN and include cell A:A31 as the range.

To include an instruction in the macro to set the recalculation mode to manual:

| **Move** | the cell pointer to cell B:B5 | *Click* | *on cell B:B5* |
| **Enter** | '/wgrm | *Enter* | *'/wgrm* |

At a later point in the macro, you enter a message prompting the user to input the code to determine whether to print the loan amortization schedule. To ensure that the range of cells used are blank when the macro executes:

| **Move** | the cell pointer to cell B:B6 | *Click* | *on cell B:B6* |
| **Enter** | '/rePROMPT~ | *Enter* | *'/rePROMPT~* |

You will create the range name PROMPT and include cells A:H31 through A:H35 as the range of cells.

To place the instructions for prompting the user to enter the principal, interest rate, and time period in your macro:

Move	the cell pointer to cell B:B7	*Click*	*on cell B:B7*
Enter	{getnumber "{Enter Principal Amount: ",PRINCIPAL}~	*Enter*	*{getnumber "Enter Principal Amount: ",PRINCIPAL}~*
Move	the cell pointer to cell B:B8	*Click*	*on cell B:B8*
Enter	{getnumber "Enter Interest Rate in Decimal Form: ",INTEREST}~	*Enter*	*{getnumber "Enter Interest Rate in Decimal Form: ",INTEREST}~*
Move	the cell pointer to cell B:B9	*Click*	*on cell B:B9*
Enter	{getnumber "Enter Time Period in Months: ",PERIOD}~	*Enter*	*{getnumber "Enter Time Period in Months: ",PERIOD}~*

You will create the range names PRINCIPAL, INTEREST, and PERIOD and include cells A:B34, A:B35, and A:B36 as the ranges, respectively.

To include a macro command for calculating the loan amortization schedule after the principal, interest rate, and time period have been input:

| **Move** | the cell pointer to cell B:B10 | *Click* | *on cell B:B10* |
| **Enter** | {calc} | *Enter* | *{calc}* |

To call the subroutine that prompts the user to enter the code for printing, then tests the value of the code, and, if appropriate, prints the loan amortization schedule:

Move	the cell pointer to cell B:B11		*Click*	*on cell B:B11*
Enter	{CKCD}		*Enter*	*{CKCD}*

To include instructions that will remove the CALC status indicator from your screen after the macro has executed and then move the cell pointer to cell A:A31:

Move	the cell pointer to cell B:B12		*Click*	*on cell B:B12*
Enter	{calc}		*Enter*	*{calc}*
Move	the cell pointer to cell B:B13		*Click*	*on cell B:B13*
Enter	{goto}BEGIN~		*Enter*	*{goto}BEGIN~*

To place a command in the macro that terminates execution of the macro:

Move	the cell pointer to cell B:B14		*Click*	*on cell B:B14*
Enter	{quit}		*Enter*	*{quit}*

At this point, you need to create the set of instructions that are included in the CKCD subroutine.

To place the subroutine name on the macro worksheet and to specify a location to enter the code:

Move	the cell pointer to cell B:A16		*Click*	*on cell B:A16*
Enter	CKCD		*Enter*	*CKCD*
Move	the cell pointer to cell B:B16		*Click*	*on cell B:B16*
Enter	{goto}PROMPT~		*Enter*	*{goto}PROMPT~*

You will create the range name CKCD and include B:B16 as its range. When the macro instruction in B:B11 is executed, control will be transferred to cell B:B16.

To include the instructions for prompting the user to input the print code:

Move	the cell pointer to cell B:B17		*Click*	*on cell B:B17*
Enter	If you wish to print the schedule:{down}		*Enter*	*If you wish to print the schedule:{down}*
Move	the cell pointer to cell B:B18		*Click*	*on cell B:B18*
Enter	type a 1 and press enter{down}		*Enter*	*type a 1 and press enter{down}*
Move	the cell pointer to cell B:B19		*Click*	*on cell B:B19*
Enter	If you do not wish to print a schedule:{down}		*Enter*	*If you do not wish to print a schedule:{down}*
Move	the cell pointer to cell B:B20		*Click*	*on cell B:B20*

| **Enter** | type a 2 and press enter{down} | | *Enter* | *type a 2 and press enter{down}* |

To include a command that causes the macro to pause and wait for the user to enter the print code:

| **Move** | the cell pointer to cell B:B21 | | *Click* | *on cell B:B21* |
| **Enter** | {?}~ | | *Enter* | *{?}~* |

After the code is input, you need to include instructions to make sure a valid code is specified. If the code is invalid, the instructions for entering the code must be repeated. If the code is valid, then the code needs to be tested to see whether or not it is appropriate to print the loan amortization schedule.

To test whether the code that was input is valid:

| **Move** | the cell pointer to cell B:B22 | | *Click* | *on cell B:B22* |
| **Enter** | {if TEST_NUM=1#or# TEST_NUM=2}{branch TEST} | | *Enter* | *{if TEST_NUM=1#or# TEST_NUM=2}{branch TEST}* |

You will create the range name TEST_NUM that contains cell A:H35 as its range.

If TEST_NUM has a value of 1 or 2, control transfers to the initial cell in range name TEST to determine whether the loan amortization schedule needs to be printed.

When the code is not valid, the input range PROMPT (A:H31..A:H35) needs to be erased and control needs to be transferred to the first instruction in the subroutine so the user can be prompted to enter the code again. To place these instructions in your macro:

Move	the cell pointer to cell B:B23		*Click*	*on cell B:B23*
Enter	'/rePROMPT~		*Enter*	*'/rePROMPT~*
Move	the cell pointer to cell B:B24		*Click*	*on cell B:B24*
Enter	{CKCD}		*Enter*	*{CKCD}*

At this point, you need to enter the instructions for testing the code. If the code has a value of 1, you do need to print the loan amortization schedule. If the code has a value of 2, you do not print the schedule.

To include the instructions for testing the code and printing:

Move	the cell pointer to cell B:A26		*Click*	*on cell B:A26*
Enter	TEST		*Enter*	*TEST*
Move	the cell pointer to cell B:B26		*Click*	*on cell B:B26*
Enter	{if TEST_NUM=2}{return}		*Enter*	*{if TEST_NUM=2}{return}*

The {if} command tests the code value to see if it is 2. When the code has the value of 2, control is transferred to the first macro command after the subroutine was called using the {return} command. In such a situation, the loan amortization schedule will not be printed. If the value in TEST_NUM (cell A:H35) is a 1, then the loan amortization schedule needs to be printed.

You will create the range name TEST and include cell B:B26 as the range.

To print the schedule:

Move	the cell pointer to cell B:B27		*Click*	*on cell B:B27*
Enter	':prsPRINT_RANGE~g		*Enter*	*':prsPRINT_RANGE~g*

You will create the range name PRINT_RANGE and include cells A:A31 through A:G105 as the range.

To include an instruction to return to the command immediately following the command that called the subroutine:

Move	the cell pointer to cell B:B28		*Click*	*on cell B:B28*
Enter	{return}		*Enter*	*{return}*

Create the following range names:

Range Name	Cell(s) to Include in the Range
BEGIN	A:A31
PROMPT	A:H31..A:H35
PRINCIPAL	A:B34
INTEREST	A:B35
PERIOD	A:B36
CKCD	B:B16
TEST_NUM	A:H35
TEST	B:B26
PRINT_RANGE	A:A31..A:G105

Your macro should look like the one illustrated in Parts 1 and 2 of Figure 17-25.

*Figure 17-25
Part 1*

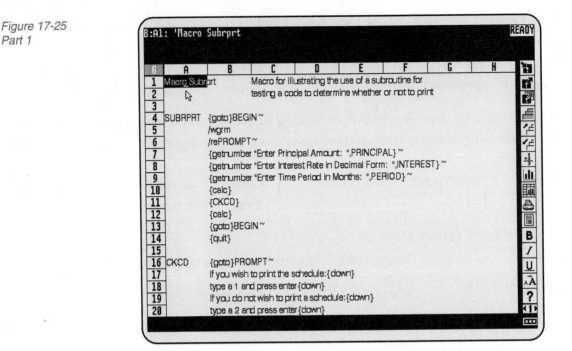

```
B:A1: 'Macro Subrprt                                            READY

        A        B        C        D        E        F        G        H
 1   Macro Subrprt      Macro for illustrating the use of a subroutine for
 2                      testing a code to determine whether or not to print
 3
 4   SUBRPRT  {goto}BEGIN~
 5            /wgrm
 6            /rePROMPT~
 7            {getnumber "Enter Principal Amount: ",PRINCIPAL}~
 8            {getnumber "Enter Interest Rate in Decimal Form: ",INTEREST}~
 9            {getnumber "Enter Time Period in Months: ",PERIOD}~
10            {calc}
11            {CKCD}
12            {calc}
13            {goto}BEGIN~
14            {quit}
15
16   CKCD     {goto}PROMPT~
17            If you wish to print the schedule:{down}
18            type a 1 and press enter{down}
19            If you do not wish to print a schedule:{down}
20            type a 2 and press enter{down}
```

*Figure 17-25
Part 2*

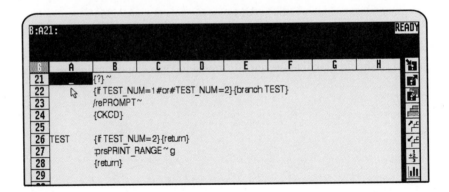

```
B:A21:                                                         READY

        A        B        C        D        E        F        G        H
21            {?}~
22            {if TEST_NUM=1#or#TEST_NUM=2}{branch TEST}
23            /rePROMPT~
24            {CKCD}
25
26   TEST     {if TEST_NUM=2}{return}
27            :prsPRINT_RANGE~g
28            {return}
29
```

Compare your macro with the one appearing in Figure 17-25, Parts 1 and 2, and make any necessary changes. Name your macro using the name SUBRPRT and include cell B:B4 as the cell in its range. Save the worksheet using the file name PRCHK.

Execute the macro SUBRPRT using $10,000 for the principal amount, 9 percent for the interest rate, and 60 months for the time period. When you are prompted for the print code, enter the number 1. Your screen should look like Figure 17-26 after the macro executes properly and you move the cell pointer to cell A:A31. You also should have printed the loan amortization schedule.

Figure 17-26

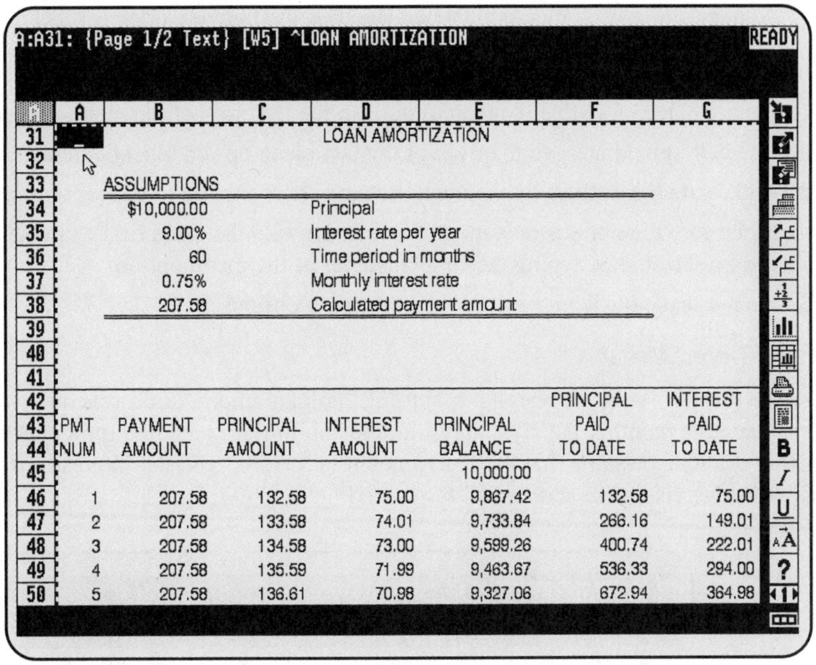

```
A:A31: {Page 1/2 Text} [W5] ^LOAN AMORTIZATION                              READY

      A      B         C         D         E          F          G
 31   =                        LOAN AMORTIZATION
 32
 33          ASSUMPTIONS
 34          $10,000.00         Principal
 35              9.00%          Interest rate per year
 36                 60          Time period in months
 37              0.75%          Monthly interest rate
 38             207.58          Calculated payment amount
 39
 40
 41
 42                                                   PRINCIPAL  INTEREST
 43   PMT    PAYMENT   PRINCIPAL INTEREST  PRINCIPAL   PAID       PAID
 44   NUM    AMOUNT    AMOUNT    AMOUNT    BALANCE     TO DATE    TO DATE
 45                                        10,000.00
 46    1     207.58    132.58    75.00     9,867.42    132.58      75.00
 47    2     207.58    133.58    74.01     9,733.84    266.16     149.01
 48    3     207.58    134.58    73.00     9,599.26    400.74     222.01
 49    4     207.58    135.59    71.99     9,463.67    536.33     294.00
 50    5     207.58    136.61    70.98     9,327.06    672.94     364.98
```

Execute the macro again, using a value of 2 for the print code. Finally, execute the macro using 3 for the print code. Notice that you are prompted for a print code until you enter a 1 or a 2. Do not save the results after the macro is executed.

Creating User-Designed Menus

In some situations, individuals may want to design their own menus using the Lotus 1-2-3 command language. The process for preparing a menu includes the following:

1. Write a *menu-processing* macro that initiates the execution of the user-designed menu.
2. Determine the entries for the menu line and the description line.
3. Write the macro commands for each menu option.

The following guidelines can be used in developing a **user-designed menu**:

1. Find a portion of the spreadsheet that has at least as many blank columns as there are menu options.
2. The first row of the user-designed menu contains the menu options as they will appear on the screen.
3. The row below the menu options includes a description of each menu option that will appear on the screen when a menu option is highlighted.
4. The macro commands for each menu option can be placed immediately below the menu item or in a range of cells at another location on the spreadsheet.

5. A menu-processing macro must be placed on the macro worksheet that contains the menu.

Some cautionary guidelines for creating menus follow:

1. Do not place more than 8 menu options in the first row of the menu you are designing.

2. The cell immediately to the right of the last menu option must be blank.

3. Make sure the options on the menu line are short enough to appear on the screen.

4. Make sure the options on a menu do not start with the same first character so that a menu option can be selected by typing the first character of the menu option.

5. Do not leave blank entries between the menu options.

Single-Tiered Menu

Suppose that you want to design a menu for the loan amortization schedule worksheet that permits you to calculate the monthly payment and print the appropriate schedule for a one- or a five-year time period. For this example, assume that the loan amount is $50,000 and the interest rate is 12 percent. When you finish this exercise, your screen will look like Figure 17-27, Part 1.

*Figure 17-27
Part 1*

The complete contents of the cells are illustrated in Figure 17-27, Part 2.

Figure 17-27
Part 2

| Macro Single | Macro for illustrating the design and use |
| | of a one tier menu |

SINGLE   {menubranch MAIN}

MAIN	1-year	Print-1	Five-year	5-Print	Stop
	1-year term	1-year sched	5-year term	5-year sched	Quit Process
	{goto}LOAN_PERIOD~	:prsPRINT_12~g	{goto}LOAN_PERIOD~	:prsPrint_60~g	/reLOAN_PERIOD~
	12~	{menubranch MAIN}	60~	{menubranch MAIN)}	{goto}BEGIN~
	{goto}BEGIN~		{goto}BEGIN~		{quit}
	{menubranch MAIN}		{menubranch MAIN}		

To complete this exercise, retrieve the AMORT file and insert an additional worksheet for the single-tiered menu macro. Make sure row 31 is the first row displayed in worksheet A and row 1 is the first row displayed in worksheet B. After you place the title and macro name on your worksheet, your screen should look like Figure 17-28.

Figure 17-28

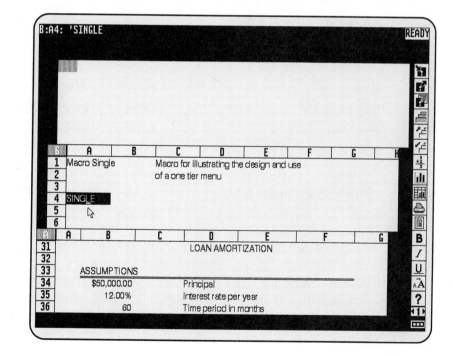

When you execute a user-designed menu macro, you must include a {menubranch} command to indicate to 1-2-3 on which menu you want to start. To include this command on the macro worksheet:

| **Move** | the cell pointer to cell B:B4 | **Click** | on cell B:B4 |
| **Enter** | {menubranch MAIN} | **Enter** | {menubranch MAIN} |

To enter the label MAIN in your macro:

| **Move** | the cell pointer to cell B:A6 | **Click** | on cell B:A6 |
| **Enter** | MAIN | **Enter** | MAIN |

The five menu options to be included are 1-year, Print-1, Five-year, 5-Print, and Stop. If the 1-year menu option is selected, then the loan amortization schedule will be computed using 12 months as the time period. When the Print-1 option is selected, the loan amortization schedule for a one-year (12 months) time period is printed.

If the Five-year menu option is chosen, the loan amortization schedule is calculated using a 60-month time period. When the 5-Print menu option is chosen, the loan amortization schedule for a five-year (60 months) time period is printed. When the Stop menu option is selected, execution of the macro will stop.

To include the five menu options in your macro:

Move	the cell pointer to cell B:B6	**Click**	on cell B:B6
Enter	'1-year	**Enter**	'1-year
Move	the cell pointer to cell B:C6	**Click**	on cell B:C6
Enter	Print-1	**Enter**	Print-1
Move	the cell pointer to cell B:D6	**Click**	on cell B:D6
Enter	Five-year	**Enter**	Five-Year
Move	the cell pointer to cell B:E6	**Click**	on cell B:E6
Enter	'5-Print	**Enter**	'5-Print
Move	the cell pointer to cell B:F6	**Click**	on cell B:F6
Enter	Stop	**Enter**	Stop

So you can see more of the information on your screen, reduce the column width of column A to 7. Then widen columns B through F so each column displays 13 characters.

At this point, you have placed the menu options on the macro worksheet. You will create the range name MAIN and include the location of the first menu option, B:B6, as its range.

The second row of your menu macro includes the description for each menu option that will appear in the control panel when the menu pointer is highlighting it. To enter the descriptive information for each of the menu options:

| **Move** | the cell pointer to cell B:B7 | **Click** | on cell B:B7 |
| **Enter** | '1-year term | **Enter** | '1-year term |

Move	the cell pointer to cell B:C7		*Click*	*on cell B:C7*
Enter	'1-year sched		*Enter*	*'1-year sched*
Move	the cell pointer to cell B:D7		*Click*	*on cell B:D7*
Enter	'5-year term		*Enter*	*'5-year term*
Move	the cell pointer to cell B:E7		*Click*	*on cell B:E7*
Enter	'5-year sched		*Enter*	*'5-year sched*
Move	the cell pointer to cell B:F7		*Click*	*on cell B:F7*
Enter	Quit process		*Enter*	*Quit process*

The macro instructions that are to be executed when a menu option is selected can appear immediately below the description of the menu option, or in a range at another location on the macro worksheet. For this example, you will place the macro instructions immediately below each menu option.

For the 1-year menu option, you need to enter macro instructions that enter the number 12 for the time period in cell A:B36, place the menu pointer in cell A:A31, and branch to the main menu.

You will create the range name BEGIN and include cell A:A31 as the range. You will also create the range name LOAN_PERIOD and include cell A:B36 as the range.

To include these instructions below the first menu option:

Move	the cell pointer to cell B:B8		*Click*	*on cell B:B8*
Enter	{goto}LOAN_PERIOD~		*Enter*	*{goto}LOAN_PERIOD~*
Move	the cell pointer to cell B:B9		*Click*	*on cell B:B9*
Enter	'12~		*Enter*	*'12~*
Move	the cell pointer to cell B:B10		*Click*	*on cell B:B10*
Enter	{goto}BEGIN~		*Enter*	*{goto}BEGIN~*
Move	the cell pointer to cell B:B11		*Click*	*on cell B:B11*
Enter	{menubranch MAIN}		*Enter*	*{menubranch MAIN}*

When the Print-1 option is selected, you must include instructions that select the proper range of cells and print a 12-month loan amortization schedule. Then, you must specify that control is to be transferred to the main menu.

You will create a range name PRINT_12 and include cells A:A31 through A:G57 as the range of cells.

To place the appropriate macro instructions under the second menu option:

Move	the cell pointer to cell B:C8		*Click*	*on cell B:C8*
Enter	':prsPRINT_12~g		*Enter*	*':prsPRINT_12~g*
Move	the cell pointer to cell B:C9		*Click*	*on cell B:C9*
Enter	{menubranch MAIN}		*Enter*	*{menubranch MAIN}*

The Five-year menu option requires the same set of instructions as the 1-year option, except the number 60 must be entered for the time period in cell A:B36.

To include the instructions that must appear below the Five-year menu option:

Move	the cell pointer to cell B:D8		***Click***	*on cell B:D8*
Enter	{goto}LOAN_PERIOD~		***Enter***	*{goto}LOAN_PERIOD~*
Move	the cell pointer to cell B:D9		***Click***	*on cell B:D9*
Enter	'60~		***Enter***	*'60~*
Move	the cell pointer to cell B:D10		***Click***	*on cell B:D10*
Enter	{goto}BEGIN~		***Enter***	*{goto}BEGIN~*
Move	the cell pointer to cell B:D11		***Click***	*on cell B:D11*
Enter	{menubranch MAIN}		***Enter***	*{menubranch MAIN}*

The set of instructions that must be included below the 5-Print menu option are the same as the Print-1 menu option, except the print range must include 60 months of data instead of 12.

You will create the range name PRINT_60 and include cells A:A31 through A:G105 as the range of cells.

To place the appropriate instructions under the 5-Print menu option:

Move	the cell pointer to cell B:E8		***Click***	*on cell B:E8*
Enter	':prsPRINT_60~g		***Enter***	*':prsPRINT_60~g*
Move	the cell pointer to cell B:E9		***Click***	*on cell B:E9*
Enter	{menubranch MAIN}		***Enter***	*{menubranch MAIN}*

The final menu option is Stop. For this menu option, you need to enter instructions to clear cell A:B36 (where you placed the time period data) and end the execution of the macro.

To place these instructions below the Stop menu:

Move	the cell pointer to cell B:F8		***Click***	*on cell B:F8*
Enter	'/reLOAN_PERIOD~		***Enter***	*'/reLOAN_PERIOD~*
Move	the cell pointer to cell B:F9		***Click***	*on cell B:F9*
Enter	{goto}BEGIN~		***Enter***	*{goto}BEGIN~*
Move	the cell pointer to cell B:F10		***Click***	*on cell B:F10*
Enter	{quit}		***Enter***	*{quit}*

Your screen should now look like Figure 17-29, Part 1.

Figure 17-29
Part 1

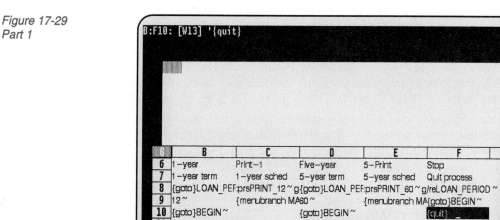

Figure 17-29
Part 2

| Macro Single | Macro for illustrating the design and use | | | |
| | of a one tier menu | | | |

| SINGLE | {menubranch MAIN} | | | |

MAIN	1-year	Print-1	Five-year	5-Print	Stop
	1-year term	1-year sched	5-year term	5-year sched	Quit Process
	{goto}LOAN_PERIOD~	:prsPRINT_12~g	{goto}LOAN_PERIOD~	:prsPrint_60~g	/reLOAN_PERIOD~
	12~	{menubranch MAIN}	60~	{menubranch MAIN}}	{goto}BEGIN~
	{goto}BEGIN~		{goto}BEGIN~		{quit}
	{menubranch MAIN}		{menubranch MAIN}		

Create the following range names:

Range Name	Cell(s) to Include in the Range
MAIN	B:B6
BEGIN	A:A31
LOAN_PERIOD	A:B36

PRINT_12	A:A31..A:G57
PRINT_60	A:A31..A:G105

After comparing the menu you designed with Figure 17-29, Part 1 with the information appearing in Figure 17-29, Part 2, make any necessary changes. Name your macro SINGLE. Include the cell B:B4 as the range for the macro SINGLE, and save the worksheet using the file name SINGLMAC.

Move the cell pointer to cell A:B36 and erase the contents of the cell. So you can see more of the worksheet, display only worksheet A. The ERR indicator appears in some of the worksheet cells. When you execute the macro SINGLE, the ERR indicator will disappear from the cells. Make sure the principal amount is $50,000 and the interest rate is 12 percent. If necessary, change the values.

Execute the macro SINGLE and select the 1-year menu option. Figure 17-30, Part 1 includes the menu when it initially appears on the screen. Figure 17-30, Part 2 illustrates the appearance of the screen after the 1-year option is selected. Note that the macro is designed so the menu will continue to appear on the screen until you select the Stop menu option. Figure 17-30, Part 3 displays the screen after the Stop option is selected from the menu.

Figure 17-30
Part 1

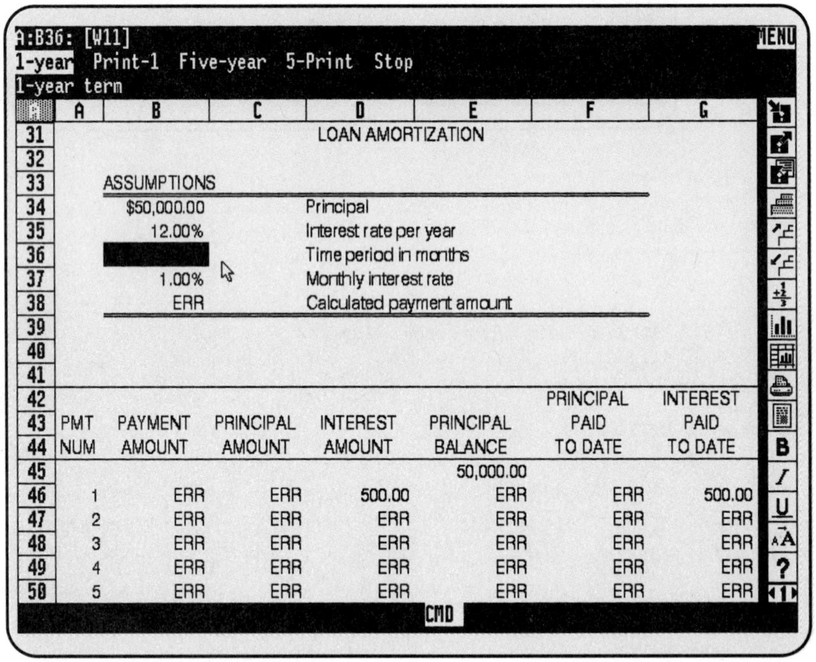

Figure 17-30
Part 2

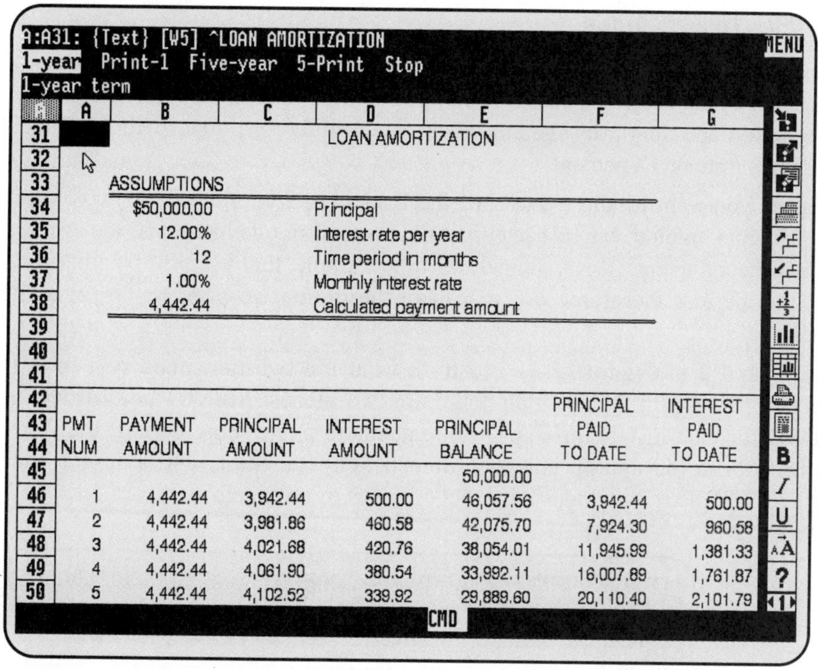

```
A:A31: {Text} [W5] ^LOAN AMORTIZATION                           MENU
1-year  Print-1  Five-year  5-Print  Stop
1-year term
```

	A	B	C	D	E	F	G
31				LOAN AMORTIZATION			
32							
33		ASSUMPTIONS					
34		$50,000.00		Principal			
35		12.00%		Interest rate per year			
36		12		Time period in months			
37		1.00%		Monthly interest rate			
38		4,442.44		Calculated payment amount			
39							
40							
41							
42						PRINCIPAL	INTEREST
43	PMT	PAYMENT	PRINCIPAL	INTEREST	PRINCIPAL	PAID	PAID
44	NUM	AMOUNT	AMOUNT	AMOUNT	BALANCE	TO DATE	TO DATE
45					50,000.00		
46	1	4,442.44	3,942.44	500.00	46,057.56	3,942.44	500.00
47	2	4,442.44	3,981.86	460.58	42,075.70	7,924.30	960.58
48	3	4,442.44	4,021.68	420.76	38,054.01	11,945.99	1,381.33
49	4	4,442.44	4,061.90	380.54	33,992.11	16,007.89	1,761.87
50	5	4,442.44	4,102.52	339.92	29,889.60	20,110.40	2,101.79

```
CMD
```

Figure 17-30
Part 3

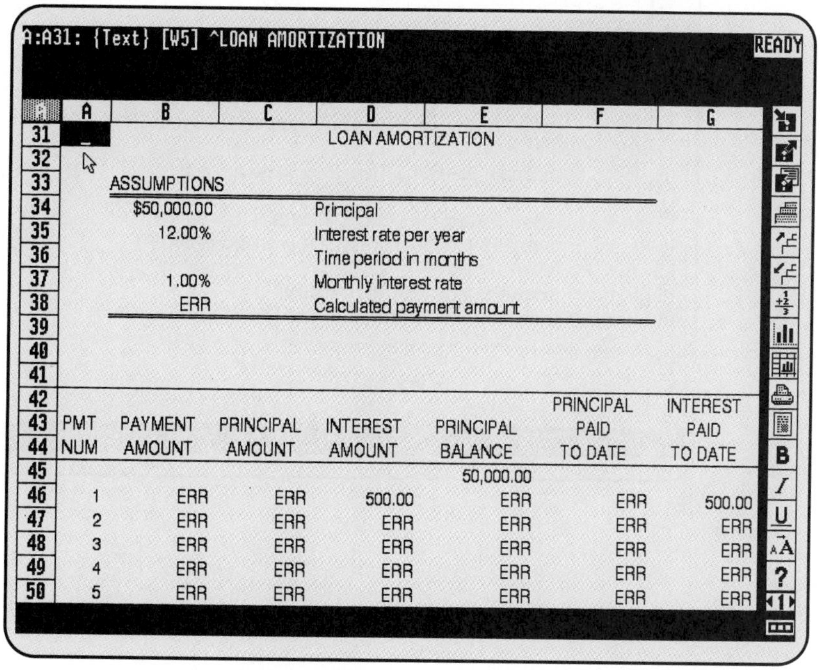

```
A:A31: {Text} [W5] ^LOAN AMORTIZATION                          READY
```

	A	B	C	D	E	F	G
31				LOAN AMORTIZATION			
32							
33		ASSUMPTIONS					
34		$50,000.00		Principal			
35		12.00%		Interest rate per year			
36				Time period in months			
37		1.00%		Monthly interest rate			
38		ERR		Calculated payment amount			
39							
40							
41							
42						PRINCIPAL	INTEREST
43	PMT	PAYMENT	PRINCIPAL	INTEREST	PRINCIPAL	PAID	PAID
44	NUM	AMOUNT	AMOUNT	AMOUNT	BALANCE	TO DATE	TO DATE
45					50,000.00		
46	1	ERR	ERR	500.00	ERR	ERR	500.00
47	2	ERR	ERR	ERR	ERR	ERR	ERR
48	3	ERR	ERR	ERR	ERR	ERR	ERR
49	4	ERR	ERR	ERR	ERR	ERR	ERR
50	5	ERR	ERR	ERR	ERR	ERR	ERR

Multiple-Tiered Menus

User-designed menus can be linked together to form a *tiered* menu structure. The example here is an extension of the single-tiered menu in the previous section that allowed you to select a one- or five-year time period and then print the amortization schedule for a loan with a principal amount of $50,000 and an interest rate of 12 percent.

Suppose you want to allow a user of the loan amortization schedule worksheet the flexibility to specify the principal amount, interest rate, and time period in one menu and then print the amortization schedule from a second menu. It is assumed, for this example, that you will be entering either 12 or 60 months for the time period; therefore, you will have the options to print a one- or a five-year loan amortization schedule.

Parts 1 and 2 of Figure 17-31 illustrate what the two-tier menu will look like when you finish this exercise. Notice in this example there are two menus: MENU1 and MENU2. The first menu includes options for entering the principal amount, interest rate, time period, transferring control to the second menu to print the appropriate loan amortization schedule, and stopping the execution of the macro. Figure 17-31, Part 3 includes the exact contents of each cell.

Figure 17-31
Part 1

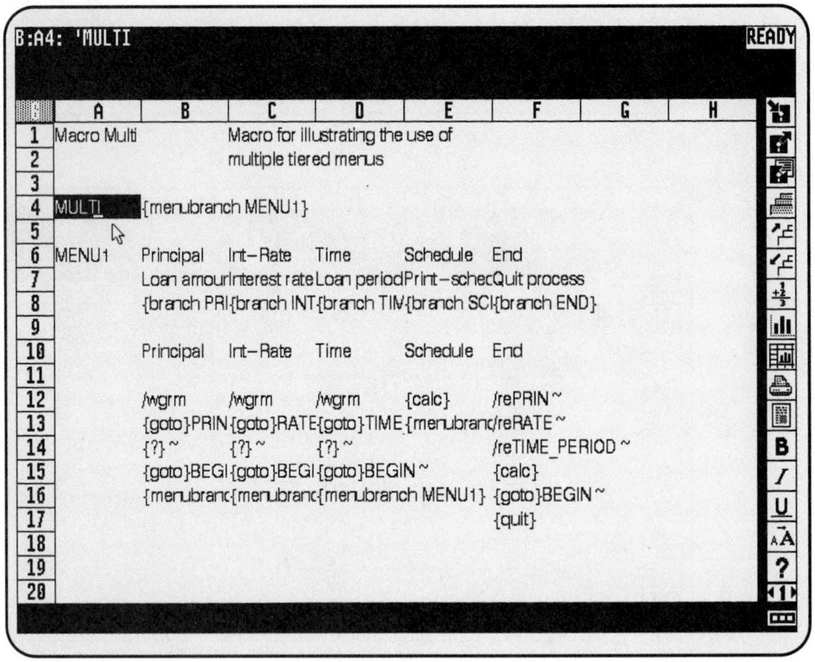

Figure 17-31
Part 2

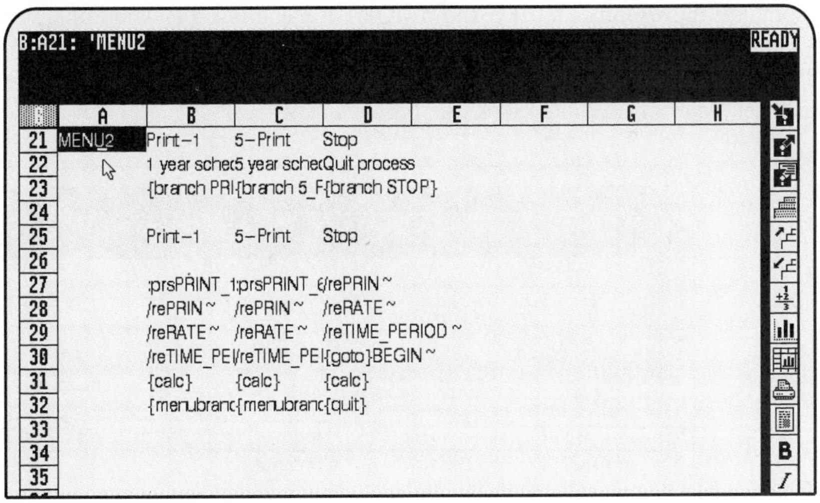

```
B:A21: 'MENU2                                                    READY

        A        B         C         D      E       F       G       H
  21  MENU2   Print–1   5–Print    Stop
  22       ▷   1 year sched 5 year sched Quit process
  23           {branch PRI{branch 5_F{branch STOP}
  24
  25           Print–1    5–Print    Stop
  26
  27           :prsPRINT_1:prsPRINT_6/rePRIN ~
  28           /rePRIN ~   /rePRIN ~   /reRATE ~
  29           /reRATE ~   /reRATE ~   /reTIME_PERIOD ~
  30           /reTIME_PEI/reTIME_PEI{goto}BEGIN ~
  31           {calc}      {calc}      {calc}
  32           {menubranc{menubranc{quit}
  33
  34
  35
```

Figure 17-31
Part 3

Macro Multi	Macro for illustrating the use of multiple tiered menus			
MULTI	{menubranch MENU1}			
MENU1	Principal	Int-Rate	Time	Schedule	End
	Loan amount	Interest rate	Loan period	Print-sched	Quit process
	{branch PRINCIPAL}	{branch INT_RATE}	{branch TIME}	{branch SCHEDULE}	{branch END}

	Principal	Int-Rate	Time	Schedule	End
	/wgrm	/wgrm	/wgrm	{calc}	/rePRIN~
	{goto}PRIN~	{goto}RATE~	{goto}TIME_PERIOD~	{menubranch MENU2}	/reRATE~
	{?}~	{?}~	{?}~		/reTIME_PERIOD~
	{goto}BEGIN~	{goto}BEGIN~	{goto}BEGIN~		{calc}
	{menubranch MENU1}	{menubranch MENU1}	{menubranch MENU1}		{goto}BEGIN~
					{quit}

MENU2	Print-1	5-Print	Stop	
	1 year sched	5 year sched	Quit process	
	{branch PRINT_1}	{branch 5_PRINT}	{branch STOP}	

	Print-1	5-Print	Stop
	:prsPRINT_12~g	:prsPRINT_60~g	/rePRIN~
	/rePRIN~	/rePRIN~	/reRATE~
	/reRATE~	/reRATE~	/reTIME_PERIOD~
	/reTIME_PERIOD~	/reTIME_PERIOD~	{goto}BEGIN~
	{calc}	{calc}	{calc}
	{menubranch MENU1}	{menubranch MENU1}	{quit}

To complete this exercise, retrieve the AMORT file and insert an additional worksheet after the AMORT worksheet for the two-tiered menu macro. Make sure row 31 is the first row displayed in worksheet A and row 1 is the first row displayed in worksheet B. After placing the title and macro name on your worksheet, your screen should look like Figure 17-32.

Figure 17-32

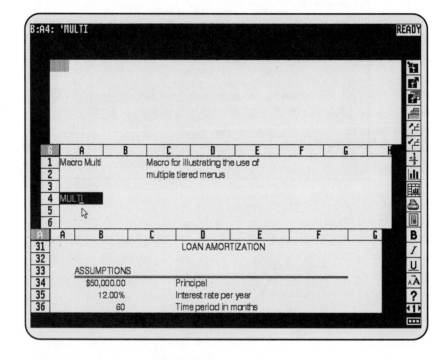

To see more of what appears in the columns, change the column widths for column A to 6 and widen columns B through F so each column will display 13 characters.

When you execute a user-designed menu macro, you must include a {menubranch} command to indicate to 1-2-3 on which menu you want to start.

To include this command on the macro worksheet:

| **Move** | the cell pointer to cell B:B4 | **Click** | on cell B:B4 |
| **Enter** | {menubranch MENU1} | **Enter** | {menubranch MENU1} |

To place the MENU1 label in your macro:

| **Move** | the cell pointer to cell B:A6 | **Click** | on cell B:A6 |
| **Enter** | MENU1 | **Enter** | MENU1 |

To include the MENU1 menu options in your macro:

| **Move** | the cell pointer to cell B:B6 | **Click** | on cell B:B6 |
| **Enter** | Principal | **Enter** | Principal |

Move	the cell pointer to cell B:C6		*Click*	*on cell B:C6*
Enter	Int-Rate		*Enter*	*Int-Rate*
Move	the cell pointer to cell B:D6		*Click*	*on cell B:D6*
Enter	Time		*Enter*	*Time*
Move	the cell pointer to cell B:E6		*Click*	*on cell B:E6*
Enter	Schedule		*Enter*	*Schedule*
Move	the cell pointer to cell B:F6		*Click*	*on cell B:F6*
Enter	End		*Enter*	*End*

At this point, you have placed the menu options for MENU1 on the macro worksheet. You will create the range name MENU1 and include the location of the first menu option, B:B6, as its range.

To place the description for each menu option that will appear in the control panel when the menu option is highlighted by the menu pointer:

Move	the cell pointer to cell B:B7		*Click*	*on cell B:B7*
Enter	Loan amount		*Enter*	*Loan amount*
Move	the cell pointer to cell B:C7		*Click*	*on cell B:C7*
Enter	Interest rate		*Enter*	*Interest rate*
Move	the cell pointer to cell B:D7		*Click*	*on cell B:D7*
Enter	Loan period		*Enter*	*Loan period*
Move	the cell pointer to cell B:E7		*Click*	*on cell B:E7*
Enter	Print-sched		*Enter*	*Print-sched*
Move	the cell pointer to cell B:F7		*Click*	*on cell B:F7*
Enter	Quit process		*Enter*	*Quit process*

In the single-tier menu example, you placed the macro instructions for each option immediately below the description of the menu option. For this exercise, you place the instructions several cells below the macro options to illustrate another approach for entering them.

To start the process for placing the instructions for the macro options:

Copy	the menu options in cells B:B6..B:E6 to cells B:B10..B:E10	*Copy*	*the menu options in cells B:B6..B:E6 to cells B:B10..B:E10*

You will create the range names for PRINCIPAL, INT_RATE, TIME, SCHEDULE, and END. Include the individual cell B:B12 through B:F12, respectively, as the range for each of the menu option range names. For example, the range name PRINCIPAL should have cell B:B12 as its range and END should have cell B:F12 as its range.

You will also create the range names PRIN, RATE, TIME_PERIOD, and BEGIN. PRIN should include cell A:B34 as its range, RATE should specify A:B35 as its range, and TIME_PERIOD should include cell A:B36 as its range. The range name BEGIN should have cell A:A31 as its range.

Now, you need to enter the instructions for the various menu options below the menu option identifiers that appear in row 10. The instructions for the Principal menu option must state that the manual calculation mode is to be used, the cell pointer needs to be moved to the cell for the user to enter the principal amount in cell A:B34, the macro must pause for the user to enter the principal value, and control is to be transferred to MENU1 after the principal amount is entered.

To place the appropriate instructions on your macro worksheet:

Move	the cell pointer to cell B:B12	*Click*	*on cell B:B12*
Enter	'/wgrm	*Enter*	*'/wgrm*
Move	the cell pointer to cell B:B13	*Click*	*on cell B:B13*
Enter	{goto}PRIN~	*Enter*	*{goto}PRIN~*
Move	the cell pointer to cell B:B14	*Click*	*on cell B:B14*
Enter	{?}~	*Enter*	*{?}~*
Move	the cell pointer to cell B:B15	*Click*	*on cell B:B15*
Enter	{goto}BEGIN~	*Enter*	*{goto}BEGIN~*
Move	the cell pointer to cell B:B16	*Click*	*on cell B:B16*
Enter	{menubranch MENU1}	*Enter*	*{menubranch MENU1}*

The macro instructions for the Int-Rate and Time menu options are exactly the same as for the Principal menu option except for the cell in which the appropriate data is to be entered.

To place the instructions for the Int-Rate menu option on your macro worksheet:

Move	the cell pointer to cell B:C12	*Click*	*on cell B:C12*
Enter	'/wgrm	*Enter*	*'/wgrm*
Move	the cell pointer to cell B:C13	*Click*	*on cell B:C13*
Enter	{goto}RATE~	*Enter*	*{goto}RATE~*
Move	the cell pointer to cell B:C14	*Click*	*on cell B:C14*
Enter	{?}~	*Enter*	*{?}~*
Move	the cell pointer to cell B:C15	*Click*	*on cell B:C15*
Enter	{goto}BEGIN~	*Enter*	*{goto}BEGIN~*
Move	the cell pointer to cell B:C16	*Click*	*on cell B:C16*
Enter	{menubranch MENU1}	*Enter*	*{menubranch MENU1}*

To include the instructions for the Time menu option in your macro:

Move	the cell pointer to cell B:D12		*Click*	*on cell B:D12*
Enter	'/wgrm		*Enter*	*'/wgrm*
Move	the cell pointer to cell B:D13		*Click*	*on cell B:D13*
Enter	{goto}TIME_PERIOD~		*Enter*	*{goto}TIME_PERIOD~*
Move	the cell pointer to cell B:D14		*Click*	*on cell B:D14*
Enter	{?}~		*Enter*	*{?}~*
Move	the cell pointer to cell B:D15		*Click*	*on cell B:D15*
Enter	{goto}BEGIN~		*Enter*	*{goto}BEGIN~*
Move	the cell pointer to cell B:D16		*Click*	*on cell B:D16*
Enter	{menubranch MENU1}		*Enter*	*{menubranch MENU1}*

For the Schedule menu option you need instructions for calculating the loan amortization schedule and transferring control to the menu for printing the schedule.

To place these instructions on your macro worksheet:

Move	the cell pointer to cell B:E12		*Click*	*on cell B:E12*
Enter	{calc}		*Enter*	*{calc}*
Move	the cell pointer to cell B:E13		*Click*	*on cell B:E13*
Enter	{menubranch MENU2}		*Enter*	*{menubranch MENU2}*

The final menu option for MENU1 to consider is END. For this menu option, you must enter instructions for erasing the principal, interest rate, and time period values, removing the CALC indicator from the screen, moving the cell pointer to cell A:A31, and stopping the execution of the macro. To incorporate these instructions on your macro worksheet:

Move	the cell pointer to cell B:F12		*Click*	*on cell B:F12*
Enter	'/rePRIN~		*Enter*	*'/rePRIN~*
Move	the cell pointer to cell B:F13		*Click*	*on cell B:F13*
Enter	'/reRATE~		*Enter*	*'/reRATE~*
Move	the cell pointer to cell B:F14		*Click*	*on cell B:F14*
Enter	'/reTIME_PERIOD~		*Enter*	*'/reTIME_PERIOD~*
Move	the cell pointer to cell B:F15		*Click*	*on cell B:F15*
Enter	{calc}		*Enter*	*{calc}*
Move	the cell pointer to cell B:F16		*Click*	*on cell B:F16*
Enter	{goto}BEGIN~		*Enter*	*{goto}BEGIN~*

| **Move** | the cell pointer to cell B:F17 | **Click** | on cell B:F17 |
| **Enter** | {quit} | **Enter** | {quit} |

Now you need to place {branch} commands in the cells immediately below the descriptions for the menu options so control will be transferred to the appropriate macro instructions for the various menu options.

To place these branch commands in the proper cells:

Move	the cell pointer to cell B:B8	**Click**	on cell B:B8
Enter	{branch PRINCIPAL}	**Enter**	{branch PRINCIPAL}
Move	the cell pointer to cell B:C8	**Click**	on cell B:C8
Enter	{branch INT_RATE}	**Enter**	{branch INT_RATE}
Move	the cell pointer to cell B:D8	**Click**	on cell B:D8
Enter	{branch TIME}	**Enter**	{branch TIME}
Move	the cell pointer to cell B:E8	**Click**	on cell B:E8
Enter	{branch SCHEDULE}	**Enter**	{branch SCHEDULE}
Move	the cell pointer to cell B:F8	**Click**	on cell B:F8
Enter	{branch END}	**Enter**	{branch END}

Create the following range names:

Range Name	Cell to Include in the Range
MENU1	B:B6
PRINCIPAL	B:B12
INT_RATE	B:C12
TIME	B:D12
SCHEDULE	B:E12
END	B:F12
PRIN	A:B34
RATE	A:B35
TIME_PERIOD	A:B36
BEGIN	A:A31

Execution is transferred to MENU2 when you select the Schedule menu option on MENU1. The Print-1 and 5-Print menu options on MENU2 provide you with the capability to print a 1-year or 5-year amortization schedule.

You are now ready to place the macro instructions for MENU2 on your macro worksheet. Use the information in Figure 17-33 to enter the macro instructions for MENU2 in cells B:A21 through B:D32.

Figure 17-33

Macro Multi	Macro for illustrating the use of multiple tiered menus			
MULTI	{menubranch MENU1}			
MENU1	Principal	Int-Rate	Time	Schedule	End
	Loan amount	Interest rate	Loan period	Print-sched	Quit process
	{branch PRINCIPAL}	{branch INT_RATE}	{branch TIME}	{branch SCHEDULE}	{branch END}
	Principal	Int-Rate	Time	Schedule	End
	/wgrm	/wgrm	/wgrm	{calc}	/rePRIN~
	{goto}PRIN~	{goto}RATE~	{goto}TIME_PERIOD~	{menubranch MENU2}	/reRATE~
	{?}~	{?}~	{?}~		/reTIME_PERIOD
	{goto}BEGIN~	{goto}BEGIN~	{goto}BEGIN~		{calc}
	{menubranch MENU1}	{menubranch MENU1}	{menubranch MENU1}		{goto}BEGIN~
					{quit}
MENU2	Print-1	5-Print	Stop		
	1 year sched	5 year sched	Quit process		
	{branch PRINT_1}	{branch 5_PRINT}	{branch STOP}		
	Print-1	5-Print	Stop		
	:prsPRINT_12~g	:prsPRINT_60~g	/rePRIN~		
	/rePRIN~	/rePRIN~	/reRATE~		
	/reRATE~	/reRATE~	/reTIME_PERIOD~		
	/reTIME_PERIOD~	/reTIME_PERIOD~	{goto}BEGIN~		
	{calc}	{calc}	{calc}		
	{menubranch MENU1}	{menubranch MENU1}	{quit}		

After you have entered the information, be sure to create range names as follows:

Range Name	Cell(s) to Include in the Range
MENU2	B:B21
PRINT_1	B:B27
5_PRINT	B:C27
STOP	B:D27
PRINT_12	A:A31..G57
PRINT_60	A31..G105

After you have compared the multi-tiered menu you designed with Figure 17-33, make any necessary changes. Name your macro MULTI. Include the cell B:B4 as the range for the macro range name MULTI and save the worksheet using the file name MULTIMAC.

Move the cell pointer to cell A:B34 and erase cells A:B34 through A:B36. So you can see more of the worksheet, display only worksheet A. The ERR indicator appears in some of the worksheet cells. When you execute the macro MULTI, the ERR indicator will disappear from the cells. Execute the macro MULTI. Figure 17-34, Part 1 includes the menu when it initially appears on the screen.

Figure 17-34
Part 1

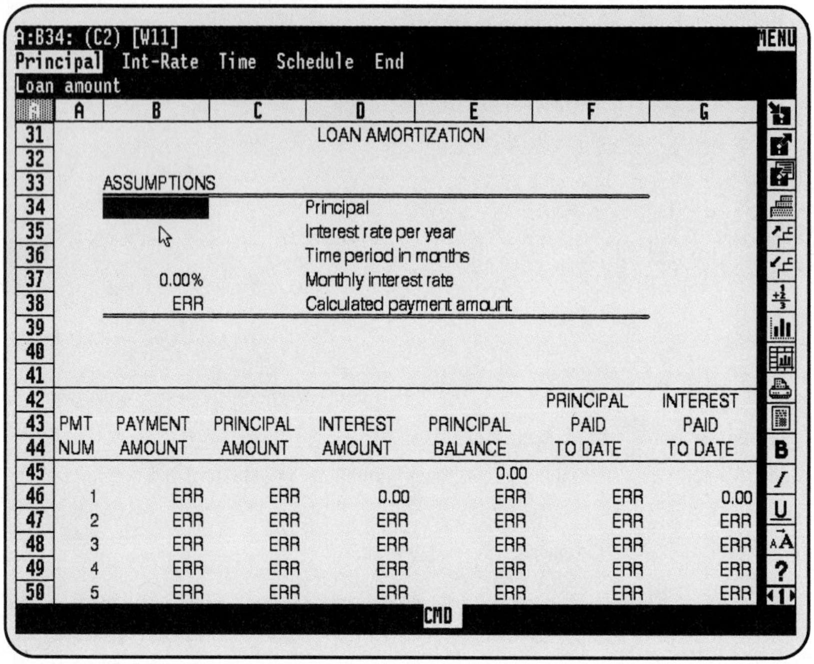

```
A:B34: (C2) [W11]                                              MENU
Principal  Int-Rate  Time  Schedule  End
Loan amount
    A        B          C          D          E          F          G
31                               LOAN AMORTIZATION
32
33          ASSUMPTIONS
34                                  Principal
35              ▷                   Interest rate per year
36                                  Time period in months
37          0.00%                   Monthly interest rate
38          ERR                     Calculated payment amount
39
40
41
42                                                        PRINCIPAL   INTEREST
43   PMT   PAYMENT    PRINCIPAL   INTEREST   PRINCIPAL      PAID         PAID
44   NUM   AMOUNT      AMOUNT      AMOUNT     BALANCE      TO DATE     TO DATE
45                                             0.00
46    1     ERR         ERR        0.00        ERR          ERR         0.00
47    2     ERR         ERR        ERR         ERR          ERR         ERR
48    3     ERR         ERR        ERR         ERR          ERR         ERR
49    4     ERR         ERR        ERR         ERR          ERR         ERR
50    5     ERR         ERR        ERR         ERR          ERR         ERR
                                          CMD
```

To illustrate the use of the macro:

Select	Principal		*Choose*	*Principal*
Enter	50000		*Enter*	*50000*
Select	Int-Rate		*Choose*	*Int-Rate*
Enter	.10		*Enter*	*.10*
Select	Time		*Choose*	*Time*
Enter	12		*Enter*	*12*

To print the resulting amortization schedule:

Select	Schedule		*Choose*	*Schedule*

Figure 17-34, Part 2 illustrates the screen after the Schedule option is selected.

Figure 17-34
Part 2

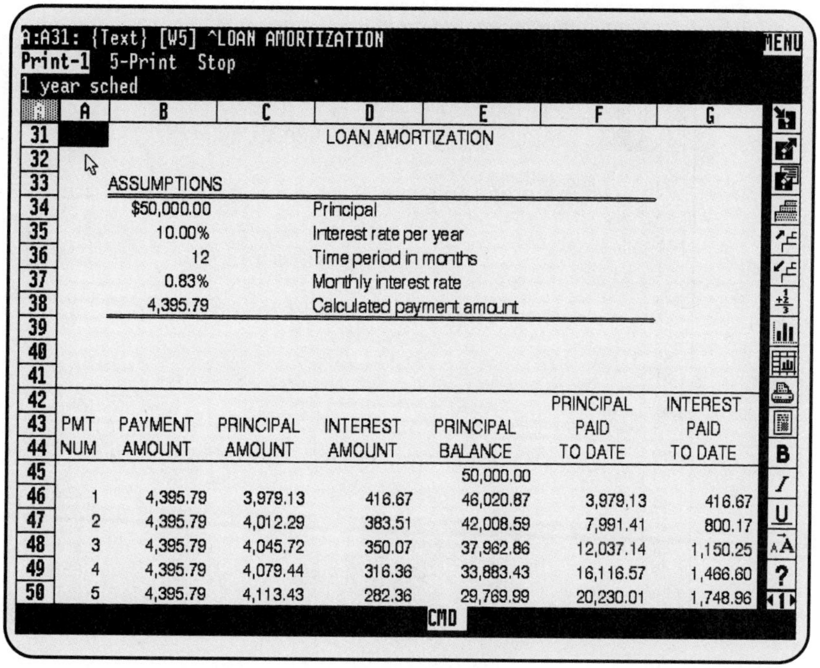

```
A:A31: {Text} [W5] ^LOAN AMORTIZATION                              MENU
Print-1  5-Print  Stop
1 year sched
```

	A	B	C	D	E	F	G
31				LOAN AMORTIZATION			
32							
33		ASSUMPTIONS					
34		$50,000.00		Principal			
35		10.00%		Interest rate per year			
36		12		Time period in months			
37		0.83%		Monthly interest rate			
38		4,395.79		Calculated payment amount			
39							
40							
41							
42						PRINCIPAL	INTEREST
43	PMT	PAYMENT	PRINCIPAL	INTEREST	PRINCIPAL	PAID	PAID
44	NUM	AMOUNT	AMOUNT	AMOUNT	BALANCE	TO DATE	TO DATE
45					50,000.00		
46	1	4,395.79	3,979.13	416.67	46,020.87	3,979.13	416.67
47	2	4,395.79	4,012.29	383.51	42,008.59	7,991.41	800.17
48	3	4,395.79	4,045.72	350.07	37,962.86	12,037.14	1,150.25
49	4	4,395.79	4,079.44	316.36	33,883.43	16,116.57	1,466.60
50	5	4,395.79	4,113.43	282.36	29,769.99	20,230.01	1,748.96

```
                                                    CMD
```

Select   Print-1 | *Choose*   *Print-1*

After the schedule is printed:

Select   End | *Choose*   *End*

Your screen should look like Figure 17-34, Part 3.

Figure 17-34
Part 3

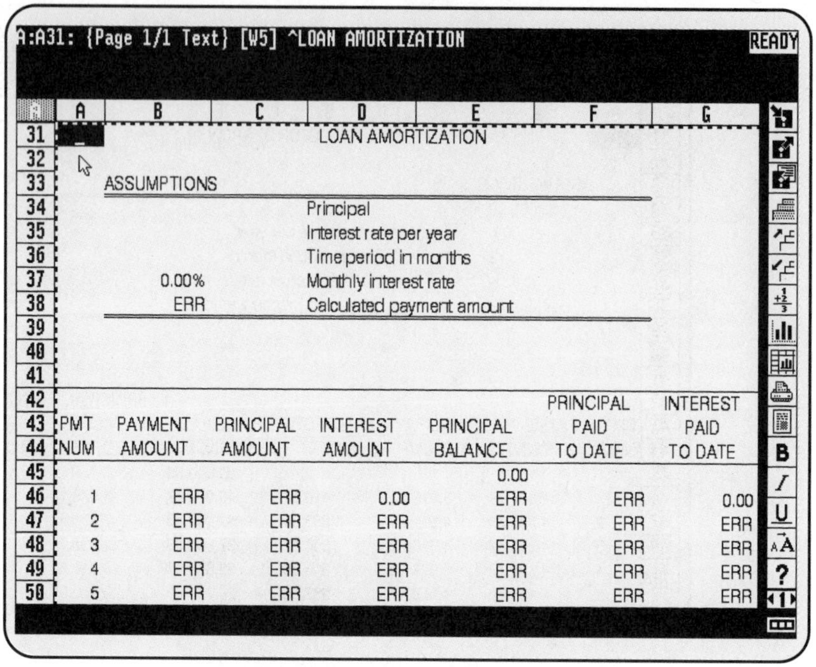

```
A:A31: {Page 1/1 Text} [W5] ^LOAN AMORTIZATION                    READY
```

	A	B	C	D	E	F	G
31				LOAN AMORTIZATION			
32							
33		ASSUMPTIONS					
34				Principal			
35				Interest rate per year			
36				Time period in months			
37		0.00%		Monthly interest rate			
38		ERR		Calculated payment amount			
39							
40							
41							
42						PRINCIPAL	INTEREST
43	PMT	PAYMENT	PRINCIPAL	INTEREST	PRINCIPAL	PAID	PAID
44	NUM	AMOUNT	AMOUNT	AMOUNT	BALANCE	TO DATE	TO DATE
45					0.00		
46	1	ERR	ERR	0.00	ERR	ERR	0.00
47	2	ERR	ERR	ERR	ERR	ERR	ERR
48	3	ERR	ERR	ERR	ERR	ERR	ERR
49	4	ERR	ERR	ERR	ERR	ERR	ERR
50	5	ERR	ERR	ERR	ERR	ERR	ERR

■ /X COMMANDS

The **/x** commands were included in Lotus 1-2-3 Release 1A. These commands provided users with some programming capability. Lotus 1-2-3 Release 3.4 has equivalent commands available that are easier to understand. The /x commands are available in later releases of 1-2-3 to maintain compatibility with macros developed using Lotus 1-2-3 Release 1A.

/xg	goto programming command
/xm	menu processing command
/xi	if-then programming command
/xn	message command to prompt user to input a number
/xl	message command to prompt user to input a label
/xc	subroutine call command
/xr	return to macro from subroutine command
/xq	quit programming command

/xg

The /xg command transfers control to a specific cell in a macro sequence. Execution then continues at the specified location.

The /xg command has the following format:

/xg location~

The equivalent advanced macro command in later versions of 1-2-3 is {branch}.

/xm

The /xm command is used to direct control to a user-designed menu in a specified location.

The /xm command has the following format:

/xm location~

The equivalent advanced macro command in later versions of 1-2-3 is {menubranch}.

/xi

The /xi command is used to execute different steps in a macro depending on a specified condition.

The /xi command has the following format:

/xi condition~

If the condition is true, the macro commands to the right of the condition are executed. If the condition is false, the macro cell in the row immediately below the /xi command is executed. The equivalent advanced macro command in later versions of 1-2-3 is {if}.

/xn

The /xn command is used to prompt an individual to enter a number that will be placed in the cell specified by the location. The prompt appears at the top of the screen.

The /xn command has the following format:

/xn message~location~

The equivalent advanced macro command in later versions of 1-2-3 is {getnumber}.

/xl

The /xl command is similar to the /xn command, except that a user is prompted to enter a string of characters. The characters are placed in the cell specified by the location. A maximum of 39 characters can be included in the message.

The /xl command has the following format:

/xl message~location~

The equivalent advanced macro command in later versions of 1-2-3 is {getlabel}.

/xc

The /xc command directs control to a location where a subroutine appears. A subroutine is a set of macro steps located outside of the main macro. Subroutines are often used when a specific condition is satisfied within a macro. The /xc command is used within the main macro to indicate where the subroutine appears on the spreadsheet.

The /xc command has the following format:

/xc location~

The equivalent advanced macro command in later versions of 1-2-3 is {subroutine}.

/xr

The /xr command is used in conjunction with the /xc command. The /xr command is used to indicate that a subroutine operation has been completed and it is time to return to the main macro. When an /xr command is encountered in a subroutine, control is transferred to the macro cell immediately following the /xc command that called the subroutine. Execution of the main macro then continues.

The /xr command has the following format:

/xr

The equivalent advanced macro command in later versions of 1-2-3 is {return}.

/xq

The /xq command stops the execution of the macro.

The /xq command has the following format:

/xq

The equivalent advanced macro command in later versions is {quit}.

Another way to stop a macro is by holding the CTRL key down and then pressing the BREAK key.

SUMMARY

Macros provide an efficient way of automating repetitive procedures. They can be used for operations such as combining files, printing a spreadsheet, completing a data query, sorting data, and restricting input to specific cells. Advanced macro commands can be used to enter sequences of numbers, to execute a loop of instructions, to prompt users to enter labels and numeric data, to create subroutines, and to develop user-designed menus. Macros provide users of Lotus 1-2-3 with immense flexibility in developing various applications.

KEY CONCEPTS

Advanced macro commands
Interactive macros
Looping through a sequence of
    macro commands
Macro key names

Multiple-tiered menus
Single-tiered menu
Subroutines
User-designed menus
/X commands

EXERCISE 1

INSTRUCTIONS: Circle T if the statement is true and F if the statement is false.

T   F   1.   You cannot use macros to place a sequence of values on a worksheet.

T   F   2.   A macro can be automatically executed when a file is retrieved by naming the macro ZERO.

T   F   3.   A series of macro instructions can be repeated only if you know how many times the instructions need to be repeated.

T   F   4.   A maximum of 10 menu options can be included in any user-designed menu.

T   F   5.   The /x commands have equivalent macro commands available in later releases of Lotus 1-2-3 that are easier to understand.

T   F   6.   Macros can be used to restrict user input to a specific set of cells.

T   F   7.   The only way to use an interactive macro is if you force the macro to execute when the file containing the macro is retrieved.

T   F   8.   Macros can be written that prompt a person to input information.

EXERCISE 2 — Creating a Macro to Query a Database Table

INSTRUCTIONS: Retrieve the PERSON file you created as an exercise in Chapter 13.

Write a macro that extracts the last names and first names for the individuals living in New York or San Antonio with the last name Adams. Include a print macro that prints the database table and the extracted records.

Place the macros for extracting the appropriate records and printing the results along with the database table on a separate worksheet. The macros should be properly documented.

Print the worksheet containing the database table and extracted records. Also, print the worksheet containing the macros you created.

EXERCISE 3 — Creating a Macro for Entering Numbers

INSTRUCTIONS: Make sure you have a blank worksheet on your screen.

Create a macro that permits you to enter numbers across a row so that you do not have to move to the next cell after you press the ENTER key. Place the macro on a separate worksheet. Document the macro properly.

Enter the numbers 100, 25, 125, and 200 in cells B10 through E10 using the macro.

Print the worksheet containing the numbers you input. Also, print the worksheet containing the macro for entering the numbers.

EXERCISE 4 — Executing a Loop of Instructions When the Number of Iterations is Known

INSTRUCTIONS: Make sure you have a blank worksheet on your screen.

Enter the following data on a worksheet.

Cell	Value
A1	10
B1	15
C1	5
A2	15
B2	20
C2	25
A3	30
B3	20
C3	10
A4	5
B4	15
C4	25
A5	15
B5	25
C5	10

Create a macro that computes for each row the sum of the cells in column A and column B and then multiplies the sum by the value in column C. Place the results in column D of each row. You can assume that you know to repeat the calculation procedure five times.

Prepare a macro that prints the worksheet with the final results. Place the macros for computing and printing the results on a separate worksheet. Document the macros properly.

Print the worksheet containing the values you entered and the resulting computations. Also, print the worksheet that includes the macros.

EXERCISE 5 — Executing a Loop of Instructions When the Number of Iterations is Unknown

INSTRUCTIONS: Make sure you have a blank worksheet on your screen.

Enter the following data on a worksheet.

Cell	Value
A1	20
B1	25
C1	15
A2	25
B2	30
C2	35
A3	40
B3	30
C3	20
A4	15
B4	25
C4	35
A5	25
B5	35
C5	20

Create a macro that for each row subtracts the value in column B from the value in column A and then divides the difference by the value in column C. Place the results in column D of each row. Assume that you do not know the number of times needed to repeat the calculation procedure.

Prepare a macro that prints the worksheet with the final results. Place the macros for computing and printing the results on a separate worksheet. Document the macros properly.

Print the worksheet containing the values you entered and the resulting computations. Also, print the worksheet that includes the macros.

EXERCISE 6 — Prompting a User to Enter Labels and Numeric Data

INSTRUCTIONS: Create an application of your own for prompting a user to enter labels and numeric data.

Print the worksheets containing the application you prepare and the macro you create. Document the macro properly.

EXERCISE 7 — Creating a Single-Tier Menu

INSTRUCTIONS: Create an application of your own for using a single-tier menu.

Print the worksheets containing the application you prepare and the single-tier menu macro you create. Document the macro properly.

EXERCISE 8 — Creating a Two-Tier Menu

INSTRUCTIONS: Create an application of your own for using a two-tier menu.

Print the worksheets containing the application you prepare and the two-tier menu macro you create. Document the macro properly.

EXERCISE 9 — Creating a Three-Tier Menu

INSTRUCTIONS: Create an application of your own for using a three-tier menu.

Print the worksheets containing the application you prepare and the three-tier menu macro you create. Document the macro properly.

APPENDIX A

LOTUS 1-2-3 SMARTICONS

The following pages show the 93 SmartIcons grouped in palettes and a brief description of each SmartIcon. The palette grouping is arranged for a VGA monitor. If you have a different monitor type, the palette arrangement may vary.

Palette 1 (Custom Palette)

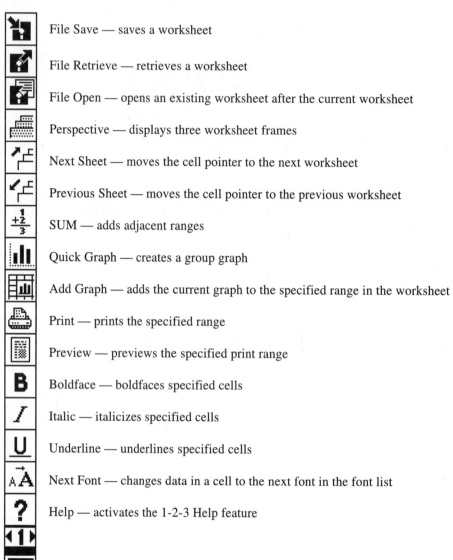

File Save — saves a worksheet

File Retrieve — retrieves a worksheet

File Open — opens an existing worksheet after the current worksheet

Perspective — displays three worksheet frames

Next Sheet — moves the cell pointer to the next worksheet

Previous Sheet — moves the cell pointer to the previous worksheet

SUM — adds adjacent ranges

Quick Graph — creates a group graph

Add Graph — adds the current graph to the specified range in the worksheet

Print — prints the specified range

Preview — previews the specified print range

Boldface — boldfaces specified cells

Italic — italicizes specified cells

Underline — underlines specified cells

Next Font — changes data in a cell to the next font in the font list

Help — activates the 1-2-3 Help feature

Palette 2

File Save — saves a worksheet

Underline — underlines specified cells

Double Underline — double underlines specified cells

Currency Format — formats a value with a $ and 2 decimal places

Comma Format — formats a value with a , and no decimal places

Percent Format — formats a value as a % with 2 decimal places

Next Font — changes data in a cell to the next font in the font list

Next Color — changes data in a cell to the next color

Next Background Color — changes the background of data in a cell to the next color

Drop Shadow — draws an outline and a drop shadow box around specified cells

Outline — draws an outline around specified cells

Shade — shades a cell

Left Align — left-aligns labels

Center — centers labels

Right Align — right-aligns labels

Help — activates the 1-2-3 Help feature

Palette 3

File Save — saves a worksheet

Row Insert — inserts row(s) above specified range

Column Insert — inserts column(s) to the left of the specified range

Row Delete — deletes specified row(s)

Column Delete — deletes specified column(s)

Sheet Insert — inserts a worksheet after the current worksheet

Sheet Delete — deletes specified worksheet

Row Page Break — inserts a page break in the row where the cell pointer is located

Column Page Break — inserts a page break in the column where the cell pointer is located

A-Z Sort — sorts in ascending order

Z-A Sort — sorts in descending order

Data Fill — fills specified cells with values

Calc — recalculates the specified cell(s)

Date — enters today's date

Zoom — enlarges or reduces the size of specified cells

Help — activates the 1-2-3 Help feature

Palette 4

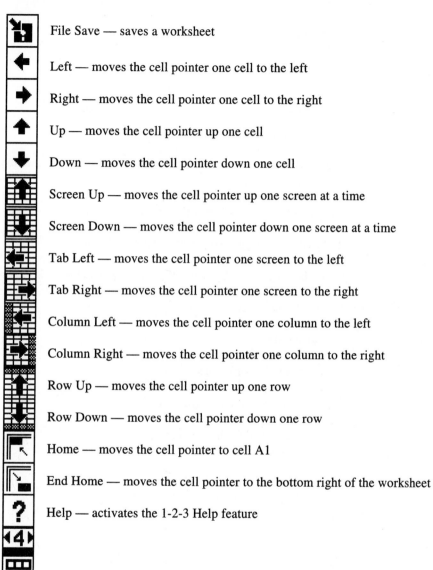

File Save — saves a worksheet

Left — moves the cell pointer one cell to the left

Right — moves the cell pointer one cell to the right

Up — moves the cell pointer up one cell

Down — moves the cell pointer down one cell

Screen Up — moves the cell pointer up one screen at a time

Screen Down — moves the cell pointer down one screen at a time

Tab Left — moves the cell pointer one screen to the left

Tab Right — moves the cell pointer one screen to the right

Column Left — moves the cell pointer one column to the left

Column Right — moves the cell pointer one column to the right

Row Up — moves the cell pointer up one row

Row Down — moves the cell pointer down one row

Home — moves the cell pointer to cell A1

End Home — moves the cell pointer to the bottom right of the worksheet

Help — activates the 1-2-3 Help feature

Palette 5

File Save — saves a worksheet

Perspective — displays three worksheet frames

Next Sheet — moves the cell pointer to the next worksheet

Previous Sheet — moves the cell pointer to the previous worksheet

End Down — moves the cell pointer down to the next cell containing data and above a blank cell

End Up — moves the cell pointer up to the next cell containing data and below a blank cell

End Right — moves the cell pointer right to the next cell containing data and left of a blank cell

End Left — moves the cell pointer left to the next cell containing data and right of a blank cell

GoTo — moves the cell pointer to a specified cell

Find — searches for or replaces data

Copy — copies the specified range to a new range

Move — moves the specified range to a new range

Copy Format — copies the current cell formats to a specified range

Undo — undoes the last command

Delete — erases the specified range

Help — activates the 1-2-3 Help feature

Palette 6

File Save — saves a worksheet

File Retrieve — retrieves a worksheet

File Open — opens an existing worksheet after the current worksheet

File New — creates a new worksheet

Print — prints the specified range

Preview — previews the specified print range

SUM — adds adjacent range

3-D SUM — adds cells directly behind the current cell when in 3-D mode

Quick Graph — creates a group graph

Add Graph — adds the current graph to the specified range in the worksheet

Graph View — displays the current graph

Edit Text — enters or edits text in a text range

Align Text — aligns labels

Circle — draws a circle around specified cells

Repeat — copies current cell to specified cells

Help — activates the 1-2-3 Help feature

Palette 7

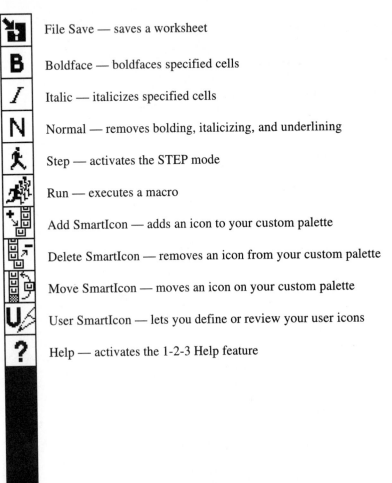

File Save — saves a worksheet

Boldface — boldfaces specified cells

Italic — italicizes specified cells

Normal — removes bolding, italicizing, and underlining

Step — activates the STEP mode

Run — executes a macro

Add SmartIcon — adds an icon to your custom palette

Delete SmartIcon — removes an icon from your custom palette

Move SmartIcon — moves an icon on your custom palette

User SmartIcon — lets you define or review your user icons

Help — activates the 1-2-3 Help feature

Palette 8

U1
U2
U3
U4
U5
U6
U7
U8
U9
U10
U11
U12

◄8►

INDEX

1-2-3 ADVANCED MACRO COMMANDS

1-2-3 FUNCTIONS